THE CAMBRIDGE HANDBOOK OF COPYRIGHT LIMITATIONS AND EXCEPTIONS

While copyright law is ordinarily thought to consist primarily of exclusive rights, the regime's various exemptions and immunities from liability for copyright infringement form an integral part of its functioning, and serve to balance copyright's grant of a private benefit to authors/creators with the broader public interest. With contributors from all over the world, this handbook offers a systematic, thorough study of copyright limitations and exceptions adopted in major jurisdictions, including the United States, the European Union, and China. In addition to providing justifications for these limitations, the chapters compare differences and similarities that exist in major jurisdictions and offer suggestions about how to improve the enforcement of copyright limitations domestically and globally. This work should appeal to scholars, policymakers, attorneys, teachers, judges, and students with an interest in the theories, policies, and doctrines of copyright law.

SHYAMKRISHNA BALGANESH is a Professor of Law at the University of Pennsylvania Carey Law School. His scholarship focuses on understanding how intellectual property and innovation policy can benefit from the use of ideas, concepts, and structures from different areas of the common law, especially private law.

NG-LOY WEE LOON is a Professor of Law at the Faculty of Law of National University of Singapore. Her main research interests are in the field of intellectual property (IP) law. She is the author of *Law of Intellectual Property of Singapore* (2nd ed., 2014).

HAOCHEN SUN is Associate Professor of Law and Director of the Law and Technology Center at the University of Hong Kong Faculty of Law. He has won the HKU Faculty of Law Research Output Prize twice, and is the co-editor of *The Luxury Economy and Intellectual Property* (2015).

The Cambridge Handbook of Copyright Limitations and Exceptions

Edited by

SHYAMKRISHNA BALGANESH

University of Pennsylvania Law School

NG-LOY WEE LOON

National University of Singapore School of Law

HAOCHEN SUN

University of Hong Kong Faculty of Law

CAMBRIDGE
UNIVERSITY PRESS

CAMBRIDGE
UNIVERSITY PRESS

Shaftesbury Road, Cambridge CB2 8EA, United Kingdom

One Liberty Plaza, 20th Floor, New York, NY 10006, USA

477 Williamstown Road, Port Melbourne, VIC 3207, Australia

314–321, 3rd Floor, Plot 3, Splendor Forum, Jasola District Centre, New Delhi – 110025, India

103 Penang Road, #05–06/07, Visioncrest Commercial, Singapore 238467

Cambridge University Press is part of Cambridge University Press & Assessment, a department of the University of Cambridge.

We share the University's mission to contribute to society through the pursuit of education, learning and research at the highest international levels of excellence.

www.cambridge.org
Information on this title: www.cambridge.org/9781009293143

DOI: 10.1017/9781108671101

First published 2021
First paperback edition 2023

A catalogue record for this publication is available from the British Library

Library of Congress Cataloging-in-Publication data
NAMES: Balganesh, Shyamkrishna, editor. | Wee Loon, Ng-Loy, editor. | Sun, Haochen, editor.
TITLE: The Cambridge handbook of copyright limitations and exceptions / edited by Shyamkrishna Balganesh, University of Pennsylvania Law School; Ng-Loy Wee Loon, National University of Singapore School of Law; Haochen Sun, University of Hong Kong Faculty of Law.
DESCRIPTION: Cambridge, United Kingdom ; New York, NY : Cambridge University Press, 2021. | Includes bibliographical references.
IDENTIFIERS: LCCN 2020016496 (print) | LCCN 2020016497 (ebook) | ISBN 9781108483049 (hardback) | ISBN 9781108671101 (epub)
SUBJECTS: LCSH: Copyright.
CLASSIFICATION: LCC K1420.6 .C36 2021 (print) | LCC K1420.6 (ebook) | DDC 346.04/82–dc23
LC record available at https://lccn.loc.gov/2020016496
LC ebook record available at https://lccn.loc.gov/2020016497

ISBN 978-1-108-48304-9 Hardback
ISBN 978-1-009-29314-3 Paperback

Contents

Contributors

Tanya Aplin, Professor of Intellectual Property Law, King's College London

Graeme W. Austin, Professor of Law, Melbourne Law School, University of Melbourne; Associate Dean, Faculty of Law, Victoria University of Wellington

Ida Madieha Azmi, Professor of Law, International Islamic University Malaysia

Arpan Banerjee, Assistant Professor, Jindal Global Law School; Scientia Doctoral Scholar, University of New South Wales

Lionel Bently, Herchel Smith Professor of Intellectual Property, Faculty of Law, University of Cambridge

Robert Burrell, Professor of Intellectual Property and Information Technology Law, Faculty of Law, University of Oxford; Professor of Law, Melbourne Law School.

Brendan Clift, Lecturer, University of Hong Kong Faculty of Law

Ben Depoorter, Max Radin Distinguished Professor, University of California Hastings College of the Law

Christophe Geiger, Professor of Law and Director of the Research Department of the Centre for International Intellectual Property Studies, University of Strasbourg

Michael Handler, Professor, Faculty of Law, University of New South Wales

Reto M. Hilty, Prof. Dr. jur., Director, Max Planck Institute for Innovation and Competition, Munich

Emily Hudson, Reader, The Dickson Poon School of Law, King's College London; Associate Professor, TC Beirne School of Law, University of Queensland

Ariel Katz, Associate Professor and Innovation Chair Electronic Commerce, Faculty of Law, University of Toronto

Alice Lee, Associate Professor and Associate Dean, University of Hong Kong Faculty of Law

Kung-Chung Liu, Lee Kong Chian Professor of Law (Practice); Director, Applied Research Centre for Intellectual Assets and the Law in Asia, Singapore Management University

Ng-Loy Wee Loon, Professor, Faculty of Law, National University of Singapore

Valentina Moscon, Dr., Senior Research Fellow, Max Planck Institute for Innovation and Competition, Munich

David Nimmer, Of Counsel, Irell & Manella LLP; Professor from Practice, UCLA School of Law

Christoph Rademacher, Associate Professor, Graduate School of Law, Waseda University

Sam Ricketson, Professor of Law, Melbourne Law School, University of Melbourne

Martin Senftleben, Professor of Intellectual Property Law, Institute for Information Law, University of Amsterdam

Daniel Seng, Associate Professor and Director, Centre for Technology, Robotics, Artificial Intelligence & the Law, Faculty of Law, National University of Singapore

Haochen Sun, Associate Professor of Law and Director, Law and Technology Center, University of Hong Kong Faculty of Law

David Tan, Professor and Vice Dean (Academic Affairs), Faculty of Law, National University of Singapore

Tatsuhiro Ueno, Professor of Law, Waseda University

Christopher S. Yoo, John H. Chestnut Professor of Law, Communication, and Computer & Information Science and Founding Director of the Center for Technology, Innovation and Competition, University of Pennsylvania

Preface

OVERVIEW

Limitations and exceptions form an integral part of copyright law's basic entitlement structure. While copyright law is ordinarily thought to consist primarily of exclusive rights, the regime's various limitations and exceptions from liability (for copyright infringement) form an integral part of its functioning and serve to balance copyright's grant of a private benefit (to authors/creators) with the broader public interest. Properly crafted limitations and exceptions are of pivotal importance to mediating copyright law's promise of providing creators with an incentive to produce new works and its devotion to affording the public access to these works, once brought into existence. They also shape a host of copyright law's additional ideals in promoting democracy and cultural progress in ways that the system's framework of exclusive rights cannot deliver on its own.

While the basic exclusive rights structure has been the subject of extensive international and comparative law discussion, including in the formation of international treaties (e.g., the Berne Convention and the TRIPS Agreement), copyright's limitations and exceptions have thus far evaded such systematic analytical investigation from an international and comparative perspective. Indeed, the World Intellectual Property Organization (WIPO) recently considered proposals to move forward on a comprehensive treaty to harmonize countries' limitations and exceptions across the world through the creation of minimum standards. Owing to objections from rights holders and WIPO member states, the proposal was eventually shelved, with the organization deciding to focus on individual areas of limitations (e.g., exceptions for the visually impaired contained in the Marrakesh Treaty).

For the first time, this volume brings together leading scholars from around the world to reflect on the comparative dimensions of copyright limitations and exceptions. The issue of comparing and contrasting countries' different approaches to copyright limitations and exceptions is still fertile academic terrain. Among other things, it reveals the normative underpinnings of the institution in different settings and jurisdictions, something that is often taken for granted and believed to be universally consistent. Copyright is today taken to be about providing authors with incentives to create; yet the manner in which copyright limitations are administered promises to illuminate the existence of additional values that have hitherto been seen as ancillary within the copyright system, such as distributive justice, social welfare, and cultural progress. In addition to the normative perspectives, an international comparison also introduces – for the first time – a deeper discussion about how copyright law and jurisprudence interfaces with other aspects of countries' legal and regulatory landscape. It sheds light on which institutional organ in a country (i.e., the legislature or the judiciary) is primarily responsible for protecting copyright in the public interest and developing jurisprudence on limitations and exceptions.

FRAMEWORK AND ORGANIZATION

Within the world of comparative copyright law and the analysis of limitations and exceptions therein, the traditional manner of framing discussions has been in terms of the divide between fair dealing jurisdictions and fair use jurisdictions – or jurisdictions with specifically delineated limitations and exceptions and those with a more general system. Much like the civil law/common law framing in general comparative law studies, this distinction tends to operate mostly as a caricature given its unidimensional focus on statutory text. It, however, ignores institutional features relating to the practice of statutory interpretation. Nor does it adequately consider a myriad of socioeconomic and political factors that impact the functioning of law in any given jurisdiction, as well as the more basic reality that the two types of exceptions might actually have converged in practice. This volume seeks to address these problems by advocating that copyright theory and policy would benefit from a more nuanced comparative approach to discussing and theorizing copyright limitations and exceptions in different jurisdictions.

The chapters in this volume cover a wide range of themes and ideas, revealing the importance and breadth of issues encapsulated within a comparative discussion of copyright limitations and exceptions. Broadly speaking, the volume presents five principal themes, each of which forms a separate part of the volume:

1 *The Theoretical Foundation of Copyright Limitations.*

While scholars continue to debate about the normative and theoretical underpinnings of copyright law as a whole, the theoretical basis of copyright's limitations and exceptions has received comparatively less attention. The first part of this volume considers the applicability of two different normative theories to the structure and function of copyright exceptions. One, the economic account, focuses on the functioning of the overall system (of exceptions), while the other – the deontologically oriented theory of self-actualization – focuses on the role of copyright exceptions in meeting individual needs for human flourishing.

2 *Internationalizing Copyright Exceptions.*

While international law has come to play an important role in the global harmonization of copyright's framework of exclusive rights, an equivalent has yet to emerge in relation to copyright exceptions. The recently concluded Marrakesh Treaty is a step in that direction. The chapters in this part explore the role of international law in facilitating the global development of a more robust set of limitations and exceptions.

These chapters examine flexibilities and constraints that may exist within today's international instruments and treaties. They also provide forward-looking and aspirational perspectives in examining what further steps in this arena might look like, and speculating toward the possibility of more tailored and systematic international efforts. As the chapters together rightly point out, internationalizing the conversation is a mixed bag, and likely to present both advantages and disadvantages, a reality that should not be forgotten or ignored.

3 *Models of Copyright Exceptions.*

As previously noted, most prior comparative discussions of copyright limitations and exceptions framed the conversation in terms of the divide between "fair use" regimes and "fair dealing" ones. Not only is this framing an oversimplification, but in focusing on the facial structure of the legal doctrine, it has ignored important institutional, political, and structural nuances about the working of the model within each jurisdiction. This part of the volume is devoted to unraveling the simplicity (and utility) of that framing.

The chapters in this part propose new models of copyright exceptions in a few different ways. Some focus on the model adopted by an individual country, to show how the jurisdiction – even if originally a fair dealing regime – has recognized the need for additional flexibility and made important steps to incorporate components of fair use. Other chapters directly challenge the utility of the distinction in the modern context, pointing to its shortcomings in recognizing the evolution of different hybridized frameworks of lawmaking and legal influence. And yet others, look to the inability of the extant framing to address the role of politics, judicial culture, and aspects of jurisdictions that a cursory examination of the law has failed to render salient.

4 *Obvious and Hidden Values in the Working of Copyright Exceptions.*

The next part of the volume addresses specific values that operate within copyright law, and influence the working of copyright exceptions – either in the abstract/general, or more specifically, through specialized and tailored rules. The values described in this part are either obvious, in being an accepted part of the conversation about copyright exceptions; or alternatively hidden, in that they are integral yet implicit in the working and structure of the doctrine.

In the former category are educational uses, parodic uses, and news dissemination, while in the latter are cultural uses (including religious uses of works), and the idea of an overarching concern for the public interest. The methodologies adopted in this part also range the gamut – from being principally doctrinal and interpretive, to the more theoretical and normative. The specific values described in these chapters should by no means be taken to imply that the ones under discussion are indeed more important than those not covered, or worse still that the ones not covered are irrelevant or absent in copyright limitations and exceptions. To the contrary, they merely reflect the particular choices of the contributors and their understanding of areas in which the scholarly literature has hitherto been lacking.

5 *Copyright Exceptions and Technology.*

The last part of the volume contains one chapter that, while focused on US fair use law, nevertheless contains a discussion of an issue that is of relevance for multiple jurisdictions: the extent to which discussions of copyright exceptions ought to countenance technological developments that are likely to undermine (or support) the core legal framework that they espouse. This chapter focuses on security measures that are central to a whole set of fair use decisions in the technological context and shows how courts have failed to grapple with the idea. It presents a wake-up call for global discussions of copyright exceptions to embrace something obvious that is beyond the domain of the law and/or of politics, namely, the influence of technology.

* * *

Together, the chapters in this volume are intended to serve as a ready guide to students, scholars, and policymakers around the world working on copyright limitations and exceptions, arousing their interest in learning more about the role of this important area of law in different legal systems. While the volume has consciously refrained from framing discussions in the traditional "comparative law" mold, it has nevertheless attempted to be exhaustive in its topical and methodological coverage, in the abiding hope that the comparative discussion of copyright limitations and exceptions will become a mainstay of intellectual property conversations and debates in the years to come.

PART I

The Theoretical Foundation of Copyright Limitations

1

The Economics of Copyright Exemptions: A Comparative Analysis

Ben Depoorter

1 INTRODUCTION TO THE ECONOMICS OF COPYRIGHT PROTECTION

Economic analysis understands intellectual property laws, including copyright law, as necessary to protect markets for information goods against an appropriation problem.[1] The core value of creative and innovative product is the information on which books, movies, and inventions are based. Information is non-excludable to the extent that once it is distributed to some, it is difficult to prevent access to others.[2]

Additionally, and increasingly also in the digital era, the costs of the imitation of a creative work are substantially lower than the costs of original creation. Since it is difficult to prevent imitators from accessing and distributing a work, prices in a competitive setting may drop to levels that prevent creators from appropriating sufficient value to recover their development costs. As a result, the incentive to create[3] and invest[4] in creative works will be socially suboptimal.[5]

Copyright law addresses the appropriation problem by creating property rights in creative works that enable copyright owners to prevent copying without permission.[6] Copyright law

[1] On the utilitarian philosophical theory of intellectual property law and for an economic account of copyright law more specifically, *see, e.g.*, PAUL GOLDSTEIN, COPYRIGHT'S HIGHWAY (1994); Gillian Hadfield, *The Economics of Copyright: An Historical Perspective*, 38 COPYRIGHT L. SYMP. 1 (1992).

[2] Oren Bracha & Talha Syed, *Beyond the Incentive–Access Paradigm? Product Differentiation & Copyright Revisited*, 92 TEX. L. REV. 1841, 1848 (2014).

[3] A growing literature shows, however, that the driving force of creativity is often motives unaffected by copyright protection. For a collection of recent work, *see* KATE DARLING & AARON PERZANOWSKI, CREATIVITY WITHOUT LAW (2017). Similarly, an ongoing literature points to ways in which authorship is commercialized outside of a copyright framework. Seminal contributions include Robert M. Hurt & Robert M. Schuchman, *The Economic Rationale of Copyright*, 56 AM. ECON. REV. 421 (1966); Arnold Plant, *The Economic Aspects of Copyright in Books*, 1 ECONOMICA 167 (1934). Empirical accounts of the effects of copyright law on creative output include Raymond Shih Ray Ku, Jiayang Sun, & Yiying Fan, *Does Copyright Law Promote Creativity? An Empirical Analysis of Copyright's Bounty*, 62 VAND. L. REV. 1669 (2009); Joel Waldfogel, *Music Piracy and Its Effects on Demand, Supply, and Welfare*, 12 INNOVATION POL'Y ECON. 91 (2012).

[4] Jonathan Barnett suggests that copyright law is essential mostly for profit-motivated intermediaries that incur the capital-intensive risks related to the creation and distribution of content. *See* Jonathan M. Barnett, *Copyright without Creators*, 9 REV. L. & ECON. 389 (2013).

[5] F. M. SCHERER, INDUSTRIAL MARKET STRUCTURE AND ECONOMIC PERFORMANCE 444 (2d ed. 1980) ("If pure and perfect competition in the strictest sense prevailed continuously ..., incentives for invention and innovation would be fatally defective without a patent system or some equivalent substitute.").

[6] On the property rights framework for intellectual property rights, *see* Harold Demsetz, *The Private Production of Public Goods*, 13 J.L. & ECON. 293 (1970). The case for strong property rights for intellectual creations is based on the notion

provides right holders with an exclusive right to copy, sell, and distribute their work. As legal monopolists, copyright owners are free to set the price of their work in a way that enables them to recoup their investments in the production of the work. A copyright holder's ability to increase the price, however, depends on the amount of substitutes for the work that are available to consumers on the market. If the copyrighted work is highly unique and desirable to consumers, the copyright owner will be able to charge a higher price than when there is competitive pressure from similar, yet non-infringing works.[7]

These higher prices, although deemed necessary to enable a creator to recoup his or her investment in the original work, may however reduce access to the work for consumers with more financial constraints. Unless the copyright owner is able to price-discriminate,[8] the overall accessibility of the work is reduced and the copyright creates so-called deadweight losses.[9] This is a first, major potential social cost related to copyright law and intellectual property rights more generally.

Additionally, copyright protection carries a second potential social cost. Because copyrighted materials are nonphysical information goods, the use and enjoyment of a copyrighted work by one does not degrade the ability of others to consume and enjoy it.[10] Due to the "non-rivalrous" nature of the consumption of information goods, the marginal costs of increasing the diffusion of information are zero. Since there is no social cost to sharing creative works, it is preferable from a welfare perspective that information goods are available free of charge.[11]

Overall then, in this utilitarian framework, society's goal is to set the scope of copyright protection so that it effectively fosters incentives without unnecessarily increasing deadweight losses and reducing access. This so-called incentives–access tradeoff has been front and center in the utilitarian philosophical theory that drives much of the academic literature on copyright law.[12]

that markets ensure efficient allocation of resources through market-based, Coasean bargaining. *See* Robert P. Merges, *Of Property Rules, Coase and Intellectual Property*, 94 COLUM. L. REV. 2655 (1994). *See also* Richard P. Adelstein & Steven I. Peretz, *The Competition of Technologies in Markets for Ideas: Copyright and Fair Use in Evolutionary Perspective*, 5 INT'L REV. L. & ECON. 209, 232–33 (1985) (suggesting that markets would find a way to overcome the high transaction costs relating to time-shifting licensing).

7 The competitive nature of entertainment markets is a topic of contention. *See, e.g.*, DEREK THOMPSON, HIT MAKERS: THE SCIENCE OF POPULARITY IN AN AGE OF DISTRACTION (2017) (describing the blockbuster effect for films and music, suggesting that entertainment markets have a winner-takes-all nature). *But see* CHRIS ANDERSON, THE LONG TAIL: WHY THE FUTURE OF BUSINESS IS SELLING LESS OF MORE (2006) (describing how the Internet has opened up potential markets for any niche product).

8 On price discrimination in copyright generally, *see, e.g.*, Julie E. Cohen, *Copyright and the Perfect Curve*, 53 VAND. L. REV. 1799 (2000); John P. Conley & Christopher S. Yoo, *Nonrivalry and Price Discrimination in Copyright Economics*, 157 U. PA. L. REV. 1801 (2008); Wendy J. Gordon, *Intellectual Property As Price Discrimination: Implications for Contract*, 73 CHI.-KENT L. REV. 1367 (1998); Glynn S. Lunney Jr., *Copyright's Price Discrimination Panacea*, 21 HARV. J.L. & TECH. 387 (2008); Michael J. Meurer, *Copyright Law and Price Discrimination*, 23 CARDOZO L. REV. 55 (2001).

9 A deadweight loss is a cost to society created by market inefficiency. In this particular instance, the higher price of the work excludes some willing buyers that the seller loses as potential purchasers. If the seller is able to engage in perfect price discrimination, each consumer would be charged the maximum price they are willing and able to pay. *See generally* PAUL SAMUELSON, FOUNDATIONS OF ECONOMIC ANALYSIS (1947).

10 *See, e.g.*, Glynn S. Lunney Jr., *Fair Use and Market Failure: Sony Revisited*, 82 B.U. L. REV. 975, 979 (2002) ("When a private good is stolen, the theft necessarily deprives the original owner of possession. Making an unauthorized copy does not.").

11 Kenneth J. Arrow, *Economic Welfare and the Allocation of Resources for Invention*, *in* THE RATE AND DIRECTION OF INVENTIVE ACTIVITY 609 (Richard R. Nelson ed., 1962).

12 This paradigm has come under recent challenge by the product differentiation approach. The important insight here is that copyright protection might increase the supply of creative works and access overall, since legal rights stimulate investments in creative industries by competitors. *See, e.g.*, Michael Abramowicz, *A New Uneasy Case for Copyright*, 79 GEO. WASH. L. REV. 1644, 1646–7 (2011); Michael Abramowicz, *An Industrial Organization Approach to Copyright Law*, 46 WM. & MARY L. REV. 33, 38 (2004); Christopher S. Yoo, *Copyright and Product Differentiation*, 79 N.Y.U. L. REV. 212, 221 (2004).

2 COPYRIGHT EXEMPTIONS: ECONOMIC JUSTIFICATIONS

Viewed through the economic lens, copyright exemptions help adjust the scope of copyright protection in the pursuit of a socially optimal tradeoff between access and incentives.

Economic accounts have suggested two primary instances where copyright exemptions are likely to be socially advantageous.[13]

First, given the non-rivalrous nature of information goods, it is socially desirable to provide free access *whenever doing so does not adversely impact the incentives of authors to create*. If there is no positive incentive effect, there is no reason to limit access by way of exclusive right to authors. Examples include situations where market failure is likely to prevent the owner from reaping any benefits from the exploitation of the copyright work.[14]

Second, it is socially desirable to restrict the exclusive right of copyright owners *if the costs of doing so are likely lower than the benefits generated by the exemption*. Examples include situations where an exemption is deemed necessary to safeguard a competing public interest, such as free speech. Exemptions may be desirable if, in the absence of an exemption, the copyright owners would be likely to exercise their exclusive right to block these socially beneficial uses. This is most likely for works that use copyrighted work for the purpose of criticism or parody.[15] Along the same lines, copyright exemptions likely produce net benefits when the incentive effects on the current copyright owners are less than the cost such protection imposes on the creation by another generation of creators.[16]

3 COPYRIGHT EXEMPTIONS AND MARKET FAILURE

The economic analysis of copyright law has focused primarily on the beneficial role of exemptions in mitigating potential allocative inefficiencies that result from copyright protection.

Although economists acknowledge the benefits of clear, strong property rights in market settings,[17] limitations to the property rights are justified when there is market failure.[18] For

[13] The seminal contribution is Wendy J. Gordon, *Fair Use As Market Failure: A Structural and Economic Analysis of the Betamax Case and Its Predecessors*, 82 COLUM. L. REV. 1600, 1601, 1614 (1982) (explaining how the US doctrine of fair use effectively permits uncompensated uses of copyrighted material where the transaction costs of licensing or other means of exchange would prevent a transfer through the market, and suggesting that copyright exemptions should apply for uses that would otherwise constitute infringement if: "(1) market failure is present; (2) transfer of the use to defendant is socially desirable; and (3) an award of fair use would not cause substantial injury to the incentives of the plaintiff copyright owner."). Economic justifications for limitations in copyright protection include, e.g., Glynn S. Lunney, Jr., *Reexamining Copyright's Incentives–Access Paradigm*, 49 VAND. L. REV. 283 (1996); Peter S. Menell, Tailoring Legal Protection for Computer Software, 39 STAN. L. REV. 1329 (1987); Peter S. Menell, *An Analysis of the Scope of Copyright Protection for Application Programs*, 41 STAN. L. REV. 1045 (1989); Peter S. Menell, *An Epitaph for Traditional Copyright Protection of Network Features of Computer Software*, 43 ANTITRUST BULL. 651 (1998) (analyzing role of limitations in addressing the market failure associated with computer software); Plant, *supra* note 3 (arguing for a narrow scope of protection for copyrighted works (limited to exact or near-exact duplication) on the grounds that broader protection would inefficiently promote investment in copyrightable endeavors at the expense of other activities in the economy); Hurt & Schuchman, *supra* note 3; Robert Kreiss, *Accessibility and Commercialization in Copyright Theory*, 43 UCLA L. REV. 1 (1995).

[14] *Id.*

[15] Robert P. Merges, *Are You Making Fun of Me?: Notes on Market Failure and the Parody Defense in Copyright*, 21 AIPLA Q.J. 305 (1993).

[16] William M. Landes & Richard A. Posner, *An Economic Analysis of Copyright Law*, 18 J. LEGAL STUD. 325 (1989). *See also* Mark A. Lemley, *The Economics of Improvement in Intellectual Property Law*, 75 TEX. L. REV. 989 (1997).

[17] R. H. Coase, *The Problem of Social Cost*, 3 J.L. & ECON. 1 (1960).

[18] Wendy J. Gordon, *Excuse and Justification in the Law of Fair Use: Commodification and Market Perspectives*, *in* THE COMMODIFICATION OF INFORMATION 149 (Niva Elkin-Koren & Neil Weinstock Netanel eds., 2002) (distinguishing between excusable cases of use under a "market malfunction" and justifiable cases of use in light of a "market limitation").

instance, markets do not clear if there are obstacles to bargaining, such as prohibitively high transaction costs, informational asymmetries, and negative externalities. When such obstacles prevent otherwise desirable transfers between copyright owners and users, the non-rival nature of information goods may favor abrogating the full exclusionary rights of the copyright owner by way of a copyright exemption.

Much of the scholarship on copyright exemptions has focused on transaction costs as a potential source of market failure and justification for copyright law. Transaction costs may create so-called negative value uses: the costs of obtaining a license might be higher than the value to the individual user. If the use of the work requires permission (for instance, using pictures in a classroom setting), the user (teacher) will elect not to use the work. In many cases, however, the use of the work would create positive externalities (education) without hurting the incentives of the author (who would otherwise not have received licensing income and would not have obtained reputation benefits/exposure).

Several contributions point out, however, that the relationship between copyright exemptions and transaction costs is complex and dynamic. First, generous copyright exemptions might prevent markets from developing the transaction-reducing institutions that could solve market failure, such as copyright collectives.[19] Second, transaction costs fluctuate over time. New technologies (interactive digital rights management technologies, etc.) might reduce transactions costs, suggesting that the importance of market failure–related copyright exemptions might diminish. Other institutional factors, such as legislative changes, might increase transaction costs. For instance, the removal of copyright formalities in the US Copyright Act has made it harder to identify copyright owners and obtain licenses.[20]

Bargaining in markets for copyrighted works is complicated also by the complementary nature of copyrighted works. In order to put together a radio program, album collection or a handbook of academic writings, it may be necessary to collect licenses on a large number of works that fit together. Such bundling requires one to obtain permission from multiple different right holders. Due to the property rule (injunctions) protection, each copyright owner effectively has a veto-right on the ideal collection of works that the licensee has in mind. In these circumstances, the market for copyrighted works has the risk of a potential tragedy of the "anticommons": the complex dynamics of negotiations might prevent mutually beneficial and socially welfare-improving bundling to take place.[21] Negotiations with multiple right holders face the familiar obstacles of transaction costs and strategic behavior. Additionally, if licensors overestimate the value of their individual contributions, a symptom documented in social science research on creators and innovators, the collective asking price might

[19] The seminal contribution on this point is Robert P. Merges, *Contracting into Liability Rules: Intellectual Property Rights and Collective Rights Organizations*, 84 Cal. L. Rev. 1293 (1996). For a discussion in the context of copyright law and copyright collectives, *see* Francesco Parisi & Ben Depoorter, *The Market for Intellectual Property: The Case of Complementary Oligopoly, in* The Economics of Copyright 162 (Wendy J. Gordon & Richard Watt eds., 2003).

[20] Wendy J. Gordon, *The Fair Use Doctrine: Markets, Market Failure and Rights of Use, in* Handbook on the Economics of Copyright 77 (Richard Watt ed., 2014). On notice costs in intellectual property systems, *see* Peter S. Menell & Michael J. Meurer, *Notice Failure and Notice Externalities*, 5 J. Legal Analysis 1 (2013).

[21] An important insight is that these impediments to bargaining exist even when transaction costs are low – for instance, due to digital technologies. Ben Depoorter & Francesco Parisi, *Fair Use and Copyright Protection: A Price Theory Explanation*, 21 Int'l Rev. L. & Econ. 453 (2003). At heart, the double monopoly problem is one of coordination between monopolists in order to reduce deadweight losses. *See, e.g.*, Norbert Schulz, Francesco Parisi, & Ben Depoorter, *Fragmentation in Property: Towards a General Model*, 158 J. Institutional & Theoretical Econ. 594 (2002).

well exceed the value of the collective work.[22] Finally, when bundling involves works that are highly complementary, a so-called Cournot-duopoly or double monopoly problem exists – if licensors do not coordinate, the increased price they individually charge makes it less likely that the collective project will come about.[23]

Given the nature of anticommons problems, the need for copyright exemptions in markets for creative works increases with (a) the number of copyright holders in it; (b) the degree of complementarity between the copyrighted inputs; and (c) the degree of independence between the various copyright holders in the pricing of their licenses.[24]

4 IMPLEMENTING COPYRIGHT EXEMPTIONS: A COMPARATIVE ECONOMIC ANALYSIS

While there is some consensus on the economic justifications for copyright exemptions, the legal implementation of exemptions is a topic of some contention. Legal systems have incorporated copyright exemptions in radically different ways. Most legal systems are situated somewhere in a continuum between two extremes: open-ended statements of permissible uses, on the one hand, and more closed, enumerated exemptions, on the other hand. These variations align with the foundational distinction in the economic analysis of law between rules and standards: the former containing more detail, where the latter are more general statements of legal norms.[25]

Most open-ended standards, the US fair use doctrine being the most famous example,[26] leave it up to judges to apply the standard to new situations and applications. Copyright exemptions that are implemented by rules usually involve statutorily provided, concrete and lists of exemption.[27]

[22] *See, e.g.*, Christopher Buccafusco & Christopher Jon Sprigman, *The Creativity Effect*, 78 U. Chi. L. Rev. 31 (2011) (describing "creativity effect"); Michael A. Heller & Rebecca S. Eisenberg, *Can Patents Deter Innovation? The Anticommons in Biomedical Research*, Science, May 1, 1998, at 698 (describing "attribution bias").

[23] For an experiment on how overvaluations by right holders can lead to price demands in excess of the total value of the bundling, *see* Ben Depoorter & Sven Vanneste, *Putting Humpty Dumpty Back Together: Experimental Evidence of Anticommons Tragedies*, 3 J.L. Econ. & Pol'y 1 (2006).

[24] Francesco Parisi, Norbert Schulz, & Ben Depoorter, *Duality in Property: Commons and Anticommons*, 25 Int'l Rev. L. & Econ. 578 (2005).

[25] On the distinction between rules and standards: "Legal norms can be precise rules, which are blueprints for action and allow for mechanical decisions by judges and civil servants. Alternatively, they can be vague, mission-oriented standards, which delegate decisions from the maker of the law to the judiciary and the administration. Rules economize on the costs of adjudication and administration. Standards economize on the costs of norm specification." Hans-Bernd Schäfer, *Rules versus Standards in Rich and Poor Countries: Precise Legal Norms As Substitutes for Human Capital in Low-Income Countries*, 14 Sup. Ct. Econ. Rev. 113, 113 (2006). There is not a binary distinction between the two categories. Rather, "[t]he difference between a rule and a standard is a matter of degree – the degree of precision." Richard A. Posner & Isaac Ehrlich, *An Economic Analysis of Legal Rulemaking*, 3 J. Legal Stud. 257, 258 (1974). *See generally* Louis Kaplow, *Rules versus Standards: An Economic Analysis*, 42 Duke L.J. 557 (1992); Pierre Schlag, *Rules and Standards*, 33 UCLA L. Rev. 379 (1985).

[26] "[T]he fair use of a copyrighted work, including such use by reproduction in copies or phonorecords or by any other means specified by that section, for purposes such as criticism, comment, news reporting, teaching (including multiple copies for classroom use), scholarship, or research, is not an infringement of copyright. In determining whether the use made of a work in any particular case is a fair use the factors to be considered shall include: (1) the purpose and character of the use, including whether such use is of a commercial nature or is for nonprofit educational purposes; (2) the nature of the copyrighted work; (3) the amount and substantiality of the portion used in relation to the copyrighted work as a whole; and (4) the effect of the use upon the potential market for or value of the copyrighted work." Copyright Act of 1976, 17 U.S.C. §107 (2007).

[27] *See* Article 5(2) of the EU Copyright Directive. 2001 O.J. (L167) at 10–19.

The comparative economic analysis of rules versus standards, as it relates to copyright exemptions, involves three main considerations: flexibility, indeterminacy, and rent seeking.

4.1 Flexibility

The unpredictable and fast-changing nature of technology[28] arguably makes open-ended standards more suitable for copyright exemptions.[29]

Open standards have a broader reach and may capture new technologies either implicitly by the broad wording or by judicial clarification in litigation. Precise legal rules, by contrast, are more quickly outdated by innovative applications of copyrighted content.[30]

Moreover, open-ended standards are more effective to counter "legal avoison."[31] Technological innovators sometimes develop novel applications that exploit the gaps between copyright rules and technologies.[32]

Technological innovators often design or create technological applications in a manner that purposefully circumvents copyright liability. For example, when the court in Napster established that copyright law implicates developers of centralized P2P technology by way of contributory liability, developers of file-sharing technology developed decentralized P2P file-sharing applications that were functionally equivalent to those explicitly prohibited in the Napster decision. By removing central servers, which gave rise to contributory liability on behalf of software developers, the developers successfully evaded the legal rule created in Napster.[33] Such acts of what has been termed legal "avoison" do violate legal rules *sensu stricto*, but nevertheless defeat the legislative intention.

[28] Take, for instance, the introduction of video cassette recording (VCR) technology. While private recordings of cable TV shows plainly violated the exclusive right of copyright holders to make copies, the flexibility of the fair use standard enabled courts to exempt the time-shifting features of VCR recorders. By allowing the record function to be maintained on VCR players, the fair use exemption arguably boosted the success of VCR technology, which eventually created a very profitable secondary market in the sale of video home system (VHS) tapes and rental movies. The fact that the VCR technology, with its dual use character, eventually boosted the revenues of copyright holders, plainly illustrates how technologies that are feared initially by copyright holders can turn out to be a blessing in disguise). See Mark A. Lemley, *Is the Sky Falling on the Content Industries?*, 9 Journal on Telecommunications and High Technology Law 125 (2011); Ben Depoorter, *Technology and Uncertainty: The Shaping Effect on Copyright Law*, 157 U. Pa. L. Rev. 1831 (2009) (discussing how it often takes many years before the social and economic consequences of new technologies become clear).

[29] On the necessity of a flexible fair use doctrine, *see, e.g.*, Dan L. Burk, *Muddy Rules for Cyberspace*, 21 Cardozo L. Rev. 121, 140 (1999) ("The 'muddy' four-part balancing standard for fair use allows courts to reallocate what the market cannot."); Michael W. Carroll, *Fixing Fair Use*, 85 N.C. L. Rev. 1087 (2007) (highlighting the context-sensitive nature of fair use); Matthew Sag, *God in the Machine: A New Structural Analysis of Copyright's Fair Use Doctrine*, 11 Mich. Telecomm. & Tech. L. Rev. 381, 435 (2005) (noting that a flexible fair use standard allows courts to adapt copyright protection to new innovations).

[30] *See, e.g.*, Ben Depoorter, *Technology and Uncertainty: The Shaping Effect on Copyright Law*, 157 U. Pa. L. Rev. 1831 (2009) (describing how rapid technological change makes open standards a better fit for copyright legislation than narrowly tailored rules).

[31] Leo Katz, Ill-Gotten Gains: Evasion, Blackmail, Fraud and Kindred Puzzles of the Law 17–30 (1996) (contrasting "avoision" of ethical rules with "avoision" of law).

[32] See in this regard Tim Wu's description of the relation between code and law: "The programmer is not unlike the tax lawyer, exploiting differences between stated goals of the law, and its legal or practical limits. He targets specific weaknesses in legal regimes . . ." Tim Wu, *When Code Isn't Law*, 89 Va. L. Rev. 679, 682 (2003).

[33] *See, e.g.*, Kristina Groennings, *Costs and Benefits of the Recording Industry's Litigation against Individuals*, 20 Berkeley Tech. L.J. 571, 573 (2005). For another notable example of a technology created to circumvent copyright provisions *see* Annemarie Bridy, *Aereo: From Working around Copyright to Thinking inside the (Cable) Box*, 2015 Mich. St. L. Rev. 465 (2015).

Bright line, narrow rules are thus easier for developers to circumvent, as they can create new adaptive technologies that does not fit within the existing rule. Because the new technology does not fit within the existing legal rule, lawmakers will need to play catch-up, reformulating substantive rules in order to capture new technologies that perform the same role in a different manner. By contrast, attempts at circumventing open standards will be more difficult given the broader sphere of application of a flexible standard. Additionally, courts can resolve ambiguities as to the applicability of the existing standard to a newly designed technology more quickly.

The choice between rules and standards also constitutes a tradeoff regarding the timing of the application of copyright exemptions. Rules are designed *ex ante* by regulators. Standards set out broader rules, allowing courts to fill in the details later on. Given the highly evolving, unpredictable innovative landscape of digital technologies, standards are a better fit for copyright exemptions.

4.2 *Indeterminacy*

The flexibility of open standards inevitably reduces the predictability of their application to new circumstances. For instance, since its inception, the US fair use doctrine[34] has been criticized for being "notoriously difficult to predict."[35] The doctrine is accused of infusing "significant ex ante uncertainty"[36] into copyright law. The lack of statutory guidance and wide discretion afforded to judges[37] are widely understood to cause substantial uncertainty.[38]

Economic analysis has highlighted how standards "trade off greater ex ante certainty for greater ex post context sensitivity."[39] When considering the desirability of flexible standards as

[34] The doctrine of fair use has been under attack for at least seventy years. *See* Dellar v. Samuel Goldwyn, Inc., 104 F.2d 661, 662 (2d Cir. 1939), in which Judge Learned Hand referred to the fair use doctrine as "the most troublesome in the whole law of copyright."

[35] Joseph P. Liu, *Two-Factor Fair Use?*, 31 COLUM. J.L. & ARTS 571, 578 (2008) (proposes reforming the current fair use doctrine by limiting the analysis to only the first and last of the four factors, instead of replacing it altogether as some other scholars have recommended).

[36] Carroll, *supra* note 29, at 1095 (citing 4 MELVILLE B. NIMMER & DAVID NIMMER, NIMMER ON COPYRIGHT §13.05 [A][1][b]); 2 PAUL GOLDSTEIN, GOLDSTEIN ON COPYRIGHT §12.2.2, at 12:34 (3d ed. 2005); WILLIAM F. PATRY, THE FAIR USE PRIVILEGE IN COPYRIGHT LAW 45 (2d ed. 1995); Gideon Parchomovsky & Kevin A. Goldman, *Fair Use Harbors*, 93 VA. L. REV. 1483, 1483 (2007) ("would-be fair-users can rarely rely on the doctrine with any significant level of confidence.") (proposing that the implementation of nonexclusive safe harbors, which expressly set forth minimum amounts of copying as fair, would work to eliminate the uncertainty and unpredictability of the current fair use doctrine in copyright law). *See also* James Gibson, *Once and Future Copyright*, 81 NOTRE DAME L. REV. 167, 192 (2005) ("Fair use . . . is too indeterminate a doctrine to provide a reliable touchstone for future conduct."); Darren Hudson Hick, *Mystery and Misdirection: Some Problems of Fair Use and Users' Rights*, 56 J. COPYRIGHT SOC'Y U.S.A. 485, 497 ("[S]ince the doctrine, as written, is open to such wide interpretation, the outcome of any legal battle that turns on the doctrine will almost always be in doubt."); Michael J. Madison, *A Pattern-Oriented Approach to Fair Use*, 45 WM. & MARY L. REV. 1525, 1666 (2004) ("Fair use is an *ex post* determination, a lottery argument offered by accused infringers forced to gamble, after the fact, that they did not need permission before."); David Nimmer, *"Fairest of Them All" and Other Fairy Tales of Fair Use*, 66 LAW & CONTEMP. PROBS. 263, 280 (2003) ("Basically, had Congress legislated a dartboard rather than the particular four fair use factors embodied in the Copyright Act, it appears that the upshot would be the same.").

[37] "Judges do not share a consensus on the meaning of fair use." Pierre N. Leval, *Toward a Fair Use Standard*, 103 HARV. L. REV. 1105, 1106 (1990).

[38] Hick, *supra* note 36. *But see* Pamela Samuelson, *Unbundling Fair Uses*, 77 FORDHAM L. REV. 2537 (2009) (showing doctrinal patterns by analyzing fair use case law in light of underlying policy concerns). *See also* Barton Beebe, *An Empirical Study of U.S. Copyright Fair Use Opinions, 1978–2005*, 156 U. PA. L. REV. 549, 554 (2008) ("much of our conventional wisdom about [US] fair use case law, deduced as it has been from the leading cases, is wrong.").

[39] Carroll, *supra* note 29, at 1100.

opposed to strict rules, the fundamental question is whether the benefits of flexibility outweigh the costs of the unavoidable higher degrees of uncertainty.[40]

It is worth noting that the application of novel technologies significantly increases the degree of legal uncertainty in copyright law.[41] Innovative leaps tend to create legal gaps, often making it difficult to rely on prior case law.[42]

Given the potential uncertainty induced by open standards in copyright law, it is important to be considerate of a number of undesirable side effects of legal uncertainty.

On the one hand, uncertainty undermines the deterrent effect of the law. Legal indeterminacy loosens the connection between behavior and enforcement. When the association between certain types of impermissible behavior and the chance of getting caught becomes more remote, individuals may decide that they might as well take the illicit action. Legal uncertainty may create the tipping point toward noncompliance,[43] as witnessed with regard to file-sharing on P2P networks or illegal video streaming.

On the other hand, if there is uncertainty about a legal standard, even individuals who attempt to act in compliance with the law will face the possibility of being held liable because of the unpredictability of the legal rule. Risk-averse individuals may react to this by "overcomplying," that is, modifying their behavior beyond the point that is socially optimal.[44] As a result, users of content that might well qualify for a copyright exemption seek out licenses or avoid using the content altogether in order to avoid the legal risk and costs associated with the uncertain application of the exemption.[45] This may have a chilling effect on creativity and authorship. Artists will avoid incorporating copyrighted materials into their creative works even when incorporating those particular works could well be considered to be fair use and non-infringing.[46] Third, uncertainty

[40] On the tradeoffs between rules and standards, *see generally* Kaplow, *supra* note 25.

[41] Depoorter, *supra* note 28.

[42] *Id.*

[43] *See* Henrik Lando, *Does Wrongful Conviction Lower Deterrence?*, 35 J. LEGAL STUD. 327, 334–35 (2006); *see also* Richard Craswell & John E. Calfee, *Deterrence and Uncertain Legal Standards*, 2 J.L. ECON. & ORG. 279, 299 (1986).

[44] Examples in the literature of overcompliance induced by uncertain application of legal standards include commentary on labor regulation and tax compliance. *See* Debra D. Burke, *Workplace Harassment: A Proposal for a Bright Line Test Consistent with the First Amendment*, 21 HOFSTRA LAB. & EMP. L.J. 591 (2004) (providing that risk-averse employers' natural reaction to the vague limits of sexual harassment laws, which prohibit employers from creating a "hostile environment," is to overcompensate by prohibiting words or conduct in the workplace that even border on harassment); Ehud Kamar, *Shareholder Litigation under Indeterminate Corporate Law*, 66 U. CHI. L. REV. 887, 889 (1999) ("[L]egal indeterminacy creates liability risk, which risk-averse fiduciaries are in a poor position to bear. Exposing corporate fiduciaries to this risk makes their services more costly and less productive to shareholders."); Kyle D. Logue, *Tax Law Uncertainty and the Role of Tax Insurance*, 25 VA. TAX REV. 339, 373 (2005) ("Legal uncertainty can induce taxpayers, especially risk-averse taxpayers, to over-comply with the law in various ways. Taxpayers could manifest over-compliance in a number of ways, such as changing the structure of their transactions, deciding not to engage in the transaction in question, or engaging the transaction as planned but without taking advantage of the more favorable tax treatment to which they are arguably – though by assumption not certainly – entitled."). Note that, when over-deterrence is not a concern, some authors have argued that uncertainty can be beneficial by inducing negotiated solutions or by increasing efficiency in law enforcement efforts. *See, e.g.*, Tom Baker, Alon Harel & Tamar Kugler, *The Virtues of Uncertainty in Law: An Experimental Approach*, 89 IOWA L. REV. 443 (2004) (positing that uncertain sanctions may be preferable on efficiency grounds because they achieve more deterrence than certain sanctions of the same expected value).

[45] Such chilling effect has also been documented in the context of investment into innovative technologies using copyright content. See Michael A. Carrier, *Copyright and Innovation: The Untold Story*, 2012 WIS. L. REV. 891.

[46] For example, documentary artists sometimes avoid including any copyrighted materials, even something as remote as a ringtone in the background of a scene. Nancy Ramsey, *The Hidden Cost of Documentaries*, N.Y. TIMES (Oct. 16, 2005), www.nytimes.com/2005/10/16/movies/the-hidden-cost-of-documentaries.html.

especially disadvantages risk-averse individuals who lack the deep pockets necessary to shoulder the prospective litigation costs involved with a fair use defense.[47]

Although very few American scholars favor disbanding the flexible, open standard approach of fair use doctrine, many have advocated infusing the doctrine with additional certainty. Examples include hybrid approaches of rules and standards where rules provide a statutory "minimal" safe harbor in copyright law in combination with a balancing test that governs potential exempted uses of copyrighted content that are outside of the bright line rules of the safe harbor. By explicitly stating a number of quantifiable permitted uses, predictable outcomes are promoted, while at the same time leaving flexibility for exempted uses outside of the safe harbor.[48]

Other more indirect approaches that seek to moderate the unintended side effects of "copyright exemption uncertainty" include proposals of copyright fee shifting against copyright holders that are unresponsive to licensing requests[49] and to withhold injunctions and limit statutory damage awards in close but unsuccessful fair use cases.[50]

4.3 *Rent Seeking*

The economic insights on standards and rules also highlight a tradeoff between the benefits of open standards (flexibility) and bright line rules (certainty). This comparative analysis is further complicated when considering the susceptibility to rent seeking.

Copyright rule exemptions are determined *ex ante* by legislators. As a result, bright line rules are likely to be subject to more intensive lobbying. The process of enumerating statutory exemptions sets out a specific timeline and target to stakeholders. By contrast, the contours of open-ended standards are set *ex post* by an independent judiciary. This is an important distinction. While the scope of copyright rule–based copyright exemptions is determined by the political influence of copyright stakeholders, copyright exemption standards will evolve based on the dynamics of litigation and the resulting judicial precedent. The influence of any particular stakeholder under either form of copyright exemption will be determined on its ability to manage either the legislative or judicial evolution of copyright exemptions.[51]

[47] Specifically, the argument is that the unpredictability of the doctrine typically induces risk-averse users of copyrighted content to obtain potentially superfluous licenses from content owners in order to minimize the risks associated with statutory damages in copyright law. John E. Calfee & Richard Craswell, *Some Effects of Uncertainty on Compliance with Legal Standards*, 70 Va. L. Rev. 965, 966 ("If the legal standard is uncertain, even actors who behave 'optimally' in terms of overall social welfare will face some chance of being held liable because of the unpredictability of the legal rule."). *See* James Gibson, *Risk Aversion and Rights Accretion in Intellectual Property Law*, 116 Yale L.J. 882 (2007). *See also* Molly Shaffer Van Houweling, *Distributive Values in Copyright*, 83 Tex. L. Rev. 1535 (2005) (discussing distributive side effects of fair use). *See generally* Uri Weiss, *The Regressive Effect of Legal Uncertainty* (Tel Aviv Univ. Law Faculty Papers, Paper No. 30, 2005), https://law.bepress.com/cgi/viewcontent.cgi?article=1030&context=taulwps (arguing that a shift from a certainty legal regime to an uncertainty legal regime transfers wealth from risk-averse parties to risk-neutral parties via settlements).

[48] Parchomovsky & Goldman, *supra* note 36, at 1511. ("We propose that for any literary work consisting of at least one hundred words, the lesser of fifteen percent or three hundred words may be copied without the permission of the copyright holder.") *Id.* at 1528. *See* Lawrence Lessig, Free Culture 295 (2004) (advocating for clearer and narrower lines demarcating the scope of protection for derivative works); Joseph P. Liu, *Regulatory Copyright*, 83 N.C. L. Rev. 87, 151–52 (2004) (suggesting that the Copyright Office could be given the regulatory authority to promulgate rules and safe harbors).

[49] Peter S. Menell & Ben Depoorter, *Using Fee Shifting to Promote Fair Use and Fair Licensing*, 102 Calif. L. Rev. 53 (2014).

[50] Pamela Samuelson, *Possible Futures of Fair Use*, 90 Wash. L. Rev. 815 (2015).

[51] While legislative processes are traditionally considered more biased, litigation and settlement dynamics are also susceptible to capture. The classic treatment is Marc Galanter, *Why the "Haves" Come Out Ahead: Speculations on the Limits of Legal Change*, 9 Law & Soc'y Rev. 95 (1974).

2

Self-Actualization and the Need to Create As a Limit on Copyright

Christopher S. Yoo[*]

INTRODUCTION

Personhood theory figures prominently in virtually every list of justifications for intellectual property in general[1] and copyright in particular.[2] Typically ascribed to the philosophical ideas of Georg William Friedrich Hegel and Immanuel Kant, this theory posits that authors have such deep connections with their creations that respect for their sense of self requires giving them a degree of ongoing control over those works.[3] In essence, works are treated as extensions of the author's person.[4] As such, certain types of interference with those works would be tantamount to intruding on a part of the author's body.

The most common legal embodiment of personhood theory in copyright law are so-called moral rights, widely recognized in continental Europe and incorporated into the 1928 revision to the Berne Convention for the Protection of Literary and Artistic Works.[5] Although the details vary from jurisdiction to jurisdiction, in general moral rights give authors control over "whether, when, by whom, and in what manner her work is presented to the public."[6]

[*] A longer version of this article is published as "Rethinking Copyright and Personhood," University of Illinois Law Review 1039 (2019).

[1] *See, e.g.*, Robert P. Merges, Peter S. Menell, & Mark A. Lemley, Intellectual Property in the New Technological Age 7–12 (2018); Stephen Breyer, *The Uneasy Case for Copyright: A Study of Copyright in Books, Photocopies, and Computer Programs*, 84 Harv. L. Rev. 281, 289–91 (1970); William Fisher, *Theories of Intellectual Property*, *in* New Essays in the Legal and Political Theory of Property 168, 171–72, 189–92 (Stephen R. Munzer ed., 2001); Seanna Valentine Shiffrin, *Intellectual Property*, *in* 2 A Companion to Contemporary Political Philosophy 653, 660 (Robert E. Goodin et al. eds., 2d ed. 2007).

[2] *See, e.g.*, Linda J. Lacey, *Of Bread and Roses and Copyrights*, 1989 Duke L.J. 1532, 1542 ("[W]orks of art are created through a person's mental labor, and thus embody more of her individual essence of being than works created through routine physical labor. Since artistic works are part of an artist's very identity, she never should be completely separated from the work.").

[3] *See, e.g.*, 1 John Henry Merryman & Albert E. Elsen, Law, Ethics, and the Visual Arts 145 (2d ed. 1987); Edward J. Damich, The Right of Personality: A Common-Law Basis for the Protection of the Moral Rights of Authors 1, 26–29 (1988); Neil Netanel, *Copyright Alienability Restrictions and the Enhancement of Author Autonomy: A Normative Evaluation*, 24 Rutgers L.J. 347, 359–61, 374–77 (1993).

[4] For an early statement, *see* Martin A. Roeder, *The Doctrine of Moral Right: A Study in the Law of Artists, Authors and Creators*, 53 Harv. L. Rev. 554, 557 (1940) ("When an artist creates, he does more than bring into the world a unique object having only exploitive possibilities; he projects into the world part of his personality and subjects it to the ravages of public use.").

[5] Berne Convention for the Protection of Literary and Artistic Works, art. 6*bis*, Sept. 9, 1886, 828 U.N.T.S. 221.

[6] Netanel, *supra* note 3, at 350. Although the term "moral rights" follows the French term *droit moral*, the concept is more accurately captured by the German term *Urheberpersönlichkeitsrecht*, which means author's rights of personality.

The result is a strong vision of copyright that gives initial authors near-absolute control over many aspects of copyright protection, including derivative works, to the exclusion of audiences and follow-on authors.[7] In many cases, personhood interests are so strong as to render moral rights inalienable.[8] In addition, the traditional approach to personhood theory values creative works only as static artifacts. The role of creativity in developing personality is limited to how the works are treated after they have been created and accords no role to the process of how works are created.

I believe that the conventional wisdom takes far too narrow a perspective on the relationship between copyright and personhood. By focusing exclusively on how creative works are treated after they have been created, the conventional wisdom ignores a broader range of ways, first suggested by the aesthetic writings of Kant and Friedrich Schiller, that creativity can develop personality. Since then, a vibrant literature in psychology, aesthetics, and philosophy has arisen that explores how the heuristic process of creating works can play a key role in self-actualization. A more encompassing conception of the relationship between personhood and creativity would regard creative works as more than mere repositories of personality and would examine how the process of creation itself can develop personality.

Reconceptualizing personhood-based theories of copyright in this manner provides a number of important insights. As an initial matter, the broader approach provides a personality-based justification for taking into account the interests of follow-on authors in using the creative process to develop their own personalities. To the extent that creativity necessarily builds on and extends the preexisting corpus of creative works, such a theory would provide an affirmative basis for insisting that follow-on authors have sufficient access to the existing corpus of prior works.

If this were all that were necessary, personhood theory would yield only a right of access for personal uses that omitted any right to share any derivative works created in this manner with anyone else. To the extent, however, that creativity must have an audience in order to be truly self-actualizing, this new approach would provide a basis for a right to disseminate works created in this manner notwithstanding the fact that they borrow from prior works.

The broader approach to personality also offers a possible response to one of the criticisms of existing copyright scholarship, which is the failure to provide a clear, affirmative theory of the public domain.[9] Indeed, even public domain advocates concede that the public domain

Id. at 383 n.162; *accord* Cyrill P. Rigamonti, *The Conceptual Transformation of Moral Rights*, 55 Am. J. Comparative L. 67, 92 (2007) (using the shorter form, *Persönlichkeitsrecht*).

[7] *See, e.g.*, Barbara Friedman, Note, *From Deontology to Dialogue: The Cultural Consequences of Copyright*, 13 Cardozo Arts & Ent. L.J. 157, 169 (1994) ("[M]odern commentators have for the most part used Hegel to defend near-absolute copyright protections, including derivative rights.").

[8] *See* Rigamonti, *supra* note 6, at 98 (tracing inalienability to the influence of 1 Otto von Gierke, Deutsches Privatrecht 756 (1895)). For a review of the inalienability of moral rights, *see* Neil Netanel, *Alienability Restrictions and the Enforcement of Author Autonomy in United States and Continental Europe Copyright Law*, 12 Cardozo Arts & Ent. L.J. 1, 48–77 (1994).

[9] Most trenchantly, Edward Samuels asks whether "the public domain [is] simply whatever is left over the after various tests of legal protection have been applied?" or whether the public domain is animated by "some compelling public policy or legal principle, that gives it a life of its own, that would tend to attribute positive aspects to it," only to conclude "that there is no such animal: the public domain is simply whatever remains after all methods of protection are taken into account." Edward Samuels, *The Public Domain in Copyright Law*, 41 J. Copyright Soc'y U.S.A. 137, 137–38 (1993); *accord id.* at 149 (concluding, after reviewing the proffered affirmative justifications for the public domain, that "it would appear that there simply is no such general theory"); *see also* Edward Samuels, *The Public Domain Revisited*, 36 Loy. L.A. L. Rev. 389, 391 (2002) (reaffirming Samuels's belief that "what I said in 1993 is essentially still correct"); Vincenzo Vinciguerra, *Contributing to the Understanding of the Public Domain*, 24 J. Marshall J. Computer & Info. L. 411, 453 (2006) (noting that "the sum of the very different approaches and theories contribute to an image of the public domain as an 'empty box,' capable of every form and meaning, and thus, with no defined form altogether").

remains defined largely in negative terms[10] and recognize the need for better articulation of affirmative theories of the public domain.[11] The revised personhood-based justification for copyright offers a basis for identifying a core of creative material that must remain in the public domain if individuals are to develop their sense of self.

Any theory providing an affirmative justification for copyright necessarily carries with it implicit limits. The reconceptualized personhood-based theory of copyright is no exception. As an initial matter, the scholarship on which it is based strongly contends that in order to be self-actualizing, creativity must exist as an end unto itself and not be instrumentally motivated to realize other objectives. This commitment strongly militates against extending the right of access and dissemination to works that are commercial in nature. It supports broader rights of access for educational purposes and more limited rights for nonchildren.

Moreover, the fact that the interests of follow-on authors must be balanced against the interests of initial authors dictates that any right of dissemination must be restricted only to the amount necessary for authors to develop their personalities. To conclude otherwise would avoid the problem of privileging the interests of initial authors over all others only to fall into the opposite trap of focusing exclusive attention on the interests of follow-on authors.

The result is a reconceptualization of personhood-theory of copyright that is more consistent with the philosophical foundations on which personhood theory is traditionally based and that takes into account a broader range of mechanisms through which creative works can promote self-actualization. It supports an affirmative basis for recognizing a right of access (and perhaps dissemination) by follow-on authors, while simultaneously balancing them against the interests of initial authors.

The chapter is organized as follows: Section 1 examines the aesthetic tradition, exploring the role that creativity serves in developing a person's faculties and personality, taking as its starting point the seminal work of Kant and Schiller exploring the role that play (*Spiel*) performs in creating personality. Although Kant and Schiller offered a passive vision of play, in which audiences simply contemplate great works of art, later psychologists, aestheticians, and philosophers articulated a more active vision in which individuals actively engage in the creative process.[12] It culminates in a theory that recognizes that individual self-actualization may depend on people becoming authors themselves. Drawing on the work recognizing that creativity often

[10] *See* James Boyle, *Foreword: The Opposite of Property*, LAW & CONTEMP. PROBS. Winter/Spring 2003, at 1, 30 ("The term 'public domain' is generally used to refer to material that is unprotected by intellectual property rights . . . ."); Jessica Litman, *The Public Domain*, 39 EMORY L.J. 965, 968, 976 (1990) (describing the public domain as "a commons that includes those aspects of copyrighted works which copyright does not protect" and "the realm comprising aspects of copyrighted works that copyright does not protect"); Tyler T. Ochoa, *Origins and Meanings of the Public Domain*, 28 U. DAYTON L. REV. 215, 217 (2002) ("Often the public domain is defined in terms of what it is not.").

[11] *See* Yochai Benkler, *Free As the Air to Common Use: First Amendment Constraints on Enclosure of the Public Domain*, 74 N.Y.U. L. REV. 354, 361–62 (1999) ("The particular weakness of the traditional definition of the public domain is that it evokes an intuition about the baseline, while not in fact completely describing it."); James Boyle, *Cultural Environmentalism and Beyond*, LAW & CONTEMP. PROBS. Spring 2007, at 5, 8 n.11 (recognizing that "we do need a better theory of the public domain," while acknowledging that the result may be multiple, overlapping theories).

[12] Other scholars have explored how play can shape personality. Julie Cohen views play as the result of interactions between the "networked self" and the cultural and architectural context in which it is situated. JULIE E. COHEN, CONFIGURING THE NETWORKED SELF: LAW, CODE, AND THE PLAY OF EVERYDAY PRACTICE 3–5, 32–33, 50–57, 82, 225–29 (2012). Madhavi Sunder sees play as an important part of a participatory culture. MADHAVI SUNDER, FROM GOODS TO A GOOD LIFE: INTELLECTUAL PROPERTY AND GLOBAL JUSTICE 71–73 (2012). This chapter views play as an intrinsic motivation that emanates entirely from the individual and is not shaped by extrinsic considerations. Examining play through the lens of philosophy, psychology, and aesthetics also provides normative content to the concept of play, which addresses one of the central limitations of Cohen's work. *See* Niva Elkin-Koren, *Affordances of Freedom: Theorizing the Rights of Users in the Digital Era*, 6 JERUSALEM REV. LEGAL STUD. 96, 103–04 (2012).

builds on prior works, this theory suggests that individual self-development may require a degree of access to the preexisting corpus of creative works. It then explores whether, in addition to being created, creative works must be read or shared with a community in order to play a role in developing one's sense of personality, which would in turn support a right of dissemination.

Section 2 explores the insights this reconceptualization yields for a personhood-based theory of copyright, discusses how it recognizes a broader range of ways that creativity develops personality, takes into account the interests of follow-on authors, and provides an affirmative theory of the public domain. It also examines the limitations implicit in the theory, discussing its emphasis on noncommercial and educational activity and providing for limits to any associated rights of dissemination.

1 TOWARD A BROADER CONCEPTION OF PERSONHOOD AND CREATIVE WORKS

In focusing narrowly on the extent to which a finished work of art embodies its creator's personality, the conventional wisdom applying personhood theory to copyright ignores the other ways that creative works can contribute to a given person's sense of self. Most importantly, creative works are important not just as artifacts that are extensions of the will of their creators. Examining German aesthetic theory rather than property theory makes clear that the heuristic experience of engaging with creative works can also promote personality. This insight is perhaps best embodied in the German aesthetic concept of play (*Spiel*), which, in the classic German dualist tradition, serves to unify the conflict between a person's rational and sensual impulses.[13] Although Kant's and Schiller's vision of play involved passive contemplation of creative works, later psychologists, aesthetic scholars, and philosophers explored how creating works can play an essential role in promoting self-actualization.

Recognizing the importance of engaging in creative activity does not by itself determine the proper scope of copyright protection. Indeed, if creativity were the sole product of the author's imagination, each person could simply pursue their own self-actualization without needing any extrinsic resources. To the extent that creative works are adaptations from the extant corpus of creative works, personhood theories arguably support structural copyright law to give individuals sufficient access to prior works to achieve self-actualization. Moreover, to the extent that such works must be read by others or be shared with a community in order to be meaningful, this theory arguably supports a right of dissemination.

A *Creativity and Self-Actualization through Play*

The fonts of modern theories of how creativity can develop personality are the work of Kant and Schiller.[14] Although many developmental psychologists focus on the consequentialist aspects of play,[15] such as a release of excess energy,[16] a safety value for discharging pent-up emotions,[17] or

[13] For an early work that hinted at this idea without developing it, *see* David Lange, *At Play in the Fields of the Word: Copyright and the Construction of Authorship in the Most-Literate Millennium*, LAW & CONTEMP. PROBS., Spring 1992, at 139.

[14] MIHAI SPARIOSU, DIONYSUS REBORN: PLAY AND THE AESTHETIC DIMENSION IN MODERN PHILOSOPHICAL AND SCIENTIFIC DISCOURSE (1989).

[15] For a survey, *see* Dorothy W. Jackson & Henry R. Angelino, *Play as Learning*, 13 THEORY INTO PRACTICE: VALUE OF PLAY FOR LEARNING 317, 318–20 (1974).

[16] Herbert Spencer.

[17] *See* Konrad Lange, *Illusion in Play and Art*, *in* A MODERN BOOK OF ESTHETICS 5 (Melvin Rader ed., 3d ed. 1960).

the practice of behaviors that will become useful later in life,[18] the German tradition values play for its ability to allow each person to develop her own sense of self rather than for its ability to promote other more consequentialist values.

i Kant

The seminal modern statement of how creative works can contribute to human self-actualization appears in the first part of Immanuel Kant's *Critique of Judgment* in a section entitled the "Analytic of the Beautiful."[19] According to Kant, humans experience the "feeling of life," described as the pleasurable experience of being endowed with and exercising a freedom that transcends the world and everything in it, only when they are in a "state of free play" completely free from any restraining concepts.[20] Human beings engage in free play when they make "judgments of beauty."[21] Beauty is not an inherent characteristic of an object, such as a statement about its shape or its color, which may not evoke any feelings of pleasure at all. Instead, judgments of beauty necessarily represent a person's visceral reactions to the object.[22]

In addition, judgments of beauty are distinct from statements of preference, which reflect the speaker's appetites and interests. Although such statements also refer to subjective experiences of pleasure produced by objects, the desire to consume or appropriate an object reflects what Kant calls an "interest" in the object. Having an interest in an object makes a person dependent on it.[23] This need draws the person along in a way that makes that person not completely free. It is only when a person's "wants" have been "appeased" that such a statement constitutes a true judgment of beauty.[24]

Judgments of beauty are also distinct from judgments of moral duty, such as the classic Kantian categorical imperative. Kant writes, "Where the moral law speaks, there is no longer, objectively, a free choice as regards what is to be done."[25] Only judgments that are exercised independently of reason and desires produce the pleasure associated with judgments of beauty. Indeed, judgments of beauty are inherently not rule-bound, since there is no rule about what is beautiful and what is not. Thus Kant concludes that art is "genuine only if it is autonomous."[26]

Instead, judgments of beauty reflect an "entirely disinterested satisfaction" that is a feeling of wholeness and integrity that is fully gratified merely by observing the object.[27] It is only when people are unconstrained by wants or rules that their cognitive faculties are in a state of free play,[28] which Kant describes as "purposiveness without purpose."[29] Indeed, conceived in this manner, aesthetic pleasure is the pleasure of freedom itself.

Although judgments of beauty are inherently subjective, the fact that they are disinterested and independent of individual preferences creates the potential for those judgments to be shared by others as well. Kant regarded judgments of beauty as invitations to others to recognize this

[18] *See* KARL GROOS, THE PLAY OF MEN (1908).

[19] IMMANUEL KANT, CRITIQUE OF JUDGMENT (J. H. Bernard trans., Hafner Publ'g Co. 1951) (1790). The discussion that follows draws on Anthony Kronman, *Is Poetry Undemocratic?*, 16 GA. ST. L. REV. 311, 318–26 (1999).

[20] KANT, *supra* note 19, at 52.

[21] *Id.* at 42.

[22] *Id.* at 56.

[23] *Id.* at 43.

[24] *Id.* at 44.

[25] *Id.* at 45.

[26] *Id.* at 62.

[27] *Id.* at 45.

[28] *Id.* at 52.

[29] *Id.* at 62, 68.

same pleasurable power in themselves.[30] Indeed, every judgment of beauty contains an aspiration toward universality that is missing from mere statements of preference or personal taste, carrying with it the expectation that others can and ought to share that judgment.[31] Sharing a judgment of beauty that has the potential to be universally communicable with others who possess the same ability to experience this freedom for themselves creates a shared experience that goes beyond two people reaching the same conclusion after conducting the same scientific experiment. The anticipated pleasure of being in the company of one's equals and in communication with them gives rise to the pleasure that Kant calls "sociability."[32]

ii Schiller

Kant's work prompted a response from Schiller. Best known as the second-leading figure of German literature (behind only Goethe), Schiller has long been overlooked as an aesthetic theorist. His early work directly challenged Kant's subjective vision of aesthetic taste, laying out a theory of art "based on principles."[33] Schiller defined beauty as the result of harmony between opposing forces: the physical and the moral, duty and inclination. He described this harmony as the *Schöne seele* ("beautiful soul"), which is the human product of the synthesis or harmony of opposing drives reconciled through a process of aesthetic education.[34]

In his *Aesthetic Letters*, Schiller focuses explicitly on the concept of play as the means for reconciling these conflicting drives. In explaining his theory of aesthetics as the path to freedom, Schiller discusses the primary elements of human experience as "impulses" (*Triebe*).[35] The form impulse (*Formtrieb*) reflects the tendency of the mind toward rational explanations and structure, while the material or sensual impulse (*Stofftrieb*) looks to concrete facts for its explanations of the world around it.[36]

The play impulse (*Spieltrieb*) is the aesthetic drive that brings these opposing drives together and holds them in tension.[37] The ultimate form of play, he states, is in contemplating the beautiful, the process described above through which the viewer can temporarily engage both drives at once, allowing moral and physical constraints to cancel each other out in a way that sets the psyche free.[38] Thus, for Schiller, the ability to play is representative of freedom. Indeed, "man ... is only fully a human being when he plays."[39] Rather than degrading beauty to a mere frivolity, the term "play" is intended to connote liberation.

Together, Kant and Schiller emphasized the importance of the idea of play in the human experience. Under this conception, play is undertaken for its own sake, which stands in stark contrast to the consequentalist visions of play that view it as an outlet for excess or compensation for deficient energy, practice for adult life, a mechanism for the assimilation of information, or some other instrumental purpose.[40] Instead, play develops the sense of self directly and is valued for itself.

30 Kronman, *supra* note 19, at 326.
31 Kant, *supra* note 19, at 59.
32 *Id.* at 139.
33 Friedrich Schiller, On the Aesthetic Education of Man in a Series of Letters, letter 26 (Reginald Snell trans., 1954) (1793).
34 *Id.* letter 12.
35 *Id.*
36 *Id.*
37 *Id.* letter 15.
38 *Id.*
39 *Id.*
40 *See supra* notes 15–18 and accompanying text.

B Toward a More Active Vision of Creativity through Play

What is particularly striking about Kant's and Schiller's views is the passiveness of their vision of play. Under this conception, play involved the appreciation of great works of art that could only be created by great masters. This so-called Romantic vision of authorship does not recognize any value to individuals' efforts to author creative works on their own, a position criticized for its attempt to justify privileging the positions of authors.[41]

Later theorists would develop more active visions of play. Most important for our purposes are the psychologists, aesthetic theorists, and philosophers who have explored the deep connections between creating expressive works and the development of personality.

i Psychology: Maslow, Rogers, and Self-Determination Theory

Psychology provides perhaps the strongest foundation for the important role that individual authorship of creative works can play in the development of personality. One prominent example is Abraham Maslow's celebrated study on the hierarchy of needs, which posited that humans are motivated by the drive to satisfy five basic needs.[42] Only after the more fundamental needs are satisfied can individuals seek to satisfy needs located higher in the hierarchy.[43] At the top of the hierarchy is the need for self-actualization, which "is not necessarily a creative urge although in people who have any capacities for creation it will take this form."[44]

Maslow's early work speaks of creative expression as if it were the unique province of artistic people,[45] suggesting that artists find the drive to create so strong that it is never satisfied.[46] His later work breaks from this limited vision of creativity, emphasizing that self-actualizing creativity was not limited to the artistic class by drawing a distinction between "special-talent creativeness" and "self-actualizing creativeness."[47] Broadening the conception of creativity permits Maslow to recast creativity as "a fundamental characteristic, inherent in human nature, a potentiality given to all or most human beings at birth."[48] Under this revised vision, cooks, hostesses, homemakers, social service workers, and clinical psychiatrists can all be creative in their own way and Maslow noted that "a first-rate soup is more creative than a second-rate painting, and that, generally, cooking or parenthood or making a home could be creative while poetry need not be."[49]

41 Indeed, a leading scholar has attributed this in large part to Schiller's desire for financial self-sufficiency and his frustration at Germany's failure to enact meaningful copyright protection. *See* MARTHA WOODMANSEE, AUTHOR, ART, AND THE MARKET: REREADING THE HISTORY OF AESTHETICS 59 (1994) (discussing Schiller's desire to promote his own self-sufficiency by promoting German adoption of copyright law); Anne Barron, *Kant, Copyright and Communicative Freedom*, 31 LAW & PHIL. 1, 26 (2012) (noting that "Kant's major concern in the 1785 Essay is in fact to legitimize the book trade ... and the profits that may be realized from it").

42 Specifically, these needs are physiological, safety, love, esteem, and self-actualization. Abraham Maslow, *A Theory of Human Motivation*, 50 PSYCH. REV. 370 (1943). He developed it further in ABRAHAM MASLOW, MOTIVATION AND PERSONALITY 80–92 (1954).

43 Maslow, *supra* note 42, at 394.

44 *Id.* at 383.

45 Maslow, *supra* note 42, at 382 ("A musician must make music, an artist must paint, a poet must write, if he is to be ultimately happy. What a man *can* be, he *must* be. This need we may call self-actualization.").

46 *Id.* at 386 ("There are other, apparently innately creative people in whom the drive to creativeness seems to be more important than any other counter-determinant. Their creativeness might appear not as self-actualization released by basic satisfaction, but in spite of lack of basic satisfaction.").

47 A. H. Maslow, *Creativity in Self-Actualizing People*, *in* CREATIVITY AND ITS CULTIVATION 83, 85 (Harold H. Anderson ed., 1959), *reprinted in* ABRAHAM MASLOW, TOWARD A PSYCHOLOGY OF BEING 135, 137 (2d ed. 1968); *and* ABRAHAM H. MASLOW, MOTIVATION AND PERSONALITY 158, 160 (3d ed. 1987).

48 *Id.* at 137.

49 *Id.* at 136.

He "learned to apply the word 'creative' … not only to products but also to people in a characterologicial way, and to activities, processes, and attitudes."[50] Indeed, self-actualizing creativeness "stresses first the personality rather than its achievements, considering these achievements to be epiphenomena emitted by the personality and therefore secondary to it."[51] Creative people "are all integrators, able to bring separates and even opposites together into unity."[52] The "inner integration of the person" is what permits creativeness to be "constructive, synthesizing, unifying, and integrative."[53] Indeed, "the creativity of [Maslow's] subjects seemed to be an epiphenomenon of their greater wholeness and integration."[54]

Maslow finds creativity "hard to define because it seems to be synonymous with health itself" and "almost synonymous with, or a *sine qua non* aspect of, or a defining characteristic of, essential humanness.[55] Although his later work adopts a similar tone,[56] it implies a more causal relationship between creativity and self-actualization, suggesting that creative expression should be part of any educational curriculum "not so much for turning out artists or art products, as for turning out better people," because the creative process plays a key role allowing people to "become full human beings" and to "move toward actualizing the potentialities that they have."[57] Maslow further describes how during "the inspirational phase of creative furore," the creative person "loses his past and his future" and becomes "utterly lost in the present."[58] When people create, they are "then *most* integrated, unified, all of a piece, one-pointed, totally organized in the service of the matter-at-hand."[59] "Creativeness is therefore systemic; i.e., a whole – or Gestalt – quality of the whole person"[60] that allows "the fusion of the person and his world."[61] It is at these moments when people are "most fully realizing themselves, most mature and evolved, most healthy, when, in a word, they are most fully human."[62]

Carl Rogers similarly regards creativity as a reflection of "man's tendency to actualize himself, to become his potentialities."[63] "It is this tendency which is the primary motivation for creativity as the organism forms new relationships to the environment in its endeavor more fully to be itself."[64] The motivation is intrinsic, not extrinsic. Although creativity may be socially beneficial, "the individual creates primarily because it is satisfying to him, because this behavior is felt to be self-actualizing."[65] Creativity is not the unique province of great works, applying equally to "creating new formings of one's personality in psychotherapy" as to "painting a picture,

50 *Id.* at 137.
51 *Id.* at 145.
52 *Id.* at 140.
53 *Id.*
54 *Id.* at 141; *see also id.* at 144 (arguing for increased emphasis "on the role of integration (or self-consistency, unity, wholeness) in the theory of creativeness").
55 *See id.* at 145.
56 Abraham H. Maslow, *The Creative Attitude*, 3 The Structurist 4, 4 (1963) ("My feeling is that the concept of creativeness and the concept of a fully-human person seem to be coming closer and closer together, and may perhaps turn out to be the same thing.").
57 *Id.* at 4.
58 *Id.* at 6.
59 *Id.* at 9.
60 *Id.*
61 *Id.* at 10.
62 *Id.* at 6; *see also* A. H. Maslow, *Emotional Blocks to Creativity*, 14 J. Indiv. Psych. 51 (1958) (describing how creativity allows the fusion of people's primary processes, which are unconscious and unbounded) and their secondary processes, which are conscious, rational and more constrained, thereby achieving the unity that characterizes self-actualized people).
63 Carl R. Rogers, Toward a Theory of Creativity, 11 Etc.: Rev. Gen. Semantics 249, 251 (1954).
64 *Id.* at 252.
65 *Id.*

composing a symphony, devising new instruments of killing, developing a scientific theory, [or] discovering new procedures in human relationships."[66] In short, creativity is a capacity that exists in every individual.

Rogers expands on these thoughts in his later work. Like Maslow's self-actualized person, Rogers views his ideal "fully functioning person" as a creative person "from whom creative products and creative living emerge."[67] In a later book chapter based on this article, he concludes that "a person who is involved in the directional process which I have termed 'the good life' is a creative person."[68] Rogers in turn defines the good life as "the process of movement in a direction which the human organism selects when it is inwardly free to move in any direction, and the general qualities of this selected direction appears to have a certain universality."[69]

These themes have found modern expression in the Self-Determination Theory (SDT) developed by Edward Deci and Richard Ryan[70] and extended to copyright by Terry Fisher.[71] SDT represents a modern version of theories that regard human behavior as motivated by the need to satisfy innate psychological needs rather than serving instrumental goals.[72] In particular, SDT posits that humans are motivated by the need to fulfill three psychological needs: competence, relatedness, and autonomy.[73]

In focusing exclusively on psychological needs, SDT excludes behaviors motivated by physiological needs.[74] In addition, SDT focuses on intrinsically motivated activities, defined as "those that individuals find interesting and would do in the absence of operationally separable consequences,"[75] such as "[a] man who, in the evening, sits at the keyboard and begins to play a piece of music, may become lost in its beauty and experience great pleasure."[76] Deci and Ryan note that "intrinsic motivation is associated with better learning, performance, and well-being."[77] Promoting intrinsic motivation in turn encourages creativity,[78] whereas introduction of external motivations reduces both the sense of self-determination and creativity.[79] Interestingly, Deci and Ryan argue that individuals can internalize extrinsic motivations in ways that are consistent with need satisfaction so that they in turn become part of their own intrinsic motivation.[80]

* * *

66 *Id.* at 250.

67 Carl R. Rogers, *The Concept of the Fully Functioning Person*, 1 Psychotherapy: Theory, Res. & Prac. 17, 23 (1963), *reprinted in* Carl R. Rogers, On Becoming a Person: A Therapist's View of Psychotherapy 183, 193 (1961). Maslow recognized the connection as well. A. H. Maslow, *A Holistic Approach to Creativity*, *in* Climate for Creativity: Report of the Seventh National Research Conference on Creativity 287, 288 (Calvin W. Taylor ed., 1971).

68 Rogers, supra note 67, at 193.

69 *Id.* at 187.

70 *See* Edward L. Deci & Richard M. Ryan, *The "What" and the "Why" of Goal Pursuits: Human Needs and Self-Determination of Behavior*, 11 Psych. Inq. 227 (2000).

71 William W. Fisher III, *The Implication for Law of User Innovation*, 94 Minn. L. Rev. 1417, 1465 (2010).

72 Deci & Ryan, *supra* note 70, at 227, 231.

73 *Id.* at 228,

74 *Id.* at 229.

75 *Id.* at 233.

76 *Id.* at 230.

77 *Id.* at 233.

78 *Id.* at 258.

79 *Id.* at 234.

80 *Id.* at 235–39.

Together these psychologists view creativity as an innate attribute of fully self-actualized individuals. These people pursue creativity as an end unto itself. Those engaging in self-actualizing creativity become lost in the moment. Indeed, any extrinsic motivation destroys the self-actualizing quality of creativity. The focus is neither on the consequences of the art nor on the tangible output, but rather on how the process of creation itself develops the sense of self.[81]

ii Aesthetics and Education

Aesthetic theorists have similarly emphasized the role that creativity can play in developing each individual's sense of self. Aesthetician Eugene Kaelin writes that "[t]he ultimate value of aesthetic expressions" lay in "the discovery of my own personality: of those feelings (some of which are forced upon me by my environment) which correlate most clearly with my true self. The self, then, must be such as to be developed by expression."[82] R. G. Collingwood similarly notes that "an artist creates in order to get his feelings clear," which in turn imparts clarity to her psychic condition.[83]

The key role that creating works can play in personal development has led many scholars to argue that art should represent a fundamental component of every child's education.[84] Some believe artistic expression allows people to explore who they are and what makes them unique.[85] Others echo Schiller by arguing that creating art permits individuals to achieve unity of body and mind.[86] Still others contend that the release of emotion and ideas through creativity permits individuals to become more fully integrated and developed as human beings.[87] This school of thought emphasizes that the process of creation matters more than the product,[88] which has become a theme echoed by modern scholars.[89]

iii Capabilities Theory: Sen and Nussbaum

Other copyright scholars see a justification for personhood theory in the "capabilities theory" pioneered by economist Amartya Sen[90] and extended by philosopher Martha Nussbaum.[91] This approach places upon the state the obligation to provide every individual with the preconditions they need to flourish and to develop their faculties meaningfully.[92]

Although some scholars suggest that human dignity only applies to needs lower in Maslow's hierarchy and does not include copyright,[93] Nussbaum's catalogue of the key aspects of the

[81] *See, e.g.*, EDWARD L. MATTIL, THE SELF IN ART EDUCATION 1 (1972) (National Art Education Association Research Monograph #5) (citing Maslow and Rogers as the basis for theories connecting creativity and personality); Willet W. Ryder, *The Role of Art in Self-Actualization*, ART EDUC., Mar. 1987, at 22, 22, 24 (same).

[82] EUGENE F. KAELIN, ART AND EXISTENCE: A PHENOMENOLOGICAL AESTHETIC 90 (1970).

[83] R. G. COLLINGWOOD, THE PRINCIPLES OF ART (1958).

[84] For an overview, *see* Ryder, *supra* note 81, at 22, 23–24.

[85] *See* MATTIL, *supra* note 81, at 12–13; Frances K. Heussenstamm, *Humanizing Higher Education*, ART EDUC., Mar. 1971, at 17, 18.

[86] *See* Kenneth R. Beittel, *The Teaching of Art in Relation to Body–Mind Integration and Self-Actualization in Art*, ART EDUC., Nov. 1979, at 18.

[87] *See* Florence Cane, *Art in the Life of the Child*, *in* CREATIVE EXPRESSION (Gertrude Hartman & Ann Shumarer eds., 1926).

[88] *See* VIKTOR LOWENFELD, CREATIVE AND MENTAL GROWTH (rev. ed. 1952).

[89] *See* LAWRENCE LESSIG, MAKING ART AND COMMERCE THRIVE IN THE HYBRID ECONOMY 25, 27, 79 (2008).

[90] *See* AMARTYA SEN, DEVELOPMENT AS FREEDOM 288 (1999).

[91] *See* MARTHA C. NUSSBAUM, WOMEN AND HUMAN DEVELOPMENT: THE CAPABILITIES APPROACH 78 (2000); MARTHA C. NUSSBAUM, FRONTIERS OF JUSTICE: DISABILITY, NATIONALITY, SPECIES MEMBERSHIP 70–76 (2006); Martha C. Nussbaum, *Constitutions and Capabilities: "Perception" against Lofty Formalism*, 121 HARV. L. REV. 4, 6 (2006).

[92] *See* SEN, *supra* note 90, at 38–39, 288; Nussbaum, *supra* note 91, at 6.

[93] Edwin C. Hettinger, *Justifying Intellectual Property*, 18 PHIL. & PUB. AFF. 31, 45 (1989).

human condition includes "Senses, Imagination, and Thought," which encompasses "being able to use imagination and thought in connection with experiencing and producing works and events of one's own choice, religious, literary, musical, and so forth."[94] In her other writings, Nussbaum also includes play, defined as "[b]eing able to laugh, to play, to enjoy recreational activities," as one of the ten basic capabilities.[95] Development of such capabilities is valued for its own sake and not for some consequentialist or extrinsic benefits. Legal scholars have built on the capabilities theory to argue that copyright should be shaped to ensure that people have the means to be creative.[96]

* * *

Although these theories are diverse, they share the common perspective that personal involvement in originating creative works plays a critical role in developing a sense of self. In the process, it replaces the passive role envisioned by Kant and Schiller with a broader conception that appreciates that personality is determined as much by the process of creating works as by how the results of those creative processes are treated. Moreover, these theories suggest that the law would be best served by providing the conditions necessary to allow individuals to engage in such self-actualizing behavior.

C The Cumulative Nature of Creativity

What would the obligation to enable individuals to develop their sense of self by engaging in creative activity entail? Courts and scholars have long recognized how creative works typically borrow from and extend the existing corpus of works. For example, Justice Story once noted:

> Virgil borrowed much from Homer, Bacon drew from earlier as well as contemporary minds; Coke exhausted all the known learning of his profession; and even Shakespeare and Milton, so justly and proudly our boast as the brightest originals, would be found to have gathered much from the abundant stores of current knowledge and classical studies in their days.[97]

Ralph Waldo Emerson similarly noted that "the debt is immense to past thought. None escapes it. The originals are not original. There is imitation, model, and suggestion, to the very archangels, if we knew their history."[98]

Copyright scholars have frequently noted the extent to which works borrow from prior works when making arguments to limit protection for derivative works.[99] In particular, a literature has developed critiquing the influence of the Romantic vision of authorship, which regards creativity as springing fully formed from the author's head.[100]

94 Nussbaum, Frontiers of Justice, *supra* note 91, at 76–78.

95 Martha C. Nussbaum, Creating Capabilities: The Human Development Approach 35 (2011); Martha C. Nussbaum, Women and Human Development: The Capabilities Approach 80 (2000).

96 *See* Cohen, *supra* note 12, at 21; Sunder, *supra* note 12, at 7–8, 89; Fisher, *supra* note 71, at 1466–76.

97 Emerson v. Davies, 8 F. Cas. 615, 619 (C.C.D. Mass. 1845) (No. 4,436) (Story, J.).

98 Ralph Waldo Emerson, *Quotation and Originality*, *in* 8 Collected Works of Ralph Waldo Emerson 93, 94 (Belknap 2010).

99 *See, e.g.*, Zechariah Chafee, Jr., *Reflections on the Law of Copyright*, 45 Colum. L. Rev. 503, 511 (1945); Paul Goldstein, *Derivative Rights and Derivative Works in Copyright*, 30 J. Copyright Soc'y U.S.A. 209, 218 (1983); William M. Landes & Richard A. Posner, *An Economic Analysis of Copyright Law*, 18 J. Legal Stud. 325, 332 (1989); Pierre N. Leval, *Toward a Fair Use Standard*, 103 Harv. L. Rev. 1105, 1109 (1990).

100 *See, e.g.*, James Boyle, *A Theory of Law and Information: Copyright, Spleens, Blackmail, and Insider Trading*, 80 Cal. L. Rev. 1413 (1992); Peter Jaszi, *Toward a Theory of Copyright: The Metamorphoses of "Authorship,"* 41 Duke L.J. 455 (1991); Mark Rose, *The Author as Proprietor: Donaldson v. Becket and the Genealogy of Modern Authorship*, 23

A classic example of this line of scholarship is Jessica Litman's article on *The Public Domain*, which observed that "[a]ll works of authorship, even the most creative, include some elements adapted from raw material that the author first encountered in someone else's works" and that "the very act of authorship in any medium is more akin to translation and recombination than it is to creating Aphrodite from the foam of the sea."[101] She notes that such observations in previous scholarship were almost invariably offered in passing without any analysis. Indeed, Jessica Litman has called the insight "such a truism that it has long been a cliché, invoked but not examined."[102] She proffers a more detailed description of the mechanism through which authors draw on other works subconsciously.[103] Authors create works without distinguishing whether the inspiration resulted from new ideas, past experiences, or works they have read.[104] Instead, works are the result of their entire range of experiences filtered through a "combination of absorption, astigmatism, and amnesia."[105] Rather than being mere "parasitism," borrowing is "the essence of authorship."[106] It also provides a justification for ensuring that current authors have sufficient access to the preexisting corpus of works.[107] Although a literature has emerged challenging how much Romantic authorship has actually influenced US copyright law,[108] these studies have not challenged the inherent cumulative nature of most (if not all) creative works.

Although Litman does not invoke the literature directly, Litman's theory finds intellectual support from poststructural critical theory, which responded to New Criticism's privileging of the work as a source of meaning by emphasizing the intertextual nature of all writings. For example, Northrop Frye admonished, "Poetry can only be made out of other poems; novels out of other novels."[109] Frye rejected the view that "imagines that a 'creative' poet sits down with a pencil and some blank paper and eventually produces a new poem in a special act of creation *ex nihilo*," noting that "[h]uman beings do not create in that way."[110] He critiqued the Romantic tendency "to think of the individual as ideally prior to his society."[111] Instead, all works are "born into an already existing order of words."[112] Each work of creativity can only be understood as part of a larger genre and the conventions surrounding that genre.[113]

Roland Barthes echoed the same themes when he argued that "a text does not consist of a line of words, releasing a single 'theological' meaning (the 'message' of the Author-God)."[114] Instead, "the text is a tissue of quotations drawn from the innumerable centers of culture .... [The writer's] only power is to mix writings, to counter the ones with the others, in such a way as never

REPRESENTATIONS 51 (1988); Martha Woodmansee, *The Genius and the Copyright: Economic and Legal Conditions of the Emergence of the "Author,"* 17 EIGHTEENTH-CENTURY STUD. 425 (1984).

101 Litman, *supra* note 10, at 966.

102 *Id.*

103 *Id.* at 1000–01.

104 *Id.* at 1010.

105 *Id.* at 1011.

106 *Id.* at 967.

107 *Id.* at 967, 1012.

108 *See* Lionel Bently, R. v. The Author: *From Death Penalty to Community Service*, 32 COLUM. J.L. & ARTS 1 (2008); Oren Bracha, The Ideology of Authorship Revisited: Authors, Markets, and Liberal Values in Early American Copyright, 118 YALE L.J. 186 (2008); Mark A. Lemley, *Romantic Authorship and the Rhetoric of Property*, 75 TEX. L. REV. 873 (1997) (book review).

109 NORTHROP FRYE, ANATOMY OF CRITICISM: FOUR ESSAYS 96 (1957).

110 *Id.* at 95.

111 *Id.* at 95–96.

112 *Id.* at 96.

113 *Id.* at 94–95.

114 Roland Barthes, *The Death of the Author*, *in* IMAGE – MUSIC – TEXT 142, 146 (Stephen Heath trans. 1977) (1967).

to rest on any of them."[115] Harold Bloom similarly noted, "The more deeply and widely we read, the more we become aware that good poems, novels, and essays are webs of allusion, sometimes consciously and voluntarily so, but perhaps to a greater degree without design."[116] Julia Kristeva similarly notes that "any text is a mosaic of quotations; any text is the absorption and transformation of another."[117]

Like Litman, literary theorists regard the process by which current works build on the preexisting literary corpus as being unconscious.[118] Borrowing moves from the subconscious to the conscious in Lawrence Lessig's most recent book, *Remix*. Through a series of anecdotes, Lessig celebrates what he calls Read/Write (RW) culture, in which people do not just consume culture; they add to it "by creating and re-creating the culture around them."[119] In contrast to the previous Read Only (RO) culture, in which "[a]rtists want their expression framed just as they intend it," RW culture "asks something more of the audience" in that "[i]t invites a response."[120] The more participatory culture surrounding RW culture creates a greater level of responsibility[121] and permits children to develop a higher degree of cultural literacy,[122] which Lessig equates to democratic literacy.[123] It has the added virtues of allowing kids to create their works within the context of a community and providing them with engaging subject matter to use as the building blocks for learning.[124]

Lessig further argues that "[r]emix is an essential act of RW creativity" and advocates preserving a right to quote or remix as a "critical expression of creative freedom" that should be preserved.[125] Although the Internet and digital technologies have opened remix expression to the masses,[126] they have simultaneously given creators of the original works a greater ability to prevent would-be remixers from obtaining access to their works.[127] Although Lessig sees value in professional creativity,[128] he warns that the enhanced level of control culture threatens to stifle the benefits of participation and responsibility associated with amateur creativity.[129] To correct this balance, Lessig advocates adopting a hybrid approach that permits commercial and sharing cultures to coexist.[130] While he speaks in terms of balance, his policy recommendations[131] and the concluding pages of his book[132] indicate that his primary concern is ensuring that would-be remixers enjoy sufficient access to the raw material they need to create their works.

115 *Id.*

116 Harold Bloom *in Plagiarism – A Symposium*, N.Y. TIMES LITERARY SUPP. (Apr. 9, 1982), at 413.

117 Julia Kristeva, *Word, Dialogue, and Novel*, *in* DESIRE AND LANGUAGE 64, 66 (Leon S. Roudiez ed., Thomas Gora et al. trans., 1980). The preexisting corpus of works was not the only extrinsic source of interpretation under poststructural theory. The other contextual source was the values and perspective brought by the reader. *See infra* notes 140–42 and accompanying text.

118 *See* Abigail Derecho, *Archontic Literature: A Definition, a History, and Several Theories of Fan Fiction*, *in* FAN FICTION AND FAN COMMUNITIES IN THE AGE OF THE INTERNET: NEW ESSAYS 61, 75 (Karen Hellekson & Kristina Busse eds., 2006).

119 LESSIG, *supra* note 89, at 28.

120 *Id.* at 84, 85.

121 *Id.* at 86; *accord id.* at 22–27.

122 *Id.* at 80–81, 114.

123 *Id.* at 107.

124 *Id.* at 77–82

125 *Id.* at 56.

126 *Id.* at 69, 82–83.

127 *Id.* at 98–105.

128 *Id.* at 84–85, 105–6, 291–92.

129 *Id.* at 86; *accord id.* at 22–27.

130 *Id.* at 225–49.

131 *Id.* at 253–73; *accord id.* at 109–14.

132 *Id.* at 293–94.

Fan fiction represents another prominent example of conscious borrowing from the existing corpus of works. Indeed, the intertextuality of fan fiction is not merely implicit. Instead, works of fan fiction consciously quote from a defined archive of works while simultaneously contributing back to it, claiming a specific relationship with that corpus and "pointedly locating themselves within the world."[133] Far from being protected by property interests, the world of fan fiction "allows, or even invites, writers to enter it, select specific items they find useful, make new artifacts using those found objects, and deposit the newly made work back into the source text's archive."[134] Indeed, the fact that an entire community is accessing the same preexisting corpus provides the common bond that holds the community of fan fiction writers together.[135]

* * *

Together these theories provide a basis for arguing that individual self-actualization depends on having sufficient access to the preexisting corpus of works. Some argue that the cumulative nature of creativity may be an inevitable aspect of the human condition. Others contend that even if borrowing from prior works is not inevitable, it provides certain benefits that are worth promoting as a matter of policy. When combined with the arguments discussed in Subsections A and B connecting creativity with the development of personality, both suggest that preventing follow-on authors from obtaining sufficient access to prior works can harm the development of individual personality. Support for this position does not depend on the extreme claim that no true works of independent creation exist. So long as derivative creativity remains an important source of self-actualization, the presence of examples of truly original inspiration would simply recalibrate the proper balance rather than eliminate all need for access to prior works.

D The Need for an Audience

The cumulative nature of all creativity provides one insight into ways that a richer conception of the relationship between personhood and creativity can shape copyright doctrine. If authoring creative works is both essential to self-actualization and requires access to the preexisting corpus of works, one might construct a theory of copyright that limits initial authors' ability to prevent follow-on authors from creating derivative works.

Such an argument would not necessarily lead to the broad type of access to preexisting works that advocates imagine. Some self-sufficient authors create for themselves and do not care if their work ever finds an audience. Indeed, if the act of creation itself is what develops personality, the need for self-actualization would be completely satisfied by a personal use right that did not include any right of dissemination. If anything, the emphasis that the psychological and aesthetic theories discussed above place on disinterestedness, intrinsic motivation, and living in the moment militate against such a right to disseminate.

That said, the idea that people will find fulfillment from authoring works that will never be read seems strange. Indeed, scholars as early as Aristotle recognized that "the poets merely follow

133 *See* Derecho, *supra* note 118, at 65; Rebecca Tushnet, *Payment in Credit: Copyright Law and Subcultural Creativity*, 70 LAW & CONTEMP. PROBS., Spring 2007, at 135, 143.

134 Derecho, *supra* note 118, at 65.

135 Letter from Rebecca Tushnet, Org. of Transformative Works, to US Copyright Office, Library of Cong. 7 (Feb. 2, 2009), *available at* www.copyright.gov/1201/2008/responses/organization-transformative-works-34.pdf.

their public, writing as its wishes dictate."[136] One branch of literary theory suggests that authors inevitably internalize their expectations of their readers' likely responses into their work.

i Internalizing the Audience's Expected Reaction

Anyone who has written or spoken in public appreciates how the nature of the audience can affect the content of the speech. Studies of the importance of an audience are best developed by the field of literary theory. Understanding this literature requires an appreciation of the overarching arc of scholarship in the field. Much of modern literary theory is a reaction to the New Criticism school that arose in the 1920s and 1930s, which focused on the close reading of texts as formal objects, independent of historical context.[137] A subsequent school known as Structuralism was similarly formal, but instead of focusing on words, it focused on the larger structures of signification that gave different words different meanings.[138] These schools shared a formal orientation and a desire to make interpretation more objective and scientific.

Structuralism in turn gave way to the cluster of schools that fit under the collective banner of Poststructuralism, with Barthes serving as a key transitional figure. While different flavors of Poststructuralism vary, they are based on the recognition that the structure that gives words meaning is a socially determined, cultural concept that can only be understood by analyzing the context in which words are used.[139] This accords audiences an important role in determining the meaning of texts.[140] Many theorists argue that meaning is the joint product of authors and readers.[141] More extreme versions of Poststructuralism give almost total primacy to audiences.[142]

By focusing on the social meaning of speech, approaches that regard the interpretation of texts as the joint product of authors and audiences (or even the exclusive province of audiences) are directed externally, as opposed to the more inward-focused concerns of self-development. This interactive conception of play is what animates the work of Hans-Georg Gadamer, in which the game plays the individual as much as the individual plays the game.[143] This conception of creativity as the joint product of authors and the contexts in which they operate is what animates Julie Cohen's exploration of interaction between play and creativity.[144]

There is a different vision of the need for an audience that is exclusively intrinsically motivated and not the joint product of both authors and audiences. One branch of reader-response theory recognizes how authors may anticipate and incorporate how readers are likely to receive their work. For example, Gerald Prince discusses the role of "narratees," the persons to

[136] Aristotle, Poetics, *in* The Rhetoric and the Poetics of Aristotle 219, 239 (W. Rhys Roberts & Ingram Bywater trans., Modern Library 1954) (originally published circa 350 BC); *see also* Aristotle, Rhetoric, *in* The Rhetoric and the Poetics of Aristotle, *supra*, at 54–56, 121–28 (emphasizing the importance of tailoring one's argument to the audience).

[137] *See, e.g.*, Monroe Beardsley, Aesthetics: Problems in the Philosophy of Criticism (1958); Roger Fowler, Linguistic Criticism (1986).

[138] The seminal work was Ferdinand de Saussure, Writings in General Linguistics (Carol Sanders et al. trans., 2006).

[139] *See supra* note 149 and accompanying text.

[140] For a brief overview, *see* Peter J. Rabinowitz, *Reader-Response Theory and Criticism*, *in* The Johns Hopkins Guide to Literary Theory and Criticism 606 (Michael Groden & Martin Kreiswirth eds., 1994).

[141] *See, e.g.*, Barthes, *supra* note 114.

[142] Stanley Fish, Is There a Text in This Class? The Authority of Interpretive Communities (1980). Note that not all reactions to structuralism focused on audiences. Other theorists advocated a return to focusing on authors' intentions. *See, e.g.*, E. D. Hirsch, Jr., Validity in Interpretation (1967); P. D. Juhl, Interpretation: An Essay in the Philosophy of Literary Criticism (1981).

[143] Hans-Georg Gadamer, Truth and Method 103, 105 (1960).

[144] Cohen, *supra* note 12, at 56.

whom authors are addressing their work.[145] Indeed, Prince envisions the narratee as a character (sometimes present only implicitly)[146] who exists internal to the text, rather than a reader who is outside the text.[147]

Similarly, Wolfgang Iser discusses how authors write for an "implied reader."[148] Unlike intended readers, which reflect the author's aims, and hypothetical informed readers, whose qualities are socially determined, Iser's implied reader has predispositions entirely laid down by the text itself "independent of any outside reality."[149] In contrast to the insight that "literary texts take on their reality by being read," the implied reader is "a textual structure anticipating the presence of a recipient without necessarily defining him" that "prestructures the role to be assumed by each recipient."[150] Quite aside from any actual reader, the implied reader is a "role offered by the text" that provides a "a frame of reference within which individual responses to a text can be communicated to others," thereby "provid[ing] a link between all the historical and individual actualizations of the text and mak[ing] them accessible to analysis."[151] From this perspective, even gaps that remain for readers to fill are part of the strategy of the author and thus under his control.[152]

Prince's and Iser's vision of the role of audiences is more consistent with the internal impact (rather than the external social meaning) that is the focus of personhood theory than is traditional reader-response theory. In essence, these audiences' roles in interpreting texts are internalized by the author and reified in the text. The environment does influence authors, but in a nonrecursive manner that authors internalize into their intrinsic motivations when authoring the work. Deci and Ryan noted, moreover, recursive processes often cause such external considerations to be internalized.[153]

This vision, however, begs an important question: is it enough for authors to internalize the role of the expected audience, or must the work actually be read in order for authorship to be self-actualizing? Prince's and Iser's focus on the external question of the interpretation of texts lead them not to offer an answer.

One possibility is that authors may be so self-directed and may have so completely internalized extrinsic motivations that they write for themselves and may not care if their work ever finds a real-world audience. If so, personhood theory would not imply any right of dissemination. Another possibility is suggested by game theory, which has long recognized the anticipation of the consequences of choices can cause equilibria to unravel.[154] Authors whose works are never read will find that the process of anticipating their audiences' reaction was an entirely hypothetical exercise. If they only realize this after the fact, they will have already gained the benefits with respect to self-actualization. More discerning authors who understand the overarching structure may be able to anticipate that the law will prevent them from sharing their works with others.

[145] Gerald Prince, *Introduction to the Study of the Narratee*, *in* Reader-Response Criticism 7 (Jane P. Tompkins ed., 1980) (reprinting article originally published in *Poétique* in 1973).

[146] *Id.* at 17–20, 22–23.

[147] *Id.* at 13 (concluding that indications of the nature of any particular narratee "whether explicit or indirect, should be interpreted on the basis of the text itself"); *see also* Rabinowitz, *supra* note 140, at 606.

[148] Wolfgang Iser, The Implied Reader: Patterns in Communication in Prose Fiction from Bunyan to Beckett (1974).

[149] Wolfgang Iser, The Act of Reading: A Theory of Aesthetic Response 34 (1978).

[150] *Id.*

[151] *Id.* at 36, 37–38.

[152] Rabinowitz, *supra* note 140, at 606.

[153] *See supra* note 80 and accompanying text.

[154] For the classic work, *see* Reinhard Selten, *The Chain Store Paradox*, 9 Theory & Decision 127 (1978).

This realization may demotivate certain authors, which in turn may prevent them from realizing the self-actualizing benefits of authorship.

ii Valuing Community

Another justification for the right to dissemination is implicit in the importance of community associated with remix and fan fiction cultures. Although saying that new works tend to build on prior works can justify a right of access to existing corpus, to the extent that the process is internal to the author, it does not imply any right to share those works. Consider the remix culture, which Lessig embraces because of the manner in which it promotes responsibility, cultural literacy, and the democratization of content creation.[155] These values could arguably be satisfied by a personal use right that authorizes access to prior works for private purposes but forbids any publication of those works.

Lessig's argument invokes a second conceptual premise to support a right of dissemination: the value of creating content in a community in which members create for one another and help each other learn how to create.[156] His success model is the anime subculture of Japan, in which children begin by making and sharing their own sketches with others and then are introduced to the larger subculture by an older child.[157] The result is that creators see themselves as participants in a self-supporting community.[158] Indeed, "the pleasures of production of transformative works are intrinsic to participating in a creative community rather than motivated by extrinsic financial rewards."[159]

Community plays an even more central role for fan fiction, whose participants define themselves by a shared interest in a common body of work.[160] Many discussions of fan fiction emphasize the distribution of authorship and the centrality of a community of interpreters, who are also authors.[161] Other members of the community provide feedback that helps new authors improve, with the shared desire for additional commentary on the common source material serving as the glue that holds the community together.[162] Engagement with this larger community is particularly important for younger authors, who learn from engaging with other members.[163] While many creators regard creating fan fiction "as an end in itself, and may only share their videos with a few close friends," many create in order to obtain recognition and status that can only be achieved through approbation by a community characterized by an elaborate subculture that is quite hierarchical and stratified and governed by a core group of elites.[164]

155 *See* LESSIG, *supra* note 89, at 80–81, 86–88, 107, 114.

156 *Id.* at 77.

157 *Id.* at 79.

158 *Id.* at 80.

159 Mizuko Ito, *The Rewards of Non-Commercial Production: Distinctions and Status in the Anime Music Video Scene*, FIRST MONDAY, May 3, 2010, at 4, www.uic.edu/htbin/cgiwrap/bin/ojs/index.php/fm/article/view/2968/2528.

160 Tushnet, *supra* note 135, at 7.

161 *See* Rebecca Tushnet, *Scary Monsters: Hybrids, Mashups, and Other Illegitimate Children*, 86 NOTRE DAME L. REV. 2133, 2140 (2011).

162 Tushnet, *supra* note 135, at 7; Tushnet, *supra* note 133, at 143 n.32 (discussing the value that fan fiction authors place on the "centrality of a community of interpreters" connected through "immediate feedback, constant discussions of underlying canon, and self-identification as members of a fandom based on particular source texts"); Karen Hellekson, *A Fannish Field of Value: Online Fan Gift Culture*, 48 CINEMA J. 113, 115–16 (2009) (describing how "[w]riter and reader create a shared dialogue that results in a feedback loop of gift exchange, whereby the gift of artwork or text is repetitively exchanged for the gift of reaction, which is itself exchanged, with the goal of creating and maintaining social solidarity"); Ito, *supra* note 159, at 12 (noting how elite fan fiction writers "look to their peers for ongoing feedback and critique" and "acknowledge the importance of social support within the creative community").

163 *See* Tushnet, *supra* note 135, at 7.

164 Ito, *supra* note 159, at 11–12.

The presence of community makes the dynamics surrounding fan fiction somewhat complex. Although peer production is often lauded for its democratic qualities and accessibility to everyone,[165] like all social practices, every community of peer production is embedded in a structure with its own sets of rules. In the case of fan fiction, the ability to participate in a larger community in which transformative works can be shared and can receive feedback plays a central role in constituting the subculture. This reasoning does not lead to a rule of access in all contests. Indeed, it only applies to subcultures in which the cycle of publication and feedback is central to the subculture. Moreover, the fan fiction community insists that any such sharing be noncommercial.[166] Subject to these limitations, the example of fan fiction does support a limited right of dissemination.

2 IMPLICATIONS FOR THE PERSONHOOD-BASED THEORIES OF COPYRIGHT

Reconceptualizing personhood-based theories in the manner I propose would place them on a sounder conceptual footing. Not only does it accord better with the philosophical writings on which personhood theory purports to be based. As discussed in Subsection A below, it recognizes that creativity can affect personality in more ways than just how the outputs of the process are treated after they have been created. It accommodates the interests of follow-on authors in a way that the conventional wisdom cannot. And it provides an affirmative basis for mandating access to the existing body of creative works.

While my theory does support those normative implications, at the same time, its logic suggests a number of important limitations, which I will discuss in Subsection B. Specifically, it suggests that any right of access be limited to noncommercial works, educational purposes, and only as much dissemination as necessary to serve the values of community.

A *Insights*

Adopting a broader sense of the ways that creative works can promote personhood yields a number of important insights. These insights in turn have important implications for copyright law.

i Creativity As a Process, Not an Artifact

The traditional view of personality theory takes a very narrow conception of the relationship between creative expression and personality that focuses exclusively on how works are treated after they have been created. In essence, this approach treats works as static artifacts that are mere repositories of their creators' personalities.

The revised conception adopts a broader view that recognizes that the process of creating works can also play an important role in developing personality. In so doing, it embodies a more heuristic view of creativity that focuses less on the results and more on the creative process itself.

165 *See* Lessig, *supra* note 89, at 84 (contrasting RW culture with the presence in RO culture with authoritative sources of interpretation); *id.* at 88 (arguing that RW culture "hides the hierarchy," unlike RO culture, which "emphasizes the hierarchy").

166 *See* Hellekson, *supra* note 162, at 114–15; Rebecca Tushnet, *Hybrid Vigor: Mashups, Cyborgs, and Other Necessary Monsters*, 6 I/S: J.L. & Pol'y for Info. Age 1, 3 (2008).

ii Greater Importance to Follow-On Authors

Another shortcoming of the conventional wisdom regarding personhood theory is that it places almost exclusive importance on the interests of the initial author. Indeed, the interest of the initial author is often regarded as being so strong as to convey absolute, inalienable control over derivative works.[167]

Kant's and Hegel's reluctance to recognize strong interests in derivative works acknowledges that derivative works reflect the personalities of follow-on authors as much as initial authors. Indeed, the process-oriented perspective on personhood reflected in the psychological, aesthetic, and philosophical literature shifts the focus away from creative works as static artifacts and instead reconceives of them as essential contributors to a dynamic process of self-actualization.[168]

iii An Affirmative Theory of the Public Domain

The final and most important advantage of my proposed reconceptualization of personality theory is its potential to provide an affirmative theory of the public domain, the absence of which both proponents and opponents of the trend toward broader copyright protection have widely regarded as a weakness.[169] As noted above, the public domain has often been defined as the residuum left after property rights have been defined. To the extent that property justifications are economically focused, the scope of fair use naturally contracts as technological advances reduce transaction costs.[170]

The broader conception I propose supports reforming copyright in ways that reflect the full range of ways that creative works can promote self-actualization. By recognizing how creating works both can develop personality and requires access to preexisting works, my approach to personality theory provides a justification for providing follow-on authors with access to the extant corpus of creativity.[171] To the extent that those works must be shared with others in order to be meaningful, it also supports a right of dissemination.

B Limits

At the same time any theory implies certain types of reform, it also necessarily suggests the natural limits of those reforms. These limits come in part from the internal logic of the theory and in part from factors external to the theory that cut in the opposite direction. The presence of these internal limits and countervailing considerations offer natural reference points for determining the proper scope of any reforms taken in the name of my revised vision of personhood theory.

i Intrinsicness and Noncommerciality

One major limit is the extent to which any personhood-based rights of access and dissemination must be noncommercial. Commerciality has long presented a puzzle for copyright law. Some early cases regarded the fact that any commercial use of a work presumptively falls outside of fair use.[172]

[167] *See supra* note 7 and accompanying text.

[168] *See also* COHEN, *supra* note 12, at 247.

[169] *See supra* notes 9–11 and accompanying text.

[170] *See, e.g.*, Robert P. Merges, *The End of Friction? Property Rights and Contract in the "Newtonian" World of On-Line Commerce*, 12 BERKELEY TECH. L.J. 115 (1997).

[171] For a related argument, *see* COHEN, *supra* note 12, at 246–47.

[172] *See* Sony Corp. of Am. v. Universal City Studios, Inc., 464 U.S. 417, 448 (1984).

Later cases clarified that the fact that a work is commercial in nature does not by itself disqualify derivative works from falling within fair use.[173]

The internal logic of how creating works can develop personality suggests limiting the right of access to noncommercial uses. Kant's initial exposition of how creative works can develop personality emphasized that the experience must be disinterested and independent of personal wants and needs.[174] Psychological theory emphasizes that individuals can only pursue self-actualization after their more instrumental needs have been satisfied and that such self-actualization can only occur when people live in the moment, creating for its own sake without any focus on the implications for the future.[175]

Lessig similarly focuses on the differences between commercial and gift cultures, emphasizing the differences in values[176] and observing that "price is poisonous" to reciprocal noncommercial cultures.[177] While Lessig would not limit access rights to noncommercial uses,[178] only noncommercial uses would be free, with those making commercial remixes having to pay a compulsory license fee.[179] Indeed, Lessig's recognition of the benefits associated with commercial creativity necessarily entails some type of balance.[180]

The rationale for allowing authors to share works created from other works also militates against including commercial works within its scope. As noted earlier, the fan fiction community has adopted a strong norm against commercial uses as inconsistent with the reciprocity of exchange.[181] Indeed, many regard commercial compensation as inconsistent with the reciprocal values that undergird fan fiction.[182]

The internal logic of this vision of personhood suggests limiting any access and dissemination rights to noncommercial uses, as the need for self-actualization would be satisfied by the noncommercial uses. Although some suggest that the distinction between these commercial and noncommercial uses may prove slippery,[183] personhood justifications do not support a broader set of reforms.

ii The Emphasis on Education

Another limitation implicit in some portions of the theory is an emphasis on youth-oriented education. For example, education plays a key role in Lessig's lauding the fact that remix allows children to learn through materials they find particularly interesting, noting that "[w]hen kids get to do work that they feel passionate about, kids (and, for that matter, adults) learn more and learn more effectively."[184] This sharing helps develop cultural literacy and serves as a form of apprenticeship in which they actually learn more.[185] Although Lessig does offer a nod toward adult learning, his rationale applies with special force to the education of children.

[173] *See* Campbell v. Acuff-Rose Music, Inc., 510 U.S. 569, 583–85 (1994).
[174] *See supra* note 27 and accompanying text.
[175] *See supra* notes 58, 65, 75 and accompanying text.
[176] Lessig, *supra* note 89, at 118, 144–49, 232, 239
[177] *Id.* at 149.
[178] *Id.* at 56.
[179] *Id.* at 254–56; *see also id.* at 110–14 (describing how compulsory licensing would have benefited remix culture).
[180] *See supra* note 128 and accompanying text.
[181] *See supra* note 166 and accompanying text.
[182] Hellekson, *supra* note 162, at 115.
[183] *See* Fisher, *supra* note 71, at 1433–35; Tushnet, *supra* note 166, at 3–4.
[184] Lessig, *supra* note 89, at 80.
[185] *Id.* at 81; *see also id.* at 27 (noting how John Philip Sousa celebrated amateur musicianship "because it produced a musical culture: a love for, and an appreciation of, the music he re-created, a respect for the music he played, and hence a connection to a democratic culture").

Rebecca Tushnet similarly emphasizes education when enumerating the benefits of fan fiction. Fan fiction creates "a unique opportunity for learning, personal expression, and individual autonomy."[186] Participation also enhances health so "that we should encourage these kinds of social institutions for youth."[187] Adapting preexisting stories also helps children develop cultural literacy.[188]

To the extent that these rationales emphasize youth-oriented education, they impose natural limits on the scope of any reforms implied by the theory. They would provide less support for extending rights of access and dissemination to noneducational contexts.

iii Implicit Limits to the Rights of Access and Dissemination

Lastly, saying that personhood theory implies a right of dissemination is not to say that such a right should be unlimited. On the contrary, the presence of countervailing considerations (such as the benefits of commercial authorship recognized by Lessig) suggests that any such rights be limited to the amount necessary to support self-actualization.

For example, any right to create derivative works must be balanced against protecting the rights of the initial authors. In recognizing that follow-on authors may make a sufficient contribution to justify trumping the interests of initial authors, both Kant and Hegel implicitly recognized that initial authors have personality interests that are not overcome until the interests of follow-on authors become sufficiently important.[189] Any other conclusion would sidestep the problems of giving exclusive primacy to the interests of initial authors only by falling into the opposite trap of giving exclusive primacy to the interests of follow-on authors.

The same could be said for any personhood-based right of dissemination. Recognizing that content must be shared with a community to be meaningful does not necessarily entail an unlimited right to disseminate. On the contrary, any such right would naturally be limited to the amount and the community needed for authorship to be meaningful. For example, while the role of the narratee and implied reader recognized by literary theory may require that the derivative work be read by someone in order to promote self-development, it does not necessarily require that the work be available to the broadest possible audience. Instead, the presence of competing interests dictates that the dissemination right would be limited to the smallest possible number of readers needed to allow the creative process to be self-actualizing. Similarly, any need to share creative works with a community would logically be limited to that community. It would not entail a right to disseminate works more broadly.

These inherent limits underscore the value of any good theory. Any arguments used to justify a position necessarily only go so far. The scope of the reasoning thus inevitably includes its own limitations. Proper application of personhood theory thus requires a clear understanding of why certain reforms are justified and a readiness to cease advocating for further reform after those rationales have been exhausted.

CONCLUSION

Personhood theory occupies a central place in copyright theory. Enshrined in the institution of moral rights, personhood theory is widely regarded as giving initial authors absolute, inalienable control over many aspects of their works.

[186] Tushnet, *supra* note 135, at 7.
[187] *Id.*
[188] *Id.*
[189] Georg Friedrich von Hegel, Hegel's Philosophy of Right ¶ 69 (T. M. Knox trans., Oxford 1952) (1821); Immanuel Kant, *On the Wrongfulness of Unauthorized Publication of Books*, *in* Practical Philosophy 23, 35 (Mary J. Gregor trans. & ed., 1996) (1785).

In this chapter, I have argued that the conventional wisdom about personhood and copyright justifications suffers from some fundamental problems. Focusing on the connection between the author and the work adopts too narrow a vision of the ways that creative expression contributes to personality. It fails to recognize how the process of creation can play a role that can be as important as how works are treated once they have been created. In so doing, the conventional wisdom adopts a view that focuses exclusively on initial authors without taking the interests of follow-on authors into account.

My reconceptualization of personhood theory accords better with the theory's purported philosophical roots. It adopts a broader conception of personhood that takes into account a broader range of ways that creativity can foster personal development. It takes the interests of follow-on authors seriously by embracing how creativity often builds on the corpus of prior works. In so doing, it offers an affirmative theory of why copyright law should provide access to existing works. The importance of readers and the need for authorship within a community arguably supports a right of dissemination.

Like any theory, the revised conception of personhood theory carries with it limits as well as justifications. It suggests that any such rights be limited to noncommercial and educational uses. Moreover, rights of access and dissemination should be limited to the amount necessary for follow-on authors to develop their personalities. As with any initial attempt to rethink an area of law, many of the ideas presented here are somewhat exploratory and will no doubt be refined, extended, and criticized in the future. I certainly expect that this will be the first rather than the last word in a long debate.

PART II

Internationalizing Copyright Exceptions

3

Displacing the Dominance of the Three-Step Test: The Role of Global Mandatory Fair Use

Tanya Aplin & Lionel Bently[*]

Article 10(1) of the Berne Convention[1] mandates a quotation exception that is broad in scope, one that is not limited by work, nor type of act, nor by purpose, and is only subject to the conditions in Article 10, namely, the work has been lawfully made available to the public, attribution, fair practice, and proportionality. We call this "global mandatory fair use." This overlooked norm in international copyright law is unaffected by and distinct from the three-step test and, as such, potentially dislodges its dominance.[2] In turn, this creates different possibilities for how to conceive of and assess copyright exceptions at the national level. To substantiate our argument, this chapter is structured in three parts. Section 1 outlines our underpinning contention, namely, that Article 10(1) creates a global mandatory "fair use" type obligation. Section 2 explains why this obligation is unaffected by the three-step test in international copyright law. Finally, in Section 3, we draw out the differences between Article 10(1) and the three-step test and illustrate the potential relevance of this for national law using the specific case of US "fair use."

1 THE CASE FOR GLOBAL, MANDATORY FAIR USE

The intellectual foundation of this chapter, namely that Article 10(1) Berne recognizes global mandatory fair use, is developed in detail elsewhere.[3] This section therefore presents only a summary of our argument. To begin, we set out the relevant provision. Article 10 is entitled "Certain free uses of works" and states:

* Thanks to Graeme Dinwoodie for his comments on an earlier version of this chapter. Thanks also to those who have debated with us the questions we engage with in this chapter: Richard Arnold, Graeme Austin, Jørgen Blomqvist, Kathy Bowrey, Robert Burrell, Richard Danbury, Thomas Dreier, Sevérine Dusollier, Niva Elkin-Koren, Hector Foucé, Suzy Frankel, Christophe Geiger, Daniel Gervais, Jane Ginsburg, Jonathan Griffiths, Emily Hudson, Ariel Katz, Brigitte Lindner, Makeen Makeen, Ryszard Markiewicz, Ansgar Ohly, Ruth Okediji, James Parish, Alexander Peukert, Sam Ricketson, Martin Senftleben, Anna Tischner, and Kim Weatherall. Finally, thanks to James Parish for his research assistance.

1 Berne Convention for the Protection of Literary and Artistic Works (1886, revised 1971) (hereafter "Berne").

2 Daniel J. Gervais, *Making Copyright Whole: A Principled Approach to Copyright Exceptions and Limitations*, 5 U. Ottawa L. & Tech. J. 1, 4 (2008) indicates that the three-step test "has become the single sieve through which all, or almost all, exceptions to exclusive copyright rights must pass to be compatible with the TRIPS Agreement."

3 T. Aplin & L. Bently, Global Mandatory Fair Use: The Nature and Scope of the Right to Quote Copyright Works (forthcoming 2020).

> It shall be permissible to make quotations from a work which has already been lawfully made available to the public, provided that their making is compatible with fair practice, and their extent does not exceed that justified by the purpose, including quotations from newspaper articles and periodicals in the form of press summaries.

Article 10(3) Berne adds a further requirement, providing that:

> [w]here use is made of works in accordance with the preceding paragraphs of this Article, mention shall be made of the source, and of the name of the author if it appears thereon.

The "global" impact of Article 10(1) Berne occurs because it binds all 183 Members of the Berne Union and, due to Article 9(1) of the TRIPS Agreement,[4] also binds the 163 Members of the World Trade Organization (WTO).

The "mandatory" quality of Article 10(1) Berne arises from the text "it shall be permissible."[5] The use of the word "shall" is imperative and Article 10(1) uses quite different language to that used in other exceptions. For example, Article 10(2) states, in relation to exceptions for education, that "it shall be a matter for legislation in the countries of the Union . . . to permit." Similar language is also found in Article 10*bis* in relation to reporting current events and Article 9(2), which allows exceptions to the reproduction right "in certain special cases." The language of Article 10(1) is distinct, and clearly reads as mandatory rather than permissive.

As well, the *travaux préparatoires* ("*travaux*") support this view. Although there is barely any reference to the mandatory nature of the exception in the Stockholm *travaux*,[6] the limitation is described in terms that reflect its basis in the entitlement of the user. The BIRPI Study group (1963), rejecting a prior formulation that limited the exception to short quotation, repeatedly referred to the exception as "the right to make quotations" or the "right of quotation,"[7] language which was carried through into the proposal for the Stockholm conference,[8] and which is entirely consistent with the mandatory formulation of Article 10(1). Moreover, it based its reasoning on the widespread acceptance of such a right in the "field of science."[9]

The *travaux* of the Stockholm Revision do not contain any discussion of the rationale for the mandatory status of Article 10(1), but they do indicate that it was acknowledged and accepted. Perhaps surprisingly, some resistance came from the United Kingdom, and, when the Committee of Government Experts met in Geneva in July 1965, the UK tabled an amendment that would have aligned the status of Article 10(1) with the various other exceptions recognized in the Convention, or then being proposed. However, despite receiving support from the Netherlands, the Committee of Governmental Experts rejected the UK proposal by 19 votes to 7, and a Swedish proposal to offer member states the freedom to establish conditions was likewise rejected, by 16 votes to 8.[10] The matter was not raised thereafter, but the special status of

[4] Agreement on Trade Related Aspects of Intellectual Property Rights (1994) (hereafter "TRIPS").

[5] The French, "sont licites," is perhaps even clearer, in that it indicates quotations are permitted rather than "permissible."

[6] Some of the *travaux* are recorded in two volumes: WIPO, Records of the Intellectual Property Conference of Stockholm, June 11 to July 14, 1967 (1971) (hereafter, "Records"). Other documents are retained at the World Intellectual Property Organization, referenced under its former acronym "BIRPI." We sourced these documents from series BT209 at The National Archives, Kew, England (hereafter "TNA").

[7] I Records, *supra* note 6, at 116.

[8] Document S/1, *Proposals for Revising the Substantive Copyright Provisions*, Arts. 1–20 (prepared by the government of Sweden with the assistance of BIRPI), *in* I Records, *supra* note 6, at 117.

[9] I Records, *supra* note 6, at 117.

[10] Report of the Committee of Governmental Experts, BIRPI: DA/22/33, [53]–[54], 10.

Article 10(1) was clear.[11] By way of contrast, at the Inter-Governmental Conference in June 1967, amendments were made to Article 10*bis*(2), which reenacted Article 9(2) from Brussels "to avoid the impression" that it was compulsory.[12] In its Brussels form (inherited from the Rome revision in 1928) Article 9(2) had stated, in mandatory terms, that "articles ... may be reproduced ... unless the reproduction thereof is expressly reserved," thus seemingly leaving no freedom to member states as to whether to adopt such an exception.[13] This was altered at Stockholm, but the form of Article 10(1) was left intact.

The view that the provision is mandatory also has the support of key commentators from both common and civil law countries.[14] For example, Professor Goldstein asserts categorically that "Article 10(1) ... obligates member countries to permit 'quotations ...'.".[15] Coauthoring with Goldstein, Professor Hugenholtz argues that Article 10(1) represents "the only instance of a mandatory limitation in an international copyright treaty."[16] Professors Ricketson and Ginsburg refer to Article 10(1) as the one Berne exception that comes closest to embodying a "user right" to make quotation: Article 10(1) exceptions are matters that *must*, rather than *may*, appear in national laws.[17] Professors Kur and Grosse Ruse-Khan also share this view, stating that the ordinary meaning of Article 10(1) "does not lend itself to any other understanding than that it is meant to be binding."[18] Similarly, Professor Xalabarder[19] and Professor Senftleben[20] see Article 10(1) as mandatory.

The fair "use" mandated relates to the "making of" quotations. It is a freedom that applies to all the rights granted by the Berne Union Member to copyright owners, not merely to rights,

[11] See Pierre Recht, *Should the Berne Convention Include a Definition of the Right of Reproduction?* 82 Copyright 84–85 (1965) ("The power to legislate freely on this point was removed from national legislations [*sic*], and the latter have had imposed on them a minimum below which they cannot go on the plea that the quotation must be short."). *See also* S. Gerbrandy and F. Klaver, *La Révision de la Convention de Berne*, 52 RIDA 5, 54 (1967) ("a coercive limitation on author's copyright" which member states cannot reduce). Professor Gerbrandy was on the Drafting Committee at the Stockholm Conference.

[12] Svante Bergström, Report of the Work of the Main Committee I (hereafter "Main Committee I Report"), [102], *in* II Records, *supra* note 6, at 1149.

[13] Sam Ricketson & Jane C. Ginsburg, International Copyright and Neighbouring Rights: The Berne Convention and Beyond [13.53], 800 (2006).

[14] However, it is also opposed by some commentators given the logic of Berne as setting out minimum standards for foreign authors and the principle of national treatment: *see* M. Ficsor, The Law of Copyright and the Internet 259 ff., [5.09] (2002); S. von Lewinski, International Copyright Law and Policy [5.163], 156 (2008); J. Blomqvist, Primer on International Copyright and Related Rights 159–60 (2014).

[15] Paul Goldstein, International Copyright: Principles, Law, Practice 303 (2001). *See also* G. B. Dinwoodie and R. C. Dreyfuss, A NeoFederalist Vision of TRIPS: The Resilience of the International Intellectual Property Regime 185 (2012) ("a mandatory quotation right"); Gervais, *supra* note 2, at 9, 20.

[16] Paul Goldstein and Bernt Hugenholtz, International Copyright: Principles, Law, Practice [11.4.1], 379 (2010). *See also* B. Hugenholtz and R. Okediji, *Conceiving an International Instrument on Limitations and Exceptions to Copyright*, Amsterdam Law School Legal Studies Research Paper No. 2012-43, 15–16 (March 7, 2012), http://ssrn.com/abstract=2017629.

[17] Ricketson & Ginsburg, *supra* note 13, at [13.42], 788–89.

[18] A. Kur and H. Grosse Ruse-Khan, *Enough Is Enough – The Notion of Binding Ceilings in International Intellectual Property Protection*, *in* Intellectual Property Rights in a Fair World Trade System: Proposals for Reform of TRIPS, ch. 8, 359–407, at 380 (A. Kur & M. Levin eds., 2011). *See also* A. Kur, *Of Oceans, Islands, and Inland Water – How Much Room for Exceptions and Limitations under the Three Step Test?*, 8 Rich. J. Glob. L. & Bus. 287, 290 (2009).

[19] Raquel Xalabarder, Study on Copyright Limitations and Exceptions for Educational Activities in North America, Europe, Caucasus, Central Asia and Israel SCCR/19/8, 19–20 (WIPO, November 5, 2009); R. Xalabarder, *On-line Teaching and Copyright: Any Hopes for an EU Harmonized Playground?*, *in* Copyright Law: A Handbook of Contemporary Research, ch. 15, 373–401, 397–398 (P. Torremans ed., 2007).

[20] M. Senftleben, *Quotation, Parody and Fair Use*, *in* A Century of Dutch Copyright: 1912–2012 354 (B. Hugenholtz, A. Quaedvlieg, & D. Visser eds., 2012).

which are required to be recognized under the Convention. This is evident from the language of Article 10(1) Berne which refers to "quotations from a work" without any restriction to the economic rights involved.[21] This may be contrasted with other provisions, such as Article 9(2) or Article 10*bis* Berne, which specify the economic rights to which the exception might apply (reproduction in the case of Article 9(2) and reproduction, broadcasting and communication to the public by wire in the case of Article 10*bis*). As such, Article 10(1) justifies quotation in the context of communication, performance, translation, adaptation, as well as in reproduction. It creates an exception applicable even to rights elaborated upon in later treaties, such as the making available right.[22] However, it does not extend to moral rights.[23]

Moreover, Article 10(1) applies to all works protected under the Berne Convention. It is not limited to quotation from literary or dramatic works. This is inferred from the absence of any such limitation in the words of Article 10(1), which refers to quotation from "a work" (in contrast with, e.g., Article 13(1) which allows for a compulsory license applicable to a subcategory of works, i.e., "a musical work and to the author of any words") and is confirmed by an examination of the *travaux*.[24] Nor is the ordinary meaning of the term "quotation" limited to quotation from literature: it is common to speak of quotation of art, music, and film. Countless examples exist of ordinary use of the term quotation to describe the inclusion of musical phrases in subsequent musical works,[25] performances or recordings, the inclusion of scenic incidents from one film in another,[26] the inclusion of paintings in films,[27] or architectural quotation.[28] The fact that the freedom includes the freedom to make quotations not just from texts, but also from music, artworks, architecture, and films, has important implications for our understanding of the

[21] *See* II RECORDS, *supra* note 6, at [769], 861 which envisages that quotation will apply to broadcasting of artistic works.

[22] APLIN & BENTLY, GLOBAL MANDATORY FAIR USE, *supra* note 3, at 55–57.

[23] The prevailing view is that, despite its form, the quotation right is *not* a limitation on the moral rights recognized under Art. 6*bis* Berne. In MAIN COMMITTEE I REPORT, it is recorded that "here too, as in the case of all uses of the work, the rights granted to the author under Art 6bis (moral rights) are reserved." [205] *in* II RECORDS, *supra* note 6, at 1165. *See* APLIN & BENTLY, GLOBAL MANDATORY FAIR USE, *supra* note 3, at 57–60.

[24] Opening discussion in Main Committee I at the Intergovernmental Conference on June 16, 1967. Judge Pierre Cavin, the Swiss representative, said his delegation approved the principle of extending the right of quotation to "all the categories of protected works": Minutes, [761], *in* II RECORDS, *supra* note 6, at 860. Later, George Straschnov, the delegate for Monaco, objected to a proposal to limit the exception to "short" quotations on the basis that this would raise particular problems in relation to the quotation of artistic works, where moral rights would be implicated if only part was used: Minutes, [769], *in* II RECORDS, *supra* note 6, at 861. For earlier references, e.g., to musical works, *see* the REPORT OF THE COMMITTEE OF GOVERNMENTAL EXPERTS p. 10, BIRPI: DA/22/33, Professor Ulmer, giving the example of "aesthetic purposes (quotation from one musical work in another musical work)." This is also recognized in the commentaries: *see, e.g.*, WILHELM NORDEMANN, KAI VINCK, PAUL HERTIN, & GERALD MEYER, INTERNATIONAL COPYRIGHT AND NEIGHBOURING RIGHTS LAW 112 (1990).*See* APLIN & BENTLY, GLOBAL MANDATORY FAIR USE, *supra* note 3, at 44–47.

[25] For an example, *see* J. PETER BURKHOLDER, ALL MADE OF TUNES: CHARLES IVES AND THE USES OF MUSICAL BORROWING 1 (1995) ("Musical quotation is one of the most characteristic facets of Charles Ives' music") and JORGE DANIEL VENECIANO, *Louis Armstrong, Bricolage and the Aesthetics of Swing, in* UPTOWN CONVERSATION: THE NEW JAZZ STUDIES 256–78, 269–70 (Robert G. O'Meally, Brent Hayes Edwards, & Farah Jasmine Griffin eds., 2004)

[26] *See, e.g.*, Anne Nesbet, *Inanimations: Snow White and Ivan the Terrible*, 50(4) FILM Q. 20, 29 n.6 (1997) (describing Eisenstein's reference to Disney's *Snow White* in *Ivan the Terrible* as "visual quotation") and INGEBORG HOESTEREY, PASTICHE: CULTURAL MEMORY IN ART, FILM, LITERATURE 47–52, 49 (2001), describing "quotations from Metropolis *that Ridley Scott pastiches in* Blade Runner."

[27] For example, MIKHAIL IAMPOLSKI, THE MEMORY OF TIRESIAS: INTERTEXTUALITY AND FILM 38 (Harsha Ram trans., 1998) (describing the shots of Picasso's painting in Jean-Luc Godard's *Breathless* as "quotations from Picasso" and explaining that "the quotes here function much like a teacher's comments in red ink.") and HOESTEREY, *supra* note 26, at 67, describing Derek Jarman's reference in his film *Caravaggio* (1986) to Jacques-Louis David's painting, *Death of Marat* (1793).

[28] For an examination from a philosophical perspective, starting from Nelson Goodman's work on quotation, *see* Remei Capdevila-Werning, *Can Buildings Quote?* 69 J. AESTH. & ART CRIT. 115–24 (2011).

breadth of the term "quotation." For example, conventions associated with literary quotation, such as the use of quotation marks, cannot be elevated into conditions for the existence of quotation within the Article 10(1) exemption, because to do so would exclude much that is ordinarily called "quotation" in art, music, or film from any possibility of exemption.

The meaning of "quotation" is also important to the notion of fair "use." We argue that quotation need not be short in itself and could, in fact, constitute the entire work. This view is supported by the ordinary meaning of "quotation" and the *travaux* accompanying Article 10(1) Berne. As a matter of ordinary meaning, it is common to speak of "lengthy quotations" or "quoting extensively." For example, David Metzer discusses Douglas Gordon's *24 Hour Psycho* (1993), which is an art piece comprising a slowed-down (and mute) rendering of Hitchcock's famous film to two frames per minute. Metzer describes this as at the "outer limit" of quotation.[29] In addition, the history of Article 10(1) is clear in not restricting quotation to short excerpts. In its 1948 Brussels version, Berne permitted the use of "short quotations," but when BIRPI drafted a text for the Stockholm revision the term "short" seems specifically to have been abandoned. The Study Group proposed that the limitation to "short quotations" be removed.[30] The Committee of Experts agreed with the removal of the qualification "short."[31] Attempts by France to restore the limitation that quotations be "short" were rejected by the Committee of Governmental Experts.[32] Thus, the text of the Proposal for consideration at the Intergovernmental Conference omitted the restriction to "short" quotations.[33] In the Main Committee I, both Switzerland and France proposed reintroducing the "short" qualification.[34] The Swiss amendment was rejected by 27 votes to 10, and, in light of this, the French amendment was not pushed.[35]

We also argue that the quotation need not be unaltered. We suggest that "quotation" might, for example, include summary or paraphrase of text, the incorporation of a phrase of music in a composition and its elaboration, or a transformative use of an artwork in a later artwork or film. This is supported by the ordinary meaning of "quotation," which seems to embrace reuse of material that has been altered. Indeed, perhaps the most widely discussed example of "quotation" among art historians concerns a case of adaptation. This is Edouard Manet's (1832–1883) most famous work *Le déjeuner sur l'herbe* (1862), which is widely acknowledged to be based upon a detail from a Marcantonio Raimondi engraving of Raphael's *Judgment of Paris*. Michael Fried calls *Déjeuner* "perhaps the most notorious instance of quotation from the Old Masters in Manet's oeuvre."[36] Fried explains "the three foregrounded figures in Manet's painting are a direct quotation from Marcantonio Raimondi's engraving."[37] Another reason to support this view is that Article 10(1) expressly includes within the concept of quotation "press summaries" and this would seem to indicate that "quotation" is not limited to verbatim reproduction.[38] Further, the fact that Article 10(1) applies to all economic rights, including translation and adaptation, implicitly indicates that "quotation" extends beyond unaltered replication.

[29] D. Metzer, Quotation and Cultural Meaning in Twentieth Century Music 217 (2003).

[30] Study Group, BIRPI: DA/20/2, p. 45.

[31] Committee of Experts, BIRPI: DA/20/3, p. 6a.

[32] Report of the Committee of Governmental Experts, BIRPI: DA/22/23.

[33] *Preparatory Documents*, S/1, *in* I Records, *supra* note 6, at 117.

[34] *Preparatory Documents*, S/45 and S/68, *in* I Records, *supra* note 6, at 688 and 690.

[35] *Minutes*, [778]–[779], *in* II Records, *supra* note 6, at 861.

[36] Michael Fried, Manet's Modernism: or, The Face of Painting in the 1860s 150 (1996).

[37] Fried, *supra* note 36, at 56 and 152. *See also* Beatrice Farwell, Manet and the Nude: A Study in Iconography in the Second Empire 255 (1981); and Carol Armstrong, *To Paint, to Point, to Pose: Manet's* Le déjeuner sur l'herbe, *in* Manet's *Le Déjeuner sur* L'herbe, ch. 4, 90–118, at 94 (P. H. Tucker ed., 1998).

[38] But cf. Ricketson & Ginsburg, *supra* note 13, at [13.41], 787 who argue that "press summaries" refers to *review* by replication of news items.

The "use" embodied in Article 10(1) is also not limited by "purpose."[39] Notably, the "proportionality" condition (discussed below) refers to the need for *a* "purpose": the extent of quotation must not exceed that justified by the *purpose*. But while the person making the quotation must have a "purpose," nowhere is there a limitation to the sorts of purpose to which the exception applies. In particular, there is no requirement to use quotation to further an argument. According to its ordinary meaning, then, there is no justification for limiting the application of the quotation exception by reference to particular types of purpose. A close look at the *travaux* reinforces this conclusion, because when proposals were made to limit the exception by reference to particular purposes, these proposals were rejected.[40] This does not mean that a user's purpose will be irrelevant: it not only affects the proportionality condition but may also be relevant to whether a quotation is "compatible with fair practice."

Finally, the "fair" use part of our argument takes account of the following conditions of the mandatory quotation exception: the work has been lawfully made available to the public, attribution, proportionality, and fair practice. According to Article 10(1), the mandatory quotation exception applies only to those works which have "already been lawfully made available to the public." This language is in fact wider than the notion of "publication" stipulated in Article 3(3) Berne because it permits making available to the public by any means and can cover situations where works have been circulated pursuant to a compulsory license.[41] The attribution requirement is contained in Article 10(3) and requires that "mention shall be made of the source, and of the name of the author if it appears thereon." The language here is flexible: for example, "mention" could encompass attributions in abbreviated form, ones that indirectly accompany the use of the quotation (e.g., in a list of credits or acknowledgments), or which are implicit (because of the recognizability of the work or source from which the quotation is taken).

The proportionality requirement is reflected in the language of Article 10(1) Berne requiring that quotations shall be permissible, "provided that … their extent does not exceed that justified by the purpose." As mentioned above, while quotation is not restricted to certain purposes, the purpose of the quotation will be relevant to judging proportionality. Further, the "extent" of the quotation refers to its amount; however, it does not preclude long quotations – it only requires them to be justified.[42] A suggested means of assessing proportionality is to ask: is the quotation capable of achieving the purpose that is claimed and would a *shorter* quotation have been as effective in achieving the purpose and less restrictive of author's rights?[43]

39 *See* Xalabarder, *supra* note 19, p. 18 Martin Senftleben, *Internet Search Results – A Permissible Quotation?*, 235 RIDA 3, 15 (2013) (no purpose requirement in Art. 10(1)).

40 While initially the Study Group proposed to broaden the exception to quotations in general, the Committee of (Non-Governmental) Experts, which met in November 1963, thought this too broad and proposed that it should be limited to quotation for "scientific, cultural, informatory or education" purposes: *see* C. Masouyé, *Perspectives de révision de la Convention de Berne*, 43 RIDA 5, 26 (1964). The Study Group rejected such a limitation, on the basis that it would not encompass "artistic purposes": BIRPI: DA.22/2, p. 54. The issue was again raised in the Committee of Governmental Experts. Here, the limitation was rejected as it would exclude from legitimate quotation citation for "judicial purposes, political purposes, aesthetic purposes and the purposes of entertainment": BIRPI: DA/22/33 p. 10.

41 *See* Ricketson & Ginsburg, *supra* note 13, at [13.41], 785; and Main Committee I Report, *in* II Records, *supra* note 6, at 1147.

42 *See Preparatory Documents*, Stockholm, *in* I Records, *supra* note 6, at 116.

43 This borrows from the broad proportionality approach used by the European Court of Human Rights. It is an adapted form of the suitability and necessity tests, i.e. whether the restriction is suitable for achieving a legitimate general aim, and whether the restriction/act is the least intrusive way of achieving this aim, but with similar efficacy. *See* Juan Cianciardo, *The Principle of Proportionality: The Challenges of Human Rights*, 3 J. Civ. L. Stud. 177, 179–80 (2010) for discussion of the Strasbourg court's approach.

Quotations must also be "compatible with fair practice." The concept, which also appears in relation to the teaching exception under Article 10(2), receives little definition in Berne. The *travaux* do not shed much light on the concept. In the early proposals, "fair practice" seems to have been considered as requiring a consideration of whether the practice was consistent with trade norms. For example, it was said to be understood among the press what was fair.[44] With the broadening out, to cover all types of quotation and all types of works, the concept seemed – at least to contemporaries – rather vague.[45] Some called it typically English,[46] but even the British content industry seemed uncomfortable with it. The Publishers Association, for example, complained.[47] The lawyer for the BBC, E. C. Robbins, said "the broadcasting authorities were regarding this article [10(1)] as their fair dealings charter to bring them in line with the press."[48] At times, it was suggested that fair use might be a preferable term.[49] In the preparatory documents for the Stockholm conference it was stated that "fair practice" must be determined "after an objective appreciation."[50] Further, the *travaux* suggest that the absence of a requirement of "short" quotations would be counterbalanced by the fair practice criterion.[51]

Given the limited guidance in Berne and the *travaux* about the meaning of "fair practice," how should this terminology be understood in the context of Article 10(1)? We argue that a normative meaning can and should be attributed to "fair practice" in Article 10(1) and that this is pluralistic in nature. This view is contrary to the view of some scholars who suggest latitude in how international copyright obligations in Berne are to be implemented. For example, Professor Dinwoodie explains that Berne allowed "significant latitude for signatory states to develop distinctive national copyright policies tailored to their own cultural or economic priorities."[52] Professors Dinwoodie and Dreyfuss have also argued that it is important to preserve the autonomy of Berne Union members.[53] Similarly, Professor Ginsburg sees international copyright conventions as providing a general framework and preserving "some national autonomy regarding the content … of copyright exceptions." Further, she suggests that "fair practice" in relation to quotation should be locally determined since "norms of fairness may differ" between states.[54]

[44] International Federation of Journalists, BIRPI: DA/22/9, p. 7.

[45] It was criticized as "vague" by some members: *see Main Committee I, Summary Minutes*, *in* II Records, *supra* note 6, at 860–61.

[46] *See* C. Masouyé, *Perspectives de révision de la Convention de Berne*, 43 RIDA 5, 26 (1964) (describing "fair practice" as "a notion of Anglo-Saxon law which seems to some too general and too vague.").

[47] Ian Parsons, Chatto and Windus Ltd, to Board of Trade, October 2, 1963 (fairness criterion "invites litigation"); Publishers Association to Wallace October 14, 1963 (want short retained as fair practice and proportionality too vague): both in TNA: BT 209/903.

[48] Third Meeting of the Copyright Committee, TNA: BT 209/908, August 11, 1966.

[49] Letter from Bernard Alton, Secretary to the Newspaper Proprietors Association, to William Wallace, Board of Trade, October 10, 1963 (suggesting "fair use" preferable to "fair practice") *in* TNA: BT 209/903; Letter from Publishers Association to William Wallace, TNA: BT209/1247, October 26, 1965.

[50] *See* Committee of Governmental Experts (1965) DA/22/2, pp. 53–54; *Preparatory Documents* S/1 (Berne Convention), *in* I Records, *supra* note 6, at 117.

[51] *Preparatory Documents* S/1 (Berne Convention), *in* II Records, *supra* note 6, at 860 per Mr Wallace from the UK and 861 per Mr Justice Hesser (Sweden), Mr O'Hannrachain (Ireland).

[52] G. B. Dinwoodie, *A New Copyright Order: Why National Courts Should Create Global Norms*, 149 U. Pa. L. Rev. 469, 491 (2000). *See also* G. B. Dinwoodie, *The Development and Incorporation of International Norms in the Formation of Copyright Law*, 62 Ohio St. L.J. 733, 742 (2001); J. Ginsburg, *International Copyright: From a "Bundle" of National Copyright Laws to a Supranational Code?*, 47 J. Copyright Soc'y U.S.A. 265, 267–68 (2000); and Ricketson & Ginsburg, *supra* note 13, at [2.02]–[2.04], 42–44.

[53] *See generally* Dinwoodie & Dreyfuss *supra* note 15.

[54] Ginsburg, *supra* note 52, at 288.

We do not take the view that Article 10(1) leaves the meaning of "fair practice" entirely to Berne Union members. Nor do we see "fair practice" as synonymous with the three-step test.[55] Instead, we argue that Article 10(1), as a mandatory obligation, has a normative content that ought to be reflected in the national laws of Berne Union countries. These are several arguments in support of this position. The first is that it seems unlikely that the framers of Article 10(1) intended "fair practice" to be without *any* content at all. This rider was seen by those participating at the Diplomatic Conference as a crucial mechanism for ensuring that the quotation exception was bounded. As such, it would seem counterintuitive for Union members to have complete latitude in determining the scope of "fair practice." Second, allowing countries complete autonomy in how they interpret "fair practice" would make little sense given the mandatory nature of the exception. Third, and perhaps most importantly, the interpretation that is proposed here is consistent with the norms set out in Articles 31 and 32 of the Vienna Convention on the Law of Treaties 1969 ("VCLT"). According to those articles, the ordinary meaning of "fair practice" must be determined according to the terms in context and in light of the treaty's object and purpose. Extrinsic aids, such as the *travaux*, can be used to confirm an interpretation resulting from Article 31 or where the meaning is ambiguous or lead to a result that is unreasonable. Thus, "harm," in an economic and moral sense, can be taken as the basis for interpreting Article 10(1) Berne because the Convention is concerned with the protection of *authors* in relation to their literary and artistic works and the rationale for this protection is grounded in either economic or moral theory. As well, the rationale for the quotation exception is linked to freedom of expression and so this should also inform the interpretation of the exception. The Berne *travaux* suggest that trade norms might sometimes be relevant. When it comes to equity or distributive justice concerns, these seem to have a basis in international copyright law, by virtue of the need to ensure that public interests are taken into account. Finally, we should be cautious about assuming the three-step test and "fair practice" are synonymous concepts.[56] In formulating Article 9(2), the Working Group on the Right of Reproduction at the Stockholm Conference preferred a general clause rather than specific exceptions to the reproduction right and, in formulating this general clause, did not consider a "fair practice" criterion.[57]

Thus, we argue that "fair practice" in Article 10(1) Berne has an autonomous and pluralistic meaning that embraces notions of moral and economic harm, distributive justice concerns, freedom of expression principles, and, in limited circumstances, custom.[58] This, in turn, translates to various factors being assessed: (i) the nature and purpose of the quotation; (ii) the size of the quotation and its proportion in relation to the source work; (iii) the actual or potential harm to the market of the source work; (iv) the integrity interests of the author of the source work and (v) the nature of the claimant's work.[59]

[55] Cf. RICKETSON & GINSBURG, *supra* note 13, at [13.41], 786.

[56] *See* RICKETSON & GINSBURG, *supra* note 13, at [13.41], 786 who suggest that the criteria of normal exploitation of the work and unreasonable prejudice to the legitimate interests of the author could be relevant to determining "fair practice."

[57] *Summary Minutes* (Main Committee I) (Stockholm), *in* II RECORDS, *supra* note 6, at 857–58, 883–85.

[58] This is because custom can be unrepresentative, so there is a need to treat custom carefully and check they are sufficiently certain, representative, and aspirational: *see* J. E. Rothman, *The Questionable Use of Custom in Intellectual Property*, 93 VA. L. REV. 1899 (2007).

[59] These pluralistic concerns and the way in which they translate into these factors are examined in detail in APLIN & BENTLY, GLOBAL MANDATORY FAIR USE, *supra* note 3, at 140–189.

2 NON-APPLICABILITY OF THE THREE-STEP TEST TO GLOBAL, MANDATORY FAIR USE

We have argued that Article 10(1) Berne creates a broad, obligatory exception – global mandatory fair use – that is only subject to the conditions contained in Article 10: the work having been made available to the public, attribution, proportionality, and fair practice. Moreover, as we will argue in this section, the three-step test – as contained in Article 9(2) Berne, Article 13 TRIPS Agreement, and Article 10 of the WIPO Copyright Treaty 1996 ("WCT") – is *inapplicable* to Article 10(1) Berne. As such, when it comes to national implementation of Article 10(1), countries do *not* have the additional burden of considering compliance with the three-step test.

To begin, it is straightforward to dismiss the relevance of the three-step test in Article 9(2) Berne to Article 10(1) Berne. This is because Article 9(2) reflects a residual discretion on Berne members to create exceptions to the reproduction right.[60] By contrast, it has often been assumed that all the exceptions permitted in the Berne Convention are subject to the three-step test embodied in Article 13 TRIPS Agreement and Article 10(2) WCT.[61] This has led some scholars to see Article 13 of TRIPS as a critical constraint on national lawmaking, casting a cloud over the legitimacy of US fair use.[62]

Article 13 TRIPS states that: "Members shall confine limitations or exceptions to exclusive rights to certain special cases which do not conflict with a normal exploitation of the work and do not unreasonably prejudice the legitimate interests of the right holder." It has been queried whether Article 13 TRIPS applies only to the additional rights recognized under TRIPS. The EU mounted this argument in the so-called "Fairness in Music Licensing case."[63] However, the Dispute Resolution Body of the World Trade Organization in the "Fairness in Music Licensing case" rejected this argument. There the panel took the view that Article 13 applied to all

60 RICKETSON & GINSBURG, *supra* note 13, at [13.10], 763. *See also* J. Hughes, *Fair Use and Its Politics – at Home and Abroad*, *in* COPYRIGHT LAW IN AN AGE OF EXCEPTIONS AND LIMITATIONS, ch. 8, 234–74, at 241 (Ruth L. Okediji ed., 2017) noting that the three-step test in Art. 9(2) Berne "might have remained an obscure component of Berne" if not for TRIPS.

61 DINWOODIE & DREYFUSS, *supra* note 13, at 185; G. B. Dinwoodie, *The Development and Incorporation of International Norms in the Formation of Copyright Law*, 62 OHIO ST. L.J. 733, 769 (2001); Michael Landau, *Fitting United States Copyright Law into the International Scheme: Foreign and Domestic Challenges to Recent Legislation*, 23 GA. ST. U. L. REV. 847, 855 (2007); Rochelle Cooper Dreyfuss & Andreas F. Lowenfeld, *Two Achievements of the Uruguay Round: Putting TRIPS and Dispute Settlement Together*, 37 VA. J. INT'L L. 275, 306 (1997); Lawrence R. Helfer, *World Music on a U.S. Stage: A Berne/TRIPS and Economic Analysis of the Fairness in Music Licensing Act*, 80 B.U. L. REV. 93, 147 (2000).

62 Paul Geller, *Can the GATT Incorporate Berne Whole?*, 12 EIPR 423, 425 (1990); Helfer, *supra* note 61, at 184; J. H. Reichman, *Universal Minimum Standards of Intellectual Property Protection under the TRIPS Component of the WTO Agreement*, 29 INT'L LAW 345, 368 (1995); R. Okediji, *Toward an International Fair Use Doctrine*, 39 COLUM. J. TRANSNAT'L L. 75, 126 *et seq.* (2000); Mary W. S. Wong, *Transformative User-Generated Content in Copyright Law: Infringing Derivative Works or Fair Use*, 11 VANDERBILT J. ENTERTAIN. & TECHNOL. L., 1075, 1102 (2009). But cf. DINWOODIE & DREYFUSS, *supra* note 13, at 186 (appearing to argue that fair use "illustrates how extensive" the freedom remains); Pam Samuelson, *Possible Futures of Fair Use*, 90 WASH. L. REV. 815, 850–53 (2015) who rebuts arguments that the US fair use doctrine is contrary to the three-step test in Berne and TRIPS and suggests they are correlative tests; and AUSTRALIAN LAW REFORM COMMISSION, COPYRIGHT AND THE DIGITAL ECONOMY 116–22 (Report No. 122) (2013) (concluding that fair use is compliant with the three-step test).

63 European Union v. United States, [6.34] WTO DS 160/R, June 15, 2000: "The principal EC argument concerning Article 13 is that it only applies to exclusive rights newly introduced under the TRIPS Agreement and that the rights conferred under Articles 1–21 of the Berne Convention (1971) as incorporated into the TRIPS Agreement can be derogated from only on the grounds of preexisting exceptions applicable under the Berne Convention (1971). In the EC view, its position is supported by Article 2.2 of the TRIPS Agreement and Article 20 of the Berne Convention (1971), which it interprets as a prohibition on any derogation from existing standards of protection under the Berne Convention (1971).

exclusive rights and that the "minor exceptions" doctrine, under which it was understood that Members of the Berne Union could operate certain minor derogations from the public performance right, was to be interpreted in line with Article 13 TRIPS Agreement.[64] Professor Ricketson also shares the view that Article 13 TRIPS is not restricted to additional rights because otherwise it would have a "very limited sphere of application, as the only non-Berne exclusive right required to be protected under TRIPs is the rental right." He adds that "as Article 9(1) of TRIPS requires members to comply with Article 1 to 21 of Berne (other than Article 6*bis*), the better view must be that Article 13 applies to all the exclusive rights listed in Berne, including that of reproduction, as well as the rental right in TRIPS."[65] Thus, it might be suggested that Article 10(1) Berne must likewise be interpreted consistently with Article 13 TRIPS.[66]

The first objection to this construction is that the WTO panel decision did *not* address the relationship between Article 13 TRIPS and Article 10(1) Berne, but rather only commented on the applicability of Article 13 TRIPS to the minor exceptions doctrine.[67] Therefore, the question of whether the mandatory quotation exception in Article 10(1) Berne must be interpreted according to the three-step test in Article 13 TRIPS remains open.[68]

A second argument is that Article 10(1) of Berne is an *obligation* on Berne Union Members and the same obligation is imposed on TRIPS Members via Article 9(1) TRIPS. It would be odd to require compliance with an obligation and yet at the same time constrain such compliance. Finally, while Article 13 TRIPS might restrict the operation of an *optional* provision, Article 2(2) TRIPS specifically indicates that nothing in Article 13 derogates from *any obligation* between the parties.[69] Effectively, Article 13 TRIPS does not purport to change Article 10(1) Berne and the relevant conditions for the quotation exception are those stipulated within Article 10.

Next, we turn to assess the applicability of Article 10 WCT to Article 10(1) Berne. As between countries that are parties to the WCT (which now number ninety-three), Article 10(2) WCT requires that "Contracting Parties shall, *when applying the Berne Convention*, confine any limitations of or exceptions to rights provided for therein to certain special cases that do not conflict with a normal exploitation of the work and do not unreasonably prejudice the legitimate interests of the author" (emphasis added). On the face of it, Article 10(2) WCT seems to require WCT contracting parties to apply the three-step test to the quotation exception in Article 10(1) Berne.[70] Upon closer

[64] WTO DS 160/R: [6.80]: "In our view, neither the express wording nor the context of Article 13 or any other provision of the TRIPS Agreement supports the interpretation that the scope of application of Article 13 is limited to the exclusive rights newly introduced under the TRIPS Agreement." *See also* [6.63].

[65] *See* S. Ricketson, WIPO Study on Limitations and Exceptions of Copyright and Related Rights in the Digital Environment SCCR 9/7, 47 (2003).

[66] *See* N. Netanel, *The Next Round: The Impact of the WIPO Copyright Treaty on TRIPS Dispute Settlement*, 37 Va. J. Int'l L. 441, 459–60 (1997), arguing that Art. 13 TRIPS imposes "some constraint on the limitations and exceptions to copyright owner rights that would otherwise be permissible under Berne."

[67] David Brennan, *The Three Step Test Frenzy – Why the TRIPS Panel Decision Might be Considered per incuriam*, 2 IPQ 212, at 219–20, 223–24 (2002), criticizing the panel for dismissing the relevance of Art. 11*bis*(2) Berne to the dispute and suggesting that the TRIPS negotiating history does not support the conclusion that Art. 13 TRIPS applies to all exceptions under Berne.

[68] J. Oliver, *Copyright in the WTO: The Panel Decision on the Three Step Test*, 25 Colum. J. L. & Arts 119, 147 (2002): the "question left open by the panel decision is whether, under TRIPs, an express Berne exception relating to free use is also subject to Article 13."

[69] TRIPS, Art. 2(2) ("*Nothing* in Parts I to IV of this Agreement *shall derogate from existing obligations that Members may have to each other under* the Paris Convention, *the Berne Convention*, the Rome Convention and the Treaty on Intellectual Property in Respect of Integrated Circuits" (emphasis added)).

[70] Pam Samuelson, *The US Digital Agenda at WIPO*, 37 Virg. J. Int'l Law 369, n.188 (1997) raised the question whether the predecessor to Art. 10(2) WCT, namely, Art. 12 in the draft WCT, would override the right of fair quotation under Art. 10(1) Berne.

analysis, however, this turns out not to be the case for two reasons. The first is that Article 10(1) of Berne is an *obligation* on Members of the Convention and the WCT imposes that same obligation on their respective parties via Article 1(4), which states, "Contracting Parties shall comply with Articles 1 to 21 and the Appendix of the Berne Convention." As was argued in relation to Article 13 TRIPS, it would be strange to require compliance with an obligation – i.e., the quotation exception in Article 10(1) Berne with the conditions specified in Article 10 – and simultaneously to prohibit such compliance by imposing additional conditions – i.e., the three-step test. More significantly, while Article 10(2) of the WCT might constrain the operation of an *optional* provision, Article 1(2) specifically indicates that nothing in the treaty derogates from *any obligation* between the parties.[71] Effectively, then, the WCT does not purport to change Article 10(1) Berne, including the obligation to allow quotation – whatever the purpose – if it meets the other conditions of Article 10.

The second reason relates to the Agreed Statement to Article 10(2) of the WCT, which states: "It is also understood that Article 10(2) *neither reduces nor extends* the scope of applicability of the limitations and exceptions permitted by the Berne Convention" (emphasis added). As Professor Ricketson explains, the fact that the Agreed Statement was adopted by consensus means that it can "be regarded as part of the context of the WCT for the purposes of Article 31(2)(a) of the Vienna Convention."[72] As such, the effect of the Agreed Statement is as follows:

> Accordingly, WCT members are not required to modify limitations and exceptions that are consistent with the present Berne text, even if these would not pass the three-step test in Article 10(2). There will, of course, be room for argument as to whether any of the existing Berne exceptions and limitations, including the minor reservations doctrine, do, in fact, go beyond the limits of the three-step test, but, to the extent that this is so, it seems clear that the three-step test cannot "trump" these existing limitations and exceptions.[73]

Therefore, it seems clear that contracting parties to the WCT must provide for a quotation exception in relation to the exclusive rights granted by Berne and that this is not subject to the three-step requirement as well. But what, then, is the role of Article 10(2) WCT? Also, what about the exclusive rights granted by the WCT in Articles 6, 7, and 8 and the effect of Article 10(1) WCT? Does the quotation exception apply to these rights and, if so, is the three-step test also applicable?

Article 10(1) WCT[74] suggests that the three-step test – as opposed to the quotation exception – would be applicable to the "new" economic rights contained in the WCT, namely, the rights of rental, distribution, and making available to the public, in Articles 6, 7, and 8, respectively.[75] Nonetheless, we argue that, in fact, the quotation exception *does* apply to the "new" WCT economic rights, as well as those contained in Berne.

Our argument relies on the impact of Article 20 Berne, which provides that special agreements can be entered into by Berne Union members "in so far as such agreements grant to

[71] WCT, Art. 1(2) ("Nothing in this Treaty shall derogate from existing obligations that Contracting Parties have to each other under the Berne Convention for the Protection of Literary and Artistic Works.").

[72] *See* RICKETSON, *supra* note 65, at 62.

[73] Id., *at* 63.

[74] "(1) Contracting Parties may, in their national legislation, provide for limitations of or exceptions to the rights granted to authors of literary and artistic works under this Treaty in certain special cases that do not conflict with a normal exploitation of the work and do not unreasonably prejudice the legitimate interests of the author."

[75] Cf. RICKETSON, *supra* note 65, at 60–61 where he says that Art. 10(1) WCT applies to the rights accorded under the WCT.

authors more extensive rights than those granted by the Convention, or contain provisions not contrary to the Convention." The WCT grants authors more extensive rights – in the form of the making available, rental, and distribution rights – but must also not be contrary to Berne. Arguably, Article 10(1) WCT requiring the application of the three-step test for economic rights granted under the WCT would be contrary to Berne insofar as it ousted Article 10(1) Berne, a mandatory exception that is not explicitly tied to any particular economic rights, but rather Berne "works."[76] Moreover, as already mentioned, Article 1(4) WCT emphasizes the requirement for contracting parties to comply with Articles 1–21 and the Appendix of Berne. It would not be possible for contracting parties to comply with the obligation in Article 10(1) Berne, which is not tied to particular economic rights but to Berne works, unless they were able to provide for a quotation exception in relation to the "new" economic rights in the WCT. Finally, as noted above, Article 1(2) WCT reiterates that nothing in the WCT "shall derogate from existing obligations that Contracting Parties have to each other under the Berne Convention" and the obligation to provide for a quotation exception contained in Article 10(1) Berne is not limited to particular exclusive rights but relates to Berne works. Therefore, the quotation exception ought to apply to *all* economic rights in the WCT *and* Berne.

But what role does this leave for the three-step test in Article 10 WCT? Although the three-step test in Article 10 WCT does not displace the quotation exception in Berne, it might constrain the operation of an *optional* exception, such as Article 10(2) or 10*bis* of Berne. As such, there does remain a role for Article 10(2) WCT.[77] Alternatively, the three-step test in Article 10(2) WCT could operate in relation to purposes or uses *not* covered by the specific exception provisions in Berne, such as Article 10 and 10*bis*. Thus, where exceptions are *not* dealing with quotation, illustration for teaching purposes, or reporting current events, but deal with uses that fall within Article 9(2) Berne, such as private use or judicial and administrative uses, and which are not simply reproductions but cover broadcasting, performance, or translation, then Article 10(2) WCT would be applicable.[78]

In relation to the "new" WCT economic rights, we have argued that the mandatory quotation exception in Article 10(1) Berne must apply to these. Even so, there is still a considerable role left for Article 10(1) WCT; in particular, for uses *other* than quotation that involve making available to the public, distribution, and rental, the three-step test as contained in Article 10(1) WCT will apply and arguably constrain the optional exceptions in Berne, such as Article 10(2) and 10*bis*.

3 THE CONSEQUENCES OF GLOBAL, MANDATORY FAIR USE FOR NATIONAL COPYRIGHT EXCEPTIONS

Having made the case for global mandatory fair use, as established by Article 10(1) Berne, and the fact that it is not constrained by the three-step test, this final section seeks to do two things. The first is to tease out the differences between Article 10(1) Berne and the three-step test; and the second is to show how this may impact on national copyright exceptions, in particular, the "fair

76 Art. 10(1) Berne states: "It shall be permissible to make quotations from a work."

77 *E.g.*, in European Union v. United States, WTO DS 160/R, [6.69] the WTO panel ruled that Art. 10(2) WCT applies the three-step test to the minor exceptions doctrine relevant to Arts. 11 and 11*bis* Berne.

78 The relationship between Art. 10(1) WCT and Art. 11*bis*(2) Berne differs. *See* Ricketson *supra* note 65, at 62: "WCT signatories are required to apply Articles 1–21 of Berne and there should be no possibility of Article 10(1) of the WCT permitting free uses to the rights specified in Article 11*bis*(1) of Berne in cases where equitable remuneration would be required under Article 11*bis*(2). This would leave open the application of free use exceptions to Article 8 WCT rights that go beyond those specified in Article 11*bis*(2) of Berne. An example would be webcasting, which would not usually be broadcasting (by wireless means) within the meaning of Article 11*bis*(1)(i)."

use" exception in section 107 US Copyright Act 1976. In so doing, we see that Article 10(1) has both a liberating and constraining effect.

There are, we suggest, several important differences between the three-step test and the mandatory quotation exception in Article 10(1) Berne. These relate to: (i) the acceptable scope of the exception; (ii) the normative value of the exception and the interests taken into account; (iii) the unpublished nature of the work that is used; (iv) the treatment of moral rights of authors; (v) the cumulative nature of the requirements; and (vi) whether the exception supports "free" exceptions. In exploring these differences, we adopt, for the sake of argument, the WTO panel's interpretation of the three-step test in the "Fairness in Music Licensing case."[79] We recognize there has been much debate about the scope of the three-step test[80] and critique of the WTO panel's decision (much of which we agree with);[81] nevertheless, we take that decision as our current benchmark for the scope of the three-step test in international copyright law.[82] We also illustrate how Article 10(1) Berne has potentially different consequences to the three-step test by utilizing the US "fair use" exception.

Acceptable Scope of the Exception

The WTO panel explicitly denied that, according to the three-step test, the purpose of exceptions must be legitimate in a "normative sense." Instead, it indicated that the scope of an exception must be "clearly defined" and "narrow in scope and reach."[83] According to the WTO panel, "clearly defined" means that the scope of an exception must be "known and particularized."[84] With regard to an exception being "narrow in scope and reach," the panel stated:

> an exception or limitation must be limited in its field of application or exceptional in its scope. In other words, an exception or limitation should be narrow in quantitative as well as a qualitative sense. This suggests a narrow scope as well as an exceptional or distinctive objective.[85]

In the context of the case, the panel decided that the "business" exception failed the first step because, although defined with certainty, it was too broad in scope.[86] Particularly pertinent was

[79] European Union v. United States, WTO DS 160/R, June 15, 2000.

[80] *See, e.g.*, C. Geiger, D. Gervais, & M. Senftleben, *The Three Step Test Revisited: How to Use the Test's Flexibility in National Copyright Law*, 29 Am. U. Int'l L. Rev. 581 (2013–14) (suggests that a global, as opposed to cumulative, approach to the three-step test should be used); Kamiel J. Koelman, *Fixing the Three Step Test*, 28(8) EIPR 407 (2006); M. Senftleben, Copyright, Limitations and the Three-Step Test: An Analysis of the Three-Step Test, in International and EC Copyright Law (2004); Christophe Geiger, Jonathan Griffiths, & Reto M. Hilty, *Towards a Balanced Interpretation of the "Three Step Test" in Copyright Law*, 30(12) EIPR 489 (2008); Huaiwen He, *Seeking a Balanced Interpretation of the Three-Step Test – An Adjusted Structure in View of Divergent approaches*, 40(3) IIC 274 (2009).

[81] *See, e.g.*, Brennan, *supra* note 67; Dinwoodie and Dreyfuss, *supra* note 13, at 80 (describing the panel's approach as formalistic, which "anatomized the exceptions provision, mistook accounting for judging, and also relied heavily on dictionary definitions"); Daniel J. Gervais, *Towards a New Core International Copyright Norm: The Reverse Three Step Test*, 9 Marq. Intell. Prop. L. Rev. 1, 14 *et seq.* (2005); Henning Grosse Ruse-Khan, The Protection of Intellectual Property in International Law [12.45], 433 (2016) (describing as "most problematic" the panel's approach of defining "all relevant terms in Article 13 in great detail – rather than limiting itself to identify the range of possible understandings that a VCLT interpretation allows"); Kur, *supra* note 18, at 323–24 (2009).

[82] As Hughes, *supra* note 60, at 245 states, "this WTO decision … serves as the pragmatic authoritative interpretation of the provision."

[83] WTO DS 160/R, [6.112].

[84] WTO DS 160/R, [6.108].

[85] WTO DS 160/R, [6.109].

[86] WTO DS 160/R, [6.131]–[6.133].

the fact that "a substantial majority of eating and drinking establishments and close to half of the retail establishments [were] covered by the exemption."[87] By way of contrast, the "homestyle" exception was seen as limited to only a small percentage of such establishments and applicable only to dramatic musical works, such as operas, operettas, and musicals.[88]

Thus, the three-step test, as interpreted by the WTO panel, requires an exception to be limited in scope and reach and to have sufficient certainty. It is on this basis that some commentators have queried the legitimacy of US "fair use" in section 107 of the US Copyright Act 1976.[89] This has led some scholars to argue that section 107 of the US Copyright Act 1976 satisfies the criterion of "certain special cases" because of the developed US case law that fits into clusters and is relatively predictable.[90] Implicit in this argument is that the first step is the domain of both the national legislature and the national courts.[91] Indeed, Justin Hughes has argued that "the fair use doctrine is a *mechanism* to allow *specific* judicially created exceptions to copyright liability" and thus credibly satisfies the three-step test.[92] Opponents argue, however, that fair use is too open-ended to satisfy the first step and query those jurisdictions that have introduced fair use, but without the jurisprudential history attaching to section 107.[93]

This debate becomes redundant once one appreciates the relevance of Article 10(1) Berne. As we have argued, this provision mandates a quotation exception, and one which is open-ended as to the range of purposes or uses of the quotation. The concept of "quotation" is broader than has often been appreciated and can encompass many forms of expressive and transformative uses that, it has been said, lie at the heart of fair use under US law.[94] Although, not every act that would count as "fair use" under section 107 of the US Copyright Act 1976 can be described as "quotation" (in particular, the technology-related uses, such as accessing interface information to ensure functional interoperability,[95] or private use), a great deal of what US fair use encompasses reflects its obligations under Article 10(1); the remainder can likely be easily justified under Article 9(2) and the other exceptions in Berne (as understood in the light of the three-step test).[96]

The Normative Value of the Exception

According to the WTO panel, the normative basis of an exception is not especially relevant to determining consistency with the first limb of the three-step test. Compatibility with the first

87 WTO DS 160/R, [6.133].

88 WTO DS 160/R, [6.143] and [6.148].

89 As Hughes, *supra* note 60, at 242: "The real issue is the first step." *See also* Okediji, *supra* note 62, at 126.

90 Michael J. Madison, *A Pattern-Oriented Approach to Fair Use*, 45 WM. & MARY L. REV. 1525 (2004); Barton Beebe, *An Empirical Study of U.S. Copyright Fair Use Opinions*, 1978–2005, 156 U. PA. L. REV. 549 (2008); Pam Samuelson, *Unbundling Fair Uses*, 77 FORDHAM L. REV. 2537 (2009).

91 M. Senftleben, *The International Three-Step Test: A Model Provision for EC Fair Use Legislation*, 1 JIPITEC 67, 76 [52] (2010).

92 Hughes, *supra* note 82, at 253–54.

93 Okediji *supra* note 62, at 150: "local judicial institutions may not be developed enough to exercise a balanced application of the doctrine." *See also* Rami Olwan, *The Adoption of the American Fair Use in Gulf States: A Comparative Analysis of Authors' Exceptions in Common Law and Civil Law Countries*, 38 EIPR 416, 432–33 expressing concern about civil law jurisdictions in Gulf states being able to utilize or develop judicial precedent (2016). Cf. David Tan, *The Transformative Use Doctrine and Fair Dealing in Singapore*, 24 SINGAPORE ACADEMY OF LAW JOURNAL 832 (2012) who argues that adopting US jurisprudence is a solution.

94 Such as parody: Campbell v. Acuff-Rose, 510 U.S. 569 (1994).

95 Sega Enterprises Ltd v. Accolade Inc. 977 F. 2d 1510 (9th Cir. 1992). *See also* Oracle Am., Inc. v. Google, Inc. 750 F.3d 1339 (2014) (certiorari denied by Supreme Court – *see* (2015) 135 S Ct 2887).

96 It would also be difficult to class private copying for the purpose of time-shifting as quotation, though this would also fall within the US fair use doctrine: Sony v. Universal City Studios, Inc. 464 US 417 (1984).

limb can occur even if an exception "pursues a special purpose whose underlying legitimacy in a normative sense cannot be discerned."[97] Even so, the panel indicated that "public policy purposes stated by law-makers when enacting a limitation or exception may be useful from a factual perspective for making inferences about the scope of a limitation or exception or the clarity of its definition."[98] Interestingly, this approach is not about assessing the normative value of the exception, but rather takes a functional approach, i.e., using the normative basis as a technique for identifying the clarity and scope of an exception. For example, in relation to the "homestyle" exemption, the WTO panel avoided making a "value judgment on the legitimacy" of the exception, but did give some weight to the public policy purposes "for drawing inferences about the scope of an exemption and the clarity of its definition."[99] In the panel's view, the legislative history, which pointed to the public policy purpose of protecting small business, often run by immigrants, women and minorities, supported the conclusion that the exception had a narrow scope.[100] In reaching this conclusion, the WTO panel did not consider the normative value of the exception relative to the interests of the right holder.[101] In this way, it stripped out possible countervailing interests of social and public importance.

Similarly, in considering the second limb of the test, the WTO panel replicated this approach. Although it pointed to empirical and normative understandings of "normal" exploitation, it focused wholly on the economic harm to the rights holder and did not actually engage in a normative assessment of "normal exploitation."[102] The panel described the empirical component as related to "areas of the market in which the copyright owner would ordinarily expect to exploit the work, but which are not available for exploitation because of this exemption."[103] The normative aspect was intended to take "into account technological and market developments"[104] and to ascertain which forms of exploitation would likely and plausibly "acquire considerable economic or practical importance."[105] The panel stressed that "not every use of a work, which in principle is covered by the scope of exclusive rights and involves commercial gain, necessarily conflicts with a normal exploitation of that work."[106] However, as already mentioned, it did not really articulate when this might be, and concentrated its attention on an empirical enquiry into the economic harm suffered by rights holders.[107] Commentators have criticized the panel's preoccupation with the interests of right holders, not least because it excludes important countervailing interests, such as access to information, promotion of competition, along with the interests of creators.[108] It has been suggested that perhaps the panel

97 WTO DS 160/R, [6.112].

98 *Id.*

99 WTO DS 160/R, [6.157].

100 WTO DS 160/R, [6.156]–[6.157].

101 *See also* Dinwoodie and Dreyfuss, *supra* note 13, at 62 referring to the fact that the panel failed to consider "the relative economic value and social importance of each use or the question of the value of a particular form of exploitation to users relative to right holders."

102 Jane C. Ginsburg, *Toward Supranational Copyright Law? The WTO Panel Decision and the "Three Step Test" for Copyright Exceptions*, 187 RIDA 3, 17 (2001).

103 WTO DS 160/R, [6.177].

104 WTO DS 160/R, [6.178].

105 WTO DS 160/R, [6.180].

106 WTO DS 160/R, [6.182].

107 WTO DS 160/R, [6.208]. This is criticized by Dinwoodie and Dreyfuss, *supra* note 13, at 63.

108 Geiger et al., *Towards a Balanced Interpretation*, *supra* note 80, at 490; Grosse Ruse-Khan, *supra* note 81, at 434–35, [12.48]. Contrast Andre Lucas, *For a Reasonable Interpretation of the Three-Step Test*, 32(6) EIPR 277, 279 (2010) arguing that the second step has always been restricted to the economic sphere and should not take into account other interests. Note that the three-step test for patent exceptions in Art. 30 TRIPS expressly refers to the legitimate interests of the patent owner *and* of third parties. The WTO panel has thus explored the scope of legitimate interests

assumed that the test would "automatically balance user and producer interests appropriately"[109] because it derived from Article 9(2) Berne, yet this ignores the ramification of transposing the measure into TRIPS, "where it applies to all user activities, to all markets, and to all of the principal intellectual property regimes."[110]

By way of contrast, Article 10(1) Berne treats the normative underpinnings of the quotation exception as particularly important. For example, as we have argued, freedom of expression and other normative justifications, relating to economic and moral harm, and distributive justice play a key role in determining fair practice. This approach of using normativity to judge what constitutes "fair practice" involves assessing the value of the use itself. Moreover, it creates a means of ensuring that the interests of users, and the public more generally, are weighed alongside the interests of authors or right holders. Whereas, the three-step test is fixated on empirical economic harm to the author or right holder, the quotation exception takes account of a range of interests, only one of which is economic harm to the right holder, in its requirement of "fair practice."

This feature of Article 10(1) Berne, when translated into a national context, such as US fair use, could point to justifications for certain considerations, such as transformative use. Transformative use is a key consideration under US fair use[111] and one that has itself undergone a transformation in the past decade or so. According to its original advocate, Pierre Leval,[112] the basis for transformative use supporting *fair* use is that it promotes copyright's rationale of stimulating creativity to the benefit of society.[113] As such, Leval argued that this requires quotation that is "of the transformative type that advances knowledge" in contrast to where it "merely repackages, free riding on another's creations."[114] This view of transformative use may be seen in decisions such as *Campbell v. Acuff-Rose.*[115] However, in more recent years, US courts have, on occasion, taken an expansionist view of what counts as transformative use and how this may be weighed as part of all four factors. An illustrative example is *Cariou v. Prince,*[116] where the Court of Appeals for the Second Circuit held that transformative use does not require "comment on the original [work] or its author," can serve purposes other than those identified in section 107,[117] and is to be judged according to how the defendant's use may "reasonably be perceived" as opposed to the defendant's stated intentions.[118] Further, in assessing the other fair use factors, the court relied heavily on the transformative *purpose* to assess whether the market

in this context: *see* Canada – Patent Protection of Pharmaceutical Products WT/DS114/R, March 17, 2000. It is perhaps, therefore, unsurprising that it did not do so in relation to Art. 13 TRIPS, which does not explicitly mention the legitimate interests of third parties.

109 Graeme B. Dinwoodie and Rochelle C. Dreyfuss, *Designing a Global Intellectual Property System Responsive to Change: The WTO, WIPO and Beyond*, 46 Houston L. Rev. 1187, 1207 (2009).

110 Dinwoodie and Dreyfuss, *supra* note 109, at 1208.

111 Indeed, some have argued that is *the* key consideration: *see* Neil W. Netanel, *Making Sense of Fair Use*, 15 Lewis & Clark L. Rev. 715, 745 (2011) describing how if the use is found to be transformative this "infuses the court's analysis of factors three and four." Contrast Beebe, *supra* note 90, at 604: "courts and commentators have exaggerated the influence of transformativeness doctrine on our fair use case law."

112 P. Leval, *Toward a Fair Use Standard*, 103 Harv. L. Rev. 1105 (1990).

113 *Id.* at 1111.

114 *Id.* at 1116. Lloyd L. Weinreb, *Fair's Fair: A Comment on the Fair Use Doctrine*, 103 Harv. L. Rev. 1137, 1140–44 (1990), criticized this view.

115 114 S. Ct 1164 (1994).

116 714 F. 3D 694 (2d Cir. 2013). Another example is Authors Guild v. HathiTrust 755 F. 3d 87 (2d Cir. 2014).

117 *Cariou*, 706. The court described the "entirely different aesthetic from Cariou's photographs" contrasting the "serene and deliberately composed portraits" with the "crude and jarring works" of Prince (706).

118 *Id.* at 707.

was harmed and to counteract the quality and quantity of what was copied.[119] Decisions such as *Cariou* have attracted criticism for collapsing the four fair use factors into a consideration of transformativeness.[120]

Transformative use or purpose sits comfortably with the notion of "quotation" in Article 10(1), according to our interpretation. When it comes to the requirement of "fair practice," there is also a place for transformative use, particularly if account is taken of freedom of expression or distributive justice considerations. Some types of transformative use may better align with freedom of expression than others, such as "directly commenting on or criticizing the original work" or "using the original work to comment on something else."[121] Whereas, changing the purpose of the work, say from an entertainment to educational purpose, or to create a social benefit, may fit better with distributive justice concerns. Importantly, however, the "fair practice" assessment in Article 10(1) Berne would not allow this one factor to "stampede" other considerations, such as economic and moral harm to the author. Therefore, to the extent that US fair use can be legitimately criticized for this "stampeding" trend,[122] we suggest this is inconsistent with "fair practice" within Article 10(1).

The Unpublished Nature of the Work That Is Used

The three-step test applies to works that are published or unpublished,[123] although the unpublished status of a work may impact on whether there is a conflict with the normal exploitation of the work and may prejudice the legitimate interests of the author (namely, her divulgation right).[124] In contrast, Article 10(1) Berne has a clear condition that the work from which the quotation is taken has lawfully been made available to the public.

For acts that fall within the scope of section 107 of the US Copyright Act 1976 and within the scope of "quotation" in Article 10(1) Berne, this means that the status of the work as not having been made available to the public is crucial. Yet, the rider to section 107 (added in 1992 by amendment)[125] states:

> The fact that a work is unpublished shall not itself bar a finding of fair use if such finding is made upon consideration of all the above factors.[126]

This provision, arguably together with the decision of the Second Circuit in *Wright v. Warner Books, Inc*[127] (which preceded the amendment to section 107), signaled a turning point which "ended the concerns about the feared possibility of a per se rule flatly prohibiting the use of unpublished material in the fair use analysis."[128] However, to ensure compatibility with

[119] *Id.* at 709–10.

[120] J. Ginsburg, *Exclusive Rights, Exceptions, and Uncertain Compliance with International Norms*, 242 RIDA 175, 251 (2014). *See also* J. Ginsburg, *Fair Use for Free, or Permitted-but-Paid?*, 29 BERKELEY TECH L.J. 1383, 1445 (2014). *See* Kienitz v. Sconnie Nation 766 F. 3d 756, 758 (7th Cir. 2014) criticizing the *Cariou* decision. *Kienitz* was referred to in TCA Television Corp v. McCollum 839 F 3d 168, 181 (2d Cir. 2016), but the Second Circuit Court of Appeal did not seek to defend its decision in *Cariou*.

[121] *See* Tan, *supra* note 93, at 846–47.

[122] Beebe, *supra* note 90, at, 605 noting that "in those opinions in which transformativeness did play a role, it exerted nearly dispositive force not simply on the outcome of factor one but on the overall outcome of the fair use test."

[123] RICKETSON & GINSBURG, *supra* note 13, at [13.28] 777–78.

[124] *Id.* at [13.29] 778.

[125] Roger L. Zissu, *Fair Use: From* Harper & Row *to* Acuff Rose, *May* 13, 1994, 42 J. COPYRIGHT SOC'Y U.S.A. 7, 10 (1994).

[126] Pub. L. No. 102-492, 106 Stat. 3145 (1992).

[127] 953 F. 2d 731, 20 U.S.P.Q. 2d 1892 (2d Cir. 1991).

[128] Zissu, *supra* note 125, at 11.

Article 10(1) Berne, there may need to be a return to the position reflected in the Supreme Court decision in *Harper & Row, Publishers Inc v. Nation Enterprises*,[129] whereby the unpublished status of the work "is a critical element of its 'nature'" and weighs heavily against fair use because of the importance of the right of first publication and the impact this would have on the market for the work.[130]

The Treatment of Moral Rights of Authors

For the three-step test as interpreted by the WTO panel, the focus of the assessment is *economic* harm to the right holder and there is only a slim possibility that authorial interests, such as moral rights, will be taken into account. Whereas, Article 10(1) Berne more explicitly and directly respects the moral rights of authors. This is done in several ways. The first is that Article 10(1) does not operate as an exception to moral rights in Article 6*bis* Berne.[131] The second is that Article 10(1) reinforces and clarifies the right of attribution via Article 10(3). Finally, in assessing "fair practice" the integrity interests of the author may be a relevant consideration.

Why, then, are moral rights virtually ignored by the three-step test, as interpreted by the WTO panel? This requires us to consider the panel's interpretation of the third step in its section 110[5] decision. The panel held that "interests" were not confined to actual or potential economic harm.[132] "Legitimate" was held to mean "lawfulness" but also to have a normative component, "in the context of calling for the protection of interests that are justifiable in the light of the objectives that underlie the protection of exclusive rights."[133] The panel indicated that "one – albeit incomplete and thus conservative – way of looking at legitimate interests is the economic value of the exclusive rights conferred by copyright on their holders," but went on to indicate that they are not "necessarily limited to this economic value."[134]

However, the panel failed to elaborate upon what may have been other legitimate interests. Rather, in defining unreasonable prejudice, it indicated that this threshold would be breached if "an exception or limitation causes or has the potential to cause an unreasonable loss of income to the copyright owner."[135] The panel maintained this economic focus in the way in which it assessed the "business" exemption.[136]

The fact that the panel indicated that legitimate interests are not "limited to right holders of the Member that brings forth the complaint"[137] might indicate that moral rights interests are pertinent.[138] This seems unlikely, however, given that Article 6*bis* Berne is specifically excluded

[129] 105 S. Ct. 2218, 2226–8 (1985), treating the unpublished nature of President Ford's memoirs as a key factor weighing against fair use.

[130] *Harper & Row*, 2232. *See further*: David B. Goroff, *Fair Use and Unpublished Works: Harper & Row v. Nation Enterprises*, 9 COLUM-VLA ART & L 325 (1984).

[131] *See* APLIN & BENTLY, GLOBAL MANDATORY FAIR USE, *supra* note 3, 57–60. Cf. RICKETSON & GINSBURG, *supra* note 13, [13.30], 778, who observe that Art. 9(2) Berne only governs exceptions and limitations to the right of reproduction and does not extend to moral rights protected under Art. 6*bis*. So, in that sense Art. 9(2) and Art. 10(1) Berne are similar.

[132] WTO DS 160/R, [6.223]

[133] WTO DS 160/R, [6.224]

[134] WTO DS 160/R, [6.227].

[135] WTO DS 160/R, [6.229].

[136] DINWOODIE AND DREYFUSS, *supra* note 13, at 64 stating that the panel "merely reiterated its arithmetic arguments."

[137] WTO DS 160/R, [6.231].

[138] Andrew F. Christie and Robin Wright, *A Comparative Analysis of the Three-Step Tests in International Treaties*, 45(4) IIC 409, 429 (2014) pointing out that the legitimate interests of a creator include moral rights, whereas transferees of copyright will not have these interests.

from incorporation into TRIPS.[139] Article 13 TRIPS may be contrasted with Article 9(2) Berne, where moral rights are clearly part of Berne (in Article 6*bis*) and thus "interests" in step three may include economic and noneconomic considerations.[140]

An impact of Article 10(1) Berne for the US fair use doctrine is that the latter may have to pay greater attention to the conditions of attribution of source and authorship. At present, attribution is not a requirement of fair use, nor does it usually tend to be weighed as part of evaluating "fairness."[141] To ensure compatibility of "quotation" uses with Article 10(1), US fair use would need to take heed of attribution of source and author. Given the open-ended nature of section 107, there would be nothing to stop courts relying on attribution as a factor in appropriate cases. However, Professor Beebe has observed that judges rarely consider factors beyond those four listed in section 107.[142] Therefore, it may be preferable to make legislative adjustments to section 107 to indicate that attribution *is* a factor that ought to be considered by courts.

More significantly, the approach to the right of integrity may need to change. Currently, the right of integrity (such as it is under US law) is subject to specific exceptions in section 106A(c) and also subject to the fair use exception in section 107.[143] Looking at the congressional history, various challenges were made to the extension of fair use to moral rights. For example, Professor Ginsburg questioned whether there was any public policy or public benefit underlying the extension of fair use to moral rights and whether it was ever fair to deny attribution or to attribute falsely.[144] Congress acknowledged that "the modification of a single copy or limited edition of a work of visual art has different implications for the fair use doctrine than does an act involving a work reproduced in potentially unlimited copies."[145] However, these differences were not explored and Congress hastily inserted the fair use limitation to federal moral rights based on an assurance from the US Copyright Office that there was no conflict between fair use, copyright, and moral rights.[146] Scholars have criticized the application of fair use to moral rights.[147] We would offer an additional, compelling reason to those cited by these scholars, namely, the fact that the mandatory quotation exception does not operate as an exception to infringement of the moral rights contained in Article 6*bis* Berne. Therefore, to ensure that "fair

139 Andre Lucas, *supra* note 108 at 277. RICKETSON & GINSBURG, *supra* note 13, at [13.104], 855.

140 RICKETSON & GINSBURG, *supra* note 13, at [13.24], 774.

141 Cf. Catherine J. Cameron, *Reinvigorating U.S. Copyright with Attribution: How Courts Can Help Define the Fair Use Exception to Copyright by Considering the Economic Aspects of Attribution*, 2 BERKELEY J. ENT. & SPORTS L. 130 (2013) who discusses the few cases where attribution has played a role in fair use.

142 Beebe, *supra* note 90, at 563–64, referring to a sample of fair use cases from 1978 to 2005.

143 *See* s. 107 "Notwithstanding the provisions of sections 106 and 106A, the fair use of a copyrighted work . . ."

144 Visual Artists Rights Act of 1989: Hearing before the Subcommittee on Courts, Intellectual Property, and the Administration of Justice of the Committee on the Judiciary, House of Representatives, One Hundred First Congress, First session, on HR 2690, p. 89, October 18, 1989. *See also* Mr Peter Karlen, Moral Rights in Our Copyright Laws: Hearings on S. 1198 and S. 1253 Before the Subcommittee on Patents, Copyrights and Trademarks of the Senate Comm. on the Judiciary, 101st Cong. pp. 105–6 (1989).

145 H.R. Rep. No. 101-514, at 22 (1990).

146 Visual Artists Rights Act of 1989: Hearing before the Subcommittee on Courts, Intellectual Property, and the Administration of Justice of the Committee on the Judiciary, House of Representatives, One Hundred First Congress, First session, on HR 2690, 77, October 18, 1989. *See also* Moral Rights in Our Copyright Laws: Hearings on S. 1198 and S. 1253 Before the Subcommittee on Patents, Copyrights and Trademarks of the Senate Comm. on the Judiciary, 101st Congress, p. 234 (1989).

147 Dane S. Ciolino, *Rethinking the Compatability of Moral Rights and Fair Use*, 54 WASH. & LEE L. REV. 33 (1997). *See also* Jane C. Ginsburg, *Copyright in the 101st Congress: Commentary on the Visual Artists Rights Act and the Architectural Works Copyright Protection Act of* 1990, 14 COLUM-VLA J. L. & ARTS 477 fn 26 (1990); Peter H. Karlen, *What's Wrong with VARA: A Critique of Federal Moral Rights*, 15 HASTINGS COMM. & ENT. L.J. 905, 912–13 (1992–93) and Rebecca Stuart, *A Work of Heart: A Proposal for a Revision of the Visual Artists Rights Act of 1990 to Bring the United States Closer to International Standards*, 47 SANTA CLARA L. REV. 645, 683 (2007).

use" is consistent with Article 10(1) Berne it would seem necessary to revisit the question of whether and, if so, to what extent, section 107 is applicable to moral rights.

The Cumulative Nature of the Requirements

Whether the three-step test is cumulative in nature, i.e., the steps are taken in sequence and each must be satisfied, has been debated by scholars. Some favor seeing the three-step test as an integrated whole. Professors Geiger, Gervais, and Senftleben, for example, argue that "While the steps can be considered sequentially … it should not be overlooked that the test constitutes a single analytical whole and serves the ultimate goal to strike an appropriate balance." As such, all steps should be considered even if one is not met.[148] Several scholars share this view of approaching the three-step test as elements in an overall, comprehensive assessment.[149] Others have suggested that in order to reflect a balanced test, the order of the steps could be reversed. This would enable a focus on "legitimate interests" of the author or right holder, which would open up a policy space in which to discuss competing interests at stake, including those linked to the underlying justification of the exception.[150] Closely linked is the suggestion that the third step should become the focal point of analysis and that this may be achieved by avoiding a narrow interpretation of steps one and two.[151] Another suggestion is to retain the cumulative, sequential structure of the three-step test, but adopt different interpretative approaches for each step.[152] Other commentators have suggested that there is undue concern about a sequential approach because, practically speaking, the second and third steps inevitably overlap and intertwine.[153] However, some scholars, such as Professor Lucas, vehemently reject a global or overlapping interpretation of the elements of the three-step test, seeing this as "directly contrary to the wording of the text" and the Stockholm revision *travaux*.[154]

The WTO panel in the "Fairness in Music Licensing case" adopted the view (albeit without there being any argument on this point) that the three-step test is cumulative in nature, so that failure to meet the first limb would be fatal.[155] Thus, the failure of the "business" exemption in section 110[5](B) of the US Copyright Act 1976 to meet the first condition in Article 13 TRIPS meant that the exception failed overall.[156] Similarly, because the "homestyle" exception complied with the first step, the panel considered it necessary to analyze and apply the second and third steps (and also found these met). In addressing these steps, the panel noted that they are "closely related" and overlap in their field of operation.[157]

Article 10(1) Berne may be contrasted with the panel's approach to the three-step test in Article 13 TRIPS. Recall that quotations shall be permissible according to Article 10(1): (i) "from a work which has already been lawfully made available to the public"; (ii) provided that their "making is

[148] Geiger D. et al. *supra* note 80, at 581, 585 (2013–14).
[149] Geiger et al., *Towards a Balanced Interpretation*, *supra* note 80, at 489, 493, 495; Kur, *supra* note 18, at 340.
[150] C. Geiger, *The Three-Step Test, a Threat to a Balanced Copyright Law?*, 37 IIC 683, 697 (2006).
[151] M. Senftleben, *supra* note 80.
[152] He, *supra* note 80, at 274.
[153] Hughes, *supra* note 60, at 242.
[154] Lucas, *supra* note 108, at 281.
[155] WTO DS 160/R, [6.74] "As both parties agree, these three conditions apply cumulatively; a limitation or an exception is consistent with Article 13 only if it fulfils each of the three conditions."
[156] WTO DS 160/R, [6.160]. Although the panel nevertheless considered steps two and three and found that they also were not met: *see* [6.190]–[6.211] and [6.237]–[6.266].
[157] WTO DS 160/R, [6.161].

compatible with fair practice"; and (iii) "their extent does not exceed that justified by the purpose"; and (iv) that according to Article 10(3) "mention shall be made of the source, and of the name of the author, if it appears thereon." We take the view, based on the text of the provisions, that each of these conditions is distinct. However, this does not mean that all the conditions must be approached sequentially and that no overlap exists between them. Granted, the conditions of a work having been lawfully made available to the public and attribution of author and source appear as straightforward prerequisites without overlap. However, overlap exists between the requirements of quotation, fair practice, and proportionality and it is important to be aware of this. As we have argued above, what constitutes a quotation should be understood broadly: it relates to all types of works, may be a transformative use, is not restricted to certain purposes and may be of any length. Proportionality targets whether the length of the quotation is justifiable according to *its* purpose. Fair practice involves a consideration of whether the quotation is consistent with a pluralistic notion of "fairness" and this may involve examining the nature or purpose of the use; the type of expressive use; the size of the quotation and its proportion in relation to the source work; harm to the market of the source work and the integrity interests of the author of the source work. From this outline, it is apparent that the length of a quotation *is* important to both the proportionality and fair practice requirements, but should not be a barrier to whether a particular use is deemed a "quotation." Further, the purpose or use of the quotation should not determine its status as "quotation," but this will be relevant to judging proportionality and also fair practice. Thus, it is important not to exclude certain uses as "quotation" based on these criteria, but instead to factor them into assessments of proportionality and fair practice. As well, the relationship between these two latter requirements is important and, logically speaking, it makes more sense to consider proportionality before fair practice. This is because, based on the *travaux*, proportionality is really only concerned with judging the appropriate length of quotations. As the *travaux* make clear, "fair practice" is also concerned with assessing the length of quotations, but this, we argue, is part of a broader assessment of whether the quoted use is *fair*. Given that the normative considerations for considering fairness are more wide-ranging, it makes sense to only apply a light filter at the proportionality stage, and to interrogate more fully the length of the quotation alongside all the other relevant factors at the fairness stage.

The impact of Article 10(1) Berne including overlapping considerations, as opposed to the WTO panel view that the three-step test is sequential or cumulative in nature, mainly relates to how national legislatures implement the quotation exception and how national courts should interpret exceptions. For national legislatures, quotation may be defined broadly (and certainly should not be restricted to short quotations for specific purposes) and their proportionality and fairness judged according to several factors. As such, an open-ended, multi-factor exception, such as fair use in section 107 of the US Copyright Act 1976, would be permissible. We might, however, as indicated above, expect a clearer indication that the "unpublished" status of the work copied and attribution of the author are relevant considerations. Moreover, we would expect courts, in interpreting such an exception consistently with Article 10(1), to engage in weighing and assessing relevant factors. Thus, an exception that is structurally organized along the lines of US fair use could give effect to Article 10(1).

Free Use Exceptions

A further distinction that can be made between Article 9(2) and Article 10(1) Berne is that the former permits free use as well as royalty based exceptions, whereas the latter is simply "free use."[158] There is nothing in the language or *travaux* to indicate that the exception in Article 10(1) must be a "royalty free" one.[159] It seems, however, that the better view is that Article 10(1) only covers an unremunerated or "free use" exception. Since nothing in the *travaux* suggests that the quotation exception would give rise to a royalty based exception. Indeed, Berne Union members have implemented Article 10(1) as an unremunerated exception.[160]

Currently, US fair use is an unremunerated exception and Article 10(1) Berne justifies this to the extent that quotation uses fall within section 107. It also provides potential resistance to the argument that certain existing fair uses should in fact be permitted-but-paid[161] and the suggestion that therefore substantial incompatibility exists between the third limb of the three-step test and US fair use.[162]

CONCLUSION

Until now, the influence of Article 10(1) Berne on copyright exceptions has been neglected. As we have argued, Article 10(1) mandates a quotation exception that may be described as global, mandatory fair use. It is global because of the reach of Berne and TRIPS. It creates a mandatory exception because of the clear language of the provision and its *travaux*. It relates to "use" that is not limited by type of work, type of act, or purpose. Finally, it is "fair" use because the conditions of Article 10, namely, the work having been lawfully made available to the public, attribution, proportionality, and fair practice, must be satisfied. In particular, the requirement of "fair practice" embraces a range of normative considerations relating to economic and moral harm, distributive justice, freedom of expression, and, in limited situations, custom.

Article 10(1) Berne, we have argued, is not subject to the three-step test, and its requirements diverge in several ways from the WTO panel's interpretation of that test. As a result, Article 10(1) provides a fresh lens through which to view national copyright exceptions and potentially displaces the dominance of three-step thinking. We have demonstrated the potential consequences of this different perspective in relation to the US fair use exception. In particular, we have shown that, according to Article 10(1), the open-ended, multi-factorial, royalty-free nature of US fair use may be justified as a matter of international copyright law. However, at the same time, to comply with Article 10(1), US fair use may need to pay greater attention to the unpublished status of works that are used and the moral rights of authors.

[158] *See* B. Hugenholtz and R. Okediji, *Conceiving an International Instrument on Limitations and Exceptions to Copyright*, Amsterdam Law School Legal Studies Research Paper No. 2012-43, at http://ssrn.com/abstract=2017629, at 51 describing quotation as an "uncompensated limitation"; Xalabarder, *supra* note 19, at 397 ("no compensation applies"); and Pascale Chapdelaine, Copyright User Rights: Contracts and the Erosion of Property 37 n.43 (2017).

[159] Ricketson & Ginsburg, *supra* note 13, at [13.41], 786 suggest that Art. 10(1), in principle, could include remunerated quotations and that this "should more readily satisfy the requirement of compatibility with fair practice than would a free use."

[160] The highly controversial so-called 'Google tax' exception in Spain: Intellectual Property Law, Art. 32(2) (introduced by Act 21 of 4 November 2014), has thus been criticised for conflicting with the 'free use' nature of the quotation right: see R. Xalabarder, The Remunerated Statutory Limitation for News Aggregation and Search Engines Proposed by the Spanish Government; Its Compliance with International and EU Law', IN3 (Internet Interdisciplinary Institute) Working Paper, available at https://papers.ssrn.com/sol3/papers.cfm?abstract_id=2504596.

[161] In particular, nonprofit educational and library uses, as opposed to private uses and mass digitization, which are the examples discussed by Ginsburg, *Fair Use for Free*, *supra* note 120, at 1445–46 (2014).

[162] Ginsburg, *Exclusive Rights*, *supra* note 120, at 261–63.

4

An International Instrument on Permitted Uses in Copyright Law

Reto M. Hilty & Valentina Moscon

INTRODUCTION

(1) International copyright law imposes a solid minimum standard of copyright protection, while requiring a very thin minimum standard of permitted uses. As the Berne Convention (BC) evolved and in 1996 subsequent international Treaties were adopted, international copyright law has increasingly strengthened protection of private rights of exclusion and eschewed setting mandatory permitted uses.[1] Also International law has been progressively interpreted as a limit for States to lay down permitted uses in their laws or to define the scope of existing provisions extensively. This is partly due to how the Three-Step Test set forth by Article 9(2) BC has been understood over time. Originally intended as a way for Berne Union countries to permit reproduction of copyrighted works, the Test has been later intended as a strict method of regulating the system of copyright permitted uses.[2]

(2) This restrictive understanding of exceptions and limitations goes hand in hand with the raising of intellectual property (IP) protection standards. In the prevailing international environment, some economically strong countries shifted the focus of their efforts from wider international *fora* to regional and bilateral agreements (mostly Free Trade Agreements), asking for more extensive protection of intellectual property rights within the scope of Article 1(1) of the TRIPS Agreement. These countries tend to negotiate for the inclusion of more protectable subject matters, broader and more extensive coverage, increased harmonization to their standards of protection, stronger enforcement mechanisms, and a weakening of flexibility and differentiation of treatment.[3]

(3) With the aim of tackling these challenges deriving from an unbalanced and inflexible copyright system, the Max Planck Institute for Innovation and Competition launched a Copyright Project in 2012. Based on an international collaboration involving

[1] Some openness toward minimum limitations to copyright may be found in the Marrakesh Treaty (*Marrakesh VIP Treaty* – Marrakesh Treaty to Facilitate Access to Published Works for Persons Who Are Blind, Visually Impaired or Otherwise Print Disabled, 2013) and in Art. 10 of the Berne Convention. *See* Berne Convention for the Protection of Literary and Artistic Works, opened for signature Sept. 9, 1886, 828 U.N.T.S. 221, S. Treaty Doc. No. 99-27, 99th Cong. (1986) (revised at Paris, July 24, 1979) [hereinafter Berne Convention], Art. 10 (articulating a right to quote).

[2] *See* SENFTLEBEN, Martin Senfteben, Copyright Limitations and the Three-Step Test. An Analysis of the Three-Step Test in International and EC Copyright Law (2004).

[3] For further discussion, *see* Ruth L. Okediji, *Reframing International Copyright Limitations and Exceptions As Development Policy, in* COPYRIGHT LAW IN AN AGE OF LIMITATIONS AND EXCEPTIONS 429 (2017).

world-renowned copyright experts,[4] this project has resulted in a legal instrument, designed to potentially become an international treaty. The proposed Instrument on Permitted Uses in Copyright Law (the Instrument) is based on broad international consensus concerning core users' prerogatives and freedoms leading toward a balanced copyright system.

(4) A first initiative in the direction of better defining the scope of permitted uses in copyright law is the "Declaration on a Balanced Interpretation of the 'three-step test' in Copyright Law" of 2008, prepared in a cooperation between the MPI[5] and the School of Law at Queen Mary University of London.[6] The Declaration opposes the increasingly restrictive understanding of the three-step test and raises concerns about its impact on the law of copyright and related rights, offering a balanced and flexible interpretation of the test in copyright law. The emerging Instrument goes a step further: it is not limited to recommendations or guidelines but provides a core of minimum permitted uses to be implemented by contracting parties in their national legislations. The Instrument includes a core of minimum permitted uses that are binding for Contracting Parties: Contracting Parties have to implement the settled minimum standards in their national legislations. This obligation places into the hands of national States a lever for tackling the political pressure that notoriously exists in international negotiations, especially in the arena of bilateral or regional agreements. In this context, the Instrument is meant to facilitate cooperation amongst countries holding different interests in international negotiations. In short, by signing an international agreement based on this Instrument, these countries would set new minimum standards of permitted uses in copyright law, which may curb the higher standards of protection claimed by certain countries in international negotiations within the scope of Article 1(1) TRIPS.

(5) In Section I, this chapter describes the international legal framework from which the idea of producing the "International Instrument on Permitted Uses in Copyright Law" derives. In Section II, it outlines the Instrument, focusing in particular on the strategy and purposes behind the Instrument.

I BACKGROUND

1 *Evolution of the Three-Step Test*

(6) Since its introduction, the scope of the three-step test has been progressively extended. Originally understood as a "counterweight to the formal recognition of a general right of reproduction,"[7] it aimed at allowing countries of the Berne Union to permit free reproduction of works "in certain special cases, provided that such reproduction does not conflict with a normal exploitation of the work and does not unreasonably prejudice the legitimate interests of the author."[8] However, the conception of the test and the

[4] The first meeting was attended by Denis Borges Barbosa, Michael Carroll, Carlos Correa, Thomas Dreier, Séverine Dusollier, Christophe Geiger, Jonathan Griffiths, Henning Grosse Ruse-Khan, Reto M. Hilty, Kaya Köklü, Annette Kur, Lin Xiuqin, Rryszard Markiewicz, Sylvie Nérisson, Gul Okutan, Alexander Peukert, Jerome Reichman, Jan Rosén, Martin Senftleben, and Raquel Xalabarder.

[5] The Institute's name at the time was the Max Planck Institute for Intellectual Property and Competition Law.

[6] *See* Christophe Geiger et al., *Declaration on a Balanced Interpretation of the 'Three-Step Test' in Copyright Law*, 6 IIC 39 (2008).

[7] *See* Geiger et al., *The Three-Step Test Revisited: How to Use the Test's Flexibility in National Copyright Law*, 29 Am. U. Int'l L. Rev. 581 (2014).

[8] *See* Berne Convention, Art. 9(2).

language used for its transposition into various legal tools has changed progressively: under the TRIPS Agreement[9] and the WIPO Treaties,[10] it has been extended to the full range of copyright and related rights.[11] In addition, the test has been enshrined explicitly in national and regional legislation and restrictively interpreted by courts, where it has mostly assumed the function of barring, rather than permitting, the adoption of new exceptions and limitations to copyright, as well as restricting the scope of application of the existing ones.[12] This evolution (or involution) is partly related to a decision of the WTO dispute settlement panel of June 15, 2000.[13] The WTO panel followed a restrictive interpretation of the test: under a rigid and mechanical sequentiality each step was treated as an independent entity. The literature on the meaning of the test after the WTO is voluminous.[14]

(7) Although the WTO panel interpretation of the three-step test has influenced its later understanding and application, this should not be considered a final ruling.[15] The restrictive interpretation of the test contrasts with both its literal wording and its historical background. The broad formulation of the test settled the question of copyright limitations in a way that countries of both the "open-clause" and the "closed-list" tradition could accept. The three-step test was initially drafted by the UK delegation at the 1967 Stockholm Conference for the Revision of the Berne Convention.[16] Therefore the test is based on language originally submitted in English, translated into the official French and subsequently retranslated into the English version of the Convention. These linguistic stages might have modified the meaning that the writers intended to give to the test.[17] At the same time, as the first draft was written by a delegation belonging to the Anglo-American copyright tradition, it is difficult to imagine that the drafters intended to establish a rule opposite to an open-ended factors test, comparable to traditional fair use legislation in common law countries.

(8) Furthermore, the Agreed Statement concerning Article 10 WCT formally adopted by the 1996 WIPO Diplomatic Conference supports the understanding of the test as an open clause and a guideline for the extension of existing limitations and exceptions, and for the

9 Agreement on Trade-Related Aspects of Intellectual Property Rights (Marrakesh, April 15, 1994), Marrakesh Agreement Establishing the World Trade Organization, Annex 1C, The Legal Texts: The Results of the Uruguay Round of Multilateral Trade Negotiations 321 (1999), 1869 UNTS 299, 33 ILM 1197 (1994), which entered into force on 1 January 1995 (hereinafter TRIPS), Art. 28.1.

10 WIPO Copyright Treaty Dec. 20, 1996 (hereinafter WCT) and WIPO Performances and Phonograms Treaty Dec. 20, 1996 (hereinafter WPPT).

11 *See* TRIPS, *supra* note 9, Art. 13; WCT, *supra* note 10, Art. 10.

12 Senftleben, *supra* note 1; Christophe Geiger, Daniel J. Gervais, & Martin R. F. Senftleben, *Understanding the "Three-Step Test"*, *in* International Intellectual Property – A Handbook of Contemporary Research 167–89 (Daniel J. Gervais ed., 2015).

13 Panel report, *Dispute Settlement [United States – Section 110(5) of the Copyright Act]* WTO Doc. WT/DS/160/R (June 15, 2000). For discussion of this report, *see* Jane C. Ginsburg, *Toward Supranational Copyright Law? The WTO Panel Decision and the "Three-Step Test" for Copyright Exceptions*, 187 Revue Internationale du Droit d'Auteur [RIDA] 3 (2001); Martin Senftleben, *Towards a Horizontal Standard for Limiting Intellectual Property Rights? WTO Panel Reports Shed Light on the Three-Step Test in Copyright Law and Related Tests in Patent and Trademark Law*, 37 IIC 407 (2006); Graeme B. Dinwoodie, *The Development and Incorporation of International Norms in the Formation of Copyright Law*, 62 Ohio St. L.J., 733 (2001).

14 For a detailed overview, *see* Senftleben, *supra* note 1.

15 *See* Geiger et al., *supra* note 7.

16 *See* Records of the Intellectual Property Conference of Stockholm: June 11 to July 14, 1967 (1971).

17 *See* Senftleben, *The International Three-Step Test: A Model Provision for EC Fair Use Legislation*, 1 J. Intell. Prop., Info. Tech. and E-Com. L. [JIPITEC] 67 para. 1 (2010), about the historical background of the three-step test. *See also* Senftleben, *supra* note 1.

introduction of new copyright permitted uses. The function of the three-step test was described as follows:

> It is understood that the provisions of Article 10 permit contracting parties to carry forward and appropriately extend into the digital environment limitations and exceptions in their national laws which have been considered acceptable under the Berne Convention. Similarly, these provisions should be understood to permit contracting parties to devise new exceptions and limitations that are appropriate in the digital network environment. It is also understood that Article 10(2) neither reduces nor extends the scope of applicability of the limitations and exceptions permitted by the Berne Convention.[18]

2 *The Drift toward an Unsustainable Application of the Three-Step Test within the European Copyright Law*

(9) European copyright law represents a clear example of the three-step test having become a strict method of regulating the system of exceptions and limitations to copyright. The Information Society Directive from 2001 (InfoSoc Directive)[19] establishes a series of broadly defined exclusive rights and subjects those rights to an exhaustive, but optional, list of permissible exceptions.[20] In addition to the stringent system of exceptions and limitations by which users are bound, the InfoSoc Directive explicitly included the restrictive three-step test: according to Article 5(5) of the InfoSoc Directive, the exceptions and limitations set out in Article 5(1) to (4) "shall only be applied in certain special cases which do not conflict with a normal exploitation of the work or other subject matter and do not unreasonably prejudice the legitimate interests the rightholder." This approach raises at least two issues. First, if national legislation adopts and specifies exceptions listed in the EU catalogue, these exceptions as implemented by member states may still be challenged on the grounds that they are incompatible with the three-step test.[21] For example, where a member state has introduced in its national law a broad exception for e-learning, such an exception might be considered noncompliant with the mentioned Article 5(3)(a) of the InfoSoc Directive (use for the purpose of illustration for teaching or scientific research) interpreted according to the EU three-step test. Second, the test might be applied to place additional constraints on national exceptions. Although neither the international legal instruments in place nor the InfoSoc Directive define the test as a principle obliging courts to interpret exceptions and limitations restrictively,[22] European national judges have increasingly applied it in an unbalanced manner, perceiving it as an "economic prejudice" test.[23] This phenomenon has become

[18] WIPO, Records of the diplomatic conference on certain copyright and neighbouring rights questions Geneva 1996, Vol. I, Geneva, 1999, p. 28, at https://www.wipo.int/edocs/pubdocs/en/wipo_pub_348_vol_i.pdf

[19] *See* Directive 2001/29 of the European Parliament and of the Council of May 22, 2001, on the harmonization of certain aspects of copyright and related rights in the information society [Official Journal L 167, 22/06/2001 P. 0010 – 0019].

[20] *See* Reto M. Hilty & Kaya Köklü, *Limitations and Exceptions to Copyright in the Digital Age. Four Cornerstones for a Future-Proof Legal Framework in the EU, in* New Developments in EU And International Copyright Law 283 (Irini A. Stamatoudi ed., 2016).

[21] *See*, Concise European Copyright Law, 469 (Thomas Dreier. P Bernt Hugenholtz eds., 2016).

[22] For a discussion, *see* Jonathan Griffiths, *The "Three-Step Test" in European Copyright Law – Problems and Solutions* (Queen Mary Sch. of L. Legal Stud. Res., Paper No. 31/2009, 2009) http://ssrn.com/abstract=1476968.

[23] In the Green Paper underlying the Information Society Directive, but not in the Directive, the European Commission had referred to the test as a guiding principle, highlighting the fact that "a number of parties suggest the 'general

progressively widespread across national courts.[24] It creates a system which offers little room for flexibilities, and is hardly adaptable to technological progress. In fact, it has become very difficult to extend free uses by analogy beyond the perimeter specified by law. One of the most widely criticized examples of the adoption of a strict standard is provided by the decision of the French Supreme Court in the *Mulholland Drive* case.[25] In this case, the French Supreme Court held that the private copy exception under French copyright law is not a positive right for users of copyright works and must be construed in accordance with the three-step test under Article 9(2) of the Berne Convention. The court stated that in the digital environment, the existence of an exception permitting the making of private copies of DVDs prejudiced the normal exploitation of the copyrighted work and therefore violated the test's second step.[26] On a similar basis, the District Court of The Hague restricted the exception for press review. The case dealt with the unauthorized scanning and reproduction of press articles for internal electronic communication in ministries. In determining whether this practice was permissible, the court considered the provision in Article 15 of the Dutch Copyright Act to be noncompliant with the requirement of the EU three-step test.[27]

(10) Decisions of national judges mingle with the Court of Justice of the European Union (CJEU) approach, which has clearly imposed an interpretation of limitations and exceptions that is in line with the three-step test. In the *Infopaq* decision, the court held that: "The exemption [in Art. 5(1) relating to transient copying] must be interpreted in the light of Article 5(5) of Directive 2001/29, under which that exemption is to be applied only in certain special cases which do not conflict with a normal exploitation of the work or other subject-matter and do not unreasonably prejudice the legitimate interests of the right holder."[28]

3 *Tensions between Formalistic and Balanced Solutions*

(11) The approach based on formalistic and abstract interpretations of the three-step test clashes with the need to adapt the legal framework in a timely manner to individual cases and technological advances. This tension emerges in a number of CJEU decisions: in some cases the court offers balanced solutions relying on a "purposive approach." For example, with regard to the exception examined in the above-mentioned *Infopaq* decision – transient copying in the sense of Article 5(1) InfoSoc Directive – in *Football Association Premier League* the court stated that: "[I]n accordance with its objective, that exception must allow and ensure the development and operation of new technologies

economic prejudice' clause in Article 9(2) Berne Convention as a point of reference." *See* European Commission, COM (1996) 586 final, at 11–12 (Nov. 20, 1996).

[24] *See* Christophe Geiger & Franciska Schönherr, *The Information Society Directive (Article 5 and 6(4))*, *in* EU Copyright Law: A Commentary, 440 (Paul Torremans & Irini A. Stadamoudi eds., 2014).

[25] *See* Cour de cassation [supreme court for judicial matters] Feb. 28, 2006, Société Studio Canal et autres c. Perquin et UFC Que Choisir (Fr.); Griffiths, *supra* note 21 (considering the development of the three-step test). For further discussion, *see* Geiger, *The Three-Step Test, a Threat to a Balanced Copyright Law?*, 37 IIC, 683 (2006).

[26] *See* Griffiths, *supra* note 21 (offering commentary on the French case).

[27] *See* Rb. Den Haag Mar. 2, 2005, case no. 192880, LJN AS 8778, m.nt. (Computerrecht 2005, p. 143). The Dutch decision has been taken into consideration in Griffiths, *supra* note 21; Senftleben, *Fair Use in The Netherlands – A Renaissance?*, 33 AMI 1 (2009). Dutch courts applied the three-step test already prior to the Information Society Directive. As early as 1990, the Dutch Supreme Court invoked the three-step test of Art. 9(2) of the Berne Convention to support its holding. *See* HR 22 June 1990, case no. 13933, NJF 1991 (Nederlandse Jurisprudentie 1991, p. 268).

[28] Case C-4/08, Infopaq International/Danske Dagblades Forening, 2009 E.C.R. 2009 I-06569, paras. 56–57.

and safeguard a fair balance between the rights and interests of right holders, on the one hand, and of users of protected works to avail themselves of those new technologies, on the other hand."[29] The court concluded that the transient copying at issue in *Football Association Premier League*, performed within the memory of a satellite decoder and on a television screen, was compatible with the three-step test of Article 5(5) InfoSoc Directive.[30] Even in the *Painer,*[31] *Deckmyn,*[32] and *Technische Universität Darmstandt*[33] decisions, the court sought to enable the effectiveness of copyright exceptions and limitations focusing on their objective.

(12) Sensitivity to a more balanced system was also shown by some national judges who have examined other avenues in search of flexibility. In some cases European national judges find normative inspiration in fundamental freedoms, such as the freedom of expression, artistic freedom, and the right of privacy;[34] in others, they circumvent the issue at stake relying on contract law. For instance, the German Federal Supreme Court stated that Google thumbnail images do not infringe copyright law.[35] The decision applies the notion of implied consent.[36] In other cases (although rarely) courts have resorted to the doctrine of misuse or abuse of copyright law in such a way as not to read the list of exceptions so rigidly.[37] Interestingly, national courts have occasionally drawn on alternative approaches to the three-step test.[38] The German Federal Supreme Court adopted an interesting approach[39] in a case involving the Technical Information Library of Hannover which had an electronic catalogue and sent copies of articles from scientific periodicals to users upon request. A representative association for publishers and booksellers claimed that such activities infringed the reproduction and distribution rights. The legal basis of this practice was the statutory limitation for personal use in Sec. 53 of the German Copyright Act. The German court admitted that the library's activity came close to that of publishers. However, instead of impeding the library's practice, the court held that authors, in order to stay below the ceiling

[29] Cases C-403/08 & C-429/08, Football Association Premier League/QC Leisure, 2011 E.C.R. 2011 I-09083, para. 164.

[30] *Cf.* Bernt P. Hugenholtz & Martin Senftleben, Fair Use in Europe: In Search of Flexibilities (2011).

[31] Case C-145/10, Eva-Maria Painer v. Standard VerlagsGmbH and Others, 2011 E.C.R. 2011 I-12533.

[32] Case C-201/13, Johan Deckmyn and others v. Helena Vandersteen and others, 2014 E.C.R. http://curia.europa.eu.

[33] Case C-117/13, Technische Universität Darmstadt/Eugen Ulmer KG, 2014 E.C.R. http://curia.europa.eu.

[34] *See, e.g.*, Bundesverfassungsgericht (BVerfG) (Federal Constitutional Court) June 29, 2000, Zeitschrift für Urheber- und Medienrecht (ZUM) 867, 2000 (Ger.).

[35] *See* Bundesgerichtshof [BGH] [Federal Court of Justice] Apr. 29, 2010, Neue Juristische Wochenzeitscshrift [NJW] 2731, 2010 (Ger.).

[36] The German Federal Court of Justice decided that a copyright owner who uploads a depiction of a copyright-protected work onto the Internet without making use of technically possible precautions to prevent that work from being searched and displayed by search engine providers had by doing so provided his/her implied consent to the reproduction of the (depiction of that) work as a thumbnail preview picture. The reproduction of the image as a preview picture in Google's preview function, while encroaching on the authors' right of presentation of their works under Art. 19a of the German Copyright Act, was therefore nonetheless not unlawful.

[37] One of the most recent and well-reasoned decisions in the field is S.T.S., Apr. 3, 2012 (R.X., No. 172) (Spain). *See* Raquel Xalabarder, *Spanish Supreme Court Rules in Favour of Google Search Engine . . . and a Flexible Reading of Copyright Statutes?*, 3 JIPITEC 162, para. 1. (2012). *See also* Caterina Sganga & Silvia Scalzini, *From Abuse of Right to European Copyright Misuse: A New Doctrine for EU Copyright Law*, 48 IIC 405 (2006); Cristophe Caron, *Abuse of Rights and Author's Rights*'(1) RIDA 176, 2–80 (1998).

[38] Paul Torremans, *Archiving Exceptions: Where Are We and Where Do We Need to Go?*, *in* Copyright and Cultural Heritage Preservation and Access to Works in a Digital World 111 (Estelle Derclaye ed., 2010).

[39] *See* Bundesgerichtshof [BGH] [Federal Court of Justice] Feb. 25, 1999, Neue Juristische Wochenzeitscshrift [NJW] 237, 2000 (Ger.).

of the normal exploitation of the work (see, three-step test), had to be remunerated in return for the uses covered by the exception.[40]

(13) Even though some attentive judges are more likely than others to apply balanced solutions in individual cases, this does not solve comprehensively the structural problem caused by the strict interpretation of the three-step test.[41] In view of this, some commentators have advanced proposals for reviewing the test in a more balanced form.[42] However, the practical difficulties of rewriting the test are self-evident: the international legislative process in this area is notoriously slow, intense, and influenced by lobbying.[43] Furthermore, a legislative revision of the three-step test may not ensure adequate results. The complexity of the review process of international treaties on intellectual property law may result in developing rules that are too detailed and therefore incapable of keeping pace with constant and rapid technological developments.

4 *"Declaration on a Balanced Interpretation of the 'Three-Step Test' in Copyright Law"*

(14) The Declaration on a Balanced Interpretation of the "Three-Step Test" in Copyright Law[44] aims at guiding the application of the three-step test. More precisely as explained by the Declaration's authors, its purpose is "to restore the three-step test to its original role as a relatively flexible standard precluding clearly unreasonable encroachments upon an author's right without interfering unduly with the ability of legislators and courts to respond to the challenges presented by shifting commercial and technological context in a fair and balanced manner." Accordingly, the three-step test should allow a comprehensive assessment of all circumstances, whereby exceptions and limitations should be interpreted in the light of their meaning and purposes, also considering all the interests involved.

(15) The Declaration is based on historic evidence and economic theories suggesting that flexibility in copyright law is recommended on at least two levels: (i) flexibility in interpretation and application of exceptions and limitations in copyright law; and (ii) freedom of states to shape copyright law to their own cultural, social and economic development needs.[45] The ideal behind the Declaration is to clarify and foster the range of flexibility already embedded in TRIPS and other treaties, in particular the Paris and Berne Conventions, demonstrating that international legislation does not need to be applied by all contracting parties in the same way. Quite the opposite, according to varying socioeconomic conditions, some differentiation is necessary. Copyright exceptions and limitations tailored to domestic needs provide the most important legal

[40] A few years later the same court followed a similar approach. *See* Bundesgerichtshof [BGH] [Federal Court of Justice] July 11, 2002, NEUE JURISTISCHE WOCHENZEITSCSHRIFT [NJW] Case I ZR 255/00.

[41] *See, e.g.*, Geiger, *From Berne to National Law, via the Copyright Directive: The Dangerous Mutations of the Three-Step Test*, 29 EUR. INTELL. PROP. REV. [EIPR] 486 (2007); Kamiel Koelman, *Fixing the Three-Step Test*, 28 EIPR 407 (2006).

[42] *See* Koelman, *supra* note 41.

[43] Antony Taubman, *Thematic Review: Negotiating "Trade-Related Aspects" of Intellectual Property Rights, in* THE MAKING OF THE TRIPS AGREEMENT 15 (Jayashree Watal & Antony Taubman eds., 2015) (describing the complexities of the negotiation process).

[44] Geiger et al., *Towards a Balanced Interpretation of the Three-Step Test for Copyright Exception*, 4 EIPR 489 (2008).

[45] *See* INTELLECTUAL PROPERTY, LEGAL AND ECONOMIC CHALLENGES FOR DEVELOPMENT (Mario Cimoli et al. eds., 2014).

mechanism for the achievement of an appropriate, self-determined balance of interests at the national level.[46]

(16) However, the Declaration, as a legal tool solely emphasizing the flexibility existing in the international legal framework may not be enough – alone – to provide a set of minimum permitted uses. This is for more than one reason, including the fact that the arguments advanced by the Declaration hardly penetrate the circles of policymakers. A further reason is that, adapting the potential flexibility inherent in the treaties presupposes a level of legal and technical proficiency that may lack in certain countries. In addition, the implementation of the principles set out in the Declaration may be problematic within the present international context. As will be explained below, high protection standards are increasingly established by free trade agreements (FTAs), thereby limiting flexible interpretations of the international treaties.

5 *From Agreed Minimum Protection Standards to "Imposed" Extensive Protection Standards*

(17) The minimum standard of protection introduced by the TRIPS Agreement served as a step in the pursuit of stronger intellectual property rights.[47] Some nations almost immediately after the introduction of the TRIPS Agreement began negotiating for broadening the scope of intellectual property rights including copyright.[48] In this process, bilateral and regional fora, allowed by Article 1(1) of the TRIPS Agreement, have taken the place of international negotiations.[49] The will of some countries pushing for the extension of intellectual property protection beyond the TRIPS standards emerges in FTAs.[50] The political failure of the Anti-Counterfeiting Trade Agreement (ACTA[51])[52] did not discourage the pursuit of further trade agreements including specific IP provisions enlarging state commitments beyond the TRIPS requirements. The scope of those so-called "TRIPS-plus" provisions usually runs contrary to the balance of interests and flexibility enshrined in TRIPS.[53]

46 Geiger et al., *supra* note 44.

47 *See* Annette Kur, *From Minimum Standard to Maximum Rules, in* TRIPS PLUS 20 – FROM TRADE RULES TO MARKET PRINCIPLES 133 (Hanns Ullrich et al. eds., 2016).

48 *See* Bryan C. Mercurio, *TRIPS-Plus Provisions in FTAs: Recent Trends, in* REGIONAL TRADE AGREEMENTS AND THE WTO LEGAL SYSTEM 215 (Lorand Bartels & Federico Ortino eds., 2006), available at http://ssrn.com/abstract=947767.

49 For a working definition of multilateral and regional agreements, *see* Sean M. Flynn et al., *The U.S Proposal for an Intellectual Property Chapter in the Trans-Pacific Partnership Agreement*, 28 AM. U. INT'L. L. REV. 105 (2012).

50 A number of recent initiatives for new multilateral IP regimes in free trade agreements include TPP, RCEP, TTIP, to name a few. *See* Kur, *supra* note 47 (providing an overview of initiatives and policy). *See generally* JOSEF DREXL ET AL., EU BILATERAL TRADE AGREEMENTS AND INTELLECTUAL PROPERTY: FOR BETTER OR WORSE? (2014).

51 On this Agreement, *see* C. Geiger, *Weakening Multilateralism in Intellectual Property Lawmaking: A European Perspective on* ACTA, 3(2) WIPO J. 166 (2012).

52 *See* Duncan Matthews & Petra Zíkovská, *The Rise and Fall of the Anti-Counterfeiting Trade Agreement (ACTA): Lessons for the European Union*, 44 IIC 626 (2013).

53 For further discussion *see* Henning Grosse Ruse-Khan, *The International Law Relation between TRIPS and Subsequent TRIPS-Plus Free Trade Agreements: Towards Safeguarding TRIPS Flexibilities*, 18 J. INTELL. PROP. L. 1 (2011) (analyzing the relationship between TRIPS flexibility provisions and TRIPS-plus FTAs); *id.*, *From TRIPS to FTAs and Back: Re-Conceptualising the Role of a Multilateral IP Framework in a TRIPS-Plus World, in* NETHERLANDS YEARBOOK OF INTERNATIONAL LAW (Fabian Amtenbrink, Denise Prévost, & Ramses A. Wessel eds., 2017); CYNTHIA M. HO, ACCESS TO MEDICINE IN THE GLOBAL ECONOMY: INTERNATIONAL AGREEMENTS ON PATENTS AND RELATED RIGHTS (2011); Peter K. Yu, ACTA *and Its Complex Politics*, 3 WIPO J. 1 (2011); Daniel Gervais, *Towards a New Core International Copyright Norm: The Reverse Three-Step Test*, 9 MARQ. INTELL. PROP. L. REV. 1 (2005).

(18) The strengthening of copyright protection is one issue; another that warrants attention is the strategy behind the "TRIPS-plus" approach and the consequences resulting therefrom. A national state willing to implement certain limitations and exceptions might be prevented from doing so through pressure from other countries or groups of countries defending high standards of copyright protection. Such standards of protection are designed by willing countries without considering the intellectual property rationale that contrariwise has been taken into account within international agreements.[54] There is no doubt that the TRIPS Agreement and the treaties concluded by the World Intellectual Property Organization (WIPO) have reached a high level of intellectual property protection. Nonetheless,[55] they are relatively balanced considering the diverse standpoints of all countries involved. Also, they convey basic principles of intellectual property law, giving an interpretative key to World Trade Organization (WTO) members.[56] Intellectual property, including copyright law, is justified as a mechanism for fostering innovation. Inherent in this "functional" rationale for creating private exclusive rights is the idea that the public interest is the most important objective. Toward this end, limiting the scope of intellectual property rights is in principle permitted by TRIPS, leaving room for interpretation to national legislatures and courts. They may benefit of it in view of the socioeconomic conditions of their countries.[57] Additionally, TRIPS includes transitional arrangements according to which some countries could benefit by delaying the application of certain provisions.

(19) Again, the international treaties in place and the TRIPS Agreement, in particular, are the result of a international, transparent contracting process. On the contrary, bilateral or regional agreements are mostly the outcome of a so-called "country club approach," which pursues interests of only some parties in a non-transparent manner.[58] In fact, within international negotiations weaker countries are likely to accept condition,[59] which stipulate standards for protecting intellectual property that go against their own interests, in exchange for certain concessions relating to free trade in goods and market preferences.[60] Such trade-off mechanisms might produce the effect of raising the standards for protecting intellectual property at the expense of the real needs of each

[54] *See* Reto Hilty, *Ways Out of the Trap of Article 1(1) TRIPS*, *in* TRIPS PLUS 20 – FROM TRADE RULES TO MARKET PRINCIPLES 185 (Hanns Ullrich et al. eds., 2016). *See also* Carlos M. Correa, *Multilateral Agreements and Policy Opportunities*, *in* INTELLECTUAL PROPERTY, LEGAL AND ECONOMIC CHALLENGES FOR DEVELOPMENT 418 (Mario Cimoli et al. eds., 2014).

[55] *See* Giovanni Dosi & Joseph E. Stiglitz, *The Role of Intellectual Property Rights in the Development Process, with Some Lessons from Developed Countries: An Introduction*, *in* INTELLECTUAL PROPERTY, LEGAL AND ECONOMIC CHALLENGES FOR DEVELOPMENT 1 (Mario Cimoli et al. eds., 2014); Jerome H. Reichman, *Intellectual Property in the Twenty-First Century: Will the Developing Countries Lead or Follow?*, 46 HOUS. L. REV. 1115 (2009). *See also* Alexander Peukert, *Intellectual Property: The Global Spread of a Legal Concept*, *in* KRITIKA – ESSAYS ON INTELLECTUAL PROPERTY 114 (Peter Drahos et al. eds., 2015) (discussing the affirmation of intellectual property standard in developing countries).

[56] *See* Hilty, *supra* note 54.

[57] Correa, *supra* note 54.

[58] *See* Yu, *supra* note 53; DANIEL GERVAIS, INTELLECTUAL PROPERTY, TRADE AND DEVELOPMENT: STRATEGIES TO OPTIMIZE ECONOMIC DEVELOPMENT IN A TRIPS PLUS ERA (2007).

[59] *See* Frederick M. Abbott, *A New Dominant Trade Species Emerges: Is Bilateralism a Threat?*, *in* THE FUTURE OF INTERNATIONAL ECONOMIC LAW 133 (William J. Davey & John Jackson eds., 2008) (discussing issues related to the effect of bilateral agreements).

[60] *See* Henning Grosse Ruse-Khan et al., *Principles for IP Provisions in Bilateral and Regional Agreements*, 44 IIC 878 (2013) (addressing this concern).

country.[61] The overall impact can be further aggravated by knock-on effects, since Articles 3 and 4 of TRIPS require equal treatment of all members, or nationals of those members, of the WTO.

Several approaches could be adopted in order to address the problems raised above. A first line is purely of a legal nature. It may be reasonable to question whether and to what extent "TRIPS-plus" agreements may be limited the existing international law and its interpretation.[62] A further related issue is whether (and how) countries that have signed bilateral agreements embedding "TRIPS-plus" standards could claim against those standards. A second approach to face the situation described above is of a strategic nature within international politics. The last one will be taken into consideration below, as the Instrument on Permitted Uses in Copyright Law may be used strategically in international negotiations.

II INSTRUMENT ON PERMITTED USES IN COPYRIGHT LAW

1 *Premise*

(20) The Instrument on Permitted Uses in Copyright Law is based on the idea that copyright protection and permitted uses of copyrighted works are two sides of the same coin. Right holders' protection and permitted uses are both equally essential in ensuring that copyright will have positive effects on the information economy and society in general. The aim of the Instrument aim is not to define a list of limitations and exceptions restraining an all-encompassing exclusive right of the copyright holder, but to foster a balanced copyright system by shifting the attention to the users' interests. Limitations and exceptions are generally understood as instruments helping to correct copyright exclusivity. But designing limitations and exceptions principally as "adjustment tools is a second-best approach" that disregards the complex needs that are essential for copyright to serve socially beneficial goals, economic growth, and development.[63] From the perspective of the authors of the Instrument, right holders' protection and permitted uses are both equally essential in ensuring that copyright can have positive effects on society and the information economy. This vision, after all, is found in the TRIPS. It suffices here to recall the principles stated in Articles 7 and 8 of TRIPS.[64] Those provisions make clear that IP rights are not unconfined rights and emphasize the obligation for members to "adopt measures necessary to protect public health and nutrition, and to promote the public interest in sectors of vital importance to their socio-economic and technological development."

[61] *See* Antonietta Di Blasé, *IP Protection in Investment Agreements, in* General Interests of Host States in International Investment Law 194 (Giorgio Sacerdoti et al. eds., 2014).

[62] *See* Henning Grosse Ruse-Khan, The Protection of Intellectual Property in International Law (2016) (addressing the technical issue concerning whether and when TRIPS flexibilities can prevail over TRIPS-plus obligations in FTAs).

[63] *See* Okediji, *supra* note 3.

[64] This argument is related to a sound understanding of copyright law, specifically the issue of the legal nature and scope of the right attributed to the creator of a work. This is an old discussion which is also related to the very notion of "intellectual property" as a property owner's right, rather than an individual right whose extension is related to its own function. *See, e.g.*, Tullio Ascarelli, Teoria della Concorrenza e dei Beni Immateriali: Istituzioni di Diritto Industriale (1957). *See also* Pierre-Emmanuel Moyse, *La nature du droit d'auteur: droit deproprité ou monopole?*, 43 McGill L.J., 50743 (1998).

(21) Precisely this idea of equal position between users' and right holders' interests has led the authors of the Instrument not to employ the expression "exceptions and limitations". The terms "exceptions and limitations," although broadly used and commonly accepted,[65] suggest a one-sided (too narrow) perspective.[66] The choice of the wording "permitted uses" is related to the fact that, the term "users' rights" is not (yet[67]) generally accepted.[68] Nonetheless the wording "permitted uses" allows prospective contracting parties to implement permitted uses in national law in the form of actual "user rights."

2 *Aims and Approach of the Project*

(22) The authors of the Instrument conceived it as an international agreement which contains concrete provisions defining a core of "minimum" permitted uses. The group of experts had previously explored the idea of creating a model law instead of a treaty. However, this solution appeared to be inappropriate and in any case less efficient than an international agreement: it would be difficult to establish a model law with worldwide applicability in the light of the various existing national copyright systems. Besides, even if a treaty approach were to fail in the end, a good draft might still help many countries to shape their domestic copyright laws according to their own needs.

The drafted treaty aims at fostering co-opertation between contracting parties. As standards of protection are based on bi- or multilateral agreements, standards of permitted uses might also be established by agreements signed by group of countries, as long as they are consistent with the three-step test. In using the flexibility allowed by international treaties with respect to the protection of copyright and related rights, contracting parties may adopt obligations aimed at achieving a minimum level of permitted uses in their national copyright laws. Thus, the primary goal of the Instrument is to allow states to support each other in carving out necessary spaces of freedom, strengthening their position in international negotiations so that they can pursue their own national interests and foster social and economic development in a coordinated manner.

(23) All countries could benefit from the introduction of minimal permitted uses, including, for example, European countries.[69] As mentioned before, those countries deal with the tight provisions of secondary EU law, which is often an obstacle to the adaptation of national copyright law to fast-paced technological developments. It is no secret that European (and generally Western) policy mostly considers the interests of the copyright industry as a priority. For this reason the path toward creating a system of permitted uses is still a challenge.

[65] *See* LUCIE GUIBAULT, COPYRIGHT LIMITATIONS AND CONTRACTS. AN ANALYSIS OF THE CONTRACTUAL OVERRIDABILITY OF LIMITATIONS ON COPYRIGHT 90 (2002) (discussing the use of the term "user's right"). *See also* LYMAN RAY PATTERSON & STANLEY W. LINDBERG, THE NATURE OF COPYRIGHT: A LAW OF USER'S RIGHT (1991).

[66] *See* Okediji, *supra* note 3.

[67] It is interesting to note that the CJEU in the above-mentioned *Painer* and *Deckmyn* referred to quotations and parodies as user "rights."

[68] *See* BALANCING COPYRIGHT – A SURVEY OF NATIONAL APPROACHES, 1 (Reto Hilty & Sylvie Nerisson eds., 2012) (explaining the use of the term "user's right" in different countries).

[69] *See, e.g.*, INTELLECTUAL PROPERTY, LEGAL AND ECONOMIC CHALLENGES FOR DEVELOPMENT, *supra* note 40, at 511. *See also* Carsten Fink & Keith E. Maskus, *Why We Study Intellectual Property Rights and What We Have Learned*, *in* INTELLECTUAL PROPERTY AND DEVELOPMENT: LESSONS FROM RECENT ECONOMIC RESEARCH (Carsten Fink & Keith E. Maskus eds., 2005); Gene M. Grossman & Edwin L. C. Lai, *International Protection of Intellectual Property*, 5 AM. ECON. REV. 1635 (2004).

(24) Furthermore, by ensuring a minimum sphere of freedom to users, the Instrument might foster a certain harmonization of the different national legislations, thus reducing differences in the availability and scope of permitted uses. In an increasingly interconnected world these differences could undermine the attainment of the primary objectives of copyright protection and thus hinder the development of the information market.[70]

3 *Effectiveness As a Key Principle of Implementation for Achieving the Instrument's Purposes*

(25) Effectiveness is a general principle of implementation of the Instrument which is crucial for achieving its objectives. This principle is explicitely established under Part B (I) of the Instrument:

1. Contracting Parties are obliged to adopt the measures necessary to ensure the effective application of this Instrument.
2. Nothing shall prevent Contracting Parties from determining the appropriate method of implementing the provisions of this Instrument within their own legal system and practice.

Contracting parties will have to comply with their international treaty obligations (*pacta sunt servanda*), and in order to do so, they will need to implement the provisions to which they agreed. Negotiating away in trade negotiations or other fora the permitted uses codified in the Instrument would entail a breach of the duty to give effect to the provisions of the Instrument.[71]

(26) At the same time, as long as the minimum permitted uses provided in the Instrument are made effectively available to users, contracting parties enjoy room for manoeuvre in establishing further permitted uses according to their domestic needs. Existing permitted uses remain intact, to the extent that they do not prevent the implementation of the Instrument provisions. The Instrument may not under any circumstances be interpreted as a ceiling of protection of permitted uses.

(27) At the same time, the principle of effectiveness does not limit the freedom of contracting parties to define the method of implementation of the Instrument. Each state is best placed to judge how the provisions on permitted uses can be given effect in a way that lives up to the principles of *pacta sunt servanda* and good faith. Thus, contracting parties may be compliant with the Instrument by both making a list of statutory permitted uses and creating open-ended clauses, such as fair use and fair-dealing. The national legislatures may consider the legal tradition of each state, including the capabilities of courts to deal with open clauses,[72] as well as cultural

[70] *See* Hugenholtz & Okediji, *supra* note 16.

[71] This explanation is included in the Explanatory Notes which form a part of the Instrument. Section 2 of part B of the Instrument concerning Effectiveness is authored by Henning Grosse Ruse-Kahn.

[72] Whether a system that attributes more deciding power to the courts is desirable is not taken into account here. However, this is a subject that certainly deserves special attention in future works, considering among other things the tendency of the civil-law legal system to approximate to the common-law tradition. *See* Craig Allen Nard, *Legal Forms and the Common Law of Patents*, 90 B.U. L. Rev. 51 (2010); Craig Allen Nard, *Rethinking International Intellectual Property Law: What Institutional Environment for the Development and Enforcement of IP Law?*, ICTSD, CEIPI (Nov. 27, 2005), www.ceipi.edu/index.php?id=14535&L=2, for discussion of this issue with particular regard to patent law.

differences. For example, the fair-use doctrine in US law, which is based on a fact-based and precedent-driven judicial enquiry mandated by sec. 107 U.S. Copyright Act, might sit uneasily with some European legal traditions.[73] Imposing a common-law approach by inserting an open clause would go beyond the bottom-line approach of the Instrument.[74]

(28) At the same time, for example, individual states are free to decide whether a permitted use can legitimately cover commercial and non-commercial use alike. In order to set up permitted uses while being compliant with the three-step test – which is embedded in the Instrument under part B(II) – it may be a decisive factor for national law to provide right holders with a statutory fee. The Instrument does not impose any specific form of statutory fee, neither in the form of equitable remuneration nor of fair compensation.[75] The Instrument simply suggests it as a tool for ensuring compliance with the three-step test.

(29) The flexibility charachterizing the Instrument is consistent with the provisions of existing international treaties. In particular, the Instrument recognizes that contracting parties have obligations to each other under treaties concerning copyright, and that nothing in the Instrument itself derogates from any such obligations or prejudices any rights that a contracting party has under any such treaties, except where the exercise of those rights would cause a serious conflict with or threat to the objectives of this Instrument.

4 *Structure of the Instrument*

The Instrument is composed of three parts: A. Permitted Uses; B. General Principles of Implementation; C. Competition; Abuse.

In Part A five groups of permitted uses are enumerated: I. Freedom of expression and information; II. Social, political and cultural objectives; III. Use of software; IV. Uses with minimal significance; and V. Free circulation. The permitted uses listed in Part A codify those included in international provisions (such as Article 10(2) BC or the Marrakesh VIP Treaty) as well as in national rules in this area.

[73] *See* Martin Senftleben, *The Perfect Match – Civil Law Judges and Open-Ended Fair Use Provisions*, 32 Am. U. Int'l L. Rev. 231 (2017) (delivering arguments supporting the possibility of introducing an open clause in European civil-law legal systems).

[74] It is interesting to note that in the "Wittem Group's European Copyright Code" an open-ended clause was introduced in chapter 5, "Limitations." In particular, chapter 5 reflects a combination of a common-law-style open-ended system of limitations and a civil-law-style exhaustive enumeration. For further discussion, *see* Jane Ginsburg, *European Copyright Code – Back to First Principles (with Some Additional Detail* (Columbia Public L. Res. Paper, Paper No. 11-261, 2011), http://ssrn.com/abstract=1747148.

[75] Within EU law the wording "fair compensation" first appeared in the InfoSoc Directive of 2001 representing a compromise solution. Indeed, when the InfoSoc Directive was introduced, several Continental European countries were already familiar with statutory "remuneration" schemes for private reproduction and similar uses, while others member states such as the UK, Ireland, Cyprus, and Malta were hesitant to introduce such remuneration rights. Therefore the use of a new concept was aimed to function as a bridge between the member states that did not have a levy system in place and those that had already provided right holders with statutory remuneration. However, the legal nature of the notion of fair compensation has been the object of attention from the CJEU, which has tried to harmonize the matter in several cases. For a summary of this development and the open issues in this field *see* Reto M. Hilty & Valentina Moscon, *Part F– Claims to Fair Compensation, in* Modernisation of the EU Copyright Rules 89–97 (Position Statement of the Max Planck Institute for Innovation and Competition, Res. Paper No. 17-12, Sept. 18, 2017), https://ssrn.com/abstract=3036787.

The conceptual structure of the rules on permitted uses in this Instrument is similar to the one characterising the provisions of the European Copyright Code (namely Chapter 5: Limitations), drawn up by a group of European academics within the Wittem Project (https://www.ivir.nl/copyrightcode/european-copyright-code/). Each rule establishes in the first place the objective pursued by the provision. For instance, the first paragraph of Part A.I. ("Freedom of expression and information") states that "Contracting Parties shall permit uses for the purpose of freedom of expression and information to the extent justified by the purpose of the use". This means that the permitted uses listed by way of example in the second paragraph of the provision are precisely meant to serve the values enunciated in the first paragraph, i.e. freedom of expression and information. Contracting parties are required to implement the listed permitted uses as a minimum standard in national law and are free to introduce further permitted uses that pursue the goal established in the first paragraph of the provision.

Part B defines general principles aimed at guiding contracting parties in the implementation of permitted uses in their national legal orders. While it is required that contracting parties apply the provisions of the Instrument effectively (Part B.I.), the Instrument helps contracting parties to be compliant with the three-step test by providing guidelines that are consistent with the interpretation given in the abovementioned "Declaration on a Balanced Interpretation of the 'Three-Step Test' in Copyright Law" (Part B.II.). In order to assure effectiveness, it is necessary that permitted uses not be limited by technology or contract. In this respect, contracting parties must ensure that no legal protection is afforded to technological protection measures where they prevent beneficiaries from enjoying permitted uses (Part B.III.) and that contractual terms do not unreasonably impede the benefits of permitted uses (Part B.IV.). In implementing the Instrument, contacting parties must pay attention to the position of creators, granting them the right of attribution in case of permitted uses (Part B.VI.) and participation in any remuneration or compensation (Part B.V.). Finally, it is clarified that permitted uses apply mutatis mutandis to related rights (in Part B.VII.).

Part C deals with competition law as an external limit to copyright. This part is based on the modern understanding that competition law and copyright law are not antagonistic but rather complementary legal fields, pursuing the objective of increasing the market offer of creative works. The Instrument clarifies that there can be no per se exemption of copyright from the general rules of competition law (Part C.I.). Notably, as a "third path" between specific permitted uses and the usual manner of monitoring and sanctioning abusive conduct under competition, the Instrument encourages the use of compulsory licenses as a remedy against abusive conduct by right holders.

5 *Status of the Project and Ways Forward*

(30) The copyright experts involved in the project met for the first time in 2012 to agree on the approach and objectives of the work that ended in the Instrument. The proposals were collected by the Max Planck Institute, which also made sure to exchange information with and gather consensus from all participants on every aspect of the Instrument. A subsequent meeting at the Institute helped to integrate the different proposals and improve on various points of the Instrument. At the time of the editorial deadline of this book, a document is presented that is substantially agreed upon in all its parts. The final document includes explanatory notes that enable readers to understand the purpose of the Instrument as a whole and each individual provision.

(31) The destiny of the Instrument is open. It would be desirable for it to find its own way into the political discussion after an initial phase of scientific debate. Although the possibilities of academic works to enter the political sphere are relatively limited, a first phase of discussion on the Instrument might see interest from a number of states. In any case, whether or not the Instrument succeeds in influencing international and national legislation, it offers at least an opportunity to consider the nature and scope of the rights covered by copyright, the purposes that a copyright system should serve and the need to grant permitted uses to achieve those purposes in compliance with a coherent interpretation of the three-step test.

5

A Copyright Limitations Treaty Based on the Marrakesh Model: Nightmare or Dream Come True?

Martin Senftleben

1 INTRODUCTION

With the adoption of the Marrakesh Treaty to Facilitate Access to Published Works for Persons who are Blind, Visually Impaired, or Otherwise Print Disabled (hereinafter "Marrakesh Treaty" or "MT"),[1] in 2013, the international copyright community has shown its willingness to take further steps in the harmonization of limitations and exceptions ("L&Es") in the field of copyright. However, the Marrakesh Treaty is only the tip of the iceberg. Its preparation and negotiation took place against the background of a much broader debate over the introduction of so-called "ceilings" in international copyright law: binding rules that set a maximum level of permissible protection.[2] While the Marrakesh Treaty had success and became reality, the bigger project of regulating the ceilings of copyright protection in an international instrument is still pending.[3]

Hence, the question arises whether the experiences with the small step of adopting the Marrakesh Treaty are encouraging enough to take the giant leap of discussing ceilings of copyright protection and establishing a general Copyright L&Es Treaty. To answer this question, the following analysis will first shed light on the peculiar configuration of the Marrakesh Treaty. The Treaty combines both very specific and very open rules on L&Es for blind and print-disabled persons with the abstract criteria of the "three-step test" known from Article 9(2) of the Berne Convention for the Protection of Literary and Artistic Works (hereinafter "Berne Convention" or "BC"),[4] Article 13 of the Agreement on Trade-Related Aspects of Intellectual

[1] World Intellectual Property Organization [WIPO], Marrakesh Treaty to Facilitate Access to Published Works for Persons who are Blind, Visually Impaired, or Otherwise Print Disabled, WIPO Doc. VIP/DC/8 (June 23, 2013), www.wipo.int/treaties/en/ip/marrakesh [hereinafter MT].

[2] *See* Annette Kur, *From Minimum Standards to Maximum Rules, in* TRIPS PLUS 20 – FROM TRADE RULES TO MARKET PRINCIPLES 133–62 (Hanns Ullrich et al. eds., 2016); Annette Kur & Henning Große Ruse-Khan, *Enough Is Enough – The Notion of Binding Ceilings in International Intellectual Property Protection, in* INTELLECTUAL PROPERTY RIGHTS IN A FAIR WORLD TRADE SYSTEM 359–407 (Annette Kur & Marianne Levin eds., 2011); Henning Große Ruse-Khan, *Time for a Paradigm Shift? Exploring Maximum Standards in International Intellectual Property Protection,* 1 J. ON TRADE, L. & DEV. 56–102 (2009).

[3] As to the conceptual contours of such an international instrument, *see* P. Bernt Hugenholtz & Ruth L. Okediji, *Conceiving an International Instrument on Limitations and Exceptions to Copyright* (Institute for Information Law Research Paper, Paper No. 2012-37, 2012), https://ssrn.com/abstract=2017629.

[4] Berne Convention for the Protection of Literary and Artistic Works, Sept. 9, 1886, *as revised* July 24, 1971, *and as amended* Sept. 28, 1979, S. Treaty Doc. No. 99-27 (1986) [hereinafter BC].

Property Rights (hereinafter "TRIPS Agreement" or "TRIPS")[5] and Article 10 of the WIPO Copyright Treaty (hereinafter "WCT").[6]

As a result of this treaty architecture, the objective to offer maximum legal certainty in respect of use privileges for blind, visually impaired, and print-disabled persons is compromised. The Marrakesh Treaty can lead to a nightmare scenario in which neither the goal of legal certainty nor the advantage of flexibility is realized. However, the Marrakesh Treaty also demonstrates how international norms could be structured to arrive at a sufficiently flexible and sustainable treaty framework for the regulation of L&Es at the national level. Certain features of the Treaty can serve as a source of inspiration for the development of a dream scenario. The following analysis begins with a discussion of the nightmare scenario (Section 2) before turning to the dream scenario (Section 3) and drawing conclusions (Section 4).

2 NIGHTMARE

In the light of the delicate political climate surrounding the establishment of further international standards in copyright law, the adoption of the Marrakesh Treaty was perceived as a miracle. Against all odds, the "Miracle of Marrakesh" shows that it is still possible to reach agreement on new international copyright rules. In terms of substance, the Treaty provides for important new mechanisms to alleviate the serious problem of the "book famine."[7] Article 4(1)(a) MT sets forth the central obligation to limit the right of reproduction, the right of distribution, and the right of making available to facilitate the availability of works in accessible format copies for blind and print-disabled persons. This obligation includes room for changes necessary to make the work accessible in the alternative format. Interestingly, Article 4(2) MT contains an exemplary provision for the implementation of the new copyright limitation at the national level. With this model provision, the Marrakesh Treaty seeks to achieve maximum clarity about the new international obligation and possible ways of implementation. The importance of a high degree of legal certainty must not be underestimated in the context of initiatives seeking to establish ceilings of protection. As Annette Kur explains:

> ... ceiling treaties bolster the position of their members vis-à-vis potential challenges already by fleshing out and concretizing the existing framework of IP provisions. In view of the difficulties TRIPS members face when appreciating the space available for legislative measures limiting the availability and scope of IP protection, the importance of such efforts should not be

[5] Agreement on Trade-Related Aspects of Intellectual Property Rights, Annex 1C of the Marrakesh Agreement Establishing the World Trade Organization, Apr. 15, 1994, 33 I.L.M. 1197 (1994) [hereinafter TRIPS].

[6] WIPO Copyright Treaty art. 10, Dec. 20, 1996, 36 I.L.M. 65 (1997) [hereinafter WCT].

[7] *Cf.* Paul Harpur & Nicolas Suzor, *Copyright Protections and Disability Rights: Turning the Page to a New International Paradigm*, 36 U.N.S.W. L.J. 745 (2013); Aaron Scheinwald, *Who Could Possibly Be Against a Treaty for the Blind?*, 22 Fordham Intell. Prop., Media & Entm't. L.J. 487 (2012). For an in-depth analysis of the Marrakesh Treaty, *see* Laurence R. Helfer et al., The World Blind Union Guide to the Marrakesh Treaty Facilitating Access to Books for Print-Disabled Individuals (2017); Mihály J. Ficsor, Commentary to the Marrakesh Treaty on Accessible Format Copies for the Visually Impaired (2013); Jonathan Band & Peter Jaszi, *Model Statute for Implementation of the Marrakesh Treaty to Facilitate Access to Published Works for Persons who Are Blind, Visually Impaired, or Otherwise Print Disabled*, InfoJustice.org (Sept. 26, 2013), http://infojustice.org/archives/30778. As to the preparatory work underlying the Treaty, *see in particular* WIPO, *Study on Copyright Limitations and Exceptions for the Visually Impaired*, Standing Comm. Copyright & Related Rights, 15th Sess., Sept. 11–13, 2006, WIPO Doc. SCCR/15/7 (Feb. 20, 2007) (prepared by Judith Sullivan), www.wipo.int/meetings/en/details.jsp?meeting_id=11264.

underestimated ... From that perspective, international rules drawing a clearer picture of what can (or must) be accepted as an exception in international IP law already for that reason are useful and welcome.[8]

Against this background, it is not surprising that Article 4 MT contains not only the general obligation to adopt a certain type of copyright limitation but also a concrete example of an appropriate mode of implementation at the national level. The model provision laid down in Article 4(2) MT makes it possible for contracting parties to successfully defend their limitation infrastructure during negotiations of free-trade agreements in which they may be urged to abandon or further restrict L&Es.[9] As there is international consensus supporting a specific way of implementing the mandatory copyright limitation following from the Marrakesh Treaty, national L&Es that are aligned with the model provision in Article 4(2) MT can survive in such a situation. Arguments against such national L&Es can be rebutted in the light of the underlying international consensus. In the words of Annette Kur, model provisions, such as Article 4(2) MT, constitute "a stronghold bolstering resistance against external pressure" which may be exerted on countries with a relatively weak bargaining position.[10]

Article 5(1) MT complements the new copyright limitation with the further obligation to allow the cross-border exchange of special format copies. If an accessible format copy is made under the new limitation in one contracting party, that copy may also be distributed and made available to beneficiaries in another contracting party.[11] Again, the Treaty seeks to ensure maximum legal certainty as to domestic implementation options by setting forth an exemplary provision in Article 5(2) MT that can serve as a model for national lawmakers.[12] It remains to be seen how difficult it is to reconcile different national concepts of "beneficiary person,"[13] "accessible format copy,"[14] and "authorized entity"[15] when it comes to the cross-border exchange of works in special format.[16] Nonetheless, the prospect of producing accessible format copies under the new copyright limitation and sharing them across borders is promising and constitutes an important step in the right direction.

However, the "Miracle of Marrakesh" came at a price. Article 11 MT makes it clear that copyright L&Es resulting from the implementation of the Treaty must be confined to certain special cases which do not conflict with a normal exploitation of the work and do not unreasonably prejudice the legitimate interests of the author or right holder.[17] The new copyright limitations in favour of blind and print-disabled persons are thus subject to thorough scrutiny in the light of the so-called "three-step test" known from Article 9(2) BC, Article 13 TRIPS, and

8 Kur, *supra* note 2, at 147.

9 *Cf.* Henning Große Ruse-Khan, *IP and Trade in a Post-TRIPS Environment*, *in* TRIPS PLUS 20 – FROM TRADE RULES TO MARKET PRINCIPLES 163–83 (Hanns Ullrich et al. eds., 2016).

10 Kur, *supra* note 2, at 146. *See id.* at 147 (pointing out that the dynamics of trade negotiations and the preferences of trade negotiators are unforeseeable. It cannot be ruled out that a country will finally renounce to a ceiling treaty in order to conclude an attractive free trade agreement.).

11 *See also* MT, *supra* note 1, art. 6 (articulating what permits the importation of accessible format copies in this context).

12 For a discussion of the practical effect of this "safe harbour option," *see* HELFER ET AL., *supra* note 7, at 43–46. As to the need for sufficient legal certainty in the field of copyright L&Es, *see* Kur, *supra* note 2, at 146–47; Kur & Große Ruse-Khan, *supra* note 2, at 367.

13 MT, *supra* note 1, art. 3.

14 MT, *supra* note 1, art. 2(b).

15 MT, *supra* note 1, art. 2(c).

16 As to this problem, *see* Marketa Trimble, *The Marrakesh Puzzle*, 45 IIC – INT'L REV. INTELL. PROP. & COMPETITION L. 768 (2014). *Cf.* Kur, *supra* note 2, at 154–56.

17 *See also* the further reference to this three-step test in art. 5(4)(b) MT (confirming the obligation to comply with the test in the context of cross-border exchange of accessible format copies).

Article 10 WCT.[18] This configuration of the Marrakesh Treaty leads to a dilemma. The Treaty combines the aforementioned specific, very detailed rules on permissible L&Es with the open-ended criteria of the three-step test in a peculiar way: the open-ended three-step test is used as a general yardstick to determine the permissibility of specific L&Es in the area of accessible format copies for blind and print-disabled persons, including specific L&Es modeled on Articles 4(2) and 5(2) MT. When it is considered that the individual criteria of the three-step test – confinement to "certain special cases," prohibition of a conflict with a "normal exploitation," prohibition of an "unreasonable prejudice" to "legitimate interests" – are open and elastic assessment factors, the resulting problem clearly comes to the fore: the open-ended three-step test may erode the legal certainty that could arise from the detailed, specific regulation of L&Es for blind and print-disabled persons, including the enhanced legal certainty that could follow from the aforementioned model provisions laid down in Articles 4(2) and 5(2) MT.[19] As the three-step test is hanging above these specific L&Es as a sword of Damocles, the whole system of precisely defined L&Es established in the Marrakesh Treaty is in danger of becoming dysfunctional: the three-step test may thwart the objective to provide maximum clarity about permissible use privileges. It reduces the added value of an international treaty exclusively devoted to a specific type of copyright limitation.

Instead of supporting the function of the three-step test to offer room for the reconciliation of copyright protection with competing social, cultural and economic interests (discussed below in Section 2.1), the Marrakesh Treaty thus confirms the constraining function of the three-step test in respect of Articles 4(2) and 5(2) MT. In the context of these specific model provisions, the test is used as a vehicle to exercise additional control in cases where a copyright limitation is already clearly defined (Section 2.2). For this reason, it is not advisable to model a general Copyright L&Es Treaty on this feature of the Marrakesh Treaty. To allow international copyright law to keep pace with the rapid evolution of new technologies and rapidly changing social, cultural and economic needs, more flexibility is indispensable.[20] Given the need for flexible lawmaking, the three-step test should be employed as a regulatory instrument to encourage and guide the process of devising new L&Es that become necessary in the digital environment (Section 2.3). Hence, the Marrakesh Treaty points in the wrong direction insofar as the regulation of the specific model provisions of Articles 4(2) and 5(2) MT are concerned (Section 2.4).

2.1 *Enabling Function of the Three-Step Test*

The inconsistency of the described configuration of the interplay between the three-step test and Articles 4(2) and 5(2) MT clearly comes to the fore when the drafting history of the three-step test is factored into the equation. The adoption of the first three-step test in international copyright law – Article 9(2) BC – followed a proposal tabled by the UK delegation at the 1967 Stockholm Conference for the Revision of the Berne Convention.[21] Having its roots in the Anglo-American

[18] For a detailed discussion of the evolution of the three-step test in international copyright law, *see* MARTIN R. F. SENFTLEBEN, COPYRIGHT, LIMITATIONS AND THE THREE-STEP TEST – AN ANALYSIS OF THE THREE-STEP TEST IN INTERNATIONAL AND EC COPYRIGHT LAW 43–98 (2004).

[19] *Cf.* Kur, *supra* note 2, at 149 (pointing out that, practically speaking, a finding of incompliance with the three-step test is unlikely in cases where a national provision is modeled on art. 4(2) MT).

[20] *Cf.* Hugenholtz & Okediji, *supra* note 3, at 42.

[21] *See* Observation of the United Kingdom, WIPO Doc. S/13, RECORDS OF THE INTELLECTUAL PROPERTY CONFERENCE OF STOCKHOLM JUNE 11 TO JULY 14, 1967, at 630 (1971) [hereinafter RECORDS 1967]. For a more detailed discussion of the drafting history, *see* SENFTLEBEN, *supra* note 18, at 47–52; Daniel Gervais, *Fair Use, Fair Dealing, Fair Principles: Efforts to Conceptualize Exceptions and Limitations to Copyright*, 57 J. COPYRIGHT SOC'Y U.S.A. 499, 510–11 (2010);

copyright tradition, it is not surprising that the three-step test consists of open-ended factors comparable to traditional fair dealing and fair use legislation in common law countries. A line between the criteria of the three-step test and the factors to be found in fair use provisions, such as the US fair use doctrine,[22] can easily be drawn. The prohibition of a conflict with a normal exploitation, for instance, recalls the fourth factor of the US fair use doctrine, "effect of the use upon the potential market for or value of the copyrighted work."[23]

Not surprisingly, the three-step test was perceived as a flexible framework at the 1967 Stockholm Conference – a framework within which national legislators would enjoy the freedom of safeguarding national L&Es and satisfying domestic social, cultural and economic needs.[24] This international *acquis* of the provision already indicates that the three-step test must not be misunderstood as a straitjacket of specific national provisions, such as specific L&Es following from the implementation of Articles 4(2) and 5(2) MT. On its merits, the flexible formula constituting the three-step test is a compromise solution allowing Berne Union members to tailor national L&Es to their specific domestic needs.[25]

Many use privileges that have become widespread at the national level are directly based on the international three-step test. A specific provision that permits the introduction of national L&Es for private copying, for instance, is sought in vain in international copyright law. It is the international three-step test[26] that creates breathing space for the adoption of this type of copyright limitation at the national level.[27] Further examples of national L&Es resting on the international three-step test can easily be found in the copyright laws of Berne Union members, such as the exemption of reproductions for research purposes, the privilege of libraries, archives and museums to make copies for the purpose of preserving cultural material, the exemption of reproductions that are required for administrative, parliamentary or judicial proceedings, or of reproductions made by hospitals and prisons.[28]

The three-step test of Article 9(2) BC, therefore, clearly has the function of creating room for the introduction of L&Es at the national level.[29] Vested with this function, it made its way into

Annette Kur, *Of Oceans, Islands, and Inland Water – How Much Room for Exceptions and Limitations under the Three-Step Test?*, 8 Rich. J. Global L. and Bus. 287, 307–8 (2009); Sam Ricketson & Jane C. Ginsburg, International Copyright and Neighbouring Rights: The Berne Convention and Beyond 759–63 (2006).

22 *See* US Copyright Act, 17 U.S.C. § 107 (2000).

23 With regard to the application of fair use analyses concerning the fourth factor in the context of the three-step test, *see* Senftleben, *supra* note 18, at 184–87.

24 *See* WIPO Doc. S/1, Records 1967, *supra* note 21, at 81.

25 *Cf.* Kamiel J. Koelman, *Fixing the Three-Step Test*, 28 Eur. Intell. Prop. R. 407 (2006); Christophe Geiger, *From Berne to National Law, via the Copyright Directive: The Dangerous Mutations of the Three-Step Test*, 29 Eur. Intell. Prop. R. 486 (2007).

26 *See* BC, *supra* note 4, art. 9(2).

27 For a discussion of limitations for private copying and accompanying levy systems in different member states of the EU, *see* Case C-467/08, Padawan v. Sociedad General de Autores y Editores de España (SGAE), 2010 E.C.R. I-10055, para. 49; Joined cases C-457/11 to C-460/11, VG Wort, ECLI:EU:C:2013:426, paras. 76–77; Case C-521/11, Amazon.com Int'l Sales, Inc. v. Austro-Mechana Gesellschaft zur Wahrnehmung mechanisch-musikalischer Urheberrechte Gesellschaft mbH, ECLI:EU:C:2013:515, para. 24; Case C-435/12, ACI Adam v. Stichting de Thuiskopie and Stichting Onderhandelingen Thuiskopie vergoeding, ECLI:EU:C:2014:254, para. 52; Case C-463/12, Copydan Båndkopi v. Nokia Danmark A/S, ECLI:EU:C:2015:144, para. 23.

28 For an example of regional copyright legislation containing these and other examples of L&Es based directly on the three-step test of art. 9(2) BC, *see* Directive 2001/29, of the European Parliament and of the Council of 22 May 2001 on Information Society 2001 O.J. (L 167) 10 (EC) on the harmonization of certain aspects of copyright and related rights in the information society.

29 *Cf.* Martin R. F. Senftleben, *The International Three-Step Test: A Model Provision for EC Fair Use Legislation*, 1 J. Intell. Prop., Info. Tech. & E-Com. L. 67 (2010). *See also* Jonathan Griffiths, *The 'Three-Step Test' in European Copyright Law: Problems and Solutions*, 9 Intell. Prop. Q. 428, 436–41 (2009) (exemplifying a flexible application of the test).

Article 13 TRIPS and played a decisive role during the negotiations of the WIPO "Internet" Treaties.[30] In Article 10(1) WCT, it paved the way for agreement on limitations of the rights newly granted under the WIPO Copyright Treaty, including the right of making available as part of the general right of communication to the public.[31] In consequence, all L&Es to the right of making available rest on the international three-step test. The room for these L&Es stems directly from Article 10(1) WCT. Considering the entire family of three-step tests in Articles 9(2) BC, 13 TRIPS and 10(1) WCT, it becomes obvious that the provision, by far, is the most important and comprehensive international basis for national L&Es.

At the same time, it is evident that the international copyright community employed the three-step test as a compromise formula whenever agreement about more specific use privileges was beyond reach. Again, the circumstances surrounding the adoption of Article 9(2) BC can serve as an example. The preparatory work for the 1967 Stockholm Revision Conference was based on the assumption that the intended perfection of the system of the Berne Union should be pursued, among other objectives, through the enlargement of the protection granted to authors by the creation of new rights or by the extension of rights which were already recognized.[32] In accordance with this approach, the establishment of the right of reproduction *jure conventionis* was regarded as one of the most important tasks of the Conference. Its accomplishment should redress the anomaly that the Convention did not contain a right of reproduction while this right held a fundamental position in national legislation.[33] The feasibility of the plan to attain the formal recognition of a general right of reproduction, however, depended on whether or not the Conference would succeed in finding a satisfactory formula for permissible limitations.[34]

In practice, the L&Es in the field of reproduction rights varied considerably throughout the Berne Union. The study group composed of representatives of the Swedish government and BIRPI which undertook the preparatory work for the Stockholm Conference noted that "domestic laws already contained a series of exceptions in favour of various public and cultural interests and that it would be vain to suppose that countries would be ready at this stage to abolish these exceptions to any appreciable extent."[35] Given these circumstances, the 1965 Committee of

[30] *See* Christophe Geiger et al., *The Three-Step Test Revisited: How to Use the Test's Flexibility in National Copyright Law*, 29 AM. U. INT'L L. REV. 581, 583–91 (2014) (regarding the evolution of this "family" of copyright three-step tests in international copyright law); SENFTLEBEN, *supra* note 18, at 43–98; Joachim Bornkamm, *Der Dreistufentest als urheberrechtliche Schrankenbestimmung – Karriere eines Begriffs*, *in* FESTSCHRIFT FÜR WILLI ERDMANN ZUM 65. GEBURTSTAG, 29 (Hans J. Ahrens et al. eds., 2002).

[31] As to the debate in the context of the WIPO "Internet" Treaties, *see* SENFTLEBEN, *supra* note 18, at 96–98; Mihály J. Ficsor, THE LAW OF COPYRIGHT AND THE INTERNET: THE 1996 WIPO TREATIES, THEIR INTERPRETATION AND IMPLEMENTATION (2002); JÖRG REINBOTHE & SILKE VON LEWINSKI, THE WIPO TREATIES 1996: COMMENTARY AND LEGAL ANALYSIS (2002).

[32] This conception was based on art. 24(1) of the Brussels Act of the Berne Convention. *Cf.* WIPO Doc. S/1, RECORDS 1967, *supra* note 21, at 80.

[33] Prior to the 1967 Stockholm Act, the right of reproduction was only implicitly recognized in the Convention. *Cf.* RICKETSON & GINSBURG, *supra* note 21, at 623–25; Mario Fabiani, *Le droit de reproduction et la révision de la Convention de Berne*, *in* LE DROIT D'AUTEUR 286 (1964); Eugen Ulmer, *Das Vervielfältigungsrecht (Art.9)*, *in* DIE STOCKHOLMER KONFERENZ FÜR GEISTIGES EIGENTUM 16 (Eugen Ulmer & Friedrich K. Beier eds., 1967). This point of view was discussed by the 1965 Committee of Governmental Experts. *Cf.* WIPO Doc. S/1, RECORDS 1967, *supra* note 21, at 81, 111–12.

[34] This is clearly stated in the WIPO Doc. S/1, RECORDS 1967, *supra* note 21, at 113.

[35] WIPO Doc. S/1, RECORDS 1967, *supra* note 21, 111–12, the study group's survey of already existing limitations on the reproduction right. *See id.* at 112, n.1 (showing that the most frequent limitations related to public speeches; quotations; school books and chrestomathies; newspaper articles; reporting current events; ephemeral recordings; private use; reproduction by photocopying in libraries; reproduction in special characters for the use of the blind; sound recordings of literary works for the use of the blind; texts of songs; sculptures on permanent display in public

Governmental Experts discussing the text proposals for the Diplomatic Conference agreed on the following draft for a separate paragraph dealing with L&Es to the envisaged general right of reproduction:

> It shall be a matter for legislation in the countries of the Union to permit the reproduction of such works (a) for private use; (b) for judicial or administrative purposes; (c) in certain particular cases where the reproduction is not contrary to the legitimate interests of the author and does not conflict with a normal exploitation of the work.[36]

At the Conference, the enumeration of specific limitations in (a) and (b) could not survive the more thorough scrutiny of the members of the Berne Union which sought for the most part either to delineate their scope more precisely or to delete them completely.[37] Italy suggested, for instance, that the term "private use" be replaced with "personal use," while France preferred the formulation "for individual or family use" to inhibit corporate bodies from claiming that their copying served private purposes.[38] In respect of the exemption provided for under (b), the Netherlands proposed the wording "for strictly judicial or administrative purposes."[39] Eventually, the UK spoke up for the abolition of paragraphs (a) and (b) altogether to avert the possible harm to authors and publishers that could flow from mention of "private use" and "administrative purposes." Instead, the UK proposed the adoption of a single general clause based on the abstract criteria set out in paragraph (c).[40] As an agreement on certain expressly listed limitations was out of reach, the catalogue of abstract criteria, provided for under (c), thus formed the groundwork for the final three-step test.

The final success of the open-ended UK proposal becomes understandable in view of the divergent views expressed by the member states. While some delegations sought to further restrict the room for L&Es, others were of the opinion that more flexibility was needed. A comparison of the various observations made during the deliberations[41] elicits the specific quality of the abstract formula which finally became the first three-step test: due to its openness, the test has the capacity to encompass a wide range of L&Es and provide a basis for the reconciliation of contrary opinions.[42] The reaction to the final text proposal underlines that this solution was a compromise indeed. While India perceived the proposed wording as narrower than the initial draft and opposed its adoption, other countries contended that the three-step test was not restrictive enough.[43]

Considering the historical background to the introduction of the three-step test in international copyright law, there can be little doubt that the application of the three-step test to the model provisions laid down in Articles 4(2) and 5(2) MT is inconsistent. The Diplomatic

places; artistic works used as a background in films and television programmes; reproduction in the interests of public safety). *Cf.* SENFTLEBEN, *supra* note 18, at 47–48.

36 WIPO Doc. S/1, RECORDS 1967, *supra* note 21, at 113.

37 *See* Observation of Denmark, RECORDS 1967, *supra* note 21, at 615.

38 *See* Observation of Italy, RECORDS 1967, *supra* note 21, at 623; Observation of France, *id.* at 615. *Cf.* in the latter the comment made by Kerever, Minutes of Main Committee I, WIPO Doc. S/81, RECORDS 1967, *supra* note 21, at 858.

39 *See* WIPO Doc. S/81, RECORDS 1967, *supra* note 21,at 691. *Cf.* Minutes of Main Committee I, WIPO Doc. S/81, RECORDS 1967, *supra* note 21, at 857.

40 *See* Observation of the United Kingdom, RECORDS 1967, *supra* note 21, at 630.

41 For such a comparison, *see* SENFTLEBEN, *supra* note 18, at 50–51.

42 *See* Minutes of Main Committee I, WIPO Doc. S/81, RECORDS 1967, *supra* note 21, at 856–58 (showing the fundamental differences). *Cf.* Christophe Geiger, *The Role of the Three-Step Test in the Adaptation of Copyright Law to the Information Society*, UNESCO E-COPYRIGHT BULLETIN 3 (Jan.–Mar. 2007), http://unesdoc.unesco.org/images/0015/001578/157848e.pdf; Hugenholtz & Okediji, *supra* note 3, at 18.

43 *Cf.* Minutes of Main Committee I, WIPO Doc. S/81, RECORDS 1967, *supra* note 21, at 883–85.

Conference that led to the adoption of the Marrakesh Treaty was convened to deal with only one specific issue: L&Es in favor of blind, visually impaired, and print-disabled persons. At the Conference, the delegations managed to achieve far-reaching agreement on permissible use privileges and the possibility of cross-border exchange. The mutual consent even went far enough to arrive at the formulation of concrete model provisions as a basis for the national implementation of the newly created international norms.[44] Hence, there was no need to invoke the three-step test as a compromise solution in a situation where WIPO members could not reach agreement on a more specific provision. By contrast, the delegations agreed on a highly specific text. The inclusion of the three-step test only diluted this highly specific result of the negotiations by adding an undesirable layer of complexity: even if a national provision is modeled on the prototypes set forth in Articles 4(2) and 5(2) MT, it is still possible to advance the argument that the national norm does not fully comply with the three-step tests listed in Article 11 MT. The three-step test was thus added as a complicating and destabilizing factor that reduces the legal certainty which the adoption of precisely defined L&Es would otherwise have guaranteed. Hence, the question arises why this regulation of the relationship between specific model provisions and the open-ended three-step test was considered – and finally even supported – at the Diplomatic Conference.

2.2 *Constraining Function of the Three-Step Test*

The answer to this question lies in the dualism that is inherent in the three-step test as a result of its appearance in different international copyright treaties.[45] As the scope of the three-step test has broadened in the course of its development in international copyright law, two distinct functions have evolved. As explained, the first three-step test, laid down in Article 9(2) BC, fulfills the function of an open clause regulating L&Es to the general right of reproduction. Within the flexible conceptual contours of Article 9(2) BC, national lawmakers are free to adopt L&Es to satisfy social, cultural, and economic needs. In this connection, the three-step test has an *enabling* function in the sense that it serves as a direct basis for the introduction of L&Es at the national level. Private use privileges in Berne Union countries, for example, can be justified internationally because of the three-step test in Article 9(2) BC. There is no other, more specific provision in international copyright law that entitles national lawmakers to limit the right of reproduction for this purpose. In the absence of Article 9(2) BC, breathing space for the adoption of private use privileges would have to be derived from other international norms, such as human rights.

In the context of the TRIPS Agreement and the WIPO Copyright Treaty, the three-step test functions in the same, enabling sense in respect of those exclusive rights that have been newly granted in these treaties. Prior to the adoption of the WIPO Copyright Treaty, for example, there was no clear international recognition of the right of making works available on the Internet in such a way that members of the public may have access from a place and at a time individually chosen by them. The adoption of a general right of communication to the public in Article 8 WCT filled this gap by adding this exclusive right to the preexisting portfolio of internationally recognized rights of communication to the public.[46] With regard to this newly granted right of making available, the three-step test of Article 10(1) WCT fulfills the same function as

[44] *See* MT, *supra* note 1, arts. 4(2), 5(2).

[45] For a more detailed discussion of this point, *see* Senftleben, *supra* note 18.

[46] *Cf.* Ricketson & Ginsburg, *supra* note 21, at 746.

Article 9(2) BC in the context of the right of reproduction: the test provides a basis for the introduction of L&Es at the national level.[47] Domestic lawmakers are free to limit the right of making available in certain respects because Article 10(1) WCT empowers them to do so. As in the case of Article 9(2) BC, there is no more specific provision in international copyright law which could serve as an alternative basis.[48]

Article 13 TRIPS and Article 10 WCT, however, also concern the regulation of L&Es to the traditional exclusive rights recognized in the Berne Convention. In the context of these rights, the three-step tests of Article 13 TRIPS and Article 10(2) WCT serve a different function. They are vehicles to exercise additional control and scrutinize more thoroughly L&Es that have been adopted by national legislators.[49] Even though these national L&Es may fully comply with the conditions set forth in specific provisions of the Berne Convention, the open criteria of the three-step test must also be taken into account and fulfilled.[50] In Article 10(2) WCT, this *constraining* function of exercising additional control – even though specific conditions of Berne provisions are already met – clearly comes to the fore:

> Contracting Parties shall, when applying the Berne Convention, confine any limitations of or exceptions to rights provided for therein to certain special cases that do not conflict with a normal exploitation of the work and do not unreasonably prejudice the legitimate interests of the author.

Hence, two different functions are assigned to the three-step test. First, it serves as a direct, enabling basis for the adoption of L&Es within the realm of several exclusive rights, such as the general right of reproduction[51] and the right of making available to the public.[52] Second, however, it functions as an additional, constraining control mechanism vis-à-vis L&Es that are imposed on the rights granted in the Berne Convention. To illustrate this constraining function, the example of implementing the right of quotation can be given: Article 10(1) BC permits the adoption of L&Es at the national level for the purpose of making "quotations from a work which has already been lawfully made available to the public, provided that their making is compatible with fair practice, and their extent does not exceed that justified by the purpose, including quotations from newspaper articles and periodicals in the form of press summaries." This is a specific entitlement of Berne Union countries to provide for a right of quotation that restricts exclusive rights granted in the Berne Convention, such as the right of reproduction. At the same time, Article 10(1) BC is the only provision in the Convention that deals with the issue of quotations. To ensure compliance with the Berne Convention, it is thus sufficient for a member state to comply with the conditions set forth in Article 10(1) BC.

If the member state is also bound by the TRIPS Agreement and/or the WIPO Copyright Treaty, however, the three-step tests of Article 13 TRIPS and Article 10(2) WCT enter the picture. As these latter provisions require additional scrutiny in the light of the open criteria of the three-step test, it becomes necessary to ascertain – on top of the specific conditions following from Article 10(1) BC – whether the right of quotation adopted at the national level constitutes a "certain special case," avoids a conflict with a "normal exploitation," and does not "unreasonably

47 *Cf.* Ricketson & Ginsburg, *supra* note 21, at 868 (drawing a line between art. 9(2) BC and art. 10(1) WCT).

48 For a more detailed description of this enabling function of the three-step test, *see* Senftleben, *supra* note 18, at 118–21.

49 *Cf.* Senftleben, *supra* note 18, at 121–24; Hugenholtz & Okediji, *supra* note 3, at 20.

50 For a detailed discussion of the relationship between specific Berne L&Es and the three-step tests of art. 13 TRIPS and art. 10(2) WCT, *see* Ricketson & Ginsburg, *supra* note 21, at 856–62, 868–73.

51 *See* BC, *supra* note 4, art. 9(1).

52 *See* WCT, *supra* note 6, art. 8.

prejudice" the "legitimate interests" of authors or right holders.[53] Hence, compliance with Article 10(1) BC is no longer sufficient. The use privilege adopted at the national level – in this case the right of quotation – may still be challenged on the ground that it does not meet the requirements following from Article 13 TRIPS and Article 10(2) WCT. While an Agreed Statement, which was formally adopted together with the text of Article 10 WCT, reduces this corrosive effect in respect of traditional L&Es that have been deemed permissible under the Berne Convention,[54] this mitigating effect of the Agreed Statement already becomes doubtful when modern adaptations of traditional use privileges to the digital environment are assessed, such as the extension of the right of quotation to automated search results generated by search engines.[55]

2.3 *Need for More Flexibility*

The described constraining function of the three-step test is highly problematic. In their study of the conceptual contours of an international instrument on L&Es in the field of copyright law, Bernt Hugenholtz and Ruth Okediji identified five minimum goals which an international treaty should realize in order to be deemed desirable:

> (i) elimination of barriers to trade, particularly in regard to activities of information service providers; (ii) facilitation of access to tangible information products; (iii) promotion of innovation and competition; (iv) support of mechanisms to promote/reinforce fundamental freedoms; and (v) provision of consistency and stability in the international copyright framework by the explicit promotion of the normative balance necessary to support knowledge diffusion.[56]

If these minimum goals are taken as a reference point, it becomes clear that a focus on the constraining function of the three-step test is not conducive to the development of an appropriate international framework for copyright L&Es. Instead, a more flexible approach is indispensable. The wording of the three-step test is far from precluding such a flexible approach. On the contrary, the reverse is true. It is striking how many open elements the provision contains. What makes a copyright limitation a "special" case? What is a "normal" exploitation of a given literary or artistic work? Which interests of authors or right holders can be deemed "legitimate?" When does the prejudice caused by any limitation reach an impermissible, "unreasonable" level?[57]

[53] *Compare* TRIPS, *supra* note 5, art. 13 (referencing to right holders), *with* WCT, *supra* note 6, art. 10(2) (referencing to authors).

[54] *See* WCT, *supra* note 6, art. 10, The Agreed Statement (stating explicitly that "Article 10(2) neither reduces nor extends the scope of applicability of the limitations and exceptions permitted by the Berne Convention."). Arguably, the three-step test of art. 10(2) is thus inhibited from making inroads into the scope of specific national L&Es based on limitation prototypes recognized in the Berne Convention, such as the right of quotation. *Cf.* Ricketson & Ginsburg, *supra* note 21, at 871 (concluding that "the three-step test cannot 'trump' these existing limitations and exceptions.").

[55] For a detailed discussion of this broadening of the scope of the right of quotation, *see* Martin R. F. Senftleben, *Internet Search Results – A Permissible Quotation?*, 235 Revue Internationale du Droit d'Auteur 3 (2013).

[56] Hugenholtz & Okediji, *supra* note 3, at 41.

[57] For a discussion of the answers given in WTO dispute settlement, *see* World Trade Organization, *United States – Section 110(5) of the US Copyright Act*, Report of the Panel, WTO Doc. WT/DS160/R (June 15, 2000). For a discussion of this WTO Dispute Settlement case, *see* Geiger et al., *supra* note 30, at 581; Martin R. F. Senftleben, *Towards a Horizontal Standard for Limiting Intellectual Property Rights? – WTO Panel Reports Shed Light on the Three-Step Test in Copyright Law and Related Tests in Patent and Trademark Law*, 37 Int'l Rev. Intell. Prop. & Competition L. 407 (2006); Senftleben, *supra* note 18, at 134–230; Mihály J. Ficsor, *How Much of What? The Three-Step Test and Its Application in Two Recent WTO Dispute Settlement Cases*, 192 Revue Internationale du Droit d'Auteur 111 (2002); Jo Oliver, *Copyright in the WTO: The Panel Decision on the Three-Step Test*, 25 Colum. J. L. & Arts. 119 (2002); David J. Brennan, *The Three-Step Test Frenzy: Why the TRIPS Panel Decision Might Be*

Evidently, the three-step test – if rightly applied[58] – has the central advantage of offering flexibility.[59] In the current situation where copyright is constantly challenged by new technological developments, services and business models, this advantage of flexibility is crucial. As Bernt Hugenholtz and Ruth Okediji also observe, the three-step test can function as a refined proportionality test in an international instrument on L&Es:

> Read in a constructive and dynamic fashion, the three-step test becomes a clause not merely limiting limitations, but empowering contracting States to enact them, subject to the proportionality test that forms its core and that fully takes into account, inter alia, fundamental rights and freedoms and the general public interest.[60]

Within a flexible framework based on the three-step test as a refined proportionality test,[61] national lawmakers can broaden and restrict the scope of L&Es to strike a proper balance between exclusive rights and competing social, cultural, and economic needs. They are rendered capable of constantly adapting the domestic copyright limitation infrastructure to new circumstances and challenges, in particular, challenges arising in the digital environment. Leaving this discretion to national lawmakers reduces the need for amendments to international legislation that is hardly capable of keeping pace with the speed of technological development. It also prevents international copyright legislation from becoming outdated and losing the social legitimacy necessary to maintain a well-functioning copyright system at the national level.

Hence, the benefits accruing from a flexible international regulation of L&Es must not be underestimated in the ongoing process of adapting copyright law to the rapid development of the Internet. Broad copyright protection is likely to absorb and restrict new possibilities of use even though this may be undesirable from the perspective of social, cultural, or economic needs.[62] User-generated content, advanced search engine services, the digitization of cultural material and automated text-and-data mining can serve as examples of current

Considered per incuriam, 2 INTELL. PROP. Q. 213 (2002); Jane C. Ginsburg, *Toward Supranational Copyright Law? The WTO Panel Decision and the "Three-Step Test" for Copyright Exceptions*, 190 REVUE INTERNATIONALE DU DROIT D'AUTEUR 13 (2001).

[58] As to the debate about the right interpretation of the open-ended three-step test, *see* Martin R. F. Senftleben, *How to Overcome the Normal Exploitation Obstacle: Opt-Out Formalities, Embargo Periods, and the International Three-Step Test*, 1 BERKELEY TECH. L.J. COMMENTARIES 1 (2014). Geiger et al., *supra* note 30, at 581; Christophe Geiger et al., *Declaration on a Balanced Interpretation of the "Three-Step Test" in Copyright Law*, 39 INT'L. R. INTELL. PROP. & COMPETITION L. 707 (2008); Hugenholtz & Okediji, *supra* note 3, at 21; Koelman, *supra* note 25, at 407; Geiger, *supra* note 42, at 19; Griffiths, *supra* note 29, at 489; Daniel Gervais, *Making Copyright Whole: A Principled Approach to Copyright Exceptions and Limitations*, 3 U. OTTAWA L. & TECH. J. 1, 30 (2008); Christophe Geiger, *The Three-Step Test, a Threat to a Balanced Copyright Law?*, 37 INT'L REV. INTELL. PROP. & COMPETITION L. 683 (2006); Thomas Heide, *The Berne Three-Step Test and the Proposed Copyright Directive*, 105 EUR. INTELL. PROP. REV. 106 (1999).

[59] As to the need for sufficient flexibility in an international treaty dealing with ceilings of protection, *see* Kur, *supra* note 2, at 148.

[60] Hugenholtz & Okediji, *supra* note 3, at 25.

[61] For a more detailed discussion of a proportionality-based approach to the three-step test, *see* SENFTLEBEN, *supra* note 18, at 243–44, 290; Geiger, *supra* note 25, at 490–91.

[62] With regard to the critical assessment of broad copyright protection, *see* GIUSEPPE MAZZIOTTI, EU DIGITAL COPYRIGHT LAW AND THE END-USER (2008); GEISTIGES EIGENTUM: SCHUTZRECHT ODER AUSBEUTUNGSTITEL? (O. Depenheuer & K. N. Peifer eds., 2008); Reto M. Hilty, *Sündenbock Urheberrecht?*, *in* GEISTIGES EIGENTUM UND GEMEINFREIHEIT 111 (Ansgar Ohly & D. Klippel eds., 2007); INTERESSENAUSGLEICH IM URHEBERRECHT (Reto M. Hilty & Alexander Peukert eds., 2004); Christophe Geiger, DROIT D'AUTEUR ET DROIT DU PUBLIC À L'INFORMATION, APPROCHE DE DROIT COMPARÉ (2004); Detlef Kröger, INFORMATIONSFREIHEIT UND URHEBERRECHT (2002); Thomas Hoeren, *Urheberrecht in der Informationsgesellschaft*, *in* GEWERBLICHER RECHTSSCHUTZ UND URHEBERRECHT 866 (1997).

phenomena requiring the reconsideration of the scope of copyright protection.[63] Without sufficient breathing space, important social, cultural, and economic benefits that could be derived from timely adaptations of the national legal framework are likely to be lost. On the basis of an elastic international three-step test, by contrast, national legislation can keep the broad grant of protection within reasonable limits and inhibit copyright from unduly curtailing competing freedoms, in particular freedom of expression and freedom of competition.[64]

2.4 *The Nightmare Scenario Revisited*

Against this background, the crux of the described Marrakesh dilemma can be brought to light: as the Marrakesh Treaty subjects the implementation of the model provisions laid down in Articles 4(2) and 5(2) MT to more thorough scrutiny in the light of the three-step test, it employs the three-step test in the problematic sense of further constraining L&Es that are already precisely defined. Article 11 MT does not fulfill the enabling function of Article 9(2) BC and Article 10(1) WCT in respect of specific national L&Es evolving from the application of Articles 4(2) and 5(2) MT. By contrast, it fulfills the constraining function that is known from Article 13 TRIPS and Article 10(2) WCT. As already pointed out, this feature of the Marrakesh Treaty reduces the legal certainty that could have followed from the precise delineation of permissible use privileges in Articles 4(2) and 5(2) MT. In addition, it means that the three-step test itself is not used as a flexibility tool in this context. With regard to Articles 4(2) and 5(2) MT, the test can only be applied to further restrict a use privilege that has been modeled on the international prototypes and, accordingly, is precisely circumscribed. Hence, the problem arises that, in respect of the model provisions of Articles 4(2) and 5(2) MT, the Marrakesh Treaty offers *neither legal certainty nor flexibility*.

The international copyright community should refrain from using this nightmare scenario as a template for a general Copyright L&Es Treaty. In comparison with the current international framework, a Copyright L&Es Treaty exposing specific L&Es to additional scrutiny under the three-step test would further restrict the room for the adoption of copyright limitations at the national level instead of enhancing flexibility. In particular, it is likely to erode the enabling function which the three-step test has in areas of crucial importance: the general right of reproduction (Article 9(1) and (2) BC) and the right of making available to the public (Articles 8 and 10(1) WCT).

63 *Cf.* Senftleben, *supra* note 55; NATALI HELBERGER ET AL., LEGAL ASPECTS OF USER CREATED CONTENT (2009), http://ssrn.com/abstract=1499333; Stef van Gompel, *Unlocking the Potential of Pre-existing Content: How to Address the Issue of Orphan Works in Europe?*, 38 INT'L REV. INTELL. PROP. & COMPETITION L. 669 (2007); D. Brad Sherman, *Cost and Resource Allocation under the Orphan Works Act of 2006: Would the Act Reduce Transaction Costs, Allocate Orphan Works Efficiently, and Serve the Goals of Copyright Law?*, 13 VA. J. L. & TECH. 12 (2007); Marco Caspers & Lucie Guibault, *Baseline Report of Policies and Barriers of TDM in Europe*, FUTURETDM (2016), www.futuretdm.eu and www.ivir.nl.

64 As to the impact of fundamental rights on international policymaking in the field of copyright, *see* Hugenholtz & Okediji, *supra* note 3, at 30–32. *Cf.* Christophe Geiger, *"Constitutionalising" Intellectual Property Law? The Influence of Fundamental Rights on Intellectual Property in the European Union*, 37 IIC: INT'L REV. INTELL. PROP. & COMPETITION L. 371 (2006); P. Bernt Hugenholtz, *Copyright and Freedom of Expression in Europe*, *in* THE COMMODIFICATION OF INFORMATION 239 (Niva Elkin-Koren & Neil W. Netanel eds., 2002); Sandro Macciacchini, URHEBERRECHT UND MEINUNGSFREIHEIT (2000); Yochai Benkler, *Free As the Air to Common Use: First Amendment Constraints on Enclosure of the Public Domain*, 74 N.Y.U. L. REV. 355 (1999); Neil W. Netanel, *Copyright and a Democratic Civil Society*, 106 YALE L.J. 283 (1996).

3 DREAM

Fortunately, the described nightmare scenario is not the only template for a general Copyright L&Es Treaty that can be distilled from the Marrakesh Treaty. As an alternative to reliance on international model provisions, Article 4(3) MT states that a contracting party may fulfill the obligation of introducing appropriate L&Es to facilitate the availability of accessible format copies "by providing other limitations or exceptions in its national copyright law" in line with the three-step tests listed in Article 11 MT.[65] Article 5(3) offers the same alternative with regard to the mechanism of cross-border exchange. Article 12(1) MT adds that a contracting party may implement in its national law "other copyright limitations and exceptions for the benefit of beneficiary persons than are provided by this Treaty having regard to that contracting party's economic situation, and its social and cultural needs, in conformity with that contracting party's international rights and obligations." As these provisions go beyond the specific use privileges reflected in the model provisions of Articles 4(2) and 5(2) MT, the three-step test can fulfill an enabling function in this context: if a national lawmaker wants to explore new avenues in the field of L&Es for blind, visually impaired, and print-disabled persons, this exploration is possible within the open-ended framework provided by the three-step test. Read in conjunction with Article 11 MT, Article 4(1) and (3) MT, for instance, establish the following international rule:

> It is not an infringement of the right of reproduction, the right of distribution, and the right of making available to the public as provided by the WIPO Copyright Treaty (WCT) [and, optionally, also the right of public performance], to facilitate the availability of works in accessible format copies for beneficiary persons and permit changes needed to make the work accessible in the alternative format, provided that such use does not conflict with a normal exploitation of the work and does not unreasonably prejudice the legitimate interests of the author.

In line with Article 4(3) MT, this rule combines the central elements of the international obligation set forth in Article 4(1) MT with the last two steps of the three-step test: the prohibition of a conflict with the normal exploitation and the prohibition of an unreasonable prejudice to legitimate interests. The first step of the three-step test – the obligation of "certain special cases" – does not apply in this context because the adoption of the Marrakesh Treaty shows unequivocally that the L&Es addressed in the Treaty are "certain special cases" in the sense of the three-step test. Otherwise, it would not have made sense to include the three-step test. Inevitably, the test would erode any limitation resulting from the implementation of the Marrakesh Treaty, if limitations for blind, visually impaired, and print-disabled persons could not even fulfill the basic threshold criterion of "certain special cases."

The above rule derived from Article 4(1) and (3) MT and Article 11 MT has the merit of establishing a flexible framework by combining an entitlement to introduce L&Es for a broadly defined purpose ("facilitate the availability of works in accessible format copies") with selected criteria of the three-step test. Following this approach, a general Copyright L&Es Treaty could apply an amalgam of open-ended assessment factors stemming from the three-step test and a general indication of legitimate purposes for the adoption of L&Es. Two objectives play a crucial role in this context: on the one hand, a general Copyright L&Es Treaty should be flexible enough to allow the copyright system to keep pace with rapid technological developments and rapidly changing social, cultural, and economic needs (discussed below in Section 3.1).[66]

[65] For a discussion of the practical effect of this "sui generis option," *see* HELFER ET AL., *supra* note 7, at 46–47.
[66] As to this core feature of a general Copyright L&Es Treaty, *see* Hugenholtz & Okediji, *supra* note 3, at 42.

On the other hand, a general Copyright L&Es Treaty should offer the legal certainty necessary to enable contracting parties with a weak bargaining position to successfully defend L&Es in trade negotiations in which they are confronted with requests to abandon or further restrict use privileges (Section 3.2).[67]

3.1 *Flexibility*

To achieve a satisfactory result with regard to the parameter of flexibility, it would not be necessary to restructure the entire edifice of international copyright law. Instead, an international instrument on L&Es could clarify the relationship between the open-ended three-step test and existing international provisions that contain permissible use privileges, such as the right of quotation in Article 10(1) BC. At the same time, it could employ the catalogue of existing international provisions with permissible use privileges as a reference point for the development of new L&Es. The following text provides a blueprint for such an international norm:

> Contracting Parties may, in their national legislation, provide for limitations and exceptions serving economic, social or cultural purposes, such as
>
> - making quotations;[68]
> - illustrating teaching;[69]
> - reporting current events;[70]
> - facilitating the availability of works in accessible format copies for blind, visually impaired or otherwise print-disabled persons;[71]
> - [further references to specific L&Es recognized at the international level];
> - [additional prototypes of specific L&Es which the Contracting Parties find desirable];
>
> provided that the use does not conflict with a normal exploitation of the work and does not unreasonably prejudice the legitimate interests of the author.

L&Es that are already recognized in international copyright law would remain unchanged under this provision. Further examples of permissible L&Es could be added to the catalogue. The proposed wording, however, would rest on the presumption that the specific L&Es listed in the catalogue, by definition, constitute "certain special cases" in the sense of the three-step test.[72] Accordingly, the requirement of certain special cases is no longer necessary. Instead, the L&Es listed in the catalogue serve as a reference point for the development of new L&Es to satisfy economic, social, or cultural needs. The catalogue of L&Es would fulfill the same function as the illustrative indication of legitimate purposes known from national fair use

[67] *Cf.* Kur, *supra* note 2, at 146–47.
[68] *Cf.* BC, *supra* note 4, art. 10(1).
[69] *Cf. id.* art. 10(2)
[70] *Cf. id.* art. 10*bis*(2).
[71] *Cf. id.* art. 4(1).
[72] This clarification can hardly be deemed a big step. In 1997, the study conducted by WIPO, *Implications of the TRIPS Agreement on Treaties Administered by WIPO*, at 22–23, WIPO Pub. No. 464(E) (1996), already noted that "[n]one of the limitations and exceptions permitted by the Berne Convention should, if correctly applied, conflict with the normal exploitation of the work and none of them should, if correctly applied, prejudice unreasonably the legitimate interests of the right holder. Thus, generally and normally, there is no conflict between the Berne Convention and the TRIPS Agreement as far as exceptions and limitations to the exclusive rights are concerned." Arguably, this statement presupposes that all specific L&Es recognized in the Berne Convention are to be qualified as "certain special cases" in the sense of the three-step test. Otherwise, these Berne L&Es would already fail the first step of the three-step test and be incompliant for this reason.

legislation. Section 107 of the US Copyright Act, for instance, refers to purposes "such as criticism, comment, news reporting, teaching . . ., scholarship, or research."[73]

In addition, the words "such as" in the proposed provision make it clear that the list of permissible L&Es serving economic, social or cultural ends is not closed. It is the very purpose of the provision to offer guidelines for the continuous adaptation of the limitation infrastructure to new circumstances. The three-step test is thus employed as an opening clause that allows national lawmakers to further develop the copyright system by devising new L&Es.[74] This aspect of the proposed provision is in line with the status quo reached under the WIPO Copyright Treaty. In the context of Article 10 WCT, the aforementioned Agreed Statement – formally adopted at the Diplomatic Conference together with the treaty text – makes it clear that the three-step test is not intended to pose obstacles to the evolution of new L&Es:

> It is understood that the provisions of Article 10 permit Contracting Parties to carry forward and appropriately extend into the digital environment limitations and exceptions in their national laws which have been considered acceptable under the Berne Convention. Similarly, these provisions should be understood to permit Contracting Parties to devise new exceptions and limitations that are appropriate in the digital network environment.

It is also understood that Article 10(2) neither reduces nor extends the scope of applicability of the limitations and exceptions permitted by the Berne Convention.[75]

Following in the footsteps of this Agreed Statement, the proposed provision would thus rely on the flexibility that can be derived from the open-ended wording of the three-step test and reinforce the enabling function which the test already has in the context of Article 9(2) BC and Article 10(1) WCT. As a result, the three-step test becomes an opening clause that allows the development of new L&Es in the light of rapid technological developments, and prevents the international treaty framework from becoming outdated soon. The proposed provision would offer the flexibility necessary to achieve these goals at the international and national level.

3.2 *Legal Certainty*

As to the remaining parameter of legal certainty, a more radical step would be necessary to avoid the nightmare scenario described above: Contracting parties would have to refrain from subjecting every element of a Copyright L&Es Treaty to scrutiny in the light of the three-step test. As explained above, it is inconsistent to use the three-step test in situations where the contracting parties have reached agreement on a specific form of implementing a copyright limitation, as in the case of Articles 4(2) and 5(2) MT. Commentators have expressed hope that Articles 4(2) and 5(2) MT will be deemed fully compliant with the three-step test. Laurence Helfer, Molly Land, Ruth Okediji, and Jerome Reichman, for instance, explain that:

[73] The list is understood as an open, non-exclusive enumeration. *See* LEON E. SELTZER, EXEMPTIONS AND FAIR USE IN COPYRIGHT: THE EXCLUSIVE RIGHTS TENSIONS IN THE 1976 COPYRIGHT ACT 19–20 (1978) (quoting Senate and House Committee Reports).

[74] For a more detailed discussion of the different purposes which a general Copyright L&Es Treaty should support, *see* Chapter 4 of this volume, by Reto Hilty and Valentina Moscon. *Cf. also* Martin R. F. Senftleben, *Comparative Approaches to Fair Use: An Important Impulse for Reforms in EU Copyright Law*, *in* METHODS AND PERSPECTIVES IN INTELLECTUAL PROPERTY 30 (Graeme B. Dinwoodie ed., 2013).

[75] *See* WCT, *supra* note 6, art. 10.

> [T]he core obligations in Articles 4, 5, and 6 of the MT provide "safe harbor" options for E&Ls that allow beneficiary persons and authorized entities to create, share, and exchange accessible format copies across borders. A state that takes advantage of these safe harbors and enacts domestic E&Ls that follow the approach set forth in the Treaty should be deemed fully compliant with the [three-step test].[76]

Similarly, Annette Kur takes the position that compliance with the three-step test is more or less self-evident:

> Of course, Article 4(2) as well operates under the condition that it is TRIPS compatible; however, different from Article 4(3), no express reference is made therein to Article 11. Neutral as it is in its actual legal effect, this regulatory detail seems to signal that TRIPS compliance is basically taken for granted, so that contracting parties espousing the model set out in Article 4(2) can feel safe about their international obligations.[77]

Indeed, it would come as a surprise if a WTO panel declared a national provision following the implementation prototypes of Articles 4(2) and 5(2) MT incompatible with the three-step test of Article 13 TRIPS. As the delegations at the Marrakesh Conference explicitly agreed on these model provisions, such a decision would imply that WIPO members erred in their assessment of the room available under the three-step test and, collectively, made the mistake of adopting excessive model provisions.

If it is true that this scenario is unlikely, it is only a small sacrifice to refrain a priori from rendering the three-step test applicable to precisely defined L&Es, such as the model provisions in Articles 4(2) and 5(2) MT. In this way, the above-described nightmare scenario could be avoided, and a Copyright L&Es Treaty could achieve both objectives: flexibility and legal certainty. To ensure a sufficient degree of flexibility, the above-described provision derived from a combination of Article 4(1) and (3) MT with assessment factors of the three-step test should become the centerpiece of the international treaty. In addition, the Copyright L&Es Treaty could provide for model provisions similar to Articles 4(2) and 5(2) MT in all cases where the contracting parties can reach agreement on a concrete, exemplary mode of implementation at the national level. These model provisions, however, should not be exposed to scrutiny under the three-step test. Otherwise, the maximum legal certainty that could follow from the adoption of concrete implementation models would be eliminated.

4 CONCLUSION

The Marrakesh Treaty contains different regulatory approaches that could serve as a starting point for the development of a general Copyright L&Es Treaty. While it is not advisable to expose precisely defined L&Es to additional scrutiny in the light of the three-step test (the nightmare scenario following from the application of the three-step test to Articles 4(2) and 5(2) MT), the combination of open-ended assessment factors stemming from the three-step test with broadly defined obligations to introduce L&Es (the dream scenario following from the application of the three-step test in the context of Articles 4(3) and 5(3) MT) could lead to a treaty framework that is flexible enough to allow international and national copyright legislation to keep pace with rapid technological developments and rapidly changing social, cultural, and economic needs. To add maximum legal certainty, the flexible international norm evolving

[76] Helfer et al., *supra* note 7, at 70–71.

[77] Kur, *supra* note 2, at 149.

from the latter approach could be supplemented with concrete model provisions that show permissible ways of implementation – without precluding the option of departing from the model provisions and adopting different L&Es at the national level that satisfy the open-ended criteria of the overarching flexible international norm.

It is important to note, however, that the three-step test must not be declared applicable to international model provisions that are intended to serve as national implementation templates. Otherwise, the application of the test will frustrate the objective of legal certainty. Model provisions should constitute true "safe harbours"[78] in the sense that national legislators should be able to rely on these implementation templates without any fear of exposure to challenges based on incompliance with the three-step test. In this way, it would be possible to realize both objectives that are central to a Copyright L&Es Treaty: flexibility and legal certainty.

[78] As to the use of safe harbour terminology in the context of the Marrakesh Treaty, *see* HELFER ET AL., *supra* note 7, at 43, 56.

6

Protection of Limitations and Exceptions in the International Copyright Framework

Sam Ricketson

IN THE BEGINNING ...[1]

The Berne Convention for the Protection of Literary and Artistic Works 1886 (Berne Convention) was the beginning of the modern system for international protection of authors' rights. It was by no means the first international treaty on this subject matter, but it was the most significant in three respects:

1. It was the first multilateral agreement to deal with authors' rights.
2. It was open to all states, without restriction.
3. It was based on the principle of national treatment, rather than any requirement of substantive reciprocity as between contracting countries.

The first and second of these are certainly worth celebrating in their own right as significant milestones in the development of public international law generally,[2] but it is the third – national treatment – which is the starting point for the subject of the present paper, namely a consideration of the provisions made for limitations and exceptions to copyright protection under the international agreements.

THE IMPLICATIONS OF THE ADOPTION OF NATIONAL TREATMENT

The principle adopted in article 2, first para, of the Berne Act 1886, provided that:

> Authors who are subjects or citizens of any of the countries of the Union, or their lawful representatives, shall enjoy in the other countries for their works, whether published in one of those countries or unpublished, the rights which the respective laws do now or may hereafter grant to natives.

With one notable addition – the words "rights specially granted" – this remains in essentially the same form in article 5(1) of the latest Act of the Berne Convention (the Paris Act 1971):

> (1) Authors shall enjoy, in respect of works for which they are protected under this Convention, in countries of the Union other than the country of origin, the rights which their respective laws do now or may hereafter grant to their nationals, as well as the rights specially granted by this Convention.

[1] The author is grateful to Professor Jane Ginsburg for her comments on an earlier version of this chapter.

[2] *See generally* Sam Ricketson, *The Emergence and Development of the International Intellectual Property System*, *in* The Oxford Handbook of Intellectual Property Law (Rochelle Dreyfuss & Justine Pila eds., 2017).

The fundamental point here is that the national treatment requirement, and the further obligation with respect to "rights specially granted," apply only to the works of authors with a Berne "country of origin" that are seeking protection in other Berne countries. The expression "country of origin" is defined at length in article 5(4) of the present text and, in general terms, refers to the country of the author's nationality or residence in the case of unpublished works or the country where publication of a work first occurs where the work is published. To give a simple example, assume that countries A, B, and C are members of the Berne Union – an easy assumption to make today in view of the near universal membership of that Union.[3] An author[4] of a literary work first published in country B[5] is concerned about infringements of her work that are taking place in each of these countries. So far as protection in countries A and C is concerned, the author will be entitled to claim whatever protection is available to nationals of those countries by virtue of the principle of national treatment under article 5(1): in effect, she is to be treated in the same way as local authors, and her treatment is assimilated to theirs, becoming for this purpose a national or resident of countries A and C. So far as protection in country B is concerned, however, the author has no claim to protection under the Berne Convention, as this is the country of origin of her work as the country of first publication. On the other hand, her entitlement to protection under the law of country B, as her country of origin, remains unaffected by anything in the Convention, notwithstanding the fact that country B itself is a member of the Berne Union. Although strictly unnecessary, this is underlined by the stipulation in the first sentence of article 5 (3): "Protection in the country of origin is governed by domestic law." It scarcely needs saying that the protection to be given here – and throughout the Convention – is positive, in the sense that it is concerned with the "rights," present and future, to be given to authors in respect of their works, and this protection extends to their successors in title, including assignees as well as heirs.[6]

This simple example, of course, masks some of the further subtleties involved in the application of national treatment, as contained in article 5(2), which provides that this protection must be free of formalities and "independent of the existence of protection in the country of origin" (in this case, country B) – a limitation that had applied under earlier versions of the Berne text.[7] Under the present formulation of article 5(2), it is, of course, even possible that the author may, for whatever reason, have no protection at all in her country of origin, but this has no effect on her ability to claim protection in countries A and C by virtue of the Berne Convention. This is underlined further by the second sentence of article 5(2) which provides that the "extent of protection, as well as the means of redress afforded to the author to protect his rights, shall be governed exclusively by the laws of the country where protection is claimed."

[3] As at June 2, 2020, 179 nations were members of the Berne Union: See the membership list at the WIPO website at: https://www.wipo.int/export/sites/www/treaties/en/documents/pdf/berne.pdf (visited July 24, 2020).

[4] This protection, of course, extends to successors in title to the author, meaning here heirs as well as assignees such as publishers, producers and the like. *See* Berne Convention for the Protection of Literary and Artistic Works art. 2(6), Sept. 9, 1886, *as revised* July 24, 1971, *and as amended* Sept. 28, 1979, S. Treaty Doc. No. 99-27 (1986) [hereinafter Berne Convention]. For ease of reference in the discussion that follows, references to the "author" should be read as including successors in title. Another term to use here would be "right holder" which is used in the Agreement on Trade Related Aspects of Intellectual Property art. 13, Apr. 15, 1994, 1869 U.N.T.S. 299, 33 I.L.M. 1197 (1994) [hereinafter TRIPS Agreement].

[5] *See* Berne Convention, *supra* note 4, art. 4(a). Of course, if the work was unpublished and the author was a national of country B, her country of origin would be the same. *See id.* art. 5(4)(c).

[6] *See* Berne Convention, *supra* note 4, art. 2(6).

[7] Under the Berne Act 1886, at a time when formalities under national laws were often still applicable, art. 2, second para., provided that "[t]he enjoyment of these rights shall be subject to the accomplishment of the conditions and formalities prescribed by law in the country of origin of the work, and must not exceed in the other countries the term of protection granted in the said country of origin."

As seen above, article 5(1) supplements the scope of protection to be granted to authors claiming national treatment under the Berne Convention (called here, for the sake of convenience, "Berne claimants," as distinct from "local or domestic claimants" who are seeking protection only in their country of origin) to include those "rights specially granted by the Convention." The expression "rights specially granted" has assumed greater significance with successive revisions of the Berne Convention,[8] and now encompasses a significant corpus of exclusive rights which must be accorded to works of Berne claimants, irrespective of what the position may be under the law of their country of origin.[9] Article 5(1) makes it clear that these are rights to be granted to works "protected under this Convention," that is, the works of Berne claimants, and this is confirmed by the language of each of the subsequent provisions of the Berne Convention in which these "rights specially granted" are specified.[10] Such rights are also buttressed by the "no formalities" requirement in article 5(1) and the minimum terms of protection specified in articles 7 and 7*bis*.

The operation of these national treatment-plus obligations can be illustrated by the following simple example. Assume that country A does not accord a right of translation or public performance to its own nationals, meaning that local works can therefore be freely translated or publicly performed within that country; it will nonetheless be required to accord such rights to Berne claimants for protection by virtue of articles 8 and 11(1), respectively. Of course, it is unlikely that country A would agree to accepting such an obligation without first extending the benefit of the same protection to its own authors, and this has generally been the trajectory of national laws of countries that have become Berne members – they will alter their domestic laws accordingly before ratifying or acceding to the different acts of the Berne Convention. It will only be in exceptional cases that a country will seek to preserve the position under its national laws, and in respect of its own authors, in the face of an obligation under the Berne Convention to apply a different standard or level of protection to Berne claimants. A striking illustration of this occurred when the USA acceded to the Berne Convention in 1989, and retained formality requirements for US authors though not for non-US authors claiming under the Berne Convention.[11] In other instances, the assumption of "rights specially granted" obligations has been in phased stages or with transitional allowances, as, for example, in the case of translation rights[12] and the term of protection for some moral rights.[13] Widely framed reservations to particular provisions were also available under earlier Berne texts, meaning that countries could accede to or ratify subsequent texts without having to comply fully in giving effect to the obligations under those provisions.[14]

8 Notably in the Berlin Act 1908 and the Rome Act 1928.

9 *See* Berne Convention, *supra* note 4, arts. 8, 9(1), 11(1), 11*bis*(1), 12, 14(1), 6*bis*(1) (exemplifying exclusive economic rights with respect to translations, reproduction, public performance and communication to the public of a performance, broadcasting and related rights, adaption, and cinematographic adaption and reproduction, and moral rights (in that order)).

10 *See id.*

11 On the other hand, Berne claimants, while entitled to protection, may receive certain procedural advantages in the event that they do register. *See* Copyright Act 1976, 17 U.S.C. §§ 411(a), 412 (1976). The above discussion, of course, is directed at states with "dualist" systems that require domestic implementation of international obligations, rather than "monist" systems where international obligations are capable of direct implementation in national courts. *See* Ricketson, *supra* note 2, at 10 [3.6].

12 At first, for a period of ten years under art. 5, first para., of the Berne Act 1886, and then for the full term of protection under the Berlin Act 1908, art. 8.

13 Under art. 6*bis*(2) of the Stockholm Act 1967, certain moral rights may be limited to the life of the author.

14 *See* Sam Ricketson & Jane Ginsburg, International Copyright and Neighbouring Rights: The Berne Convention and Beyond 107 [3.26] (2d ed. 2006). The scope for the making of reservations was an issue that caused

More important, for present purposes, are provisions of the Berne Convention dealing with limitations of, and exceptions to, the protection to be granted to Berne works.[15] In the absence of such provisions, it might be supposed that the granting of "rights specially granted" would have had to be without restriction insofar as each of the relevant articles speaks of the "enjoyment of the exclusive right" in question, such as translation, reproduction, and so on. Prior to the adoption of any particular right "specially granted," protecting countries would have been free to protect such a right in whatever way they wished by virtue of the principle of national treatment – or even not at all. And while considerable latitude may still have been allowed to Berne members in the way they defined the scope of such rights once adopted in the Berne text,[16] no exception or immunity to them would have been allowable once they had been so defined. Furthermore, reliance on the principle of national treatment would not have been possible, in the event that there were exceptions to protection applicable under domestic law, as this would have involved a clash between the two limbs of article 5(1), namely the obligation to provide national treatment *plus* the rights specially granted.[17] At this point, limitations or exceptions otherwise available to users under national treatment would have to give way to protection of the right now "specially granted." For this reason, the Berne Convention has long contained provisions allowing for particular limitations in the case of works to be protected and exceptions to the protection of rights "specially granted" in the case of Berne claimants. The principal of these limitations in the case of works to be protected are to be found in articles 2(2) (unfixed works), 2(4) (official texts), 2(8) (exclusion of protection for "news of the day"), and 2*bis* (limitations with respect to certain speeches and addresses). In the case of exceptions or permitted uses, the principal provisions are to be found in articles 9(2) (the "three-step" test in respect of reproduction rights), 10 (quotations and uses in teaching), and 10*bis* (various press and broadcasting uses, and the reporting of current events).[18] There is also a provision for remunerated exceptions in relation to mechanical reproduction rights (article 13), broadcasting and certain public communications (article 11*bis*(2)), and reproduction and translation rights in the case of developing countries (appendix to the Paris Act 1971), while there is a body of permissible implied exceptions that have been agreed to in past revision conferences, albeit not expressed formally in the Berne text.[19] While these limitations and exceptions have arisen in a piecemeal

much concern at later revision conferences, and the scope for them now under the Stockholm Act 1967 and the Paris Act 1971 is much more limited.

[15] In the discussion which follows, "limitations" is used to refer to situations where no protection is required, while "exceptions" is used to refer to uses which are permitted in situations where protection would otherwise be required.

[16] For example, the meaning of "public" and "to the public" in the case of exclusive performance rights under art. 11 and the meaning of such terms as "adaptations, arrangements, and other alterations" in the case of art. 12. By contrast, the scope of the reproduction right under art. 9(1) was broad, including reproduction "in any manner or form," but this left the issue of transient or temporary reproductions at large, while it was thought necessary to make specific provision for the case of sound or visual recordings under art. 9(3).

[17] This, indeed, was the flashpoint of debate over the introduction of the exclusive reproduction right into the Berne Convention at the time of the Stockholm Revision Conference of 1967. Absent any express requirement in the Berne Convention to protect reproduction rights, Berne members were free to have whatever exceptions to this they wanted under national laws which could then apply to Berne works under the principle of national treatment. Once, however, the exclusive reproduction right became a right "specially granted," it was necessary for the Convention to make specific provision for exceptions, leading ultimately to the adoption of the three-step test in art. 9(2). *See* Ricketson & Ginsburg, *supra* note 14, at 759 [13.03]; Martin Senftleben, Copyright, Limitations and the Three-Step Test: An Analysis of the Three-Step Test in International and EC Copyright Law (2004).

[18] Articles 10 and 10*bis* are expressed more generally with respect to the rights covered, but variously include uses by way of reproduction, public performance, broadcasting, and communication to the public by wire. *See* Ricketson & Ginsburg, *supra* note 14, at 783 [13.38]–[13.55].

[19] These are the implied "minor reservations" doctrine and the implied exceptions that are allowable with respect to translations. *Id.* at Ricketson & Ginsburg, *supra* note 14, at 830 [13.78]–[13.87].

and ad hoc fashion, they nonetheless have a number of characteristics in common, which, at the risk of repetition, are worth emphasizing:

1. They are obviously directed at limitations or exceptions to the protection to be granted to works of Berne claimants and are not concerned with the domestic law of the protecting country: they are directed solely to the scope of protection to be granted to Berne claimants under the twin limbs of article 5(1), namely national treatment and "rights specially granted." This potentially leaves the protecting country free to pursue a different policy with respect to such limitations or exceptions in the case of their own authors if this is thought to be appropriate, for example, to reflect specific national cultural concerns or traditions. While such domestic limitations or exceptions will obviously be part of the law of any Berne member in which protection is claimed by a Berne claimant, they will not fall within the scope of the national treatment principle in article 5(1): see further article 19, which permits the making of claims for the benefits of "any greater protection" under the laws of Berne members, but clearly cannot authorize the imposition of "lesser protection" through the application of any wider limitations or exceptions adopted domestically (see further discussion of article 19 below).
2. For the most part, these provisions set the outer limits as to what such limitations or exceptions may contain, as well as stating conditions for their application, rather than stipulating specifically framed exceptions. Thus, considerable flexibility is left to national legislators to determine the scope of the exceptions that may be applied. This is particularly so in the case of the three-step test under article 9(2), where it is possible that even compulsory licences in specific circumstances may be justified if its requirements are satisfied.[20] As noted above, in other specified circumstances, the Berne Convention also explicitly provides for remunerated uses or compulsory licenses.[21]
3. For the most part, there is no obligation on Berne members to apply these limitations or exceptions in their protection of Berne claimants. They are framed permissively, other than the quotation exception in article 10(1), which appears to be framed in mandatory language.[22] Hence, the scope and content of such limitations or exceptions may be calibrated along a scale up to the maximum limits of what is permitted under these provisions; equally, it is open to Berne members to opt not to have any exception at all in relation to any or all of these possible uses (with the exception of quotations).
4. Bearing in mind that these provisions apply only to the works of Berne claimants, this provides a sharp contrast to many other public international instruments which do require implementation under domestic laws so far as the citizens or residents of those countries are concerned, for instance, human rights instruments, environment protection, maritime and marine pollution treaties, telecommunications and postal agreements, and so on. This essential difference is sometimes lost sight of in the general discourse about authors' rights and exceptions to those rights, to say nothing of the ongoing debate about "user rights." A guarantee of free speech or freedom from arbitrary arrest would mean little under human rights instruments if only directed at foreigners seeking protection in a contracting country rather than locals – domestic observation and implementation lies at the heart of

[20] *See id.* at 775 [13.25]–[13.26].

[21] *See id.* at 776 [13.26].

[22] *See* Berne Convention, *supra* note 4, art. 10(1): "It shall be permissible to make quotations from a work ..." (the word "shall" indicating that *Berne* countries must provide for such an exception). *See also* Tanya Aplin & Lionel Bently, Chapter 3 in this volume.

such agreements which seek to universalize the protection of individual human rights, and the same is true of a wide number of other treaties on different topics. By contrast, the Berne Convention, like its counterpart the Paris Convention on the Protection of Industrial Property, has always been concerned with a quite different objective, namely the protection of authors in countries other than their own.

These general observations about the role of limitations and exceptions under the Berne Convention apply equally, with one exception discussed further below, to the later international agreements dealing with authors' rights, namely the WIPO Copyright Treaty of 1996 (WCT) and the TRIPS Agreement of 1994 (which is concerned more broadly, among other things, with the protection of "rightholders"). Both agreements require compliance with the substantive provisions of the Berne Convention (articles 1–21),[23] and are therefore not concerned with domestic claimants for protection, but only with those claiming protection from outside by virtue of these agreements which, in turn, is to be provided on the basis of national treatment, together with the "rights specially granted" under the Berne Convention and certain further exclusive rights provided for in the WCT and the TRIPS Agreement, respectively.[24] Both agreements also contain provisions, based on the three-step test derived from article 9(2) of the Berne Convention, that limit the scope of limitations to, or exceptions to, the rights that they confer.[25] As under the Berne Convention, these restrictions apply only to claimants from outside, leaving contracting states, in theory at least, free to retain their own national copyright laws and cultural policies and traditions while providing the level of protection required for foreign claimants. International harmonization of standards is therefore limited to foreigners, albeit with the likely consequence that these will be extended to domestic claimants either before, or at the time, their countries agree to become bound by the agreements in question on the basis that few, if any, countries will want to treat foreign claimants more generously than they treat their own. Furthermore, although prescriptive in their terms, the "rights specially granted" under the Berne Convention and the other exclusive rights to be protected under the WCT and the TRIPS Agreement contain within them a degree of flexibility as to their implementation in national laws in providing the required protection of foreigners.[26]

NEW DEPARTURES ...

In historic terms, the adoption of the principle of national treatment at the birth of the Berne Union represented a significant break from earlier and more idealistic attempts to create overarching obligations in the form of an international copyright code embodying the same standards of protection applicable in each country.[27] But earlier and even less ambitious efforts to promote international protection across borders based on reciprocal obligations had also failed, other than at the bilateral level.[28] Accordingly, the adoption of national treatment as a

[23] *See* WIPO Copyright Treaty arts. 1(4), 3, Dec. 20, 1996, S. Treaty Doc. No. 105-17 (1997) [hereinafter WCT] (which applies arts. 2–6 *mutatis mutandis* of the Berne Convention), and the Agreed Statement Concerning Article 3; TRIPS Agreement, arts. 3.1, 9.1 (but note art. 9.2 which excludes any obligation to protect moral rights under art *6bis* of the Berne Convention).

[24] *See* WCT, *supra* note 23, art. 6 (right of distribution), art. 7 (right of rental), and art. 8 (right of communication to the public); TRIPS Agreement, art. 11 (limited obligation in relation to rental rights).

[25] *See* WCT, *supra* note 23, art. 10 and Agreed Statement Concerning Article 10; TRIPS Agreement, art. 13.

[26] *See further supra* note 16.

[27] *See, e.g.*, the 1858 Literary Congress in Brussels: RICKETSON & GINSBURG, *supra* note 14, at 44 [2.05].

[28] *See id.* at 27 [1.29].

starting point was a pragmatic way of breaking the logjam and moving into the multilateral plane. More recent efforts at international norm formulation in relation to copyright, however, appear to have reverted to attempts to influence these standards directly at the domestic level, rather than doing so indirectly, over time, through increased "rights specially granted" or further rights accorded under separate treaties such as the WCT.

Notable here is the Marrakesh Treaty to Facilitate Access to Published Works for Persons Who Are Blind, Visually Impaired, or Otherwise Print Disabled 2013 (Marrakesh Treaty), which contains obligations explicitly addressed to national laws and what happens at the domestic level. Thus, article 4(1) provides:

> (a) Contracting Parties shall provide in their national copyright laws for a limitation or exception to the right of reproduction, the right of distribution, and the right of making available to the public as provided by the WIPO Copyright Treaty (WCT), to facilitate the availability of works in accessible format copies for beneficiary persons.[29] The limitation or exception provided in national law should permit changes needed to make the work accessible in the alternative format.
>
> (b) Contracting Parties may also provide a limitation or exception to the right of public performance to facilitate access to works for beneficiary persons.

Further provisions under article 4 extend and define these obligations with respect to uses by "authorized entities" acting on behalf of beneficiary persons, while articles 5 and 6 apply to cross-border exchange and importation of versions of works in accessible formats. Countries are left free to implement and apply these obligations "within their own legal system and practice"[30] and a further provision stipulates that these exceptions are to comply with the obligations that contracting parties have under the respective provision on the three-step test in the Berne Convention, the WCT, and the TRIPS Agreement.[31] Article 12 also contemplates that other

[29] Defined in Marrakesh Treaty art. 3 as follows:

A beneficiary person is a person who: (a) is blind;

(b) has a visual impairment or a perceptual or reading disability which cannot be improved to give visual function substantially equivalent to that of a person who has no such impairment or disability and so is unable to read printed works to substantially the same degree as a person without an impairment or disability; or

(c) is otherwise unable, through physical disability, to hold or manipulate a book or to focus or move the eyes to the extent that would be normally acceptable for reading; regardless of any other disabilities.

[30] *See* Marrakesh Treaty art. 10(2), (3).

[31] *Id.*, art. 11

("In adopting measures necessary to ensure the application of this Treaty, a Contracting Party may exercise the rights and shall comply with the obligations that that Contracting Party has under the Berne Convention, the Agreement on Trade-Related Aspects of Intellectual Property Rights and the WIPO Copyright Treaty, including their interpretative agreements so that:

(a) in accordance with Article 9(2) of the Berne Convention, a Contracting Party may permit the reproduction of works in certain special cases provided that such reproduction does not conflict with a normal exploitation of the work and does not unreasonably prejudice the legitimate interests of the author;

(b) in accordance with Article 13 of the Agreement on Trade-Related Aspects of Intellectual Property Rights, a Contracting Party shall confine limitations or exceptions to exclusive rights to certain special cases which do not conflict with a normal exploitation of the work and do not unreasonably prejudice the legitimate interests of the rightholder;

(c) in accordance with Article 10(1) of the WIPO Copyright Treaty, a Contracting Party may provide for limitations of or exceptions to the rights granted to authors under the WCT in certain special cases, that do not conflict with a normal exploitation of the work and do not unreasonably prejudice the legitimate interests of the author;

(d) in accordance with Article 10(2) of the WIPO Copyright Treaty, a Contracting Party shall confine, when applying the Berne Convention, any limitations of or exceptions to rights to certain special cases that do not conflict with a normal exploitation of the work and do not unreasonably prejudice the legitimate interests of the author.").

limitations and exceptions in favor of “beneficiary persons” may be adopted by contracting countries in particular circumstances:

1. Contracting Parties recognize that a Contracting Party may implement in its national law other copyright limitations and exceptions for the benefit of beneficiary persons than are provided by this Treaty having regard to that Contracting Party’s economic situation, and its social and cultural needs, in conformity with that Contracting Party's international rights and obligations, and in the case of a least developed country taking into account its special needs and its particular international rights and obligations and flexibilities thereof.
2. This Treaty is without prejudice to other limitations and exceptions for persons with disabilities provided by national law.

The status of these last-mentioned provisions is unclear. Article 12.1 has very little meaning if it is directed to what national laws may do with respect to their own works – they should be able to do this in any event – while any other limitations or exceptions directed at foreign-sourced works will obviously need to comply with the restrictions imposed under the Berne Convention, including the Appendix on Developing Countries, the WCT, and the TRIPS Agreement respectively, quite apart from the specific requirement to observe the three-step test under the Marrakesh Treaty, article 11. Article 12.2 is likewise uncertain in its application, unless it is intended to preserve non–Marrakesh compliant exceptions under domestic law (see further below).

There may, of course, be uncertainty in the first place as to whether the Marrakesh provisions are directed at the works of domestic, rather than nondomestic, claimants for protection. The repeated words “in its national law” suggest that the exceptions are to apply to both categories of work without differentiation, and, for the sake of the following discussion, this might be called the “broad interpretation.” However, a stricter interpretation of article 4 might be that the rights of reproduction, distribution and public communication referred to in that article mean only those rights covered by the Berne Convention or the WCT[32] and therefore the mandatory exceptions required of national laws under that article apply only to the treatment of non-domestic works (this might be called the “narrow interpretation”). In truth, the wording of the Marrakesh Treaty as a whole elides these questions, and either interpretation has significant consequences in view of the mandatory nature of these obligations. In this regard, the Marrakesh Treaty is unique among international copyright treaties in imposing obligations that contracting countries *must* implement in their domestic laws with respect to works entitled to protection under those laws, whether confined to non-domestic works or not. A similar approach appears to be contemplated in the other work on exceptions for libraries, archives, and educational uses that is occurring under the auspices of the WIPO Standing Committee on Copyright and Related Rights.[33]

[32] In this regard, it might be noted that art. 4(1)(a) of the Marrakesh Treaty (set out in the main text) refers only to the right of making available to the public as provided for in the WCT, but it is not clear if this qualification applies to the rights of reproduction or distribution also mentioned in that article. Distribution rights are, of course, provided for in the WCT under art. 6, but reproduction rights fall under art. 9 of the Berne Convention, so the absence of any reference to the Berne Convention here might lead to the conclusion that art. 4(1)(a) of the Marrakesh Treaty is referring to reproduction rights generally that are protected under domestic laws with respect to domestic as well as nondomestic claimants.

[33] WIPO, Standing Committee on Copyright and Related Rights, 23rd Sess., Nov. 21–25, 28, 29 & Dec. 2, 2011, Conclusions, SCCR/23/REF/CONCLUSIONS (Dec. 2, 2011), www.wipo.int/meetings/en/doc_details.jsp?doc_id=190903, for an early discussion of treaty proposals on exceptions and limitations for libraries and archives, and for educational and research institutions. Outside of WIPO, *see* Reto Hilty & Valentina Moscon, Chapter 4 in this volume.

The implications of this new tendency toward mandatory exceptions require careful consideration, particularly so far as the interactions between the Marrakesh Treaty and the earlier authors' rights treaties are concerned. While membership of none of these older agreements is required for a country to become a contracting party to the Marrakesh Treaty, the latter proceeds on the unspoken assumption that this will be the case – not unreasonably, in view of the large current memberships of these agreements – and article 1 of the Marrakesh Treaty provides that nothing in the Treaty is to "derogate from any obligations that Contracting Parties have to each other under any other treaties, nor shall it prejudice any rights that a Contracting Party has under any other treaties." Central to each of these older treaties is the obligation of national treatment, raising the question of whether, on both the broad and narrow interpretations posited above, the specific exceptions in favor of blind and visually impaired persons required by the Marrakesh Treaty would need to be applied to foreign works from non-Marrakesh countries under the Berne Convention and the WCT as they now form part of the national law of each Marrakesh country. The interaction between national treatment obligations and these new Marrakesh obligations is a complicated issue, and is best examined by reference to the situations before and after a country ratifies or accedes to the Marrakesh Treaty. Consider, first, the situation applying before a country joins the Marrakesh Treaty.

Assume country A, a member of the Berne Union, the WCT and the WTO, has a significant domestic population of blind and visually impaired persons. These persons desire readier and more convenient access to protected works, some of which are by local authors who are protected in any event under the domestic laws of country A, while others, perhaps the bulk, are by foreign authors whose entitlement to protection in country A arises by virtue of its obligations under the Berne Convention, the WCT, and the TRIPS Agreement. Country A now implements a system of exceptions under its domestic law that allows generously for free use without restriction of all of this material in whole or in part, and extends these, in turn, to a category of readers whose disability is intellectual rather than physical.[34] It is likely that these exceptions would go beyond what would be permitted under the various criteria in articles 9(2), 10 and 10*bis* of the Berne Convention, article 10 of the WCT, and article 13 of the TRIPS Agreement, but this will not be a problem so far as domestic claimants under the law of country A are concerned, as country A remains free to treat the works of its own nationals as it wishes, and, in this instance would be able to pursue a domestic policy of exceptions that favors the interests of users over domestic right holders.

What, then, is the position with respect to foreign claimants? Could it be argued, for example, that under the principle of national treatment these wider exceptions will become applicable to them on the basis that they are now part of national law? In the case of the Berne Convention, there are two provisions, which might, on their face, be relevant in this regard:

Article 19 Protection Greater than Resulting from Convention

The provisions of this Convention shall not preclude the making of a claim to the benefit of any greater protection which may be granted by legislation in a country of the Union.

Article 20 Special Agreements Among Countries of the Union

The Governments of the countries of the Union reserve the right to enter into special agreements among themselves, in so far as such agreements grant to authors more extensive rights than those granted by the Convention, or contain other provisions not contrary to this Convention. The provisions of existing agreements which satisfy these conditions shall remain applicable.

[34] This was formerly the case in Australia. *See Copyright Act* 1968 (Cth) pt. VB, div. 4 (Austl.) (copying and communicating of works for persons with an intellectual disability) (now repealed).

Both provisions, however, are concerned with grants of protection to claimants under the Convention that are "greater" (article 19) than they would otherwise receive under article 5(1) or the grant of rights under special agreements that are "more extensive" or contain provisions that are "not contrary" to the Convention (article 20) (noting, of course, that there is no special bilateral or other agreement present in the example postulated here). It is therefore difficult to see how they can be relevant in the case of provisions of national legislation that would provide for lesser protection in the form of wider exceptions or derogations from what is allowed in the case of works of Berne claimants under such provisions as articles 9(2), 10, or 10*bis*. Neither the WCT nor the TRIPS Agreement contains counterparts to articles 19 and 20 of the Berne Convention, but article 1 of the WCT links this agreement tightly to the Berne Convention, with the opening statement that it is a special agreement within article 20 of the Berne Convention,[35] that it is not to derogate from existing obligations that contracting parties have to each other under the Berne Convention,[36] and, more specifically, that contracting parties are to comply with articles 1 to 21 of the Berne Convention.[37] A similar non-derogation obligation and a further obligation to comply with articles 1 to 21 of the Berne Convention are contained in the TRIPS Agreement.[38] These non-derogation obligations are directly relevant to the specific rights that contracting countries undertake to protect under these agreements, in particular, reproduction rights under the Berne Convention and communication and distribution rights under the WCT, and the exceptions contained in such provisions as articles 9(2), 10, and 10*bis* of Berne and the three-step test in article 10 of the WCT and article 13 of the TRIPS Agreement that apply to these rights. As already noted above, these "rights specially granted" must be accorded in addition to whatever else may be required by or encompassed by the principle of national treatment,[39] meaning that exceptions to such rights under domestic laws cannot be extended to foreign claimants under these agreements by virtue of national treatment if they go beyond what provisions such as article 9(2) allow. If this reasoning is correct, country A remains free to adopt whatever exceptions it thinks fit with respect to blind or visually impaired persons where locally authored works are concerned, but in applying these exceptions to foreign right holders will need to do so within the limits allowable under the Berne Convention, the WCT and the TRIPS Agreement with respect to "rights specially granted." Country A in this scenario would also be free to have no exceptions at all with respect to foreign right holders, as no compulsion to have such exceptions arises under either the Berne Convention or the WCT, other than in the case of quotations under article 10(1) of the Berne Convention.

Consider, secondly, the situation where country A (a Berne, WCT, and WTO member) now joins the Marrakesh Treaty. If it has not already done so, it must adopt exceptions in favor of blind and visually impaired readers in its national laws with respect to both locally produced and foreign-sourced works (on the broader interpretation above) or with respect to foreign-sourced works alone (on the narrow interpretation). The following questions then arise:

1. If country A already has exceptions of this kind in force relating to domestic works, but these are wider than those contemplated by the Marrakesh Treaty, will it be allowed to retain these? In the pre-Marrakesh situation, this would have been possible (see above), but

[35] WCT, *supra* note 23, art. 1(1).
[36] *See id.* art. 1(2).
[37] *See id.* art. 1(4).
[38] *See* TRIPS Agreement, *supra* note 4, arts. 2.2, 9.1.
[39] *See* WCT, *supra* note 23, art. 3; TRIPS Agreement, *supra* note 4, art. 3.

it may be that article 11 of the Marrakesh Treaty suggests otherwise once that Treaty comes into operation, as the three-step test criteria listed there appear directed at national legislation generally, rather than just exceptions and limitations that affect foreign-sourced works (the broader interpretation). Against this, and consistently with the narrow interpretation suggested above, it might be argued that article 11 does not go so far as this, as it is expressed as being concerned only with the "obligations" that a contracting party has under the conventions listed (the Berne Convention, the WCT, and the TRIPS Agreement) and is not otherwise concerned with what national laws must contain. It might also be said that it is unlikely that the proponents of the Marrakesh Treaty intended so to limit the options of contracting countries with respect to the limitations and exceptions that might be imposed on domestic authors. The language of the Marrakesh Treaty, however, is ambiguous on this issue, and either interpretation is arguable.[40] It may also be here that the Marrakesh Treaty, article 12.2 (referred to above), could be called in aid to sustain wider exceptions previously imposed in relation to works of domestic authors.

2. If country A has no exceptions at all with respect to blind and visually impaired persons, its accession to the Marrakesh Treaty obviously means that such exceptions must now be adopted and, on the broad interpretation above, applied to both domestic and foreign authors alike, unlike the previous position where such exceptions were permissive under the Berne Convention, the WCT, and the TRIPS Agreement, and did not need to be applied to foreign, let alone local, authors. Under the Marrakesh Treaty, each contracting country must now have such a set of exceptions. Wider exceptions, however, will not be allowable, as, for example, suggested above, where the works may be copied in their entirety – these are unlikely to pass Marrakesh muster, although a case in support might be made if they are subject to remuneration.[41]
3. Having adopted Marrakesh-consistent exceptions, are these to be applied only to works of authors from other Marrakesh countries, or should they also be applied to works from non-Marrakesh countries that are Berne, WCT, or WTO members now that they are part of the national law of the Marrakesh country in which protection is sought? In contrast to the position before a country ratifies or accedes to the Marrakesh Treaty, the exceptions adopted will be, by definition, Berne-consistent, as well as WCT- and TRIPS-consistent, and there should be no issue if that country now extends them more widely to non-Marrakesh countries. Indeed, such an extension would not be a matter of choice but would be mandated under the national treatment obligations in these earlier agreements. On the other hand, the non-Marrakesh country would be under no obligation to apply corresponding exceptions in respect of works whose country of origin is a member of the Marrakesh Treaty.

Various scenarios therefore arise from the interaction between the Marrakesh exceptions regime, the older copyright treaties, and the principle of national treatment contained in those treaties. These may be summarized as follows:

[40] A possible further argument is that a treaty extending to domestic authors that is negotiated under the auspices of WIPO would be outside the jurisdiction of WIPO under the terms of its own treaty, namely, the Convention Establishing the World Intellectual Property Organization 1967. But it is not WIPO that is negotiating the treaty, but the parties themselves, and it must be the case that the latter are free to determine for themselves the scope of the obligations they are discussing. However, the fact that they have such "plenary" power among themselves hardly answers the question of which of the two interpretations posited above is the correct one.

[41] *See* Marrakesh Treaty art. 4(5).

1. For a non-Marrakesh country bound by the older treaties, it can impose whatever exceptions or limitations it likes with respect to domestic works and uses relating to blind and visually impaired persons. So far as foreign works are concerned, exceptions will be applicable only within the limits presently set by the Berne Convention, the WCT, and the TRIPS Agreement: more generous exceptions cannot be imposed.
2. For a Marrakesh country, exceptions in the case of blind and visually impaired readers are now mandated and are to be within the parameters set by the three-step test and otherwise within the framework contained in the Marrakesh Treaty itself. On the broad interpretation, these are to be applied to domestic as well as foreign works, but on either the broad or narrow interpretation, there is no longer any national discretion as to whether to have such exceptions in the first place – or, indeed, to have wider ones. Article 12.2, however, might serve to preserve wider exceptions in favor of users of domestic works.
3. Exceptions applied in accordance with the Marrakesh Treaty will be applicable to works from non-Marrakesh countries on the basis that they will also be consistent with the exceptions regimes of the Berne Convention, the WCT, and the TRIPS Agreement, and, as part of national law, this is now required as a matter of national treatment under those agreements.

SOME BROADER IMPLICATIONS: DOES ALL THIS REALLY MATTER?

The ultimate issue here, of course, is the desirability of having mandatory exceptions in the first place, regardless of whether or not they apply also to domestic works. Exceptions in favor of blind and visually impaired persons may well be a special case, where all will be agreed that the exceptions are justifiable from a policy perspective, particularly given the incidence of blindness and visual impairment in developing countries. Accordingly, it can be said that making them mandatory for this category of users, while a departure from the traditional position, can be readily accommodated in our international framework for the protection of authors and their works. Indeed, it might be argued that mandatory exceptions in cases such as this provide a clear and, perhaps, much-needed direction to national legislators. Extending this approach further to other categories of users, however, is a development that requires more careful consideration, and may not be as benign – or "as good an idea" – as may first appear. The following questions and comments may help to clarify the issues in play here:

1. *What is the harm with mandatory obligations with respect to exceptions in the first place?* This is a perfectly reasonable question to begin with, particularly when it is understood that under the present international framework, outside the Marrakesh Treaty, some perfectly desirable exceptions in areas other than those concerned with blind and visually impaired persons may be contained in some national laws but not in others. Here, the would-be beneficiaries of such exceptions can rely only upon national treatment, as modified by the relevant articles of the Berne Convention, the WCT, and the TRIPS Agreement in the case of foreign-sourced works, and will have to grin and bear it in those countries which do not have such exceptions, or perhaps receive something less generous. Mandatory obligations therefore should ensure that users receive a modicum of uniform treatment in whichever country they seek to invoke those exceptions. Uniformity of expectations and certainty are in themselves desirable goals in any policy- and lawmaking, whether at the national or international levels. Harmonization of standards, whether in terms of positive norms or exceptions to those norms, must therefore be of assistance to both right holders and users alike, and has become a striking feature of regional intellectual property

arrangements, as in the European Communities, and at the procedural level, as witnessed by recent WIPO initiatives in the industrial property sphere.[42] Harmonization, in the sense of "minimal limitations," lies also at the heart of the interesting project on a new international instrument on permitted uses that is being carried out under the auspices of the Max Planck Institute for Innovation and Competition in Munich and which is described in some detail by Reto Hilty and Valentina Moscon in their chapter in the present volume.[43]

2. *One size fits all?* Against this, at the broader multilateral level, it may be argued that uniform, mandatory exceptions are unnecessarily restrictive, and unrealistically assume that one model or style of exception will suit all countries at all times. This leaves less room for national responses that better reflect local conditions and cultural traditions, while responding to the same overall objective. Permissive obligations allow for more tailored responses, while setting outer boundaries as to what may be done. In this regard, it can be argued that the solutions contained in the Marrakesh Treaty were already encompassed within the bounds of the three-step test in article 9(2) of the Berne Convention, article 10 of the WCT, and article 13 of the TRIPS Agreement. Working within these parameters, countries had considerable discretion as to how they approached these issues, including the imposition of compulsory licenses where the requirements of the three-step test were satisfied. It is not altogether clear what advance the Marrakesh provisions embody in this regard, apart from the simple prescription that there should be limitations and exceptions dealing with these uses in national laws. Indeed, given that the Marrakesh provisions are made subject to the three-step discipline in any event, it might be argued that, to the extent that these prescribe one particular way of achieving compliance, they implicitly preclude countries adopting other ways of doing the same thing. It will be suggested below that the Marrakesh Treaty, in fact, falls short of prescribing a specific model for the limitations and exceptions it mandates, but the point remains: the more closely that such exceptions are defined in treaty language, the less latitude is afforded to contracting countries to craft their own solutions.
3. *The existing Conventions are too general in their scope*: Leaving aside their obvious lack of compulsion (with the exception of article 10(1) of the Berne Convention), it may nonetheless be argued that the existing conventions are too general and incomplete in their language, in that only a few kinds of justifiable uses are referred to, such as illustration in teaching and reporting of current events in articles 10 and 10*bis* of the Berne Convention, while the three-step test refers only to "certain special cases." National laws therefore receive comparatively little guidance as to the areas in which free and/or remunerated exceptions might be desirable or even necessary. Moreover, the limiting criteria in each of these provisions leave much to the judgment of individual contracting states, such as "that justified by the purpose" and compatibility with "fair practice" (articles 10(1) and (2) of the Berne Convention), "conflict with normal exploitation" and "not unreasonably prejudice the legitimate interests of the author/right holder" (article 9(2) of the Berne Convention; article 10 of the WCT, and article 13 of the TRIPS Agreement), and "appropriately extend" and "appropriate in the digital network environment" (agreed statements to article 10 of the WCT). But these general purposes and criteria are also a source of strength, in that they provide a degree of latitude

[42] *See, e.g.*, Patent Law Treaty, June 1, 2000, 39 I.L.M. 1047; Trademark Law Treaty, Oct. 27, 1994, 2037 U.N.T.S. 298; Singapore Treaty on the Law of Trademarks, Mar. 27, 2006, S. Treaty Doc. No. 110-2.

[43] *See* Reto M. Hilty & Valentina Moscon, Chapter 4 in this volume.

to contracting states to determine their own responses to particular issues as they arise rather than containing a prescribed model that must be adopted in such cases.[44] The need for such flexibility as to implementation is, of course, acknowledged in the provisions of the Marrakesh Treaty itself,[45] which is also open to the criticism that the model offered in the Treaty is a contingent one in that it is made ultimately dependent upon compliance with the obligations of contracting parties under the earlier copyright agreements, in particular the three-step test.[46] It might fairly be said that, while purporting to provide a clear set of directions to contracting parties in terms of requiring them to provide for limitations and exceptions providing for "access" to blind and visually impaired persons in the form of "accessible formats" that may be made by "beneficiary persons" and "authorized institutions," and for cross-border exchange and importations, the question of whether such exceptions in national law comply with the three-step test is left ultimately for each national law to determine for itself in the light of its other treaty obligations.[47] Contracting parties are therefore left with no clearer guidelines as to what will comply than was previously the case pre-Marrakesh. Accordingly, the Marrakesh Treaty is hardly a good example of the phenomenon of mandatory exceptions that is being criticized here, although it may serve as an illustration of the difficulties involved in trying to put such matters into treaty language.[48] While the amelioration of the plight of blind and visually impaired readers may be justified as a worthy, one-off case for doing so (on the assumption that this is, indeed, possible), extension of mandatory exceptions into other spheres significantly intrudes into a sphere where national laws have traditionally been free to pursue their own solutions. Even on the narrow interpretation suggested above, this is a significant departure from the traditional approach adopted in the international copyright treaties, and represents the first concerted attempt at international harmonization of standards in the area of exceptions.

4. *Loss of national autonomy?* As already noted, on the broader interpretation suggested above, mandatory exceptions applicable at the domestic level and subject to such conditions as are imposed by the three-step test have a direct impact on what that country can do vis-à-vis its own citizens. Hitherto, such national autonomy might have been thought to be an advantage that would allow countries to adopt exceptions policies to meet local needs and cultural traditions, even if the requirements for foreign claimants under the conventions meant that any less generous treatment of local authors would have to be modified consistently with the conditions contained in the three-step test and other articles of the Berne Convention, the WCT, and the TRIPS Agreement. Mandatory conditions at the domestic level therefore limit this sphere for differential national responses.

[44] *See further* Jane Ginsburg, *Do Treaties Imposing Mandatory Exceptions to Copyright Violate International Copyright Norms?* Media I. Intell. Prop. Issues (Feb. 27, 2012). *See also* Sam Ricketson and Jane Ginsburg, *The Berne Convention: Historical and Institutional Aspects*, *in* International Intellectual Property: A Handbook of Contemporary Research (Daniel Gervais ed., 2015), 31–36.

[45] *See* Marrakesh Treaty arts 4(3) and 10(2).

[46] *See id.* art. 11.

[47] In this regard, note that art 4(3) provides Contracting Parties with the option of fulfilling the obligation under art 4(1) through providing *other* limitations or exceptions in its national copyright law, subject to compliance with arts 10 and 11.

[48] In this regard, it is interesting to note that the title of this treaty eschews the description of being a treaty on limitations and exceptions, being more tactfully labeled as a treaty to "facilitate access to published works . . ." An earlier version of the draft treaty was more explicit. WIPO, *Draft Text of an International Instrument/Treaty on Limitations and Exceptions for Visually Impaired Persons/Persons with Print Disabilities*, VIP/DC/3 REV (April 20, 2013), www.wipo.int/edocs/mdocs/diplconf/en/vip_dc/vip_dc_3_rev.pdf.

5. *Inconsistency with protection of the rights of authors?* At a more fundamental level, there is a clear inconsistency with the approach embodied in the Marrakesh Treaty, and its projected progeny, and that embodied in the older agreements (the Berne Convention and the WCT) and even the TRIPS Agreement.[49] The latter are concerned with protection of the rights of authors/right holders, whereas the Marrakesh Treaty is quite explicitly concerned with limiting those rights. While it may be argued that such a treaty is necessary to restore "balance" in the international protection of authors' rights, this overlooks the fact that the Berne Convention and the other treaties already contain their own internal balancing mechanisms as explained above. Indeed, even at the outset of the Berne Convention, the need for such balance was emphasized in the oft-quoted statement of Numa Droz, one of the leading figures at the first Berne drafting conference of 1884, that "limits to absolute protection are rightly set by the public interest."[50] Separate treaties embodying mandatory exceptions therefore are profoundly at odds with the history and tradition of the Berne Convention.

OTHER WAYS OF PROCEEDING? SOME CONCLUDING REMARKS

The discussion above suggests that there are difficulties involved in the approach embodied in the Marrakesh Treaty and in its foreshadowed successors. These embody a paradigm shift from the traditional copyright treaties, as they move into the sphere of regulating copyright norms at the national level, particularly on the broad interpretation suggested above.[51] But even on the narrow interpretation, where these obligations apply only to foreign claimants, their mandatory character represents a considerable erosion of national legislative autonomy. While the Marrakesh Treaty might be treated as a special and one-off case not to be repeated, "erosion" in a more meaningful sense is increasingly likely to occur where mandatory exceptions are adopted in other areas of more general activity, such as libraries, archives and education, to mention only those that are currently under consideration within the WIPO. In the author's view, mandatory exceptions serve rather to confuse and complicate, and a better way forward would be to work within the existing framework of international copyright protection. How might this be done?

A useful starting point is to recognize that negotiating new treaties to deal with these issues is usually a time-consuming and frustrating process. While the Marrakesh Treaty was completed in a comparatively short period of time, this has not been true of other recent treaty initiatives in the copyright sphere,[52] as evidenced by the languor that has accompanied efforts to

[49] *See* Ginsburg, *supra* note 44 (putting this point even more strongly, writing before the adoption of the Marrakesh Treaty that "... mandatory exceptions treaties are profoundly inconsistent with the history and spirit of the Berne Convention because they would, for the first time, create an international instrument whose *sole purpose is to diminish the rights of authors*."). *See also* International Literary and Artistic Association, *Report of the ALAI Ad Hoc Committee on the Proposals to Introduce Mandatory Exceptions for the Visually Impaired* (Feb. 27, 2010), www.alai.org/en/assets/files/resolutions/report-mandatory-exceptions.pdf.

[50] Actes du Congrès de Berne de 1884, 67.

[51] "Paradigm shift" may be too drastic a term to describe this development, which, it must be admitted, is only in its infancy. Nonetheless, its implications for the future are profound, and embody a potentially new and different approach in the sense that would be understood by Thomas Kuhn, the originator of the expression. *See* Thomas T. Kuhn, *The Structure of Scientific Revolutions*, *in* 2 INTERNATIONAL ENCYCLOPAEDIA OF UNIFIED SCIENCE 1 (2d enlarged ed. 1970).

[52] It is pertinent to note here the comparatively short period of preparations involved in the run-up to the adoption of the so-called Internet Treaties (the WCT and the WIPO Performances and Phonograms Treaty) in 1996, effectively beginning in 1994, although the initial work on a possible protocol to the Berne Convention began in 1991.

complete a broadcasters' treaty,[53] the time that elapsed in the case of the audiovisual performers' treaty,[54] and the period that has passed since proposals for exceptions for libraries and archives were put on the agenda of the WIPO Standing Committee on Copyright and Related Rights.[55] Moreover, as noted above, it may be doubted that the contingent character of the Marrakesh exceptions really achieves much advance on the pre-Marrakesh position under the Berne Convention, the WCT, and the TRIPS Agreement, apart from highlighting, perhaps, the desirability of having such exceptions. Treaty negotiation is essentially an extended and often convoluted exercise in give and take, corridor discussions, and positioning by regional groups, with the making of concessions and the "fudging" of texts so as to mask continuing differences between contracting parties. In this regard, the Marrakesh Treaty is no different from many of its predecessors. A better and more effective usage of this time and human effort therefore would be to pitch discussions at a less contentious level where the parties formulate model provisions that are accepted as meeting three-step compliance or compliance with other existing treaty provisions, but are suggestive or indicative only. Such instruments, although not binding, could have the greater advantage of being agreed, and declared, to be presumptively compliant with earlier treaty obligations, such as the three-step test, rather than being made an overriding condition for compliance, as under the Marrakesh Treaty – and then leaving this as a matter for each contracting party to determine for itself. "Soft law" approaches have been taken in other areas of WIPO's competence, such as trademarks, and can be quietly effective over time in guiding developments at the national level while not prescribing a particular solution.[56] Exhortation, rather than compulsion, is more likely to ensure more uniform practice among states, with a wide range of "soft law" options that may be adopted and that would be capable of providing guidance to national legislators and policymakers.[57] In this regard, the standing committee and working group machinery of WIPO provides a meaningful forum in which these issues can be debated and worked through between state representatives, with contributions from experts and interested observer parties, but in a less contentious atmosphere than occurs where the focus is upon specific treaty language and hard-edged diplomatic negotiation. At this level, consensus may be more readily achieved, with a continuous feedback loop being established between international discussions and national practice.

[53] Still underway in 2019. *See* para. 22 of the chairman's report for the 39th session of WIPO, Standing Committee on Copyright and Related Rights, 39th Sess., *Oct. 21–25, 2019. SCCR/39/Summary by the Chair (October 25, 2019). See* Sam Ricketson, *The Draft Broadcaster's Treaty: Latecomers to International Protection – Or Perhaps None at All, in* THE FUTURE OF COPYRIGHT: A EUROPEAN UNION AND INTERNATIONAL PERSPECTIVE 77 (Irini A. Stamatoudi ed., 2016).

[54] This treaty, the Beijing Treaty on Audiovisual Performances, was not completed until 2012; it was adopted on June 24, 2012.

[55] Beginning in 2004; *See further* WIPO, Standing Committee on Copyright and Related Rights, 12th Sess., SCCR/12 (Nov. 17–19, 2004), www.wipo.int/meetings/en/details.jsp?meeting_id=6312 (listing the meeting documents).

[56] *See, e.g.*, the WIPO Recommendations on well-known trademarks and the use of trademarks on the Internet; *see further Standing Committee on the Law of Trademarks, Industrial Designs and Geographical Indications (SCT)*, WIPO, www.wipo.int/policy/en/sct (last accessed June 6, 2019). History is also a good teacher here, and it is worth recalling the various "Model Laws" for developing countries that WIPO, and its predecessor BIRPI, promulgated some decades ago, for example, on inventions (1965), trademarks, trade names and acts of unfair competition (1967), designs (1970), appellations (1975), copyright (1976), computer software (1978), and patents (1979); *see further WIPO Model Laws for Developing Countries*, WIPO, ftp://ftp.wipo.int/pub/library/ebooks/ModelLaws (last accessed June 6, 2019). All of these were designed with Paris and Berne compliance in mind, as the case may be, and provide useful reference points even now.

[57] *See* BERNT HUGENHOLTZ & RUTH OKEDIJI, OPEN SOCIETY INSTITUTE, CONCEIVING AN INTERNATIONAL INSTRUMENT ON LIMITATIONS AND EXCEPTIONS TO COPYRIGHT: FINAL REPORT 44–55 (2008).

Admittedly, this is a modest and less ambitious approach than others presently under consideration, particularly in the academic sphere.[58] It assumes, first of all, that sensible outcomes can be achieved within the existing international framework of authors' rights protection rather than seeking to do so outside in a way that may ultimately lead to an irreconcilable collision of norms, for example, through a human rights paradigm that takes users' rights as a starting point or through approaches based on trade disciplines or on competition or consumer law.[59] It assumes, too, that the criteria presently contained in the Berne Convention, the WCT, and the TRIPS Agreement, and notably the three-step test, are workable and capable of providing the necessary framework within which sets of compliant model provisions and guidelines on limitations and exceptions may be slotted. The history of the adoption of the three-step test for reproduction rights under the Berne Convention and its subsequent trajectory suggest that this is, indeed, the case. Thus, the range of existing exceptions "grandparented" at the time of the adoption of article 9(2) of the Berne Convention was both rich and diverse, and unchallenged, while the great bulk of subsequent exceptions adopted in national laws can usually, with care, be justified under this test or the other exceptions allowed under the Berne Convention, the WCT, or the TRIPS Agreement. Room is left for national variation according to local tradition and needs, and, of course, the scope for domestic exceptions of wider effect is preserved. Indeed, much of the debated differences between the virtues of an open-ended exception such as fair use (in, for example, the US) and a closed list of exceptions (in, for example, the EU) demonstrates the latitude allowed by the three-step test and its associated exceptions – all can be accommodated within the wider umbrella they provide. Moving to mandatory exceptions in specific areas therefore detracts from this flexibility, particularly if these are to become applicable at the domestic level, thereby representing a significant shift in our international copyright policy and treaty making. Sadly, perhaps, we are a long way from harmonizing copyright standards and limitations and exceptions globally, and must work within the existing framework. Nonetheless, with care and effort, a lot can be achieved within that framework, while preserving national policies and traditions.

[58] This is not to say that the limitations involved in an academic project, such as that described by Hilty and Moscon in Chapter 4 in this volume, are not fully acknowledged by the authors. Indeed, Hugenholtz and Okediji pointed out the difficulties involved in formulating a specific treaty on limitations and exceptions, and ultimately argued for soft law options that worked within the existing system, *id.*

[59] For further discussion, and dismissal, of these possibilities *see id* at 29.

PART III

Models of Copyright Exceptions

7

Debunking the Fair Use vs. Fair Dealing Myth: Have We Had Fair Use All Along?

Ariel Katz[*]

1 INTRODUCTION

Eleven decades ago, on December 16, 1911, the Imperial Copyright Act of 1911 received royal assent, codifying fair dealing for the first time, and thus explicitly recognizing it, in the imperial copyright legislation.[1] Ten years later, the same fair dealing provision would appear in the Canadian Copyright Act and would remain the basis of the current fair dealing provisions. Tragically, what was supposed to be an exercise in the codification of a dynamic and evolving common law principle, usually referred to as "fair use," ended up – with a few notable exceptions – in a hundred years of solitude and stagnation.[2] Misinterpreting the 1911 Act, some courts and commentators in the UK and other Commonwealth countries adopted a narrow and restrictive view of fair dealing. Meanwhile, in the United States, fair use, the same common law concept that English and American courts developed, remained uncodified for most of the twentieth century. When the United States finally codified fair use in 1976, Congress left no doubt that the codification would not alter its common law basis and ought not hinder its flexibility and adaptability. Thus, toward the end of the twentieth century, a noticeable split in Anglo-American copyright law emerged: an open, flexible, and general fair use regime in the United States, and a seemingly rigid and restrictive fair dealing tradition in the Commonwealth countries.[3]

[*] This chapter is adapted from Ariel Katz, *Fair Use 2.0: The Rebirth of Fair Dealing in Canada, in* The Copyright Pentalogy: How the Supreme Court of Canada Shook the Foundations of Canadian Copyright Law 93 (Michael Geist ed., 2013).

[1] Australia enacted a short-lived fair dealing provision in the Copyright Act 1905 (Cth) s 28 (Austl.) providing that "a book shall not be infringed by a person making an abridgement or translation of the book for his private use (unless he uses it publicly or allows it to be used publicly by some other person), or by a person making fair extracts from or otherwise fairly dealing with the contents of the book for the purpose of a new work, or for the purposes of criticism, review, or refutation, or in the ordinary course of reporting scientific information." This provision was apparently taken from the failed UK Copyright Bill 1900, H.L. Bill [295]. The 1905 Act was replaced with Australia's Copyright Act 1912 which adopted the UK's 1911 Act. *See* Alexandra Sims, *Strangling Their Creation: The Courts' Treatment of Fair Dealing in Copyright Law since 1911*, 2010 Intell. Prop. Q. 192, 192–224.

[2] *See* Sims, *supra* note 1.

[3] According to Sean Flynn and Michael Palmedo, fair use is open, flexible, and general in the following sense: *open*, since the user right can be applied to an open, as opposed to a defined (a.k.a. closed), list of purposes, uses, works, or users; *flexible*, since the user right is applied through a flexible proportionality test that balances the interests of the rights holder with those of the user and general public; and *general*, since the exception promotes uniform application by applying a single flexible test to a group of multiple uses or purposes. *See* Sean Flynn & Michael Palmedo, The User Rights Database: Measuring the Impact of Copyright Balance (2017).

However, at the turn of the twenty-first century, fair dealing was reborn in Canada. In 2004, the Supreme Court of Canada heard *CCH v. Law Society of Upper Canada*,[4] its first-ever case involving fair dealing, and unanimously declared that fair dealing is a users' right, which is as integral to copyright law as the rights of copyright owners and therefore should be given large and liberal interpretation.[5] Eight years later, the Court rejected attempts to roll back its historic 2014 decision and handed down two judgments reaffirming its holdings from *CCH* and clarifying that they were applicable to a wider range of activities.[6] In doing so, the court corrected a century-long misconception of fair dealing, reunited it with its historical roots, and brought it closer to its American counterpart. Moving in the same direction, and shortly before the Supreme Court handed down its judgments, the Parliament of Canada passed the Copyright Modernization Act, which explicitly recognized education, parody, and satire as purposes that could qualify as fair dealing[7] (as well as a series of other specific exceptions, addressing issues such as user-generated content, copying for private purposes, time-shifting or temporary copying).[8]

Still, both the Court and Parliament stopped short of explicitly adopting an open-ended approach to fair dealing, seemingly unable to decide whether Canada is better off clinging to a burdensome colonial British past or embracing an imperfect (North) American present. This chapter shows, however, that this dilemma is false: while fair dealing has ossified under current British law,[9] the colonial copyright past that Canada inherited is not quite as burdensome as it is commonly perceived to be.

The chapter will recount the history of fair use and fair dealing and show that, contrary to conventional wisdom, the enactment of the Imperial Copyright Act of 1911 – and subsequently the enactment of the Canadian Copyright Act of 1921 – was not designed to cause any major alteration in the common law of fair dealing, and the explicit recognition of five enumerated purposes in the (then) newly enacted fair dealing provision was not intended to limit the principle of fair dealing exclusively to those five purposes. Moreover, despite abundant contemporary literature that highlights a seeming dichotomy between the open-ended US-style fair use, and the supposedly close-ended fair dealing,[10] this dichotomy is false.

Canada is now poised to fully embrace an open-ended fair dealing, and there are very good reasons for doing that. This was indeed one of the major recommendation in the report of a parliamentary committee that reviewed the Copyright Act in 2019.[11] While amending the

[4] *See* CCH Canadian Ltd. v. Law Society of Upper Canada, [2004] 1 S.C.R. 339 (Can.).

[5] *See id.* paras. 48, 51.

[6] *See* Soc'y of Composers, Authors and Music Publishers of Can. v. Bell Can., [2012] 2 S.C.R. 326 (Can.); Alberta (Education) v. Canadian Copyright Licensing Agency (Access Copyright), [2012] 2 S.C.R. 345 (Can.).

[7] *See* Copyright Act, R.S.C. 1985, c C-42, § 29 (Can.).

[8] *See id.* §§ 29.21, 29.22, 29.23, 30.71.

[9] Since this chapter focuses on Canada, I will leave the question of whether fair dealing has been irrevocably ossified in the UK to others.

[10] *See, e.g.*, David Vaver, Intellectual Property Law: Copyright, Patents, Trade-marks 234 (2d ed. 2011); Lior Zemer, *Copyright Departures: The Fall of the Last Imperial Copyright Dominion and the Case of Fair Use*, 60 DePaul L. Rev. 1051, 1068 (2011); Louis Grilli et al., *Fair Dealing or Fare Stealing?: Implications of Canadian Copyright Law Reform on the Online Classroom*, 7 Can. J. L. Tech. 267 (2010); Giuseppina D'Agostino, *Healing Fair Dealing? A Comparative Copyright Analysis of Canada's Fair Dealing to U.K. Fair Dealing and U.S. Fair Use*, 53 McGill L.J. 309, 314 (2008); David Bradshaw, *Fair Dealing As a Defence to Copyright Infringement in UK Law: An Historical Excursion from 1802 to the* Clockwork Orange *Case 1993*, 10 Denning L.J. 67, 73 (1995). Until recently, I echoed this view, too. *See* Ariel Katz, *What Can Canada Learn from Israel about Copyright Reform?*, U. of Toronto L. Sch. Fac. Blog (Dec. 10, 2007), http://web.archive.org/web/20071210161010/http://utorontolaw.typepad.com/faculty_blog/2007/12/what-can-canada.html.

[11] Committee Report No. 16: Statutory Review of the Copyright Act, Report of the Standing Committee on Industry, Science and Technology (Ottawa, ON: House of Commons of Canada, 2019) at 69.

Copyright Act to that effect could add a welcome clarity, strictly speaking, no legislative change is required, because, as the rest of this chapter demonstrates, we have had an open, flexible, and general fair dealing/use all along.

2 THE FAIR USE VS. FAIR DEALING MYTH

According to conventional wisdom, a fundamental difference exists between the American fair use doctrine and the Canadian (or Commonwealth) fair dealing doctrine. American fair use can apply potentially to any purpose. This conventional wisdom rests principally on the language of section 107 of the US Copyright Act, which states that "the fair use of a copyrighted work . . . for purposes such as criticism, comment, news reporting, teaching (including multiple copies for classroom use), scholarship, or research, is not an infringement of copyright."[12] The words "such as" clarify the illustrative nature of the enumerated purposes, ensuring that fair use could apply to other purposes as well. In contrast, sections 29 and 29.1 of the Canadian Copyright Act (like other descendants of the 1911 UK Copyright Act) do not contain the magic words "such as." Therefore, the argument goes, the list of enumerated purposes is exhaustive,[13] and accordingly, "[d]ealings for other purposes are not covered by the exception, even if they would otherwise be fair."[14]

In addition to this statutory difference, several other arguments are sometimes invoked to prove the supposed fundamental distinction between fair use and fair dealing: that "fair use" is an American concept, developed by American courts, and therefore is alien to the legal traditions of the British Commonwealth, where the doctrine is called "fair dealing";[15] and that the distinct histories and origins of Commonwealth and American copyright laws, including differences in their constitutional foundations, reflect disparate conceptions of copyright and hence justify, or at least explain, differences in substantive rules concerning fair dealing or fair use.[16] Lastly, it is sometimes suggested that the terms "dealing" versus "use" in themselves signify such fundamental differences.

This conventional wisdom is flawed. As the rest of this chapter shows, fair use is not an American invention. The concept of fair use originated in the English courts and continued to develop during the nineteenth century by English and American judges who mutually influenced and cross-referenced each other. Its first codification in the UK 1911 Copyright Act was not meant to limit its application to the five enumerated purposes. While some courts assumed that the list was exhaustive, and judicial dicta and commentary supporting this proposition can easily be found, the proposition that the list of allowable purposes is exhaustive has never been the *ratio* of any decided and reported case.[17]

Why the UK Parliament chose the term "dealing," as opposed to "use," remains a mystery.[18] However, the legislative history indicates that in codifying the doctrine, the UK Parliament did not intend to change the nature of the doctrine or narrow its potential scope. It is also telling that when the Parliament of Canada enacted the same provision ten years later, the English version used the term "fair dealing," while the French version, which is equally authoritative, referred to

[12] Copyright Act, 17 U.S.C. § 107 (2012).

[13] *See*, *supra* note 10.

[14] Alberta (Education) v. Canadian Copyright Licensing Agency (Access Copyright), [2009] C.B.D. No. 6, para. 77 (Can.), *rev'd*, Alberta (Education) v. Canadian Copyright Licensing Agency (Access Copyright), [2012] 2 S.C.R. 345 (Can.).

[15] *See, e.g.*, D'Agostino, *supra* note 10, at 359.

[16] *See* Barry Sookman & Dan Glover, *Why Canada Should Not Adopt Fair Use: A Joint Submission to the Copyright Consultation*, 2 Osgoode Hall Rev. L. Pol'y 139, 158 (2009).

[17] The closest case is Hawkes & Son (London), Ltd. v. Paramount Film Service, Ltd. [1934] 1 Ch. 593 (CA) (Eng.).

[18] *See* Bradshaw, *supra* note 10, at 72.

"fair dealing" as "utilisation équitable,"[19] as it still does. One would be hard-pressed to find any difference between "utilisation" and "use."[20]

The arguments that the distinct histories and origins of Commonwealth and American copyright laws, as well as differences in their constitutional foundations, reflect disparate conceptions of copyright and hence justify, or at least explain, differences in substantive rules, are equally misconceived.[21] This historical account is inaccurate, as the copyright acts of both countries are descendants of the Statute of Anne and the jurisprudential developments that followed in Britain and the US.

Attributing differences in the area of fair dealing to differences in the constitutional foundations is equally flawed. The US Constitution empowers Congress "[t]o promote the Progress of Science and useful Arts, by securing for limited Times to Authors and Inventors the exclusive Right to their respective Writings and Discoveries,"[22] and this clause is generally understood to impose some limitations on congressional legislative power in this area.[23] In contrast, the argument goes, the Constitution Act, 1867 gives the Parliament of Canada exclusive jurisdiction over Patents of Invention and Discovery and over Copyrights,[24] but mentions no substantive limitation on the content of such laws.

However, the lack of language similar to that of the US Constitution does not necessarily imply any differences in how copyright (and patent) laws were conceived when those constitutional documents were drafted. Indeed, the notion that copyright and patent laws should promote the progress of science and the useful arts was not invented by the framers of the US Constitution, but rather reflected the common conception of the era. It is easy to see that the title of the Statute of Anne, the first copyright statute, contained the three elements found in the American Constitutional clause. The Statute of Anne's long title was "an act for the encouragement of learning, by vesting the copies of printed books in the authors or purchasers of such copies, during the times therein mentioned." Both combine a public policy goal (compare "for the encouragement of learning" and "to promote the Progress of Science") to be achieved by granting private exclusive rights (compare "by vesting the copies of printed books in the authors or purchasers of such copies" and "by securing ... to Authors exclusive Right to their ... Writings") and a duration limitation (compare "during the times therein mentioned" and "for limited Times").[25]

[19] *See* Copyright Act 1921, 11–12 Geo. V, c 24, § 16(1)(i) (Can.).

[20] Indeed, elsewhere in the French version of the Act, the word "utilization" is used where the English Act uses the word "use." *See, e.g.*, *id.* § 16(1)(ii).

[21] *See, e.g.*, Compo Co. v. Blue Crest Music Inc., [1980] 1 S.C.R. 357 (Can.). In that case, Justice Estey noted (not in the context of fair dealing) that "United States court decisions, even where the factual situations are similar, must be scrutinized very carefully because of some fundamental differences in copyright concepts which have been adopted in the legislation of that country. The United States statutes have not been based upon the international copyright treaties of the 19th and 20th centuries, being the Berne Convention of 1886 and the Rome Copyright Convention of 1928, as the United States of America did not become signatories thereto." While it is true that when that decision was written the US was not a member of the Berne Convention, the suggestion that this fact demonstrates fundamental differences in copyright concepts ignores the history of the legislation. International treaties may explain some differences and later developments, but those treaties have not altered the fundamental concepts and key doctrines.

[22] U.S. Const. art. I, § 8, cl. 8.

[23] There is no consensus, however, about the nature and scope of those limitations. *See, e.g.*, Jeanne C. Fromer, *The Intellectual Property Clause's External Limitations*, 61 Duke L.J. 1329 (2011). *See also* Dotan Oliar, *Making Sense of the Intellectual Property Clause: Promotion of Progress as a Limitation on Congress's Intellectual Property Power*, 94 Geo. L.J. 1771 (2005).

[24] *See* Constitution Act 1867, 30 & 31 Vict., c 3, §§ 91(22), 91(23) (UK).

[25] Oren Bracha, *The Adventures of the Statute of Anne in the Land of Unlimited Possibilities: The Life of a Legal Transplant*, 25 Berkeley Tech. L.J. 1427, 1445 (2010). Bracha also describes how the first US Copyright Act, enacted in 1790, was a mere copy of the Statute of Anne, and had the same title. *See also* Michael D. Birnhack, *The Idea of Progress in Copyright Law*, 1 Buffalo Intell. Prop. L.J. 3, 36 (2001) (noting that the term "science" in 1790 had a broader meaning than today and was synonymous with "knowledge" or "learning").

"Progress" was a buzzword in the eighteenth century and reflected the contemporaneous ideals of the Enlightenment.[26] While the US Constitution might be considered as one of the highlights of the Enlightenment, those ideals were not invented by the framers and did not originate in the American colonies. Those ideas were prevalent in Britain, and it is not surprising that they would also appear in contemporaneous English judicial decisions.

In 1785 (four years before the adoption of the US Constitution), Lord Mansfield warned that:

> We must take care to guard against two extremes equally prejudicial; the one, that men of ability, who have employed their time for the service of the community, may not be deprived of their just merits, and the reward of their ingenuity and labour; the other, that the world may not be deprived of improvements, nor the progress of the arts be retarded.[27]

Indeed, in *Cary v. Kearsley* from 1802, considered to be the first pronouncement of fair use, Lord Ellenborough tied fair use to the notion of progress of science and the public interest when he wrote the following:

> That part of the work of one author is found in another, is not of itself piracy, or sufficient to support an action; a man may *fairly adopt* part of the work of another: he may so make use of another's labours for the promotion of science, and the benefit of the public: but having done so, the question will be, Was the matter so taken *used fairly* with that view, and without what I may term the *animus furandi*?[28]

Thus, when Justice Souter of the US Supreme Court explained that "[f]rom the infancy of copyright protection, some opportunity for fair use of copyrighted materials has been thought necessary to fulfill copyright's very purpose, '[t]o promote the Progress of Science and useful Arts . . .'"[29] his historical account of fair use was as accurate with respect to American law as it was true to English and Canadian law, notwithstanding the absence of explicit "progress" language in the Canadian written or the British unwritten constitutions.

Likewise, the notion that copyrights, like patents for inventions, were limited grants of statutory exclusive rights, justified in the name of the public interest, was common to both jurisdictions, and evolved in corresponding steps in Britain and the US. This meaning harks back at least to *Darcy v. Allen* from 1603[30] and the Statute of Monopolies from 1624.[31] As Oren Bracha writes, "By the end of the eighteenth century, the principle of limited duration of monopolies had been a staple of English political thought for two centuries."[32]

What prompted the framers of the US Constitution in 1789 to include the specific language in clause 8 is not entirely clear, and what their precise intention was is equally obscure. However, the lack of similar language in the Canadian Constitution Act provides very poor evidence for fundamental differences in the conception of copyright between the two countries.

Similarly, arguments that American fair use reflects the First Amendment protection of free speech overstate the point inasmuch as they suggest that open, flexible, and general fair use is

[26] *See* Birnhack, *supra* note 24.

[27] Sayre v. Moore (1782) 102 Eng. Rep. 139 (KB). *Cf.* Théberge v. Galerie d'Art du Petit Champlain Inc., [2002] 2 S.C.R 336 (Can.), para 32 (stating that "[e]xcessive control by holders of copyrights and other forms of intellectual property may unduly limit the ability of the public domain to incorporate and embellish creative innovation in the long-term interests of society as a whole, or create practical obstacles to proper utilization").

[28] Cary v. Kearsley (1802) 170 Eng. Rep. 679, 680 (emphasis added).

[29] Campbell v. Acuff-Rose Music, Inc., 510 U.S. 569, 575 (1994).

[30] *See* Darcy v. Allen (1603) 11 Co. Rep. 84 b (Eng.).

[31] *See* Statute of Monopolies 1624, 21 Jac I, c. 3 (Eng.).

[32] Bracha, *supra* note 24, at 1450.

a uniquely American invention. The US Supreme Court recently described fair use (and the idea/expression dichotomy) as "built-in First Amendment accommodations" within the Copyright Act.[33] This could mean that that courts must construe and apply fair use in line with First Amendment strictures,[34] and that Congress may not expand or extend copyright protection in a way that avoids or diminishes these doctrines.[35] However, this recent "constitutionalization" of US fair use tells very little about the doctrine's historical development and how it compares to fair dealing. It might be true that in the absence of entrenched constitutional protection for freedom of expression (e.g., in Canada before the Charter of Rights and Freedoms, in the UK before the Human Rights Act, or in Australia) courts and legislators may not be constitutionally *bound* to recognize similar "free speech accommodations." However, the lack of such a constitutional imperative only means that Parliament could choose to enact copyright law that does not accommodate free speech. It does not imply that Parliament chose to override free speech or was oblivious to its importance.

In sum, the claim that differences between American fair use and Canadian fair dealing arise from different constitutional structures reflecting divergent ideological views about copyright does not have any historic support.

3 THE HISTORY OF FAIR DEALING

A *Common Law Origins*

Fair use and fair dealing were not born by statute. The concept of fair use developed as judge-made law, first by English and then by American judges, who mutually influenced and cross-referenced each other.[36] The prehistory of fair use and fair dealing has been documented by several scholars[37] and need not be repeated here fully, but a few highlights are worth mentioning.

First, as Bill Patry writes, "unlike Athena, the doctrine of fair use did not spring forth fully formed."[38] Its scope and contours developed gradually, although "the basic foundation and rationale were established [by English judges] remarkably early."[39] By 1841, when the doctrine made its full appearance in the United States in *Folsom v. Marsh*,[40] American courts already had a developed body of English case law to draw upon. During the nineteenth century, fair use was a broad concept that encompassed several issues that today would often be treated separately, such as copying of non-protectable facts and ideas as distinct from protectable expressions,[41] the copying of nonsubstantial parts of protected expressions,[42] as well as the permissible copying of substantial parts of protected expressions. While current doctrine tends to treat these issues as

[33] *See* Golan v. Holder, 132 S. Ct. 873, 890 (2012) (quoting Eldred v. Ashcroft, 537 U.S. 186, 219 (2003)).

[34] *See* Neil W. Netanel, *First Amendment Constraints on Copyright after* Golan v. Holder: *Melvin B. Nimmer Memorial Lecture*, 60 UCLA L. REV. 1082, 1105 (2013).

[35] *See id.* at 1103.

[36] *See, e.g.*, Scott v. Stanford (1867) L.R. 3 Eq. 718, 722 (quoting Justice Story's famous formulation of fair use in American law from Folsom v. Marsh 9 F. Cas. 342 (C.C.D. Mass. 1841)), and noting that "[t]he general principles guiding the court in cases of this description could hardly be found better stated" than in that case).

[37] *See, e.g.*, Matthew Sag, *The Pre-History of Fair Use*, 76 BROOKLYN L. REV. 1371 (2011); Alexandra Sims, *Appellations of Piracy: Fair Dealing's Prehistory*, 2011 INTELL. PROP. Q. 3 (2011); WILLIAM F. PATRY, THE FAIR USE PRIVILEGE IN COPYRIGHT LAW (2d ed. 1995).

[38] PATRY, *supra* note 36, at 3.

[39] *Id.*

[40] *See* Folsom v. Marsh, 9 F. Cas. 342 (C.C.D. Mass. 1841).

[41] *See* E. J. MACGILLIVRAY, THE COPYRIGHT ACT, 1911, ANNOTATED 29 (1912).

[42] *See* Chatterton v. Cave [1878] 3 AC 483 (HL) 492.

conceptually distinct, and confine fair dealing to the third, the three are not entirely separate. The tests used for determining "substantiality" involve similar questions to those that are asked in determining "fairness,"[43] and whether the work is mainly factual or expressive may influence the outcome of the fairness analysis.[44]

Second, the common terminology in English copyright law prior to 1911 was often "fair use,"[45] just like the American terminology, but it was also common to use the term "fair" as an adjective to describe specific activities, such as "fair quotation,"[46] "fair criticism," "fair refutation,"[47] and, in the earlier cases, "fair abridgement."[48] Sometimes courts would not use the term "fair" but its synonyms, such as "bona fide imitations, translations and abridgements."[49] The switch to "fair dealing" in Commonwealth jurisdictions seems to simply follow a terminology adopted when the doctrine was codified in 1911 in the UK, but, as will be discussed in greater detail below, there is no evidence that the switch from "use" to "dealing" was intended to reflect any change in the law or its direction.

Third, the English judges who created fair use should not necessarily be seen as champions of users' rights and the public interest, reining in overly expansive copyrights – as might be seen through contemporary spectacles. Rather, recognizing fair use allowed judges to actively expand the scope of copyright protection, beyond the original exclusive right to print or reprint books.[50]

Still, even before the Supreme Court of Canada declared in *CCH* that fair dealing is a "users' right,"[51] courts and commentators often referred to the ability to use another's work without permission as a users' right and employed the term "the right of fair user."[52] Similarly, the connection between fair use, the scope of protection, and the public interest was not invented in Canada's *CCH* case, or in the US, but had been recognized two centuries earlier in England. For example, as already noted, in *Cary v. Kearsley*, decided in 1802, Lord Ellenborough explained that:

> [A] man may fairly adopt part of the work of another: he may so make use of another's labours for the promotion of science, and the benefit of the public; but having done so, the question will be, Was the matter so taken used fairly with that view, and without what I may term the *animus furandi*?

Then, after further elaboration, he put the question for the jury to consider as:

> [W]hether what so taken or supposed to be transmitted from the plaintiff's book, was fairly done with a view of compiling a useful book, for the benefit of the public, upon which there has been a totally new arrangement of such matter – or taken colourable, merely with a view to steal the copy-right of the plaintiff?[53]

And by the end of the nineteenth century, in the famous *Hanfstaengl v. Empire Palace* case, the Court of Appeal described copyright as "a monopoly restraining the public from doing that

[43] *See* Vaver, *supra* note 10, at 187–88.
[44] *See* Cambridge University Press v. Becker, 863 F. Supp. 2d. 1190, 1225 (N.D. Ga. 2012).
[45] Lewis v. Fullarton (1839) 48 Eng. Rep. 1080. *See also* Bradshaw, *supra* note 10, at 68.
[46] Wilkins v. Aikin (1810) 34 Eng. Rep. 163, 164.
[47] Lord Perceval v. Phipps (1813) 2 V. & B. 19 (Eng.).
[48] Gyles v. Wilcox (1740) 26 Eng. Rep. 489, 490.
[49] Millar v. Taylor (1769) 98 Eng. Rep. 201, 205. *See generally* Saul Cohen, *Fair Use in the Law of Copyright*, 6 Copyright L. Symp. 43, 48 (1955).
[50] *See* Robert Burrell & Allison Coleman, Copyright Exceptions: The Digital Impact (2005).
[51] CCH Canadian Ltd. v. Law Society of Upper Canada, [2004] 1 S.C.R. 339, paras. 12–13 (Can.).
[52] J. M. Easton, The Law of Copyright in Works in Literature, Art, Architecture, Photography, Music and the Drama by the Late Walter Arthur Copinger 144 (5th ed. 1915).
[53] Cary v. Kearsley (1802) 170 Eng. Rep. 679, 680.

which, apart from the monopoly, it would be perfectly lawful for them to do." The court explained that the "monopoly is itself right and just, and is granted for the purpose of preventing persons from *unfairly* availing themselves of the work of others . . ."[54] The court recognized the need to limit the scope of copyright lest it be turned into an "instrument of oppression and extortion" and explained that on the basis of such considerations courts recognized various limitations on the scope of copyright, before concluding that infringement occurs only if one "copies more than is fair, so that his copy may be used as a substitute for the original."[55] The House of Lords affirmed the decision. In his judgment, Lord Macnaghten similarly described the case as one "in which there has been no unfair use and no copying of anything which the artist can claim as his."[56]

Therefore, to the extent the *CCH* may be seen as revolutionary, it is only revolutionary when viewed through a very narrow historical perspective, but viewing it with a longer historical gaze suggests that if *CCH* departed from earlier case law, it only brought back the law to its historical path.

B The Codification of Fair Use

Fair use remained a common-law principle in the UK until the enactment of the Copyright Act, 1911, which for the first time included a statutory fair dealing provision. Section 2(1)(i) of the 1911 Act provided that "Any fair dealing with any work for the purposes of private study, research, criticism, review, or newspaper summary" shall not constitute an infringement of copyright. It was supplemented by additional, specifically tailored exceptions. The same provision would appear a decade later in Canada, where its language would remain unchanged until 1993.[57] In the US, the doctrine remained uncodified until 1976.

Consistent with the view that section 2(1)(i) of the 1911 Act only codified an already existing principle, courts in the UK continued to understand copyright as a right that did not extend to exclude others from making fair use of a work and to describe infringement as the making of only an *unfair use* of the work.

In *Francis, Day, & Hunter v. Feldman & Co*,[58] a case from 1914, the plaintiff was the copyright owner in a popular song, which had been met by what was described as an answer or reply song. Justice Neville noted that while "it is clear that an answer need not necessarily be an infringement of the words of the original song . . . a song may well be an answer and yet an infringement of the original work"; what needs to be considered is "whether fair use has been made of the expression of ideas in the plaintiffs' song, or whether that use has been excessive and such as to amount to a colourable imitation of the original song."[59] Applying this test, Justice Neville concluded that the defendant's song was merely a colourable imitation of the plaintiff's song and

[54] Hanfstaengl v. Empire Palace [1894] 3 Ch. 109 (CA) 128 (Eng.), *aff'd*, Franz Hanfstaengl v. H. R. Baines & Co. (1895) AC 20 (HL).

[55] *Id.*

[56] *Hanfstaengl v. Baines* (1895) AC at 30.

[57] North American Free Trade Agreement Implementation Act, S.C. 1993, c 44, § 64(1) (Can.) (adding an attribution requirement to criticism, review and newspaper summary). In 1997, "newspaper summary" was replaced with the wider "news reporting", the phrase "private study or research" was modified to "research or private study" (apparently to preempt an interpretation that would limit research to private settings), and the reference to "work" was deleted to expand fair dealing to sound recordings, performers' performances and communication signals. *See* An Act to amend the Copyright Act, S.C. 1997, c 24, § 18(1) (Can.).

[58] *See* Francis, Day, & Hunter v. Feldman & Co. [1914] 111 LT 521 (CA) (Eng.).

[59] *Id.* at 523.

held in favour of the plaintiff. Although there was no verbatim copying, he described the defendant's song as "an obvious attempt ... to catch the particular expression of ideas that appear in the first song ..." In his view, the many words from the first song that were put in the defendants' song, including their context and collocation, showed "that what was aimed at really was a copying of the plaintiffs' song, with such alterations as, in the author's opinion, would exonerate him from a charge of infringing the copyright."[60] The Court of Appeal did not take issue with the test for infringement yet disagreed with its application. It reversed the decision and held that there had been no colourable imitation of the song, and therefore no infringement of the plaintiffs' copyright by the defendants.[61]

Four years later, the court in *Educational Company of Ireland v. Fallon Brothers and Getz*[62] approached the issue of infringement in the same way. One of the defendants, Professor Getz, wrote a book for school use, assigned the copyright to the plaintiffs, and agreed not to publish any similar work during the subsistence of the agreement. He subsequently wrote a similar book on the same topic, adopting the same system, repeating the same kind of lessons, intended practically for the same class of pupils, and which the other defendants published and sold at a low price.

The defendants argued that there was no copyright in the plaintiff's work because it lacked sufficient originality as it was merely a compilation of existing and common materials. The court noted that under the 1911 Act, copyright could clearly subsist in an original compilation of non-original materials and explained that the test for infringement is "whether the author of the later work has made an unfair use of the prior work."[63] The court then held that infringement took place because the second book substantially reproduced everything of value in the earlier book; it was merely a substitute for the first, calculated to supersede it and harm its market.[64]

These cases are noteworthy for several reasons. First, the fairness analysis seems to center around the question of whether the defendant created merely a substitute – a colourable imitation – of the plaintiff's work, in which case the use would be unfair, or whether it has done something sufficiently different, which does not merely supersede the plaintiff's work, in which case it would be fair. This analysis echoes the focus on whether the use is transformative or merely substitutive, which has become the crux of American fair use doctrine in recent years.[65]

Second, although the cases were decided under the 1911 Act and interpret some of its provisions, none of them refer to the newly enacted statutory "fair dealing" provision. Rather, they revolve around fair use (or lack thereof) as an underlying principle, applying the same tests from the pre-1911 case law.

Third, like the US fair use jurisprudence, the decisions focused on fairness and were not preoccupied with determining whether the purpose of the defendant's use fell under any of the enumerated purposes in the fair dealing provision (which were not even mentioned).

These decisions indicate that the enactment of section 2(1)(i) of the 1911 Act was not perceived as introducing any change in the law of fair use or in the understanding of what constitutes infringement. As I discuss below, this view was common among commentators at the time and the one that emerges from the legislative history.

[60] *Id.*
[61] *Id.*
[62] Educational Company of Ireland v. Fallon Brothers and Getz [1919] 1 IR 62 (Ch.) (Ir.).
[63] *Id.* at 68.
[64] *Id.* at 68, 71.
[65] *See, e.g.*, Authors Guild v. Google, Inc., 804 F.3d. 202 (2d Cir. 2015).

Nevertheless, as noted above, contemporary conventional wisdom holds that the enactment of the 1911 Act was meant to create an exhaustive list of allowable purposes. However, this view is biased by hindsight. It confuses a narrow and erroneous *subsequent* interpretation of the 1911 Act with the *intended* effect of the 1911 codification, and it also wrongly deduces, from the inclusion by US Congress of the explicit words "such as," that their absence from the UK 1911 legislation *necessarily* reflects Parliament's desire to limit fair dealing only to the enumerated purposes. As I explain below, a small number of early English courts misinterpreted Parliament's intent, adopting a restrictive but erroneous view of fair dealing, a view which has never been seriously challenged. Moreover, the legislative history of section 107 in the US indicates that the decision of Congress to add the words "such as" reflects a lesson learned from the failed earlier British attempt at codification.[66]

C *Fair Dealing's Decline*

A few early cases have set the law of fair dealing in the UK and the Commonwealth on a restrictive trajectory from which it has not yet recovered. Of these cases, *University of London Press*, *British Oxygen*, and *Hawkes and Son* are particularly noteworthy: the first, not for what it had held, but for how its holding was later misinterpreted, and the other two for their holding and reasoning. Overall, with some exceptions, these decisions misconstrued Parliament's intent and set the tone for a castrated version of fair dealing: first by confining fair dealing to the list of enumerated purposes and then by construing them narrowly.

i University of London Press

University of London Press Ltd v. University Tutorial Press Ltd.[67] was one of the first reported cases decided under the 1911 Act, and the first case involving the newly enacted fair dealing provision. This, perhaps, explains its enduring influence, despite being only a trial level decision. The outcome of the case does not seem to be particularly controversial or revolutionary – not in retrospect, and probably also not at the time it was decided – but some of its dicta and the misinterpretation of some of its holdings have turned it into an important milestone in the takeover of an owner-centric view of copyright in UK law.

The defendants published a book entitled *London Matriculation Directory*, which contained several matriculation papers copied from a prior publication of the plaintiff, a subsidiary of the University of London, that were written by examiners hired by the university. The defendants' publication also included "answers to the questions in [some of] the papers ...; and it also comprise[d] a short criticism of the construction of the various papers, ... intended for the guidance of future examiners rather than for the edification of possible students."[68] The court found that both publishers recognized that students and teachers derived significant utility from samples of previous examination questions, and to satisfy that demand, both publishers had

[66] The Latman Study, one of the preliminary studies that led to the enactment of section 107, reviewed previous attempts to codify fair use since the passage of the US Copyright Act of 1909. Some proposals explicitly suggested adopting the UK provision. One of them, from 1940, proposed a provision protecting "fair dealing" for "the purpose of private study, research, review or newspaper summary." The entire section was deleted after the Joint Committee on Materials for Research, apparently considering "the position of the scholar more favorable under the case law, convinced all other interested groups except the book publishers that the attempt to codify the doctrine of fair use had been unsuccessful." Allen Latman, Subcommittee on Patents, Trademarks, and Copyrights of the Committee on the Judiciary, 86th Cong, Study 14: Fair Use of Copyrighted Works 21 (Comm. Print 1960).

[67] *See* Univ. of London Press Ltd. v. Univ. Tutorial Press Ltd., [1916] 2 Ch. 601 (Eng.).

[68] *Id.* at 613.

decided to compete in that market. Even though the defendants' publication was not identical to the plaintiffs' and added its own content, copying a significant amount from one publication for the purpose of publishing a competing publication would hardly make an easy case for fair dealing, either today or a century ago. MacGillivray, who acted as co-counsel for the defendants, probably recognized that fair dealing would be an uphill battle and focused most of its defense on other issues. Fair dealing was the last line of defense, pleaded in the alternative, should other arguments fail.

Justice Peterson's judgment reflected the same view of the importance of the issues. He devoted only one paragraph to the fair dealing argument, which he easily dismissed without much elaboration. After describing how both publishers sought to compete in the same market, how there was very little in the defendants' work that could be seen as criticism, and how the partial answers provided by the defendant to some of the questions provided relatively little added value, he concluded that:

> It could not be contended that *the mere republication* of a copyright work was a "fair dealing" because it was intended for purposes of private study; *nor, if an author produced a book of questions for the use of students, could another person with impunity republish the book with the answers to the questions.* Neither case would, in my judgment, come within the description of "fair dealing." In the present case the paper on more advanced mathematics has been taken without any attempt at providing solutions for the questions, and the only way in which the defendants have dealt with this paper is by appropriating it, except that there are eleven lines of criticism of it, dividing the questions into easy, troublesome, and difficult questions. To the questions in the other two papers answers are provided. *Both publications are intended for educational purposes and for the use of students,* and in my judgment the defendants have failed to bring themselves within the protection of s. 2, sub-s. 1 (i.), of the Act.[69]

When read in context, it is clear that *University of London* only stands for the unremarkable proposition that the *mere* republication of a work, by a competing publisher, without adding anything substantial, does not make a credible fair dealing case – a proposition that, on the reported facts of the case, does not seem to be highly controversial.[70]

Contrary to a persistent, self-perpetuating, yet erroneous reading of the judgment, Justice Peterson did not hold that the term "private study" applied only to copying made by students for their own private use. In fact, he accepted that the defendant's book had been intended for "private study," and that like the plaintiff's book, it was intended for "educational purposes and for the use of students." While the phrase "private study" might seem somewhat enigmatic today, there was nothing remarkable in accepting the argument that the books, the defendant's and the plaintiff's alike, were indented for "private study." At the time, it was common for publishers of educational books to describe and promote them as suitable for private study.[71]

Nor did Justice Peterson rule that fair dealing could not apply to other purposes, beyond those explicitly mentioned in the Act (a question that was not before him and need not have been). The question in the case was whether the dealing, although for private study, was fair. He rejected the fair dealing defense on the basis that the dealing was not fair, not on the basis that

[69] *Id.* at 613–14.

[70] This was also the conclusion in *Educational Company of Ireland v. Fallon Brothers and Getz* [1919] 1 IR 62 (Ch.) (Ir.), which involved a similar type of dispute.

[71] *See, e.g.*, Hermann Lange, Lange's New German Method Adapted for Class Teaching and Private Study: In Four Volumes (1876); Alfred Hix Welsh, Essentials of English for Schools, Colleges, and Private Study (1884); William Benjamin Smith, Elementary Co-ordinate Geometry for Collegiate Use and Private Study (1886).

the defendant's purpose did not amount to "private study" or that its educational purpose was not specifically mentioned in the Act.

Nevertheless, for almost a century, this case has been misinterpreted, and was frequently cited as an authority supporting the very propositions that it does not stand for. The first misinterpreter seems to be F. E. Skone James, who, as the editor of the sixth edition of *Copinger*, cited *University of London* as authority for the proposition that private study "only covers the case of a student copying out a book for his own use, but not the circulation of copies among other students."[72] And until the Supreme Court of Canada's ruling in *Alberta (Education)*, Canadian courts repeated this error.

For example, the Federal Court of Appeals (FCA) in *CCH* posited that "British courts have held that use in an educational institution was not for the purpose of private study," but despite the reference to "British courts" in plural, provided a single reference, *University of London Press*.[73] The FCA further added that "the Court in *University of London Press, supra* interpreted private study as not including educational purposes, and therefore did not allow professors to claim an exemption based upon their students' purposes."[74] But *University of London* did not make any of those holdings. It did not deal with "professors [claiming] an exemption" or with "use in an education institution" but rather with two competing commercial publishers. Therefore, it did not hold and could not have held that "use in an educational institution was not for the purpose of private study."

The Copyright Board in *Alberta (Education)* repeated the same errors. It stated "[a]lmost a century ago, British courts established a dichotomy between private study and teacher–student classroom interaction" and concluded that "[i]t therefore seems impossible that a copy made by a teacher for his or her class can be for the purpose of private study ..."[75] Like the FCA, it referred to "British courts" in plural while citing only *University of London*, and in a similar erroneous fashion suggested that *University of London* was a case about a classroom setting.

On appeal, the FCA endorsed the Copyright Board's interpretation. But ultimately, the Supreme Court declined to repeat these errors and noted that the *University of London* had very little bearing on the meaning of "private study" and does "not stand for the proposition that 'research' and 'private study' are inconsistent with instructional purposes."[76]

[72] F. E. Skone James, Copinger on the Law of Copyright 123 (6th ed. 1927).

[73] *See* CCH Canadian Ltd. v. Law Society of Upper Canada, [2002] 4 F.C.R. 213, para. 129 (Can. C.A.).

[74] *Id.* para. 130.

[75] Alberta (Education) v. Canadian Copyright Licensing Agency (Access Copyright), [2009] C.B.D. No. 6, para. 90 (Can.).

[76] *Id.* para. 21. This interpretation of *University of London* was one of the key arguments in the Intervener Factum that the Centre for Innovation Law and Policy filed in *Alberta (Education)* and of which I was one of the coauthors, Alberta (Education) v. Canadian Copyright Licensing Agency (Access Copyright), [2012] 2 S.C.R. 345) (Can.) (Factum of the Intervener, The Centre for Innovation Law and Policy ("CILP")). In that Factum we also included two earlier decisions in which private study and instruction were considered as complementary or even synonymous rather than contradictory. In *Caird v. Sime* [1878] 12 App. Cas. 326 (HL), the House of Lords held that a university professor had not forfeited his right of first publication of his lectures by delivering them to his students in the classroom. The majority reasoned that the professor's duty as a teacher was not to address the public at large, but "to give personal instruction to the individuals composing his audience." The court held that the professor's lectures were "private, inasmuch as the author [did] not by their delivery communicate his ideas and language to the public at large." Similarly, in *Dickens v. Hawksley* [1935] Ch. 267 (Eng.), the terms "instruction" and "private study" were used interchangeably by different judges, and were distinguished from "public" and "publication." The case involved a dispute between heirs of Charles Dickens over the copyright in his unpublished manuscript about the life of Jesus Christ. Justice Bennett described the manuscript as "written for the ***instruction*** of the author's children and ... not intended by him for publication." On appeal, Lord Maugham described the work as one "written by the author ***not for publication but*** for the benefit of his family, and ... for their ***private*** study." *Id.* at 301 (emphasis added).

ii British Oxygen

British Oxygen v. Liquid Air[77] involved two competitors: the plaintiff, who manufactured and sold oxygen gas, and the defendant, who manufactured equipment for producing oxygen gas. Both were competing for the same customers. To persuade a customer not to buy the defendant's equipment, the plaintiff offered that customer a deep discount conditional on a long-term exclusivity commitment. The details of the offer were communicated in a letter sent to the customer. The defendant obtained the letter from that customer, reproduced twelve copies, and sent one of them to a firm of stockbrokers on the London Stock Exchange, together with a letter complaining about the plaintiff's competitive tactics. The plaintiff filed a lawsuit claiming copyright infringement.

The defendant challenged the copyrightability of such a letter, but argued that if such a letter was a literary work within the meaning of the 1911 Act, then its reproduction was permitted as fair dealing for the purpose of criticism. The defendant also relied on earlier cases that found that a person was entitled to publish a letter when it was necessary to protect his character.

Justice Romer rejected all those arguments. He indicated that he was in agreement with the plaintiff's view that "criticism" within the meaning of the Act meant criticism of the work as such but thought that he did not have to actually decide this matter because fair dealing simply could not apply to criticizing an unpublished literary work. Subjecting an unpublished literary work to public criticism, review, or newspaper summary, without the consent of the copyright owner, would be, in his mind, "manifestly unfair." He further doubted that the right to publish a letter to vindicate one's good name survived the passage of the 1911 Act and held that in any event that defense was inapplicable.

iii Hawkes & Son

Hawkes & Son involved the unauthorized use by Paramount Film of twenty seconds of the musical work "Colonel Bogey" (which lasted four minutes in total) in a newsreel reporting the opening of the Royal Hospital School by the Prince of Wales.[78] At trial level, the defendants argued that the part copied was not substantial and that in any event fair dealing applied because "[t]hese news films are in effect a pictorial form of newspaper. The case comes within … fair dealing for the purposes of private study, research, criticism, review, or newspaper summary … The sound film is an audible and pictorial newspaper summary."[79] Justice Eve, the trial judge, held that no substantial part of the work had been reproduced, and that if he was wrong about that then "the acts of the two defendants constitute a fair dealing with the work … it is impossible that what has been done can inflict any substantial injury on the plaintiffs' monopoly, or invade any market of the plaintiffs, actual or problematic."[80]

The Court of Appeals reversed. On appeal, the defendant's lawyers conceded that the part taken was substantial but maintained that fair dealing applied. They emphasized that the reproduction was made for the sole purpose of indicating what happened when the Prince of Wales opened the school, and maintained, based on the case law prior to 1911, that the purpose of the reproduction had always been "of vital importance for the purpose of ascertaining whether there has been an infringement."[81] MacGillivray, who acted as co-counsel for the defendant,

77 *See* British Oxygen v. Liquid Air [1925] 1 Ch. 383 (Eng.).
78 *See* Hawkes & Son (London), Ltd. v. Paramount Film Service, Ltd. [1934] 1 Ch. 593 (CA) (Eng.).
79 *Id.* at 595.
80 *Id.* at 598.
81 *Id.* at 600.

must have been familiar with the legislative history, and his argument that "the matters specified in the proviso to s. 2, sub-s. l, are merely examples of 'fair dealing'"[82] is entirely consistent with that history.[83]

However, Lord Hanworth MR decided "simply to look at the statute" and to interpret it according to its purpose, which in his view was "the necessity for the protection of authors whether of musical or of literary compositions."[84] In interpreting the Act as if that was its only purpose, he adopted a very strong owner-centric view of copyright, ignored its public interest goals, and dismissed the relevance of any consideration of whether the defendant's actions caused any harm to the plaintiff.[85] Remarkably, the authority he relied on to support these propositions was the same paragraph from *Hanfstaengl v. Empire Palace*, where the court described copyright's purpose as preventing persons from *unfairly* availing themselves of the work of others, and noted that infringement occurs only if one "copies more than is fair, so that his copy may be used as a substitute for the original."[86] In an extremely narrow interpretation of the statute, he held that "the collocation of the words 'criticism, review, or newspaper summary' clearly points to the review or to notices of books which appear in newspapers, and not to anything of the nature that was done in the present case."[87] This holding was a clear departure from pre-1911 case law, which did not limit "review" to those narrow settings, and recognized that "criticism" did not apply solely to criticism of the copied work, but could extend to criticizing the views contained in it.[88]

Lord Slesser agreed and added a few interesting remarks. While he acknowledged that the notion of "substantial part" appeared in the statute for the first time in 1911, he emphasized the continuity with the pre-1911 case law and the fact that Parliament explicitly codified what had already been decided by the courts under the previous legislation.[89] However, when considering the defense of fair dealing, he chose to ignore any similar continuity with the previous case law. He took the view that "this [fair dealing] proviso must be dealt with strictly, and when it says 'newspaper summary' it means newspaper summary and nothing else."[90]

Lord Romer, despite showing some sympathy to the defendants, who caused no harm to the plaintiffs, was equally dismissive of their legal arguments. He joined the view that the plaintiffs' harm – or lack thereof – was irrelevant because the plaintiffs were simply asking the court to enforce their legal rights. The plaintiffs were entitled to have their rights enforced, regardless of the interests of the defendant or of the audience.[91]

The strong proprietary and owner-centric language used by the judges makes it difficult to speculate whether the outcome of *Hawkes & Son* would have been different under an explicitly open-ended fair dealing provision, or one that used a different term from "newspaper summary." In any event, while the owner-centric legacy of *Hawkes & Son* continued to burden Commonwealth

[82] *Id.* at 599.
[83] *See infra* Part IV.B.
[84] *See* Hawkes & Son (London), Ltd. v. Paramount Film Service, Ltd. [1934] 1 Ch. 593 (CA) 602–3 (Eng.).
[85] *See id.* at 603. *Cf.* Society of Composers, Authors and Music Publishers of Canada v. Bell Canada, [2012] 2 S.C.R. 326, paras. 9–10 (Can.) (acknowledging the shift in the court's approach, away from an "author-centric view which focused on the exclusive right of authors and copyright owners to control how their works were used in the marketplace" to focusing "instead on the importance copyright plays in promoting the public interest, and emphasiz[ing] that the dissemination of artistic works is central to developing a robustly cultured and intellectual public domain.").
[86] *See* Hanfstaengl v. Empire Palace [1894] 3 Ch. 109 (CA) 128 (Eng.).
[87] Hawkes & Son [1934] 1 Ch. at 604.
[88] *See* Sims, *supra* note 1, at 197–99.
[89] *See* Hawkes & Son [1934] 1 Ch. at 603–8.
[90] *Id.* at 608.
[91] *Id.*

law for many years, some of its harsh consequences were relieved through legislative change. In 1956, the UK changed the term "newspaper summary" to "reporting current events"[92] – Canada would do the same in 1997, by replacing "newspaper summary" with "news reporting."[93] Subsequent amendments in both countries also exempted "incidental inclusion."[94]

Not all cases followed the same restrictive, owner-centric, approach to fair dealing. Even before the Supreme Court of Canada declared in 2004 that fair dealing is a users' right and should be given large and liberal interpretation,[95] some courts, on occasion, approached fair dealing in a more liberal way. For example, in *Hubbard v. Vosper*, Lord Denning MR declined to interpret fair dealing as narrowly as the plaintiff suggested, and did not follow an earlier case suggesting that "criticism" was limited to "criticism of the work as such" or that fair dealing could not apply to criticizing unpublished works.[96] Moreover, his canonical statement that "[i]t is impossible to define what is 'fair dealing'"[97] reflects a vision of flexibility and common law adjudication rather than one that sees courts as strictly bound by the confines of the statutory provision. A year later, the holding in *Hubbard v. Vosper* led the court to recognize that a common law "public interest" defense may "override the rights of the individual (including copyright), which would otherwise prevail and which the law is also concerned to protect."[98]

Nevertheless, it appears that the restrictive view articulated in *Hawkes & Son*, according to which fair dealing was confined to the explicitly enumerated purposes, has never been challenged, and accordingly courts did not have the opportunity to thoroughly consider it. When courts found a dealing fair, they also found that it fell within one of the enumerated purposes, and when they rejected the defense, they characterized the dealing as unfair, even if it was for an enumerated purpose. But there is no reported case where a court found that a defendant's dealing with a work was fair but nonetheless infringing solely because the purpose was not specifically enumerated. Until such a reasoning becomes the *ratio decidendi* of a Supreme Court ruling, the exhaustiveness of the list of enumerated purposes remains an open one.

4 INTERPRETING THE 1911 ACT

Recall that not too long before the UK Parliament enacted the 1911 Act, the House of Lords affirmed the Court of Appeal's decision in *Hanfstaengl v. Empire Palace*, which had stated copyright's purpose as only preventing persons from *unfairly* availing themselves of the work of others, and noted that infringement would occur only if a defendant "copies more than is fair, so that his copy may be used as a substitute for the original."[99] The crucial question, therefore, is what was Parliament's intent when it enacted the fair dealing provision in 1911? Did Parliament intend to replace the common law doctrine with an exhaustive statutory regime but without changing its scope, or did it contemplate a limited statutory regime that coexists with the common law? Did Parliament intend to amend the common law of fair use or fair dealing by confining the doctrine to the five enumerated purposes or was Parliament's intention merely to clarify that the doctrine existed without restraining courts' power to continue developing it?

92 Copyright Act 1956, 4 & 5 Eliz. 2, c. 74, § 6(3) (UK).
93 An Act to amend the Copyright Act, S.C. 1997, c 24, § 18(1) (Can.).
94 Copyright, Designs and Patents Act 1988, c. 48, § 31 (UK); Copyright Act, R.S.C. 1985, c C-42, § 30.7 (Can.).
95 *See* CCH Canadian Ltd. v. Law Society of Upper Canada, [2004] 1 S.C.R. 339, paras. 48, 51 (Can.).
96 Hubbard v. Vosper [1972] 2 QB 84, 94 (Eng.).
97 *Id.*
98 Beloff v. Pressdram Ltd., [1973] F.S.R. 33 (Ch.) 38 (Eng.).
99 Hanfstaengl v. Empire Palace [1894] 3 Ch. 109 (CA) 128 (Eng.), *aff'd*, Franz Hanfstaengl v. H. R. Baines & Co. (1895) AC 20 (HL) (Eng.).

While a plain reading of the statutory language might support the interpretation that Parliament replaced and restricted the common law doctrine, other principles of statutory interpretation, including the legislative history, indicate that the replace-and-restrict interpretation is the least likely one.

This part begins with discussing the restrictive interpretation, largely based on the supposed plain meaning of the fair dealing provision, and then proceeds to refute it.

A *The Restrictive Interpretation*

i Expressio unius

The strongest support for the interpretation that the fair dealing clause in section 2 of the UK 1911 Act[100] (and its subsequent iterations in the Canadian legislation) confines fair dealing to the five enumerated purposes and excludes all other purposes is implied exclusion, based on an inference from the Act's language. Arguably, if Parliament intended to allow courts to apply fair dealing to other, non-enumerated purposes, it would have said so. Parliament could have added the words "such as" (as the US Congress did in 1976) or could have used similar drafting techniques to clarify that the enumerated purposes are illustrative rather than exhaustive. In other words, *expressio unius est exclusio alterius*: "to express or include one thing implies the exclusion of the other."[101]

While *expressio unius* is helpful in determining a text's linguistic meaning, it does not necessarily ascertain its legal meaning.[102] As Aharon Barak writes:

> [L]ogic governs the scope of this canon [of interpretation]. If I say that people are mortal, you should not infer that animals live forever. Even when it is possible to infer "no" from "yes," that choice does not necessarily become the text's legal meaning. Perhaps the "yes" itself is included merely as a precaution, to remove doubt (*ex abundanti cautela*); perhaps it is only an example; perhaps it reflects sloppy writing.[103]

Therefore, "[l]ike the other presumptions relied on in textual analysis, implied exclusion is merely a presumption and can be rebutted."[104]

In 1929, the Supreme Court of Canada noted that:

> The maxim, *expressio unius est exclusio alterius*, enunciates a principle which has its application in the construction of statutes and written instruments, and no doubt it has its uses when it aids to discover the intention; but, as has been said, while it is often a valuable servant, it is a dangerous master to follow. Much depends upon the context. One has to realize that a general rule of interpretation is not always in the mind of a draughtsman; that accidents occur; that there may be inadvertence; that sometimes unnecessary expressions are introduced, ex *abundanti cautela*, by way of least resistance, to satisfy an insistent interest, without any thought of limiting the general provision; and so the axiom is held not to be of universal application.[105]

One of the cases that the Court relied on, *McLaughlin v. Westgarth*,[106] is particularly noteworthy because it was decided by the Privy Council in 1906, five years before the passage

100 *See* Copyright Act 1911, 1 & 2 Geo. 5, c. 46, § 2(1)(i) (UK).
101 *See* Aharon Barak, Purposive Interpretation in Law 8 (2005).
102 *Id.*
103 *Id.* at 108–9.
104 Ruth Sullivan, Statutory Interpretation 193 (2d ed. 2007).
105 Turgeon v. Dominion Bank, [1930] S.C.R. 67, 70–71 (Can.).
106 *See* McLaughlin v. Westgarth [1906] UKPC 33 (appeal taken from Austl.).

of the 1911 Act. In delivering the judgment of the Privy Council, Lord Halsbury observed that modern statutes might often be drafted "with great particularity and minuteness."[107] Unfortunately, he explained, this mode of drafting encourages "any body of persons, seeing a possibility of liability on their part, [to] apply to Parliament to have special provisions inserted for their protection."[108] Parliament often complies with such application, which, in turn, leads the plaintiffs to argue "that anybody who is not included in the enumeration of the particular persons so inserted must be taken to be excluded by the operation of the statute from protection just because they are not included and others are."[109] He held that "[t]he doctrine applicable to all such cases is that a great many things are put into a statute ex *abundanti cautela*, and it is not to be assumed that any body not specifically included is for that reason alone excluded from the protection of the statute."[110]

Moreover, he further noted that "[t]heir Lordships, however, state this general position rather in view of the construction of statutes in general than as being specially relevant to this particular case."[111] This holding, therefore, serves as a backdrop against which the Act passed five years later should be evaluated. It provided a clear directive from the highest court that the exemption of one class of persons from liability should not, without something more, be interpreted as denying protection from all others not specifically exempted.

Therefore, if there were any presumption that the express enumeration of specific purposes in the fair dealing clause excludes all others, it can be easily rebutted in the present context. Moreover, as the proceeding analysis shows, there is no evidence in the legislative history to support the *expressio unius* interpretation. It instead reflects Barak's three possibilities: some of the purposes may have been included to remove doubt; all of them, read together, stand in synecdochically for a variety of permissible uses; and in retrospect, the omission of "such as" reflects sloppy writing.

ii Two Notes on Plain Meaning

Even though the *expressio unius* interpretation assumes that the statute's meaning is clear, it must be noted that the meaning of the fair dealing provision is not as clear as those who adhere to this view pretend it to be. The notion that fair dealing applies only to certain allowable purposes implies that "[d]ealings for other purposes are not covered by the exception, *even if they would otherwise be fair*."[112] Accordingly, proponents of this view call upon us to assume that in enacting the words "[a]ny fair dealing with any work for the purposes of private study, research, criticism, review, or newspaper summary... shall not constitute an infringement of copyright," the UK Parliament in 1911 (and Canada's in 1921) intended that any dealing with a work for any other purpose, even though the dealing may otherwise qualify as fair, would still constitute an infringement of copyright.

While grammatically plausible, this interpretation is paradoxical. The adjective "fair" usually stands for something that is "just or appropriate under the circumstances."[113] It would seem rather peculiar for a legislator to adopt a provision that intentionally holds unlawful dealings that

[107] *Id.*
[108] *Id.*
[109] *Id.*
[110] *Id.*
[111] *Id.*
[112] Alberta (Education) v. Canadian Copyright Licensing Agency (Access Copyright), [2009] C.B.D. No. 6, para. 77 (emphasis added).
[113] *Fair*, OxfordDictionaries.com, https://en.oxforddictionaries.com/definition/fair (last accessed Dec. 21, 2018).

would be "just or appropriate under the circumstances." Why would a legislator wish to outlaw acts that would be just or appropriate? Wouldn't such legislation be unjust and inappropriate? If the intent had really been to confine the exception only to the five enumerated purposes while excluding all others, and further limit it to the subset of those dealings (those that are both within these enumerated purposes and that are fair), it would have been open to say so directly. For example, Parliament could have provided that "it shall not constitute an infringement of copyright to deal with any work for the sole purposes of private study, research, criticism, review, or newspaper summary, and provided that any such dealing is fair." Such a provision would have indeed clarified that the exception of fairness could apply only to one of the enumerated purposes and to no other purpose.

Moreover, the closed-list view of fair dealing commits the logical error of confusing the conditional (If P, then Q) with the biconditional (If P and only if P, then Q). A biconditional statement or rule includes both a conditional statement (If P, then Q) and its inverse (If Not-P, then Not-Q).[114] But the conditional "If P, then Q" should not be mistaken for including its inverse (the biconditional). The statement "if it's raining, then the sky is gray" is a true statement, but it does not mean that the sky is gray only if it's raining (or that if it's not raining then the sky isn't gray). After all, the sky may be gray even when it's not raining.

Or consider the legal meaning of a rule such as "no dogs allowed in restaurant", whose scope might vary depending on the mischief that the rule was intended to address. If the purpose of the rule was to prevent the potential disruption caused by dogs that enter the restaurant, then the rule might be interpreted as not applying to seeing-eye dogs that are trained to be well behaved.[115] Thus understood, the rule might even be interpreted as applying to other potentially disrupting animals even if they are not dogs. However, if the "no dogs allowed" rule was promulgated because the restaurant specifically seeks to serve customers with severe allergies to dogs, then the rule should be interpreted as preventing the entry of a seeing-eye dog, while permitting the entry of any non-dog animal.

Legislated texts are imperfect, and their legal meaning cannot be based solely on their textual meaning; they should be aided by resort to the legislative history and other interpretative principles, which are discussed below.

B *Legislative History of the 1911 Act*

"The legislative evolution and history of a provision may often be important parts of the context to be examined as part of the modern approach to statutory interpretation."[116] Understanding the meaning of fair dealing also requires understanding the law that existed prior to 1911 and what changes, if any, the 1911 Act intended to effect.[117] The Copyright Act of 1911 was "[a]n Act to amend and consolidate the Law relating to Copyright." As early as 1878, consolidation of the law was recommended by a Royal Commission, which found the existing law "wholly destitute of any sort of arrangement, incomplete, often obscure, and, even when intelligible upon long study, so ill-expressed that no one who did not give such study to it could expect to understand it."[118]

114 *See* Adam N. Steinman, *To Say What the Law Is: Rules, Results, and the Dangers of Inferential* Stare Decisis, 99 VA. L. REV. 1737, 1803 (2013).

115 *Id.*

116 Canada (Canadian Human Rights Commission) v. Canada (Attorney-General), [2011] 3 S.C.R. 471, para 43 (Can.).

117 *See* FRANCIS BENNION, STATUTORY INTERPRETATION 458 (3d ed. 1997) ("The interpreter cannot judge soundly what mischief an enactment is intended to remedy unless he or she knows the previous state of the law, the defects found to exist in that law, and the facts that caused the legislator to pass the Act in question.").

118 ROYAL COMMISSION ON COPYRIGHT, REPORT OF THE ROYAL COMMISSION ON COPYRIGHT, 1878, xxiv, C.2036, para. 7 (UK).

Some additional amendments were also required in order to comply with the Berne Convention for the Protection of Literary and Artistic Works signed in 1908.

In addition to extending the term of copyright protection, its application to new subject matter, and the abolition of mandatory registration, the new Act broadened the definition of what copyright was, expanded the definition of what constituted infringement, and enlarged the scope of remedies that might be available to the plaintiff under the Act, in comparison to what was contained in the Copyright Act, 1842. Many of those changes were not entirely revolutionary and reflected developments already recognized in the case law. Still, their explicit recognition in the new statute removed any doubt that the rights and remedies were considerably broader than those explicitly stated in the 1842 Act. This fact helps us understand the motivation for legislating a fair dealing provision instead of continuing to rely on judge-made fair use rulings.

Indeed, a simple explanation might be that since the 1911 Act was mainly a project of consolidation of different acts and codification of different common law rules, it seemed prudent not to leave fair use without any statutory basis. Even though the Royal Commission in 1878 recommended against legislating a specific fair use provision and preferred letting the court continue to apply the doctrine on a case-by-case basis,[119] it is possible that the drafters of the 1911 Act had a different view and thought that their ambitious project of codification and consolidation would be incomplete without mentioning the doctrine in the statute.[120]

Another explanation is a possible concern that if the Act recognized only the expansion of the copyright but remained silent about limitations to those expanded rights, courts might have interpreted that as a signal that Parliament had decided to abolish fair use.[121]

Of course, Parliament could have achieved this result by simply stating that any fair dealing with any work does not constitute infringement, without specifying particular purpose. This, however, might have been considered too vague, and it would make sense to give some illustration.

Alternatively, the purpose of specifying the five categories might have extended beyond removing doubts that fair dealing applied to the purposes already recognized in the case law, but also to ensure that it applied to those who lacked solid grounding in the case law. In particular, the addition of "research," "newspaper summary," and "private study" categories that had no direct precedent in the case law can support this explanation.[122]

[119] *See id.* para. 67.

[120] Interestingly, in 1909, the US Congress consciously decided to leave the determination of fair use entirely to the courts and the Act of 1909 remained, like its predecessors, entirely silent on this issue. *See* Latman, *supra* note 65.

[121] MacGillivray, in his 1912 commentary, offered an explanation along those lines:

"The protection granted under the general definition of copyright in sect. 1 is so absolutely prohibitive of any use in the nature of a reproduction of the whole or any part of the author's work, that it is necessary to introduce the exceptions specified in sub-section (i) [of s 2]. It would hardly have been safe to have left it entirely to the Court to say what exceptions should or should not be admitted upon the analogy of the case law decided under the Copyright Act, 1842." MacGillivray, *supra* note 40, at 27.

See also Ariel Katz, *Fair Use 2.0: The Rebirth of Fair Dealing in Canada, in* The Copyright Pentalogy: How the Supreme Court of Canada Shook the Foundations of Canadian Copyright Law 93, 122 (Michael Geist ed., 2013).

[122] Although commentators such as MacGillivray noted that "[t]he liberty of fair dealing by way of research [was] probably intended to express the whole of the existing case law on the meaning of fair use," MacGillivray, *supra* note 40, at 28 there does not seem to be prior case law dealing with research as such, possibly because reproduction for the purpose of research that did not involve publication or distribution was not a reason for concern and might not have even been actionable under the previous Act. "Newspaper summary" did not appear in the bill, but was added in committee, and "private study" might have been added to overrule, or at least narrow the scope of, the holding in *Novello v. Sudlow* and its progeny. *See also* Katz, *supra* note 120, at 122, and the references therein.

By contrast, it is theoretically possible that by specifying the five enumerated categories, Parliament intended to abolish the common law on fair use, and replace it with a limited statutory fair dealing provision that applies only to those categories, and further prevents the courts from recognizing additional ones. This view has been accepted lately as conventional wisdom, although it is the least likely of all explanations. As we shall see below, there is no evidence supporting this explanation, and sufficient evidence to reject it.

i The Legislative Record

While the legislative record may not be rich enough to unequivocally determine Parliament's intent in 1911, it contains enough to refute the claim that the codification of fair dealing was intended to confine it to the five enumerated purposes or impose a limit on the common law doctrine. In fact, the record contains sufficient evidence to the contrary.

When the bill was introduced to the House of Commons, Mr. Buxton, the president of the Board of Trade (the ministry responsible for drafting the legislation), surveyed the main changes in the proposed Act.[123] If the bill contemplated major reform with respect to fair dealing, it would have been expected that such change was mentioned, but it was not. Nor did Viscount Haldane, who introduced the bill to the House of Lords, mention any contemplated change with respect to fair dealing. In fact, in objecting to a motion "to confine to literary and dramatic works the doctrine of fair dealing which has been laid down by the Courts, and not to extend it to pictures,"[124] Viscount Haldane emphasized the judge-made nature of the doctrine of fair dealing and stated:

> All we propose to do is to declare that for the future the principle of fair dealing which the Courts have established is to be the law of the Code. … The principle of fair dealing is a principle which the Courts have applied with the greatest care. … All that is done here is to make a plain declaration of what the law is and to put all copyright works under the same wording.[125]

This statement proves illuminating in several respects. First, it recognizes fair dealing as a *principle*, and shows that the purpose was to codify a *general principle*, applicable to a wide range of circumstances, as opposed to legislating specific rules that articulate specific exceptions, tailored to specific circumstances. Second, it clarifies that there was no motivation to effect any change in the nature of that principle, only to declare its existence. Third, it shows that there was no concern that the application of this principle by the courts had caused any mischief and that legislation was required to limit their discretion. Instead, the statement evinces trust in the way courts have applied the principle and confidence in their continued ability to do the same in the future.

The parliamentary debates provide additional evidence. One of the debates concerned the status of copyright in written letters. One Member of Parliament proposed adding an explicit exception permitting the publication of private letters in the public interest, or to protect the recipient's reputation.[126] He was concerned that the new bill might be interpreted as taking away a right previously recognized by the courts.[127] The Solicitor General opposed the amendment on the basis that there was no need for an explicit exception because the courts could be trusted

[123] *See* 23 Parl Deb HC (5th ser.) (1911) cols. 2587–663 (UK).
[124] 10 Parl Deb HL (5th ser.) (1911) col. 117 (UK).
[125] *Id.*
[126] *See* 28 Parl Deb HC (1911) col. 1951–56 (UK).
[127] *See id.*

not to enjoin or not to award damages against a person who published a letter when the publication was justified.[128] The subsequent withdrawal of the proposed amendment confirms that Parliament did not consider the fair dealing clause as preventing courts from finding certain uses to be fair, even if not mentioned explicitly.[129]

It appears, therefore, that section 2(1)(i) was meant to codify the *principle* of fair dealing, without restricting or limiting courts' ability to apply, adapt, and adjust it according to the circumstances of particular cases. By specifying instances of dealings and subjecting them to an overarching principle of fair dealing, Parliament intended to guarantee the continued vitality of the doctrine. As Isabella Alexander writes, rather than to restrict, the five enumerated purposes "were intended to be understood synecdochically as standing in for a variety of permissible uses."[130]

ii Additional Extrinsic Evidence

In addition to the legislative record, other contemporaneous extrinsic aids support the view that the 1911 Act was not meant to restrict fair dealing and confine it to the five enumerated purposes. Several commentaries followed the enactment of the 1911 Act. All of them offer a general overview of the 1911 Act, survey the motivations for enacting it, and discuss the main changes relative to earlier law. None of them mentions fair dealing as a major change compared to previous law. All of them, when discussing the various provisions of the 1911 Act, including the issue of infringement, refer to earlier case law, thus clearly indicating that they did not regard the 1911 Act as a revolution, but as an evolution of a previous body of statutory rules and common law interpretation.

Reporting on the legislative process in the fall of 1911, the *Law Times* noted that the bill, which was expected to be approved soon, on the one hand would widen the type of acts that could constitute infringement, but on the other hand "expressly seeks to exclude from the penalties of infringement fair dealing with a work by way of newspaper summary or research [and other exceptions]."[131] In other words, the fair dealing proviso was added to make explicit a limitation on liability which otherwise might be implied.

In the same vein, MacGillivray suggested that the fair dealing proviso was simply added out of abundance of caution.[132] Similarly, J. M. Easton, the author of the fourth and fifth editions of *Copinger on Copyright*, the leading treatise on copyright, noted that "[a]ny fair dealing with any work for the purposes of private study, research, criticism, review, or newspaper summary is also *expressly permitted* by the Act,"[133] but wondered why it was even necessary to include an explicit fair dealing provision for the enumerated purposes, because "fair dealing for other purposes has always been . . . permitted and, presumably, it was not intended to cut down the rights of fair use previously enjoyed under the old law."[134] Further, when introducing section 2(1), which contained six exceptions (fair dealing in section 2(1)(i) and five additional ones), Easton described all of these "six acts [as] examples of what might be considered 'fair dealing' with the original work."[135]

[128] *See id.* at the reply of Solicitor General Sir J. Simon.
[129] Yet *British Oxygen* shows that not all judges interpreted the Act in that manner.
[130] Isabella Alexander, Copyright Law and the Public Interest in the Nineteenth Century 284 (2010).
[131] *Legislation and Jurisprudence*, 131 Law Times 569, 581 (1911).
[132] *See* MacGillivray, *supra* note 40.
[133] Easton, *supra* note 51, at 144.
[134] *Id.*
[135] *Id.* at 134.

Richardson's general observation about the 1911 Act is also consistent with Easton's. He noted that "parts of the law which are practically judge-made such as the questions as to infringement by a new work other than an exact copy have remained to any great extent unaltered."[136] Then, in discussing what constitutes an infringement, he summed up explaining that "[c]opyright then consists in the right to prevent an unfair use of the work."[137]

Likewise, L. C. F. Oldfield's commentary did not seem to read section 2(1)(i) as limiting the common law of fair use. In his introduction, he stated that when an Act of Parliament has received judicial construction, and a later Act *in pari materia* uses the same words, it is presumed that those words retain their meaning, unless there was indication to the contrary.[138] His discussion of fair dealing reveals that he did not see anything in the 1911 Act suggesting alteration of the law on fair use. He explained that "[w]hat is fair dealing with a work depends upon the circumstances of each particular case," and quoted a paragraph from an American case, which he regarded as giving "an excellent summary of the law."[139] Tellingly, he wrote that "[i]t is submitted that the present Act does not alter the law with respect to abridgements, and that if *bona fide* and original, although made without the original author's consent, they are not infringements."[140] The fact that abridgement was not mentioned in section 2(1)(i) did not bother him.

Robertson's commentary discusses fair dealing rather briefly, noting that "[t]his exception is couched in very wide terms, and its limits are not easy to define."[141] He appears to be one of the few commentators that did consider the new Act to have somewhat limited the doctrine of fair dealing. At one point he stated that reproduction allowed under the fair dealing provision "must not be dealt with for any other purpose than one of those specified in the proviso"[142] but failed to notice that the conclusion was inconsistent with other statements that he made.[143]

[136] J. B. Richardson, The Law of Copyright xi (1913).

[137] *Id.* at 99. *See also id.* at 112 ("[c]opyright may be infringed by making an unfair use of an earlier work in composing a new one. The question as to what constitutes a fair use of an earlier work is by no means easy to answer; it varies with the nature of the subject. and it has also varied with the same subject from time to time."). Richardson mentioned "fair dealing" twice, in both cases to emphasize that the fair dealing provision did not effect a change in the law. *Id.* at 37, 137. In discussing whether making a private copy of an artistic work constituted infringement, he noted that "[p]robably the true view was that where a single person made sketches for his own private amusement and not for sale or gratuitous distribution, this did not constitute an invasion of copyright; but where the copies were made for sale or gratuitous distribution it was illegal, as this might interfere with the commercial value of the prints. Under The Copyright Act, 1911, it is expressly provided that any fair dealing with a copyright work for the purpose of private study or research is permissible. Thus, it would seem that the copying of an artistic work by a student in the course of study would now be legitimate; but if the copy was made for any other purpose, it would be an infringement of copyright." *Id.* at 137. While the last statement might seem to endorse the *expressio unius* view, this was not the issue that Richardson discussed.

[138] *See* L. C. F. Oldfield, The Law of Copyright 6 (1912).

[139] *Id.* at 57 ("As a question of strict law, apart from exceptional cases, the privilege of fair use accorded to a subsequent writer must be such, and such only, as will not cause substantial injury to the proprietor of the first publication; but cases frequently arise in which, though there is some injury, yet equity will not interpose by injunction to prevent the further use, as where the amount copied is small and of little value, if there is no proof of bad motive, or where there is well-founded doubt as to the legal title, or where there has been long acquiescence in the infringement, or culpable laches and negligence in seeking redress, especially if it appear that the delay has misled the respondent.") (citing Lawrence v. Dana, 4 Cliff. 1, 83 (1869)).

[140] *Id.* at 58.

[141] George Stuart Robertson, The Law of Copyright 107 (1912).

[142] *Id.* at 119–20.

[143] For example, in the immediately preceding paragraph he explained that "fair dealing for [the enumerated] purposes … covers the cases, which have caused some difficulty in the minds of judges, where a reproduction of an artistic work is made by hand for the purpose of private study or amusement." *Id.* "Amusement," which he claims to be covered by the proviso, is actually not specified in it. In discussing abridgements, he conceded that the issue was unsettled, and suggested that "whether there is likelihood of competition between the infringing work and the work infringed [would be] an important factor in deciding whether a fair use has been made of the latter or not," without

In sum, if by enacting the fair dealing provision Parliament had intended to modify the existing doctrine of fair use by confining it to five enumerated categories exclusively, most of the contemporaneous commentators failed to notice that intention. The parliamentary debates do not support this view either. In Canada, the debates in 1921 do not contain any meaningful discussion of fair dealing.

The view that Parliament had intended to restrict fair dealing to the five enumerated purposes began appearing later. In 1927, the sixth edition of *Copinger* was published by a new publisher. This edition was no longer authored by Easton, but penned by F. E. Skone James. The sixth edition's view about the scope of fair dealing was entirely different and considerably more restrictive. In Skone James's view, the principle embodied in section 2(1)(i) limited "the right to fair use to purposes which in their nature are likely to differ from those of the works from which extracts are taken." He regarded the enumeration of the five purposes as a "limitation of purposes in regard to which the defence of fair dealing can be set up," claiming that the new provision "has probably not altered the law, but it has prevented any attempt to extend the defence to new purposes."[144] Skone James provided no authority to support this restrictive interpretation and failed inexplicably to acknowledge that a contrary view was expressed in the previous edition. Perhaps it was the status of *Copinger* as the leading treatise on copyright that entrenched the restrictive view of fair dealing.

A leading Canadian treatise has witnessed a similar inexplicable reversal of view on fair dealing. Writing in 1944, Harold Fox, in his first treatise on Canadian copyright law, took it for granted that a statutory fair dealing coexisted with a common law fair use.[145] In numerous other places, he referred to fair use, relying indiscriminately on pre-1911 English and American cases.[146] Nowhere did he suggest that the UK 1911 Act or the Canadian 1921 Act rendered the common law concepts of fair use obsolete or that by enacting the fair dealing provision, Parliament intended to enact a more limited fair use regime than that found in the United States. His view was that the statutory fair dealing allowed only the enumerated purposes, and that "[t]hose terms will no doubt be construed strictly."[147] But "[a]t the same time it would seem that the 'substantiality' of the amount copied is still a test for infringement and that the court still has jurisdiction notwithstanding [the fair dealing provision] to hold that a substantial part of the work has not been taken where the part or parts taken can be justified as fair use or fair quotation."[148] Thus, the statutory fair dealing would apply even when substantial part was taken, and "affords additional protection to defendants," that is, even beyond what might be permitted as fair use.[149] While his view of what the common law of fair use had permitted might be restrictive, the crucial point is that he viewed the statutory right as expanding upon it. Fox's second edition from 1967 repeats the same view.[150]

suggesting the fair use was limited to the five enumerated purposes, or noticing that abridgment is not among them. *Id.* at 106. In discussing parodies, he noted the difficulty that they might present but added that "[i]t has never been suggested, for instance, that the brilliant parody of *Tannhäuser* was a breach of copyright," without noticing that "parody" is not mentioned in § 2(1)(i), or without arguing that it is a form of criticism. *Id.* at 112.

[144] Skone James, *supra* note 71, at 122.

[145] *See* Harold G. Fox, The Canadian Law of Copyright 423–25 (1st ed. 1944).

[146] *See id.* at 348–65.

[147] *Id.* at 346. Fox did not offer support for the notion that those terms would be construed strictly, and elsewhere in the book he actually suggested that the term criticism should be given "its broadest sense as meaning a critical use of the material for the promotion of the art or science to which it pertains." *Id.* at 430.

[148] *Id.*

[149] *Id.* at 425.

[150] *See* Harold G. Fox, The Canadian Law of Copyright and Industrial Designs (2d ed. 1967).

Fox died in 1969. The third edition of his treatise, by John McKeown, was published in 2000.[151] The discussion in the previous editions of the pre-1911 case law on fair use all but disappeared. When discussing what constitutes infringement, McKeown concluded that the approach taken to "fair use" by the courts prior to 1911 was, "[i]n light of subsequent cases and the current provisions of the Act ... no longer appropriate."[152] McKeown did not refer to any specific subsequent cases or any current provision of the Act to support this proposition. Moreover, he failed to address Fox's account of fair use or provide reasons for his different view of the relevance of pre-1911 cases.

In any event, most recent and present discussions about copyright and about copyright reform in Canada and other Commonwealth jurisdictions have taken it for granted that fair dealing cannot apply beyond the enumerated purposes. This assumption was shared both by those advocating replacing the current fair dealing regime with a non-exhaustive provision as well as by their opponents. Proposals to amend the Act in this direction never came to fruition,[153] and the preferred approach in all recent rounds of copyright reform was to specify additional exceptions.[154]

It would be tempting to say that Parliament did not adopt those proposals for reform because it correctly recognized that the existing provisions were never intended to be exhaustive and reform was unnecessary. But this would be inaccurate. The truth is that while Parliament recognized a need to expand the exceptions, it chose not to open up the fair dealing provision. But even if this choice reflects the way that recent Parliaments interpreted the existing provision, this perception does not change the meaning of the original provisions. Parliament enacts laws, but it does not interpret them,[155] and any subsequent amendment in a statute cannot be deemed to be or to involve any declaration as to the previous state of the law or that the law under that enactment was different from the law as it is under the enactment as amended.[156]

C Additional Principles of Statutory Interpretation

i The Mischief Rule

The mischief rule, traced back to *Heydon's Case* of 1584, instructs courts to discern and consider the following: (1) what was the common law prior to the enactment of the statute; (2) what was the mischief and defect for which the common law did not provide; (3) the remedy that Parliament proscribed for that mischief; and (4) "[t]he true reason of the remedy; and then the office of all the judges is always to make such construction as shall supress the mischief, and advance the remedy."[157]

[151] *See* John S. McKeown, Fox Canadian Law of Copyright and Industrial Designs (3rd ed. 2000).

[152] *Id.* at 439. Later in the same text, he referred to the same case law and added "[a]t the time these cases were decided there were no express exceptions from infringement in the relevant legislation and the concept was linked to whether a substantial part of a work had been taken. This was a common law equitable doctrine which was referred to as 'fair use' or 'fair dealing.' Cases dealing with this doctrine must be applied with care." *Id.* at 546.

[153] *See, e.g.*, Barry Torno, Fair Dealing: The Need for Conceptual Clarity on the Road to Copyright Revision 71 (1981); Judy Erola et al., From Gutenberg to Telidon: A White Paper on Copyright: Proposals for the Revision of the Canadian Copyright Act 39–40 (1984).

[154] *See* Sookman & Glover, *supra* note 15, at 153.

[155] *See* Barak, *supra* note 101, at 348–49. It should also be noted that even though the current provision is not identical to the original fair dealing provision from 1921, the changes have been minor, and, with the exception of the insignificant attribution requirements that were added in 1993, all other changes expanded the scope of fair dealing.

[156] *See* Interpretation Act, R.S.C. 1985, c L-21 (Can.).

[157] Sullivan, *supra* note 103, at 201 (citing Heydon's Case (1584) 76 Eng. Rep. 637, 638).

However, as the previous discussion makes clear, there is no indication that the way courts handled the doctrine was considered to be a mischief. There is no indication that legislation was required to remedy such mischief by limiting courts' discretion with regard to the purposes to which fair dealing might apply. Therefore, if Parliament did not consider the existing doctrine of fair use to cause any mischief, there is no reason to presume that Parliament had intended to restrict its application.

ii Presumption That an Enactment Does Not Change Existing Law without Clear Indication

The conclusion that Parliament had no intention to prevent the application of fair dealing to other purposes is further supported by the "presumption that the legislature does not intend to change existing law or to depart from established principles, policies or practices" unless it expresses its "intentions to do so with irresistible clearness, failing which the law remains undisturbed."[158]

As Sullivan writes, "despite the constitutional primacy of the legislature... it is presumed that the legislature does not intend to change the common law, to introduce exceptions to general principles (which often originate in the common law), to interfere with common law rights and freedoms, or to take away the jurisdiction of common law courts."[159]

Recall that in *Hanfstaengl*, decided not long before the 1911 Act, the House of Lords affirmed the decision of the Court of Appeal which described copyright as "a monopoly restraining the public from doing that which, apart from the monopoly, it would be perfectly lawful for them to do" and that its scope is limited to "preventing persons from *unfairly* availing themselves of the work of others . . ."[160] This formulation is significant for two reasons: first, because it affirms that copyright itself entails derogation from the common law rights of individuals, and second, because it limits the scope of copyright to preventing only unfair uses of works.

Accordingly, while Parliament, by enacting copyright legislation, restricted the common law right to use works for any purpose, the legislation did not take away the right of any member of the public to engage in fair use of works, and this forms the common law backdrop against which the provisions of the 1911 Act (and any subsequent legislation) have to be assessed.[161] In other words, interpreting the 1911 Act as limiting the right of fair use recognized prior to its passage would require the interpreter to find an irresistibly clear expression of such a legislative intent. As noted above, the legislative record and other extrinsic evidence do not support such a finding.

The principle that abrogation of common law rights and principles requires explicit language was well recognized at the time of the enactment of the 1911 Act.[162] Indeed, the drafters of the Act applied this principle. When they intended to abrogate existing common law rights, they made their intention explicit. For example, section 31 of the 1911 Act was titled "Abrogation of common law rights." This provision was meant to settle once and for all the uncertainty with respect to whether there existed a "common law copyright" independent of the statute. At the

[158] Parry Sound (District) Social Services Administration Board v. OPSEU, [2003] 2 S.C.R. 157, para. 39 (Can.) (citing Goodyear Tire & Rubber Co. of Canada v. T. Eaton Co., [1956] S.C.R 610, 614 (Can.)).

[159] SULLIVAN, *supra* note 103, at 314.

[160] Hanfstaengl v. Empire Palace [1894] 3 Ch. 109 (CA) 128 (Eng.) (italics added).

[161] *Cf.* Ariel Katz, *Intellectual Property, Antitrust, and the Rule of Law: Between Private Power and State Power*, 17 THEORETICAL INQUIRIES IN L. 633, 681–707 (2016) (discussing how the understanding of copyright as a legal monopoly restricting the common law rights of individuals has shaped doctrines such as exhaustion and contributory liability).

[162] *See, e.g.*, WILLIAM FEILDEN CRAIES, A TREATISE ON STATUTE LAW 301–3 (1911).

same time Parliament clarified "that the abrogation of common law rights only applie[d] to the common law proprietary right"[163] but did not affect other common law causes of action.[164]

While section 31 explicitly abrogated some common law rights, section 6(1) of the 1911 Act explicitly invited courts to resort to the common law when deciding the proper remedy when infringement has been found.[165] Notably, neither section 31 nor section 6(1) limited any common law rights of users or any common law defense that might be applicable. If Parliament was interested in restricting users' rights or limiting the common law defenses that may be applicable to them, it would have done that explicitly.

Moreover, the choice of the terms "fair" or "fair dealing" also indicates the legislative intent to maintain continuity with the pre-enactment case law. Notably, in the 1937 case of *Johnstone v. Bernard Jones*, both parties agreed that while the case had to be decided according to the statutory provision, the previous case law on what constituted "fair use" was relevant and helpful.[166]

iii Avoiding Absurd Consequences

Among other considerations, the legal interpreter is directed to avoid an interpretation that produces absurd consequences.[167] "[A]n interpretation can be considered absurd if it leads to ridiculous or frivolous consequences, if it is extremely unreasonable or inequitable, if it is illogical or incoherent, or if it is incompatible with other provisions or with the object of the legislative enactment."[168]

A few examples will suffice to show that the view that the list of enumerated purposes is exhaustive leads to such absurd consequences. Consider, for example, the common – and indeed indispensable – practice in judicial proceedings whereby litigants make several copies of the authorities they rely on and submit them to the court and to all other parties. There is no explicit provision in the Copyright Act that permits this action, and the making of such copies does not easily fit any of the enumerated fair dealing provisions. Interestingly, the current UK legislation includes explicit provisions that permit the making of such copies,[169] but they did not exist in 1911, and cannot be found in the Canadian Act. Yet, in *CCH* the Supreme Court did not hesitate to endorse the Great Library's policy, a policy which explicitly permitted the making of copies "required for the purposes of research, review, private study and criticism, *as well as use in court, tribunal and government proceedings*"[170] and concluded that "the Law Society's dealings with the publishers' works satisfy the fair dealing defence."[171] Even though Parliament never explicitly exempted this activity, the Court effectively recognized an additional implied fair dealing exception for this purpose, and rightly so. Doing otherwise would be utterly absurd.

Or consider time-shifting. In 1984, the US Supreme Court ruled, in the landmark *Sony v. Universal* case, that it was fair use – and therefore not an infringement of copyright – for individuals to use a video cassette recorder to tape television shows in order to view them at a later time. At the end of the majority opinion, after providing a detailed doctrinal analysis, Justice Stevens wrote the following epilogue: "One may search the Copyright Act in vain for any sign

[163] MacGillivray, *supra* note 40, at 159–60.
[164] *See id.*
[165] *See* Copyright Act 1911, 1 & 2 Geo. 5 c. 46, § 34(1) (UK).
[166] Johnstone v. Bernard Jones Publications (1937) 1 Ch. 599, 602 (Eng.).
[167] *See* Rizzo & Rizzo Shoes Ltd., [1998] 1 S.C.R. 27, para. 27 (Can.).
[168] *Id.*
[169] *See* Copyright, Designs and Patents Act 1988, c. 48 (UK).
[170] CCH Canadian Ltd. v. Law Society of Upper Canada, [2004] 1 S.C.R. 339 (Can.).
[171] *Id.* para 73.

that the elected representatives of the millions of people who watch television every day have made it unlawful to copy a program for later viewing at home."[172]

Should we assume that because time-shifting was explicitly recognized as non-infringing only in 2012,[173] the elected representatives of millions of Canadians who have watched television every day and have taped TV shows for the better part of the prior three decades have made it unlawful to videotape TV shows?

And what about a person who made two copies of a TV show: to begin watching one at home, and continue watching it on an iPad at the gym? The new time-shifting exception in section 29.23(c) covers only the making of one reproduction. Does the second one necessarily makes that person an infringer? Such a result seems plainly absurd.

Or consider section 29.4, permitting common classroom activities, such as writing a poem on a blackboard or incorporating an image into an overhead presentation. This provision was enacted in 1997, meaning that until that year, there was no explicit provision permitting those activities. While PowerPoint presentations did not exist in 1911, chalk, blackboards, and poems clearly did. It would be absurd to think that for the better part of the twentieth century, writing a poem on a blackboard in a classroom required the permission of the copyright owner, and that Parliament intended this result, but changed its mind in 1997.

Moreover, the notion that fair dealing applies only to certain allowable purposes implies that other purposes, even if they would otherwise be fair, are not covered by fair dealing. This means that, in 1911, when Parliament provided that "[a]ny fair dealing with any work for the purposes of private study, research, criticism, review, or newspaper summary ... shall not constitute an infringement of copyright," it meant that dealings with works for other purposes may still be regarded as fair, but nonetheless shall constitute an infringement of copyright. As noted above, this is a paradoxical result.[174]

Finally, and more generally, the notion that Parliament intended to exclude the possibility of applying fair dealing to non-enumerated purposes necessarily means one of the following two alternative assumptions is true: one, that Parliament believed that it had canvassed the entire universe of uses that were known at the time of the enactment, as well as those that might be known and possible sometime in the future, and concluded that only the five (and now eight) enumerated purposes were capable of qualifying as fair dealing; or two, that Parliament was aware it could not foresee all potential future uses, but still decided in advance that no matter what those uses might be they ought to be categorically excluded.

The first alternative is inconsistent with the "basic assumption that the legislature is a competent institution acting in the public interest."[175] No competent legislature could believe that it could foresee all types of future uses and predetermine that they could not possibly be fair. Indeed, "if an item which on the application of the *expressio unius* principle would be excluded is of a class which came into existence only after the passing of the enactment, it is probably right to disregard the principle as an aid to construction."[176]

The absurdity of the alternative assumption necessarily points to the conclusion that fair dealing must be a flexible standard for it to achieve its purposes of balancing the public interest with the rights of authors. Fair dealing has a purpose: to allow the unauthorized use of works in a

[172] Sony Corp. of America v. Universal City Studios, Inc., 464 U.S. 417, 456 (1984).
[173] *See* Copyright Act, R.S.C., 1985, c L-42, § 29.23 (Can.).
[174] *See supra* Part IV.A.2.
[175] SULLIVAN, *supra* note 103, at 211.
[176] F. A. R. BENNION, BENNION ON STATUTE LAW 202 (3d ed, 1990) (citing A-G for Northern Ireland's Reference (No 1 of 1975) [1977] AC 105 (HL) 132).

manner that promotes the public interest in the encouragement and dissemination of works of the arts and intellect, when the dealing does not seriously undermine the copyright owner's opportunity to obtain a just reward.[177]

Yet, even though it is possible to identify the *principle* that fair dealing stands for, articulating a precise legal *rule* that implements it is notoriously difficult, if not impossible. The Royal Commission on Copyright, whose 1878 report was one of the bases for the enactment of the Copyright Act, 1911, stated that "no principle which we can lay down, or which could be defined by the Legislature, could govern all cases that occur" and that ultimately these can be decided only on a case-by-case basis by "the proper tribunals."[178] Almost a century later, the US Congress House Committee reached a similar conclusion, noting that "since the doctrine is an equitable rule of reason, no generally applicable definition is possible, and each case raising the question must be decided on its own facts."[179] Lord Denning, in *Hubbard v. Vosper*,[180] the Supreme Court of Canada, in *CCH Canadian*, made similar observations, as did the US Supreme Court in *Campbell*.[181]

Similarly, at the international level, attempts to draft a precise rule regarding limitations and exceptions to copyright proved futile, and resulted in the intentionally vague three-step test, such as the one incorporated in the Berne Convention.[182]

Once the central role that fair dealing plays in calibrating the rights of owners with the rights of users and the public interest is recognized, the view that fair dealing applies only to the explicitly enumerated purposes becomes tenuous, because it requires one to believe that those specific purposes encompass the entire universe of dealings that could justify using a work without getting the copyright owner's permission. If the purpose of the Copyright Act is to encourage future innovation and creativity, fair dealing must be flexible and unlimited with respect to the purposes to which it could apply, otherwise this purpose would be undermined. Rule makers cannot foresee all the types of future uses that justify exemption, and inevitably, a system that relies exclusively on *ex ante* proscribed rules will be tailored to allow only the interests of existing users who had enough political clout to lobby for an exemption.[183] By definition, however, truly new innovations in technology or in cultural expression, those that do not yet exist and may not even be thought of, have no one advocating for them.[184] Without a possibility of relying on a flexible fair dealing standard, the law might prevent these innovations from ever being created. A system that permits only the uses that were able to bargain their way at the legislative negotiation table but excludes all others is doomed to cultural and technological stagnation. While a flexible fair dealing does not guarantee that all socially beneficial uses will be permitted, at least it allows the new uses, those that were not even thought of, or that had no one lobbying for them during the legislative process, to have their day in court and argue,

[177] *See* Théberge v. Galerie d'Art du Petit Champlain Inc., [2002] 2 S.C.R 336 (Can.). *See also* Authors Guild, Inc. v. Google Inc., 954 F. Supp. 2d. 282, 293 (S.D.N.Y, 2013) (finding that Google Books project was fair use because it "provides significant public benefits. It advances the progress of the arts and sciences, while maintaining respectful consideration for the rights of authors and other creative individuals, and without adversely impacting the rights of copyright holders.").

[178] Royal Commission on Copyright, *supra* note 117, para. 67.

[179] H.R. Rep. No. 94-1476, at 65 (1976).

[180] *See* Hubbard v. Vosper [1972] 2 QB 84, 94 (Eng.).

[181] *See* Campbell v. Acuff-Rose Music, Inc., 510 U.S. 569 (1994).

[182] *See* Martin Senftleben, Copyright, Limitations, and the Three-Step Test: An Analysis of the Three-Step Test in International and EC Copyright Law 50–1 (2004).

[183] *See* Peter DiCola & Matthew Sag, *An Information-Gathering Approach to Copyright Policy*, 34 Cardozo L. Rev. 173, 241 (2012).

[184] *See* Thomas B. Nachbar, *Monopoly, Mercantilism, and the Politics of Regulation*, 91 Va. L. Rev. 1313, 1375 (2005).

"we're fair!" It allows innovators to use their scarce resources on recruiting the most talented developers before they need to hire the lobbyists.[185]

Leaving room to individual litigants and the courts to apply fair dealing to circumstances unforeseen by Parliament is not a "far less effective, less democratic and less principled way to approach copyright reform"[186] than the alternative. Quite the contrary: it is more effective, more democratic, and more principled, because it enables policymaking based on evidence and arguments that are inherently incapable of having a voice in the legislative process.[187] It is a feature, not a bug.

Moreover, specific rule-based exceptions, whose main advantage is the certainty that they are purported to promote, are vulnerable to rigidity. Without an overarching principle to guide them, their application tends to "hinge on arcane debates over taxonomy[, making them] perennially uncertain."[188] In contrast, an open, flexible, and general fair dealing avoids this rigidity, and increases certainty over time, as the contours of owners' and users' rights in unforeseen circumstances are determined through litigation,[189] and subsequent legislative amendments when necessary.

5 CONCLUSION

When fair dealing was codified a century ago, there was no intention to restrict or limit its application, adaptation, and adjustment by the courts. Parliament sought to codify a principle, a flexible *standard*, not precise rules. Unfortunately, the English courts in a series of early post-codification cases failed to recognize this point, and so sentenced fair dealing to a hundred years of stagnation. Fortunately, at the turn of the twenty-first century the Supreme Court of Canada declined to follow that restrictive path. Parliament's decision to explicitly recognize additional purposes and add specific exceptions moves Canadian law in the same direction. The Court's rulings and Parliament's action have entrenched fair dealing and provided a necessary correction that allows fair dealing to resume the role it was always supposed to play. But if conventional wisdom is correct, some uses, present or future, are still categorically excluded. This is not a recipe for progress. In a legal environment that outlaws novel ways of using, reusing, and disseminating works outright, fewer new forms of expression will emerge.

However, there is no serious indication that this is what Parliament intended when it legislated fair dealing, and there are very good reasons to challenge the view that it did have such intentions. "All we propose," declared Viscount Haldane before the House of Lords in 1911, "is to declare that for the future the principle of fair dealing which the courts have established is to be the law of the Code."[190] All I propose is that we follow that law.

Open, flexible, and general fair dealing is here. It always has been.

[185] *See* Ariel Katz, *Where Will the Next Google Come From?*, ARIEL KATZ BLOG (Mar. 14, 2011), http://arielkatz.org/archives/1000.
[186] Sookman & Glover, *supra* note 15, at 163.
[187] *See* DiCola & Sag, *supra* note 184, at 241.
[188] Matthew Sag, *Fair Use in the Internet Age* (draft manuscript, on file with the author).
[189] *See id. See also* Niva Elkin-Koren & Orit Fischman-Afori, *Rulifying Fair Use*, 59 ARIZ. L. REV. 161 (2017).
[190] 10 Parl Deb HL (5th ser.) (1911) col. 117 (UK).

8

Fair Use As an Advance on Fair Dealing? Depolarizing the Debate

Michael Handler & Emily Hudson

1 INTRODUCTION

Over the last dozen or so years, countries with laws based on the Copyright Act 1911 (UK) have prioritized the issue of copyright exceptions in their law reform agendas. In each of these countries, a central question has related to the desirability of injecting greater flexibility into exceptions, most notably through the introduction of a "fair use" provision in addition to, or perhaps replacing much of, the existing closed-list system.[1] The resulting statutory reforms have varied. Sri Lanka and Israel, for example, have both adopted a US-style fair use defense, along with a small number of specific exceptions, in their new copyright laws of 2003 and 2007.[2] Singapore has also enacted an open-ended provision, albeit in the form of extended fair dealing rather than fair use. This was achieved by amending one of the purpose-limited fair dealing exceptions to allow it to apply to (almost) any use, with the many closed-list exceptions otherwise retained.[3] In contrast, the reforms of Canada and the UK have – in terms of drafting

Our thanks go to Robert Burrell and Kim Weatherall, the coauthors of our Submissions 278 and 716 to the Australian Law Reform Commission's *Copyright and the Digital Economy* inquiry, on which this chapter builds. All submissions to the *Copyright and the Digital Economy* inquiry cited in this chapter are available at www.alrc.gov.au/inquiry/copyright-and-the-digital-economy/submissions-received-by-the-alrc-4/.

[1] As will be discussed in this chapter, the classification of an exception as a "standard" or a "rule" is more complicated than simply reading the statutory text; furthermore, we use the phrases "open" and "closed" somewhat differently to "standard" and "rule." By closed-list system, we mean an exhaustive set of exceptions in which each provision focuses on a specific act or is otherwise limited in scope, especially through being restricted to a particular purpose. Under this nomenclature, we count fair dealing as a "closed" exception, although we recognize that it may operate more broadly than other provisions. In contrast, an open-ended exception could in theory apply to any use by any user, with the key test relating to fairness or an equivalent concept. Fair use in US law and elsewhere is therefore an "open" exception, as is the extended version of fair dealing in Singapore, discussed *infra*, note 3.

[2] In Sri Lanka, *see* Intellectual Property Act, Act No. 36 of 2003, ss. 11–12. In Israel, *see* Copyright Act 2007, Arts. 19–32. *See also* Tamir Afori, *Israel's New Fair Use Provision, in* Intellectual Property Law and Policy Volume 11, at 264, 267 (Hugh Hansen ed., 2010) (on the political background).

[3] *See* Copyright Act 1977, ss. 35(1) and 109(1) (Sing.) (amended by the Copyright (Amendment) Act 2004). We say "almost" any use as dealings for the purposes of criticism, review, and reporting current events remain covered by other fair dealing provisions in ss. 36–37 and 110–11. For discussion of the approach in Singapore, *see* Ng-Loy Wee Loon & Andy Leck, *Protection of Intellectual Property Rights, in* Developments in Singapore Law between 2001 and 2005, at 242 (Teo Keang Sood ed., 2006), and Singapore Ministry of Law and Intellectual Property Office of Singapore, Public Consultation on Proposed Changes to Singapore's Copyright Regime 28–29 (2016), available at https://www.mlaw.gov.sg/files/news/press-releases/2019/01/PublicConsultationPaperOnProposedChangesToCopyrightRegimeInSingaporeAugust2016.pdf (considering amending the open-ended provision so that it more closely aligns with US law). The existing Singaporean approach has been recommended in Ireland. *See* Copyright Review Committee, Modernising Copyright 89–97 (Oct. 2013) (recommending an open-ended "fair use" defense

choices – stayed closer to the existing infrastructure, with the addition of new fair dealing purposes directed to education, parody, and (in the UK) caricature, pastiche and quotation, and the introduction of new detailed exceptions to accommodate specific practices such as user-generated content, private copying, and data mining.[4] The Australian reform experience has been less fruitful. After some expansion of exceptions (albeit within the closed-list model) in 2006, an impasse arose following strong calls for fair use from two major law reform inquiries. Despite the level of attention already given to copyright exceptions, the Australian government initiated yet another round of consultation in relation to reform options in 2018. There may finally be some progress, as the Australian government announced in August 2020 that it intends to make a series of reforms to the Australian copyright statute, including a new fair dealing exception for non-commercial quotation, a limitation on liability for use of orphaned works, and reforms to certain specific exceptions.

In this chapter we seek to explore the reasons for this impasse and to revitalize the debate around the desirability of alternative options for reform, such as the addition of new fair dealing purposes or the development of other closed provisions that utilize a less prescriptive drafting style. We start from the premise that the exceptions regime in Australia has fundamental problems and is in need of reform.[5] Our aim is to assess the value of a model that maintains but expands and improves upon a closed-list system, compared to one based around an open-ended "fairness" exception. We are therefore interested in exploring the relative merits of a country like Australia adopting the approach of Canada and the UK (that have expanded fair dealing); or joining the US, Israel or Sri Lanka (fair use), or Singapore (extended fair dealing); or moving somewhere between these groups.

We start this task in Section 2 by observing how exceptions debates in Australia and elsewhere have come to be characterized by two camps, one arguing forcefully in favor of fair use and the other decrying the problems of such an approach and defending the structure of the existing system. We note that this focus on fair use, while it is to be welcomed for challenging the status quo and highlighting inadequacies of the closed-list system, has led to the ousting of any meaningful consideration of alternative approaches. In Section 3 we turn to consider substantive arguments in favor of fair use and the status quo, noting how those arguments tend to converge into debates over "certainty versus flexibility." Here we see the repetition of certain tropes, for instance that closed exceptions provide greater certainty in outcomes and practice but are

to be added to the closed list of exceptions, and a non-exhaustive list of eight factors to be taken into account in considering "fairness"). For comment, *see* Mark Hyland, *At a Crossroads: Irish Copyright*, 37 EUR. INTELL. PROP. REV. 773 (2015).

[4] In Canada, *see* Copyright Modernization Act, S.C. 2012, c 20 (expanding the key "fair dealing" exception in the Copyright Act, R.S.C. 1985, c C-42, s. 29 to cover education, parody, and satire, and adding complex new exceptions for non-commercial user-generated content, private copying, time shifting, and the making of backup copies). In the UK, a number of reforms to the Copyright, Designs and Patents Act 1988, c. 48 were introduced in 2014, expanding the "fair dealing" defenses to cover quotation, parody, pastiche, caricature, and illustration for instruction, and adding new defenses covering computational analysis, assisting people with disabilities and library copying. In 2015, the new s. 29B, covering private copying, was quashed. *See* British Academy of Songwriters, Composers and Authors v. Secretary of State for Business, Innovation and Skills [2015] EWHC 1723 (Admin). For consideration of the new exceptions, *see* LIONEL BENTLY ET AL., INTELLECTUAL PROPERTY LAW ch. 9 (5th ed. 2018). For the background, *see* GOWERS REVIEW OF INTELLECTUAL PROPERTY (2006) (recommending new, specific exceptions but also that the EU Information Society Directive be amended to permit domestic exceptions for transformative use), and IAN HARGREAVES, DIGITAL OPPORTUNITY: A REVIEW OF INTELLECTUAL PROPERTY AND GROWTH (2011) (expressing concerns as to whether "fair use" would be consistent with EU law, and instead recommending the adoption of new, specific exceptions).

[5] We have made our case in detail in Robert Burrell et al., *Submission 278 to Australian Law Reform Commission: Discussion Paper 79*, at 10–35 (Dec. 14, 2012). Similar arguments may also apply to the exceptions regimes in other countries.

unresponsive to changing conditions, while fair use affords a greater degree of flexibility and adaptability but is unpredictable. As we explain, although these observations bring to mind some of the literature on standards and rules, they are based on an oversimplified set of assumptions regarding the desirability and effect of different forms of legal drafting.[6] We seek to depolarize this aspect of the debate by providing a fuller account of what "increasing flexibility" actually entails, including by reference to recent experiences in Canada and the UK that demonstrate how closed systems may exhibit benefits usually associated with a fair use approach.

We remain of the view that fair use is the best reform option for a country such as Australia. However, taking a pragmatic perspective, we are also aware of the political challenges in implementing fair use, and that other reform options have the potential to improve greatly on the existing suite of exceptions. We therefore argue that it is important not to overestimate the merits of fair use in comparison with a substantially rehabilitated closed-list model. Expanded fair dealing, coupled with a range of specific exceptions, remains a viable option and is worthy of careful consideration. It ought not to be marginalized or repudiated in the rush to make a case that a country's system of exceptions should be liberalized.

2 THE POLARIZED DEBATE OVER EXCEPTIONS REFORM

A *The Recent Australian Experience*

Copyright exceptions have been considered in Australia in three major government inquiries since 2005. The first led to reform largely within the existing environment of detailed, closed exceptions. The other two – both of which recommended more far-reaching reform – have not yet been acted on (although given the Australian government's announcement in August 2020, this may change in 2021).[7] We start by providing an overview of each inquiry and of the increasingly polarized viewpoints that have been presented by stakeholders; in Section 2B we explore the change in status of expanded fair dealing from one limb of the 2006 reforms to a "second best" alternative to fair use.

In the first inquiry of 2005, the Commonwealth Attorney-General's Department, operating under a conservative government, concluded that Australia should retain its closed-list model but introduce a range of new exceptions. The proximate cause for this review was the 2004 United States–Australia Free Trade Agreement,[8] and in particular the concern that whilst the copyright aspects of that Agreement had required Australia to strengthen rights and expand enforcement mechanisms, there was no mention of balancing aspects of US law such as fair

[6] Such a critique has also been made in ROBERT BURRELL & ALLISON COLEMAN, COPYRIGHT EXCEPTIONS: THE DIGITAL IMPACT 270–71 (2005), and Emily Hudson, *Implementing Fair Use in Copyright Law: Lessons from Australia*, 25 INTELL. PROP. J. 201 (2013).

[7] Without making any reference to any of these inquiries, the Australian government undertook relatively minor exceptions reform in 2017, notably by providing new exceptions for use of copyright material by people with disabilities or those assisting such people, and new preservation copying provisions for libraries and archives. *See* Copyright Amendment (Disability Access and Other Measures) Act 2017 (Austl.). As noted in the Introduction, in August 2020 the Australian government announced a proposal to introduce a new fair dealing exception for non-commercial quotation as well as other reforms, including amendments to the libraries, archives and education exceptions. See Australian Government, Department of Infrastructure, Transport, Regional Development and Communications, *Copyright Access Reforms* (Aug. 13, 2020), available at www.communications.gov.au/departmental-news/copyright-access-reforms. The government has indicated that it will release draft legislation later in 2020, and will engage in further stakeholder consultation.

[8] Free Trade Agreement, U.S.–Austl., May 18, 2004, 43 I.L.M. 1248.

use.[9] Rather than allowing these concerns to slow down parliamentary approval of the Agreement, the government promised, as part of its reelection policies for the imminent federal election, to hold an inquiry in relation to fair use.[10] The government was reelected in October 2004 and the review commenced the following May. Respondents were invited to address two key questions: whether existing exceptions were adequate in the digital age,[11] and how any new exceptions should be drafted, including whether Australia should introduce an open-ended provision similar to fair use.[12]

Among those representing user constituencies, there were recurring complaints that Australia's existing exceptions were inflexible, outdated, and not up to the job.[13] However, it is fair to say that among these respondents, there was also a lack of clarity and consensus regarding the form any amendments should take. Some opposed fair use,[14] while others favored the introduction of a range of reforms that seemed to countenance more of everything: new specific exceptions, new fair dealing purposes and a new fair use provision.[15] A number of submissions referred to a "hybrid" approach that seemed to be based on the expansion of fair dealing, although the precise suggestion was not particularized.[16] All these positions were underpinned by a concern that certainty should not be sacrificed in a shift toward flexibility.

In 2006, and in the absence of any final report, the government passed legislation that reformed some exceptions, notably by adding parody and satire as fair dealing purposes, and accommodating specific practices within new and amended closed exceptions.[17] This legislation also added an autochthonous exception for educational institutions, libraries and archives, and users with a disability.[18] Overall, it can be said that the government agreed that reform was necessary but drafted amendments that accorded with existing drafting approaches. One might speculate whether this was partly in response to – or at least not helped by – the inconsistent and unenthusiastic reception given to fair use by those who would conceivably be its strongest supporters.

[9] Attorney-General's Department, Fair Use and Other Copyright Exceptions: An Examination of Fair Use, Fair Dealing and Other Exceptions in the Digital Age: Issues Paper ¶¶ 6.9–6.15 (May 2005) ("Fair Use Issues Paper") (describing recommendations from the Parliamentary Joint Standing Committee on Treaties and the Senate Selection Committee on the United States–Australia Free Trade Agreement in relation to fair use or equivalent amendments). The Fair Use Issues Paper also noted earlier calls for expanded fair dealing: *id.* ¶¶ 6.3–6.8 (referring to Copyright Law Review Committee, Simplification of the Copyright Act 1968: Part 1: Exceptions to the Exclusive Rights of Copyright Owners (1998)). For further discussion, *see* Robert Burrell & Kimberlee Weatherall, *Exporting Controversy? Reactions to the Copyright Provisions of the US–Australia Free Trade Agreement: Lessons for US Trade Policy*, 2008 U. Ill. J.L. Tech. & Pol'y 259.

[10] Liberal Party of Australia, Strengthening Australian Arts 22 (2004).

[11] Fair Use Issues Paper, *supra* note 9, ¶¶ 11.1–11.21.

[12] *Id.* ¶¶ 1.1–1.7, 14.1–14.14.

[13] *See, e.g.*, the submissions to the Fair Use Issues Paper made by the Australian Broadcasting Corporation, Australian Digital Alliance, Australian Vice-Chancellors' Committee, Internet Industry Association, Electronic Frontiers Australia, Copyright in Cultural Institutions Group, and Australian Film Commission (copies on file with the authors).

[14] *See, e.g.*, the Australian Film Commission's submission (copy on file with the authors).

[15] *See, e.g.*, submissions by the Australian Broadcasting Corporation, Australian Vice-Chancellors' Committee, and Copyright in Cultural Institutions Group (copies on file with the authors).

[16] A key protagonist for this was the Australian Digital Alliance, which recognized that within the time frame of the review it was not in a position to provide a draft of its proposed model. Others to endorse a hybrid approach included the Australian Society of Archivists and the National Archives of Australia (copies on file with the authors).

[17] *See* Copyright Amendment Act 2006, sched. 6 (Austl.). For general discussion, *see* Kimberlee Weatherall, *Of Copyright Bureaucracies and Incoherence: Stepping Back from Australia's Recent Copyright Reforms*, 31 Melb. U. L. Rev. 967 (2007).

[18] *See* Copyright Amendment Act 2006, sched. 6, item 10 (Austl.) (adding a new s. 200AB to the Copyright Act 1968). For discussion, *see* Emily Hudson, *The Copyright Amendment Act 2006: The Scope and Likely Impact of New Library Exceptions*, 14 Austl. L. Librarian 25 (2006).

The second inquiry was the product of the new Labor government's reference to the Australian Law Reform Commission (ALRC) in 2012 to examine whether Australia's exceptions were "adequate and appropriate in the digital environment."[19] In announcing receipt of the final terms of reference, the president of the ALRC stated that whilst recent amendments to the Copyright Act had sought to respond to digital developments, "these changes occurred before the digital economy took off. The ALRC will need to find reforms that are responsive to this new environment, and to future scenarios that are still in the realm of the imagination."[20] The ALRC was therefore tasked with revisiting many of the issues considered just seven years earlier in relation to the scope of copyright exceptions. In contrast with the legislative outcome of the 2005 review, which implicitly rejected fair use, the primary recommendation made in the ALRC's 2013 *Copyright and the Digital Economy* report was that Australia should adopt a fair use defense closely resembling section 107 of the US Copyright Act of 1976 but with a longer list of illustrative purposes.[21] The ALRC's secondary recommendation was that if fair use was not adopted, Australia should significantly expand its fair dealing defenses to cover a range of purposes expressed at a high level of abstraction, such as "criticism or review," "quotation," "non-commercial private use," "incidental or technical use," "library or archive use," and "education," without any further qualifications.[22] In either case, the ALRC recommended the repeal of the nine existing fair dealing provisions and over twenty specific exceptions covering format and time shifting, temporary uses, library preservation copying, and educational use, leaving only a small number of subject-matter-specific exceptions in place.[23] The ALRC's Final Report was met with near silence by a changed, conservative government.

Immediately before the ALRC's Final Report was publicly released, the government announced an independent, comprehensive review of Australia's competition policy. One of the concerns expressed in the final report of this review, published in 2015, was that "there is no overarching IP policy framework or objective guiding changes to IP protection," and that there was a "need for an overarching review of IP."[24] In response, the government asked the Productivity Commission, its independent research and advisory body on economic matters, to conduct a review of all of Australia's intellectual property laws within a year. The Productivity Commission handed down its *Intellectual Property Arrangements* report in late 2016. It agreed with the substance of the ALRC's primary recommendation as to fair use,[25] but did not consider whether existing exceptions ought to be repealed or retained, or the relative merits of expanding the scope of the current closed list of exceptions. At the same time the government made the Productivity Commission's report publicly available, it released a commissioned cost–benefit analysis of the ALRC's primary and secondary recommendations, undertaken by Ernst & Young. This analysis concluded that both fair use and expanded fair dealing would generate net benefits compared with the status quo, with fair use generating the larger benefits.[26] In 2017, the government responded to the Productivity Commission's fair use

[19] *See* Australian Law Reform Commission, Report No. 122, Copyright and the Digital Economy 7 (Nov. 2013) ("ALRC Final Report").

[20] *See* Australian Law Reform Commission, *Terms of Reference Received for the ALRC Copyright Inquiry* (June 29, 2012), available at www.alrc.gov.au/news-media/media-release/terms-reference-received-alrc-copyright-inquiry.

[21] *See* ALRC Final Report, *supra* note 19, at 14 (Recommendations 4-1, 5-1, 5-2, and 5-3).

[22] *Id.* at 14 (Recommendation 6-1).

[23] *See id.* at 14–16 (Recommendations 5-4, 10-1, 11-1, 12-1, and 14-1).

[24] Competition Policy Review, Final Report 104 (Mar. 2015).

[25] *See* Productivity Commission, Report No. 78, Intellectual Property Arrangements ch. 6 (Sept. 2016).

[26] *See* Ernst & Young, Cost Benefit Analysis of Changes to the *Copyright Act 1968* (2016), available at www.communications.gov.au/documents/cost-benefit-analysis-changes-copyright-act-1968.

recommendation by stating that it "will publicly consult on more flexible copyright exceptions"; this consultation took place in 2018.[27] It did not make comments on the Ernst & Young analysis.

One of the most notable features of these Australian reviews, albeit something that has come to characterize debates about the scope of copyright more generally,[28] has been the increasingly polarized positions adopted by different copyright stakeholders.[29] As noted above, numerous respondents argued in 2005 that Australia's existing exceptions were in need of reform, but no clear consensus emerged among those respondents as to what changes should be made. By the time of the ALRC and Productivity Commission inquiries, this group – which consisted of a loose coalition of internet intermediaries, telecommunications companies, consumer associations and advocacy groups, cultural institution representatives, government organizations, peak education bodies, universities, and IP academics – had come to advocate consistently for a shift to fair use. These organizations and individuals focused their attention on the benefits of fair use, portraying it as a flexible, adaptable, and workable doctrine that would facilitate socially beneficial conduct and provide broad economic benefits for Australia, as well as overcoming many of the problems with the existing closed-list system. Arguing in favor of the status quo was a second camp whose underlying position remained largely unaltered from the 2005 review. This group – which comprised content producers, most broadcasters, sports rights holders, collecting societies, and publisher/author associations and advocacy groups – resisted any departure from the existing closed system and supported only minor technical reforms. In their formal submissions and public statements, they painted fair use in almost exclusively negative terms, as an alien, uncertain, and risky concept whose implementation would reduce incentives to create and would generate substantial costs.[30]

This polarization is, to some extent, unsurprising, given the forums in which these views have been ventilated. Public consultation processes encourage stakeholders to advocate for the strongest version of whatever position they support, in the hope of convincing the reform body to recommend that particular course of action.[31] Consistency of position is also important if disagreement between those in the reform camp – even if it relates only to the mechanics in which change is to be effected – may be used to weaken the case for a new paradigm. Given this backdrop, and with the second camp barely acknowledging the limitations of the existing state of the law, those pushing for reform could hardly have been expected to take a cautious approach, engaging critically with a range of reform options and pointing out their potential strengths and weaknesses. This might have given ammunition to those on the other side or have led to a diluted set of recommendations. Indeed, from the time the ALRC first expressed its preference for a shift to fair use in its 2013 Discussion Paper, it is possible to see the pro-reform first camp as "doubling down" on its advocacy for fair use in subsequent submissions to the ALRC and Productivity Commission,

[27] *See* Australian Government Response to the Productivity Commission Inquiry into Intellectual Property Arrangements 7 (Aug. 2017), available at www.pc.gov.au/inquiries/completed/intellectual-property/intellectual-property-government-response.pdf; Australian Government, Department of Communications and the Arts, Copyright Modernisation Consultation Paper (Mar. 2018), available at www.communications.gov.au/have-your-say/copyright-modernisation-consultation. The Australian government announced in August 2020 that it proposes to introduce reforms to the Copyright Act 1968: *see supra* note 7.

[28] *See generally* Jane C. Ginsburg, *How Copyright Got a Bad Name for Itself*, 26 Colum. J. L. & Arts 61, 71 (2002).

[29] *See* Patricia Aufderheide & Dorian Hunter Davis, *Stakeholders and Arguments in Australian Policy Debates on Fair Use and Copyright*, 11 Int'l J. Comm. 522 (2017) (mapping stakeholder participation in the two inquiries). *See also* Gary Lea, *Fair Use Not Fair? Australian "Copyright and the Digital Economy" Report Receives a Cool Response*, 19 Comm. Laws 51, 53 (2014).

[30] For a more detailed analysis of the stakeholders and their arguments, *see* Aufderheide & Davis, *supra* note 29.

[31] Or, at least, they encourage parties to put forward ambit claims, in the expectation that the reform body will settle on a compromise position once all stakeholder views have been considered.

recognizing that this option was gaining some traction[32] – an approach that, in turn, only served to mobilize the second camp in increasing its public opposition to fair use.

Nonetheless, it remains striking that the exceptions debate in Australia has become reduced to the binary question of whether or not fair use should be adopted. Few of the contributors to the recent Australian inquiries argued for reform *within* the existing closed-list framework, for instance by downplaying the purported differences between fair use and an expanded fair dealing regime, or devising broadly worded, forward-looking exceptions to cover uses that ought to be permissible. This is notwithstanding: (i) the scope of the matters addressed in the ALRC's initial Issues Paper, which included fifty-five questions, of which only two pertained specifically to fair use;[33] (ii) the political challenges in making the case for fair use; and (iii) the recent experiences of Canada and the UK, where there has been expansion of exceptions through a fair dealing paradigm. The handful of contributors to the ALRC inquiry that sought to engage with the desirability of staying within a fair dealing framework expressed only faint support for the idea, classifying it as a "poor alternative"[34] to fair use or a "second best reform option."[35] This accords with the broader Australian literature on copyright exceptions, which reveals few contemporary attempts to make the case that an expanded fair dealing model might offer similar benefits to, or even have some advantages over, fair use.[36]

B *Fair Dealing: A Second Best Reform Option?*

A key matter with which we wish to engage in this chapter is whether it concedes too much to accept that expanded fair dealing is inferior to fair use.[37] In answering this question, we start by describing the ALRC's approach to its secondary recommendation in relation to fair dealing. This recommendation has received next to no attention in the scholarship or in subsequent debates, a matter that is not surprising given its presentation by the ALRC. Whilst fair use was front and centre in the ALRC's Final Report and the focus of sustained analysis, its defense of fair dealing was shorter and much less emphatic. The ALRC did not, therefore, attempt to prosecute the case that its expanded fair dealing model might have advantages over fair use,

32 This, to some extent, characterizes our own shift as contributors to these inquiries. *Compare* Burrell et al., *Submission 278*, *supra* note 5, *with* Robert Burrell et al., *Submission 716 to Australian Law Reform Commission: Discussion Paper 79* (July 31, 2013), and Isabella Alexander et al., *Submission 505 to Productivity Commission, Intellectual Property Arrangements: Draft Report* (June 3, 2016), available at www.pc.gov.au/__data/assets/pdf_file/0010/201520/subdr505-intellectual-property.pdf.

33 *See* Australian Law Reform Commission, Issues Paper 42, Copyright and the Digital Economy 5–10 (Aug. 2012), covering questions in relation to, e.g., the guiding principles for reform, internet use and digitization, data mining, private use, transformative use, use by educational and cultural institutions, the statutory licenses and the current fair dealing exceptions. The central question asked in the Attorney-General's Terms of Reference to the ALRC was "whether the exceptions and statutory licences in the Copyright Act 1968 are adequate and appropriate in the digital environment." ALRC Final Report, *supra* note 19, at 7. The Terms of Reference also stated that the ALRC should consider, among other things, "whether further exceptions should recognise fair use of copyright material; allow transformative, innovative and collaborative use of copyright materials to create and deliver new products and services of public benefit; and allow appropriate access, use, interaction and production of copyright material online for social, private or domestic purposes": *id.*

34 Intellectual Property Committee, Business Law Section, Law Council of Australia, *Submission 765 to Australian Law Reform Commission: Discussion Paper 79*, at 5 (Aug. 8, 2013).

35 Universities Australia, *Submission 754 to Australian Law Reform Commission: Discussion Paper 79*, at 16 (July 2013).

36 *Cf.* Melissa de Zwart, *Fairness and Balance: Lessons from Canada for the Proposed Australian Law of Fair Use*, 24 Austl. Intell. Prop. J. 129, 143–44 (2014) (touching on this issue).

37 As noted earlier, our chapter starts from the premise that reform is required, a position that is clearly contested by some stakeholders.

instead describing this proposal as "a pragmatic second-best option"[38] and a potential gateway to fair use.[39] In contrast, the ALRC identified a number of reasons why fair use would be superior to expanded fair dealing.[40]

As noted in Section 2A, the ALRC's secondary recommendation was to consolidate fair dealing into a single provision. This new provision would include the existing purposes of research or study, criticism or review, parody or satire, reporting news and giving professional advice, along with six new purposes: quotation, noncommercial private use, incidental or technical use, library or archive use, education, and access for people with a disability.[41] The provision would also contain guidance in relation to fairness, these factors being the same as those recommended for fair use (namely, language tracking closely section 107 of the US Copyright Act).[42] The case for expanded fair dealing was made in a very short chapter[43] that followed two extensive ones that argued for fair use.[44]

Despite its clear preference for fair use, the ALRC identified some common benefits between fair use and expanded fair dealing. First, it noted the similar operational character of both provisions, namely that they are "flexible standards, rather than prescriptive rules," they revolve around an assessment of fairness, and (on its proposed model) they utilize the same fairness factors.[45] As discussed in further detail below, whilst there is nuance in the characterization of a provision as a standard or rule, it is fair to say that both fair use and expanded fair dealing have standard-like features, although it could be argued that fair use sits further along the spectrum toward a pure standard due to its non-exhaustive list of purposes.

Secondly, the ALRC claimed that expanded fair dealing and fair use would each produce incentive effects, in terms of encouraging socially productive and transformative uses, and discouraging harmful unlicensed uses.[46] The subsequent Ernst & Young analysis attempted to quantify the economic benefit conferred by each model, concluding that both would be superior to the status quo, but that fair use would yield greater net benefits than expanded fair dealing.[47] There are serious challenges for such a project, as much is dependent on the framing questions, available evidence, and underlying assumptions. Some questions may be imponderable or unlikely to elicit any meaningful answers.[48] However, we can, at least, take from this analysis the proposition that both expanded fair dealing and fair use would generate net benefits

[38] ALRC Final Report, *supra* note 19, ¶ 6.40.

[39] *See id.* ¶ 6.41 (stating that "[a] new fair dealing exception could be a step towards fair use. The Australian Government could introduce the exception recommended in this chapter, and then later consider whether to remove the limitation to the listed purposes, so that the exception became an open-ended fair use exception."). In a footnote to this text, the ALRC identified issues with such a two-stage approach, including the need for two reform processes, and the potential time wasted in seeking to demarcate the limits of the prescribed purposes.

[40] *See id.* ¶¶ 6.18–6.28.

[41] *See id.* at 14 (Recommendation 6-1) and ¶ 6.6.

[42] *See id.* ¶ 6.29.

[43] *See id.* at ch. 6 (pp. 161–69).

[44] *See id.* at chs. 4–5 (pp. 87–160).

[45] *See id.* ¶ 6.14.

[46] *See id.* ¶ 6.15.

[47] *See* Ernst & Young, *supra* note 26, at 98–99.

[48] For a similar critique of a UK Consultation Paper that called for evidence about the potential economic effect of a parody exception, described as consisting "mainly of statements of the blindingly obvious or questions which cannot possibly be answered either at all or quantitatively," *see* Sir Robin Jacob, *Parody and IP Claims: A Defence? – a Right to Parody?*, *in* Intellectual Property at the Edge: The Contested Contours of IP 427, 433–34 (Rochelle Cooper Dreyfuss & Jane C. Ginsburg eds., 2014). For discussion of the use of empirical techniques in intellectual property law generally, see Emily Hudson & Andrew Kenyon, *Intellectual Property Law and Empirical Research*, *in* Across Intellectual Property: Essays in Honour of Sam Ricketson (Graeme W. Austin et al. eds., 2020).

through their encouragement (or at least facilitation) of the circulation and reuse of existing works.

Finally, the ALRC noted that fair use and expanded fair dealing would each enjoy greater inbuilt responsiveness to new conditions when compared with prescriptive exceptions.[49] The essence of this argument, as it relates to fair dealing, is that if the prescribed purposes are described at a sufficiently high level of generality, they will be able to apply to new technology and uses without the need for legislative intervention. In addition to reducing the need for ongoing rounds of law reform, this would also prevent the legislature from having to predict, in advance, the precise uses that ought to come within the scope of an unremunerated exception.[50]

Some suggestion of fair use and expanded fair dealing yielding similar benefits was also made implicitly in the Final Report, most notably through the ALRC's lack of differentiation between the two approaches in chapters dealing with specific uses and stakeholder constituencies. These chapters included discussion of the new purposes to which fair use and expanded fair dealing might apply, but with fairly cursory examination of the difference in outcome between each model. To illustrate, in chapter 12 the ALRC stated that further consultation may be necessary to consider the scope of fair dealing for "library or archive use" if the government adopted expanded fair dealing, but that given the same fairness factors were proposed for that and fair use, "[a]pplying ... fair use or amended fair dealing to library or archive uses should ... produce the same result."[51] In chapter 14, in relation to education, the ALRC likewise discussed fair dealing only briefly, repeating its earlier point that this would be "a second best option, but it is more likely to enable educational institutions to make use of new digital technologies and opportunities than the existing or amended specific exceptions."[52]

There were two main points where the ALRC's analysis of fair use and expanded fair dealing diverged. One was in relation to the ability of individuals to "contract out" of exceptions, where it was recommended that fair use *not* be subject to a limitation on contracting out, but that such a restriction should apply to expanded fair dealing.[53] This conclusion was based on concerns that restricting freedom of contract may have unintended consequences for fair use,[54] and that fair use – as an open-ended defense – would not inevitably be applied to uses "which serve important public interests."[55] In contrast, the ALRC was of the view that the existing fair dealing exceptions *did* cover important interests, and that a restriction on contracting out should also apply to the new recommended purposes, thus producing a consistent approach across the various categories.[56] The other point of divergence was in the analysis of quotation in chapter 9. Here, the ALRC included a relatively sustained analysis of quotation as a fair dealing purpose, this being addressed primarily to the impact, if any, of Article 10 of the Berne Convention on the wording of this aspect of the proposed exception. It was concluded that Article 10 did not render it necessary to spell out any further qualifying limbs, either because the Berne requirements were

[49] The ALRC included as an illustration the failure of time-shifting exceptions to apply to cloud-based services. *See* ALRC Final Report, *supra* note 19, ¶ 6.16. Although the Final Report does not cite this case, this would seem to countenance the decision of the Full Court of the Federal Court in Nat'l Rugby League Invs. Pty. Ltd. v. Singtel Optus Pty. Ltd. (2012) 201 F.C.R. 147 (Austl.). For a critique of that decision, *see* Rebecca Giblin, *Stranded in the Technological Dark Ages: Implications of the Full Federal Court's Decision in NRL v Optus*, 34 EUR. INTELL. PROP. REV. 632 (2012).

[50] *See* ALRC Final Report, *supra* note 19, ¶ 6.17.

[51] *Id.* ¶ 12.47.

[52] *Id.* ¶ 14.82.

[53] *See id.* at 18 (Recommendation 20-2).

[54] *See id.* ¶ 20.92.

[55] *Id.* ¶ 20.94.

[56] *Id.* ¶¶ 20.97–20.99.

dealt with via the fairness factors, or were a minimum standard that could be exceeded.[57] No such analysis was included for fair use, plus there was some suggestion that the boundaries of quotation may be more significant under fair dealing than fair use:

> The [fair dealing] exception would require consideration of whether the use is fair, having regard to the same fairness factors that would be considered under the fair use exception. Applying the two exceptions to instances of quotation should, therefore, produce the same result. However, there will be some transformative uses of copyright materials that are not quotation, in that there is no attempt to reference the original work. These may be protected by the fair use exception, but not by a fair dealing quotation exception.[58]

Overall, the structure and emphasis of the Final Report suggests that expanded fair dealing was included if not as an afterthought then at least as a second best option. The bulk of the ALRC's intellectual energies went into making the case for fair use, with expanded fair dealing being seen as a way to capture some of these benefits, but not to the same degree. It seems that the ALRC was of the view that even a generous closed list of purposes would result in expanded fair dealing being "less flexible and less suited to the digital age than an open-ended fair use exception" and would lead to the situation where "many uses that may well be fair . . . continue to infringe copyright, because the use does not fall into one of the listed categories of use."[59] The ALRC also noted the argument that fair dealing may be seen as more certain than fair use because of the exhaustive purposes, but cited the submission (admittedly made by us) that "Australia's current system of exceptions only provides 'certainty' in the sense that we can be confident that a whole raft of socially desirable re-uses of copyright material are prohibited."[60] It attempted a short rehabilitation of fair dealing in response to criticisms of "confined exceptions," emphasizing that fair dealing did not necessarily require a narrow construction and could be made more similar to fair use by adding more purposes.[61] In sum, however, the attitude of the ALRC toward fair dealing seemed to reflect the approach of those calling for reform: the key question was whether Australia should adopt fair use, with fair dealing being presented as the very much next best option if fair use was thought to be a bridge too far.

3 DEPOLARIZING THE FAIR USE DEBATE

In Section 3 we seek to rehabilitate expanded fair dealing as a reform option by analyzing it as a worthwhile model in its own right rather than as a variant of fair use. We start by considering how fair use morphed from an unattractive option that in 2005 failed to garner significant support to the preferred option in 2012–13 of those favoring the liberalization of exceptions in Australia. We suggest that this shift was in part due to the rejection of an oversimplified account that emphasized the unpredictability of fair use when compared to the certainty offered by specific exceptions. In Section 3B we build the case for expanded fair dealing as a model that also enjoys predictability and responsiveness. We use the standards and rules literature along

[57] *Id.* ¶¶ 9.53–9.80. Art. 10(1) states: "It shall be permissible to make quotations from a work which has already been lawfully made available to the public, provided that their making is compatible with fair practice, and their extent does not exceed that justified by the purpose, including quotations from newspaper articles and periodicals in the form of press summaries." Art. 10(3) states: "Where use is made of works in accordance with the preceding paragraphs of this Article, mention shall be made of the source, and of the name of the author if it appears thereon."

[58] ALRC Final Report, *supra* note 19, ¶ 9.83.

[59] *Id.* ¶ 6.19.

[60] *Id.* ¶ 6.22, citing Robert Burrell et al., *Submission 716*, *supra* note 32, at 4.

[61] *See* ALRC Final Report, *supra* note 19, ¶¶ 6.24–6.28.

with experiences in Canada and the UK to make this out, before concluding with some remarks about what a viable expanded fair dealing exception might look like.

We preface these observations by again noting that we remain of the view that Australia should enact a fair use provision, as argued in our submissions to the ALRC Review and the Productivity Commission.[62] However, we are motivated to reconsider expanded fair dealing for a number of reasons. As noted above, there are many political impediments to adopting fair use, and the signals from the current Australian government are that it is still not minded to introduce such a reform. Although fair use is our preferred position for Australia, we are cognizant of the warning that one should not let the perfect be the enemy of the good. But furthermore, we are keen to explore the differences between fair use and expanded fair dealing for this reason: might supporters of fair use have overstated, even if inadvertently, the superiorities of a fully open-ended model?

A *How We Got Here*

As seen in Section 2, those supporting the status quo have retained a consistent position over the years, with the key movement occurring among those who believe that Australia's suite of exceptions is in need of fundamental reform. We believe that a number of factors have led to the improved reception of fair use. One factor is organizational, and relates to better communication and cooperation between different user representatives. This has resulted in greater sophistication and consistency in the viewpoints of those calling for change. A second factor relates to the makeup of this group, and in particular the involvement of internet intermediaries and telecommunications companies such as Google, Yahoo, Optus, and Telstra.[63] This has been significant politically as it demonstrates that reform to exceptions is not just the preserve of educators, librarians, and other "fringe" groups but is supported by economically significant players and those involved in digital innovation. Thirdly, we suspect that a "Groundhog Day" effect has arisen: the sense that a closed-list system of copyright exceptions will require the attention of repeated law reform inquiries, followed by endless rounds of statutory amendment to update provisions. It is understandable that in such an environment, stakeholders might become increasingly amenable to the view that an entirely new paradigm is required.

A fourth reason why fair use has become far more palatable is growing acceptance that fair use can embody both flexibility *and* certainty. As noted above, debates regarding the drafting of exceptions often feature well-worn tropes regarding the characteristics said to be associated with general and specific provisions, for example, that the application of detailed, closed exceptions is more predictable but that such provisions lack responsiveness to changed conditions, whilst open-ended drafting permits flexibility and fact-specific determinations but at the expense of *ex ante* certainty. Important scholarship over the last ten to fifteen years has been breaking down

[62] *See* Burrell et al., *Submission 278, supra* note 5; Burrell et al., *Submission 716, supra* note 32; Alexander et al., *supra* note 32. In 2018, one of us made a submission to the Copyright Modernisation consultation which sought to summarize lessons from the UK experience that were relevant to the specific questions addressed in that consultation. This submission supported the introduction of new fair dealing purposes. It noted the authors' support of fair use, but also that this 'should not be taken as inferring that we have rejected other reforms, such as expansion to fair dealing' as 'new fair dealing purposes ... could do much to improve experiences and deal with copyright overreach.' See Emily Hudson, Tanya Aplin & Robert Burrell, *Submission to the Copyright Consultation: Department of Communications and the Arts* (July 4, 2018), available at https://www.communications.gov.au/sites/default/files/submissions/hudson_aplin_and_burrell.pdf.

[63] ALRC Final Report, *supra* note 19, ¶ 4.40. Telstra and Optus are Australia's two largest telecommunications providers.

this dichotomy in a number of ways.[64] For instance, scholars in the US have undertaken systematic analysis of fair use case law to identify patterns in decision-making,[65] thus pushing back against concerns that fair use is merely the "right to hire a lawyer."[66] This chimes with interview-based fieldwork at US cultural institutions, where participants repeatedly reported a comfort in relying on fair use as part of their copyright management strategies, with those describing new applications of fair use reasoning (for instance, to cover low-resolution images in online collection databases) able to argue from the case law and first principles to explain their viewpoints.[67] In contrast, for areas mediated by closed libraries and archives provisions, reported experiences among interviewees in Australia, Canada, and the US cast doubt on whether those exceptions inevitably deliver certainty, given drafting problems, the use of ambiguous language, the pace of technological change, and so forth.[68] Overall, copyright debates are becoming grounded in a more nuanced and empirically informed vision of copyright exceptions that moves beyond an oversimplified choice between flexibility and certainty, instead asking how language and the interpretative practices of judges, lawyers, and users bear upon the operation of exceptions in practice.

B Rehabilitating Fair Dealing

Despite these shifts in the intellectual underpinnings of copyright debates, it is notable that the positive qualities said to be associated with open-ended drafting have caused the stocks of fair use to rise, but without a noticeable spillover into fair dealing. This may reflect a doctrinal view that fair use is superior to fair dealing, or a pragmatic view that it is important to agitate for the most far-reaching reform option on the basis that a more limited version is likely to emerge from a contested law reform process. It may also be that support for fair dealing has not actually declined, but that it seems that way due to the high level of attention being paid to fair use. In this subsection we reassess the reasons why expanded fair dealing might be attractive as a reform option in its own right: that it may capture many of the same benefits as fair use, and may be superior to a provision modeled on section 107 of the US Copyright Act or some other fully open-ended exception.

To make out these arguments, it is useful to start by elaborating on some lessons from the literature on standards and rules. This scholarship rests on the proposition that legal drafting can take two overarching forms: it can be specific and rule-like, setting out in advance the legal consequences of a particular behaviour or set of facts; or it can be less prescriptive and more standard-like, providing guidance regarding the appropriate legal response but leaving

64 For one of the leading contributions, *see* BURRELL & COLEMAN, *supra* note 6.

65 *See* Barton Beebe, *An Empirical Study of US Copyright Fair Use Opinions, 1978–2005*, 156 U. PA. L. REV. 549 (2008); Pamela Samuelson, *Unbundling Fair Uses*, 77 FORDHAM L. REV. 2537 (2009); Matthew Sag, *Predicting Fair Use*, 73 OHIO ST. L.J. 47 (2012). *See also* PATRICIA AUFDERHEIDE & PETER JASZI, RECLAIMING FAIR USE: HOW TO PUT BALANCE BACK IN COPYRIGHT (2011).

66 This sentiment was expressed by LAWRENCE LESSIG, FREE CULTURE: HOW BIG MEDIA USES TECHNOLOGY AND THE LAW TO LOCK DOWN CULTURE AND CONTROL CREATIVITY 141–42 (2004).

67 *See* EMILY HUDSON, DRAFTING COPYRIGHT EXCEPTIONS: FROM THE LAW IN BOOKS TO THE LAW IN ACTION ch. 5 (2020).

68 *See id.* ch. 4 (also noting that at times these provisions offer too much certainty, in terms of being under-inclusive as judged by their own policy goals or stated aims). *See also* Emily Hudson & Andrew T. Kenyon, *Digital Access: The Impact of Copyright on Digitisation Practices in Australian Museums, Galleries, Libraries and Archives*, 30 UNSW L.J. 12 (2007); KYLIE PAPPALARDO ET AL., IMAGINATION FOREGONE: A QUALITATIVE STUDY OF THE REUSE PRACTICES OF AUSTRALIAN CREATORS (Nov. 2017), available at https://eprints.qut.edu.au/115940/8/QUT-print.pdf.

that determination to a judge or other adjudicator.[69] Although the difference between standards and rules has been described as the "degree of precision,"[70] another explanation emphasizes the timing of decision-making relative to the occurrence of the relevant behaviour or trigger: for rules the legal consequences have been specified *ex ante*, whilst for standards any legal consequences are determined *ex post*.[71] It has therefore been observed that rules can reflect a preference for legislative decision-making and tend to reduce judicial discretion, whilst standards can reflect a preference for judicial decision-making and tend to increase judicial discretion.[72] To illustrate this model, a rule might render it an offence to drive above 60 km/h on a particular stretch of road, while a standard might prohibit driving at an "excessive" speed.[73]

Echoes of the standards and rules literature can be seen in copyright debates that highlight the respective merits of certainty versus flexibility in the drafting of exceptions, with the former usually associated with detailed closed-ended provisions and the latter with exceptions that are more general or adopt open-ended drafting. However, standards and rules thinking is far more sophisticated than a mere binary distinction between two forms of drafting, or between certainty and flexibility. For instance, it is clear that standards and rules exist on a spectrum[74] and that they may be simple or complex, as measured by the number of relevant considerations.[75] To the extent that certainty is associated with rules, it is more accurate to say that the relevant characteristic is *ex ante* certainty. Standards also involve a search for certainty, albeit with this certainty generated via some court process or litigation. This judge-made certainty can be relevant to two audiences. Most obviously it is relevant to the parties to the case, as it describes the precise legal consequences of the facts before the court. But by discussing relevant considerations, it can also provide guidance regarding the application of the standard in other situations, and indeed the accumulation of precedent over time can cause judicial rules to develop beneath an overarching standard. While language provides initial clues as to whether a particular legal command operates as a standard or a rule, ultimately this is a matter of interpretative practices.[76] In addition to the interpretations of judges, relevant interpretations can come from lawyers and academics, and from those regulated by the law (whom we will call users), both individually in their own practices and collectively via industry codes and agreed policies. When all these interpretative practices are taken into account, gaps can emerge between the textual cues in a provision and how it operates in practice, and between

69 For an overview of the literature on standards and rules and its lessons and predictions for copyright exceptions, *see* Hudson, Drafting Copyright Exceptions, *supra* note 67, ch. 2. The legal rulemaking literature has also used other categories and nomenclature to describe sources of law, e.g., presumptions, factors, principles, analogies, etc. *See, e.g.*, Cass R. Sunstein, *Problems with Rules*, 83 Cal. L. Rev. 953, 959–68 (1995).

70 Isaac Ehrlich & Richard A. Posner, *An Economic Analysis of Legal Rulemaking*, 3 J. Legal Stud. 257, 258 (1974).

71 *See* Louis Kaplow, *Rules versus Standards: An Economic Analysis*, 42 Duke L.J. 557 (1992).

72 *See, e.g.*, Ehrlich & Posner, *supra* note 70, at 261.

73 This example recurs in the literature on standards and rules. *See, e.g.*, *id.* at 257; Kaplow, *supra* note 71, at 560; Russell Korobkin, *Behavioral Analysis and Legal Form: Rules vs. Standards Revisited*, 79 Or. L. Rev. 23, 23 (2000).

74 *See, e.g.*, Ehrlich & Posner, *supra* note 70, at 258.

75 Thus, a simple rule might involve a single consideration, such as the law prohibiting driving above 60 km/h, whilst a complex rule might use a detailed algorithm to determine the maximum permissible speed. *See* Kaplow, *supra* note 71, at 565.

76 *See* Sunstein, *supra* note 69, at 959–60 (observing that classification of legal regulation "cannot be decided in the abstract. Everything depends on the understandings and practices of the people who interpret the provision. Interpretative practices can convert an apparently rule-like provision into something very unrule-like. . . . The content and nature of a legal provision cannot be read off the provision. It is necessary to see what people take it to be.").

the interpretative preferences of different constituencies.[77] For instance, one of us observed in 2013 that:

> [T]he seemingly rule-like preservation copying exceptions for libraries and archives in Australian and US law have numerous restrictions, including [in some provisions] a three copy limit on the number of reproductions that can be made. Presumably, then, once an institution makes a fourth copy, it must turn to another exception or to licensing. And yet, in interviews conducted with staff at leading Australian and US institutions, it was repeatedly reported that this restriction was ignored, without a second thought. It seems that institution staff, having internalized norms about good preservation and archival practices, recognize that such practices – especially when performed with digital technologies – often require the production of greater than three copies. Many, therefore, read the language of "three copies" as a proxy for "a reasonable number of copies."[78]

The standards and rules literature does not posit that any one form of drafting is preferable to another. Rather, it judges the best form of drafting as dependent on the context, as judged by matters including the frequency and homogeneity of behaviour to be regulated, the knowledge and risk profile of users, the operation of any relevant social norms, and the costs of compliance and enforcement.[79] Applying this to copyright exceptions, it must therefore be emphasized that "[f]air use should not be seen as inevitably superior to specific exceptions, or the endpoint of a mature copyright system . . . there will be times when a simple rule is superior; instances when a multi-factor standard is preferable; and still other times when the best approach is a well-drafted complex rule."[80] Nevertheless, if one is amenable to arguments regarding the virtues of fair use, it might be asked whether such benefits – and perhaps even other ones – might be captured in other forms of drafting that, whilst not completely open-ended, would seem to operate on the standard-like end of the spectrum. The answers to these questions will depend on doctrinal and empirical analysis.

Starting with textual cues, we see parallels in the language and structure of fair use and fair dealing: both are judged by reference to fairness and to listed purposes, the latter being exhaustive in the case of fair dealing and non-exhaustive in the case of fair use. This factor, along with the inclusion in fair dealing provisions of additional requirements (e.g., for sufficient acknowledgments), makes fair use look like it involves a higher level of judicial discretion than fair dealing. It is therefore not surprising that in crafting a consolidated and expanded fair dealing provision, the ALRC sought to bolster its standard-like qualities by adding new purposes, eliminating other requirements,[81] and urging a liberal interpretation of the provision.[82]

77 This latter is illustrated by the response to CCH Canadian Ltd. v. Law Soc'y of Upper Canada [2004] 1 S.C.R. 349 (Can.). Whilst the academic reaction was overwhelmingly positive, the response of cultural institutions was far more muted, despite the strong philosophy underpinning the Canadian Supreme Court's decision and the facts of that case involving a library. *See further* HUDSON, DRAFTING COPYRIGHT EXCEPTIONS, *supra* note 67, ch. 7.

78 Hudson, *Implementing Fair Use*, *supra* note 6, at 214–15. The three-copy limitation that existed in some of the Australian preservation copying provisions was removed in reforms introduced by the Copyright Amendment (Disability Access and Other Measures) Act 2017 (Austl.).

79 *See* Hudson, *Implementing Fair Use*, *supra* note 6, at 219–21.

80 *Id.* at 226.

81 For example, recommendation 6-1 refers to one of the prescribed purposes being "criticism or review," without any mention of the qualifying words currently found in the Australian statute ("whether of that work or of another work, and a sufficient acknowledement of the work is made"). *See* Copyright Act 1968, s. 41 (Austl.) (and similar in s. 103A). Of course, failure to acknowledge the authorship or source of a work might be relevant to the question of fairness.

82 ALRC Final Report, *supra* note 19, ¶¶ 6.24–6.28.

One of the key lessons from standards and rules, however, is the importance of interpretative practices in classifying and assessing legal regulation. One claim made by those who support fair use is that its randomness has been overstated:[83] that US judges operate in predictable ways, and have created a doctrine that makes principled use of the flexibility that inheres in the statutory language.[84] In contrast, there has been criticism of the interpretative paradigms of judges in countries such as the UK and Australia on the basis that those judges have preferred unduly narrow interpretations of fair dealing and have paid short shrift to user considerations.[85] One argument that has therefore been made in favor of fair use is that it would mark a clear signal to judges (and others) that these narrow conceptions must be abandoned when applying the new fair use provision.

But is fair use essential for a shift in attitude to occur? The obvious counterpoint is Canada, where fair dealing was given a judicial reboot by the Supreme Court in its 2004 decision in *CCH Canadian Ltd. v. Law Society of Upper Canada*.[86] This decision was underpinned by a strong vision of exceptions operating as users' rights, a philosophy that manifested in a number of ways, including the prescribed purposes being given a large and liberal interpretation. One may question how much *CCH* translated into new user practices, as the interpretation preferred by the Supreme Court departed radically from prevailing understandings of exceptions,[87] resulting in some initial suspicion about its longevity.[88] However, with the Supreme Court confirming in the "pentalogy" of 2012 that it meant what it said about fair dealing,[89] and the Canadian legislature expanding (not contracting) fair dealing in the Copyright Modernization Act of 2012,[90] it is now clear that *CCH* was not an outlier or aberration. Instead, the Canadian experience illustrates that judicial attitudes are not immutable, and that judges can interpret fair dealing in ways that emphasize its breadth and standard-like attributes. Glimpses of similar possibilities can be seen in Australian case law[91] and in statements

83 For examples of literature that doubts the coherence of fair use, *see, e.g.*, William W. Fisher, III, *Reconstructing the Fair Use Doctrine*, 101 HARV. L. REV. 1659 (1988); David Nimmer, *"Fairest of Them All" and Other Fairy Tales of Fair Use*, 66 LAW & CONTEMP. PROBS. 263 (2003); Michael J. Madison, *Rewriting Fair Use and the Future of Copyright Reform*, 23 CARDOZO ARTS & ENT. L.J. 391 (2005).

84 *See supra* note 65 and surrounding text.

85 For examples of such critiques, *see* BURRELL & COLEMAN, *supra* note 6; Michael Handler & David Rolph, *"A Real Pea Souper": The* Panel Case *and the Development of the Fair Dealing Defences to Copyright Infringement in Australia*, 27 MELB. U. L. REV. 381 (2003).

86 [2004] 1 S.C.R. 349.

87 *See, e.g.*, Cie générale des établissements Michelin – Michelin & Cie v. CAW-Canada (1996) 71 C.P.R. 3d 348 (Can. F.T.C.D.); Boudreau v. Lin (1997) 150 D.L.R. (4th) 324 (Can. Ont. Gen. Div.); Hager v. ECW Press Ltd. [1999] 2 F.C. 287 (Can. F.T.C.D.); CCH Canadian Ltd. v. Law Soc'y of Upper Canada [2000] 2 F.C. 451 (Can. F.T.C.D.).

88 Thus, even among those who agreed with the Supreme Court's approach, there were concerns that *CCH* might operate as a short-lived high water mark in fair dealing jurisprudence, being unwound by later case law or legislative intervention. *See generally* HUDSON, DRAFTING COPYRIGHT EXCEPTIONS, *supra* note 67, ch. 6.

89 Relevantly, these cases included Soc'y of Composers, Authors & Music Publishers of Canada v. Bell Canada [2012] 2 S.C.R. 326 (Can.), and Alberta (Minister of Educ.) v. Canadian Copyright Licensing Agency (Access Copyright) [2012] 2 S.C.R. 345 (Can.). *See generally* THE COPYRIGHT PENTALOGY: HOW THE SUPREME COURT OF CANADA SHOOK THE FOUNDATIONS OF CANADIAN COPYRIGHT LAW (Michael Geist ed., 2013).

90 *See supra* note 4. The pentalogy and the Copyright Modernization Act occurred in the midst of a long-standing dispute between Access Copyright and Canadian universities in relation to Access's proposed tariff for educational copying. This dispute has resulted in a shift in copyright management at many Canadian universities, including greater reliance on fair dealing. For a description, see HUDSON, DRAFTING COPYRIGHT EXCEPTIONS, *supra* note 67, at 267–75.

91 *See, e.g.*, Fairfax Media Publ'ns Pty. Ltd. v. Reed Int'l Books Australia Pty. Ltd. (2010) 189 F.C.R. 109, ¶¶ 130–44 (Austl.) (defining "reporting of news" to include the activity of a media monitoring service, and observing, in relation to fairness, that the abstracts prepared by the service were a transformative use (citing Am. Geophysical Union v. Texaco, Inc., 60 F.3d 913 (2d Cir. 1995) (U.S.)). There has not been a great deal of Australian case law on fair dealing, and analysis often goes back to statements in TCN Channel Nine Pty. Ltd. v. Network Ten Pty. Ltd. (2001)

emanating from the Court of Justice of the European Union (albeit in relation to exceptions generally rather than fair dealing).[92] There may also be some judicial impetus to recalibrate exceptions in response to the expansionist tendencies that have characterized the trajectory of copyright law.[93]

The next question is whether, in rewriting fair dealing, it is possible to include textual cues that a robust approach is to be preferred. Again, one argument in favor of fair use is that such signals are inbuilt (especially if the statute utilizes language from section 107 of the US Copyright Act) and can be bolstered by the legislature in explanatory materials. But once again it is possible to imagine similar cues in a reform environment that expands fair dealing. An obvious starting point would be in the drafting of fair dealing itself: the statute could avoid any unnecessary limitation of statutory language;[94] the permitted purposes could be drafted at a high level of abstraction but nevertheless have meaning; and any definition of "fairness" could reinforce the intention to create a robust and flexible operation. In Canada, for example, fair dealing has been expanded to include education, parody, and satire,[95] whilst in the UK, reforms in 2014 included new fair dealing exceptions for quotation,[96] caricature, parody, and pastiche,[97] and illustration for instruction.[98] The quotation exception is an obvious candidate for expansive interpretations, with academics identifying room to manoeuvre within such a provision,[99] and some even arguing that Article 10 of the Berne Convention mandates a kind of global fair use provision.[100] There is also potential for the much-overlooked pastiche exception to emerge as a broadly operating exception that enjoys substantial overlaps with what US judges describe as transformative use.[101] In terms of fairness, if one wanted to encourage forward-leaning interpretations through the definition of what is

108 F.C.R. 235 (Austl.), *rev'd in part* (2002) 118 F.C.R. 417 (suggesting a liberal interpretation of the fair dealing purposes should be taken).

92 *See, e.g.*, Cases C-403/08 and C-429/08, Football Ass'n Premier League Ltd. v. QC Leisure, 2011 E.C.R. I-9083 (Grand Chamber) (noting at ¶¶ 162–63 that although the CJEU case law indicates the copyright exceptions should be interpreted strictly, interpretations should also "enable the effectiveness of the exception thereby established to be safeguarded"); Case C-201/13, Deckmyn v. Vandersteen, 2014 E.C.D.R. 21 (Grand Chamber) (emphasizing the need for a "fair balance" in the application of the exception for parody permitted under Art. 5(3)(k) of the Information Society Directive).

93 *See, e.g.*, EMI Songs Australia Pty. Ltd. v. Larrikin Music Publ'g Pty. Ltd. (2011) 191 F.C.R. 444 (Austl.). That case centered on the flute riff in the Men at Work song "Down Under," which was held to infringe copyright in the iconic work "Kookaburra Sits in the Old Gum Tree," written in the 1930s by Marion Sinclair. The case raised a number of doctrinal and policy issues, including in relation to the lack of a quotation exception in Australian law. For instance, Emmett J observed at ¶ 100 that "[i]f, as I have concluded, the relevant versions of Down Under involve an infringement of copyright, many years after the death of Ms. Sinclair, and enforceable at the behest of an assignee, then some of the underlying concepts of modern copyright may require rethinking." At ¶ 101 he further wondered "whether the framers of the *Statute of Anne* and its descendants would have regarded the taking of the melody of Kookaburra in the Impugned Recordings as infringement, rather than as a fair use that did not in any way detract from the benefit given to Ms. Sinclair for her intellectual effort in producing Kookaburra."

94 For instance, "criticism" and "review" should not be limited to criticism or review of the work being copied, or of another work. *Cf.* Copyright Act 1968, s. 41 (Austl.).

95 *See* Copyright Act, R.S.C. 1985, c C-42, s. 29 (Can.).

96 *See* Copyright, Designs and Patents Act 1988, c. 48, s. 30(1ZA) (UK).

97 *Id.* s. 30A.

98 *Id.* s. 32(1). *See, e.g.*, Emily Hudson & Paul Wragg, *Proposals for Copyright Law and Education during the COVID-19 Pandemic*, 71 N. IRELAND L. Q. OA35 (2020).

99 *See, e.g.*, Elizabeth Adeney, *Appropriation in the Name of Art: Is a Quotation Exception the Answer?*, 23 AUSTL. INTELL. PROP. J. 142 (2013).

100 As discussed by Tanya Aplin and Lionel Bently in this volume.

101 *See* Emily Hudson, *The Pastiche Exception in Copyright Law: A Case of Mashed-Up Drafting?*, 2017 INTELL. PROP. Q. 346.

"fair," one possibility might be to import the six fairness factors from Canadian law,[102] although as we discuss below there is one risk with this approach.

Despite all this, the ALRC stated in its Final Report that "a confined fair dealing exception will be less flexible and less suited to the digital age than an open-ended fair use exception" and that "with a confined fair dealing exception, many uses that may well be fair will continue to infringe copyright, because the use does not fall into one of the listed categories of use."[103] However, we wonder whether this statement about the coverage of an expanded fair dealing exception is empirically accurate and, even if it is, whether it reflects remediable issues with the ALRC's proposed list of purposes. As noted earlier, in its chapters focusing on particular uses and constituencies, the ALRC frequently stated that outcomes under fair use and its expanded fair dealing exception would be the same. If right, then the key question is the degree to which fair use reaches beyond fair dealing's prescribed purposes.

This brings us to the question of whether expanded fair dealing might be *superior* to fair use, if one's drafting approach for the former is designed to capture the standard-qualities of the latter. Here we observe that those who support open-ended drafting generally call for fair use as modeled on US law rather than a new, autochthonous exception. The standards and rules literature helps provide a reason for this. By design, standards require case law in order for certainty to emerge. When the US Copyright Act was passed in 1976, section 107 was a codification of an existing common law doctrine, meaning that there were already judicial indications regarding its scope and application.[104] To be clear, users can draw from other sources when interpreting standards, including their own intuitive understandings of the policies behind the law, case law from other jurisdictions, statutory indications, and industry guidelines and codes of practice.[105] However, we risk a period of uncertainty if existing understandings are swept away in a "blank canvas" approach to statutory drafting; for instance, the failure of the bespoke Australian section 200AB exception can in part be attributed to the lack of comprehensibility of its drafting, which "served to oust intuitive understandings and industry norms, and put in their place a series of concepts that neither institutional users nor their professional advisors feel confident to interpret."[106]

One attraction of fair use, therefore, is that a provision modeled on section 107 may have greater initial clarity, as users (and eventually judges) can point to US case law for indications regarding the operation of the exception. However, this benefit could prove illusory in the longer term if Australian law is tied to that of the US, and the latter develops in ways that are objectionable or unsuited to Australian conditions. As such, expanded fair dealing may be attractive as a reform that builds on the existing domestic approach whilst also signalling that a broader, more standard-like approach is intended. To that end, one issue with using

[102] *See* CCH Canadian Ltd. v. Law Soc'y of Upper Canada [2004] 1 S.C.R. 349, ¶¶ 65–72 (the purpose of the dealing; the character of the dealing; the amount of the dealing; alternatives to the dealing; the nature of the work; and the effect of the dealing on the work).

[103] ALRC Final Report, *supra* note 19, ¶6.19.

[104] For a comprehensive overview of the process leading up to the 1976 Act, *see* William F. Patry, The Fair Use Privilege in Copyright Law (2d ed. 1995).

[105] *See* Hudson, *Implementing Fair Use*, *supra* note 6, 226–27.

[106] *Id.* at 227. Section 200AB was originally available only to three nominated user groups: bodies administering a library or archives; educational institutions; and users with a disability and those assisting such people. In judging whether a particular use fell within the exception, the relevant matters included factors said to have the "same meaning" as Art. 13 of the TRIPS Agreement. *See* Copyright Act 1968, s. 200AB (Austl.). One of the reforms of the Copyright Amendment (Disability Access and Other Measures) Act 2017 (Austl.) has been to set out a new fair dealing regime to facilitate access to copyright material by persons with a disability. This has replaced that part of s. 200AB dealing with disabled users.

the six Canadian fairness factors (as we suggest above) may be to repeat the problem of hitching Australian law to another jurisdiction.[107] If the Canadian factors were to be used, there would need to be a clear statement about the interpretative significance of this choice,[108] and perhaps other language or drafting cues (whether in the prescribed purposes or elsewhere) to give the new provision a local flavor. Applying this analysis to the ALRC's proposed model for expanded fair dealing, it would seem to us that the suggested drafting – which would use US-inspired fairness factors – is the least desirable option, due to its capacity to confuse as to the relevance of US law. We would therefore suggest a different set of factors, based either on concepts in Australian law or, with relevant caveats, that of Canada.

4 CONCLUSION

In this chapter we have sought to respond to the increasingly polarized debate in relation to exceptions reform by revisiting one option that, in Australia at least, seems to have disappeared from the agenda: expanding fair dealing. Whilst we remain of the view that fair use is the best option for Australian law, we recognize that there are political and doctrinal impediments to such a change. In this chapter we have therefore asked whether fair dealing has the ability to capture benefits said to be associated with fair use. We have used standards and rules analysis to argue that expanded fair dealing may not be a lowly second-best to fair use but a decent reform option in its own right, if any such provision has appropriately drafted fairness factors, sufficiently broad purposes, and makes limited reference to additional requirements. Turning to the secondary recommendations of the ALRC in relation to expanded fair dealing, we note two ways in which the proposed model might be improved: revision of the prescribed purposes, if these leave a significant gap between expanded fair dealing and fair use; and replacing the proposed US fairness factors with others more suited to a fair dealing environment.

[107] For instance, those who believe that fair dealing can be used by universities for material posted in online learning environments may have some concern about the outcome in Canadian Copyright Licensing Agency (Access Copyright) v. York Univ., 2017 F.C. 669 (Can.).

[108] For example, the extent to which the six Canadian factors differ from those currently contained in the "research or study" exceptions in ss. 40(2) and 103C(2) of the Copyright Act 1968 (Austl.).

9

The Changing Judicial Politics of Copyright Exceptions in the UK

Robert Burrell

INTRODUCTION

In an article written some years ago, I expressed the concern that those who were in favor of the United Kingdom (UK) and other Commonwealth countries moving to a fair use model of copyright exceptions were not paying sufficient attention to how judges would react to the introduction of such a defense.[1] The universal assumption seemed to be that the problem lay solely with the quality of the legislative tools available to judges. In contrast, I sought to demonstrate that if judges were unable to protect users, this was in large part because they had divested themselves of tools that could have been used to provide such protection. I argued that, viewed over a long sweep of history, judges in the UK had demonstrated a reluctance to protect user interests. My argument was that without a change in judicial attitudes a fair use defense would be applied parsimoniously and hence users would see little, if any, benefit. This argument gained some traction, and the observation that we need to think about exceptions reform not merely in terms of drafting choices, but also in terms of judicial culture, now appears to be broadly accepted.[2]

Reflecting on my earlier work almost twenty years later, I had intended to look at subsequent trends in UK case law to see whether there had been a discernible change in judicial attitudes. Might there now be reason to be more confident about the transformative potential of a fair use defense? Asking this question seemed timely. The desirability or otherwise of switching to a fair use model will take on renewed importance in the the UK after Brexit, provided (as now seems likely) copyright reverts to being a matter for national policymaking. The intervening period had also seen several rounds of legislative reform and in 2014 the UK completed the most significant liberalization of the exceptions in more than a century. Was there any evidence that judges had responded to this as a signal that they should also push a liberalization agenda, as would be essential if fair use were to be transplanted successfully into UK law? Was there any evidence that unrelenting criticism of the state of current copyright law from academics and civil society groups had impacted on interpretive practices?

[1] Robert Burrell, *Reining in Copyright Law: Is Fair Use the Answer?* 2001 Intellectual Property Quarterly 361 (2001).

[2] *See, e.g.*, Carys Craig, Copyright, Communication and Culture: Towards a Relational Theory of Copyright Law 160–61 (2011); *id.* at 180; Emily Hudson, *Implementing Fair Use in Copyright Law: Lessons from Australia*, 25 Intellectual Property Journal 201, 208 (2013); *id.* at 215–18.

A review of the relevant decisions soon suggested, however, that the issues dominating the case law did not map comfortably onto a pro-user/pro-owner dichotomy. Rather, the decisions were being dominated by difficult questions around the relationship between national rulemaking and EU law. This observation is itself instructive. It reminds us that some of the shifts that have occurred in the copyright landscape over the past twenty years relate not so much to *what* is being decided but more to *who* is making the decisions. In the UK, recent legislative reform has been entirely dominated by the executive. This has been possible as a consequence of the way in which EU and UK law have been understood to intersect. However, the observation that there has been a shift in the locus of copyright rulemaking is not one that is confined to the UK. Kimberlee Weatherall has noted that in Australia new and significant discretion has been conferred on the executive. Those empowered range from the attorney-general to agencies such as the Australian Competition and Consumer Commission and the Australian Communications and Media Authority.[3]

A shift in where and how rules are made must impact on the way judges approach matters of interpretation. We expect judges to scrutinize rules made by the executive quite differently to how they scrutinize primary legislation. This is particularly true if an executive agency appears to be stretching its power to achieve ends that are outside those originally envisaged when the power was granted. It is also particularly true in fiercely contested areas of policymaking – a category into which copyright unquestionably now falls – where the judiciary has an important role in ensuring that an agency has treated stakeholders fairly and weighed evidence appropriately. This chapter therefore argues that changes in the policymaking landscape have had a largely unnoticed impact on the judicial politics of making decisions around copyright exceptions. It reminds us that when we are thinking about reform we need to think about matters of manner as well as substance, since the former may weigh at least as heavily on judicial interpretation. If we are going to take questions of judicial culture and mind-set seriously, as I think we must, we need to widen our scope of inquiry to think about the broader range of obligations that fall on judges.

This chapter begins by providing an overview of legislative developments in the UK over the past few years. It then turns in the second substantive section to demonstrating, by means of two case studies, that recent developments in the UK around exceptions have been driven by concerns that do not map comfortably onto a pro-owner/pro-user dichotomy. In the conclusion, this chapter turns to consider what its analysis might mean for the desirability of fair use. I suggest that although it does nothing to suggest that fair use is desirable per se, it casts doubt on the merits of one of the most promising alternatives to fair use, namely, that we institute a new rulemaking procedure to allow the exceptions to be rapidly "updated" to deal with technological change and new artistic practices.

RECENT REFORMS: BACKGROUND AND OVERVIEW

As suggested in the introduction, 2014 saw the most important reform of exceptions in the UK since the Copyright Act 1911. A number of new exceptions have been introduced into the Copyright, Designs and Patents Act 1988 (CDPA), and many of the existing provisions have been amended. This is not the place to provide a detailed account of these reforms, but to provide a flavor of the amendments the following, in particular, might be noted:

[3] Kimberlee Weatherall, *Of Copyright Bureaucracies and Incoherence: Stepping Back from Australia's Recent Copyright Reforms*, 31 MELBOURNE UNIVERSITY LAW REVIEW 967 (2007).

- Data mining: a new provision allows a person with lawful access to a work to copy it in order to carry out a computational analysis of anything recorded in the work for the purpose of noncommercial research.[4]
- Parody: a new provision allows fair dealing with a work for the purposes "of caricature, parody or pastiche."[5]
- Quotation: a new right to quote from a work has been added to an existing exception that allowed fair dealing for the purpose of criticism, review, and reporting current events. As with the existing exception, the quotation provision is dependent on the defendant providing a "sufficient acknowledgement" of the work copied and is only available for works that have been lawfully made available to the public.[6]
- Copies for use by persons with a disability. The CDPA 1988 already contained provisions to facilitate the production of copies of works that would be accessible to people with a visual impairment. The new provisions have a more general field of application.[7]
- Educational copying: the original and very limited educational copying defense has been replaced by a much broader exception that allows for fair dealing with a work for the purpose of illustration for instruction.[8]

The above reforms, alongside more minor amendments (such as the updating of the libraries and archives provisions to take account of technological developments), mark a significant and welcome shift in attitudes toward the exceptions. Viewed alongside similar legislative developments and proposals in other countries, it seems that one part of copyright policymaking is finally moving in a sensible direction. It is, however, important to understand something of how these reforms were implemented since they did not, as one might expect, result from Parliament enacting an amendment to the CDPA 1988.

The story of how the UK got to its current position begins with the Information Society Directive 2001.[9] One of the most important features of this Directive is that it seeks to harmonize copyright exceptions throughout the European Union. The Directive did not immediately succeed in creating common exceptions throughout Europe, and in this respect harmonization looked to have failed. Indeed, failure was a more-or-less inevitable consequence of the way member states approached the negotiations, with each country seeking to preserve its preexisting list of exceptions, rather than seeking to agree on a new set of provisions that would apply across Europe. The result was a long list of optional provisions that were sufficiently broadly worded that member states felt justified in doing little more than tweaking their existing exceptions.

The immediate effect of the Directive was, therefore, limited. Insofar as it had any impact on UK law, its influence was detrimental in that the UK merely layered a number of additional constraints on an already tightly constrained set of provisions (e.g., the exception allowing for fair dealing for research or private study was in general retained, but commercial research was excluded from the ambit of this provision to make it compliant with the Directive). For critics of the Directive (and there were many at the time), this result was entirely unsurprising and reflected the antipathy of the European legislature to copyright exceptions. Here it might be

[4] Copyright, Designs and Patents Act 1988 c.48, § 29A.

[5] *Id.* § 30A.

[6] *Id.* § 30.

[7] *Id.* § 31A *et seq.*

[8] *Id.* § 32.

[9] Directive 2001/29/EC of the European Parliament and of the Council of May 22, 2001, on the Harmonisation of Certain Aspects of Copyright and Related Rights in the Information Society.

noted that early versions of the Directive contained a highly circumscribed list of exceptions.[10] However, what critics failed to acknowledge was that the desire of member states to preserve their existing exceptions had resulted in a final text that contained a large number of surprisingly broad provisions.

Recognition that the Directive might actually provide a platform for liberalization came as a result of domestic reform initiatives. In December 2006, the *Gowers Review of Intellectual Property* was published.[11] In a wide-ranging report, the committee called for an overhaul of exceptions, including through the introduction of new parody and format-shifting defenses,[12] and the broadening of existing defenses, in particular those relating to copying by librarians and archivists. The first consultation process on the Gowers recommendations closed in April 2008. Unsurprisingly, this process revealed marked differences between copyright owners and copyright users. This led the Labour government of Gordon Brown to commit itself to holding a second consultation process in the latter part of 2009, but by the time this second consultation process commenced the government had already been convinced to abandon many of the Gowers proposals. Most notably, the introduction of a format-shifting exception was rejected on the grounds that it was too difficult to reach a consensus, with support instead being expressed for a European solution; and the introduction of a parody exception was rejected on the ground that the committee had not been convinced of the need for such a provision. The government did, however, signal its intention to press ahead with some reform of the library and educational copying provisions. The most important of these would have been the introduction of an orphaned works scheme (that is, a provision that would have allowed for the reproduction of works where the copyright owner cannot be located).[13] Provisions to allow for the introduction of such a scheme were included in the Digital Economy Bill 2010, but parliamentary opposition in the run up to the general election of that year led to the orphaned works provisions being abandoned. The fate of the Gowers recommendations followed a pattern that can be traced back many decades, whereby official bodies charged with reviewing the state of UK copyright law become convinced of the need to free up the exceptions, only to find many of their recommendations watered down or ignored entirely.

However, another possibility for reform opened up when the coalition government led by David Cameron announced its support for a further review of copyright law. The resulting report of Professor Ian Hargreaves, *Digital Opportunity: A Review of Intellectual Property and Growth*, was published in May 2011.[14] This reiterated the broad thrust of many of the suggestions made by the Gowers Committee. Importantly, the Hargreaves review concluded that the UK should "realise all the opportunities within the EU framework, including format shifting, parody, non-commercial research, and library archiving."[15]

[10] *See Proposal for a European Parliament and Council Directive on the Harmonisation of Certain Aspects of Copyright and Related Rights in the Information Society* (98/C 108/03) COM(1997) 628 final (submitted by the Commission on 21 January 1998). This draft contained a closed list of eight optional exceptions.

[11] Andrew Gowers, Gowers Review of Intellectual Property (2006), *available at* www.gov.uk/government/uploads/system/uploads/attachment_data/file/228849/0118404830.pdf

[12] The latter would allow, for example, the copying of tracks from a CD onto an MP3 player. *Id.* at 5.

[13] The UK Intellectual Property Office, Taking Forward the Gowers Review of Intellectual Property: Second Stage Consultation on Copyright Exceptions, 2009. For discussion, *see* Ronan Deazley, *Copyright and Parody: Taking Backward the Gowers Review?*, 73 The Modern Law Review 785 (2010).

[14] Ian Hargreaves, Digital Opportunity: A Review of Intellectual Property and Growth (2011), *available at* www.gov.uk/government/uploads/system/uploads/attachment_data/file/32563/ipreview-finalreport.pdf.

[15] *Id.* at 99.

In August 2011, the government indicated broad support for the Hargreaves recommendations, but decided to embark on a further consultation process. This process closed in March 2012. In July 2012, the government published a policy statement in which it indicated its intention to press ahead with legislation to deal with orphaned works and to make provision for extended collective licensing.[16] Implementing legislation for the Hargreaves recommendations came as part of the Enterprise and Regulatory Reform Act 2013. As regards exceptions, the bill originally sought to introduce a new section 28ZA into the CDPA 1988. This would have given the secretary of state the power to repeal or introduce new exceptions. The inclusion of this provision generated significant concern among copyright owner lobbyists and it was dropped from the final version of the legislation. However, the government took the view that to the extent that its plans for exceptions reform involved implementing additional provisions of the Directive, it had the power to introduce new provisions through secondary legislation under the aegis of the European Communities Act 1972. The significance of this decision is discussed in detail, below. Following protracted political negotiations and a last-ditch effort by copyright owners to scupper the reforms, the first group of amendments (dealing with exceptions for research, education, use by libraries and archives, use for the benefit of persons with a disability, and public administration) entered into force on June 1, 2014. The new quotation and parody exceptions came into force on October 1, 2014.[17] As part of this second set of reforms the government also tried to introduce a new format-shifting exception. However, as is discussed in detail in the final substantive section of this chapter, this provision was the subject of a successful challenge before the High Court.

THE BASIS AND NATURE OF RECENT REFORMS

The point that is worth underscoring is that government took the view that it could make amendments to the CDPA 1988 without direct recourse to Parliament. The legal basis for this position was said to be section 2(2) of the European Communities Act 1972. This empowered the designated minister by "order, rules, regulations or scheme" to make provision "for the purpose of implementing any EU obligation of the United Kingdom, or enabling any such obligation to be implemented." Importantly, such orders, rules, regulations, or schemes allowed the minister to amend or repeal an Act of Parliament. Section 2(2) of the 1972 Act formed a central plank of how EU law was incorporated into the UK's domestic legal system: when EU legislation was promulgated, UK law could be adapted quickly through an executive rulemaking process.[18] Although it is hard to question the efficacy of this procedure or to argue that membership of the EU did not require some such arrangement, it had obvious implications for parliamentary sovereignty. The fact that executive orders made using this process received some degree of parliamentary scrutiny, in that they would generally be laid before Parliament giving the legislature the opportunity to reject (but not to amend) them, mitigated, but did not resolve, the problem.

[16] HM Government, The Government Response to the Hargreaves Review of Intellectual Property and Growth, 2011

[17] The Copyright and Rights in Performances (Quotation and Parody) Regulations 2014.

[18] In the constitutional parlance of the UK (and some other Commonwealth countries) provisions that confer a power on ministers to amend primary legislation are generally known as "Henry VIII" clauses. This has its origins in the Statute of Proclamations 1539, which gave the king the power to legislate by royal decree. But *see infra* n. 23 as to the suggestion that § 2(2) is *sui generis*.

Wherever one comes out on the desirability of the system set up by the 1972 Act – and without wanting in any way to descend into the merits or demerits of Brexit – it does have to be acknowledged that the way in which the government employed its powers to reform the exceptions had little to do with how the operation of section 2(2) of the 1972 Act was normally explained and justified. By the time of the 2014 reforms, UK law had already been amended by ministerial order to make it compatible with the Information Society Directive.[19] The 2014 regulations were prompted not by a court decision that suggested that the earlier implementing regulations were defective, but rather by a decision that the government would prefer to introduce some additional and purely optional exceptions found in the Directive. The government thus rewrote an Act of Parliament not because of some legal imperative, but rather out of a policy preference; and this from a government accused of having unduly close links with Google,[20] which has lobbied for exceptions reform internationally.[21]

It would take a myopic focus on the improvement of copyright law for the above not to raise concerns. It is notable, but entirely unsurprising, that the view that any reform should have proceeded by way of primary legislation was aired in the Lords during the debate on the Quotation and Parody Regulations.[22] In doctrinal terms, moreover, it is clear that the judiciary's obligations when reviewing secondary legislation are quite different from when reviewing primary legislation. As the Supreme Court has recently reiterated, in scrutinizing secondary legislation carefully the judiciary is protecting parliamentary sovereignty. Most significantly, the Supreme Court emphasized:

> When a court is considering the validity of a statutory instrument made under a Henry VIII power, its role in upholding Parliamentary supremacy is particularly striking, as the statutory instrument will be purporting to vary primary legislation passed into law by Parliament.[23]

A second doctrinal reason for the courts adopting a cautious approach to the 2014 reforms relates to the form of legislative drafting adopted by the 2014 regulations. In order to explain this point, it is necessary to provide some context. One of the criticisms levelled at the way in which the UK transposed intellectual property directives into national law is that it showed a marked

[19] *See* The Copyright and Rights in Performances (Quotation and Parody) Regulations 2014.

[20] *See, e.g.*, Rowena Mason and Rajeev Syal, *Cameron too close to Google, say critics, after £130m tax deal*, THE GUARDIAN, Jan. 27, 2016, www.theguardian.com/politics/2016/jan/27/cameron-too-close-to-google-say-critics-130m-tax-deal.

[21] This is true, for example, in Australia where Google has pushed for the introduction of a US-style fair use defense. In some quarters the Hargreaves review was dubbed the "Google review" of copyright. *See, e.g.*, Andrew Orlowski, *Government's 'Google Review' Copyright Rules Become Law*, THE REGISTER (July 30, 2014), www.theregister.co.uk/2014/07/30/govts_google_review_copyright_rules_become_law/.

[22] 29 July 2014, Parl Deb HL col. 1568.

[23] R (On the Application of the Public Law Project) v. Lord Chancellor [2016] UKSC 39 (UK), at 25. Admittedly, in Oakley Inc v. Animal Ltd [2005] EWCA (Civ) 1191 (UK), concerning the validity of regulations implementing the *Designs Directive*, the Court of Appeal accepted the attorney-general's submission that § 2(2) of the 1972 Act is *sui generis* and that the normal approach to the interpretation of Henry VIII clauses could not be applied. *Oakley* no doubt helped convince the government that it could proceed as it did with the 2014 Regulations. In particular, *Oakley* makes it clear that § 2(2) could allow for the implementation of purely optional provisions of a Directive and the fact that something can be characterized as a "policy choice" is not a basis for limiting the scope of ministerial power. Nevertheless, it is clear that the 2014 Regulations go considerably beyond anything that was before the court in that case (in *Oakley* the question was about the scope of ministerial power to introduce transitional provisions in reliance on an optional provision of a directive). There is therefore a good argument that a court would be right to approach the 2014 Regulations with caution despite *Oakley*. This is to say nothing of the increasing political controversy that has attached to § 2(2) in the period since that case was decided, something that was true even before the 2016 Brexit referendum, and it is now hard to imagine a court accepting that this provision is not to be classified as Henry VIII power.

reluctance to transpose the text of the corresponding directive without amendment. The practice was for the national regulations to adopt similar, but not quite identical, language to that used in the directive or for the national regulations to add limitations, qualifications or "clarifications" that have no basis in the corresponding provisions of EU law. This left national courts in a difficult position. If they ignored the domestic implementing legislation they failed to respect the domestic legislative/political process and rendered nugatory the idea that member states have a degree of freedom when deciding how to transpose a directive into national law.[24] Conversely, if they gave weight to the domestic text they risked undermining the harmonization process (a point to which we will have cause to return) and exposing the UK to a claim for damages from persons who suffered a loss as a consequence of the failure to transpose the Directive correctly.[25]

The original regulations implementing the Information Society Directive could not, however, fairly be said to reflect the above trend. As has already been noted, the regulations took a *de minimis* approach to exceptions reform. The UK left all of its existing provisions in place and merely tinkered with them to ensure that they complied with any restrictions set up by the Directive. This approach reflected the view, widely shared at the time, that the Directive preserved considerable policymaking freedom for member states when it came to the exceptions. As recently as 2010, Advocate General Trstenjak could state that Article 5 of the Directive "allows the Member States considerable flexibility."[26] This view reflects the negotiating history of the Directive. It also receives support from the text of the Directive itself. Most obviously, the final provision in the shopping list of permissible exceptions set out in Article 5 states the member states may provide for exceptions "in certain other cases of minor importance where exceptions or limitations already exist under national law, provided that they only concern analogue uses and do not affect the free circulation of goods and services within the Community . . ."[27] This "minor exceptions" provision seems to speak to the sort of broad policy latitude that Advocate General Trstenjak and most academic commentators (including myself) had taken for granted. More generally, it has been argued that the exceptions in Article 5 are not capable of being transposed into national law: they are not "a workable code of permitted acts" and the "optional provisions listed in Art 5(2) and 5(3) cannot easily be converted into self-contained exceptions suitable for direct application by a national court."[28] This is because they do not, as written, have the requisite degree of specificity or offer the courts an appropriate degree of guidance.

If the Directive leaves member states with a broad degree of freedom, then national legislatures are, for example, free to transpose part of an exception into national law. Take, for instance, the provision of the Directive that allows a member state to introduce an exception for "use for the purpose of caricature, parody or pastiche."[29] On the broad view this provision would allow a

[24] *See* Consolidated Version of the Treaty on the Functioning of the European Union art. 288, Oct. 26, 2012, 2012 O.J. 326 ("A directive shall be binding, as to the result to be achieved, upon each Member State to which it is addressed, but shall leave to the national authorities the choice of form and methods.").

[25] Usually referred to as "Francovich damages" after Case C-6/90 Francovich v. Italy, 1991 E.C.R. I-00467. For a recent example of such damages being awarded *see* Ogieriakhi v. Minister for Justice and Equality (No. 2) [2014] IEHC 582 (H. Ct.)(IR).

[26] Case C-467/08 Sociedad General de Autores y Editores (SGAE) v. Padawan S. L., 2010 E.C.R. I-10055).

[27] Directive 2001/29/EC of the European Parliament and of the Council of 22 May 2001 on the Harmonisation of Certain Aspects of Copyright and Related Rights in the Information Society art. 5(3)(o).

[28] Jonathan Griffiths, *Fair Dealing after Deckmyn – The United Kingdom's Defence for Caricature, Parody or Pastiche, in* Research Handbook on Intellectual Property in Media and Entertainment (Megan Richardson and Sam Ricketson eds., 2017).

[29] Directive 2001/29/EC of the European Parliament and of the Council of 22 May 2001 on the Harmonisation of Certain Aspects of Copyright and Related Rights in the Information Society art. 5(3)(k).

Member State to introduce an exception that only covered parody. It would also be permissible on this view for a member state to introduce additional limitations on the scope of an exception. For example, France would be justified in preserving the limitation that uses for the purpose of parody, pastiche and caricature must "observe the rules of the genre."[30] More controversially, it might be open to a member state to create an exception drawing on elements of different provisions of the Directive. For example, the UK might have tried to justify its public interest defense through some combination of Article 5(3)(c) (reporting current events), Article 5(3)(e) (public security), and Article 5(3)(o) (minor exceptions).[31]

In some respects, the 2014 Regulations adopt a very different approach to the original implementing regulations. Whereas the original regulations adopted a bare compliance approach, the 2014 Regulations look to the Directive as a platform for liberalization. In the language of the Hargreaves review, the aim was for the UK to "realise all the opportunities within the EU framework." This shift to thinking about the Directive as setting up opportunities was unquestionably important. For present purposes, however, it is equally important to note that the 2014 Regulations still rest on the broad view of the policy freedom left to member states. The 2014 Regulations do not transpose exceptions into national law without qualification or amendment. Rather, they seek to adapt the provisions of the Directive to the UK's legislative framework. The new quotation and parody exceptions are thus situated within the UK's "fair dealing machinery."[32] The intention was that this would provide courts with immediate guidance as to how to approach the new exceptions. Most obviously, it was a steer that they should draw on the traditional fairness factors articulated by Lord Denning in *Hubbard v. Vosper.*[33]

The difficulty for UK courts, and the heart of the second reason they have for approaching the 2014 reforms with caution, is that it is now clear that the broad view of the freedom left to member states needs to be qualified.

Specifically, the CJEU has emphasized that the degree of discretion left to Member States in how they transpose exceptions into national law varies according to the provision of the Directive in question. In some instances, Member States do indeed enjoy significant latitude. Some provisions of the Directive do not constitute "measures of full harmonisation" and allow Member States "significant discretion allowing them to strike a balance between the relevant interests".[34] In other cases, however, the Directive is not to be treated as preserving very broad policy freedom, but rather as presenting member states with something closer to a binary choice. That is, that they are free either to implement or to not implement a provision in the form that it is set out in the Directive. The extent of the freedom left to Member States is determined not merely by the wording of the provision of the Directive, but also by the extent to which an exception impacts on 'the smooth functioning of the internal market'.[35]

The operation of the binary-type model can be seen most clearly in *Deckmyn v. Vandersteen.*[36] In that case the CJEU emphasized that "parody" had to be regarded as an "autonomous

[30] Code de la Propriété Intellectuelle [Intellectual Property Code], art. L-122 5.

[31] *See* Jonathan Griffiths, *Pre-empting Conflict: A Re-examination of the Public Interest Defence in United Kingdom (UK) Copyright Law*, 34 Legal Studies 76 (2014).

[32] Emily Hudson, *The Pastiche Exception in Copyright Law: A Case of Mashed-Up Drafting?*, 2017 Intellectual Property Quarterly 346 (2017), 346.

[33] (1972)2 Q.B. 84.

[34] C-516/17 Spiegel Online GmbH v Volker Beck, 2019 ECLI:EU:C:2019:625, [24]–[29].

[35] *Id.* at [25] and see Directive 2001/29/EC of the European Parliament and of the Council of May 22, 2001, on the Harmonisation of Certain Aspects of Copyright and Related Rights in the Information Society recital 31.

[36] Case C-201/13, 2014 ECLI:C:2014:2132.

concept of EU law," that is, one with a uniform interpretation throughout the Union. The CJEU therefore articulated how parody was to be understood and provided other guidance as to how various rights and interests are to be balanced when the exception is being applied. There can be little question that the binary model is potentially helpful to persons who wish to distribute a parody throughout as much of the EU as possible without seeking a license. Users do not have to concern themselves with the nuance of different national parody defenses. Rather, users only have to worry about the scope of the harmonized parody exception and then whether any given Member State has chosen to implement that exception.

The CJEU is thus promoting true harmonization of the exceptions in some areas. This has advantages for users who are seeking to rely on an exception to make and distribute a derivative work.[37] It also reflects the core institutional function of the CJEU in ensuring the smooth operation of the single market. But it also means that it is going to fall to the CJEU to flesh out much of the detail, since at the moment we do not even know for certain which provisions of the Directive are to be regarded as measures of full harmonisation.[38] As will be seen in the next section, this creates difficult questions for national courts, particularly in cases where referring a question to the CJEU would be inappropriate. Importantly, moreover, Brexit complicates rather than resolves the underlying tension. The authority for the 2014 Regulations still has to be traced back to the Directive and insofar as some of the new provisions (such as the parody exceptions) rest on an erroneous view of the freedom left to member states, UK courts will be confronted with hard choices in how to proceed.

THE CHALLENGE FOR UK COURTS

The previous section set up two reasons why the UK courts cannot be expected to approach interpretation of the exceptions in the same way that we might have wanted them to have done in 1989 or, for that matter, 1912.[39] The first is that the 2014 amendments rest on a forward-leaning interpretation of the scope of executive rulemaking power. The second is that the relationship between national and EU law is still very much in flux and Brexit does not solve the difficult questions that arise as a consequence. To illustrate the significance of these issues, this section is built around two case studies. Specifically, it considers the decisions in *Academy of Songwriters, Composers and Authors Musicians' Union v. Secretary of State for Business, Innovation and Skills*[40] and *Forensic Telecommunications Services Ltd v. Chief Constable of West Yorkshire Police.*[41] In the former case Green J quashed the statutory instrument that sought to bring in a new format-shifting exception. In the latter case Arnold J. indicated that the research exception has to be read narrowly as extending only to "scientific research." At first sight, these cases appear to continue the trend of UK courts reading exceptions narrowly, an approach that contributed to copyright law becoming seriously misshapen over the course of the twentieth century. On closer

[37] This point does not hold for other types of exception, such as those relating to private use. This is a point that has been developed at length elsewhere. See ROBERT BURRELL & ALLISON COLEMAN, COPYRIGHT EXCEPTIONS: THE DIGITAL IMPACT 303–4 (2004).

[38] See Griffiths, supra note 31 and Eleonara Rosati, *Just a Laughing Matter? Why the Decision in Deckmyn Is Broader Than Parody*, 52 Common Market Law Review 511. See also EMILY HUDSON, DRAFTING COPYRIGHT EXCEPTIONS – FROM THE LAW IN BOOKS TO THE LAW IN ACTION 23–24 (2020) (doubting the capacity of the CJEU to develop sufficiently detailed guidance to ensure conformity between Member States).

[39] That is, respectively, when the CDPA 1988 and the Copyright Act 1911 came into force.

[40] [2015] EWHC (Admin) 2041.

[41] [2012] FSR 15.

inspection, however, these cases are not to be readily categorized as demonstrating a continuation of this unwelcome pattern. Rather, the outcomes in these cases can only be understood by reference to the two interpretive issues set out in the preceding section.

(a) *Academy of Songwriters*

The first case worth exploring in detail is *Academy of Songwriters, Composers and Authors Musicians' Union v. Secretary of State for Business, Innovation and Skills*. The background to that case was that the claimants brought a challenge to the defendant's decision to introduce section 28B into the CDPA. This provision contained a so-called "format-shifting" exception. It would have allowed persons who legitimately acquired content, such as an e-book or a digital copy of a film or sound recording, to copy that work for his or her own private use.[42] In introducing this provision the government was relying on Article 5(2)(b) of the Directive. This allows member states to introduce an exception "in respect of reproductions on any medium made by a natural person for private use and for ends that are neither directly nor indirectly commercial." The Directive also generally requires that any such exception should be on the "condition that the rightholders receive fair compensation." It was envisaged that this provision would allow for the continuation of private copying schemes, widespread among EU member states, that allow for such copying in conjunction with a private copying levy on blank media and/or recording equipment. However, the Directive also provides that "[i]n certain situations where the prejudice to the rightholder would be minimal, no obligation for payment may arise."[43] The introduction of a private copying levy has long been a controversial topic in the UK, and the government took the view that it did not want to reopen this issue.[44] Consequently, it did not introduce a levy in conjunction with section 28B, taking the view that its proposed scheme fell within the "minimal prejudice" concession. An important part of the government's case was that owners would seek to "price-in" unremunerated copying by fixing a higher price for the original. As a consequence, a significant part of the case was concerned with whether there was likely to be a market failure that would prevent owners from using this strategy successfully (it being obvious that in a hypothetical perfect market this would be how owners would respond).

In a decision handed down in June 2015, Green J held that the claimant's application for judicial review succeeded. This did not automatically result in the relevant statutory instrument being quashed, and hence section 28B being struck down, since the government could, inter alia, have decided to revisit the levy question.[45] However, in the subsequent hearing on remedies and costs, the government submitted that the regulations should indeed be quashed and Green J made an order to that effect.[46] This was the first time that an exception had been struck down by a UK court and is hardly suggestive of the judiciary developing a more sympathetic attitude toward users. Moreover, the decision seems to speak to an otherworldliness in copyright policymaking. There has been no attempt by the government to introduce a new provision. As a consequence, many acts of private copying continue to be technically

[42] The exception did not, therefore, allow the transfer of the work to a friend or family member.

[43] Recital 35.

[44] In taking this view the government was also influenced by the "Kretschmer report," which identified significant inconsistencies and problems with levy schemes in Europe. Martin Kretschmer, Private Copying and Fair Compensation (2011) *available at* www.gov.uk/government/publications/private-copying-and-fair-compensation.

[45] [2015] EWHC 2041, [21].

[46] British Academy of Songwriters, Composers and Authors Musicians' Union v. Secretary of State for Business, Innovation and Skills [2015] EWHC 2041 (Admin).

illegal in the UK, but users can carry on regardless, safe in the knowledge that there is virtually no prospect of an action being brought against them. It also serves to perpetuate a model that causes so much frustration among copyright reformers with relatively modest agendas. When users who have purchased lawful copies are told that they cannot use make ordinary and fair use of their perfectly lawful digital devices the entire copyright system is brought into disrepute. Take a person who has bought a DVD boxset of *Game of Thrones*. This person may want to watch this series on their iPad while traveling and hence will need to convert the DVDs into a series of digital video files, import these files into iTunes, and then sync their iPad with iTunes. To tell this person they are infringing copyright creates a result that fails to chime with how we naturally interact with digital content. Still worse, it sends a signal to this user that they are no different from the person who decided to download the series unlawfully. That so many owner representatives seem indifferent to the need to avoid the copyright system falling (deeper) into disrepute is surprising; that the judiciary has seemingly furthered this trend is disheartening.

Academy of Songwriters is not, however, to be categorized as readily as the above account suggests. The single most important legal issue in the case was the standard of review to be applied. The government's position was that given the complexity of the socioeconomic issues involved and the broad discretion left to member states by Article 5(2)(b) of the Directive, the court should exhibit a very high degree of deference. Indeed, the government went as far as to suggest that the court was not competent to determine whether the government had acted in error.[47] In contrast, the claimants argued that the court was required to apply a full merits review and decide the issues on a "correct or incorrect" basis, without affording any margin of appreciation to the government.[48] Green J came down much closer to the claimants' position, concluding that the government only had a "modest" discretion over the evaluation of the evidence.[49] Two factors, in particular, motivated this conclusion. The first was that the text of the Directive sets up a right to compensation as a general precondition for the creation of any exception by reference to Article 5(2)(b). For the scheme established by section 28B to be justified it had to fall within a narrow concession, namely, that if owners are likely to suffer *de minimis* harm then no compensation had to be paid.[50] Second, the proprietary nature of the claimants' interests placed the court under a further obligation to review the evidence used to justify the decision carefully.[51] Green J was also at pains to emphasize that the mere fact that the decision turned on the assessment of economic evidence was not a sufficient reason to adopt a different position, stating:

> It is an error to suggest that simply because the subject matter of a decision, or the evidence used to justify it, is "economic" or "technical" that courts should recoil in terror and move gratefully into judicial reticence mode by reference to "margin of appreciation."[52]

47 [2015] EWHC 2041, [127].
48 *Id.*
49 [2015] EWHC 2041, [135].
50 [2015] EWHC 2041, [143].
51 [2015] EWHC 2041, [147] ("... the consequence of the Defendant making an error is to strip proprietors of valuable and important property rights; because it is in the best interests of the economy for rightholders to be properly rewarded and protected since this is integral to the system of rewards for creativity which intellectual property laws respect; because copyright is a right protected under Article 1 of the First Protocol to the ECHR [European Convention on Human Rights] and under the Charter and it is EU policy to ensure observance of that principle.")
52 [2015] EWHC 2041, [144].

In taking this stance he noted that the Supreme Court had warned against judicial timidity in judicial review cases[53] and that decisions that are of enormous significance to individuals and companies can often be characterized as economic or technical.[54]

It is hard to fault the above reasoning. We cannot expect courts to be sanguine about the executive (i) adopting a forward-leaning interpretation of its right to pass secondary legislation (under the European Communities Act); (ii) to introduce a provision that can only be justified within the terms of the underlying directive if it complies with strict criteria (minimal prejudice); (iii) so as to limit the scope of a constitutionally protected set of rights (under both the European Convention on Human Rights (ECHR) and the European Charter). Despite this, Green J sided with the government's interpretation of a number of important issues, including the government's measure of how loss or harm to the claimants was to be calculated.[55] More generally, he did not strike an unsympathetic tone to the defendant's position.[56] Ultimately, however, Green J was faced with the fact that the government had run a consultation process that was seriously flawed. Most strikingly, the government did not address what it took *de minimis* harm to mean; it accepted that the "likelihood of harm" question could only be answered by empirical evidence, but then relied on evidence that did not focus specifically on the *de minimis* question; it purported to rely on other evidence which when read closely just raised further questions or explained why some lines of inquiry had not been pursued; and it seemingly just ignored some evidence.

(b) Forensic Telecommunications

The second case that is worthy of close attention is *Forensic Telecommunications Services Ltd v. Chief Constable of West Yorkshire Police*. The claimant in that case had developed a system for extracting deleted data from mobile phones. This system was primarily intended to be used in connection with the investigation and prosecution of criminal offences. The claimant had developed specialist software for accessing the data quickly and had compiled a list of permanent memory absolute addresses or "PM Abs addresses," in essence, information that identified where in the memory, for any given model of phone, the user-generated data was stored. The claimant had licensed its system to the security services, but not to police forces. A member of the security services was seconded to the defendant's police force during the course of a major antiterrorism operation. This security service officer had a copy of the claimant's system on his laptop. During the course of the investigation the security service officer provided a police officer in the defendant's employ with a partial set of PM Abs addresses derived from the claimant's system, seemingly in light of a conversation where the recipient police officer revealed that he was working on a rival system. These lists were then posted by the recipient on a website that acted as an information exchange for those interested in mobile phone data retrieval and were subsequently incorporated into a rival system.

The claimant brought actions for breach of confidence, infringement of database right, and infringement of copyright. The claimant was successful in its confidence and database right

[53] Citing R (on the application of Rotherham Metropolitan Borough Council and others) v. Secretary of State for Business, Innovation and Skills [2015] UKSC 6, [65]. Although it might be noted that this warning comes immediately before a reiteration by Lord Neuberger that "the rule of law is not served by judges failing to accord appropriate respect to the primary policy-making and decision-making powers of the executive." *Id.*

[54] [2015] EWHC 2041, [144].

[55] Specifically, the court accepted that the government was entitled to adopt a "lost sales" approach to calculating harm, rather than a lost "licensing fee" approach.

[56] *See, in particular,* his strong rejection of the claimants' contention that the Secretary of State had predetermined the outcome of the consultation process. [2015] EWHC 2041, [274]–[281].

claims. However, the claim for infringement of copyright was rejected on the basis that the PM Abs addresses list compiled by the claimant did not constitute an original literary work. Nevertheless, Arnold J. went on to consider the other elements of the copyright claim, including the defendant's argument that posting the PM Abs addresses list fell within fair dealing for the purpose of research. Arnold J. stated that he would have rejected this defense. In reaching this conclusion, he indicated his support for the view (conceded by the defendant) that the research exception in the CDPA 1988 must be narrowly interpreted as limited to "scientific research," this being derived from Article 5(3)(a) of the Directive. He indicated further that the notion of "scientific research" could not be extended to "the forensic purpose of enabling [the defendants] and others to extract data from mobile phones for use in criminal investigations."[57] Two other points are also worthy of attention. First, Arnold J. indicated that he was leaving open the question of whether the scope of the research exception had to be read still more narrowly as being confined not merely to "use for the purposes of scientific research" but rather to "illustration for the purposes of scientific research." Secondly, he indicated that the use was in any event not fair dealing. Insofar as this conclusion rested on the likely commercial harm to the claimant, this element of the decision is relatively uncontroversial.[58] However, Arnold J. also indicated that this conclusion was bolstered by the fact that the PM Abs addresses list was an unpublished work.

Forensic Telecommunications, even more than *Academy of Songwriters*, could readily be characterized as providing another chapter in the long and undistinguished history of the judiciary failing to give adequate weight to user interests in the UK. Here we have a case where the court was under no obligation to address the defendant's argument that its conduct fell within the research and private study exception, but where the court nevertheless went out of its way to signal (i) that the claimant was correct in taking the view that only scientific research was within the exception; (ii) that the notion of "scientific" research was itself to be read narrowly; (iii) the question of whether the exception should be confined still further to cases of "illustration for scientific research" was being left open; (iv) that the test of fairness *as applied to the research and private study* exception should apply more restrictively to unpublished works, a point never properly tested in the UK case law[59]; and (v) that the PM Abs addresses list was properly characterized as an unpublished work, despite it being reproduced in the manuals that the claimant provided to licensees of its system.

On closer inspection, however, *Forensic Telecommunications* is not necessarily quite what it seems. The reason this case has attracted attention is not because of Arnold J's treatment of the exceptions or even because of his conclusion that PM Abs addresses list did not attract copyright protection. Rather, its significance has been thought to lie in the fact that it contains a detailed and thoughtful consideration of how the CDPA 1988 is to be interpreted in light of the Information Society Directive and subsequent guidance from the CJEU. It was decided shortly after the CJEU had begun to signal that it was prepared to step in and push the harmonization of the exceptions beyond the political compromise reflected in the text of the Directive. Arnold J. noted that the CJEU had already begun to lay down general interpretive guidelines: such that

[57] [2011] EWHC 289, [109].

[58] Here it might be noted that the defendant's actions were subsequently blamed in the media for having caused the claimant's collapse. *See, e.g.*, Jim Armitage, *The Scandal of How the Police Ruined a Private Forensics Firm That Helped Catch the Failed London Bombers of* 2005, THE INDEPENDENT (Sept. 29, 2017), www.independent.co.uk/news/business/analysis-and-features/police-forensics-scandal-terrorism-bombing-west-yorkshire-phone-fts-a7973286.html.

[59] The point being that for research and private study there will be many cases where the only person who will see the copy made is the student or researcher (as, for example, with many types of archival research). In these cases, the work will very often be unpublished and it is arguable that a presumption against being allowed to copy unpublished works is unnecessary and inappropriate.

exceptions must be interpreted strictly[60] whilst enabling the effectiveness of the exception to be established[61]; that authors were entitled to "legal certainty" as regards their rights[62]; and that courts were to have direct regard to Article 5(5) of the Directive, which sets out a variant of the three-step test.[63]

In light of this guidance, Arnold J. anticipated the CJEU's direction of travel. In insisting that the research exception must be limited to "scientific research," Arnold J. was doing no more than moving the UK closer to the binary model considered in the previous section, under which member states either have or do not have a *harmonized* exception. In leaving open the question of whether the exception had to be further restricted to "illustration for the purposes of scientific research" Arnold J. was not signaling that he was uncertain as a normative matter as to whether this interpretation would be desirable. He was not signaling that he would need the benefit of submissions from counsel before reaching a position on which interpretation would be best. Rather, he was merely leaving open the question of whether the ambiguously worded Article 5(3)(a) of the Directive should be read disjunctively as allowing (i) illustration for teaching and (ii) scientific research; or conjunctively as allowing "illustration for (i) teaching and (ii) scientific research." On the binary model such a question could only be satisfactorily answered by the CJEU and Arnold J. was unquestionably right to leave it open.

Other elements of the judgment are to be explained as Arnold J. doing his best to anticipate how the CJEU might be likely to approach certain matters. The litigation was of relatively low value and it would have been difficult to have concluded (and neither side suggested) that a refence to the CJEU was appropriate. Most obviously, Arnold J. would have been aware that the CJEU would have had little reason to interpret "scientific research" in such a way as to catch the defendant's use. This is because the defendant's conduct fell much more comfortably within the optional exception set out in Article 5(3)(e) of the Directive, which, inter alia, allows for "use for the purposes of public security." Arnold J. thus had to confront a problem with the way in which the UK has implemented the Directive, a problem that has not been entirely eliminated by the recent reforms.[64] If the government had transposed the entire list of exceptions from the Directive into national law the defendant in *Forensic Telecommunications* would have had an excellent chance of being able to establish that its use fell within a protected purpose. The question would then have switched to whether the taking had gone beyond what was permissible, with this question presumably to be determined under a binary model by reference to the three-step test in Article 5(5).[65]

Arnold J. was therefore occupied by the difficult question of how to reconcile national law with the Information Society Directive, and not by a belief in the primacy of owners' rights. In this respect it is notable that he appeared frustrated by the fact "that counsel for the Defendants did not advance any defense to FTS's claims arising out of WYP's status as a public authority or law enforcement agency."[66] Arnold J. presumably had in mind the fact that he had not been

60 Case C-5/08 Infopaq International A/S v Danske Dagblades Forening 2009 E.C.R. I-06569.

61 Joined Cases C-403/08 & C-429/08 Football Association Premier League Ltd v QC Leisure 2011 ECR I-09083.

62 *Id.*

63 *Id.*

64 I.e. because even after the 2014 reforms we do not see all of the exceptions permitted under the Directive being transposed into national law.

65 It might, however, be noted that it is far from certain that the CJEU would treat Art 5(3)(a) Directive as measure of full harmonisation. The language of this provision is perhaps apt allow it to be classified in this way, but it would be hard to argue that the smooth functioning of the single market demands a high level of harmonisation of teaching and research exceptions.

66 [2011] EWHC 289, [142].

given the opportunity to consider whether, despite appearances to the contrary, Article 5(3)(e) of the Directive should be deemed to have been transposed into national law, most obviously by reference to section 171(3) CDPA 1988, which preserves a common law public interest defense, with the scope of this defense then being reinterpreted to make it compliant with the Directive.

CONCLUSION

Drafting choices are unquestionably important when contemplating reform of the exceptions, but there is now a general recognition that getting the language of the legislation right is only part of the battle. One of the reasons why the standards and rules literature provides such a useful lens through which to explore how exceptions should be crafted is that this literature reminds us that the character of a legal norm can change over time.[67] Standards can ossify, most commonly as they become an umbrella for a finite set of judge-made rules. Conversely, rules can be interpreted flexibly and so become more like standards. This helps suggest that fair use is not necessarily a panacea for copyright's ailments and nor is it the only option that might produce meaningful reform.

If I have become more supportive of the introduction of fair use over time, particularly in Australia, it is because fair use has taken on such a totemic status in debates about reform that its introduction could only be taken by the judiciary as a signal that they should adopt a different position. In other words, fair use would hopefully produce the critical change in judicial attitudes as well as more textual flexibility. At the same time, however, I have never been of the view that fair use is the only model for reform. Two other models also demand attention. The first involves sticking closer to the fair dealing approach, with protection for users being built around a series of generously interpreted and broadly worded (but not entirely open-ended) provisions. Rather than having a single meta-standard one would instead have a series of standard-like provisions that, taken together, would provide users with an appropriate degree of protection. That such a model might be made to work appears to be borne out by the transformation of fair dealing in Canada in the post-*CCH* period.[68] It also remains the most promising model for change in the EU,[69] and writing in this volume Michael Handler and Emily Hudson argue that if the political obstacles to fair use prove insurmountable in Australia then this model demands reconsideration.[70]

The second model that deserves consideration when thinking about options for reform is to stick much closer to a rules-based model of exceptions, that is, to persevere with a long list of provisions, all of which are relatively narrow in scope. One objection to this approach is that legislative processes tend to be slow and cumbersome. The other is that the principal advantage of this model, namely that it offers users certainty, is often illusory in that the application of even narrow exceptions will often turn on criteria that can only be determined *ex post*: was the taking "fair," was the inclusion really "incidental,"[71] etc. These objections might, however, be overcome through the establishment of a rulemaking process: an executive agency might be able to

67 *See* Hudson, *supra* note 2, and the sources cited therein.

68 That is, in the period since the Supreme Court of Canada handed down its decision in *CCH Canadian v. Law Society of Upper Canada* [2004] SCC 13.

69 The argument being that the Information Society Directive contains a sufficiently long list of broadly worded provisions that they would be capable of forming a satisfactory set of users' rights. *See* Burrell & Coleman, *supra* note 35, ch. 10.

70 Michael Handler & Emily Hudson, *supra* Chapter 8 in this volume.

71 Cf. CDPA 1988, § 31; Information Society Directive, Art 5(3)(i).

respond relatively quickly as problems present themselves and rulemaking might extend to deeming certain uses to be "fair" or "incidental." Such a scheme is not without precedent. As was noted earlier in this chapter, in the UK the bill that became the *Enterprise and Regulatory Reform Act 2013* originally contained a provision that would have given the secretary of state the power to repeal or introduce new exceptions, albeit that this would only have been possible within the boundaries established by European law. The South African Copyright Act 1978 contains a provision that allows for the creation of new exceptions by regulation,[72] and in a similar vein the Israeli Copyright Act 2007 provides that "the Minister may make regulations prescribing conditions under which a use shall be deemed a fair use."[73] Most recently, writing in the context of Australian law, David Brennan has argued that the Copyright Tribunal of Australia should be given delegated legislative power to allow it to "periodically determine new public interest exceptions."[74] Any suggestion that might break the current impasse in copyright reform in Australia deserves a serious hearing. Moreover, Brennan's preferred scheme has a number of interesting features and has much to recommend it over a delegation of power to a government minister.

The argument presented here should, however, remind us that this sort of delegation of legislative power comes at a cost. Courts are obliged to scrutinize delegated legislation carefully. If such legislation introduces limitations on property rights, courts are, in essence, required to adopt a pro-owner position. Copyright is not of such central importance to the legal system or to society that we should want or expect courts to jettison this position. None of this is to conclude that the rules-based model of exceptions reform is necessarily to be rejected, but it does mean that when thinking about the constitutional implications of this model we need to do more than merely satisfy ourselves that there is no constitutional impediment to such a model being established.

More generally, the analysis presented here is intended to remind us that the comprehensive changes that have taken place in the copyright landscape over the past fifteen to twenty years may require us to think in somewhat different ways about the obligations that fall on the judiciary. Judges in copyright cases may not be merely weighing the interests of copyright owners and users. They may also be involved in the ultimately more important tasks of holding the executive to account, setting the limits of executive rulemaking and establishing the relationship between national law and supranational legal obligations.

72 South African Copyright Act 98 of 1978, § 13.

73 Copyright Act, 2007, § 19(c) (Isr.).

74 David Brennan, *The Copyright Tribunal As Exception-Maker: Are Both Flexibility and Certainty Achievable?*, 28(3) AUSTRALIAN INTELLECTUAL PROPERTY JOURNAL 83–96 (2018).

10

"Fair Use" through Fundamental Rights in Europe: When Freedom of Artistic Expression Allows Creative Appropriations and Opens Up Statutory Copyright Limitations

Christophe Geiger

1 INTRODUCTION

It is often assumed that an open-ended limitation to copyright, such as the fair use defense, is alien to the civil law tradition as it gives too much power to judges to design the contours of copyright law on a case-by-case basis.[1] However, the increasing use of fundamental rights in copyright disputes in many civil law countries is challenging that assumption, raising the question of whether a sort of "fair use" limitation is not already being wielded through the weighing of interests and use of the proportionality test, both of which are required when the judiciary is applying fundamental rights.[2] It will be shown in this chapter that even in France, traditionally considered an exemplar of civil law reasoning in copyright matters, a recent and highly commented-upon decision of the French Supreme Court concerning the balancing of freedom of artistic expression with copyright has paved the way for a judicial *in concreto* assessment of copyright limitations.[3] This change in approach by the courts can be witnessed not only in France but also in many other civil law jurisdictions across Europe,[4] and even by the

The author is very grateful to Luisa Pieroni, legal intern at the the Centre for International Intellectual Property Studies (CEIPI), University of Strasbourg (France),for her great editorial support and her research assistance while elaborating this chapter.

[1] P. Bernt Hugenholtz & Martin R. F. Senftleben, *Fair Use in Europe: In Search of Flexibilities* 4 (Amsterdam Law Sch. Research Paper No. 2012-39; Inst. for Info. Law Research Paper No. 2012-33, 2012) ("[F]air use in Europe is often regarded as an oxymoron or even a taboo in classic author's rights doctrine.").

[2] Already advocating that the use of fundamental rights opens up the closed list of statutory limitations through the use of the proportionality requirement, creating an open-ended limitation to copyright law, *see* Christophe Geiger, Droit d'auteur et droit du public à l'information: Approche de droit comparé 391 (2004). For further discussion about the principle of proportionality and its consequences, *see* Jonas Christoffersen, *Human Rights and Balancing: The Principle of Proportionality, in* Research Handbook on Human Rights and Intellectual Property 19, 19–39 (Christophe Geiger ed., 2015); Orit Fischman Afori, *Proportionality – A New Mega Standard in European Copyright Law*, 45 Int'l Rev. Intell. Prop. & Competition L. 889 (2014); Christophe Geiger & Elena Izyumenko, *Intellectual Property before the European Court of Human Rights, in* Intellectual Property and the Judiciary 9 (Christophe Geiger et al. eds., 2018); Christophe Geiger & Elena Izyumenko, *Shaping Intellectual Property Rights through Human Rights Adjudication: The Example of the European Court of Human Rights*, 46 Mitchell Hamline L. Rev. 527 (2020).

[3] Cour de Cassation [Cass.] [supreme court for judicial matters] 1e civ., May 15, 2015, Bull. Civ. 1, No. 13/27391 (Fr.). Discussing this case and the recent case law in France with regard to creative appropriations, *see also* Christophe Geiger, *Appropriation créative et droit d'auteur: Réflexions sur les évolutions récentes de la jurisprudence française à la lumière du droit de l'Union et du droit comparé, in* Mélanges en l'honneur du Professeur Claude Witz 327–47 (2018).

[4] *See generally* Christophe Geiger & Elena Izyumenko, *Copyright on the Human Rights Trial: Redefining the Boundaries of Exclusivity through Freedom of Expression*, 45 Int'l Rev. Intell. Prop. & Competition L. 316 (2014). *See also infra* Sections 2 and 3.

Court of Justice of the European Union (CJEU),[5] thus strengthening the argument for the introduction of an open clause for limitations in EU copyright law.[6]

In fact, important rulings often result from concrete and simple situations to which judges are required to respond as appropriately and fairly as possible. In this context, the judiciary is increasingly playing a crucial role in the intellectual property arena, allowing the legislative framework to adapt to both technological developments and new social and economic practices.[7] At a time when legislative solutions are very slow to emerge, and often manifest difficult compromises, the courts can allow a legal field to develop by proposing innovative solutions that amount to a break with established practices. This was certainly the case with the groundbreaking ruling rendered by the French Supreme Court on May 15, 2015, in *Klasen v. Malka* addressing the relationship between copyright and freedom of artistic expression. That decision constitutes the point of departure for this chapter, as it is symptomatic of a larger trend in civil law countries to legitimize creative uses based on fundamental rights beyond those allowed by statutory limitations to copyright law.[8]

[5] The cases are too numerous to be cited here. For further references, *see* Christophe Geiger, *The Role of the Court of Justice of the European Union: Harmonizing, Creating and Sometimes Disrupting Copyright Law in the European Union, in* New Developments in EU and International Copyright Law 435 (Irini Stamatoudi ed., 2016); Jonathan Griffiths, *Taking Power Tools to the Acquis: The Court of Justice, The Charter of Fundamental Rights and European Union Copyright Law, in* Intellectual Property and the Judiciary, *supra* note 2, at 144; Stijn van Deursen and Thom Snijders, *The Court of Justice at the Crossroads: Clarifying the Role for Fundamental Rights in the EU Copyright Framework*, 49 Int'l Rev. Intell. Prop. & Competition L. 1080 (2018). The importance of fundamental rights when interpreting EU copyright law has been reiterated by the CJEU in a trilogy of decisions rendered on 29 July 2019, *Funke Medien NRW GmbH v. Bundesrepublik Deutschland*, C-469/17; *Pelham GmbH and Others v. Ralf Hütter and Florian Schneider-Esleben*, C-476/17; and CJEU, *Spiegel Online GmbH v. Volker Beck*, C-516/17, excluding however that fundamental rights can serve as external limitations when none of the existing exceptions is applicable (see *infra* on this issue note 8).

[6] Calling for the introducing of an open-ended limitation in EU copyright law, *see, e.g.*, Martin Senftleben, *The Perfect Match: Civil Law Judges and Open-Ended Fair Use Provisions*, 33 Am. U. Int'l L. Rev. 231 (2017); P. Bernt Hugenholtz, *Flexible Copyright: Can EU Author's Rights Accommodate Fair Use?, in* New Developments in EU and International Copyright Law, *supra* note 5, at 417; Christophe Geiger, *Flexibilising Copyright – Remedies to the Privatisation of Information by Copyright Law*, 39 Int'l Rev. Intell. Prop. & Competition L. 178 (2008); Christophe Geiger, *Copyright as an Access Right, Securing Cultural Participation through the Protection of Creators' Interests*, in What if We Could Reimagine Copyright? 102 sq. (Rebecca Giblin & Kimberlee Weatherall eds., 2016); Christophe Geiger & Elena Izyumenko, *Towards a European "Fair Use" Grounded in Freedom of Expression*, 35 Am. U. Int'l L. Rev 1–74 (2019); Martin Senftleben, *Comparative Approaches to Fair Use: An Important Impulse for Reforms in EU Copyright Law, in* Methods and Perspectives in Intellectual Property 30 (Graeme Dinwoodie ed., 2014); Hugenholtz & Senftleben, *supra* note 1; Christophe Geiger et al., *The EU Commission's Proposal to Reform Copyright Limitations: A Good but Far Too Timid Step in the Right Direction*, 40 Eur. Intell. Prop. Rev. 4 (2018). Detailed on this issue, see T. Rendas, *Exceptions in EU Copyright Law, In search of A balance between flexibility and Legal Certainty*, PhD thesis defended at the Universidade Catolica Portuguesa, Lisbon, Sept. 2020.

[7] On the role of the judiciary in IP law, *see* the various chapters in C. Geiger, C. A. Nard and X. Seuba (eds.), Intellectual Property and the Judiciary, *supra* note 2, in particular the introduction to the volume p. 1 *sq.*

[8] This approach has recently been explicitly endorsed by the advocate general (AG) of the Court of Justice of the European Union. In his opinion in Case C-469/17, *Funke Medien NRW GmbH v. Federal Republic of Germany*, delivered on October 25, 2018 (EU:C:2018:870), AG Szpunar considered that there are circumstances when the exclusive rights "*must yield to an overriding interest relating to the implementation of a fundamental right or freedom*" – an explicit admittance (for the first time at EU level) of the admissibility of an external limitation to copyright by freedom of expression [at 40]. In his two subsequent Opinions in the "Pelham" and "Spiegel Online" cases, dealing with the question of the admissibility of an external freedom-of-expression limitation beyond the list of codified exceptions in EU copyright law, the AG specified that there is such an "exceptional circumstance" when the "essence of a fundamental rights" is at stake. *See* Opinion of Advocate General Szpunar in Case C-476/17, *Pelham and Others*, delivered on December 12, 2018, EU:C:2018:1002, [94]; and Opinion of Advocate General Szpunar in Case C-516/17, *Spiegel Online*, delivered on January 10, 2019, EU:C:2019:16, [62]. On these opinions, *see* Christophe Geiger & Elena Izyumenko, *Freedom of Expression As an External Limitation to Copyright Law in the EU: The Advocate General of the CJEU Shows the Way*, 41 Eur. Intell. Prop. Rev. 131 (2019). Unfortunately, however, the CJEU in these cases

The facts of the case are as follows. The painter Peter Klasen incorporated into his paintings three photographs from an Italian fashion journal showing the face of a young model after coloring them blue. Klasen's process is relatively banal for anyone familiar with the artistic movements of the past forty or fifty years, in which collages incorporating a range of uses and reworkings of famous trademarks, consumer objects, advertising, fictional characters, and popular works are legion.[9] In fact, many artists make frequent use of such a process, primarily by reworking elements protected by intellectual property rights (copyright, trademark, or designs rights) for the purpose of criticism or homage, their aim being to trigger artistic reflection on society and its current icons.[10] Appropriation plays a central role in the modern and contemporary art movements, even if original works are sometimes modified or transformed. Fortunately, most creative appropriations are not subject to copyright infringement litigation[11] because, given their frequency, such litigation would likely lead to seizure of the contemporary art collections of many of the world's major museums.[12]

However, such cases occasionally end up before the courts, usually when two factors are present, sometimes in combination. The first is extrinsically linked to the success of the derivative work in question. If it is successful, the author of the appropriated work is likely to consider him or herself legitimately entitled to a share of the fruits of that success. The second is

decided not to follow the AG on this point. Despite showing a favorable position to the possibility of interpreting EU copyright in the light of fundamental rights norms, the Luxembourg court considered in fact that is not possible to go beyond the exhaustive list of limitations by using an external freedom of expression-exception (CJEU, *Funke Medien NRW GmbH v. Bundesrepublik Deutschland*, C-469/17, 29 July 2019, EU:C:2019:623 (*"Funke Medien"*, at para. 64); CJEU, *Pelham GmbH and Others v. Ralf Hütter and Florian Schneider-Esleben*, C-476/17, 29 July 2019, EU: C:2019:624 (*"Pelham"*, at para. 65); and CJEU, *Spiegel Online GmbH v. Volker Beck*, C-516/17, 29 July 2019, EU: C:2019:625 (*"Spiegel Online"*, at para. 49). On these very important decisions see Christophe Geiger & Elena Izyumenko, *The Constitutionalization of Intellectual Property Law in the E.U. and the* Funke Medien, Pelham *and* Spiegel Online *Decisions of the CJEU: Progress, But Still Some Way to Go!*, 51 Int'l Rev. Intell. Prop. & Competition L. 282 (2020).

9 On these artistic movements, *see, e.g.*, Irving Sandler, Art of the Postmodern Era: From the Late 1960s to the Early 1990s (1996). The movement that made use of this approach the most was beyond doubt the one known as "Appropriation Art." *See* Appropriation (David Evans ed., 2009); Emprunts et citations dans le champ artistique (Pierre Beylot ed., 2005).

10 Several scholars have analyzed the intellectual property problems posed by appropriation art, in particular in the context of US copyright law, as in the US a certain number of copyright cases dealt with the delicate issue of what can be appropriated or not in the copyright context. *See, e.g.*, Lynne A. Greenberg, *The Art of Appropriation: Puppies, Piracy and Post-Modernism*, 11 Cardozo Arts & Ent. L.J. 1, 23–33 (1992); Peter Jaszi, *Is There Such a Thing As Postmodern Copyright?*, 12 Tul. J. Tech. & Intell. Prop. 105 (2009); Judith Bresler, *Begged, Borrowed or Stolen: Whose Art Is It Anyway? An Alternative Solution of Fine Art Licensing*, 50 J. Copyright Soc'y USA 15 (2003); William M. Landes, *Copyright, Borrowed Images, and Appropriation Art: An Economic Approach*, 9 Geo. Mason L. Rev. 1 (2000); Darren Hudson Hick, *Appropriation and Transformation*, 23 Fordham Int. Prop. Media & Ent. L.J. 1155 (2013); Jacqueline Morley, *The Unfettered Expansion of Appropriation Art Protection by the Fair Use Doctrine: Searching for Transformativeness in* Cariou v. Prince *and Beyond*, 55 IDEA 385 (2015); Amy Adler, *Fair Use and the Future of Art*, 91 NYU L. Rev. 559 (2016). For a comparative approach, *see* Christophe Geiger, *Freedom of Artistic Creativity and Copyright Law: A Compatible Combination?*, 8 U.C. Irvine L. Rev. 101 (2018); André Lucas & Jane Ginsburg, *Copyright, Freedom of Expression and Free Access to Information (Comparative Study of American and European Law)*, 249 RIDA 5 (2016); Paula Westenberger, Cultural Palimpsests: Artistic Reuses in Brazil in the Context of Copyright and Human Rights (2018) (unpublished Ph.D. dissertation, Queen Mary University of London).

11 According to one scholar, this could also be the result of the uncertain legal situation with regard to appropriation art, inducing self-censorship in the art world, *see* Adler, *supra* note 10, at 566 (underlining that "the disparate results in these cases, not to mention the high costs of litigating against a backdrop of uncertainty, help explain why a climate of 'self-censorship' has taken hold in the art world"). *See also* Patricia Aufderheide et al., *Copyright, Permissions, and Fair Use in the Visual Arts Communities: An Issues Report* 5 (Feb. 2015), http://cmsimpact.org/wp-content/uploads/2016/01/fair_use_for_visual_arts_communities.pdf (stating that artists "pay a high price for copyright confusion and misunderstanding. Their work is constrained and censored, most powerfully by themselves, because of that confusion and the resulting fear and anxiety.").

12 Museums can in addition to the artists also be liable for copyright infringement, as an exhibition can be considered as an act of communication to the public.

when the appropriation harms the reputation of, or is contrary to the idea behind, the original work or is simply objected to by the original author. The latter occurs primarily in cases in which the derivative work contains a criticism of the primary work. Both factors were present in *Klasen v. Malka*, in which a fashion photographer brought an action against the painter for infringement of his copyright on the photographs in question. In justifying the appropriation, Klasen, a member of the artistic movement known as Narrative Figuration,[13] explained that the objective of his artistic approach was to use advertising images in his paintings to provoke reflection by the spectator, thereby putting the initial work in a new context and expressing something entirely new and unexpected. He emphasized that the photographs had been integrated into his work as symbols of excessive consumption.

On the legal side, the painter raised in his defense a series of arguments ranging from the photographs' lack of originality, the quotation, parody, and incidental use exceptions, and, finally, the freedom of artistic expression laid down in Article 10 of the European Convention on Human Rights (ECHR). Although in the first instance the Paris District Court held in effect that the photographs lacked originality,[14] the Paris Court of Appeal overruled that decision, finding that the choices made by the photographer reflected genuine aesthetic decisions that were an imprint of his personality as author and, consequently, that the photographs at issue were deserving copyright protection.[15] The parody, quotation, and incidental/accessory use exception defenses[16] were all rejected, which is unsurprising given the excessively restrictive interpretation of limitations that has traditionally prevailed in the French copyright system.[17] The sole defense the painter had left was to claim that the use was legitimated by his right to freedom of artistic expression. However, the Court of Appeal dismissed that argument, holding that there was no higher public interest that would justify the rights of a derivative artist prevailing over those of an original work's author. The court held that freedom of expression can be limited to protect other individual rights and that the reworking of visual material in Klasen's work could not reasonably permit him to ignore the rights of the original photographer. In other words, the Court of Appeal considered the photographer's copyright to limit the painter's freedom of artistic expression.

Klasen appealed the decision, arguing that the limitation on his exercise of artistic expression was disproportionate in comparison with legislators' objective and that the court ought to have assessed the proportionality of the infringement in light of the factual circumstances of the case rather than in an abstract manner.[18] The French Supreme Court supported his argument, and

[13] This movement often intends to give art a political dimension. On this art movement, *see* JEAN-LOUIS PRADEL, LA FIGURATION NARRATIVE (2008); SARAH WILSON, THE VISUAL WORLD OF FRENCH THEORY: FIGURATIONS (2010).

[14] Tribunal de Grande Instance [TGI] [ordinary court of original jurisdiction] Paris, Jan. 31, 2012, No. 10/02898 (Fr.).

[15] Cour d'appel [CA] [regional court of appeal] Paris, Pole 5, 1st Chamber, Sept. 18, 2013, No. 12-02480 (Fr.).

[16] On this limitation for "accessory" use created in France by the judiciary without legal basis and allowing the reproduction or representation of a work when it is not the main subject and it is included in the "scenery" of a picture, *see* Christophe Geiger, *Creating Copyright Limitations without Legal Basis: The "Buren" Decision, a Liberation?*, 36 INT'L REV. INTELL. PROP. & COMPETITION L. 842 (2005). The limitation for incidental use is also foreseen in Art. 5(3)(i) of the InfoSoc Directive of 2001.

[17] For a criticism of this restrictive interpretation of limitations and exceptions often used by national courts or the CJEU, but which is not mandated by the copyright legal framework nor the rationale of copyright law, *see* Christophe Geiger & Franciska Schönherr, *Limitations to Copyright in the Digital Age*, *in* RESEARCH HANDBOOK ON EU INTERNET LAW 110 (Andrej Savin and Jan Trzaskowski eds., 2014); Christophe Geiger, *Promoting Creativity through Copyright Limitations: Reflections on the Concept of Exclusivity in Copyright Law*, 12 VAND. J. ENT. & TECH. L. 515 (2010).

[18] *See* also in this sense the advocate general of the CJEU in his Opinion in *Funke Medien NRW*, *supra* note 8, [at 31]), stating that "any balancing of copyright against fundamental rights which goes beyond merely interpreting the provisions of copyright law, an exercise on the borderline between the interpretation and application of the law, must ... be carried out having regard to the circumstances of each individual case," that is to say, on a case-by-case basis which is a standard approach of the human rights courts and ECtHR in particular. According to the advocate

consequently reversed the Court of Appeal ruling based on Article 10 of the ECHR. The Supreme Court criticized the appellate judges for not having explained "*in the specific case* the manner in which the search for a fair balance between the rights at issue required the decision as pronounced" (emphasis added). With this simple sentence, the French Supreme Court finally put an end to a debate that had been raging for over fifteen years on the application of fundamental rights in the intellectual property arena and, more precisely, on the manner in which a fair balance is to be struck between copyright and freedom of expression.[19]

The aims of this chapter are to discuss the evolution in jurisprudential understanding in the EU, and more specifically in France, of the relationship between copyright and freedom of artistic expression and to analyze the courts' apparent acceptance of a sort of "fair use" approach through the application of fundamental rights as external limitations to copyright law. The chapter is divided into three sections following this introduction. The first discusses the application of freedom of artistic expression to copyright law on a case-by-case basis, showing that, although long contested, such an approach is now mandated by the courts, thus significantly "flexibilizing" the legal framework in this area; the second is dedicated to finding a balance between fundamental rights and copyright, with particular attention paid to the weight the judiciary should afford freedom of artistic expression versus copyright in cases of creative appropriation; and the final section discusses and evaluates the growing need for legislative reform to render freedom of artistic expression fully compatible with copyright law in cases of creative reuse.

2 FAIR USE THROUGH THE APPLICATION OF FREEDOM OF ARTISTIC EXPRESSION TO COPYRIGHT ON A CASE-BY-CASE BASIS: A QUESTION (FINALLY) RESOLVED

France was, surprisingly, one of the first countries in which first instance judges accepted an argument based on freedom of expression to limit copyright law beyond statutory limitations. In a highly debated decision rendered at the end of the 1990s by the Paris District Court[20] in the *Utrillo* case, the judges decided, based on Article 10 of the ECHR, that it was permissible for a television channel to film a number of paintings by Maurice Utrillo when reporting on the opening of an art exhibition dedicated to the artist's work, even if the use exceeded the scope of available exceptions to copyright in that case.[21] The court considered that showing some of the

general, "[t]hat case-by-case approach enables the principle of proportionality to be applied as accurately as possible, thereby avoiding unjustified interferences with both copyright and fundamental rights." (*Id.*)

[19] *See generally* P. Bernt Hugenholtz, *Copyright and Freedom of Expression in Europe*, *in* EXPANDING THE BOUNDARIES OF INTELLECTUAL PROPERTY: INNOVATION POLICY FOR THE KNOWLEDGE SOCIETY 343 (Rochelle Dreyfuss et al. eds., 2001); DROIT D'AUTEUR ET LIBERTÉ D'EXPRESSION: REGARDS FRANCOPHONES, D'EUROPE ET D'AILLEURS (Alain Strowel & François Tulkens eds., 2006); Christophe Geiger, *'Constitutionalizing' Intellectual Property Law? The Influence of Fundamental Rights on Intellectual Property in Europe*, 37 INT'L REV. INTELL. PROP. & COMPETITION L. 371 (2006); GEIGER, *supra* note 2. For an overview, drawing on the case law of the ECtHR and the CJEU, of the influence of the right to freedom of expression and information on European copyright law in the digital context, *see* Elena Izyumenko, *The Freedom of Expression Contours of Copyright in the Digital Era: A European Perspective*, 19 J. WORLD INTELL. PROP. 115 (2016). The debate about the admissibility of a case-by-case approach when evaluating the impact of a copyright restriction on freedom of expression has however been since revitalized by the CJEU in its 3 seminal decisions of July 29, 2019 (*supra* note 8), declaring inacceptable an external freedom of expression-assessment beyond the codified limitations in EU copyright law, in contradiction with the case-law of the European Court on Human Rights on this matter.

[20] Tribunal de Grande Instance (TGI).

[21] Tribunal de Grande Instance [TGI] [ordinary court of original jurisdiction] Paris, 3d Chamber, Feb. 23, 1999, No. 98-7053 (Fr.). For a comment, *see* Pascal Kamina, *Le droit du public à l'information peut-il justifier une exception au droit d'auteur?*, RECUEIL DALLOZ 580 (1999). This was the case because of the excessively narrow interpretation of the quotation exception under the French law. More generally on this question *see* Christophe Geiger, *Author's Right,*

paintings was inevitable in communicating information about the art exhibition and that it would have been impossible for the channel not to use copyright-protected images when informing the public of the artist's work.[22] Interestingly, a specific limitation allowing this type of use for information purposes was later introduced, in 2006, in the French Intellectual Property Code[23] during the implementation process of the Directive on the Harmonisation of Copyright in the Information Society of 2001 (the so-called InfoSoc Directive),[24] but it was not available at the time of the *Utrillo* judgment.

The case went up to the French Supreme Court, which disagreed with externally limiting copyright law through the application of ECHR Article 10, and held that because the legislature had already taken the balancing of fundamental rights into consideration when drafting the copyright law, going beyond that legislative equilibrium was not permissible.[25] In other words, in the Supreme Court's view, it is impossible to refer to freedom of expression as an external limitation to copyright because that fundamental right had already been internally acknowledged by legislators in drafting the list of exceptions laid down in the French Intellectual Property Code. The same approach was also followed by the Belgian Supreme Court in a judgment on September 25, 2003, in which it held in an abstract manner that "the freedom of expression guaranteed by Article 10 of the European Convention on Human Rights and by Article 19 of the International Treaty concerning Civil and Political Rights does not prevent the protection of a literary or artistic work by copyright."[26]

A number of scholars have rightly pointed out that this approach is not compatible with the European legal system and that a fair and proportionate application of fundamental rights requires an appreciation on a case-by-case basis, striking a balance between the specific rights at issue by means of a proportionality test.[27] In parallel, a number of national judges in several EU countries have indeed embraced the possibility of restricting copyright beyond its internal limits, whether by relying directly on freedom of expression or by combining it with an existing copyright exception, thereby permitting a reevaluation of the limits of copyright protection in light of fundamental

Copyright and the Public's Right to Information, *in* New Directions in Copyright Law 24 (Fiona Macmillan ed., 2007) (problematizing the relationship between the author and the recipient of information as it is enshrined in the freedom of expression and the right to information).

[22] Michel Vivant & Jean-Michel Bruguière, Droit d'auteur et droits voisins 586 n.1 (3d ed. 2015).

[23] Code de la Propriété Intellectuelle [C. Propr. Intell.] art. L. 122-5 (Fr.), *translation available at* http://www.wipo.int/edocs/lexdocs/laws/en/fr/fr467en.pdf [https://perma.cc/HD7H-G9BP], introduced by law No. 2006-961 of August 1, 2006, concerning copyright and neighboring rights in the information society. On the scope of this new exception *see* Christophe Geiger, *The New French Law on Copyright and Neighbouring Rights of 1 August 2006: An Adaptation to the Needs of the Information Society?*, 38 Int'l Rev. Intell. Prop. & Competition L. 401 (2007).

[24] Directive 2001/29/EC of the European Parliament and of the Council of 22 May 2001 on the Harmonisation of Certain Aspects of Copyright and Related Rights in the Information Society, 2001 O.J. (L 167) 10 [hereinafter InfoSoc Directive].

[25] Cass. 1e civ., Nov. 13, 2003, Bull. Civ. I, No. 01-14385 (Fr.). For a comment, *see* Christophe Geiger, *France: Intellectual Property Code, Art.L.122-5-3; European Convention on Human Rights, Art.10 – "Utrillo"*, 35 Int'l Rev. Intell. Prop. & Competition L. 716 (2004).

[26] Cass., 25 Sept. 2003, Auteurs et médias 2004, p. 29. For a combined comment on the two rulings, *see* André Lucas, *Droit d'auteur, liberté d'expression et "droit du public à l'information"*, 2005 Auteurs & Média 13 (2005).

[27] Pascal Kamina, *Droit d'auteur et Article 10 de la Convention européenne des droits de l'Homme*, 25 Légicom 15 (2001); Christophe Geiger, Droit d'auteur et droit du public à l'information, Approche de droit comparé 391–408 (2004). More generally on the use of the proportionality test in copyright disputes, *see* Geiger & Izyumenko, *supra* note 4. However, some scholars are very critical of the introduction of the proportionality requirement within copyright law, *see, e.g.*, Lucas & Ginsburg, *supra* note 10, at 78 (stressing with further references the "dangers of the proportionality test . . .; they are particularly formidable in the field of copyright because the diversity of interest that the courts have to weight increases the need for subjective assessments, a situation which, in the European context, creates legal uncertainty that is harmful both for rightholders and users of works.").

rights.[28] In some instances, even when the assessment of specific facts did not justify the legitimization of the use at issue, judges have still insisted on imperatively taking the facts of the case into account, stressing that an external conflict between freedom of expression and copyright can arise in certain circumstances. In *Ashdown v. Telegraph Group*, for example, the London Court of Appeal considered it "necessary for the court to look closely at the facts of individual cases" to accommodate fundamental rights because, under rare circumstances, the right of freedom of expression can "come into conflict with the protection afforded by the Copyright Act."[29] In the United States, where the fair use exception allows considerably more flexibility than in the majority of European countries,[30] the Supreme Court has held that there are circumstances in which a defense based on the First Amendment to the US Constitution, which protects freedom of speech, may be justified. In this respect, even though copyright is traditionally considered "categorically immune" to free speech,[31] the US Supreme Court softened its position in *Eldred v. Ashcroft*,[32] holding that copyright is only "generally immune to free speech," thereby expanding the possibility of using freedom of expression as a limitation in exceptional circumstances.

In Europe, in contrast, the Treaty of Lisbon, which entered into force in 2009, has influenced the use of fundamental rights in the intellectual property area to a considerable extent,[33] leading to an adjustment to judicial practice in multiple national jurisdictions. In effect, along with the Lisbon Treaty, the Charter of the Fundamental Rights of the European Union and all of its rights, freedoms, and principles have acquired the same legal value as the Treaties of the European Union,[34] thus integrating the core of EU primary law. Therefore, national judges are required to interpret their internal laws in the light of the fundamental rights afforded by the EU system and, by means of a proportionality test, to ensure a fair balance between the rights in question.[35] The CJEU has been very clear about this matter. In *Promusicae v. Telefónica*,[36] for example, the CJEU emphasized that EU law demands that member states pay extra attention when implementing directives

> ... to rely on an interpretation of [directives] which allows a fair balance to be struck between the various fundamental rights protected by the Community legal order. Further, when implementing the measures transposing those directives, the authorities and courts of the Member

[28] *See, e.g.*, the "Medienprofessor" Case, Austrian Supreme Court 12 June 2001, [2002] GRUR Int. 341, 33 Int'l Rev. Intell. Prop. & Competition L. 994; Hague Court of Appeals, Church of Scientology v. XS4ALL, 4 September 2003, 6 AMI 222 (2003); Supreme Court of the Canton of Zurich, Sept. 9, 2004, MEDIALEX 231 (2004); German Constitutional Court, Germania 3, 29 June 2000, GRUR INT. 149 (2001).

[29] *See, in particular*, Ashdown v. Telegraph Group Ltd. [2002] EWCA (Civ) 1142 (Eng.) ("Rare circumstances can arise where the right of freedom of expression will come into conflict with the protection afforded by the Copyright Act, notwithstanding the express exceptions to be found in the Act ... This will make it necessary for the court to look closely at the facts of individual cases.").

[30] In the context of appropriation art, *see* Morley, *supra* note 10. For a comparison with the situation in the EU, *see* Lucas & Ginsburg, *supra* note 10, at 32; Geiger, *supra* note 10, at 119.

[31] Harper & Row Publishers Inc. v. Nation Enterprise, 471 U.S. 539 (1985).

[32] Eldred v. Ashcroft, 537 U.S. 28 (2003).

[33] Christophe Geiger, *Intellectual "Property" after the Treaty of Lisbon: Towards a Different Approach in the New European Legal Order?*, 32 Eur. Intell. Prop. Rev. 255 (2010).

[34] Treaty of European Union (TEU) art. 6(1), July 29, 1992, 1992 O.J. (C 191).

[35] Christophe Geiger, *Copyright's Fundamental Rights Dimension at EU Level, in* Research Handbook on the Future of EU Copyright 27 (Estelle Derclaye ed., 2009); Dirk Voorhoof, *Freedom of Expression and the Right to Information: Implications for Copyright, in* Research Handbook on Human Rights and Intellectual Property 331 (Christophe Geiger ed., 2015); Bernd Justin Jütte, *The Beginning of a (Happy?) Relationship: Copyright and Freedom of Expression in Europe*, 38 Eur. Intell. Prop. Rev. 11 (2016).

[36] Case C-275/06, Productores de Música de España (Promusicae) v. Telefónica de España SAU, 2008 E.C.R. I-271, [2008] 2 CMLR 17.

> States must not only interpret their national law in a manner consistent with those directives but also make sure that they do not rely on an interpretation of them which would be in conflict with those fundamental rights or with the other general principles of Community law, such as the principle of proportionality.[37]

National judges are thus expected to interpret their own national legislation and review the scope of their jurisdiction's exceptions to copyright in light of the fundamental rights that are affected. Nevertheless, in some cases such an interpretation might not be possible if no specific statutory exception is available. In these cases, judges must have direct recourse to a fundamental right as a legal basis to legitimate the use at hand and limit copyright "from the outside." Such a situation is particularly likely to arise in EU countries where national intellectual property legislation does not take sufficient account of the fundamental rights in question, particularly where exceptions to copyright are constructed too narrowly.

The European Court of Human Rights (ECtHR) finally eliminated any remaining doubts about this subject in *Ashby Donald*.[38] In that case, the Strasbourg judges determined that a prohibition on the communication of works on the Internet, even in breach of copyright, might constitute a violation of freedom of expression. Hence, even in a situation in which there has been clear copyright infringement, it is always necessary to evaluate whether the resulting restriction to freedom of expression is "necessary in a democratic society" so as to strike a fair balance between the different rights at issue. After pointing out that "freedom of expression constitutes one of the essential bases of a democratic society, one of the basic conditions for its progress and the development of each individual," the ECtHR confirmed that "it involves exceptions that in any event require a narrow interpretation, and the need to restrict it must be established convincingly."[39] The court thus made it clear that intellectual property rights must be interpreted as exceptions to freedom of expression and that, given the great importance of that freedom within the framework of a democratic society, judges need to be very careful indeed in the presence of a restriction, particularly when it comes to political and artistic speech.[40]

Following these decisions at European level, the development of French case law seemed inevitable. Accordingly, perfectly in line with the ECtHR approach, the French Supreme Court in *Klasen* demanded that the Court of Appeal explain "concretely the manner in which the search for a fair balance between the rights in question required the decision that it rendered."[41] It is interesting to note that, at approximately the same time in the Netherlands, the Dutch

[37] *Id.* ¶ 70.

[38] Ashby Donald v. France, App. No. 36769/08 (Eur. Ct. H.R. Jan. 10, 2013); *see also* the so-called "Pirate Bay" decision (Neij & Sunde Kolmisoppi v. Sweden, App. No. 40397/12 (Eur. Ct. H.R. Feb. 19, 2013)). For a joint comment, *see* Geiger & Izyumenko, *supra* note 27.

[39] Ashby Donald v. France, App. No. 36769/08, ¶ 38 (Eur. Ct. H.R. Jan. 10, 2013). However, by refusing to take into account freedom of expression beyond the limited list of exceptions in EU copyright law, the CJEU contradicts this position (see *supra* note 8). It remains to see how this conflict between the approach of both courts will be resolved, in particular in the light of the future pending accession of the EU to the European Convention on Human Rights. In any case, as it has been emphasized, it "raises the questions of the "constitutionality" of the Luxemburg Court's position in the sense of its compatibility with the EU treaties and the fundamental rights order in the EU" (Christophe Geiger & Elena Izyumenko, *The Constitutionalization of Intellectual Property Law in the E.U. and the* Funke Medien, Pelham *and* Spiegel Online *Decisions of the CJEU: Progress, But Still Some Way to Go!*, *supra* note 8, at p. 301).

[40] In this sense, *see* Christophe Geiger, *Fundamental Rights, a Safeguard for the Coherence of Intellectual Property Law?*, 35 Int'l Rev. Intell. Prop. & Competition L. 268 (2004) (recalling that copyright has to be considered "as an island of exclusivity in a sea of freedom" (freedom of expression, freedom of competition)); Helle Porsdam, *On European Narratives of Human Rights and Their Possible Implications for Copyright*, in 6 New Directions in Copyright Law 335 (Fiona Macmillan ed., 2007).

[41] Cass. 1e civ., May 15, 2015, Bull. Civ. 1, No. 13-27391 (Fr.). For a comment, *see* Christophe Geiger, La Semaine Juridique 967 (2015).

Supreme Court reached a similar conclusion in a remarkable judgment issued on April 3, 2015.[42] In the case concerned, the Dutch Supreme Court criticized the Court of Appeal for deciding that copyright constitutes a limitation to the freedom of expression established in Article 10 of the ECHR and that only in exceptional circumstances can freedom of expression justify the use of a copyright-protected work beyond the internal limits imposed by law. The Court of Appeal had ruled that exceptional circumstances were not satisfied in the case at issue without explaining why. Hence, the Supreme Court reversed the decision, stating that the appellate court ought to have explained – and verified *in the specific case* – the manner in which the restriction of freedom of expression was not only proportionate to achieve its results, but also necessary in a democratic society.

3 FAIR USE THROUGH FUNDAMENTAL RIGHTS BALANCING: WEIGHING FREEDOM OF ARTISTIC EXPRESSION AND COPYRIGHT IN CASES OF CREATIVE APPROPRIATION

A. *Finding a Fair Balance between Copyright and Freedom of Artistic Expression in National Courts: Towards the Legitimization of Creative Reuses of Copyrighted Works*

Two highly influential decisions of the Federal Constitutional Court of Germany (BVerfG) also pertain to the issue of creative appropriation and deserve a brief examination here. In *Germania 3* and *Metall auf Metall*, the BVerfG gave important guidance on how to balance copyright and freedom of artistic expression. *Germania 3*[43] concerned a playwright, Heiner Müller, who had extensively quoted, in italics, from the work of Bertolt Brecht in his play entitled *Germania 3*. The dispute was brought to the constitutional court, which decided that the use of four pages in total of quoted material from Brecht did not constitute an infringement of copyright because the quotation in question was part of a new creative and artistic work. The BVerfG further stated that legal understanding of the quotation exception needs to be expanded and interpreted more extensively to guarantee the protection of artistic freedom.[44] In addition, it reinforced the notion that copyright exceptions have to be read in the light of such freedom to strike a balance between various interests.[45]

The highly commented-upon case of *Metall auf Metall*[46] centered on the hip-hop song "Nur Mir," which sampled a continuously repeating two-second rhythm sequence from "Metall auf

[42] HR 3 April 2015, m.nt. EE (GS Media BV/Sanoma Media Netherlands BV and Others) (Neth.). *See, in particular*, para. 5.2.5 of the judgment.

[43] Bundesverfassungsgericht [BVerfG] [Federal Constitutional Court], June 29, 2000, 3 GRUR INT. 149, § 22 (2001) (Ger.). For nonofficial English translation, *see* Elizabeth Adeney & Christoph Antons, *The Germania 3 Decision Translated: The Quotation Exception before the German Constitutional Court*, 35 EUR. INTELL. PROP. REV. 646 (2013).

[44] In paragraph 27 of the decision, the BVerfG clarified that the great mistake of the Court of Appeal was that it "gives no particular artistic weight to how it is worked into the drama and its position in the play." *See* Adeney & Antons, *supra* note 43.

[45] *See* Adeney & Antons, *supra* note 43 ("The Court states that 'the prohibition placed on the quotation of these two passages represents [the complainants allege] a crude attack on the integrity of Heiner Müller's art work and therefore also on Art 5(3) of the Basic Law' [freedom of art]"); for more decisions that contest the lack of flexibility of the copyright system, *see* Hugenholtz and Senftleben, *supra* note 1 (stating that in *Germania 3* the court "held that . . . the quotation right deserves broad application with respect to artistic works. Authors must, to a certain degree, accept that works of art gradually enter the public domain. Copyright exemptions should be interpreted accordingly, and reflect a balancing of relevant interests. In the case at hand, the Court considered, the commercial interests of the copyright owner should give way to the user's interest in providing artistic commentary.").

[46] Federal Constitutional Court, First Senate, *Metall auf Metall*, 31 May 2016, 1 BvR 1585/13 (Ger.). For the press release in English, *see* Federal Constitutional Court, *The Use of Samples for Artistic Purposes May Justify an Interference with Copyrights and Related Rights* (May 31, 2016), https://www.bundesverfassungsgericht.de/SharedDocs/Pressemitteilungen/EN/2016/bvg16-029.html. For a comment, *see* Ines Duhanic, *Copy This Sound! The Cultural Importance of*

Metall," a composition by the famous German band Kraftwerk. The Federal Court of Justice (BGH) initially considered the sampling to be an infringing use, and held that the takeover of even the smallest part of a musical composition constituted interference with the rights of the phonogram producers if the reproduction was intended to sound like the original composition.[47] The BGH also held that simply appropriating a music sample without adding one's own version of it falls outside the limit of free use that could have legitimized the appropriation.[48] The BVerfG, however, reversed this decision, ruling that the courts have to search for a fair balance between protecting the property interests of phonogram producers and protecting the freedom of artistic creativity, to ensure that the latter is not disproportionally affected. The constitutional judges also held that the presumption that the inclusion of any sound sequence in a work interferes with the phonogram producers' rights affords no attention to artistic freedom, and hence is unsuitable for seeking a fair balance between the interests involved.[49] Finally, the BVerfG ruled that submitting sampling to the authorization of the right holder would potentially restrict free artistic activity and cultural development, thereby creating a degree of legal uncertainty for artists.[50]

Sampling for Hip Hop Music in Copyright Law: A Copyright Law Analysis of the Sampling Decision of the German Federal Constitutional Court, 11 Gewerblicher Rechtsschutz und Urheberrecht internationaler Teil [GRUR int.] 1007 (2016); Marc D. Mimler, *"Metall auf Metall" : The German Federal Constitutional Court Discusses the Permissibility of Sampling Music Tracks*, 7 Queen Mary J. Intell. Prop. 119 (2017); Neil Conley & Tom Braegelmann, *Metall auf Metall: The Importance of the Kraftwerk Decision for the Sampling of Music in Germany*, 56 J. Copyright Soc'y U.S.A. 1017 (2009); Mathias Leistner, *Die "Metall auf Metall"-Entscheidung des BVerfG - Oder: Warum das Urheberrecht in Karlsruhe in Guten Händen ist*, 8 Gewerblicher Rechtsschutz und Urheberrecht [GRUR] 772 (2016); Rupprecht Podszun, *Postmoderne Kreativität im Konflikt mit dem Urheberrechtsgesetz und die Annäherung an "Fair Use"*, Zeitschrift für Urheber- und Medienrecht 606 (2016).

47 *See* the two decisions in this case by Bundesgerichtshof [BGH] [Federal Court of Justice] Nov. 20, 2008, Case I ZR 112/06, *Metall auf Metall I, translated in* Neil Conley & Tom Braegelmann, *Metall auf Metall: The Importance of the Kraftwerk Decision for the Sampling of Music in Germany Part III: Case Translation*, 56 J. Copyright Soc'y U.S.A. 1017, 1034 (2009); and BGH Dec. 13, 2012, Case I ZR 182/11, *Metall auf Metall II, translated in* AF, *Germany: "Metall auf Metall"*, 48 Int'l Rev. Intell. Prop. & Competition L. 343 (2017).

48 Gesetz über Urheberrecht und verwandte Schutzrechte [Urheberrechtsgesetz] [UrhG] [Copyright Act], Sept. 9, 1965, BGBl. I § 24 (Ger.). The free use ("freie Benutzung") limitation permits the author to freely exploit a work created on the basis of another work, provided that "the personal characteristics of the first work are lost in the derived work." Detailed on Art. 24 of the German Copyright Act, *see* Duhanic, *supra* note 46; Veronika Fischer, Digitale Kunst und freie Benutzung, Systematisierung und Flexibilisierung (2018). From an international perspective, *see* Paul Edward Geller, *A German Approach to Fair Use: Test Cases for TRIPs Criteria for Copyright Limitations?*, 57 J. Copyright Soc'y U.S.A. 553 (2010). *See also* Urheberrechtegesetz [UrhG] [Federal Law on Copyright in Works of Literature and Art and on Related Rights] Bürgerliches Gesetzbuch [BGBl] No. 111/1936, § 5(2) (Austria).

49 Overall, the BVerfG stated that "if the freedom of art development interferes with the rights of phonogram producers only slightly, the interests of the latter should bend in favour of the freedom of art," as *translated in* Chenguo Zhang, *'Sampling' Is Freedom of Art: The German Federal Constitutional Court Deliberates on the Acceptability of Music Sampling in the 'Metall auf Metall' Case*, 33 Computer L. & Sec. Rev. 870, 871 (2017).

50 Note however, that the same case went back to the German Federal Supreme Court, which submitted it on August 4, 2017, to the CJEU for Opinion. As it concerns freedom of artistic creativity in particular at issue, Advocate General Szpunar came to a different conclusion than the German Constitutional Court, considering that, as the EU law stands now, (unlicensed) music sampling should be regarded as a violation of the exclusive rights of phonogram producers and, consequently, as not covered by the "essence" of the right to freedom of expression and freedom of the arts. According to the Advocate General, such stance of EU law toward music sampling and artistic creativity in general might change in the future, but this is a step for the EU legislature, not the court, to undertake (*see* Opinion of Advocate General Szpunar in *Pelham and Others* [at 98]). In its "Pelham" decision, the Court of Justice is more nuanced, as is allows sampling if it is non-recognisable, and considers further that the quotation exception could potentially cover recognisable, but "dialogic" use of the original work, subject to certain other conditions (see *supra* note 8). The exclusion of an external "freedom of art"-review remains however problematic from a fundamental rights perspective; detailed in this sense *see* C. Geiger, *Freedom of Artistic Creativity and Copyright Law: A Compatible Combination?*, 8 U.C. Irvine L. Rev. 413 (2018).

The German Constitutional Court thus demonstrated far-sighted comprehension of musical development and the particularities of different music styles, as subjecting a use to the exclusive right of phonogram producers would render the use of past sound recordings far more difficult in the future.[51] Both of these BVerfG decisions demonstrate the court's serious concern for the need to safeguard freedom of artistic expression when developing new musical styles and to determine how a proportional and fair balance must be sought between this fundamental right and the protection of intellectual property rights.[52] The court also clearly acknowledged the fragility of artistic freedom in the copyright context in these cases, and seemed to recommend that national courts exercise caution when dealing with cases involving creative reuses of copyrighted works.

In the Netherlands, the Hague Court of Appeal also had an opportunity to render a judgment in a 2011 case concerning a conflict between design rights and freedom of artistic expression.[53] The Danish painter Nadia Plessner had portrayed an African child holding a Louis Vuitton bag, to draw attention to the woeful manner in which the Western media was treating the humanitarian crisis in the Darfur region of Sudan – affording more attention to celebrity gossip than to the ongoing genocide (the painting, entitled *Darfurnica*, also made reference in its structure and title to Picasso's famous *Guernica*) – prompting the luxury fashion house to bring an action for infringement of its design rights on the depicted bag. The Hague court found in favor of the artist on the basis of freedom of artistic expression, holding that the luxury product depicted in the artwork in this concrete case was being used as a vehicle to express a critical political view endowed with great social significance and, accordingly, that freedom of expression should prevail.[54]

All of these important cases clearly demonstrate that intellectual property law is not weakened when freedom of expression is prioritized. On the contrary, the intellectual property system actually gains legitimacy when exclusive rights are not used to prevent artistic activities and criticism in the form of art.[55] Moreover, important safeguards exist, most notably the proportionality test conducted to prevent abusive uses of freedom of expression by litigants. It goes without saying that in the *Klasen* case discussed above, free artistic expression would have been impeded if a prior obligation had been imposed on the painter to contact the owner of the original photographs to ask for permission for the intended use. It is also highly unlikely that the photographer would have been willing to grant such permission, particularly if the artist had explained that his photographs had been chosen to illustrate and criticize the superficiality of the fashion world and the excesses of a consumption-based society! In addition to these practical difficulties, it must be noted that it is not always easy to identify the rights holder in the case of photography, as photographers (particularly when they work for magazines) often assign their

[51] On further discussion on music sampling and mashups, *see* Bernd Justin Jütte & H. Maier, *A Human Right to Sample – Will the CJEU Dance to the BGH-Beat?*, 12 J. INTELL. PROP. L. & PRACT. 784 (2017). More generally and on user-generated contents and the enabling of a legal mashup culture, *see* Bernd Justin Jütte, *The EU's Trouble with Mashups: From Disabling to Enabling a Digital Art Form*, 5 J. INTELL. PROP. INFO. TECH. & ELEC. COM. L. 172 (2014).

[52] Surprisingly, in the case of music, on the other side of the Atlantic the flexible fair use defense seems to have been rarely successful in cases of nonparodic uses. *See* detailed on the issue Edward Lee, *Fair Use Avoidance in Music Cases*, 59 B.C. L. REV 1873 (2018).

[53] Rb. 's-Gravenhage, 4 May 2011, IER 2011, 39 m. nt. W. Sakulin (Plesner/Louis Vuitton) (Neth.).

[54] *See* on this case Jani McCutcheon, *Designs, Parody and Artistic Expression: A Comparative Perspective of* Plesner v Louis Vuitton, 41 MONASH UNIV. L. REV. 192 (2015); Lucie Guibault, *The Netherlands: Dafurnica, Miffy and the Right to Parody!*, 2 J. INTELL. PROP. INFO. TECH. & ELEC. COM. L. 236 (2011).

[55] For a fundamental reflection on this, *see* the fascinating work of GIANCARLO FROSIO, RECONCILING COPYRIGHT WITH CUMULATIVE CREATIVITY: THE THIRD PARADIGM (2018) (examining the long history of creativity in order to demonstrate disparity between cumulative mechanics of creativity and modern copyright policies, and proposing options to reconcile both).

rights to third parties. Therefore, placing the burden of locating rights holders on the authors of derivative works imposes very high transactional costs.

In fact, it is difficult to imagine Andy Warhol requesting permission from the rights holder of the Campbell trademark before producing his famous *Campbell's Soup Cans* with the intention of mocking American consumer society. Or indeed Marcel Duchamp seeking permission from the potential holders of the design rights on the ready-mades he displayed as works of art. Or Jeff Koons asking for the consent of the creators of advertisements to make use of their posters as a way of scorning the messages they wished to communicate. More generally, would it really have been reasonable to require Pablo Picasso – and the many other artists who subsequently adapted his work – to ask Édouard Manet's heirs for permission to paint his version of *Le Déjeuner sur l'herbe* (a painting whose composition incidentally derived from an engraving by Marcantonio Raimondi, an engraving that was itself based on a drawing by Raphael)? Numerous similar examples can be drawn from the annals of art history.[56] In a 2007 case, the French Supreme Court had an opportunity to demonstrate the sensitivity of such questions, and did not hesitate to base its decision on freedom of artistic expression in permitting the publication of a sequel to *Les Misérables*, despite an attempt to prevent it by the heirs of Victor Hugo based on the perpetual moral rights of the renowned writer.[57]

Decisions based on fundamental rights reasoning are becoming increasingly frequent in EU member states, and it is thus anticipated that the importance of seeking a fair balance between copyright and freedom of artistic expression will soon be recognized and affirmed by a majority of Europe's highest courts. Moreover, the use of a proportionality test seems to be the means envisioned by the courts in all of the aforementioned rulings for achieving a fair such balance in light of the factual circumstances of each case. Therefore, it seemed clear that the claim that the conflict between copyright and freedom of expression has been internalized and that no judicial review beyond the existing exceptions is possible belonged to the past. However, as we have noted previously, the CJEU in 2019 has taken a conflicting position, so that this debate has now been revived in the EU. Moreover, the acknowledgment of the relevance of striking a fair balance between the interests at stake by several of the highest courts in EU member states has still not translated into general application by courts of lower instance. Such resistance to change is clearly illustrated by developments subsequent to the *Klasen* decision in France.

B. *Resistance to Change: Paris District Court Decision in* Koons v. Bauret *and Judgment of Remittal in* Klasen

As previously discussed, applying the principle of proportionality in copyright cases has the potential to legitimize freedom of artistic expression in diverse situations of creative appropriation.[58] However, a number of trial judges in France have continued to support a more restrictive approach despite the *Klasen* decision by the French Supreme Court in 2015. The Paris District Court judgment in *Koons v. Bauret* and remittal decision of the Versailles Court of

[56] Only the visual arts are mentioned here, but this exercise could easily be transposed to all kinds of art, from music, to cinema, to literature, etc.

[57] Cass. 1e civ., Jan. 30, 2007, Bull. Civ. I, No. 125 (Fr.). For a summary of the case in English, *see* D.W., *Copyright Law: France – Victor Hugo II*, 38 INT'L REV. INTELL. PROP. & COMPETITION L. 736 (2007). For a comment, *see* Christophe Geiger, *Copyright and the Freedom to Create: A Fragile Balance*, 38 INT'L REV. INTELL. PROP. & COMPETITION L. 707 (2007).

[58] *See* Christophe Geiger, *Freedom of Artistic Creativity and Copyright Law: A Compatible Combination?*, 8 U.C. IRVINE L. REV. 101 (2018).

Appeal in *Klasen* are exactly such cases. As these two decisions were the first to apply *in concreto* balancing and use of the proportionality test, as mandated by a correct application of fundamental rights in the context of appropriation art, they are worthy of detailed analysis. Furthermore, they are also important for a general assessment of this art form from a copyright perspective at the national and international levels.

i) The Judgment of the Paris District Court on March 9, 2017, in Koons v. Bauret

Koons v. Bauret[59] centered on a postcard featuring a black-and-white photograph of two naked children holding hands, taken in 1970 by Jean-François Bauret, that the American artist Jeff Koons had used as inspiration in 1988 in designing the porcelain sculpture *Naked* as part of his "Banality" series. The photographer's heirs brought an action for copyright infringement against Koons and the Centre Pompidou,[60] arguing that the sculpture reproduced the protected photograph in full. Koons did not contest that argument, even though he had added elements not present in the original photograph to the sculpture (such as the colored base with flowers and small flower bouquet held by the boy) and cited numerous other sources of inspiration. Many arguments were brought forward as part of the defense, the main one being that the use was legitimated by freedom of artistic expression as protected by Article 10 of the ECHR. A liberal reading of the existing exceptions in EU law, particularly of the right of quotation, would probably have justified the use in question, thus permitting recognition under French law of artistic quotation in the context of a creative reuse of copyright in the interest of protecting artistic discourse. However, because the French courts traditionally have a very narrow understanding of the quotation exception, Article 10 of the ECHR seemed like the best means of legitimating the use under French copyright law.[61]

The Paris District Court welcomed the argument that Article 10 protects freedom of artistic creativity and clarified that assessing the facts on a case-by-case basis is required to guarantee a fair balance between copyright and freedom of expression. This stance was clearly a consequence of the aforementioned *Klasen* decision, with which the court complied. However, in appreciation of the particularities of the case, and after making a clear reference to fundamental-rights balancing mechanisms, the court came to the conclusion that the creative use in question should not be allowed, as Koons had failed to justify the imperative necessity of using Bauret's photograph without seeking the photographer's prior authorization.

Although the decision can be criticized, it must be noted that it shows real progress, as French courts in the past had frequently limited their analysis to an abstract appreciation of the conflict between copyright and freedom of expression, an approach that is not compliant with the method required to balance fundamental rights. An example of this lack of appreciation of the particularities of each concrete case can be seen in the *Klasen* decision reached by the Appellate Court of Paris.[62] The court considered, without any further explanation, the copyright protection of the photograph as imposing a limit on the painter's freedom of expression and, as a result, rejected the defendant's argument based on such freedom, as "the rights in the alleged

[59] Tribunal de Grande Instance [TGI] [ordinary court of original jurisdiction] Paris, 3d Chamber, Mar. 9, 2017, No. 15-01086 (Fr.). For a comment *see* Jean-Michel Bruguière, 348 LÉGIPRESSE 177 (2017); Jean-Michel Bruguière, 64 PROPR. INTELL. 69 (2017). The Paris Court of Appeal in a decision of Dec. 17, 2019 (No. 152/2019), confirmed the decision of the Paris District without much argumentation, far from a proper proportionality analysis required by article 10 ECHR.

[60] In fact, the work of art in question was part of the catalogue of an art exhibition devoted to Koons in 2014 by Centre Pompidou.

[61] On the (very contestable) restrictive interpretation of exceptions by courts at national level, in particular in France, *see supra* Section 2 of the chapter.

[62] CA Paris, Pole 5, 1st Chamber, Sept. 18, 2013, No. 12/02480.

infringing work could not, without a higher interest, outweigh the rights of the works from which they were derived."[63] The decision was eventually reversed by the French Supreme Court, resulting in the remittal of the case to a lower instance court for an assessment of the concrete facts therein, thus effecting a clean break with previous case law holding that any argument based on a violation of Article 10 of the ECHR that went beyond the scope of existing exceptions should be considered invalid.[64]

Returning to *Koons v. Bauret*, the Paris District Court began its justification of its ruling by highlighting that, according to the ECtHR, the weight to be afforded the right to freedom of expression is intrinsically linked to the type of discourse used in the given circumstance (political speech enjoying greater protection than commercial speech). The judges considered it necessary to ascertain whether the situation concerned the reuse of copyright for commercial intent or for a higher public interest purpose in order to properly measure the impact on that fundamental right.[65] In fact, as discussed above, making such a distinction is a very important step when striking a fair balance between the rights at stake, as it permits appreciation of the effects of an eventual restriction on freedom of artistic creativity. It remains evident, nevertheless, that the appropriation at issue was not exclusively a form of commercial expression, which would be the case, for example, in an advertising campaign.[66] As rightly emphasized by the court, and also in full alignment with the reasoning of the ECtHR,[67] the fact that Jeff Koons earns money from his art does not lead to the conclusion that his artistic creations have a commercial purpose.[68]

However, the court surprisingly reversed the burden of proof, based on its understanding that for freedom of expression to outweigh property rights, the interest being protected must be legitimate and proportional to the ends being achieved and the benefit of a democratic society. This seems to be an incorrect understanding of how ECHR Article 10 is to be applied in copyright cases. Under the rationale of that article, the order in which the burden of proof is analyzed is inverted. Because in this case it was the enforcement of the copyright on the photograph that resulted in the restriction of the American artist's freedom of artistic creativity, it should have been left to the photographer, not the creator of the artistic reuse, to prove that the restriction was indeed necessary and imperative for the benefit of a democratic society. It is evident that freedom of expression holds a privileged position in the EU legal system, and should thus be seen in the context of artistic creativity as a principle from which copyright protection departs.[69]

The court continued its analysis by assessing the justification given by Koons for his use of the specific photograph concerned. Neither the argument that the creative reuse was made with the intention of reflecting upon society nor that Koons's artistic expression had gained a high degree of public acceptance would have been rejected by the court as long as the artist had succeeded

[63] CA Paris, Pole 5, 1st Chamber, Sept. 18, 2013, No. 12/02480.

[64] French Supreme Court, 1st Civil Chamber, Nov. 13, 2003, *supra* note 25; For a critical comment, *see* Geiger, *supra* note 23.

[65] TGI Paris, Mar. 9, 2017, No. 15-01086 (Fr.).

[66] Case C-71/02, Herbert Karner Industrie-Auktionen GmbH v, Troostwijk GmbH, [2004] E.C.R. I-03025, ¶ 51 ("When the exercise of the freedom does not contribute to a discussion of public interest and, in addition, arises in a context in which the Member States have a certain amount of discretion, review is limited to an examination of the reasonableness and proportionality of the interference. This holds true for the commercial use of freedom of expression, particularly in a field as complex and fluctuating as advertising (*see*, to that effect, Case C-245/01 RTL Television [2003] ECR I-12489, paragraph 73; judgments of the ECHR of 20 November 1989, Markt intern Verlag GmbH and Klaus Beermann, Reports of Judgments and Decisions series A No 165, paragraph 33; and of 28 June 2001, VGT Verein gegen Tierfabriken v. Switzerland, Reports of Judgments and Decisions 2001 -VI, paragraphs 69 to 70).").

[67] *See* Geiger & Izyumenko, *supra* note 2, at 31.

[68] In the same sense, the mere fact that a newspaper is sold to its readers does not amount to a commercial expression.

[69] *See* more detailed Geiger & Izyumenko, *supra* note 27.

in proving that he had conveyed a new and enriching message that would contribute to the development of contemporary art. However, the court considered that the artist had failed to explain in a sufficiently concrete manner the necessity of using the two children in the photograph concerned to spread his message. It seems, in fact, that the court penalized Koons both for his failure to explain why he could not have designed the work differently and for making use of a number of details depicted in the photograph.

The former part of the court's decision is of great importance, as the judges essentially required the artist to provide a convincing justification of his creative process. However, neither the argument concerning the particularities of the artistic movement of which the work of art was a part nor the description of the aim of the individual sculpture or series of sculptures was evaluated with the attention it deserved. Instead, the Paris judges came rather close to judging the artistic merits of the sculpture in question, and even the pertinence and legitimacy of the art movement to which Koons belongs. Indeed, by asking the artist to justify his creative choices, the judges seemed to be assessing his art rather than limiting themselves to matters of law.[70] It is extremely difficult to evaluate "why an artist could not have done the work of art differently" without entering an area outside legal discourse. This sort of appreciation exceeds a mere request for further information concerning an artistic process of creation.[71] In any case, it is clear that imposing the burden of proof on an artist in this manner entails a strong risk of interfering in the artistic process, potentially leading to a denial of the artist's intellectual and creative freedom. Therefore, judges should be extremely prudent in their rulings when asking for artistic justifications.[72] That said, in an *a contrario* interpretation, it could also be deduced that the photograph's reuse might have been deemed legitimate by the court if Koons had been better able to explain the necessity of that reuse.

In *Koons v. Bauret*, the Paris District Court also made use of another surprising element in establishing the primacy of the photograph's copyright over the derivative work, that is, the fact that it is essential for the public to have knowledge of the primary work in order for the appropriated work to provoke reflection in spectators. Because the photograph was unknown to the general public, such reflection was not possible in this case. The judges thus introduced a distinction between works that are well known, which can easily be appropriated in a lawful

[70] Sharing this concern, *see* Edouard Treppoz, *Retour sur la dénaturation contextuelle du Dialogues des Carmélites* Comment on Cass. 1re civ., June 22, 2017, *G. Bernanos et a. c/ D. Techerniakov, Bel Air Media et a.*, 352 LÉGIPRESSE 438, 440 (2017) (emphasizing the need "for a fruitful dialogue between the art world and the legal world . . . . In the world of art, it is important to analyse the works in question so that the judge can take this analysis into consideration when qualifying the work. In the same sense that a judge is not a technical expert in patents, requiring the help of an expert, the judge is also not an art specialist, which justifies the use of experts in the field." Therefore, this author concludes that the judge has to make his/her decision taking into account the artistic analysis that is subjected to him/her.).

[71] It is conceivable that Jeff Koons might even be unable to explain how the use of this particular photograph was necessary for the creation of the work in question. It is possible to imagine that the use of this photograph was so obvious for the artist, in such a way that is not even possible for him to explain the reasons behind this obviousness. To ask an artist to expose or to dissect his creative reasoning and thus to justify his inspiration as to allow judges to appreciate it seems a very problematic step to us, as this sort of appreciation is definitely outside any legal scope.

[72] This was also the position of the United States Court of Appeals for the Second Circuit in the *Cariou v. Prince* decision, considering that creative appropriation by Richard Prince of the photographs by Patrick Cariou was covered by the fair use exception. Cariou v. Prince 714 F. 3d 694 (2d Cir. 2013). The court was of the opinion that Cariou had not to justify his creative choices: "What is critical is how the work in question appears to the reasonable observer, not simply what an artist might say about a particular piece of work. Prince's work could be transformative even without commenting on Cariou's work or on culture, and even without Prince's stated intention to do so," *id.* at 707. Commenting on this passage, *see* Lucas & Ginsburg, *supra* note 10, at 46 ("[T]he Court's refusal to require artists to explain themselves is certainly compatible with freedom of expression. Artist are not critics – no more than judges are – and the copyright law should let their works speak for themselves.").

manner, and unknown works, for which such a possibility cannot be recognized. Such a distinction is difficult to justify.[73] It is also contrary to the rationale of the appropriation art movement, whose aim is to cast light on forgotten, outdated, and kitsch works, as well as on any other image or cultural material of a particular time and place that is not expected to be an object of commercial exploitation (for example, a 1970s-era postcard bought at a second-hand shop or flea market or a limited advertising campaign). It thus seems that the Paris court mixed up the requirements of the parody exception, for which a reference to the original work is of major importance, with those of artistically creative reappropriation, which is protected under Article 10 of the ECHR.[74]

In fact, the court reached the surprising conclusion in this case that the artist had used the photograph for personal reasons, that is, to avoid having to be creative himself. Accordingly, it concluded that such use should not have been made without the authorization of the photograph's author and the owner of the copyright on the postcard on which it appeared. The judges seemed to imply that Koons had run out of inspiration and wanted to save himself the effort of creating something new. As previously noted, this conclusion fails to understand the process behind creative appropriation in which the core of a new work is based on an existing work of art. Such appropriation *is* the creative act (or at least a part of it), and without it the work would lose its raison d'être. Once again, a cautious approach is needed if we are to avoid having the courts define what *is* or *is not* a work of art deserving of copyright protection. Assessing the elements that justify a restriction on freedom of artistic expression would have sufficed for the case in question to have arrived at a very different outcome. Moreover, the court completely failed to identify the interests of Bauret's heirs and those of Jeff Koons and to strike a fair balance between their interests and the public interest. Further, no evidence was provided by the deceased photographer's heirs to justify the imperative need to prohibit the public display of Koons's sculpture. Such a prohibition would not only deprive French spectators of access to a major piece of art by a renowned twentieth-century artist, but would also prevent the artist from publicly conveying his artistic message.

ii) Decision to Remit Klasen to the Versailles Court of Appeal

The decision on the *Klasen* case by the Versailles Court of Appeal on March 16, 2018,[75] raises the same concerns and reservations about implementation of the proportionality test in assessing freedom of artistic expression on a case-by-case basis in copyright cases. The Versailles Court deemed the use of the photographs included in Klasen's painting to be illegal[76] based on the two rather surprising arguments also used by the Paris District Court

[73] In this sense, *see also* Bruguière, *supra* note 59, at 72 n.63 ("Why should works of art that are unknown enjoy a supplementary protection in comparison to well-known works?").

[74] This same surprising argument was reused by the Paris Court of First instance (TGI) in a decision of 8 November 2018, *Koons and Centre Georges Pompidou v. Davidovici*, in which it was considered that Jeff Koons had infringed the copyright of a photographer when using the image of an advertisement campaign as a point of departure for one of his sculptures. The court found no violation of Art. 10 ECHR and no disproportionate restriction of the artist's freedom of artistic expression, as no artistic dialogue was possible since the original work was unknown and thus considered that the artist just wanted to spare a creative effort.

[75] CA Versailles, 1e ch., Mar. 16, 2018, No. 15/06029. For comments, *see* Jean-Michel Bruguière, La Semaine Juridique, Mar. 16, 2018, at 513; Valérie-Laure Benabou, Dalloz IP/IT, 2018, at 300; Christophe Caron, Comm. com. Électr, 2018, comm. 32; Pierre Noual, Revue Lamy Droit de l'Immatériel 5193 (2018). For further a comment in English, *see* Eleonora Rosati, *Not Sufficiently 'Transformative' Appropriation of a Photograph Held Infringing by French Court*, 13 J. Intell. Prop. L. & Prac. 525 (2018).

[76] On the facts of the case, *see supra* Section 2.

in *Koons v. Bauret*. First, the court stated that it was up to Peter Klasen, who had invoked his freedom of expression in defense, to establish the extent to which a fair balance between the protection of his rights and those of the original work's right holder should be sought to justify his failure to obtain authorization for use of that work. Second, because of that failure,[77] the court considered that Klasen's unauthorized use of the photographs in question had not been indispensable for the exercise of freedom of expression he was claiming. As previously noted, this reversal of the burden of proof can be contested under Article 10 of the ECHR, which establishes that the burden of proof rests with the party seeking to restrict such freedom and who, for that purpose, needs to demonstrate that the restriction is imperative and not disproportional. Klasen explained sufficiently well that his rationale for using the photographs was to expose how cultural materials convey a message about consumer society. In fact, the use of advertisements has long been the core of pop culture and, more generally, of contemporary art. Nevertheless, in the eyes of the court, this justification was not sufficient. It held that the painter had failed to explain exactly why he had chosen these particular photographs, even though his explanation made it clear that the appropriated material was part of his creative process, if not the heart of his artistic speech. As previously emphasized, such a position taken by the courts risks diminishing the artistic choices that artists should have in exercising their creative freedom.

The Versailles Court then proceeded to analysis of a scholarly position[78] put forward by the defendant concerning the legal treatment of appropriation art, and arrived at the unexpected conclusion that photographs that are not well known to the public cannot serve as the substrate of such art. This reasoning brings to mind the Paris District Court's decision in *Koons v. Bauret*,[79] in which the court held that a primary work had to be known to the public to be used as an object of artistic appropriation. As Valérie-Laure Benabou has pointed out, the judges in these two cases seemed alarmingly interested in assessing the merits of particular works of art, which has traditionally been considered undesirable when it comes to copyright, as judges are not to play the role of art critics.[80] This is exactly what judges are doing when court decisions consider artistic appropriation legitimate only if the derivative work makes use of a well-known primary work.[81] Prof. Benabou emphasized that using notoriety as a yardstick to measure the level of protection a work of art deserves is rather odd.[82] In reality, it is not the notoriety of a piece of art that might permit its appropriation, but rather the artistic reasoning behind that appropriation. If this stance had been adopted in the two aforementioned cases, the uses would undoubtedly have been deemed permissible.

77 On the contrary, the artist even confirmed that the primary work was perfectly capable of being substituted by any other advertising photographs of similar kind for achieving the same means.

78 Interestingly, the passage discussed in the ruling of the Court of Appeal was extracted from the comments on the decision of the French Supreme Court written by the author of this chapter. *See* Christophe Geiger, comment on the decision of the French Supreme Court, May 15, 2015, *supra* note 3, at 1623.

79 TGI Paris, Mar. 9, 2017, No. 15-01086 (Fr.).

80 This fear had already been voiced in 1903 by Justice Holmes in Bleistein v. Donaldson Lithographing Co., 188 U.S. 239 (1903) ("it would be a dangerous undertaking for persons trained only to the law to constitute themselves final judges of the worth of pictorical illustrations, outside the narrowest and most obvious limits. At the one extreme some works of genius would be sure to miss appreciation."). *See also* Greenberg, *supra* note 10, "[I]t is apparent that judges could misconstrue the requirement and deny copyright protection to controversial or innovative works. The requirement does not operate as an incentive for artists to create, but rather discourages new forms of creation.").

81 Benabou, *supra* note 75, at 301.

82 *Id.* at 302.

4 BEYOND FAIR USE: RENDERING FREEDOM OF ARTISTIC EXPRESSION FULLY COMPATIBLE WITH COPYRIGHT PROTECTION THROUGH LEGISLATIVE REFORM

The French Supreme Court's decision in *Klasen* and other national high court decisions applying freedom of artistic expression to limit intellectual property rights have confirmed that the judiciary always needs to adopt a case-by-case approach, even if the use in question lies outside the scope of an exception. However, as we have seen, the debate is not entirely closed as the CJEU decided that limiting copyright beyond the admitted catalogue of exceptions laid out in the InfoSoc Directive is incompatible with EU law.[83] The recent position of the CJEU risks relaunching another (no less fundamental) discussion on the necessary space devoted to freedom of artistic expression within copyright law, thereby encouraging EU legislators to intervene by exempting certain uses for creative purposes from the scope of protection for an exclusive right. Could such an exemption be achieved by expanding the legal understanding of the existing list of exceptions (specifically, the coverage of quotation and parody) to cover creative appropriations? In fact, the wording of the InfoSoc Directive[84] is in many respects considerably more flexible than that of many national laws, as the right of quotation was drafted at the EU level as an open concept. It could thus very well allow an assessment of the facts on a case-by-case basis.

Another possibility would be the creation of an entirely new creative use exception to copyright, such as that implemented in Canada[85] in 2012. Although, as we have seen, the question of allowing the creative use of copyright-protected content remains an extremely sensitive topic in Europe, Canadian legislators did not hesitate in resolving the problem by creating a specific exception for "content not commercially generated by the user." Thus, according to Article 29.21 of the Canadian Copyright Act, "it is not an infringement of copyright for an individual to use an existing work or other subject-matter or copy of one, which has been published or otherwise made available to the public, in the creation of a new work or other subject-matter in which copyright subsists" provided that a certain number of criteria are fully satisfied. The most important criteria are the noncommercial nature of the derivative work and "the absence of a substantial adverse effect, financial or otherwise, on the exploitation or potential exploitation" of the first work, "including that the new work or other subject matter is not a substitute for the existing one."[86] Although these criteria carefully limit permitted uses, their reading gives the impression that they will be difficult to implement. In reality, the distinction between commercial and noncommercial use is not always easy to draw, and the absence of an important adverse effect on the exploitation of the first work is subject to a diversity of interpretations. In this respect, one might recall the endless discussions generated by the

[83] CJEU, 29 July 2019, "*Funke Medien*", "*Pelham*", and "*Spiegel Online*", *supra* note 8. These decisions were rendered upon the request of the Bundesgerichtshof (Federal Supreme Court), Request for a preliminary ruling, *Pelham GmbH and Others*, Case C-476/17. For a discussion, *see* European Copyright Society, *Opinion of the European Copyright Society in Relation to the Pending Reference before the CJEU in Case C-476/17, Hutter v Pelham*, https://europeancopyrightsocietydotorg.files.wordpress.com/2018/03/opinion-metall-auf-metall-fin4.pdf (last accessed January 16, 2019). In his Opinion on this case, Advocate General Szpunar considers that an external limitation is only admissible in "exceptional circumstances" when the "essence of a fundamental right" is at stake, but estimates that unlicensed music sampling is not covered by the "essence" of the right to freedom of expression and freedom of the arts (Opinion in *Pelham and Others*, *supra* note 8, [98]). For a comment *see* Geiger & Izyumenko, *supra* note 8.

[84] InfoSoc Directive, art. 5.3(d).

[85] Copyright Act, R.S.C. 1985, c C-42, s. 29.21 (Can.).

[86] *Id.* ss. 29.21 (1)(a) and (d), respectively.

condition laid down by international law[87] that an absence of conflict with the normal exploitation of a work is necessary for a copyright exception to be permitted.[88] Such a condition also seems to be reflected in the wording proposed by the Canadian legislature.[89] At the same time, however, the condition[90] also reminds us of one of the four factors that need to be considered in the fair-use defense framework according to US copyright law, namely, the influence of the proposed creative use on the potential market for the protected work.[91]

One might well wonder which of the foregoing solutions is the most worthy of adoption. Without embarking on in-depth analysis of Canadian copyright law,[92] it could be pointed out that the exception in Article 29.21 of the Canadian Copyright Act constitutes an attempt to internalize the conflict between freedom of expression and copyright within a particular legislative provision. Thus, the Canadian approach responds directly to certain commentators' preoccupation with the multiplication of conflicts outside copyright law, i.e., in the field of fundamental rights or competition law. However, such internalization through the implementation of a new exception for uses made for creative purposes is not a new idea.[93] In fact, it was clearly considered to be a potentially viable option by the European Commission[94] a good decade ago, and was also envisaged as a possibility by the European Parliament in a resolution dated July 9, 2015.[95] In the same spirit, a group of European academics working on the

[87] Namely the second condition of the three-step test, "provided that such reproduction does not conflict with a normal exploitation of the work."

[88] Specifically Art. 9.2 of the Berne Convention (for the right of reproduction), Art. 13 of the Agreement on Trade-Related Aspects of Intellectual Property Rights (TRIPS) (for all property rights) and Arts. 10 and 16 of the WIPO treaties on Copyright (WCT) and Performing Rights and the Rights of producers of Phonograms (WPPT), laying down the so-called three-step test. *See* on this question Christophe Geiger et al., *The Three-Step-Test Revisited: How to Use the Test's Flexibility in National Copyright Law*, 29 AM. U. INT'L L. REV. 581 (2014); *see also* Christophe Geiger, *The Role of the Three-Step Test in the Adaptation of Copyright Law to the Information Society*, UNESCO E-COPYRIGHT BULLETIN, Jan.–Mar. 2007, *available at* http://unesdoc.unesco.org/images/0015/001578/157848e.pdf.

[89] Which however has not prevented certain commentators from arguing that Art. 29.21 does not respect the criteria imposed by international law. *See* on this question Peter Yu, *Can the Canadian UGC Exception Be Transplanted Abroad?*, 26 INTELL. PROP. J. 175 (2014) (putting forward very serious arguments in favor of the compatibility of the provision with the three-step test).

[90] On the conditions for the fair use defense in copyright matters, *see* Jütte, *supra* note 51.

[91] Art. 107 of the American 1976 Act. It must be noted that in the *Campbell v. Acuff Rose* judgment, the Supreme Court held that the reuse of a chorus from the song "Pretty Woman" by a hip-hop group parodying the famous song by Roy Orbison constituted fair use, holding that the fourth criterion was not necessarily the most important and that all the criteria should be applied in the light of the objective pursued by copyright, namely the promotion of progress in science and useful arts. Campbell v. Acuff-Rose Music, Inc., 510 U.S. 569 (1994). The lawful use for creative purposes was thus admitted despite the fact that this was a "commercial" use, mainly because the work was of a "transformative" nature.

[92] *See*, in particular, among the many commentaries, Theresa Scassa, *Acknowledging Copyright's Illegitimate Offspring: User-Generated Content and Canadian Copyright Law*, *in* THE COPYRIGHT PENTALOGY: HOW THE SUPREME COURT OF CANADA SHOOK THE FOUNDATIONS OF CANADIAN COPYRIGHT LAW 431 (Michael Geist ed., 2013).

[93] More generally, the idea that copyright, through the many exceptions that it includes, already regulates within itself all the conflicts that could oppose it to other rights, is moreover advanced to dismiss the idea that such conflicts can be taken into account outside the legal provisions. But, who can seriously believe in a legislature that has foreseen everything? For this reason, the Advocate General of the CJEU has recently admitted that there are exceptional circumstances that justify an external limitation of copyright through fundamental rights, while still considering that "in the normal scheme of things, the internal limits on copyright make it possible to reconcile, in a satisfactory way overall, fundamental rights and freedoms with the exclusive rights of authors as regards the use of their works." *See* Opinion in Case C-469/17, *Funke Medien*, *supra* note 8, Par. 40. On this issue *see* detailed Geiger & Izyumenko, *supra* note 8.

[94] Green Paper of the Commission of the European Communities, Copyright in the Knowledge Economy, COM 466 (2008).

[95] European Parliament Resolution of July 9, 2015, on the implementation of Directive 2001/29/EC of the European Parliament and of the Council of May 22, 2001, on the harmonization of certain aspects of copyright and related rights in the information society P8_TA-PROV(2015)0273, in which the European Parliament "notes with interest the

European Copyright Code project proposed the adoption of a general clause covering all uses justified by freedom of expression that are not provided for by existing EU legislation.[96] Recently, scholars have proposed to implement a new use privilege for User-Generated Content which combined with the obligation to pay equitable remuneration would satisfy all requirements of international copyright law such as the three-step test and create a new revenue stream for creators.[97] Other more classical options have also been considered. In France, for example, the "Lescure" report suggested the development of existing exceptions (the quotation and parody exceptions in particular) as a way to "ease the conditions in which the protected works can be reused in order to create derived works and to distribute them within a non-commercial framework"[98] while still complying with InfoSoc Directive.[99]

Whatever solution is adopted, it would be desirable to increase the flexibility of and role granted to freedom of artistic expression within copyright law to better adapt legal provisions to the factual circumstances of various art movements. The failure of copyright law to take sufficient account of fundamental values such as freedom of expression ultimately risks the rejection of the entire system by creators and the general public alike if no appropriate solution is implemented.[100] In this context, the argument put forward by several scholars that flexible exceptions are not within the continental tradition, and risk increasing legal uncertainty, is not convincing as numerous other open norms can be found in continental legal systems.[101] Moreover, the uncertainty that an open provision can generate should not be overestimated. Even in the United States, whose copyright system is often presented as difficult to predict owing to the fair use clause, empirical studies over the past decade have shown that the solutions adopted by the courts can be forecast in most cases, largely disproving certain preconceived ideas

development of new forms of use of works on digital networks, in particular transformative uses, and stresses the need to examine solutions reconciling efficient protection that provides for proper remuneration and fair compensation for creators with the public interest for access to cultural goods and knowledge" (paragraph 42). For a comment, *see* Christophe Geiger et al., *The Resolution of the European Parliament of 9 July 2015: Paving the Way (Finally) for a Copyright Reform in the European Union?* 37 Eur. Intell. Prop. Rev. 683 (2015).

[96] The Wittem Project: *European Copyright Code*, art. 5.2 (April 2010), www.copyrightcode.eu. *See, in particular*, Thomas Dreier, *The Wittem Project of a European Copyright Code, in* Constructing European Intellectual Property: Achievements and New Perspectives 292 (Christophe Geiger ed., 2013).

[97] *See* Martin Senftleben, *User-Generated Content : Towards a New Use Privilege in EU Copyright Law, in* Research Handbook on Intellectual property and Digital Technologies, p. 136 sq (Tanya Aplin ed., 2020); Joao Pedro Quintais, Copyright in the Age of Online Access: Alternative Compensation System in EU Law (2017) (in particular, ch. 6, pp. 365–406); and from the same author: *Rethinking Normal Exploitation: Enabling Online Limitations in EU Copyright Law*, AMI - tijdschrift voor auteurs-, media- en informatierecht 2017/6, pp. 197–205.

[98] Pierre Lescure, Mission «Acte II de l'exception culturelle»: Contribution aux politiques culturelles à l'ère numérique 36 (2013).

[99] The Directive in fact proposes the right of quotation as an open concept, permitting an assessment on a case-by-case basis (Art. 5.3 d requires the use to be "in accordance with fair practice, and to the extent required by the specific purpose"). This is very close to a "fair use" condition. In this line, some scholars have actually defended recently the idea that the right of quotation as included in international copyright law is very similar to a "fair use" provision. *See* Chapter 3 by Tanya Aplin & Lionel Bently in this volume.

[100] *See in this sense* Christophe Geiger, *Reconceptualizing the Constitutional Dimension of Intellectual Property: An Update, in* Intellectual Property Law and Human Rights 117 sq (Paul L.C. Torremans ed., 4th ed. 2020).

[101] For example, the French author's right tradition often accommodates itself very well with open concepts. As an example, the extremely subjective criterion of originality is frequently the source of uncertainty, often making it impossible to know in advance if a work will be protected by copyright or not (it is then necessary to wait for the judge to make a decision, often at the end of very long proceedings; *see* on this question Vivant & Bruguière, *supra* note 22, at 260; these authors also ask whether originality is not an "elusive concept," *id.* ¶ 258. Open norms constitute the special feature of any law that claims to be dynamic and adaptable. Continental civil laws are full of it, far beyond the field of copyright, *see* Céline Castets-Renard, Notions à contenu variable et droit d'auteur (2004).

on the matter.[102] The fact that more than forty countries worldwide have adopted open clauses within the copyright arena,[103] and that many of those countries boast flourishing cultural industries, should serve to mitigate concerns and definitively permit a different view concerning open-ended clauses to limit copyright. However, the mere transplant of a US-type fair use provision would admittedly not be ideal, as the copyright systems on the two sides of the Atlantic, despite certain convergences,[104] remain different in scope and spirit.[105] Thus, as has been recently proposed, a more promising way forward – and one that is more compatible with the EU legal system – might be to codify the criteria already used by judges when balancing fundamental rights and copyright law and introduce a European fair use provision based on freedom of expression in the EU *acquis* in addition to the existing list of exceptions.[106]

More fundamentally, it might be necessary to think ahead and carry out a more in-depth review of the mechanism of exclusivity in the context of a derivative creation, even if doing so means considering other options for the remuneration of a work's original authors.[107] This fascinating, albeit complex, issue is beyond the scope of this chapter. Whatever solution is adopted, it must necessarily guarantee that copyright (and, more generally, intellectual property law) cannot under any circumstances be misused for the purpose of censorship, regardless of whether the expression in question has political, cultural, or artistic intent.[108] All in all, one thing appears quite obvious: it can hardly be considered compatible with free artistic creativity in a democratic society to demand that artists seek authorization before creating a new work.

[102] Matthew Sag, *Predicting Fair Use*, 73 Ohio St. L.J. 47 (2012); Barton Beebe, *An Empirical Study of U.S. Copyright Fair Use Opinions*, 1978–2005, 156 U. Pa. L. Rev. 549 (2008); Pamela Samuelson, *Unbundling Fair Uses*, 77 Fordham L. Rev. 2537 (2009).

[103] For the list of these countries and their legislation, *see* Jonathan Band & Jonathan Gerafi, *The Fair Use/Fair Dealing Handbook* (Mar. 2015), http://infojustice.org/wp-content/uploads/2015/03/fair-use-handbook-march-2015.pdf [https://perma.cc/489F-MYUK].

[104] *See* Gillian Davies, *The Convergence of Copyright and Authors' Rights: Reality or Chimera?*, 26 Int'l Rev. Intell. Prop. & Competition L. 964 (1995).

[105] *See* in this sense Paul L. C. Torremans, *The Perspective of the Introduction of a European Fair Use Clause*, *in* Codification of European Copyright Law: Challenges and Perspectives 319 (Tatiana-Eleni Synodinou ed., 2012).

[106] *See* detailed for such a proposal Christophe Geiger & Elena Izyumenko, *Towards a European "Fair Use" Grounded in Freedom of Expression*, 35 Am. U. Int'l L. Rev 1–74 (2019).

[107] *See* on this issue Christophe Geiger, *Les limites au droit d'auteur en faveur de la création dérivée*, *in* Copyright and Freedom of Expression: Proceedings of the ALAI Study Days 338 (2008); Christophe Geiger, *Promoting Creativity through Copyright Limitations, Reflections on the Concept of Exclusivity in Copyright Law*, 12 Vand. J. Ent. & Tech. L. 515 (2010); Christophe Geiger, *Statutory Licenses as Enabler of Creative Uses*, *in* Remuneration of Copyright Owners, Regulatory Challenges of New Business Models 305 (Kung-Chung Liu & Reto M. Hilty eds., 2017). *See* Christophe Geiger, *Freedom of Artistic Creativity and Copyright Law: A Compatible Combination?*, 8 U.C. Irvine L. Rev. 101 (2018) (advocating a "limitation based"-statutory remuneration system for commercial creative uses, administrated by an independent regulation authority which could solve *ex post* disputes between original and derivative creators on the price to be paid for the transformative use via mediation, taking into account the existing and expected revenue streams for the derivative work).

[108] For a reflection in this sense in order to redesign copyright as an access right, *see* Christophe Geiger, *Copyright As an Access Right: Securing Cultural Participation through the Protection of Creators' Interests*, *in* What If We Could Reimagine Copyright? 73 (Rebecca Giblin & Kimberlee Weatherall eds., 2016).

11

Limitations and Exceptions in Copyright Law across the Taiwan Strait

Kung-Chung Liu

1 INTRODUCTION

Copyright, like any form of intellectual property (IP), is subject to exceptions and limitations, and the interpretation and application of which are highly uncertain owing to changing technical and business environments. In addition, provisions on exceptions and limitations are either vague or constantly in flux, particularly in civil law jurisdictions, where frequent revisions by legislatures take place to keep abreast of evolving needs in balancing the interests of copyright owners, copyright industry, users of copyrighted works, and the general public.

Ever since mainland China's opening up, the country has been receptive to legal regimes from Taiwan, particularly in the civil code, IP, and competition law arenas, as the two sides share the same cultural roots and are on different levels of development, which allows passing on experiences to the later comer. Taiwan's experiences with "modernization" are of great reference value to mainland China.[1] Further, the geographical proximity, relatively cheap elements of production, and massive domestic market of mainland China have lured Taiwanese businesses to establish close economic ties with the mainland.[2] Although both sides have been members of the World Trade Organization (WTO) since 2002, neither considers the other a "foreign country," and thus neither brings disputes against the other to the WTO. Therefore, there is a greater than normal need for mainland China and Taiwan to strengthen mutual understanding and cooperation to protect IP and to negotiate the resolution of problems relevant to both. As a result, the Cross-Strait Agreement on Intellectual Property Right Protection and Cooperation, signed by the Strait Exchange Foundation (representing mainland China) and the Association for Relations Across the Taiwan Strait (representing Taiwan), took effect on September 12, 2010. In the years since, a coordination and assistance mechanism for law enforcement, including the enforcement of copyright law, has also been established. The IP offices on both sides of the Strait meet regularly and maintain a working relationship.

Consequently, the copyright regimes of the two jurisdictions have a number of features in common, such as the indefinite protection of moral rights, the nontransferability of moral rights an open-ended approach to fair use, and no collection of levies for it. There are also a number of common issues, such as weak collective management organizations, the lack of cooperation between collective management organizations from both sides, the collection of fees for the

[1] One recent example is that mainland China follows the Taiwan IP Court model to establish its IP courts. For more, *see infra* Section 2.2.

[2] Mainland China has become the biggest export market for Taiwan, overtaking the US, since 2003.

commercial exploitation of copyrighted works produced on the other side of the Strait, and the mutual control of audio-video imports.[3]

Ironically, the 2017 International IP Index of the American Chamber of Commerce,[4] a notorious interest group, places the copyright regimes of both jurisdictions in the same group of relatively low performers. According to the IP Index, Taiwan scores 2.03 out of 6 for the item "Copyrights, Related Rights, and Limitations,"[5] and mainland China scores only slightly and yet surprisingly better 2.28 out of 6.[6]

For the above-mentioned reasons Taiwan and mainland China make a good pair for comparison and contrast. Thus, studying how Taiwan and mainland China fare in dealing with copyright exceptions and limitations and their similarities and differences makes an intriguing area of research. This is what drives the writing of this chapter. The chapter will first make general observations concerning the relevant aspects of the two jurisdictions (Section 2). It will then examine how the two sides deal with copyright exceptions and limitations and set out their similarities and differences (Section 3), explore ways to improve the copyright exception and limitation regime across the Taiwan Strait to ensure universal applicability (Section 4) and conclude by pointing out two topics for further study (Section 5).

2 SOME GENERAL OBSERVATIONS AND CONTRASTS

2.1 *IP Offices*

As in many other jurisdictions, IP offices are undoubtedly in the driver's seat in the development of copyright law on both sides of the Taiwan Strait. Taiwan is home to one centralized IP office, the Taiwan Intellectual Property Office (TIPO), which operates under the Ministry of Economic Affairs and deals with issues concerning patents (invention patents, utility model patents, and design patents), trademarks, copyright, integrated circuit layouts, and trade secrets, albeit excluding plant variety rights. The activism exhibited by TIPO and its technocrats is rivaled by that of their counterparts in mainland China, albeit for different reasons: Taiwan's activism is aimed primarily at alleviating pressure from its dominant ally, the United States, whereas mainland China's is directed at boosting the national innovation-based economy. TIPO regularly initiates IP law revisions, thereby preempting the judiciary's limited efforts to streamline, systemize, and strengthen the IP regime and threatening to destabilize IP statutory law itself. As a

[3] The Taiwan Association for Copyright Protection (TACP) was designated and recognized by mainland China as the authentication organization for Taiwan's audiovisual products to be marketed in mainland China. Movies, videos, and broadcast programs of mainland China have to be approved by the Taiwan Ministry of Culture in advance and in the specified amount before export to Taiwan.

[4] Global Innovation Policy Center, US Chamber of Commerce, *International IP Index: "Infinite Possibilities,"* www.theglobalipcenter.com/ipindex2017-details/?country=tw (last accessed Dec. 12, 2018).

[5] The breakdown of the score is as follows: Copyrights (and related rights) term of protection 0.53; Legal measures that provide necessary exclusive rights that prevent infringement of copyrights and related rights (including Web hosting, streaming, and linking) 0.25; Availability of frameworks that promote cooperative action against online piracy 0.25; Scope of limitations and exceptions to copyrights and related rights 0.50; Digital rights management legislation 0.50; and Clear implementation of policies and guidelines requiring proprietary software used on government ICT systems to be licensed software 0.00.

[6] The breakdown of the score is as the following: Copyrights (and related rights) term of protection 0.53; Legal measures that provide necessary exclusive rights that prevent infringement of copyrights and related rights (including Web hosting, streaming, and linking) 0.25; Availability of frameworks that promote cooperative action against online piracy 0.50; Scope of limitations and exceptions to copyrights and related rights 0.25; Digital rights management legislation 0.25; and Clear implementation of policies and guidelines requiring proprietary software used on government ICT systems to be licensed software 0.50.

consequence, the development of IP law in Taiwan is largely equivalent to "new amendments" to statutory IP law. The virtuous circle between statutory IP law and IP case law has yet to be established.

Mainland China currently lacks a centralized IP office. Instead, it has the State Administration of Press, Publication, Radio, Film and Television (SAPPRFT) in charge of copyright; the State Administration of Industries and Commerce overseeing trademarks; and the State Intellectual Property Office with responsibility for patents. Admittedly, there are not only divergent sectorial interests among the different agencies, but also conflicts of interest within a specific IP agency. For example, SAPPRFT has a number of dominant content providers as its direct subordinate units, including China Central Television, Central People's Radio, the China Film Group Corporation, and People's Publishing House, to name just a few. SAPPRFT is at the same time both regulator (referee for market competition) and market player, as it is tasked with the development of the content industries. Conflicts of interest are inevitable when the interpretation and application of exceptions and limitations affect the status and interests of such state-run/-owned enterprises.

2.2 *Judges, Courts, and IP Courts*

Both Taiwan and mainland China are civil law jurisdictions, with the latter less so. Rather ironically, however, Taiwanese judges, who operate with more judicial independence under the more "advanced and experienced" jurisdiction of the two, seem to exhibit an extreme tendency to "adjudicate strictly in accordance with statutes," turning a blind eye to individual injustices in concrete cases. Unsurprisingly, in a recent poll conducted by a leading Taiwanese business monthly, judges received the lowest confidence score of the tencareers listed.[7] Although the so-called "precedent system"[8] still exists in Taiwan according to Article 57 of the Court Organization Act, despite being scaled back and even frozen in recent years, there has never been any precedent set on the Copyright Act and Copyright Collective Management Organization Act, which to some extent indicates that the Supreme Courts have failed to clarify the ambiguous provisions therein to further develop copyright law.

Taiwan's one and only IP Court was established in 2008. It deals with all IP laws and the Fair Trade Act (which incorporates the laws governing cartels and unfair competition), including civil (first and second instances), criminal (second instance), and administrative cases ("three in one").[9] Judges in Taiwan are not trained to treat IP differently from tangible property, and, unfortunately, IP judges are no exception. The calculation of damages could be the defining

[7] According to a "Survey on Social Trust in Taiwan" conducted in 2016 by the Common Wealth (published in Taiwan in Chinese language), judges rank as the least trustworthy (28.4 percent of the surveyed expressed trust, while 65.4 percent expressed distrust) out of ten careers, followed by reporters, congressmen, government officials, city counselors, business bosses, policemen, low-level civil servants, primary and middle school teachers, and doctors. *See Taiwan Shehui Xinrendu Diaocha Faguan Jizhe Xinrendu Diaochewei* (台灣社會信任度調查 法官、記者信任度吊車尾) *[Survey on Social Trust in Taiwan Lowest Trust in Judges and Journalists]*, CommonWealth Mag. (May 24, 2016), www.cw.com.tw/article/article.action?id=5076475.

[8] The precedent regime works like the *stare decisis* principle in the common law, which allows the Supreme Courts (including the Supreme Court, Supreme Administrative Court, and Public Functionary Disciplinary Sanction Commission) to choose some precedents from the decisions they rendered and bestow upon them legal binding force on all courts until the Supreme Courts decide otherwise. However, the Judicial Yuan, the highest judicial organization, intends to abolish the precedent regime in the draft amendment bill to the Court Organization Act.

[9] Taiwan IP Court has an all-inclusive jurisdiction, which is broader than that of its counterparts in mainland China, Germany (Patentgericht), Japan (IP courts), Korea (Patent Court), and the US (Court of Appeals for the Federal Circuit).

issue. As the Supreme Court clings on to the traditional mind-set and continues to demand detailed proof or at least an explanation of how exactly the IP Court has arrived at the damages awarded, IP Court judges tend to award only small damage amounts in order to avoid their decisions being rescinded, and their performance evaluations and subsequent promotion to the Supreme Court negatively affected.[10] One 2015 study shows that the damages awarded in the majority of cases of copyright infringement range from NT$10,000–50,000[11] (in 44 out of 112 cases), followed by damages of NT$100,000–500,000 (in 42 out of 112 cases).[12] The same study also shows that winning plaintiffs, on average, receive just 37.1% of the damages they claim, with 53.6% of winning plaintiffs receiving just 0–25% of what they claim.[13] Such small damage amounts naturally lead copyright owners to question the usefulness of litigating in Taiwan and to refrain from filing lawsuits with the IP Court.[14]

Judges in mainland China, in contrast, have much greater room to maneuver, as statutes are generally less detailed because the National People's Congress convenes just once a year for approximately eleven days and does not function as an active parliament. Accordingly, mainland judges have to deal with many thorny issues in the absence of law, and the numerous deficiencies in law mean that laws can only "guide" rather than bind judges. The Supreme People's Court (SPC) is a prominent example, as it has issued a number of guidelines on the application of IP laws,[15] and even some "regulations."[16] Moreover, judicial activism on the local government level is also fueled by the fact that most cases,[17] including IP cases, are decided by the provincial courts,

[10] Taiwan adopts a centralized government system. Therefore, judges are appointed and promoted by the Judicial Yuan and follow the hierarchy of government to pursue promotion to higher courts, which pay higher salary.

[11] The exchange rate between the US$ and NT$ is circa 30:1.

[12] Kao Kai-Chun (高愷均), Taiwan Zhihui Caichan Fayuan Sunhai Peichang Panjue Shizheng Yanjiu (臺灣智慧財產法院損害賠償判決實證研究) [Empirical Study on Damage Award of Taiwan Intellectual Property Court] 120 (2015) (unpublished LL.M. thesis, National Taiwan University), http://handle.ncl.edu.tw/11296/ndltd/28154799530012695996.

[13] *Id.* at 121.

[14] The newly filed first-instance civil cases with the IP Court decreased from 899 in 2010 to 664 in 2015 and further down to 628 in 2016. However, the number bounced back to 679 in 2017. *See* http://ipc.judicial.gov.tw/ipr_english/doc/Statistics/10704-2.pdf [broken link]

[15] *See, e.g.*, Zuigao Renmin Fayuan Guanyu Shenli Ginfan Zhuanliquan Jiufen Anjian Yingyong Falu Ruogan Wenti De Jieshi (Er) (最高人民法院关于审理侵犯专利权纠纷案件应用法律若干问题的解释(二)) [Interpretation (II) of the Supreme People's Court on Several Issues concerning the Application of Law in the Trial of Patent Infringement Dispute Cases] (promulgated by the Supreme People's Court, Mar. 21, 2016, effective Apr. 1, 2016) (China); Zuigao Renmin Fayuan Guanyu Shangbiao Fa Xiugai Jueding Shihang Hou Shangbiao Anjian Guanxia He Falu Shiyong Wenti De Jieshi (最高人民法院关于商标法修改决定施行后商标案件管辖和法律适用问题的解释) [Interpretation of the Supreme People's Court on Issues concerning the Jurisdiction over Trademark Cases and Application of Law after the Entry into Force of the Decision on Amending the Trademark Law] (promulgated by the Supreme People's Court, Mar. 25, 2014, effective May 1, 2014) (China).

[16] *See, e.g.*, Zuigao Renmin Fayuan Guanyu Shenli Zhuanli Jiufen Anjian Shiyong Falu Wenti De Ruogan Guiding (2015 Xiuzheng) (最高人民法院关于审理专利纠纷案件适用法律问题的若干规定 (2015修正)) [Several Provisions of the Supreme People's Court on Issues concerning the Application of Law in the Trial of Cases on Patent Disputes (2015 Amendment)] (promulgated by the Supreme People's Court, Jan. 29, 2015, effective Feb. 1, 2015) (China).

[17] The SPC has discretion to decide which cases provincial courts can hear according to the amount of monetary value of the litigation object as threshold. For example, according to the "Notice of the Supreme People's Court on Adjusting the Standards for the Jurisdiction of the Higher People's Courts and Intermediate People's Courts over Civil and Commercial Cases of the First Instance" (May 1, 2015), High People's Courts and Intermediate People's Courts in Beijing, Shanghai, Guangdong, Jiangsu, and Zhejiang can try first instance civil and criminal cases which have a monetary value of up to RMB 500 million and RMB 100 million, respectively. *See* Zuigao Renmin Fayuan Guanyu Diaozheng Gaoji Renmin Fayuan He Zhongji Renmin Fayuan Guanxia Diyishen Minshang Shi Anjian Baozhun De Tongzhi (最高人民法院关于调整高级人民法院和中级人民法院管辖第一审民商事案件标准的通知) [Notice of the Supreme People's Court on Adjusting the Standards for the Jurisdiction of the Higher People's Courts and Intermediate People's Courts over Civil and Commercial Cases of the First Instance] (promulgated by the Supreme People's Court, Apr. 30, 2015, effective May 1, 2015) (China).

namely, the Intermediate Courts and High Courts, and seldom reach the SPC, although the SPC can act as appellate court to review decisions by lower courts when they pass the threshold and even act as the court of first instance in cases likely to exert major impact on the country as a whole.[18] Furthermore, budgets for provincial courts do not come from the central government, but from provincial governments. Hence, provincial courts are dependent on the governments of the provinces in which they are located, which increases the risk of "localism" and even "local protectionism." At the same time, however, judges sitting on the bench of provincial courts do not normally look forward to promotion to the SPC, as living expenses are prohibitively high in Beijing, which bestows upon them a certain degree of autonomy from the SPC.

In mainland China, IP Courts were established in Beijing, Shanghai and Guangzhou in 2014 as intermediate courts for a test period of three years. The three IP Courts have jurisdiction over civil and administrative cases concerning patents, plant variety rights, integrated circuit layouts, technological secrets, computer softwares, administrative appeals against administrative decisions concerning copyright, trademark, and unfair competition, and civil cases concerning the recognition of well-known marks, but are excluded from hearing criminal and cartel law cases.[19] The IP Courts also hear appeals against civil and administrative decisions made by the Local People's Courts in cases concerning copyright, trademark, technology contracts, and unfair competition.[20]

While promoting the establishment of the three IP Courts, the SPC has also designated fifteen provincial courts as specialized courts to deal with cross-regional IP cases. As the three-year test period draws to an end in 2017, the SPC recently announced in its 2017 White Paper on Judicial Protection of IP that "(To establish) Appeal Mechanism for IP Courts" is now one of its judicial reform projects.[21]

3 HOW THE TWO SIDES HAVE DEALT WITH COPYRIGHT EXCEPTIONS AND LIMITATIONS

3.1. *The Current Regimes*

3.1.1 *Taiwan*

A STATUTORY PROVISIONS

Subsection 4, section 4 (Economic Rights) of chapter III (Authors and Copyright) of Taiwan's Copyright Act, entitled "Limitations on Economic Rights," outlines at least eighteen types of

[18] Art. 20 of the Civil Procedure Law in mainland China provides: The Supreme People's Court shall have jurisdiction as the court of first instance over the following civil cases: (1) cases that have major impact on the whole country; and (2) cases that the Supreme People's Court deems it should try. Art. 22 of the Criminal Procedure Law in mainland China provides: The Supreme People's Court shall have jurisdiction as the court of first instance over major criminal cases that pertain to the whole nation. Art. 17 of the Administrative Procedure Law in mainland China provides: The Supreme People's Court shall have jurisdiction as a court of first instance over grave and complicated administrative cases in the whole country.

[19] Zuigao Renmin Fayuan Guanyu Beijing, Shanghai, Guangzhou Zhishi Chanquan Fayuan Anjian Guanxia De Guiding (最高人民法院关于北京、上海、广州知识产权法院案件管辖的规定) [Provisions of the Supreme People's Court on the Jurisdiction of the Intellectual Property Courts of Beijing, Shanghai and Guangzhou over Cases] (promulgated by the Supreme People's Court, Oct. 31, 2014, effective Nov. 3, 2014), art. 1.

[20] *Id.*, art. 6.

[21] *See Zuigaofa Fabu 2017 nian Zhishi Chanquan Sifa Baohu Zhuangkuang Baipishu Zinshou Zhezuoquan Znshuliang Zengzhang Jin Liu Cheng* (最高法发布2017年知识产权司法保护状况白皮书 新收著作权案数量增长近六成) *[The Supreme Court Publishes 2017 White Paper on the Status of Intellectual Property Judicial Protection. The Number of Newly Received Copyright Cases Has Increased by Nearly 60 percent]* Economic Daily (Apr. 19, 2018), www.ce.cn/xwzx/gnsz/gdxw/201804/19/t20180419_28886103.shtml.

limitation on the economic rights of copyright owners: 1. government and judicial use (Articles 44–45); 2. school and preparation of pedagogical text use (Articles 46–47); 3. public cultural institution use (Article 48); 4. archive use (e.g., abstracts appended to academic works; Article 48-1); 5. use in news reporting (Article 49); 6. use of government works (Article 50); 7. personal use (Article 51, including the reproduction of computer programs [Article 59]); 8. quotations (Article 52);[22] 9. use for the visually impaired and learning disabled (Article 53); 10. examination use (Article 54); 11. nonprofit public performances (Article 55); 12. temporary recordings by broadcasting organizations (Article 56); 13. rebroadcasts by community antenna (Article 56-1); 14. the public display of artworks and outdoor display of artistic or architectural works (Articles 57–58); 15. domestic (national) exhaustion of copyright, which allows transfer (Article 59-1) and rental (excluding sound recordings and computer programs) of lawful copies (Article 60); 16. use of commentary on daily events (Article 61); 17. use of public speeches (Article 62); and 18. the translation of works allowed under Articles 44, 45, 48(iii), 48-1 through 50, 52–55, and 61–62; adaptation of works allowed under Articles 46 and 51; and distribution of works allowed under Articles 46–50, 52–54, 57(2), 58, and 61–62 (Article 63). The second last article of subsection 4, namely Article 65, summarizes the above-mentioned limitations as fair use and defines its legal effect, i.e., "Fair use of a work shall not constitute infringement on economic rights in the work (Paragraph 1),[23]" and then lists the four-factor test for determining compliance with Articles 44 through 63 and "other conditions of fair use" (paragraph 2).

Article 65(2) began as a verbatim translation of the four fair use factors under section 107 of the US Copyright Act and was introduced under pressure from the United States in 1993 to guide the interpretation and application of Articles 44–63.[24] It was then revised in 1998 into an open-ended general clause that allows "other conditions of fair use."[25] In addition, subsection 4 is followed by subsection 5, which provides for the compulsory licensing (CL) for domestic use of the sound recording of a musical work (Articles 69–70). Furthermore, since 2010, Article 24 of the Law for the Development of the Cultural and Creative Industries empowers TIPO to grant CL to use "orphan works" upon the payment of compensation.[26]

[22] The Taiwan High Court decided in *2000 Shang-Zi No. 716* (Taiwan High Ct., Apr. 24, 2001) that to include a published newspaper commentary by the other into his own collected essays, though related in their concerns, did not qualify for "quotation" and was illegal reproduction.

[23] Art. 65(1) was added in 1998 based on the simple reasoning: "The legal effect of fair use was negligently not provided for, and Paragraph 1 was added based on the reference to Section 107 of the US Copyright Act." As Shieh Mingyan rightly points out: "Article 44 et al are provisions of limitation, which as the term limitation suggests are beyond the reach of the economic (copy)rights, and no longer belong to the realm of rights of rights holders; once the use of other's works complies with those Articles, it of course does not constitute infringement on economic rights in the work, and has not only the effect of preventing the illegality of the act of use." *See* Shieh Mingyan (謝銘洋), Zhihui Caichanquan Fa (智慧財產權法) 241 (2008).

[24] In adopting the US four-factor test, section 35(2)(e) of the Singapore Copyright Act also adds a fifth factor for the consideration of fair dealing: the possibility of obtaining the work or adaptation within a reasonable time at an ordinary commercial price.

[25] Art. 65(2) provides: In determining whether the exploitation of a work complies with the reasonable scope referred to in the provisions of Arts. 44 through 63, or other conditions of fair use, all circumstances shall be taken into account, and in particular the following facts shall be noted as the basis for determination: 1. The purposes and nature of the exploitation, including whether such exploitation is of a commercial nature or is for nonprofit educational purposes. 2. The nature of the work. 3. The amount and substantiality of the portion exploited in relation to the work as a whole. 4. Effect of the exploitation on the work's current and potential market value. In Asia an increasing number of countries (civil law jurisdiction such as Korea and common law jurisdiction such as Singapore and Malaysia) are adopting an open-ended general fair use clause in their copyright acts.

[26] However, the TIPO provides strict procedural requirements for such use and a uniform fee of NT$5,000 for each use, which leads to no use of orphan works.

The legislation stipulated in subsection 4 is flawed in some respects. (1) It never mentions the three-step test, simply because the technocrats at the TIPO have never acknowledged the three-step test, nor the need to introduce it into the Copyright Act. (2) It fails to make clear the conceptual distinction between free fair use and statutory CL in Article 47, which stipulates the payment of compensation for use of works. And (3) although Article 65(2) functions as a general clause of fair use, many articles of subsection 4 still contain the term "within a reasonable scope" (Articles 44–47 and 50–52) or "necessary" (Articles 44–46, 48, 49, 52, and 59), which seems to suggest a double limitation (or marginalization), as these terms will have to be interpreted again in the context of the general "fair use" clause.

B JUDICIAL PRACTICE

Few court decisions to date have dealt with the provisions of subsection 4. The following are a few of the exceptions.

Reiterated Article 65(2) As an Open-Ended General Fair Use Clause The Taiwanese Supreme Court, in a criminal ruling in 2002, reiterated that Article 65(2) is an open-ended general fair use clause:

> The limitations of economic rights (referred to by the academics as fair use) of the old provisions (amended and publicized on 24 April 1993) were limited only to Articles 44 through 63, and Article 65 was set as an evaluation standard for the applicability of Articles 44 through 63 to exploitations of works in question. However, with the complication of the modes of exploitation, the scope of fair use delineated by Articles 44 to 63 has already become rigid, unable to cope with practical needs. In order to expand the scope of fair use, the new provisions (amended and publicized on 21 January 1998) have revised this Article into a general clause, so that exploitations that do not satisfy Articles 44 to 63, yet are *similar to or of minor nature* compared to the situations prescribed in Articles 44 to 63, and reasonable measured by the standards of this Article, can still constitute fair use.[27]

Exemption Provision Is Different from Fair Use In a 2014 civil case, the Supreme Court made a conceptual distinction between exemption and fair use without fully explaining its reasons for doing so:

> Exemption provision is different from fair use. Exemption provision sets limit to the category of works and the kinds of exclusive rights, and courts can exempt conduct that satisfies the legal requirements, without having to take into consideration other factors used for evaluating fair use. Article 49[28] is an exemption provision, which allows newspapers and networks to exploit works that are seen or heard in the course of the report within the scope necessary to the report, does not provide "within a reasonable scope," and excludes illegality; consequently, courts do not need to take into consideration factors contained in Article 65(2).[29]

Following the logic of this decision, it seems that the articles in subsection 4 that contain "within a reasonable scope" constitute a fair use clause, and thus need to take into consideration the factors in Article 65(2) when applied, whereas those that do not contain that wording constitute an exemption clause, and thus do not need to take those factors into account when

[27] 2002 Tai-Shang-Zi No. 837 (Taiwan Sup. Ct., Feb. 7, 2002). Emphasis added.

[28] Art. 49 provides: "When reporting current events by means of broadcasting, photography, film, newspaper, network, or otherwise, works that are seen or heard in the course of the report may be exploited within the scope necessary to the report."

[29] 2014 Tai-Shang-Zi No. 1352 (Taiwan Sup. Ct., July 3, 2014).

applied. Presumably, this approach is meant to avoid the aforementioned double-marginalization problem (i.e., "necessary" to be further interpreted by "fair use").

Taking Other Factors Such As Transformative Use into Consideration In addition to the four factors listed in Article 65(2), Taiwanese courts have also taken a number of other factors, such as transformative use,[30] into account by adopting the negative formulation that the disputed use was "substitutive" rather than "transformative" in nature, and therefore not fair use. Consequently, transformative use has a greater chance of being recognized as fair use than substitutive use.

Fair Use Can Be for Profit or Not Educational In a 2005 criminal case decision the Supreme Court resorted to Article 1 of the Copyright Act[31] to argue that fair use can be for profit or not educational:

> in deciding the first factor of Article 65(2), namely "the purposes and nature of the exploitation, including whether such exploitation is of a commercial nature or is for nonprofit educational purposes," it is appropriate to interpret the purpose of use from the raison d'être of the Act foreseen from Article 1, rather than adopting a simple dichotomy of either commercial or non-commercial (or educational[32]). In other words, if the purpose and nature of use of the user is conducive to the balance of public interest of the society or to the development of national culture, such use is to be viewed positively, even if its purpose is not educational.[33]

Copy Shops Copying for a Fair User Are Not Infringing Copyright In its capacity as the second instance court, Taiwan IP Court ruled in *2010 Xing-Zhi-Shan-Yi-Zi 61* (decided on September 27, 2010) that a copy shop which makes copies for customers who have commissioned it to do so within the scope of fair use is not committing copyright infringement, and thus acquitted the copy shop in question of criminal responsibility.

C OVERALL ASSESSMENT

Copyright law in Taiwan is dominated by and has been distorted by the rampant number of criminal cases brought by right holders, a situation caused by the lack of discovery process in civil procedures and the stringent criminal rule of three years' imprisonment for any and all copyright infringement. The ratio of criminal to civil cases in the copyright arena is disproportionately high. In June 2016 alone, prosecutors brought 361 charges against individuals suspected of copyright infringement (a total of 1,749 such charges from January to June of that year). Fair use principle does not really work to the benefit of the users, because, once warned of the possibility of criminal charges, the accused tend to settle hurriedly and even overpay the rights holders. What also makes one worry is that when Taiwanese courts applied fair use principle to criminal cases, it is unclear whether it is a legitimate interpretation of the copyright regime per se or rather a manipulation to avoid the harsh criminal punishment, which weakens its convincing power and even legitimacy.

30 2009 Min-Zhu-Shan-Zi No. 5 (Taiwan High Ct., May 27, 2009); 2009 Min-Zhu-Shan-Yi-Zi No. 3 (Taiwan High Ct., May 27, 2009); and 2011 Min-Zhu-Su-Zi No. 55 (Taiwan IP Ct., Sept. 26, 2012).

31 Art. 1 provides: "This Act is specifically enacted for the purposes of protecting the rights and interests of authors with respect to their works, balancing different interests for the common good of society, and promoting the development of national culture. Matters not provided for herein shall be governed by the provisions of other acts."

32 Shieh Mingyan is of the same opinion. *See supra* note 23, at 243.

33 2005 Tai-Shang-Zi No. 7127 (Taiwan Sup. Ct., Dec. 16, 2005).

3.1.2 *Mainland China*

A STATUTORY PROVISIONS ON "LIMITATIONS ON RIGHTS"

Section 4 of chapter II (Copyright) of mainland China's Copyright Act is entitled "Limitations on Rights" and allows twelve types of copyright limitations (in Article 22), as well as statutory licensing (Article 23) in the case of textbooks for the nine-year compulsory education and national education programs. In addition, there are also four statutory licensing provisions in chapter IV (Publication, Performance, Recording, and Broadcast): the republication of published works by other newspapers (Article 33(2)[34]), reproduction of recorded musical works (Article 40(3)), broadcast of published works, and broadcast of published recordings (Articles 43(2) and 44).

B PROVISIONS ON THE "LIMIT" TO IMPOSE "LIMITATIONS ON RIGHTS": FROM TWO-STEP TO THREE-STEP TEST

Article 21 of the Implementation Rules on the Copyright Act adopts the two steps (or prongs) of the international norm on the limit to impose "limitation on rights" of the three-step test,[35] namely (fair) use does not conflict with a normal exploitation of the work and does not unreasonably prejudice the legitimate interests of the author. However, it is noteworthy that the SPC unexpectedly adopts the entire three-step test and combines it with the four-factor test in paragraph 8 of "Opinions of the Supreme People's Court on Issues concerning Maximizing the Role of Intellectual Property Right Trials in Boosting the Great Development and Great Prosperity of Socialist Culture and Promoting the Independent and Coordinated Development of Economy":

> Under *the special circumstances of actual necessity to facilitate technological innovation and commercial development*, and after taking into consideration the purposes and nature of the exploitation, the nature of the used work, the amount and substantiality of the portion used from the work and the effect of the exploitation on the work's potential market or value, if the use of work does not conflict with a normal exploitation of the work and does not unreasonably prejudice the legitimate interests of the author, then it can be recognized as fair use.[36]

Since the first step, namely "in certain special cases," has not been defined by the Berne Convention and TRIPS Agreement, then according to point 3 of the Declaration, "A Balanced Interpretation of the 'Three-Step' Test in Copyright Law," advocated by the German Max

[34] Art. 33 (2) of the Chinese Copyright Act provides: "Except where the copyright owner has declared that reprinting or excerpting is not permitted, other newspaper or periodical publishers may, after the publication of the work by a newspaper or periodical, reprint the work or print an abstract of it or print it as reference material, but such other publishers shall pay remuneration to the copyright owner as prescribed in regulations. In (2016) Min-Zai-Zi No. 86 decision (June 28, 2016), the SPC reiterates: "Statutory license according to Article 33 of the Copyright Act is premised on the conditions that the copyright holder has submitted his work to a newspaper or journal, and the latter has published the work."

[35] The three-step test was first established by Art. 9(2) of the Berne Convention for the Protection of Literary and Artistic Works (Berne Convention) in 1967 to restrict the reproduction right of the author: "It shall be a matter for legislation in the countries of the Union to permit the reproduction of such works *in certain special cases*, provided that such reproduction *does not conflict with a normal exploitation of the work* and *does not unreasonably prejudice the legitimate interests of the author*." (Emphases added.) The test is later adopted by Arts. 13 (copyright), 26 (industrial design) and 30 (patent) of the TRIPS Agreement.

[36] Zuigao Renmin Fayuan Guanyu Chongfen Fahui Zhishi Chanquan Shenpan Zhineng Zuoyong Tuidong Shehui Zhuyi Wenhua Da Fazhan Da Fanrong He Cujin Jingji Zizhu Xiediao Fazhan Ruogan Wenti De Yijian (最高人民法院关于充分发挥知识产权审判职能作用推动社会主义文化大发展大繁荣和促进经济自主协调发展若干问题的意见) [Opinions of the Supreme People's Court on Issues concerning Maximizing the Role of Intellectual Property Right Trials in Boosting the Great Development and Great Prosperity of Socialist Culture and Promoting the Independent and Coordinated Development of Economy] (promulgated by the Supreme People's Court, Dec. 16, 2011, effective Dec. 16, 2011) (China). Emphasis added.

Planck Institute (MPI) for Innovation and Competition and endorsed by many eminent IP scholars from around the world,[37] "the three-step test's restriction of limitations and exceptions to exclusive rights to certain special cases does not prevent legislatures from introducing open ended limitations and exceptions, so long as the scope of such limitations and exceptions is reasonably foreseeable." Consequently, it is perfectly legitimate for the SPC to phrase the first step as "under *the special circumstances of actual necessity to facilitate technological innovation and commercial development*."

B JUDICIAL PRACTICE

This section focuses more on examining the decisions of mainland China's IP Courts and the SPC, as they are leading either in IP expertise or legal hierarchy.[38]

THE SPC

Further Use for Profit-Making Purposes Can Still Be Fair Use In 2002, the SPC issued"Interpretations on the Application of Law in Copyright Civil Dispute Cases," which briefly touches upon fair use. Article 18 of the Interpretations interprets Article 22(1)(x) of the Copyright Act (copying, drawing, photographing or video recording of an artistic work located or displayed in an outdoor public place) as follows:

> (1) Artistic works in outdoor public place as Article 22(1)(x), Copyright Act provides mean statutes, paintings, calligraphies etc. located and displayed in outdoor place for social activities of the public. (2) The person who conducted the copying, drawing, photographing or video recording of the above-mentioned artistic work may further exploit his results by reasonable means and within reasonable scope, without constituting infringement.

Paragraph 8 of the 2011 "Opinions of the Supreme People's Court on Issues concerning Maximizing the Role of Intellectual Property Right Trials in Boosting the Great Development and Great Prosperity of Socialist Culture and Promoting the Independent and Coordinated Development of Economy" by the SPC further clarifies that the further exploitation by reasonable means and within reasonable scope can be recognized as fair use, irrespective whether it is for commercial purposes.[39]

Government Agencies Bear a Greater Duty of Care in Supplying Authors' Names on Publicly Displayed Work In *2013 Min-Ti-Zi 15* (December 24, 2014), there was controversy over whether the defendant, i.e., the Water Resources Bureau of Shaoxing City, was right to rely on the indication of the author's name on the displayed outdoor artistic work in question or whether it bore an obligation to investigate whether that work derived from the work of another author and, if so, whether it should have given the latter's name in the tourism booklets it

[37] Declaration, Christophe Geiger et al., A Balanced Interpretation of the "Three-Step Test" in Copyright Law, www.ip.mpg.de/fileadmin/ipmpg/content/forschung_aktuell/01_balanced/declaration_three_step_test_final_english1.pdf (last accessed Dec. 12, 2018).

[38] For other court decisions on fair use, *see* Yu Yu (于玉), Zhezuoquan Heli Shiyong Zhidu: Yanjiu Yingdui Shuzi Wangluo Huanjing Tiaozhan (著作权合理使用制度研究: 应对数字网络环境挑战) 255–88 (2012).

[39] In an appeal-rejecting ruling (2013 Min-Shen-Zi No. 2091) the SPC reiterated the same opinion. However, in a decision handed down on January 27, 2015 (2014 Shen-Zhong-Fa-Zhi-Min-Zhong-Zi No. 827) the Shenzhen Intermediate People's Court stated without any further elaboration that fair use, as stipulated in Art. 22 of the Copyright Act, is for nonprofit educational purposes only. In other words, the court took the categorical stance that any use that is for-profit in nature is not fair use. Shenzhen is considered by many as the most innovative city in mainland China, and many important IP cases are litigated there, such as the well-known *Huawei v. InterDigital* case in 2013. Therefore, decisions rendered there deserve special attention.

published to satisfy the fair use requirement of "mentioning the name of the author and the title of the work." In its ruling concerning the controversy, which was widely reported by the local news media, the SPC held that the Bureau should have been aware of the identity of Mr. Wang Jushian. Further, given that the Bureau was the construction and management unit of the Luhuyuan Scenic Area, it was charged with providing a comprehensive introduction to the area through the tourism booklets it published, including the names of all authors of works therein. In sum, the SPC ruled that government bureaus are different from the general public, and thus bear a much heavier duty of care in providing accurate authors' names for publicly displayed works.

IP COURTS AND OTHER COURTS

Confirming the Openness of Article 22 of the Copyright Act It could be argued whether Article 22 of mainland China's Copyright Act is a closed or open-ended clause. However, courts tend to take the latter view. The trend started with a 2008 decision by the Chao Yang District People's Court of Beijing,[40] which was selected and published in the Gazette of the SPC, signaling some recognition by the SPC.[41] Then the Beijing First Intermediate Court in *Beijing Sogou Information Service Co., Ltd. v. Wenhui Cong* (*2013 Yi Zhong Min Zhong Zi No. 12533*), affirms that it is legally permissible to recognize a fair use of a copyrighted work even though such use falls outside the ambit of Article 22.[42] The Beijing People's High Court further emphasizes in its *2013 Gao Min Zhong Zi No. 1211* decision that establishing fair use outside statutory enumeration calls for thorough investigation into the complex body of relevant factors and that the user bears the burden of proof with respect to those factors.[43]

Conflicting Views on the "Appropriate Quotation" Fair Use China's IP Courts have divergent views on "appropriate quotation" fair use (Article 22(1)(ii)).[44] For instance, the Shanghai IP Court in *2015 Hu-Zhi-Min-Zhong-Zi* 730 (decided on April 25, 2016) developed a US four-factor test and adopted the transformative use concept: in applying the three-step test, courts are to make an overall consideration of the purpose of the cited work's use, the percentage of the new work that the cited work accounts for, whether the normal exploitation of the rights holders has been affected, and whether unreasonable harm has been inflicted upon the rights holders. The court stated:

> Quotation for the purpose of explaining some issue means that quotation of work is to explain other issues and not to solely display the artistic value of the quoted work while the original artistic value and function of the quoted work has transformed in the new work[45]; the quotation

[40] (2008) Chao-Min-Chu-Zi 13556, *cited in* Wu Weiguang (吴伟光), Zhezuoquan Fa Yanjiu: Guoji Tiaoyue, Zhongguo Lifa Yu Sifa Shijian (著作权法研究: 国际条约、中国立法与司法实践) 394 (2013).

[41] Li Chen (李琛), Zhezuoquan Jiben Lilun Pipan (著作权基本理论批判) 198 (2013).

[42] For detailed discussion of the decision, *see* Haochen Sun & Jonny Xuyang Han, *Requirements for Recognizing a New Type of Fair Use under Chinese Copyright Law*, *in* Leading Copyright Cases in Major Asian Jurisdictions (Kung-Chung Liu ed., 2019).

[43] For more discussion of the decision, *see* Sampsung Xiaoxiang Shi & Qian Wang, *China's Fair Use Doctrine after the Google Book Search Project*, *in id*. Academic opinions on the issue diverge. Liu Chuntian et al. take a negative view based on the strict interpretation of the three-step test. *See* Liu Chuntian (刘春田) et al., Zhishi Chanquan Fa (知识产权法) 115 (2009). Li Chen also takes a negative view on the ground that Art. 22 of the Copyright Act adopts the close-ended approach. *See* Li, *supra* note 41, at 198. However, Weiguang Wu takes a positive stance based on the implied exceptions recognized by the Berne Convention and the complicated situations that justify fair use etc. *See* Wu, *supra* note 40, at 393.

[44] Art. 22(1)(ii) provides: appropriate quotation from a published work in one's own work for the purposes of introduction to, or comments on, a work, or demonstration of a point.

[45] The decision, however, seems to misunderstand the concept of transformative use, which sees value in the new work that it transforms, rather than dead-copying the original work into something different and/or new.

in the new work is not limited to the extent of where it is necessary, and even if the quotation in the new work is not necessary, it can nevertheless constitute fair use.

The Beijing IP Court, in contrast, determined in *Jing-Zhi-Min-Zhong-Zi* 98 (decided on January 19, 2015) that the defendant's use of the plaintiff s ten photos was not necessary for the introduction of or comments on those ten photos or for explaining certain issues pertaining to them, but rather was intended to enhance the attractiveness of the defendant's own work (a discussion of the health of infants and pregnant women), and therefore did not constitute a fair use. The Guangzhou IP Court came to the same conclusion in *2015 Yue-Zhi-Fa-Zu-Min-Zhong-Zi 108* (decided on May 9, 2015). Finally, in *2016 Jing-Min-Zhong* 53 (decided on March 31, 2016), the Beijing IP Court expressed the same narrow reading of the "appropriate quotation" fair use:

> The purpose of "quotation" should be limited to "introduction to, or comments on, a work, or demonstration of a point", rather than simply showing to readers the quoted works as such, which would lead to competition between the new work and the original work.

Views on the News Reporting Fair Use In *2015 Jing-Zhi-Min-Zhong-Zi 1699* (December 29, 2015), the Beijing IP Court determined that a report entitled "AIDS-infected Boy from Sichuan Provence Went to Shanxi Province for Schooling after Being Expelled by Villagers" published by the *Beijing News* (in Chinese) was licensed to the plaintiff and that the defendant had uploaded it to its own "value-added service," namely, China Mobile Phone News – Morning and Evening News, without permission. It further held that because the report was not an objective work appearing at the time the reported event occurred, its use by the defendant did not constitute the use of a work by another during the reporting of an event, and therefore did not constitute the fair use stipulated in Article 22(1)(iii) of the Copyright Act.[46]

In *2017 Yue-Min-Zhong 12* (decided on March 21, 2017) the Guangzhou IP Court took a narrow view of the "news reporting" fair use and applied the three-step test to interpret such use: "fair use constitutes a limitation of and exception to the exclusive right of copyright holders, and is premised on the conditions that it be allowed only in special circumstances, does not conflict with the normal use of the work, and does not unreasonably prejudice the legitimate interests of the right holder." The court concluded that the plaintiff had acquired the work at issue through the payment of a fee, whereas the defendant had exploited the work on its commercial website without a license from the right holder, thereby exceeding the boundary of fair use and infringing upon the plaintiffs legitimate interests.

C OVERALL ASSESSMENT

Copyright fair use regime in mainland China is rather complete and in line with international treaties. Judging from the content of the few decisions by the three IP Courts, it is fair to say that specialized IP judges' understanding of fair use is in a nascent stage, as their reasoning why a particularly use is or is not recognized as fair use was scarce or even nonexistent. The SPC has done far more quasi-legislation than actual adjudication. The quasi-legislation by the SPC has been largely persuasive and conforming to the international mainstream.

46 Art. 22(1)(iii) provides: unavoidable inclusion or quotation of a published work in the media, such as in a newspaper, periodical and radio and television program, for the purpose of reporting current events. Admittedly, the reasoning of this decision is rather hard to understand.

3.2 Copyright Amendment Proposals

3.2.1 Taiwan

For the first time in at least three decades, TIPO, on its own initiative rather than under US pressure, began revising Taiwan's Copyright Act in 2010. However, the resulting deliberations dragged on until 2016 due to the status quo thinking and the inability of technocrats to reconcile divergent interests of civil society.[47] On November 20, 2017, the Executive Yuan (Cabinet) resolved a Copyright Act Amendment Bill. With regard to copyright limitations, the draft is of the opinion that the current individually listed items of fair use can no longer cope with the needs of the Internet and digital era. Therefore, in addition to revising the current items, the draft recognizes two additional fair use items: distance learning and digital archiving by the National Library. Moreover, it also deals with the double-marginalization problem by deleting "within a reasonable scope" from the other articles of subsection 4, thereby rendering it unnecessary to apply Article 65(2) to interpret those articles.[48]

However, the draft does not include the many court opinions cited in section 3.1.1, such as the transformative nature of the use, and adopts a rather liberal approach of rejecting the simple dichotomy of commercial or noncommercial (or educational or noneducational). Given the comprehensive nature of the draft, it will likely take years to pass it, although the ruling party control two-thirds of the seat in the parliament.

3.2.2 Mainland China

In an unprecedented fashion, SAPPRFT's predecessor, the National Copyright Administration (NCA), in 2011 commissioned three eminent IP institutions to draft a comprehensive copyright law amendment proposal separately.[49] The NCA submitted its fourth draft to the State Council in 2014, along with 1,500 pages of collected opinions. In June 2014 the Legislative Affairs Office of the State Council then invited public comments on the draft within one month. No progress has been achieved since.

Article 43 of the draft essentially leaves the current Article 22 intact, but added (1) an open-ended, and even sweeping, clause for fair use to paragraph 1: (xiii) Other Circumstances; and (2) a new paragraph 2 to codify the three-step test. A rather new development is the new provisions, rather than being put under Article 43, on the use by the legal licensee of computer programs for the purpose of (1) installing onto computer hardware, making a backup copy, making the necessary changes of the program to fit the actual working environment or to fulfill the program's function (Article 44); (2) studying the design concept and principle of the program (Article 45); and (3) acquiring the necessary compatibility information (Article 46).

[47] In August 2016, the Executive Yuan decided on a partial amendment to the Copyright Act to help Taiwan's bid for the second round negotiation of the Trans Pacific Partnership (TPP) Agreement, which foresees 1. Subjecting acts circumventing technological protection measures to criminal penalties. 2. Indicting certain contraventions, which are liable for criminal penalties without a complaint. 3. Introducing protection of encrypted program-carrying satellite and cable signals. Worth pointing out is the fact that the Executive Yuan did not extend the term of protection for copyright to seventy years after the death of the author of the work. However, with the US abandoning the TPP in 2017, the TPP was transformed into Comprehensive and Progressive for TPP (CPTPP; the eleven members signed the CPTPP on March 8, 2018, which will enter into force sixty days after at least six of the signatories have notified the Depositary (NZ) of the completion of ratification procedures), which suspends most of the IP clauses of TPP. The amendment bill was dropped and instead the Executive Yuan resolved a Copyright Act Amendment Bill in 2017.

[48] Intellectual Property Office, R.O.C., www.tipo.gov.tw (last accessed Dec. 12, 2018).

[49] IP School of Renmin University, Institute of Legal Study of the Chinese Academy of Social Sciences, and Zhongnan University of Economics and Law.

The divergent interests of the budding civil society in mainland China and the conflicting sectorial interests within various government agencies can arguably be the major stumbling blocks for the enactment of the draft. It is understood that passing the draft is not high on the agenda of the National People's Congress.

3.3 *Comparison*

For twenty-five years, Taiwan's Copyright Act has imported the US four-factor test to judge open-ended fair use, which is complemented by twenty-two articles on specific instances of fair use. However, judges, even specialized IP judges, show a general tendency to interpret these provisions narrowly, as they are exceptions to the copyright protection and exceptions need to be interpreted narrowly. That leads to infrequent use of the fair use regime and only a small number of court decisions, making fair use not a workable balancing mechanism and copyright law unpopular among the public. Equally worrying is that copyright law development in Taiwan is very much distorted by prevalent criminal sanctions, evidenced by the fact that two of the only three Supreme Court decisions cited and discussed above are criminal. The Copyright Act Amendment Bill seems to be complacent and foresees little substantial change. The Copyright Act never mentions or intends to incorporate the three-step test.

In contrast, mainland China's Copyright Law from its enactment in 1990 (effective since 1991) contains Article 22, basically untouched by the two amendments, which shows it is more home-grown than the result of foreign pressure. In addition, judges in China are not only less bound by the civil law doctrinal disciplines, but are even required by the SPC to "insist on active judiciary."[50] The SPC itself is active in expressing many opinions on fair use, not via decisions but through issued opinions and interpretations, including the introduction of the general three-step test and the specific four-factor test. Therefore, it is expected that mainland China would more likely develop a workable fair use regime that suits the local needs through the judiciary than Taiwan. More importantly, Articles 44–46 of the Copyright Law amendment draft show its ability to reflect on and accommodate the actual needs of technological development in mainland China. If passed, the tide might change for Taiwan to learn from mainland China.

4 MOVING FORWARD: FIXING FAIR USE

As stipulated in the Agreed Statement to the WIPO Copyright Treaty (WCT), the WCT permits countries "to carry forward and appropriately extend into the digital environment limitations and exceptions in their national laws which have been considered acceptable under the Berne Convention," and to "devise new exceptions and limitations that are appropriate in the digital network environment." In the WIPO Performances and Phonograms Treaty (WPPT), too, the limitations on or exceptions to the exclusive rights granted to phonogram performers and producers are extended to the digital environment. Therefore, this chapter offers suggestions on how the mainland Chinese and Taiwanese copyright fair use regimes can be improved to accommodate the digital environment.

[50] *See* Opinions of the Supreme People's Court, *supra* note 36.

4.1 Optimizing Individual Fair Use Clauses

4.1.1 Avoiding Double Marginalization

Individual fair use clauses need to be clear-cut, easy to apply, and not subject to yet another general fair use clause. Consequently, in Taiwan, the terms "within a reasonable scope," contained in Articles 44–47 and 50–52, and "necessary," contained in Articles 44–46 and 48, 49, 52, and 59, of the Taiwanese Copyright Act should be deleted. In mainland China, the terms "appropriate," "a small quantity of copies," and "within proper scope" contained in Article 22(I)(ii)(v)(vii) of the Copyright Act should also be done away with.

4.1.2 Recognizing New Forms of Fair Use That Are Appropriate in the Digital Network Environment

The features of the digital network environment include at least the ubiquitous use of software, the compelling need to study the design concepts and principles of dominant software, and the indispensability of being compatible and inter-connectable (Internet and Internet of things etc.). Articles 43–46 of China's Copyright Law amendment draft are a timely addition to the pool of fair use and worth adopting.[51] Moreover, the digital network environment makes the borrowing of other's content and the sharing of one's own content a daily fact, therefore there needs to be a special fair use clause for so-called user generated content (UGC).[52]

4.2 Softening the Three-Step Test with the Proportionality Principle

The three-step test, one of the general principles for the limitation and exceptions to copyright, industrial design and patent, can be rather strangling in practice, as the cumulative reading of the three factors can unnecessarily narrow the scope of limitations. To mitigate, the MPI's 2008 "A Balanced Interpretation of the 'Three-step Test'" Declaration advocates an interpretation of the test to ensure a proper, balanced application of limitations and exceptions;[53] further, the 2010 "Proposals for Amendment of TRIPS" by leading IP institutions in Europe suggest clarifying copyright limitations by replacing the abstract three-step test with a number of concrete mandatory limitations.[54] This chapter shares the same view and is promoting the idea of returning IP law to the normal legal network also in the fair use context by using the widely accepted *proportionality principle (in balancing copyrights and their exceptions and limitations)* to summarize or even replace the three-step test to avoid the accumulative and therefore misleading reading of it which leaves little room for "fair use."

[51] For similar opinion, *see* Wu Handong (吴汉东), Zhezuoquan Heli Shiyong Zhidu Yanjiu (著作权合理使用制度研究) 293 (3d ed. 2013).

[52] Section 29.21 (1) of the Canadian Copyright Act provides exception for creative use: It is not an infringement of copyright for an individual to use an existing work or other subject-matter or copy of one, which has been published or otherwise made available to the public, in the creation of a new work or other subject-matter in which copyright subsists and for the individual – or, with the individual's authorization, a member of their household – to use the new work or other subject-matter or to authorize an intermediary to disseminate it for noncommercial purposes.

[53] However, the leading Chinese IP scholar Wang Qian finds no difficulty in following the rigid three-step test. *See* Wang Qian (王迁), Zhezuoquan Fa (著作权法) 321 (2015).

[54] In 2001 the University of Stockholm launched the "Intellectual Property in Transition" project in cooperation with the Institute for Civil Law at the University of Copenhagen, IPR University Center in Helsinki, and Max Planck Institute (MPI) for Innovation and Competition in Munich, which led to the proposals. *See* Intellectual Property Rights in a Fair World Trade System: Proposals for Reform of TRIPS (Annette Kur ed., 2011).

4.3 No Contracting-Out Exceptions and Limitations

The copyright universe is increasingly constructed by private contracts, most of them standardized and adhesive. If exceptions and limitations can also be contracted out, such as agreements that prohibit reverse engineering,[55] then many public policy considerations will be hollowed out. Copyright law needs to prevent that from happening, as the total privatization of copyright law would mean an escape into contract law to circumvent control and oversight. Public policy considerations are nonnegotiable and must prevail.

5 CONCLUSION

Looking forward, two research topics are worth further exploration, not just by two sides of the Taiwan Strait, but perhaps the world over. First, the fairness of "fair use." Oftentimes the traditional rationale for free fair use is premised on the unspoken understanding that to ask for license and charge royalty for this kind of use was simply impractical; for example, to charge private personal use is practically impossible. However, in the Internet world, this impossibility has been overcome to certain degree as every use of work on the Internet is recorded and every user is paying for such use, directly or indirectly. Continuous blanket free use based on fair use could seem unfair. Some "fared use" mechanisms must be found to better remunerate the copyright owners.[56]

Second, the exercise of the essential copyright could, like the exercise of the essential patent, constrain market competition. Although both sides of the Taiwan Strait have put in place a mechanism to deal with this issue in their respective competition law,[57] what is lacking is a copyright law internal mechanism to regulate the refusal of a copyright owner to grant licenses on reasonable terms and the necessary adjustment of the anti-competitive license conditions. In this regard, section 144 of the Copyright, Designs and Patents Act 1988, UK, offers a good reference point for future study: relevant public authorities can "cancel or modify license conditions and, instead or in addition, grant compulsory license in respect of the copyright."[58]

[55] For more detailed discussion, *see* Wu, *supra* note 40, at 382–88.

[56] *See generally* Kung-Chung Liu, *Individual Licensing Models and the Role on Internet Platform Providers, in* Remuneration of Copyright Owners – Regulatory Challenges of Business Models 227 (Kung-Chung Liu & Reto Hilty eds., 2017).

[57] Art. 45 of Taiwan's Fair Trade Act provides a vague solution: No provision of this Act shall apply to any proper conduct in connection with the exercise of rights pursuant to the provisions of the Copyright Act, Trademark Act, or Patent Act. In contrast, Art. 55 of China's Antimonopoly Act provides a more concrete solution: This Law does not govern the conduct of business operators to exercise their intellectual property rights under laws and relevant administrative regulations on intellectual property rights; however, business operators' conduct to eliminate or restrict market competition by abusing their intellectual property rights shall be governed by this Law.

[58] Copyright, Designs and Patents Act, 1988, c. 48, § 144 (Eng.)
("Powers exercisable in consequence of report of Competition and Markets Authority.
Subsection (1A) applies where whatever needs to be remedied, mitigated or prevented by the Secretary of State or (as the case may be) the Competition and Markets Authority ... consists of or includes – (a) conditions in licences granted by the owner of copyright in a work restricting the use of the work by the licensee or the right of the copyright owner to grant other licences; or (b) a refusal of a copyright owner to grant licences on reasonable terms.
(1A) The powers conferred by Schedule 8 to the Enterprise Act 2002 include "power to cancel or modify those conditions and, instead or in addition, to provide that licences in respect of the copyright shall be available as of right.").

12

A General Clause on Copyright Limitations in Civil Law Countries: Recent Discussion on Japanese-Style Fair Use Clause

Tatsuhiro Ueno

1 INTRODUCTION

The 1970 Japanese Copyright Act (JCA)[1] basically adheres to the *droit d'auteur* system.[2] In common with the practice in most civil law countries, it contains a detailed catalogue of specific provisions on the limitations on and exceptions to copyright[3] rather than a general or open-ended clause covering such limitations/exceptions. Over the years, the detailed list of enumerated provisions in the JCA has frequently been revised to adapt to technological development and social change. In fact, a large number of specific copyright limitation provisions were introduced in the 2009 and 2012 JCA,[4] which include specific provisions for web search engines (Article 47*sexies*[5]), Internet auctions (Article 47*bis*), text and data mining for commercial or noncommercial purposes (Article 47*septies*[6]), and experimental exploitations for the purpose of developing technology (Article 30*quater*[7]). There is no doubt that specific provisions on copyright limitations, and their continual revision, will remain indispensable to copyright law in Japan.

However, the question we must ask is whether this approach is sufficient to meet the needs of the real world and to resolve the various issues likely to arise in the future. In my eyes, enumerated provisions are often too detailed and rigid to respond flexibly to technological development and social change. What is needed is thus some kind of general or open clause on copyright limitations. The purpose of this chapter is to present the recent discussion in Japan concerning the possibility of introducing more flexible provisions or a general clause or general provision on copyright limitations that would be appropriate for civil law countries.

1 Translations of the JCA are available at www.cric.or.jp/english/clj/ and www.japaneselawtranslation.go.jp/law/detail/?id=1980&vm=2&re=&new=1.

2 For an outline in English of the JCA and major cases, *see* Tatsuhiro Ueno, ch. 22 (Japan), *in* COPYRIGHT THROUGHOUT THE WORLD (Silke von Lewinski ed., loose-leaf updated 2019); Teruo Doi & Tatsuhiro Ueno, ch. (Japan), *in* INTERNATIONAL COPYRIGHT LAW AND PRACTICE (Lionel Bently ed., loose-leaf updated 2019); JAPANESE COPYRIGHT LAW: WRITINGS IN HONOUR OF GERHARD SCHRICKER (Peter Ganea, Christopher Heath & Hiroshi Saito eds., 2005).

3 In this chapter, I use the term "limitations" to refer to both limitations on and exceptions to rights.

4 Regarding the 2009 amendment, *see* Copyright Division, Commissioner's Secretariat, Agency for Cultural Affairs, Explanation of the revision of the copyright act in 2009, 03/2010 Journal of the Japanese Group of AIPPI 81.

5 Art. 47*sexies* was amended by the 2018 amendment and became Art. 47*quinquies*(1)(i) as a result of the enactment on January 1, 2019.

6 Art. 47*septies* was amended by the 2018 amendment and became Art.30*quater*(ii) as a result of the enactment on January 1, 2019.

7 Art.30*quater* was amended by the 2018 amendment and became Art.30*quater*(i) as a result of the enactment on January 1, 2019.

2 GENERAL CLAUSE ON COPYRIGHT LIMITATIONS

A *Fair Use or Fair Dealing Clause in Common Law Countries*

As is well known, many common law countries have a general or open clause on copyright limitations. US-style fair use provisions can be seen in some of the common law countries, including Israel (Article 19) and the Philippines (Article 185.1), whereas others have opted for UK-style fair dealing provisions as a quasi-general clause.[8] Others still have a mixture of fair dealing provisions for some purposes and fair use provisions for others, Singapore being a notable example (Article35(2)).

B *General Clause on Copyright Limitations in Civil Law Countries?*

Most civil law countries such as Japan, in contrast, lack any general (open-ended) clause on copyright limitations such as a fair use or fair dealing clause because such clauses are traditionally considered ill-matched to the civil law legal system.

i Korea, Taiwan, and China

However, there are exceptions. Korea and Taiwan, both of which are civil law jurisdictions, have introduced a US-style fair use clause. The Korean Copyright Act (KCA) was amended in 2011 to introduce a general provision on copyright limitations (Article 35*ter*)[9] that seems to combine a US-style fair use provision with the three-step test. That provision (KCA Article 35*ter*) was then revised on March 22, 2016,[10] to remove two parts (including "for news reporting, criticism, education and research etc."), and enacted on September 23, 2016. This amendment was presumably intended to expand the scope of application of the Korean fair use clause. The 1992 Taiwan Copyright Act also includes a US-style fair use clause (Article 65).

China is in the process of reviewing revisions to the Chinese Copyright Act and released a draft amendment in 2014 that introduces a subparagraph (13) named "other circumstances" (其他情形) as a general "basket clause" at the end of a catalogue of specific provisions on copyright limitations.

ii Japan

In Japan, there have been ongoing discussions on the introduction of a general clause on copyright limitations in addition to the catalogue of specific provisions (what can be dubbed a Japanese-style fair use clause) since 2007, despite the traditional view that such a clause is not suitable for civil law countries.[11]

It was proposed at a June 18, 2008, meeting of the Intellectual Property Strategic Program of the Intellectual Property Strategy Headquarters of the Japanese Government that the introduction of a general clause on copyright limitations be considered.[12] A subsequent report issued by the Task Force on Intellectual Property System in the Age of Digital Networks on November 27, 2008, stated that "it would be appropriate to add to those provisions a general

[8] *See* Jonathan Band & Jonathan Gerafi, Fair Use/Fair Dealing Handbook (May 7, 2013), *available at* http://infojustice.org/wp-content/uploads/2013/05/fair-use-handbook-05072013.pdf.

[9] Act No. 11110 of December 2, 2011.

[10] Act No. 14083 of March 22, 2016.

[11] *See* Tatsuhiro Ueno, *Rethinking the Provisions on Limitations of Rights in the Japanese Copyright Act: Toward the Japanese-Style "Fair Use" Clause*, 07/2009 Journal of the Japanese Group of AIPPI 159 (2009).

[12] A translation is available at www.kantei.go.jp/jp/singi/titeki2/keikaku2008_e.pdf.

clause on limitation of rights [Japanese-style 'fair use' clause] that comprehensively permits fair use of a work to the extent that does not unreasonably prejudice the legitimate interests of right holders."

After discussions of the issue by the Subcommittee on Legal Affairs of the Subdivision on Copyright of the Council for Cultural Affairs, four specific provisions on copyright limitations (Article 30*bis*, Article 30*ter*, Article 30*quater*, and Article 30*quater*) were introduced in 2012. However, the proposed general clause was not incorporated into the JCA because of strong objections from copyright holders.

Four years later, in 2016, the issue arose again, with heated debate over whether to introduce more flexible provisions or a general provision on copyright limitations into the JCA. The Intellectual Property Strategy Headquarters issued the Intellectual Property Strategic Program 2016 on May 9, 2016, in which it was proposed that the possibility of introducing flexible provisions on copyright limitations be considered to promote new innovations in the digital network era. The following year, a report issued by the Subcommittee on Legal and Fundamental Affairs of the Subdivision on Copyright of the Council for Cultural Affairs on February 24, 2017, recommended introducing such provisions.

iii My Opinion

The questions I pose here are whether it is possible to introduce a general clause on copyright limitations in civil law countries and what provision would be appropriate and acceptable in those countries.

(1) POSSIBLE GENERAL CLAUSE IN CIVIL LAW COUNTRIES

In my view, one idea would be to introduce a combination of specific provisions and a general basket clause on copyright limitations.

(a) Combination of Specific Provisions and a General Clause I believe that it would be more acceptable to introduce a general basket clause at the end of a catalogue of specific provisions on copyright limitations than to replace specific provisions with a single general clause.

In fact, the 2010 European Copyright Code[13] contains a general basket clause on copyright limitations for "[a]ny other use that is comparable to the uses enumerated in art. 5.1 to 5.4(1)." Called "Further limitations," the clause appears after the four categories of specific provisions on such limitations (Article 5.5). According to a footnote in the Code, this style of copyright limitations "reflects a combination of a common law style open-ended system of limitations and a civil law style exhaustive enumeration."[14]

(b) Factors to Be Considered If we are to introduce a general clause on copyright limitations, it is important that we also provide the factors to be considered in that clause. Such factors can foster legal certainty to a certain extent while maintaining flexibility. A general basket clause that specifies particular factors to be considered is by no means alien to the JCA. Article 20(2) of the JCA, the provision on the right of integrity, initially lists three specific provisions defining the types of modifications that shall not be considered to constitute an infringement of that right, and, in addition, provides a general basket clause for "other unavoidable

[13] www.copyrightcode.eu/.

[14] *See* footnote 48 of the European Copyright Code.

modifications," taking into account such factors as "the nature of a work as well as the purpose of and the manner of its exploitation."

(2) PROPOSAL FOR A GENERAL CLAUSE ON COPYRIGHT LIMITATIONS IN JAPAN

I have elsewhere proposed the following provision as an example of a general basket clause on copyright limitations that specifies certain factors to be considered and can be added to a catalogue of specific provisions (Articles 30 through 49 of JCA) under the term "Japanese-style fair use."[15]

(Further limitations)

Article 49*bis* of Japanese Copyright Act

In addition to the acts listed in [specific provisions on copyright limitations], an exploitation of a work shall be permitted if such exploitation is considered to be fair [reasonable/unavoidable] in light of the nature of a work as well as the purpose of and the manner of its exploitation; provided, however, that the foregoing shall not apply in the case where such exploitation is likely to unreasonably prejudice the interests of the copyright holder.

One potential criticism is that introducing a general clause would render the criteria for copyright infringement unclear. However, the raison d'être of a general clause lies in its ambiguity, with the flexibility it affords making it possible to respond to variety and change.

iv Small "Basket" Clause Introduced by the 2018 Amendment

The Japanese government submitted the bill to the 196th ordinary Diet session on February 23, 2018. The bill was passed in the Diet session on May 18, 2018 (Law No. 30 of 2018), and came into force on January 1, 2019.

This 2018 amendment introduced three flexible provisions on copyright limitations (Article 30*quater*, Article 47*quater* and Article 47*quinquies*) by aggregating some preexisting provisions such as the specific provisions for web search engines (Article 47*sexies*), text and data mining (Article 47*septies*), and experimental exploitations for the purpose of developing technology (Article 30*quater*) and newly adding a small "basket" clause for any other equivalent use of works in each provisions (the main paragraph of Article 30*quater* as well as Article 47*quater*(1)(2) and Article 47*quinquies*(1)(iii)), instead of introducing a general clause on copyright limitations.

In my view, these flexible provisions are considered to follow the style of a combination of specific provisions and a "basket" clause on copyright limitations and might therefore be helpful for civil law countries other than Japan.

3 CONCLUSION

The limitations on and exceptions to copyright play a significant role in achieving an appropriate balance between the protection and exploitation of copyrighted work. A detailed catalogue of specific provisions on copyright limitations, and the continuous revision thereof, will

[15] *See also* Ueno, *supra* note 11 at 191; Tatsuhiro Ueno, *Kenriseigen no Ippankitei* [A general clause on copyright limitations], *in* SHINAYAKA NA CHOSAKUKENSEIDO NI MUKETE [Toward the flexible copyright system] (Nobuhiro Nakayama ed., 2017) (in Japanese).

It should be noted that the term "Japanese-style fair use clause" does not necessarily imply that we should try to copy the US-style fair use provision.

undoubtedly remain essential in civil law. However, enumerated provisions are often too detailed and rigid to permit flexible responses to technological development and social change.

It is therefore argued here that what is needed in both common law countries and civil law countries such as Japan is some kind of general or open clause on copyright limitations. In my opinion, the combination of a detailed catalogue of specific provisions and a general basket clause on copyright limitations would be both an acceptable and appropriate option for civil law countries.

The flexible provisions introduced by the 2018 amendment are considered to follow the style of a combination of specific provisions and a "basket" clause on copyright limitations.

I hope that recent discussions and developments in Japan concerning this option and the issues surrounding it will provide a meaningful example for other civil law countries.

13

Bridging Fair Dealing and Fair Use Concepts: Malaysia's Transition to a Hybrid System

Ida Madieha Azmi

1 INTRODUCTION

In 2012, Malaysia moved from a pure fair dealing system to a hybrid fair dealing and fair use system. The transition was made possible with the incorporation of section 13(2A) into the Copyright Act 1987.[1] The section provided for the weighing of four fair use factors in considering whether a particular conduct amounts to a fair dealing under section 13(2)(a) and (b) of the Copyright Act 1987. In so doing, the four fair use factors played an instrumental role in defining the parameters of acceptable conduct as fair dealing.

Traditionally, fair dealing is viewed as distinct from the concept of fair use, leading to the question whether the concepts of fair dealing and fair use are divergent from or convergent with each other. Despite the perceived divergence, there seem to be common roots in the assessment of fairness as well as legitimate purposes in both concepts. This chapter discusses the factors influencing the decision of the courts in arriving at a finding of fair dealing in the UK and in Malaysia, and a finding of fair use in the US. The rest of the chapter begins with the historical antecedent to the incorporation of fair use factors into the Malaysian Copyright Act. Section 3 makes a cursory comparison between the concepts of fair dealing and fair use, and Section 4 inquires into whether there are common factors considered by the courts in both the fair use and fair dealing systems. Section 5 deals with the question of whether the inroads of fair use into the fair dealing system necessarily make significant changes to the ideational basis of the system. Using the factors identified by the Malaysian court as instrumental to the make-up of a fair dealing defense in *MediaCorp*,[2] the maiden and only Malaysian case on fair dealing, the chapter analyzes whether the court would have decided differently using the four fair use factors.

2 THE HISTORY OF FAIR DEALING AND PERMISSIBLE USES IN MALAYSIA

Malaysia promulgated its first indigenous copyright legislation in 1969. The 1969 Act was short lived and replaced by the 1987 Act which remains operative until now. From thereon, the range

[1] Section 13(2A) reads: For the purposes of paragraph (2)(a), in determining whether a dealing constitutes a fair dealing, the factors to be considered shall include – (a) the purpose and character of the dealing, including whether such dealing is of a commercial nature or is for non-profit educational purposes; (b) the nature of the copyright work; (c) the amount and substantiality of the portion used in relation to the copyright work as a whole; and (d) the effect of the dealing upon the potential market for or value of the copyright work.

[2] MediaCorp News Pte Ltd & Ors v. Mediabanc (Johore Bharu) Sdn Bhd & Ors [2010] 4 AMR 1; [2010] 1 LNS 296 (Malay.).

of permissible uses under the law have been added on, broadened, and diversified. Malaysia essentially practices a fair dealing system, whereby certain usage for specified purposes is tolerated.[3] Incrementally, these exceptions grew to extend to fair dealing for review and typographical use of a copyright work in 1990.[4] That was the year that saw a range of exceptions being introduced, including incidental inclusion in a broadcast, use for the purpose of setting an exam question, time shifting, performance for charitable purposes, and use for legal and judicial purposes. Another major revision took place in 1997, when a specially crafted provision allowing certain usage of copyright work for the disabled community was added.

Five years after that, the 2012 amendment followed suit by introducing one new exception and fine-tuning four more provisions. The new exception related to the making of a transient and incidental electronic copy of a work following the standard set under the WIPO Copyright Treaty 1996. The first revision related to nonprofit research as one of the specified uses under the fair dealing provisions and was extended to all types of research. In addition, the provision allowing recording made for the use of schools, universities, or educational institutions was extended to all reproductions made for the use of those institutions. The third revision related to the exception for the disabled community and was expanded to enable format shifting to allow the visually or hearing impaired to enjoy content in any form suitable for them. Lastly, the making of transient copies for purposes of broadcasting was extended to cover all broadcasting stations regardless of whether they are affiliated with the government or not.

These incremental additions to the exceptions and limitations indicate that the scope of permissible use must move along with technological changes and public interest. Regardless, among the provisions, fair dealing remains the broadest allowance in terms of usage. The relevant provisions on fair dealing in Malaysia are sections 13(2)(a) and (b) of the Copyright Act 1987. Despite being one of the oldest exceptions in the history of copyright law in Malaysia, this provision has not been tested by the courts, with the exception of one rare instance in a case involving media reporting service. The unexplored contours of the fair dealing provisions render the concept as enigmatic as ever since the scope of the fair dealing provisions depends substantially on the court's interpretation.

To that extent, the sole case decided in Malaysia would be instrumental in shedding some light on how the Malaysian court construes conceptions of fairness under the broad concept of fair dealing. The maiden case is *MediaCorp News Pte Ltd & Ors v. Mediabanc (Johore Bharu) Sdn Bhd & Ors*,[5] a case decided by the High Court of Malaya. In this case, a company based in Johor Bahru that provided media monitoring service in the form of recordings of certain television broadcasts from Singapore was sued for copyright infringement. The company raised the defense of fair dealing for the purposes of nonprofit research and private study. Pursuant to requests made by clients, the company contended that continuous and substantial off-air recordings were done to enable them to determine which parts were relevant to the clients. As only the relevant excerpts in the form of news clips and segments of broadcasts were provided to the clients, the company claimed that there had not been substantial reproductions of the broadcast. In addition, the company contended that their services were not in competition with the broadcast stations nor were their services considered to be a substitute for the broadcast.

[3] These specified purposes are (i) nonprofit research; (ii) private study; (iii) criticism; (iv) review; (v) reporting of current events; (vi) parody; (vii) pastiche; and (viii) caricature.

[4] Copyright (Amendment) Act 1990, which took effect on 1 October 1990.

[5] [2010] 4 AMR 1; [2010] 1 LNS 296 (Malay.).

In determining the defense of fair dealing, the presiding judge, Justice Nallini Pathmanathan, was guided by UK case law as to the relevant factors that made up "fair dealing." Specifically, six factors were examined. First and foremost, the purpose of the dealing and whether it fell within the specified purposes under section 13(2)(a) and (b) was evaluated. In assessing the first factor, the learned judge was mindful of the claim that the company was not charging anything for the excerpts of the broadcasts provided to clients and thereby not making money at the expense of the latter. The only fee charged by them was for their services in the compilation, editing and delivery, which they claimed fell within the rubric of research. Without such research, there was no way in which the company would be able to identify content that met the demand of their clients. On this point, the presiding judge was not convinced by the defendant's story as she felt that the company was providing a service for a fee. The judge felt that the whole operation of the company should be viewed in totality. The research part of the operation could not be isolated from the commercial part and this militated against the finding of nonprofit research.

The second relevant factor was the nature of the work, and whether the work was a valuable creative expression which took substantial effort to put together. The works in question were broadcast programs produced by the plaintiff that took substantial financial and human investment to put together. This essentially meant that the work was worth protecting from unscrupulously being purloined by others. The third factor was the substantiality of the alleged reproduction, on which the court found in the affirmative as there had been wholesale copying of the plaintiff's broadcasts. Fourthly, the court raised the issue as to whether there has been an express acknowledgment of the source of the material where the excerpts were taken. On this point, the presiding judge was of the view that acknowledgment alone was not sufficient. Judging from the substantial reproduction, the judge was of the view that the conduct could not simply be forgiven by the mere act of acknowledgment.

The fifth factor focused on the motive of the party dealing with the work. If the reproduction had been made for legitimate educational needs, that would have been forgiven. Yet what happened in this case was clearly for commercial purposes that were alien to a sense of morality and justice. The final factor weighed by the judge was the effect of the dealing on the market of the copyright owner. In the estimation of the judge, this last factor also went against the defendant. In her view, as a result of the media monitoring service, the copyright owner was deprived of sales and there might be instances where the public would associate the service provided by the company with the plaintiff's broadcast services.

Even though media reporting and broadcasts are two entirely different markets and not rivals to each other, the court clearly took the commercial nature of the service as indicative of an effort to profiteer from someone else's work, a notion which is contrary to fair dealing.

MediaCorp was instrumental in shedding some light on the conception of fair dealing as construed from the perspective of the Malaysian court. As it is the maiden and only case on fair dealing, it will be used as a vantage point from which a fair estimation can be reached as to whether it would have been decided differently using the fair use concept. The next section reviews the concepts of fair use and fair dealing in order to establish the links between the two concepts.

3 FAIR USE VERSUS FAIR DEALING: IS THE DISTINCTION ILLUSORY?

Striking the right balance between the right holder and users without unnecessarily jeopardizing the economic incentives to which the copyright owners are entitled is essential. in consequence, much ink has been spilled on examining the optimum model for copyright exceptions.[6] On this score, many academics are of the view that the US fair use model is more robust and flexible than the fair dealing model currently being practiced in the UK and other common law countries.[7] In drawing a comparison between the two, the Australian Law Reform Committee (ALRC), for example, in its report entitled *Copyright and the Digital Economy: Final Report*, highlights the strengths of the fair use system as being, among others, that it is flexible and technology-neutral.[8] As a result, it promotes public interest and transformative uses, assists innovation, and better aligns with reasonable consumer expectations.

Malaysia and Singapore have migrated from the pure fair dealing system to a hybrid one involving the US fair use factors. In Malaysia, the four fair use factors are to be used in the assessment of the fair dealing exception. This leads to the issue as to whether fair dealing and fair use are contradictory to each other or if the latter is to be used to supplement the former. In order to gauge the impact of the infusion of the fair use concept into fair dealing, we need to understand how the two concepts have been depicted by academics and the courts.

Fair dealing has been described as an "elusive concept" which is difficult to describe with precision.[9] Judges have portrayed the concept as a "matter of fact, degree or impression."[10] Fair use on the other hand has been described as being too broad, unclear and uncertain, making it risky to both the copyright owner and the user.[11] Both fair use and fair dealing are invoked by way of defenses which justify it being labeled as "affirmative defense or a user privilege."[12] So ingrained is fair use in US copyright law that it is considered as its great white whale.[13]

In this context, it is apt to quote Lord Denning in *Hubbard v. Vosper* to illustrate the UK courts' approach to the assessment of fair dealing:

> You must first consider the number and extent of the quotations . . . Then you must consider the use made of them. If they are used as a basis of comment, criticism or review, that may be fair dealing. If they are used to convey the same information as the author, for a rival purpose, they may be unfair. Next, you must consider the proportions. To take long extracts and attach short comments may be unfair. But short extracts and long comments may be fair. Other considerations may come to mind also. But . . . it must be a matter of impression.[14]

Patterson describes fair use as the right to make a limited use of another's copyright.[15] The rationale of the doctrine stems from the realization that certain limited forms of copying should be allowed to support the growth of knowledge. Another theory is that fair use should be allowed as it is a "solution to market failure," i.e., a remedy to resolve the problem of getting clearance and the possibility of high transaction cost.[16]

6 Steven O'Heany, *Fair is Fair: Fair Dealing, Derivative Rights and the Internet*, 12 Asper Rev. Int'l Bus. & Trade L. 75 (2012).

7 Seagull Haiyan Song, *Reevaluating Fair Use in China: A Comparative Copyright Analysis of Chinese Fair Use Legislation, the US Fair Use Doctrine and the European Fair Dealing Model*, 51 IDEA: Intell. Prop. L. Rev. 453 (2011).

8 Terry Flew, *Fair Use and the Future of Copyright*, 17(2) Internet L. Bulletin 41 (2014).

9 Graeme W. Austin, *Four Questions about the Australian Approach to Fair Dealing Defenses to Copyright Infringement*, 57 J. Copyright Soc'y 611 (2010).

10 Hubbard v. Vosper [1972] 2 QB 84 (Eng.).

11 Joseph P. Liu, *Two Factor Fair Use?*, 31 Colum. J. L. & Arts 571 (2007–8).

12 Michael D. Brittin, *Constitutional Fair Use*, 20 Wm. & Mary L. Rev. 85 (1978–79).

13 Paul Goldstein, *Fair Use in Context*, 31 Colum. J. L. & Arts 433 (2007–8).

14 [1972] 2 QB 84; [1972] 1 All ER 1023 (Eng.), *per* Lord Denning MR at 94.

15 L. Ray Patterson, *Understanding Fair Use, Law and Contemporary Problems*, 55 L. & Contemp. Probs. 249 (1992).

16 Wendy J. Gordon, *Excuse and Justification in the Law of Fair Use: Commodification and Market Perspectives*, *in* The Commodification of Information 149, 152 (Nina Elkin-Koren & Neil Weinstock Netanel eds., 2012).

Like fair dealing, fair use originated from case law. The first judicial testimony to fair use was *Folsom v. Marsh*,[17] an 1841 case concerning the abridgement of George Washington's biography. In arriving at a finding of fair use, Justice Story asserted that in abridging the work from twenty volumes to two, the author had created a new work altogether.[18] In that case, the factors used by the court to determine fair use were "the nature and objects of the selections made, the quantity and value of the materials used, and the degree in which the use may prejudice the sale, or diminish the profits, or supersede the objects, of the original work."[19]

From its origin as case law–based, in 1976 the US Congress codified the fair use factors to what is currently known, i.e.,

(i) the purpose and character of the use;
(ii) the nature of the copyrighted work;
(iii) the amount and substantiality of the portion used in relation to the copyrighted works as a whole; and
(iv) the effect of the use upon the potential market value of the copyrighted work.

The four fair use factors are synonymous with the US style of weighing the fairness of a conduct involving copyright materials. These factors have been the subject of a century-old critical appraisal, not only by the courts but also by legal academics.

Besides the four statutorily designated fair use factors, the courts have also taken into account other factors such as whether the copyright infringer has acted in good faith.[20]

Unlike the US approach of codifying the fair use factors, in the fair dealing systems of some countries like the UK, India and pre-2012 Malaysia the factors that go into the fairness inquiry are developed by the courts on a case-by-case basis. Some fair dealing countries like Australia, New Zealand and Hong Kong have codified the factors. From the century-old jurisprudence, several factors can be distilled. Holyoak & Torremans (2010) summarized the relevant factors in the assessment of fair dealing from case law as follows[21]:

(i) For what purpose was the work copied? The degree to which the defendant's use competes with the exploitation of the copyright by its owner is an important consideration.
(ii) What is the proportion of the copied part in relation to the whole work? The weight given to this factor depends very much on the particular circumstances of the case.
(iii) What motive led to the copying? If the motive was to compete with the original work, this is likely to render the defendant's use of the work unfair.
(iv) What is the status of the work copied? If the work is not published or confidential, the defense is unlikely to succeed.

Laddie et al.[22] mention an additional factor: whether the exploitation of the copyright work constitutes a substitute for or competes with the original material.

As the assessment of fairness in both systems is made through the court, to that extent both fair use and fair dealing suffer from the same limitation, i.e., uncertainty.[23] This could have been the

[17] Folsom v. Marsh, 9 F. Cas. 324 (C.C.D. Mass. 1841).

[18] Patterson, *supra* note 15.

[19] D. R. Jones, *Commerciality and Fair Use*, 15 Wake Forest J. Bus. & Intell. Prop. L. 620 (2015).

[20] Simon J. Frankel & Matt Kellog, *Bad Faith and Fair Use*, 60 J. Copyright Soc'y 1 (2012).

[21] Paul Torremans, Holyoak & Torremans Intellectual Property Law 288 (8th ed. 2016).

[22] Hugh Laddie et al., The Modern Law of Copyright and Designs (3d ed. 2000), cited with approval by Hart J in IPC Media Ltd v. News Group Newspapers Ltd [2005] EWHC 317 (Ch), [13] (Eng.).

[23] Michael J. Madison, *Madisonian Fair Use*, 30 Cardozo Arts & Ent. L.J. 39, 44 (2012).

result of courts' interpretation of "fairness" and "purpose" of the conduct which calls for a case-by-case analysis.[24]

On that score, the factors taken into account by the US courts bear a lot of similarities with those taken into account in fair dealing by the UK and Commonwealth courts. Holyak & Torreman's first fair dealing factor is categorically the same in genre as the first fair use factor. The second fair dealing factor deals with the substantiality of reproduction, which is the third fair use factor. The third fair dealing factor that deals with motive falls within the first fair use factor. The status of the work which was identified by Holyak & Torremans finds its equivalence in the second fair use factor. Finally, the additional factor identified by Laddie et al. corresponds to the fourth fair use factor.

4 MORE IN COMMON THAN AT ODDS WITH EACH OTHER?

At the basic level, both fair dealing and fair use attempt to accomplish the same goal,[25] i.e., that copyright should not hinder the wider public interest in the free flow of information and educational needs.[26] Despite the legislative differences between the two systems, the established purposes considered to be legitimate under both the fair dealing and the fair use system share commonalities, i.e., criticism, comment, news reporting, teaching, scholarship, or research.[27] In this section, we examine the sum of common factors considered on both sides to determine whether there is a divide between them.

4.1 *The Purpose of the Usage*

As the pre-2012 Malaysian as well as the UK fair dealing exceptions are tied down to the eight stipulated purposes in the statute, much debate goes into whether a particular action falls within them or not. The common law courts have repeatedly said that the use must squarely fall within one of the specified purposes. This can be counterproductive, as a substantial amount of time is spent in establishing the purpose as well as whether the conduct is justifiable or not. In *Pro Sieben Media AG v. Carlton UK Television Ltd*,[28] a substantial amount of time was spent examining whether a documentary criticizing the practice of cheque book journalism could be considered as current news as opposed to being of historical interest or concern.[29] At the trial level, Laddie J was of the view that the inclusion of the copyright materials in the documentary was ancillary to the main purpose of the documentary, i.e., criticizing cheque book journalism, and therefore did not fall within the domain of criticism.[30] Walker J on appeal, however, ruled that the phrase should be interpreted liberally and be given a "wide and indefinite scope."[31] As a result, even though copyright materials reproduced were only illustrative of cheque book journalism and were not the main focus of the criticism, the conduct fell within the scope of criticism.[32]

[24] *See* Jones, *supra* note 19, at 620.
[25] *See* O'Heany, *supra* note 6, at 75, 89.
[26] K. K. Puri, *Fair Dealing with Copyright Material in Australia and New Zealand*, 13 Victoria U. Wellington L. Rev. 277, 298 (1983).
[27] *See* Campbell v. Acuff-Rose Music, 510 U.S. 569 (1994).
[28] [1998] FSR 43 (Eng.).
[29] Lorna Caddy et al., *The European Approach to Fair Dealing – Harmony or Discord?*, 57 J. Copyright Soc'y U.S.A. 573 (2009–10).
[30] [1998] FSR 43 (Ch) 54 (Eng.).
[31] [1999] FSR 610 (CA) 620 (Eng.).
[32] Jonathan Griffiths, *Fair Dealing in the Law of Copyright*, 8 Nottingham L.J. 54 (1999).

With regard to the purpose of the reproduction, when the purpose is not to criticize or review the part taken but only to use it as leverage for marketing purposes such as comparative advertising, then it is questionable whether this could be considered as criticism, or even "in the context of" or "as part of an exercise in" or "for the purpose of" criticism or review. In *IPC Media Ltd v. News Group Newspapers Ltd*,[33] the defendant relaunched its television magazine by reproducing the front cover of the plaintiff's magazine in order to promote its own magazine. The court decided that whilst the defendant's reproduction could arguably be characterized as criticism, this kind of criticism did not constitute criticism "of the [claimant's] work or another work within the meaning of section 30(1) of the UK Copyright Act 1988." The finding was made even though the presiding judge alluded to the fact that "a high value [was] placed upon competitiveness in the marketplace and the right of the consumer to information."[34] Eventually, the case was dismissed because the presiding judge noted that such comparative advertising could have been achieved without resorting to the reproduction of the copyright work. On the other hand, in *Prince of Wales v. Associated Newspapers Ltd*,[35] the publication of contents of private journals belonging to the prince had little to do with a current event or with criticism or review.

In *Newspaper Licensing Agency Ltd & Ors v. Meltwater Holding Bv and Others*,[36] the defendants ran a media monitoring service using a software that "reads" the contents of websites and produces an index of the words in the sites. Clients were then able to identify contents which were useful to them, in the form of a hyperlink to the relevant article, headline from the article, the opening words, and an extract from the article. The defendants were sued by the Newspaper Licensing Agency and several newspaper publishers, claiming that this amounted to copyright infringement as they had acted without license from the licensing body. In holding for infringement, the court found that headlines were original literary works and the extracts produced by the media reports constitute a substantial part of the literary work. In addition thereto, headlines were created through such careful choice of words, sequence and combination of words that that expression could be considered as intellectual creation capable of protection as copyright subject matter. More fundamentally, the service provided by Meltwater could not be considered as criticism, as none of the content was the subject of criticism of the reporting of current events. On that basis, the usage by Meltwater was not considered to fall within the rubric of fair dealing.

The purpose of the reproduction is also the first fair use factor in the US and other countries that have adopted the fair use system, including Malaysia. The first factor requires a two-pronged inquiry, i.e., as to the purpose and character of the use. It is with this factor that the inquiry whether the defendant's use is commercial or whether that use was transformative comes into the picture. In that sense, in the US, both the purpose and fairness of the conduct are subsumed in the first character. The fair dealing system, on the other hand, first investigates whether the alleged conduct falls within the stipulated purpose, before the second inquiry as to the whether the alleged conduct is fair or not.[37]

4.2 *Nature of the Work*

With regard to the nature of the work, the fact that a work is fictional would render more protection afforded to it. That means the courts are more inclined to give more leeway to copy

[33] [2005] EWHC 317 (Ch) (Eng.).
[34] *Id.* at [18].
[35] [2006] EWHC 522 (Ch) (Eng.).
[36] [2011] EWCA Civ 890 (Eng.).
[37] *See* Catherine Colston, *Fair Dealing: What is Fair?*, 10 Denning L.J. 91 (1995).

from factual works than from fictional works. Equally treated with more protection are unpublished works.[38] The rationale is that suchunpublished content is equivalent to confidential information that should be protected against leaks. In *Ashdown v. Telegraph Group Ltd.*,[39] the publication of contents of minutes of meetings which have never been disclosed to the public was not acceptable, as the main purpose was to criticize the prime minister and not to criticize the minutes. The decision reinforced the position in *Beloff v. Pressdram Ltd & another*,[40] where certain leakage of an internal office memorandum was considered as unfair conduct which did not justify a finding of fair dealing. Similarly, in *HRH Prince of Wales v. Associated Newspapers Ltd.*,[41] the publication of content of private journals belonging to the prince was held to be a breach of confidence, in which the prince had a reasonable expectation of privacy. This factor connects somehow with the fourth factor, i.e., the manner in which the work is being obtained.

The nature of the work is also the second fair use factor. This factor also involves a two-pronged inquiry, i.e., as to how creative is the plaintiff's work and whether the work has been published or otherwise exposed to the public. In *Love v. Kwitny*,[42] a reproduction of an unpublished manuscript was considered to be an unfair use. So is the act of reproducing excerpts of former President Gerald Ford's unpublished memoirs.[43]

4.3 *The Amount Taken from the Work*

The extracts reproduced must be proportionate to the purpose of the usage. The classic case for this is *British Broadcasting Corp v. British Satellite Broadcasting Ltd.*[44] In this case, the Chancery Division outlined the restriction on use for it to qualify as fair dealing. The excerpts taken must be short and as in this case each excerpt lasted between fourteen and thirty-seven seconds whilst the "menu" excerpts were even shorter, lasting from only four and five seconds each. Such reproductions were considered to be justifiable and proportionate to the purpose of reproduction, i.e., reporting of current news in this case.

This also constitutes the third fair use factor. If the amount of reproduction is substantial, it may implicate that the defendant is trying to take advantage of the copyright material to his benefit. In *Twin Peaks v. Publications Int'l, Ltd.*,[45] a guidebook on the television show *Twin Peaks* which contained detailed descriptions of plot, character, and setting was not found to be a fair use. The same conclusion was reached in the case of *Religious Technology Center v. Lerma* where the materials used by the defendant constituted the entire publications of the Church of Scientology.[46] The production of a book of trivia questions based on the characters and events of the *Seinfeld* television production was found to involve substantial reproduction as the actual dialogue of the show had been used.[47] If the part taken constitutes the heart of the copyright

[38] *See* Harper & Row Publishers Inc. v. Nation Enterprises, 471 U.S. 539 (1985).
[39] [2001] All ER (D) 07.
[40] [1973] 1 All ER 241 (Eng.).
[41] [2006] EWHC 522 (Ch) (Eng.).
[42] 772 F. Supp. 1367 (S.D.N.Y. 1989).
[43] Harper & Row Publishers Inc. v. Nation Enterprises, 471 U.S. 539 (1985).
[44] [1991] 3 All ER 833 (Eng.).
[45] 996 F. 2d 1366 (2d Cir. 1993).
[46] 40 U.S.P.Q. 2d 1569 (E.D. Va. 1996).
[47] Castle Rock Entertainment, Inc. v. Carol Publ. Group, 150 F.3d 132 (2d Cir. 1993).

materials, the court may be persuaded to find against fair use as in *Roy Export Co Estab. of Vaduz v. Columbia. Broadcasting Sys., Inc*,[48] where one minute and fifteen seconds of a Charlie Chaplin movie was reproduced by a television news program in a report about the latter's death. Although the reproduction was minimal, it was found to contain the fundamental portion of the copyrighted content.

Naturally, if the amount of reproduction is minimal, such as 1 percent of unpublished letter and journal entries used by the biographer of the author Richard Wright[49] or in the case of usage of forty-one seconds of film of a boxing match involving Muhammad Ali for the purpose of production of his movie biography,[50] this does not amount to excessive copying and is thus allowed.

4.4 *The Manner in Which the Work Is Obtained*

The conduct of the defendant must also be fair. The unlawful manner in which the work was acquired, failure to acknowledge the author of the work, unlawful disclosure of confidential information, whether permission was initially sought and refused by the copyright owner, or the use distorts the content of the work – all are factors that can amount to bad faith and may weigh against the finding of fair dealing. The clean hands requirement has been extrapolated in *Prince of Wales v. Associated Newspapers Ltd.*,[51] where contents of a copy of a journal written by a member of the British royal family were published with an intent of throwing open a debate as to his suitability to ascend to the throne. The court found that there was no possibility of the claim of criticism succeeding, as the journal had been leaked through a breach of confidential information. The judgment of Blackburne J was further endorsed on appeal by the English Court of Appeal.[52]

On the contrary in *Time Warner Entertainment Co. Ltd. v. Channel 4 Television Corp.*[53] reproduction was allowed even if the materials were acquired without the consent of the copyright owner. The laser disks of the film had been obtained in an underhand manner, thus causing the act of acquisition of the work to be alleged as unfair conduct. Neil LJ, however, was of the view that with a work which was already in the public domain, the method of acquisition of the work would not be "rendered unfair because of the method by which the copyright material was obtained."[54] The same issue arose in *Fraser Woodward Ltd v. British Broadcasting Corporation and Another.*[55] In this case, photographs of a famous celebrity were reproduced by the plaintiff in a television program without the consent of the copyright owner. The testimony from the photographer was that he explicitly refused consent to the use of his photographs for the television program for fear of the residual value of his photographs. The testimony was, however, not accepted by the presiding judge who viewed the issue to be irrelevant as clearly the defendant was relying on a fair dealing defense.

48 627 F.2d 1095, 1100 (2d Cir. 1982).
49 Salinger v. Random House, 811 F.2d 90 (2d Cir. 1987).
50 Monster Communications, Inc. v. Turner Broadcasting Sys. Inc., 935 F. Supp. 490 (S.D.N.Y. 1996).
51 [2006] EWHC 11 (Ch) (Eng.).
52 [2007] 2 All ER 139 (CA) (Eng.).
53 [1994] EMLR 1 (CA) (Eng.).
54 This finding was accepted by the other presiding judge, Henry LJ.
55 [2005] EWHC 472 (Ch) (Eng.).

The position seems to be the same in the United States. Bad faith on the part of the defendant may be used against his plea of fair use.[56] Once there is a finding of bad faith, in most instances, the defense of fair use will fail as elaborated in Section 4.2 above.

4.5 *The Effect of the Use to the Market As Well As Whether There Exist Alternatives to the Dealing*

If the alleged fair dealing is in competition with the original works, then the likelihood of the conduct being upheld as fair will be slim. Laddie et al.[57] describe this as the most important element – whether the exploitation of the copyright work constitutes a substitute or is competing with the original material. The extrapolation of this principle can be seen in two cases: *IPC Media v. News Group Newspapers Ltd.*[58] and *Newspaper Licensing Agency v. Meltwater Holding BV and Others.*[59] In *IPC Media v. News Group Newspapers Ltd.*,[60] the court reasoned that since the main purpose of the use was to reduce sales of the competitor's product in order to advance one's own product, this did not constitute a dealing that was fair. The finding was made without any clear evidence that the effect of the use was to substitute for or compete with the plaintiff's copyright material. In *Newspaper Licensing Agency*,[61] the court considered whether allowing a media reporting service to operate without license from the copyright holders amounted to unjustifiable profiteering from the copyright materials. The fact that there existed licensing bodies that regulated such activities indicated that only licensed collection and reproduction of media reports was allowed under the law. The finding of unjustifiable profiteering was arrived at despite the fact that the defendant's product could not foreseeably compete with the market of the newspaper agencies.

The effect of the defendant's conduct on the plaintiff's market constitutes the fourth fair use factor in the United States. Mathew Sag posits that this inquiry appears to be an objective factual investigation, but in actual fact it is a highly subjective assessment.[62] In undertaking this line of inquiry, there is a need to understand the effect of the given use on the potential market in the first place.[63] However, using empirical means, Sag argues that the predictability of fair use outcomes in litigation can be assessed systematically. Accordingly, Sag advanced the view that using the factors of fair use as variables as well as a number of doctrinal assumptions, the consequence of a fair use claim can be fairly predicted.

If the reproduction causes minimal effect on the potential market then the conduct is not prohibited, as in the case of the reproduction of thumbnail images of photographs in *Kelly v. Arriba-Soft.*[64] The thumbnail versions were perceived to be of lower quality and thus would not constitute meaningful competition to or substitution for the original copies. Likewise with "time-shifting" by way of home videotaping of a television broadcast as was held in *Universal*

[56] Simon J. Frankel & Matt Kellog, *Bad Faith and Fair Use*, 60 J. Copyright Soc'y 1 (2012).
[57] Laddie et al., *supra* note 22, cited with approval by Hart J in IPC Media Ltd v. News Group Newspapers Ltd [2005] EWHC 317 (Ch), [13] (Eng.).
[58] [2005] EWHC 317 (Ch) (Eng.).
[59] [2011] EWCA Civ 890 (Eng.).
[60] [2005] EWHC 317 (Ch) (Eng.).
[61] [2011] EWCA Civ 890 (Eng.).
[62] Matthew Sag, *Predicting Fair Use*, 73 Ohio St. L.J. 47, 63 (2012).
[63] *Id.*
[64] 03 C.D.O.S. 5888 (9th Cir. 2003).

City Studios v. Sony Corp.[65] In the estimation of the Supreme Court, delayed viewing would not in any way have rivaled the original broadcast.[66]

5 TRANSFORMATIVE USE AND THE GULF BETWEEN FAIR USE AND FAIR DEALING SYSTEMS

One major distinction between the fair dealing and fair use concepts is in relation to the treatment of derivative work.[67] The US Copyright Act contains a list of examples of derivative work, but their role is for purposes of mere illustration.[68] The most important feature is that the work has been recast, transformed, or adapted. In *Campbell*,[69] the Supreme Court defines a "transformative use" as "a use that does not merely supersede the objects of the original creation, but rather instead adds something new, with a further purpose or different character."[70] Whilst parody has often been touted as a classic example of transformative use, there are many uses where the original work has been mashed up or remixed to create new value for the original work.[71] In so doing, the Supreme Court departed from a prior presumption that "a commercial or profit making purpose" would be "presumptively unfair."[72] This is where the fair dealing system and fair use system depart. When transformative use is pleaded, other factors are simply overlooked.[73] It no longer matters that the work is fictional or the amount of copying is wholesale or the purpose of the use is commercial.[74] The focus is on the creation of a new value which can be marketed, and not competition with the original work.[75] Mathew Sag, for example, suggests that for a work to be considered a "transformative use" there must be substantial difference with the original work.[76] Among the issues considered for the transformative factor is whether "new expression or meaning" has been created, i.e., whether new value has been created from the old work to the extent that new information, new aesthetics, new insights and new understandings result from the effort. This is more so in the digital environment where there are enormous opportunities for the transformation of copyright materials into other forms.

In a series of cases, the US courts found fair use for an internet search engine, even if the entire works have been copied. In *Kelly v. Arriba Soft Corporation*,[77] the court found in favor of

65 Kelly v. Arriba-Soft, 464 U.S. 417 (1984).

66 Universal City Studios v. Sony Corp., 464 U.S. 417 (1984).

67 *See* O'Heany, *supra* note 6, at 75.

68 *See* US Copyright Act of 1976 § 101, 17 U.S.C. § 107 (2012) ("a derivative work is a work based upon one or more pre-existing works, such as a translation, musical arrangement, dramatization, fictionalization, motion picture version, sound recording, art reproduction, abridgment, condensation, or any other form in which a work may be recast, transformed or adapted").

69 Campbell v. Acuff-Rose Music, Inc, 510 U.S. 569 (1994).

70 Randall P. Bezanson & Joseph M. Miller, *Scholarship and Fair Use*, 33 COLUM. J.L. & ARTS 409 (2010).

71 *See, e.g.*, Fisher v. Dees, 794 F. 2d. 432 (9th Cir. 1986), a parody of a song where the original lyric line and six bars of the song were borrowed; Elsmere Music, Inc. v. National Broadcasting Co., 482 F. Supp. 741 (S.D.N.Y) *aff'd by* 632 F. 2d. 252 (2d Cir. 1980), where only the words "I Love" and four musical notes were taken from the original work; Leibovitz v. Paramount Pictures Corp., 137 F. 3d 109 (2d Cir. 1998), where a movie impersonated a photograph of a pregnant celebrity in front of a well-known magazine and was found to constitute a parody.

72 Justice Stevens's decisions in Sony Corp. of Am. v Universal City Studios, Inc., 646 U.S. 417 (1984); Harper & Row Publishers, Inc. v. Nation Enters., 471 U.S. 539, 562–63 (1985).

73 *See* Campbell v. Acuff-Rose Music, Inc, 510 U.S. 569 (1994); Bill Graham Archives v. Dorling Kindersley Ltd., 448 F.3d 605 (2d Cir. 2006).

74 *See* Jones, *supra* note 19, at 620, 654.

75 Barton Beebe, *An Empirical Study of U.S. Copyright Fair Use Opinions*, 1978–2005, 15 U. PA. L. REV. 549 (2008).

76 *See* Sag, *supra* note 62, at 73.

77 336 F.3d 811 (9th Cir. 2003).

Ariba for providing copyright materials in thumbnail version even though in so doing Ariba had reproduced the whole image.

The scope of transformative use was further extended in *Google v. Perfect 10*,[78] where the court upheld the transformative use of a search engine that compressed original photographs protected under copyright in a thumbnail version as by doing so a new use of the original work was created.

A further testimony to the concept of transformative use is the Google library project, *Authors Guild*,[79] where Google scanned about 20 million books protected under copyright with the full or partial assistance of public libraries. In this case, the court justified the transformative nature of the conduct on the basis that Google is now making books more accessible to readers. Although the whole book is scanned, readers can only view snippets consisting of a few sentences before and after the search term. In addition, the presiding judge viewed the online materials as not being a substitute for the original work, hence there was no danger that the commercialization of the original work would be affected. They could in fact further increase the demand for the original work.

It is interesting to note that in all three internet cases, the court assumed that the new service provided by the search engine was in no way competing with the original work in the same market. This is in contrast with media reporting cases in the UK, where the substantiality of the reproduction will stand against any finding of fairness. In that context, Jonathan Band (2008) believes the current form of search technology implicates higher chances of liability as the software robots or spiders copy a substantial amount of content and not the metadata as they crawl the web pages in search of useful materials.[80]

The limitation of the fair dealing concept is that the usage must strictly fall within the stipulated purposes. In some instances this has led to an unreasonable expansion of the copyright user's exclusive right to legitimate business which he is not involved in nor in competition with nor is it within his contemplation. In *Newspaper Licensing Agency Ltd and Others v. Meltwater Holding BV and Others*,[81] the service of media clipping which came complete with index, hyperlink, headline, opening words, and extract from the article was found not to amount to criticism or review. In the court's estimation the practice of the industry and the availability of license for press clipping agencies rendered the defendant's conduct inexcusable as it would deprive the copyright owner of what is rightfully theirs. However, in hindsight, the effect is the expansion of the copyright holder's interest to a secondary market and this is surely not the true objective of copyright. In that case, the presiding judge proceeded to examine whether the end user in asking the press clipping service was actually doing it for the purpose of reviewing them, for which the court found to the negative as "the End User does not apply his critical faculties at all to the work, whether the article or the text extracts. The purpose of Meltwater News is merely to enable the End User to decide whether he want to see the content of the articles."

Even an internal newspaper cutting service which does not run in competition with the news agency service was considered unacceptable as fair dealing. In *Newspaper Licensing Agency Ltd v. Marks & Spencer Ltd*,[82] an internal newspaper cutting service run by Marks & Spencer which was made available only to their employees was found not to be within the "reporting of current events" and hence infringing.

[78] Google v. Perfect 10, 508 F.3d 1146 (9th Cir. 2007).

[79] Authors Guild v. Google, Inc., No. 05-8136, 2009 U.S. Dist. LEXIS 102837 (S.D.N.Y. Nov. 4, 2009).

[80] Jonathan Band, *Google and Fair Use*, 3 J. Bus. & Tech. L. 1, 3 (2008).

[81] [2011] EWCA Civ 890 (Eng.).

[82] [1999] EMLR 369 (Ch) (Eng.).

Both *Newspaper Licensing Agency Ltd and Others v. Meltwater Holding BV and Others*[83] and *Newspaper Licensing Agency Ltd v. Marks & Spencer Ltd*[84] illustrate the UK court's hesitance to look beyond the mundane findings of quantum of reproduction and commercial interest in order to examine the critical issue as to whether the reproduction has actually impeded the market of the copyright materials. The court also ignored the issue as to whether it was justifiable to expand the exclusive rights to cover secondary use of the materials.

Steven O'Heany argues that expanding the right holders' interest to cover derivative work could lead to "a loss of creative input." In his view, most intellectual creative activity is derivative in nature. Naturally, when one composes a song, a novel, or even a factual work, reference must be made to existing work. In actuality, it is impossible for a work to be created from nothing as all new creations ultimately are built on other work that has evolved prior to them. Therefore, having a proper understanding of transformative use could bring a balance between the interests of copyright owners and the expansion of science and arts.[85]

6 CONCLUSION

Striking a balance between the copyright owner's interests and the wider public interest is no easy feat. Even if the court claims to want to strike a balance, the system is tilted in favor of the copyright owner. What else do property-like exclusive rights serve if not the protection of the economic interests of the copyright owner? So the right holders argue.

To that extent the concept of fair dealing has been described as too rigid and not accommodative of the creation of a new or potential market. On this point, as far back as 1977, the report of the Whitford Committee on the Law of Copyright and Designs had recommended that the scope of the "fair dealing" defense, which it states to be of particular interest to the publishers, the press, and to the public at large, should be extended, and no longer restricted to particular works (thereby excluding copies of typographical arrangements), particular forms ("criticism or review" or "reporting current events"), or particular media (newspapers, magazines, periodicals, broadcasting or cinematograph films); and that there should be a general defense of "fair dealing" which does not conflict with normal exploitation of the work or subject matter and does not unreasonably prejudice the legitimate interests of the copyright owners.[86]

Is the distinction between fair dealing and fair use really illusory? To a certain extent yes. Many common factors are adopted by the court in determining the fairness of the conduct as well as the purpose of the conduct on both sides. Both are equally elusive and difficult to draw with precise extrapolation. However, the major strength of fair use is that it is not restricted to any specified purposes. The fair use system is based on an open norm with a list of purposes which are non-exhaustive. To that extent, the migration from a fair dealing system to a fair use system in 2012 is a welcome development in Malaysia. Rather than trying to fit into delineated purposes and looking at the fairness of the conduct, the fair use system is more flexible and may give more room for the courts and the users to explore and maneuver.[87] Adopting the more expansive fair use would be more in touch with technological advances such as social media and evolving digital and online tools and services. Most of this User Generated Content (UGC) may initially

83 [2011] EWCA Civ 890 (Eng.).
84 [1999] EMLR 369 (Ch) (Eng.).
85 *See* O'Heany, *supra* note 6, at 75.
86 *Id.* at para. 677.
87 *See* Caddy et al., *supra* note 29, at 573.

be noncommercial in nature[88] but eventually may be used to generate income and solely on that basis may be considered to be outside the domain of fair dealing.[89]

In the final analysis, it has to be accepted that both the determination of fair dealing and fair use are established *post ante*, after disputes have arisen and been brought to the court. To that extent, users and consumers relying on these decisions run the risk that later courts may distinguish these decisions. This is unlike a situation where guidelines are developed based on a uniform set of rules, easily understood by users, as to what would be considered "fair dealing" or "fair use." The position is worse in countries such as the UK which do not have a statutory definition of "fair dealing," because this confers very wide discretionary powers on judges.[90] It would appear that neither "fair dealing" nor "fair use"provides certainty to the users even though there has been an attempt to come up with guidelines on fair use. In this respect the suggestion made by Pamela Samuelson for the Copyright Office to prepare opinion letters as to permissible and nonpermissible conduct is worth adopting.[91] The range of transformative uses recommended by her extended beyond the normal conceptions. She recommended that comparative advertising, private noncommercial use, and even market failures as a result of difficulties in clearing rights be acceptable. If copyright is to play its role in the promotion of education and science then surely the debate as to what amounts to legitimate use should be extended beyond the known purposes.[92]

Even more fundamental, the belief that copyright should solely serve the interests of the copyright owners belongs to yesteryear. The main preoccupation is not whether copyright should give more prominence to the property owner, but whether other competing stakeholders are restricted from making use of the work. This need not necessarily mean that we are moving to a user-centric copyright, but rather a system which is friendly to users. The concern is that copyright should not be used as a platform to undermine the creation of a new or potential market. Theoretically when a work is transformed into another work, it is as if a new work has been created altogether and therefore the interests of the original copyright owner ceased.

Coming back to the Malaysian case of *MediaCorp*, would it be decided differently under the concept of fair use? Would the provision of a media monitoring service be considered as a new or potential market that should not be inhibited by the copyright owner? As conceded by the presiding judge, the service was in no way competing with the plaintiff's market, i.e., broadcasting services. Would the case be decided differently if there was never any form of licensing system for the usage of off-air broadcast signals for other services, as is the case with Malaysia? Surely, here there is no issue at all of a potential market in media monitoring services by the broadcasting organizations as there is no possibility of legitimate licensing of the contents of a broadcast.

Even if media monitoring services cannot be considered a transformative use, could the usage by the defendant be subjected to compulsory licensing as the issue is one of competition rather than copyright infringement? Surely the idea is not to foreclose the creation of a new service or market or any means of monetizing content that does not go to the extent of profiteering from

88 Michael Fraser, *Fair Is Foul and Foul Is Fair: From Analogue to Digital Fair Dealing*, 9 J. L. & Info. Sci. 93 (1998).

89 Sophia Christou & Abi Paramaguru, *User Generated Content, Copyright and Fair Dealing*, 12 Internet L. Bulletin 57 (2009).

90 Catherine Colston, *Fair Dealing: What is Fair?*, 10 Denning L.J. 91 (1995).

91 Pamela Samuelson, *The Copyright Principles Project: Directions for Reform*, 25 Berkeley Tech. L.J. 1175, 1206 (2010).

92 *See also* Michael W. Carroll, *Fixing Fair Use*, 85 N.C.L. Rev. 1087 (2006–7), for a discussion on setting up of a Fair Use Board in the US Copyright Office whose task is to declare a proposed use of another's copyrighted work to be a fair use.

other's content without justification. Can the court instruct the copyright owner to compulsorily grant a license to the offender in these cases rather than trying to fit them into fair dealing or fair use exceptions? As adverted to by Gervais, this is a classic case where such uses should be allowed but against the payment of negotiated remuneration, where the use is indispensible to compete in a derivative market. The problem that can arise is when the license is unavailable, leading to elimination of creation of a derivative market.[93] These are some of the nascent concerns that would have cropped up if the fair use factors had been read into the fair dealing provisions. That would have led to a very interesting analysis indeed.

[93] Daniel Gervais, *Fair Use, Fair Dealing, Fair Principles: Efforts to Conceptualize Exceptions and Limitations to Copyright*, 57 Copyright Soc'y USA 499 (2010).

PART IV

Obvious and Hidden Values in the Working of Copyright Exceptions

14

Creating a Public Interest Principle for the Adjudication of Fair Use and Fair Dealing Cases

Haochen Sun

INTRODUCTION

Fair use is an awkward creature. It has been hailed as a legal invention that is essential for human and societal development.[1] At the same time, fair use has become something of a legal monster, causing no end of troubles owing to its vague and shifting contours. Hence, lamentations that fair use is the most troublesome[2] yet least determinate[3] doctrine in copyright law are hardly surprising.

Accordingly, fair use is fraught with legal dilemmas. Although high hopes are attached to its potential to protect the public interest, fair use has suffered a number of setbacks worldwide. Domestic laws governing fair use are variegated, and, worse still, individual judges may interpret and apply those laws differently.[4] The confluence of these various problems is posing increasingly grave threats to both copyright holders and users of their works domestically and globally, given that the protection and exploitation of copyrighted works now transcends national boundaries more than ever thanks to the liberalization of international trade and development of digital technology.

Against this backdrop, I put forward a public interest principle that I believe would guide courts toward better-informed decisions in fair use cases. At first blush, the public interest

[1] *See, e.g.*, Barton Beebe, *Does Judicial Ideology Affect Copyright Fair Use Outcomes?: Evidence from the Fair Use Case Law*, 31 COLUM. J.L. & ARTS 517, 522 (2008); William W. Fisher III, *Reconstructing the Fair Use Doctrine*, 101 HARV. L. REV. 1661, 1661 (1988); Ruth L. Okediji, *Reframing International Copyright Limitations and Exceptions As Development Policy*, *in* COPYRIGHT LAW IN AN AGE OF LIMITATIONS AND EXCEPTIONS 445 (Ruth L. Okediji ed., 2017); Pamela Samuelson, *Unbundling Fair Uses*, 77 FORDHAM L. REV. 2537, 2540 (2009); Haochen Sun, *Fair Use As a Collective User Right*, 90 N.C. L. REV. 125, 201 (2011); Rebecca Tushnet, *Intellectual Property As a Public Interest Mechanism*, *in* THE OXFORD HANDBOOK OF INTELLECTUAL PROPERTY LAW 95, 99 (Rochelle Dreyfuss & Justine Pila eds., 2018).

[2] Dellar v. Samuel Goldwyn, Inc., 104 F.2d 661, 662 (2d Cir. 1939) (stating that "the issue of fair use ... is the most troublesome in the whole law of copyright"); *see also* Monge v. Maya Magazines, Inc., 688 F.3d 1164, 1170 (9th Cir. 2012) (quoting *Dellar*, 104 F.2d at 662).

[3] Paul Goldstein, *Goldstein on Copyright* § 12:3 (3d ed. Supp. 2019) (arguing that "[n]o copyright doctrine is less determinate than fair use"); Princeton Univ. Press v. Mich. Document Servs., Inc., 99 F.3d 1381, 1392 (6th Cir. 1996) (quoting Time Inc. v. Bernard Geis Assocs., 293 F. Supp. 130, 144 (S.D.N.Y. 1968)) ("Fair use is one of the most unsettled areas of the law. The doctrine has been said to be 'so flexible as virtually to defy definition.'"); Haochen Sun, *Overcoming the Achilles Heel of Copyright Law*, 5 NW. J. TECH. & INTELL. PROP. 265, 283–91 (2007) (discussing how and why the US fair use doctrine is indeterminate).

[4] RUTH L. OKEDIJI, THE INTERNATIONAL COPYRIGHT SYSTEM: LIMITATIONS, EXCEPTIONS AND PUBLIC INTEREST CONSIDERATIONS FOR DEVELOPING COUNTRIES 20 (2006), *available at* https://unctad.org/en/Docs/iteipc200610_en.pdf.

principle is grounded in the legitimacy of copyright law as the long-entrenched guardian of the public interest. The Statute of Anne, the very first copyright statute, was designed as "An Act for the Encouragement of Learning, by vesting the Copies of Printed Books in the Authors or purchasers of such Copies . . . ."[5] The Copyright Clause of the American Constitution grants Congress the power to confer copyright upon authors for the purpose of "promot[ing] the Progress of Science and useful Arts."[6] According to the US Supreme Court, "'Progress of Science' . . . refers broadly to 'the creation and spread of knowledge and learning.'"[7]

Internationally, copyright treaties have also enshrined the public interest as a guiding principle,[8] lending strong support to the adoption of the proposed principle. For instance, the Agreement on Trade-Related Aspects of Intellectual Property Rights (TRIPS Agreement)[9] states the public interest objectives of intellectual property protection.[10] Article 8 of the TRIPS Agreement adopts the public interest principle by stipulating that intellectual property protection should "promote the public interest in sectors of vital importance to [countries'] socio-economic and technological development."[11] Moreover, the Preamble of the WIPO Copyright Treaty emphasizes "the need to maintain a balance between the rights of authors and the larger public interest, particularly education, research and access to information. . . ."[12]

I argue that the public interest principle would legally upgrade fair use from serving as an "engine of free expression"[13] to serving as an engine of public interest protection. As I will

[5] 8 Anne, ch. 19 (1710). Influenced by this legislative tradition, the Canadian Copyright Act, for instance, is structured as "a balance between promoting the public interest in the encouragement and dissemination of works of the arts and intellect and obtaining a just reward for the creator . . . ." L. T. C. Harms, The Enforcement of Intellectual Property Rights: A Case Book 181 (3rd ed. 2012).

[6] U.S. Const. art. I, § 8, cl. 8.

[7] Golan v. Holder, 565 U.S. 302, 324 (2012); *see also* Eldred v. Ashcroft, 537 U.S. 186, 245 (2002) (Breyer, J., dissenting) (describing "the basic Clause objective" as "'promot[ing] the Progress of Science,' *i.e.*, knowledge and learning"); Feist Publ'ns, Inc. v. Rural Tel. Serv. Co., 499 U.S. 340, 349–50 (1991) (holding that "[t]he primary objective of copyright is not to reward the labor of authors, but '[t]o promote the Progress of Science and useful Arts.' To this end, copyright assures authors the right to their original expression, but encourages others to build freely upon the ideas and information conveyed by a work.") (citations omitted); Orrin Hatch & Thomas Lee, *"To Promote the Progress of Science": The Copyright Clause and Congress's Power to Extend Copyrights*, 16 Harv. J.L. & Tech. 1, 7 (2002) ("Everyone agrees that the notion of 'science' in the founding era referred generally to all forms of knowledge and learning.").

[8] *See, e.g.*, Daniel Gervais, *Fair Use, Fair Dealing, Fair Principles: Efforts to Conceptualize Exceptions and Limitations to Copyright*, 57 J. Copyright Soc'y U.S.A. 499, 518 (2010) (concluding that "'public interest' . . . has always formed part of international copyright law and policy"); Ruth L. Okediji, *Toward an International Fair Use Doctrine*, 39 Colum. J. Transnat'l L. 75, 81–82 (2000) (finding that "the negotiators and drafters of the [TRIPS] Agreement . . . were primarily concerned with . . . the public interest principles that serve as a basis for copyright").

[9] Agreement on Trade-Related Agreements of Intellectual Property Rights, art. 13, Apr. 15, 1994, Marrakesh Agreement Establishing the World Trade Organization, Annex 1C, 33 I.L.M. 1197 (1994) [hereinafter TRIPS Agreement].

[10] Art. 7 of the TRIPS Agreement states the public interest objectives as follows:

> The protection and enforcement of intellectual property rights should contribute to the promotion of technological innovation and to the transfer and dissemination of technology, to the mutual advantage of producers and users of technological knowledge and in a manner conducive to social and economic welfare, and to a balance of rights and obligations.

Id. at art.7; *see also* Peter K. Yu, *The Objectives and Principles of the TRIPS Agreement*, 46 Hous. L. Rev. 979, 1007 (2009) (pointing out that the official view of Art. 7 is that it is "intended to strike a balance that more widely promotes social and economic welfare").

[11] TRIPS Agreement, *supra* note 9, at art. 8.

[12] World Intellectual Property Organization Copyright Treaty, Dec. 20, 1996, 36 I.L.M. 65 (1997).

[13] Harper & Row Publishers, Inc. v. Nation Enters., 471 U.S. 539, 558 (1985); *see also* Eldred v. Ashcroft, 537 U.S. 186, 219, 221 (2003) (describing fair use as a "free speech safeguard[]" and a "First Amendment accommodation[]").

demonstrate, adoption of the principle would modify the judicial application of the fair use doctrine in two major ways.

First, the public interest principle would offer two substantive legal standards. It would create a public interest use standard for courts to utilize in weighing the first fair use factor without applying the dichotomy of transformative and non-transformative use. Meanwhile, it would also require courts to employ the significant market harm standard when considering the fourth fair use factor.

Second, the public interest principle would also modify the procedural rules concerning the assignment of the burden of proof in fair use cases. It would place only the burden of proving a public interest use under the first factor on the user who is the defendant in judicial proceedings. At the same time, it would shift the burden of proving market harm and the other fair use factors to the copyright holder, the plaintiff who has demonstrated prima facie copyright infringement in judicial proceedings.

Moreover, I also examine the implications of the public interest principle for dealing with the differences between the fair use and fair dealing doctrines. Commentators and policymakers alike have explored ways of reforming fair dealing by taking advantage of the open-ended, flexible qualities of fair use[14] and of reforming fair use by injecting the certainties that fair dealing affords.[15] In this chapter, I argue that the public interest principle can be used to develop a meaningful alternative that bridges the gaps between the two doctrines. By largely preserving the existing attributes of both, the principle would serve as a commonly shared principle for adjudicating cases and developing further legislative reforms in both fair use and fair dealing jurisdictions.

Given the venerable goal of upholding the socially beneficial function of copyright law,[16] I further propose that as long as courts apply the public interest principle in deciding fair use cases, copyright law will serve as an engine of public interest protection. Accordingly, in Sections 3 and 4 of this chapter, I discuss how the public interest principle should be adopted and applied both substantively and procedurally under the fair use doctrine. I further consider the principle's feasibility for guiding the fair dealing doctrine in Section 5.

1 CREATING TWO SUBSTANTIVE STANDARDS FOR THE PUBLIC INTEREST PRINCIPLE

In this section, I consider how the public interest principle can lead to the adoption of the "public interest use" and "significant market substitution" standards in judicial inquiries into fair use.

[14] *See, e.g.*, Anupam Chander, *How Law Made Silicon Valley*, 63 Emory L.J. 639, 677 (2014) (arguing that the fair dealing regimes in the European Union "proved less flexible in responding to technological developments than American fair use"); Robert Burrell & Allison Coleman, Copyright Exceptions: The Digital Impact 249–75 (2005).

[15] *See, e.g.*, Barton Beebe, *Fair Use and Legal Futurism*, 25 Law & Literature 10, 15 (2013) (pointing out that "[t]he very malleability that was once a virtue of fair use doctrine now leaves it exposed to powerful efforts to constrict its scope"); Sun, *supra* note 3, at 283 ("The condition that requires copyright limitations [to] be 'clearly defined' and 'narrow in scope and reach' calls into question whether the first prong of the three-step test [as required by Article 13 of the TRIPS Agreement] will strike down [fair use doctrine that is] by nature flexible and open-ended."); P. Bernt Hugenholtz & Martin Senftleben, *Fair Use in Europe: In Search of Flexibilities* 9 (Amsterdam Law School Research Paper No. 2012-39; Institute for Information Law Research Paper No. 2012-33, 2012), https://papers.ssrn.com/sol3/papers.cfm?abstract_id=2013239 (contending that "the rule of fair use as it presently exists and is applied in the United States has always attracted criticism, particularly for its presumed lack of predictability").

[16] *See* Rebecca Giblin & Kimberlee Weatherall, *If We Redesigned Copyright From Scratch, What Might It Look Like?*, *in* What If We Could Reimagine Copyright? 7 (Rebecca Giblin & Kimberlee Weatherall eds., 2017) (reviewing "[t]he fundamental societal goals commonly described as constituting the public interest in copyright"); Pierre N. Leval, *Toward a Fair Use Standard*, 103 Harv. L. Rev. 1105, 1107 (1990) ("The copyright is not an inevitable, divine, or natural right that confers on authors the absolute ownership of their creations. It is designed rather to stimulate activity and progress in the arts for the intellectual enrichment of the public.").

A Public Interest Use

In applying the first fair use factor, namely, "the purpose and character of the use,"[17] courts should instead utilize the public interest use standard to examine whether an unauthorized use of a work primarily benefits the public interest in character. Such utilization would require courts to dismantle the dichotomy between transformative and non-transformative uses. The public interest standard not only treats transformative use as a typical public interest use, but also weighs non-transformative uses in light of the public interest. If a non-transformative use promotes that interest, then it should be deemed to be in compliance with the first fair use factor.

i Transformative Use

Since the US Supreme Court's ruling in *Campbell*,[18] transformativeness has been the predominant legal standard for weighing the first fair use factor.[19] In *Campbell*, the court opined that the "the more transformative the new work, the less will be the significance of other factors, like commercialism, that may weigh against a finding of fair use."[20]

Transformative use, by its very nature, protects the public interest. Of course, the immediate beneficiary is the copier who uses the work for the transformative purpose concerned. For instance, by making transformative use of copyrighted books, Google received the immediate benefit of creating Google Library. However, the ultimate beneficiaries are members of the public. By adding a "new expression, meaning, or message"[21] or function[22] to the original work, a transformative use communicates a new work or the original to the public with benefits that the copyright holder of the original work did not intend to offer.[23] Therefore, it ultimately "enrich[es] public knowledge."[24]

[17] 17 U.S.C. § 107 (2018).

[18] 510 U.S. at 585 ("[T]he fact that even the force of that tendency will vary with the context is a further reason against elevating commerciality to hard presumptive significance.").

[19] *See* Barton Beebe, *An Empirical Study of U.S. Copyright Fair Use Opinions*, 1978–2005, 156 U. PA. L. REV. 549, 606 (2008) (pointing out that "a finding of transformativeness may be dispositive of the outcome of the fair use test"); Neil Netanel, *Making Sense of Fair Use*, 15 LEWIS & CLARK L. REV. 715, 768 (2011) ("Since 2005, the transformative use paradigm has come to dominate fair use case law . . . ."); Matthew Sag, *Predicting Fair Use*, 73 OHIO ST. L.J. 47, 84 (2012) (concluding that "transformative use by the defendant is a robust predictor of a finding of fair use"); Rebecca Tushnet, *Copy This Essay: How Fair Use Doctrine Harms Free Speech and How Copying Serves It*, 114 YALE L.J. 535, 555 (2004) (arguing that "fair use law has been realigned around transformative use").

[20] 510 U.S. at 579; *see also* Mattel Inc. v. Walking Mountain Prods., 353 F.3d 792, 800 (9th Cir. 2003) ("The Supreme Court has recognized that parodic works, like other works that comment and criticize, are by their nature often sufficiently transformative to fit clearly under the fair use exception."); Kelly v. Arriba Soft Corp., 336 F.3d 811, 818 (9th Cir. 2003) ("The more transformative the new work, the less important the other factors, including commercialism, become."); Suntrust Bank v. Houghton Mifflin Co., 268 F.3d 1257, 1271–74 (11th Cir. 2001) ("[C]onsideration of [the transformative nature of the parody] certainly militates in favor of a finding of fair use, and, informs our analysis of the other factors.").

[21] 510 U.S. at 579.

[22] *See, e.g.*, Perfect 10, Inc. v. Amazon.com, Inc., 508 F.3d 1146, 1165 (9th Cir. 2007) ("[M]aking an exact copy of a work may be transformative so long as the copy serves a different function than the original work." (citing *Kelly*, 336 F.3d at 818–19)). The court found a search engine's copying of website images in order to create an internet search index transformative because the original works "serve[d] an entertainment, aesthetic, or informative function, [whereas the] search engine transforms the image into a pointer directing a user to a source of information." *Id.*

[23] Authors Guild v. Google, Inc., 804 F.3d 202, 214 (2d Cir. 2015) (concluding that "transformative uses tend to favor a fair use finding because a transformative use is one that communicates something new and different from the original or expands its utility, thus serving copyright's overall objective of contributing to public knowledge").

[24] *Id.*

Transformative use, as required by the first fair use factor, is one of the key reasons the US courts ruled in favor of Google.[25] When weighing the search function afforded by Google Library, the Second Circuit took pains to examine the public benefits that Google's transformative use produced:

> As with HathiTrust (and iParadigms), the purpose of Google's copying of the original copyrighted books is to make available significant information about those books, permitting a searcher to identify those that contain a word or term of interest, as well as those that do not include reference to it. In addition, through the Ngrams tool, Google allows readers to learn the frequency of usage of selected words in the aggregate corpus of published books in different historical periods. We have no doubt that the purpose of this copying is the sort of transformative purpose described in *Campbell* as strongly favoring satisfaction of the first factor.[26]

The purpose of Google's reproduction of copyrighted books, according to the Second Circuit, was to add an information search function to the books, a function that the copyright holders did not offer. That function ultimately benefits readers and researchers, who are members of the public, enabling them to efficiently locate information contained in a book and learn the frequency of select word usage.

Google Library's snippet view function was similarly deemed by the Second Circuit to constitute a transformative use on the same grounds:

> Google's division of the page into tiny snippets is designed to show the searcher just enough context surrounding the searched term to help her evaluate whether the book falls within the scope of her interest … . Snippet view thus adds importantly to the highly transformative purpose of identifying books of interest to the searcher.[27]

The above passage shows that the ultimate beneficiaries of the snippet view function are information searchers, who again are members of the public. As a transformative use, the function serves their interest in evaluating the content surrounding search words, thereby providing them with a better understanding of search results extracted from a vast pool of information.

A series of other fair use rulings lend support to transformative use being identified as a type of public interest use. Take parodic use cases as an example.[28] In *Campbell*, the US Supreme Court ruled that parody transforms a work for the purpose of humorous comment or criticism, thereby "provid[ing] social benefit, by shedding light on an earlier work, and, in the process, creating a new one."[29] In *Suntrust v. Houghton Mifflin Co.*, the US Court of Appeals for the Eleventh Circuit grounded its ruling on parodic use in policy considerations, writing that "the public interest is always served in promoting First Amendment values and in preserving the public domain from encroachment."[30]

ii Non-transformative Use

The public interest use standard also protects non-transformative uses of works that promote the public interest. It requires courts to treat transformative and non-transformative uses

[25] *Id.*

[26] *Authors Guild*, 804 F.3d at 217.

[27] *Id.* at 218.

[28] *See* David Tan, *The Lost Language of the First Amendment in Copyright Fair Use: A Semiotic Perspective of the "Transformative Use" Doctrine Twenty-Five Years On*, 26 Fordham Intell. Prop. Media & Ent. L.J. 311, 345 (2016) (pointing out that parody "advanc[es] democratic debate on matters of public interest through the use of irreverent humor").

[29] Campbell v. Acuff-Rose Music, Inc., 510 U.S. 569, 579 (1994).

[30] 268 F.3d 1257, 1275 (11th Cir. 2001).

equally when they are made in the public interest. The non-transformative use of a work utilizes "the same 'overall function'" of the work from which the user copied.[31] For instance, preparing coursepacks by copying textbooks published by others does not alter the function of the copyrighted materials and therefore constitutes a non-transformative use.[32] Given that such use serves the same purpose or function as the original work,[33] courts have routinely disfavored shielding it, and therefore have generally treated it as tantamount to an infringing use.[34]

Although a non-transformative use can be made for a user's personal interest, it can also be made in the public interest, that is, to benefit others. Commentators have found many instances in which non-transformative use promotes democratic progress and educational development through the wider dissemination of information.[35] Professor Rebecca Tushnet, for example, has convincingly demonstrated how various non-transformative uses not only protect freedom of expression by positively facilitating copiers' free speech activities,[36] but also promote larger social values by affording audiences access to copiers' speech.[37]

Similarly, several landmark copyright cases have demonstrated the necessity of legalizing non-transformative uses that protect the public interest. For instance, *Authors Guild, Inc. v. HathiTrust*[38] epitomizes cases in which non-transformative use may promote social justice. The Second Circuit decided that HathiTrust's reproductions of works to facilitate access to them by the print-disabled constituted a non-transformative use.[39] However, it still ruled in favor of HathiTrust under the first fair use factor by recognizing the public benefits accruing to print-disabled readers from the access afforded them.[40] Relying on the legislative history of US law, the court asserted that providing access to works for the print-disabled "assure[s] equality of opportunity, full participation, independent living, and economic self-sufficiency for such individuals."[41]

Cambridge University Press v. Patton is another leading case that marks a watershed in valuing the social function of non-transformative uses in promoting education. In this case, the Eleventh Circuit ruled that Georgia State University's operation of an electronic reserve system that allowed its professors to make digital copies of excerpts of copyrighted books available to their

[31] Cambridge Univ. Press v. Patton, 769 F.3d 1232, 1262 (11th Cir. 2014) (citing Peter Letterese & Assocs., Inc. v. World Inst. of Scientology Enters., 533 F.3d 1287, 1311 (11th Cir. 2008)).

[32] *See id.* at 1264 ("In the coursepack cases, … the first factor weighed against a finding of fair use when the nontransformative, educational use in question was performed by a for-profit copyshop, and was therefore commercial. In a more recent case, a district court refused to allow a commercial copyshop to sidestep the outcome of the coursepack cases by requiring its student customers to perform the photocopying themselves (for a fee) when assembling paper coursepacks from master copies held by the copyshop.") (citations omitted).

[33] *See* Sun, *supra* note 1, at 188 (noting that the transformative uses are differentiated from non-transformative uses because the latter "simply copy the original copyrighted works and thereby make no new contributions to enrich culture").

[34] *See, e.g.*, L.A. Times v. Free Republic, No. CV 98-7840 MMM (AJWx), 2000 U.S. Dist. LEXIS 5669, at *75 (C.D. Cal. Mar. 31, 2000) ("Conversely, the amount and substantiality of the copying and the lack of any significant transformation of the articles weigh heavily in favor of plaintiffs … .").

[35] Tushnet, *supra* note 19, at 566.

[36] *Id.* at 565–66.

[37] *Id.* at 562 (contending that "[pure] copying is of value to audiences who have access through copying to otherwise unavailable speech. It also enhances copiers' ability to express themselves; to persuade others; and to participate in cultural, religious, and political institutions.").

[38] 755 F.3d 87 (2d Cir. 2014).

[39] *Id.* at 101–2.

[40] *Id.* at 102 ("We conclude that providing access to the print-disabled is still a valid purpose under Factor One even though it is not transformative.").

[41] *Id.* (citing Congress's statement in the Americans with Disabilities Act).

students did not constitute a transformative use. According to the ruling, such use did not add new meaning[42] or purpose[43] to the excerpts concerned. Rather, it served the same function as the excerpts, that is, constituting course reading material for university students.[44] The Eleventh Circuit ruled, however, that because the non-transformative use was made by a university, that is, by a nonprofit educational institution, it deserved favorable protection under the first fair use factor.[45] This opinion followed the legislative intention of ensuring the proper treatment of educational use as a paradigmatic example of fair use.[46] It also recognized the value of educational use in fulfilling copyright law's goal of furthering the public interest.[47]

I have demonstrated that the traditional dichotomy between transformative and non-transformative use serves to undervalue certain legitimate public interests. Both can promote the public interest, provided that the ultimate beneficiaries of the use in question are members of the public. As Justice Blackmun wisely ascertained, there is a "humanitarian impulse" built into the first fair use factor because its intent "is to encourage users to engage in activities the primary benefit of which accrues to others."[48] Therefore, guided by the public interest principle, courts should replace the dichotomy between transformative and non-transformative use with the public interest use standard in the first fair use factor inquiry. At the same time, given the application of that standard, courts may also consider removing the commerciality standard from the first factor.[49] As demonstrated earlier in this subsection, cases involving transformative and non-transformative uses of works for commercial purposes can actually serve the public interest. Therefore, both commercial and noncommercial uses can promote the public interest.[50] Given that the ultimate goal of the first factor is to consider the public interest, it is unnecessary for courts to consider the commerciality standard.

42 Cambridge Univ. Press v. Patton, 769 F.3d 1232, 1262 (11th Cir. 2014) ("Although a professor may arrange these excerpts into a particular order or combination for use in a college course, this does not imbue the excerpts themselves with any more than a *de minimis* amount of new meaning.").

43 *Id.* at 1263 ("Nor do Defendants use the excerpts for anything other than the same intrinsic purpose – or at least one of the purposes – served by Plaintiffs' works: reading material for students in university courses.").

44 *Id.* (quoting Campbell v. Acuff-Rose Music, Inc., 510 U.S. 569, 579 (1994) ("Although an electronic reserve system may facilitate easy access to excerpts of Plaintiffs' works, it does nothing to transform those works .... Rather, Defendants' use of excerpts of Plaintiffs' works 'supersede[s] the objects of the original creation.'").

45 *Id.* at 1267 ("Furthermore, we find this sufficiently weighty that the first factor favors a finding of fair use despite the nontransformative nature of the use.... [W]e are persuaded that, despite the recent focus on transformativeness under the first factor, use for teaching purposes by a nonprofit, educational institution such as Defendants' favors a finding of fair use under the first factor, despite the nontransformative nature of the use.").

46 *Id.* ("Congress devoted extensive effort to ensure that fair use would allow for educational copying under the proper circumstances and was sufficiently determined to achieve this goal that it amended the text of the statute at the eleventh hour in order to expressly state it.").

47 *Id.* ("[A]llowing latitude for educational fair use promotes the goals of copyright."); *id.* at 1282 ("Nonprofit educational uses are more likely to be fair because they promote the ultimate aims of copyright – the creation and dissemination of knowledge.").

48 Sony Corp. of Am. v. Universal City Studios, Inc., 464 U.S. 417, 496 (1984) (Blackmun, J., dissenting).

49 In fact, the US Supreme Court has downgraded the importance of the commerciality standard for transformative use. In *Sony*, the court stated that "every commercial use of copyrighted material is presumptively an unfair exploitation of the monopoly privilege that belongs to the owner of the copyright." 464 U.S. at 451. In Harper & Row Publishers, Inc. v. Nation Enterprises, the court further explicated commercial use, noting that it is a "factor that tends to weigh against a finding of fair use" because "the user stands to profit from exploitation of the copyrighted material without paying the customary price." 471 U.S. 539, 562 (1985). However, in *Campbell*, the Supreme Court refuted its earlier rulings in *Sony* and *Harper & Row* with regard to the commerciality standard, instead ruling that "the more transformative the new work, the less will be the significance of other factors, like commercialism, that may weigh against a finding of fair use." 510 U.S. at 579.

50 *See, e.g.*, MADHAVI SUNDER, FROM GOODS TO A GOOD LIFE: INTELLECTUAL PROPERTY AND GLOBAL JUSTICE 118 (2012) (pointing out that "the history of fair use is replete with commercial uses").

iii Identifying Group-Based and Society-Based Public Interests

How then do courts identify a public interest use under the first fair use factor? I propose that they can do so by ascertaining whether the use of a work has produced either group-based or society-based interests.[51]

Group-based interests can be recognized on the basis of the identities of the group members who take part in various social and cultural activities.[52] Examples of groups whose activities constitute fair use include researchers, educators, and journalists. The importance of protecting group-based interests can be inferred from a number of judicial rulings. In *Sega Enterprises Ltd. v. Accolade, Inc.*,[53] for example, courts applied the fair use doctrine to protect the public interest in reverse engineering technology that allows software engineers as a group of users to achieve the interoperability of different software programs.[54] Similarly, in *A.V. ex rel. Vanderhye v. iParadigms, LLC*,[55] the interests of students as a group of users in copying works in their entirety for use in an antiplagiarism database were protected.[56]

Courts may first identify either the identity-based group to which the users of copyrighted works belong or the larger social benefits that may be generated by the unauthorized use of such works. In doing so, courts would place themselves in a better position to consider the extent to which the unauthorized use of copyrighted works affects the protection of group members' interests more widely or promotes the creation of social benefits. For instance, research as a permitted fair use encompasses not only an individual research activity but also research as "a practice or system,"[57] which is a collective activity that many participate in as a group of researchers.

The society-based interests involved in the use of a work are designed to ensure that "the public as a whole can live in a free and just society."[58] These interests are related to the overall economic, political, and cultural needs of the society to which that public belongs. The emergence of Internet-related technologies resulted in a host of new copyright disputes. Relying on the legal concept of transformative use, courts have moved to protect the public interest in benefiting from progress in such technologies. In *Kelly v. Arriba Soft Corp.*,[59] *Field v. Google Inc.*,[60] and their progeny,[61] the US courts ruled that the reproduction in their entirety of numerous photographs or web pages to create and operate internet search engines constitutes fair use. The US courts ascertained that because they were created by search engines serving as

[51] *See* Sun, *supra* note 1, at 177 ("Both types of collective rights allow the public to enjoy freedom in asserting collective interests in utilizing copyrighted works.").

[52] *Id.* at 178.

[53] 977 F.2d 1510 (9th Cir. 1992).

[54] *Id.* at 1523 (ruling that reverse engineering "has led to an increase in the number of independently designed video game programs offered for use with the [plaintiff's] console"); *see also* Pamela Samuelson & Suzanne Scotchmer, *The Law and Economics of Reverse Engineering*, 111 YALE L.J. 1575, 1608–09 (2002) ("From this approximation of source code, reverse engineers can discern or deduce internal design details of the program, such as information necessary to develop a program that will interoperate with the decompiled or disassembled program.").

[55] 562 F.3d 630 (4th Cir. 2009).

[56] *Id.* at 639 (ruling that "iParadigms' use of plaintiffs' works [in a plagiarism detection database] had an entirely different function and purpose than the original works").

[57] CCH Canadian Ltd. v. Law Soc'y of Upper Can., [2004] 1 S.C.R. 399 (Can.), ¶¶ 48, 51, 63 (emphases added), *available at* http://scc.lexum.org/en/2004/2004scc13 /2004scc13.pdf.

[58] Sun, *supra* note 1, at 180.

[59] 336 F.3d 811 (9th Cir. 2003).

[60] 412 F. Supp. 2d 1106 (D. Nev. 2006).

[61] *See, e.g.*, Perfect 10, Inc. v. Amazon.com, Inc., 508 F.3d 1146, 1168 (9th Cir. 2007) (ruling that the display of thumbnail images of the copyrighted photographs constituted fair use).

an electronic reference tool, such reproductions benefited society as a whole by improving public access to information.[62]

Accordingly, courts should apply transformativeness as a means of identifying either a group- or society-based public interest. For example, by first recognizing the new functions that Google Library added to the books it reproduced, the US courts considered how such transformative uses could bring about a society-based public interest. Consequently, they treated Google Library as itself constituting a technological breakthrough in opening up new functions for books. More importantly, they also regarded it as a scheme for enhancing the societal interests in knowledge acquisition and sharing through such technological progress.

However, the utilization of transformativeness does not foreclose the possibility of any inquiry into whether a non-transformative use furthers the public interest identified through the group- and society-based approach. Instead, courts still enjoy the latitude to consider how and why a non-transformative use promotes a group- or society-based public interest. As discussed earlier, the US court rulings on HathiTrust Digital Library exemplify such an application of the group- and society-based approach. Courts determined that HathiTrust's non-transformative use served the interest of the print-disabled as a group of readers in accessing books.[63]

B Significant Market Substitution

The second component of the public interest principle requires the application of the "significant market substitution" standard, which should guide courts to apply the fourth factor of the fair use doctrine, namely, "the effect of the use upon the potential market for or value of the copyrighted work."[64] To do so, courts should exclude the public interest use of a work from the full spectrum of the work's market share. Put differently, when courts deal with the fourth factor, they should require copyright holders to legally tolerate public interest uses of their works to the extent that those uses do not cause significant market substitutions of their works.

i Assessing Market Harm Properly

According to the US Supreme Court, an unauthorized use of a work runs counter to the fourth factor only when it "act[s] as a substitute for"[65] the work. Following from that logic, the fourth factor triggers two inquiries about how such a use would cause harm to both the current and potential market value of the work.[66] Despite the large number of fair use cases heard over the years, uncertainty still surrounds the fourth factor itself and its relation to the other factors.[67] In *Campbell*, the Supreme Court attempted to clarify, stating that "when ... the second use is transformative, market substitution is at least less certain, and market harm may not be so readily inferred."[68] Although this is an authoritative interpretation of the fourth factor, the approach

[62] *Id.* at 1165 (ruling that "a search engine provides social benefit by incorporating an original work into a new work, namely, an electronic reference tool").

[63] *See supra* text accompanying notes 38–41.

[64] 17 U.S.C. § 107 (2018).

[65] Campbell v. Acuff-Rose Music, Inc., 510 U.S. 569, 591 (1994) (deciding that "cognizable market harm" is limited to "market substitution").

[66] *Id.* at 590 (quoting 3 M. Nimmer & D. Nimmer, *Nimmer on Copyright* § 13.05(A)(4) (1993)) (concluding that under the fourth factor, courts should "consider not only the extent of market harm caused by the particular actions of the alleged infringer, but also 'whether unrestricted and widespread conduct of the sort engaged in by the defendant ... would result in a substantially adverse impact on the potential market'").

[67] *See* Sun, *supra* note 3, at 290.

[68] *Campbell*, 510 U.S. at 591.

proffered by the court suffers from two problems. First, the court did not consider whether a non-transformative use that serves the public interest should be treated on the same footing as a transformative use under the fourth factor.

Second, the court utilized the copyright holder–based approach to determine the scope of the protectable market shielded by copyright. It correctly pointed out that a transformative use is unlikely to cause a market substitutive effect because it "usually serve[s] different market functions."[69] However, it erred by determining the scope of the protectable market by whether the use would generally create or license others to create derivative works. According to the Supreme Court, critical review and parody do not fall within the ambit of a protectable market because copyright holders would not license others to use their works in those particular transformative ways.[70] The court's treatment of a copyright holder's protectable market here fails to capture the essence of fair use. By nature, fair use legally permits unauthorized uses of works in the public interest, provided that they do not violate the fair use factors.[71] Copyright holders are not supposed to enjoy proprietary control over all public interest uses of their works through any of their potential licensing arrangements.[72] Such proprietary control, regardless of whether it incentivizes copyright holders to create works, would be detrimental to public interest protection.[73]

Third, when it comes to fair use such as a critical comment on or parody of a work, neither of these public interest uses of the work would significantly substitute its market because those uses serve the public interest in openly discussing issues relating to the work. They do not intend to replace sales of the work in the marketplace. From this perspective, courts do not need to consider whether the copyright holder would license others to use the work for the purpose of

[69] *Id.*; *see also* Authors Guild v. HathiTrust, 755 F.3d 87, 99 (2d Cir. 2014) (citing Billy Graham Archives v. Dorling Kindersley Ltd., 448 F.3d 605, 614 (2d Cir. 2006)) ("In other words, under Factor Four, any economic 'harm' caused by transformative uses does not count because such uses, by definition, do not serve as substitutes for the original work.").

[70] *Campbell*, 510 U.S. at 592 ("This distinction between potentially remediable displacement and unremediable disparagement is reflected in the rule that there is no protectible derivative market for criticism. The market for potential derivative uses includes only those that creators of original works would in general develop or license others to develop. Yet the unlikelihood that creators of imaginative works will license critical reviews or lampoons of their own productions removes such uses from the very notion of a potential licensing market.").

[71] As Judge Leval correctly pointed out, it is presumptively valid for a fair use to cause a certain amount of harm to the market value of the work concerned. He argues that "[b]y definition every fair use involves some loss of royalty revenue because the secondary user has not paid royalties .... [I]f an insubstantial loss of revenue turned the fourth factor in favor of the copyright holder, this factor would never weigh in favor of the secondary user." Leval, *supra* note 16, at 1124–25.

[72] Professor Shyamkrishna Balganesh argues that it is legally and socially undesirable to define an overly broad scope of copyright, thereby allowing copyright holders to control market share to an extent that disincentivizes them to create new works. Hence, he concludes that "[c]opyright ... needs to internalize the idea that incentives have limits and develop a mechanism by which to eliminate unincentivized gains from a creator's entitlement, especially when including them in the entitlement is likely to produce more costs than benefits." Shyamkrishna Balganesh, *Foreseeability and Copyright Incentives*, 122 Harv. L. Rev. 1569, 1574 (2009). He further contends that the conventional practice of fair use has allowed copyright holders to "internalize all possible benefits, until the fair use determination concludes otherwise." *Id.* at 1585. Therefore, as he further points out, "[i]n focusing on this presumptive entitlement by itself, fair use does very little in practice to link the defendant's actions (that is, copying) with the creator's original incentive." *Id.*

[73] According to Professor Mark Lemley, all "[e]fforts to permit [copyright] owners to fully internalize the benefits of their creativity [through their proprietary control] will inevitably get the balance [of copyright protection] wrong." Mark A. Lemley, *Property, Intellectual Property, and Free Riding*, 83 Tex. L. Rev. 1031, 1032 (2005). Professor James Boyle also points out that fair use serves as a limitation on the scope of copyrights. *See* James Boyle, The Public Domain: Enclosing the Commons of the Mind 66 (2008) ("When society hands out the right to the copyright holder, it carves out certain areas of use and refuses to hand over control of them.").

critical review or parody.[74] Therefore, the fourth factor should be read as having already divorced public interest uses from the market of copyright holders. What courts should consider under the fourth factor is whether public interest uses of works would in turn significantly substitute the market of those works. If they would, then courts are very likely to rule in favor of the copyright holders.[75] If they would not, courts are very likely to rule in favor of users.[76]

The significant market substitution standard can resolve the aforementioned problems through a new approach that directly allows courts to exclude a public interest use of a work that is permissible under the first fair use factor from the ambit of the work's market under the fourth factor. Stemming from the public interest principle, the significant market substitution standard guides courts to more effectively weigh the extent of market harm. To that end, it requires courts to utilize public interest considerations in evaluating the harm to a work's current and potential market value. If courts can identify a public interest use under the first fair use factor, they should then apply the significant market substitution standard, which sets a higher threshold for establishing market harm.

The Second Circuit ruling in the Google Library case sheds light on how this new standard can be applied. Although the fourth fair use factor is intended to protect the market value of a work, the Second Circuit examined it in light of public interest considerations and then applied the significant market substitution standard, which allows the public to benefit from limited uses of copyrighted works to the extent that such uses do not exert a significant substitutive effect on those works' market value. The Second Circuit stated:

> We recognize that the snippet function can cause *some* loss of sales. There are surely instances in which a searcher's need for access to a text will be satisfied by the snippet view, resulting in either the loss of a sale to that searcher, or reduction of demand on libraries for that title, which might have resulted in libraries purchasing additional copies. But the possibility, or even the probability or certainty, of some loss of sales does not suffice to make the copy an effectively competing substitute that would tilt the weighty fourth factor in favor of the rights holder in the original. There must be a meaningful or significant effect "upon the potential market for or value of the copyrighted work."[77]

Here, the Second Circuit filled the vacuum left by the Supreme Court's *Campbell* ruling, casting new light on how to ascertain the probability of market substitution in light of the public

[74] *See, e.g.*, William F. Patry, *Patry on Copyright* § 10:151 (2018) ("Too broad an interpretation of the potential market, however, presents its own considerable dangers. If taken to a logical extreme, the fourth factor would always weigh against fair use since there is always a potential market that the copyright owner could in theory license.") (citations omitted); Rebecca Tushnet, *Content, Purpose, or Both*, 90 Wash. L. Rev. 869, 891(2015) ("Transformativeness, despite its potential ambiguities, has the capacity to recognize the uses that we find valuable and that we believe copyright owners shouldn't control.").

[75] *See Campbell*, 510 U.S. at 593 ("Evidence of substantial harm to [a derivative market] would weigh against a finding of fair use."); Harper & Row Publishers, Inc. v. Nation Enterprises, 471 U.S. 539, 566–67 (1985) ("Fair use, when properly applied, is limited to copying by others which does not materially impair the marketability of the work which is copied."); Cambridge University Press v. Patton, 769 F.3d 1232, 1276 (11th Cir. 2014) ("The central question under the fourth factor is not whether Defendants' use of Plaintiffs' works caused Plaintiffs to lose some potential revenue. Rather, it is whether Defendants' use – taking into account the damage that might occur if 'everybody did it' – would cause *substantial* economic harm such that allowing it would frustrate the purposes of copyright by materially impairing Defendants' incentive to publish the work.").

[76] *See* Sony Corp. of Am. v. Universal City Studios, Inc., 464 U.S. 417, 454 (1984) (ruling that fair use "requires the copyright holder to demonstrate some likelihood of harm"); Authors Guild v. Google, Inc., 804 F.3d 202, 224 (2d Cir. 2015) (deciding that a violation of the fourth fair use factor could be found if the defendant caused "a meaningful or significant effect" on the market value of the plaintiff's work).

[77] *Authors Guild*, 804 F.3d at 224.

interest principle. The Second Circuit was fully aware of instances in which the provision of snippet views by Google Library would cause some loss of sales to the affected works. However, it ruled that such market harm is nonetheless permitted under the fair use doctrine as long as it does not lead to "meaningful or significant"[78] market substitution of the works. In other words, the fair use doctrine tolerates a moderate degree of market harm caused by a transformative use that is socially beneficial. The doctrine protects such a socially beneficial use as long as it does not cause market harm sufficient to significantly replace the copyright holder's work in the marketplace. With regard to a non-transformative use that protects the public interest, the Second Circuit decided that copyright holders should not be vested with market control over their works to the extent that those works are used by digital libraries providing the print-disabled with access to them.[79]

To follow the public interest principle, courts should first determine whether the use of a work is socially beneficial, and then ensure that such use would not cause significant market substitution.[80] Again, the Second Circuit showed how courts should handle these two steps in weighing the fourth factor. For the first step, the Second Circuit concluded that snippet views promote the public interest in locating information, such as a historical fact that is not protected by copyright law. It offered the plausible case of a student writing a research paper who would benefit from the snippet view of *The Making of Franklin D. Roosevelt* generated by the entry of search words to discover the historical fact that Roosevelt had been stricken with polio.[81] With regard to the second step, the Second Circuit found that snippet views of copyrighted books did not cause significant market substitution to the books because Google had endeavored to make those views short, disjointed, and incomplete.[82]

ii Evaluating Market Harm but Not Benefits

In weighing the fourth fair use factor, some US courts have considered the benefits that the authorized use of a work can confer upon its market value. For example, the District Court approvingly weighed the market benefits accrued from Google Library in its assessment of the fourth factor.[83] A number of leading commentators have contended that both the Supreme Court's fair use rulings and practical needs lend support to a consideration of market benefits.[84]

[78] *Id.*

[79] *See* Authors Guild v. HathiTrust, 755 F.3d 87, 103 (2d Cir. 2014) ("The fourth factor also weighs in favor of a finding of fair use. It is undisputed that the present-day market for books accessible to the handicapped is so insignificant that 'it is common practice in the publishing industry for authors to forgo royalties that are generated through the sale of books manufactured in specialized formats for the blind . . . .'" (quoting Final Form Br. and Special App. for Pls.-Appellants at *34)).

[80] *See* Jeanne C. Fromer, *Market Effects Bearing on Fair Use*, 90 WASH. L. REV. 615, 633 (2015) ("[T]here may be societal benefits from a use without concomitant market benefits to the copyright owner, but when there are market benefits to the copyright owner, there tends also to be societal benefit. All in all, policies weighing in favor of fair use suggest that market benefits to the copyright holder offer a signal that there is a societal benefit favoring fair use, which might also benefit the copyright holder.").

[81] *Authors Guild*, 804 F.3d at 224.

[82] *Id.* at 224–25.

[83] *See* Authors Guild v. Google Inc., 954 F. Supp. 2d 282, 293 (S.D.N.Y. 2013); *see also* Kelly v. Arriba Soft Corp., 336 F.3d 811, 821 (9th Cir. 2003) (discussing defendant's use of the plaintiff's images in thumbnail version in the defendant's search engine brought benefits to the plaintiff); Nat'l Ctr. for Jewish Film v. Riverside Films, LLC, No. 5:12-cv-00044-ODW (DTBx), 2012 U.S. Dist. LEXIS 131831, at *13–14 (C.D. Cal. Sept. 14, 2012) (ruling in favor of the defendants because their films would cause "a newfound interest in Plaintiff's copyrighted films").

[84] *See, e.g.*, Fromer, *supra* note 80, at 641 ("In sum, *Campbell*'s fair use analysis ought to be read to require consideration of both market harms and benefits – so long as these harms and benefits surpass a certain degree of speculativeness – to determine the market effects bearing on fair use. The statute, copyright policy, and business realities justify this understanding of the fourth fair use factor."); Pamela Samuelson, *Possible Futures of Fair Use*, 90 WASH. L. REV. 815,

As shown in the preceding subsection, however, the significant market substitution standard does not necessitate judicial inquiry into whether the unauthorized use of a work may benefit its market value. Instead, it requires courts only to evaluate the harm to the work's market value caused by the unauthorized use.[85]

Contrary to these commentators' inference from leading precedents, the US Supreme Court's fair use rulings should not be read as providing judicial support for a consideration of market benefits under the fourth factor. In *Sony*, the court did turn its attention to how the reproduction of works for the time-shifting purpose conferred market benefits upon the copyright holder concerned and public benefits in the form of wider access to television programs.[86] However, it then shifted its attention and emphasized that what the fourth factor really requires is for a copyright holder to "demonstrate some likelihood of harm" to refute the contention that a reproduction of his or her work constituted a fair use.[87] Without weighing up whether the said market benefits could mitigate the potential market harm, the court then directly concluded that the copyright holders in question had failed to prove on the merit of the fourth factor that the reproduction at issue had "cause[d] any likelihood of nonminimal harm to the potential market for, or the value of, their copyrighted works."[88] Relying on *Sony*, the Supreme Court later asserted in *Harper & Row Publishers, Inc. v. Nation Enterprises* that inquiry into the fourth factor is concerned merely with market harm.[89] It did not consider whether the unauthorized publication of excerpts from former President Nixon's memoirs had produced market benefits by bringing the public's attention to the memoirs prior to their publication. Instead, the court implied that it was improper to consider market benefits.[90]

Similarly, the *Campbell* ruling should not be read as setting a precedent on judicial consideration of market benefits under the fourth factor. In a footnote to its ruling, the court offered the following analysis:

> Even favorable evidence, without more, is no guarantee of fairness. Judge Leval gives the example of the film producer's appropriation of a composer's previously unknown song that turns the song into a commercial success; the boon to the song does not make the film's simple copying fair. This factor, no less than the other three, may be addressed only through a "sensitive balancing of interests." Market harm is a matter of degree, and the importance of this factor will vary, not only with the amount of harm, but also with the relative strength of the showing on the other factors.[91]

823 (2015) ("After *Campbell*, it is acceptable for courts to take into account possible market benefits of a defendant's use of the plaintiff's work in weighing market effects, not just possible negative effects. Campbell has opened the door to considering possible benefits and harms together in a holistic way, as well as in relation to the other factors.").

[85] *See, e.g.*, 4 Melville B. Nimmer & David Nimmer, *Nimmer on Copyright* § 1305[A][4] (2018) ("The fourth factor looks to adverse impact only by reason of usurpation of the demand for plaintiff's work through defendant's copying of protectable expression from such work."); Folsom v. Marsh, 9 F. Cas. 342, 348 (C.C.D. Mass. 1841) (ruling that fair use defenses should "look to ... the degree in which the use may prejudice the sale, or diminish the profits, or supersede the objects, of the original work."); Wendy J. Gordon, *The Concept of "Harm" in Copyright*, *in* Intellectual Property and the Common Law 30 n.81 (Shyamkrishna Balganesh ed., 2015) ("The fourth fair use factor ... has been interpreted both as referring to plaintiff's private harm, and as referring to impact on incentives.").

[86] Sony Corp. of Am. v. Universal City Studios, Inc., 464 U.S. 417, 454 (1984).

[87] *Id.*

[88] *Id.* at 456.

[89] 471 U.S. 539, 568 (1985) ("This inquiry must take account not only of harm to the original but also of harm to the market for derivative works.").

[90] The court ruled that "[a]ny copyright infringer may claim to benefit the public by increasing public access to the copyrighted work. But Congress has not designed, and we see no warrant for judicially imposing, a 'compulsory license' permitting unfettered access to the unpublished copyrighted expression of public figures." *Id.* at 569 (citations omitted).

[91] Campbell v. Acuff-Rose Music, Inc., 510 U.S. 569, 590 n.21 (citations omitted).

To some commentators, this observation is the epitome of the Supreme Court's endorsement for incorporating a consideration of market benefits into analysis of the fourth factor.[92] In my opinion, however, the observation is not intended to open the door to any such additional consideration for several reasons.

First, despite its mention of "the boon" to the copyright holder's market, the court did not examine the market benefits of parodies that accrued to copyright holders, as commentators have alleged.[93] Rather, it solely analyzed the various scenarios in which parodies might cause harm to copyright holders and then decided to insulate the fourth factor from consideration of those hypothetical harms.[94]

Second, by the "sensitive balancing of interests" quoted from *Sony*, the court did not intend to weigh both the positive benefits and harmful effects that an unauthorized use could bring to a copyright holder's market. Instead, it meant to show its concurrence with the part of the *Sony* ruling in which interests were weighed under the confluence of all four fair use factors,[95] the first factor in particular.[96]

Third, when the court concluded that the degree of market harm must be balanced with "the other factors," it was by no means referring to market benefits as factors. Again, it situated its analysis of market harm in the scrutiny of transformativeness under the first factor. Indeed, the court made it crystal clear that transformativeness serves as a countervailing consideration against the market harm assessment under the fourth factor.[97]

On the other hand, the proposed consideration of market benefits is fraught with problems, making its incorporation into application of the fourth factor undesirable indeed. First, measuring market benefits is infeasible in practice. Virtually any unauthorized use of a work could hypothetically benefit the copyright holder to a certain extent. For example, as unauthorized uses can promote the visibility or popularity of a work to various degrees,[98] they might result in increased sales for the copyright holder.[99] However, it would be difficult indeed to put an exact figure on such benefits, and it would be nearly impossible to calculate exactly how many people purchased a given work because an authorized copy thereof had aroused their interest. Nor

[92] *See, e.g.*, Fromer, *supra* note 80, at 629.

[93] *Id.* (arguing that "the Court hints that some parodies might even confer market benefits").

[94] *Campbell*, 510 U.S. at 591–92 ("Indeed, as to parody pure and simple, it is more likely that the new work will not affect the market for the original in a way cognizable under this factor, that is, by acting as a substitute for it . . . . We do not, of course, suggest that a parody may not harm the market at all, but when a lethal parody, like a scathing theater review, kills demand for the original, it does not produce a harm cognizable under the Copyright Act.").

[95] Sony Corp. of Am. v. Universal City Studios, Inc., 464 U.S. 417, 454–55 (1984) ("When [fair use] factors are all weighed in the 'equitable rule of reason' balance, we must conclude that this record amply supports the District Court's conclusion that home time-shifting is fair use.").

[96] In footnote 40 of the *Sony* ruling that the court cited, it was stated that courts should particularly weigh the first factor which triggers an inquiry of the character of use as being productive and nonproductive with the fourth factor. *Sony*, 464 U.S. at 455 n.40.

[97] *Campbell*, 510 U.S. at 591 (ruling that "when . . . the second use is transformative, market substitution is at least less certain, and market harm may not be so readily inferred.").

[98] *See* David Fagundes, *Market Harm, Market Help, and Fair Use*, 17 Stan. Tech. L. Rev. 359, 379 (2014) ("Infringement can, however counterintuitively, serve as a source of publicity and drive up demand in a way that more than makes up for the lost sales of some copies.").

[99] Judge Leval gives an example of how "[q]uotation of the original may substantially augment its value and yet be a clear infringement." He pointed out that "[t]his would occur, for example, if a famous disc jockey, without authorization, regularly used an obscure song as the theme melody of her program. The value of the copyright for the song would be greatly enhanced." Pierre N. Leval, *Nimmer Lecture: Fair Use Rescued*, 44 UCLA L. Rev. 1449, 1459 (1997); *see also* Patry, *supra* note 74, § 6:14 (pointing out that "a search engine's retrieval and display of excerpts from a copyrighted book will likely lead to increased sales, as well as providing valuable information to the individual who initiated the query").

would it be an easy task to measure the reputational benefits accruing to a work through an unauthorized use.[100] More difficult still would be to calculate those benefits in dollars. Given these difficulties, it would be unrealistic to determine the market benefits to a work first and then weigh those benefits against the market harm.

Second, the proposed separation between market benefits and harm is likely to be circular in nature, which may result in unintended negative consequences for copyright holders. Market benefits, if ascertained exogenously without taking a closer look at copyright holders' legitimate intentions, are in turn very likely to be harmful to their interests protected under the fourth factor. In these circumstances, so-called market benefits would actually equate to market harm to copyright holders. *Monge v. Maya Magazines, Inc.*[101] epitomizes just this kind of adverse circumstance for copyright holders. The defendant, Maya Magazines, had published photos of the wedding of the Monges, a celebrity couple who wished to keep their marriage secret. Before the unauthorized publication, Maya Magazines had bought the photos in question from the Monges' chauffeur, who had tried but failed to extort money from the Monges for the photos' return. Maya Magazines' publication of the photos might have been considered to confer market benefits on the couple by increasing demand for their wedding photos and other photos and burnishing their reputation as celebrities. However, it is crystal clear that the Monges never wished to enjoy such questionable benefits, having vehemently objected to any publication of their wedding photos. Hence, the wider the circulation of the photos, the greater the harm – rather than benefits – inflicted upon them.

There were two kinds of harm to the Monges associated directly with the market benefits derived from the unauthorized initial publication of the photos and their subsequent circulation. First, there was significant market harm caused directly to their proprietary control over the market for their wedding photos,[102] as their publication limited the couple's exercise of their exclusive right to publish,[103] further distribute,[104] and prepare derivative works.[105] Second, there was indirect harm to other of the Monges' personal interests relating to the market for their wedding photos. The forced opening up of that market by Maya Magazines not only impinged upon their privacy but also negatively affected their reputation as unmarried celebrities.[106] All in

[100] Similarly, a search engine's reproduction and display of a work may increase the reputation of the work on the Internet.

[101] 688 F.3d 1164 (9th Cir. 2012).

[102] In my view, it would have been better for courts to rule that the unauthorized initial publication concerned caused harm to the right to control the market for the photos rather than to the photos' potential market value. Such an approach would have alleviated any doubt over whether the copyright holders in the case had any wish to publish their photos, meaning that the photos' potential market value was uncertain. The right to control the market for a work does not require consideration of the potential value of that market. For the court's ruling in this regard, *see id.* at 1182 ("Maya's un-authorized 'first and exclusive' publication of the images substantially harmed the potential market because the publication directly competed with, and completely usurped, the couple's potential market for first publication of the photos.").

[103] 17 U.S.C. § 106(3) (2018). The US Supreme Court concluded that "Clause (3) of section 106, establishes the exclusive right of publications. . . . Under this provision the copyright owner would have the right to control the first public distribution of an authorized copy . . . of his work." Harper & Row, Publishers, Inc. v. Nation Enters., 471 U.S. 539, 552 (1985) (citing H.R.Rep. No. 94-1476, p. 62 (1976), U.S. Code Cong. & Admin. News 1976, p. 5675). It also ruled that "[t]he right of first publication encompasses not only the choice whether to publish at all, but also the choices of when, where, and in what form first to publish a work." *Id.* at 564.

[104] 17 U.S.C. § 106(3).

[105] *Id.* § 106(2).

[106] *See* Patrick R. Goold, *Unbundling the 'Tort' of Copyright Infringement*, 102 VA. L. REV. 1833, 1837 (2016) (finding that "[w]hile some courts conceptualize harm as lost revenue from the defendant, others require proof of consumer demand diversion, and occasionally courts also find a cognizable nonfinancial injury to privacy, reputation, or creative control"); David Ladd, *The Harm of the Concept of Harm in Copyright*, 30 J. COPYRIGHT SOC'Y U.S.A. 421,

all, *Monge v. Maya Magazines, Inc.* demonstrates the infeasibility of considering market benefits under the fourth factor, given that such "benefits" can in reality impose harm on copyright holders if their works are being used in a manner contrary to their legitimate intentions.

Hence, I agree with commentators who state that courts should consider the larger social benefits accruing from unauthorized uses of a work,[107] but respectfully disagree with them that such benefits should be considered under the fourth fair use factor. Instead, social benefits should be considered under the first fair use factor with the public interest use standard I suggest above.

2 MODIFYING THE PROCEDURAL RULE BY REALLOCATING THE BURDEN OF PROOF

The assignment of burden of proof is of critical importance.[108] In some circumstances, it can determine the outcome of a fair use case, thereby profoundly affecting protection of the public interest. For example, as discussed in Section 2, the Chinese courts placed the burden of proving fair use on the accused infringers in copyright disputes. Therefore, the Beijing High Court simply rejected Google's assertion of fair use on the grounds that the company had failed to submit evidence proving fair use.[109] By strictly following such a procedural rule, the court failed to consider any public interests involved in the provision of Google Library. At the same time, although the US courts properly protected the public interest in the Google Library case, there are still problems with the fair use doctrine they invoked, specifically with their procedural treatment of fair use as an affirmative defense.

In this section, I first identify the major inadequacies of assigning the burden of proof in the way required by the affirmative defense approach to fair use. I then explore how the public interest principle can lead to the redefinition of fair use as a collective user right, thereby triggering a major modification of the procedural rule for burden of proof allocation. I argue that users should be required to bear only the burden of proving whether their use meets the first fair use factor, the public interest use standard thereunder in particular. When it comes to the three other fair use factors, copyright holders should shoulder the burden of proof.

A *Major Problem with the Affirmative Defense Approach*

Under the fair use doctrine, the burden of proving fair use is placed on the alleged infringers who have used copyrighted works.[110] In *Harper & Row*, for example, the US Supreme Court treated fair use as "an affirmative defense requiring a case-by-case analysis,"[111] thereby refuting

422 (1983) (pointing out that "[t]he [mere] notion of economic "harm" as a prerequisite for copyright protection is mischievous"); *cf.* Gordon, *supra* note 85, at 51 ("Subjective distress may be 'harm' in some contexts, such as the tort of intentional infliction of emotional distress, but should not count as such in copyright.").

[107] *See* Fromer, *supra* note 80, at 633 (concluding that "there may be societal benefits from a use without concomitant market benefits to the copyright owner, but when there are market benefits to the copyright owner, there tends also to be societal benefit").

[108] Shyamkrishna Balganesh, *Copyright as Market Prospect*, 166 U. Pa. L. Rev. 443, 497 (2018) ("A major unresolved controversy of some significance in copyright jurisprudence is whether fair use should be a part of the plaintiff's prima facie case, or instead an affirmative defense.").

[109] *See* Robert P. Merges & Seagull Haiyan Song, Transnational Intellectual Property Law: Text and Cases 456 (2018), at 456.

[110] *See* Sun, *supra* note 1, at 146 ("By treating fair use as an affirmative defense, courts place the burden of proving fair use on the allegedly infringing users in copyright disputes.").

[111] 471 U.S. 539, 561 (1985).

the existence of presumptive categories of fair use.[112] In *Campbell*, the court further clarified that "[s]ince fair use is an affirmative defense, its proponent[s] would have ... the burden of demonstrating fair use."[113] Following this judicial characterization of fair use as an affirmative defense,[114] users are procedurally required to bear the burden of producing the requisite evidence and persuading courts that said evidence is sufficiently probative to demonstrate that their use of the copyrighted work in question satisfies all fair use factors.[115] In *Perfect 10, Inc. v. Amazon.com, Inc.*,[116] the US Court of Appeals for the Ninth Circuit further explicated the way in which the burden of proving fair use should be handled as a matter of procedure in the different stages of judicial proceedings:

> At trial, the defendant in an infringement action bears the burden of proving fair use. Because "the burdens at the preliminary injunction stage track the burdens at trial," once the moving party has carried its burden of showing a likelihood of success on the merits, the burden shifts to the non-moving party to show a likelihood that its affirmative defense will succeed.[117]

Placing the burden of proving fair use on users as an affirmative defense, however, has given rise to a number of unintended negative consequences. First, users are not by any means in a better position to prove the fourth fair use factor, which in many cases is the key determining factor in the case outcome. The US Supreme Court has exhibited sympathy for the difficulty defendants experience in obtaining sufficient evidence to prove fair use under the fourth factor.[118] However, it has not reversed the burden of proof by requiring plaintiffs to demonstrate market harm. Instead, it has merely defied practice to presume market harm if a commercial use is found.[119]

Second, the affirmative defense approach places an onerous procedural burden on users, which may deter members of the public from asserting their fair use privilege. A fair use inquiry is a complex combination of law and fact without bright line rules.[120] As a highly sophisticated body of copyright law, the fair use doctrine is known for its ambiguity, with all four fair use factors still ill-defined.[121] Therefore, defendants must rely on legal professionals to assist them

112 *Id.* ("The drafters resisted pressures from special interest groups to create presumptive categories of fair use, but structured the provision as an affirmative defense requiring a case-by-case analysis.").

113 Campbell v. Acuff-Rose Music, Inc., 510 U.S. 569, 590 (1994).

114 *See, e.g.*, Peter Letterese & Assocs. v. World Inst. of Scientology Enters., 533 F.3d 1287, 1307 n.21 (11th Cir. 2008) ("The affirmative defense of fair use is a mixed question of law and fact as to which the proponent carries the burden of proof."); Am. Geophysical Union v. Texaco Inc., 60 F.3d 913, 918 (2d Cir. 1994) ("Fair use serves as an affirmative defense to a claim of copyright infringement, and thus the party claiming that its secondary use of the original copyrighted work constitutes a fair use typically carries the burden of proof as to all issues in the dispute."); Columbia Pictures Indus. v. Miramax Films Corp., 11 F. Supp. 2d 1179, 1187 (C.D. Cal. 1998) (holding that "because fair use is an affirmative defense, Defendants bear the burden of proof on all of its factors").

115 *See* Ned Snow, *Proving Fair Use: Burden of Proof as Burden of Speech*, 31 CARDOZO L. REV. 1781, 1784 (2010) (pointing out that to prove the existence of fair use, a user is required to "produce the necessary evidence (even where the inquiry is speculative) and to persuade the court that her interpretation of the evidence reflects fact (even where the inquiry is subjective)").

116 508 F.3d 1146 (9th Cir. 2007).

117 *Id.* at 1158 (quoting Gonzales v. O Centro Espirita Beneficente Uniao do Vegetal, 546 U.S. 418, 429 (2006)).

118 *Campbell*, 510 U.S. at 590 ("Since fair use is an affirmative defense, its proponent would have difficulty carrying the burden of demonstrating fair use without favorable evidence about relevant markets.") (citation omitted).

119 *Id.* at 591 (citing Sony Corp. of Am. v. Universal City Studios, Inc., 464 U.S. 417, 451 (1984)) (distinguishing *Sony*'s ruling that "[i]f the intended use is for commercial gain, that likelihood may be presumed. But if it is for a noncommercial purpose, the likelihood must be demonstrated").

120 Harper & Row, Publishers, Inc. v. Nation Enters., 471 U.S. 539, 560 (1985) ("Fair use is a mixed question of law and fact.").

121 *See, e.g.*, Sun, supra note 3, at 291 ("Judging from section 107's legislative purpose and structure and the discrepancies in courts' approaches to apply the four factors, the fair use doctrine is indeed vague, flexible and open-ended.").

with collecting and then utilizing evidence to demonstrate that a fair use claim prevails on the basis of all four factors. Because of these onerous procedural and evidentiary requirements, the process of proving fair use is very likely to incur a six-figure attorney fee.[122] Faced with the high cost of defending the fair use privilege, users, particularly the less well-off and not-for-profit entities, may prove unwilling to assert the legality of their uses before courts.[123] Consequently, commentators have lamented that fair use has been unduly reduced to "the right to hire a lawyer to defend [one's] right to create."[124]

Third, the affirmative defense approach has impaired such public interests as free speech and education, which are crucial to a free and equal society. Free speech activities, to a greater or lesser extent, involve the copying of copyrighted works.[125] In the various stages of copyright litigation proceedings – from the preliminary injunction to courtroom hearing to voluntary settlement – the difficulty of collecting evidence to prove market harm and the high litigation costs involved impose an undue burden on users who wish to defend their free speech right.[126] Worse still, the fear of failing to tackle such difficulties successfully might deter people from asserting their free speech right even prior to the commencement of judicial proceedings. The affirmative defense approach can therefore exert a chilling effect on free speech in everyday life.[127] Such a chilling effect can also be seen in educational settings, raising serious concerns over whether fair use can deliver on its promise to promote education.[128]

B Transforming Fair Use into a Collective User Right

In response to the problems with reducing fair use to an affirmative defense, several commentators have contended that the nature of fair use should be redefined in line with the legislative intent of section 107 of the US Copyright Act, which governs fair use analysis.[129] At the same time, the redefinition should also alleviate the burden on users of proving fair use.[130] Although such an approach has merit, I believe that a better approach would be to follow the public interest principle by redefining fair use as a collective user right and subsequently reallocating the burden of proof between the user and copyright holder.

[122] *See, e.g.*, Kevin M. Lemley, *I'll Make Him an Offer He Can't Refuse: A Proposed Model for Alternative Dispute Resolution in Intellectual Property Disputes*, 37 AKRON L. REV. 287, 311 (2004) ("Intellectual property litigation typically spans several years with total costs commonly exceeding hundreds of thousands or even millions of dollars. A 2001 survey . . . calculated the average cost through trial of typical patent disputes . . . at $1,499,000; $699,000 for similar trade secret disputes; $502,000 for trademark disputes; and $400,000 for copyright disputes.") (footnotes omitted).

[123] *See, e.g.*, Sun, *supra* note 1, at 192; James Gibson, *Risk Aversion and Rights Accretion in Intellectual Property Law*, 116 YALE L.J. 882, 890 (2007).

[124] LAWRENCE LESSIG, FREE CULTURE: THE NATURE AND FUTURE OF CREATIVITY 187 (2004).

[125] *See* Tushnet, *supra* note 19, at 567.

[126] Lydia Pallas Loren, *Fair Use: An Affirmative Defense?*, 90 WASH L. REV. 685, 691, 709–10 (2015) ("Treating fair use as an affirmative defense places an unnecessary and inappropriate burden on free speech. Placing the burden of proving or disproving fair use may play a significant role in the outcome of a litigated case at a variety of stages, from the issuance of a preliminary injunction to the ultimate determination of infringement liability. And, of course, who bears the burden of proving a use was (or was not) a fair use affects the settlement posture of the parties, as well as the behavior of potential fair users even prior to the filing or threat of litigation.") (citation omitted).

[127] *Id.* at 710; Eugene Volokh, *Freedom of Speech and Intellectual Property: Some Thoughts after Eldred, 44 Liquormart,* and *Bartnicki*, 40 HOUS. L. REV. 697, 719–22 (2003) (arguing that placing the burden of proof on the defendant violates First Amendment due process rights).

[128] *See, e.g.*, Sun, *supra* note 3, at 321–22.

[129] Loren, *supra* note 126, at 695 ("The committee believes that any special statutory provision placing the burden of proving fair use on one side or the other would be unfair and undesirable.") (internal quotation marks omitted).

[130] *Id.* at 702.

i Fair Use As a Statutory Right

By characterizing fair use as an affirmative defense, the US courts have turned a blind eye to the statutory definition of fair use. The US Copyright Act explicitly embraces fair use as a statutory right. Section 108 states that "[n]othing in this section . . . in any way affects the right of fair use as provided by section 107, or any contractual obligations assumed at any time by the library or archives when it obtained a copy or phonorecord of a work in its collections."[131] As this statutory language is crystal clear, fair use should be regarded as a right.

However, what remains unclear is whether it is a substantive right, a procedural right, or both. As a substantive right, fair use is more akin to a positive right.[132] It is supposed to entitle members of the public to make fair use of copyrighted works on their own decisions. As a procedural right, however, fair use serves as a negative right entitling a user to sufficient judicial protection in various stages of legal proceedings that prevent copyright holders from unduly interfering with fair use.[133] According to a report by the US Copyright Office, sections 107 and 108 define fair use as a substantive right. The report further reads section 108 as a "fair use savings clause," entitling "libraries and archives to make fair use of works to the same extent as any other user of a copyrighted work" under section 107.[134] Therefore, fair use is a substantive right that entitles the public to take the positive action of using a work without permission from the copyright holder.[135]

ii Fair Use As a Judicially Recognized Right

Because fair use has been judicially defined as an affirmative defense, courts have increasingly deviated from the practice of considering fair use as a substantive, positive right. The US Court of Appeals for the Eleventh Circuit actually ventured to redefine fair use as an "affirmative right" in its *Suntrust Bank v. Houghton Mifflin Co.* ruling.[136] In that case, the Eleventh Circuit grounded the fair use right in the constitutional right to free speech under the First Amendment:

> [F]air use should be considered an affirmative *right* under the 1976 Act, rather than merely an affirmative defense, as it is defined in the Act as a use that is not a violation of copyright. However, fair use is commonly referred to as an affirmative defense, and, as we are bound by Supreme Court precedent, we will apply it as such. Nevertheless, the fact that the fair use right must be procedurally asserted as an affirmative defense does not detract from its constitutional significance as a guarantor to access and use for First Amendment purposes.[137]

131 17 U.S.C. § 108(f)(4) (2012).

132 Isaiah Berlin, *Two Concepts of Liberty*, *in* LIBERTY 178 (2002) ("The 'positive' sense of the word 'liberty' derives from the wish on the part of the individual to be his own master. I wish my life and decisions to depend on myself, not on external forces of whatever kind.").

133 *Id.* at 174 ("The defence of liberty consists in the 'negative' goal of warding off interference.").

134 US COPYRIGHT OFFICE, SECTION 108 OF TITLE 17, at 9 (2017), www.copyright.gov/policy/section108/discussion-document.pdf.

135 Loren, *supra* note 126, at 698 ("The language of Section 108, identifying the 'right of fair use,' furthers the textual argument that the statute does not treat fair use as an affirmative defense in the style of 'confession and avoidance.' A defense is any reason that the plaintiff should not prevail. On the other hand, an affirmative defense is relevant only once the plaintiff's prima facie case has been proven. If fair use is 'not an infringement,' then the plaintiff has not met its burden to demonstrate a prima facie case of infringement without overcoming the argument that the use is a fair use.") (citations omitted).

136 268 F.3d 1257 (11th Cir. 2001).

137 *Id.* at 1260 n.3 (citations omitted). In this footnote, the judge cited Bateman v. Mnemonics, Inc., 79 F.3d 1532 (11th Cir. 1996), which also defined fair use as a right:

> Although the traditional approach is to view "fair use" as an affirmative defense, this writer, speaking only for himself, is of the opinion that it is better viewed as a right granted by the Copyright Act of 1976. Originally, as a judicial doctrine without any statutory basis, fair use was an infringement that was

Similarly, the US Court of Appeals for the Second Circuit also attempted to redefine fair use as a right in *NXIVM Corp. v. Ross Institute*, undergirding that right with the Copyright Clause of the US Constitution:

> Fair use is not a doctrine that exists by sufferance, or that is earned by good works and clean morals; it is a right – codified in § 107 and recognized since shortly after the Statute of Anne – that is "necessary to fulfill copyright's very purpose, [t]o promote the Progress of science and the useful arts. . . ."[138]

The foregoing quote from the Copyright Clause is largely understood to justify copyright protection as a means to the end of promoting the public interest. For example, the US Supreme Court and lower federal courts alike have repeatedly stressed that protection of the public interest is the primary objective of US copyright law.[139] Therefore, as long as fair use is invoked in the public interest, copyright law should also protect it as a positive right.[140]

In attempting to redefine fair use as a right, courts did not further propose altering the procedural rules for fair use cases by shifting the burden of proving fair use to the plaintiff.[141] Nevertheless, in *Lenz v. Universal Music Corp.*,[142] the US Court of Appeals for the Ninth Circuit decided to deviate from the affirmative defense approach:

> [Characterizing fair use as an affirmative defense] conflates two different concepts: an affirmative defense that is labeled as such due to the procedural posture of the case, and an affirmative defense that excuses impermissible conduct. Supreme Court precedent squarely supports the conclusion that fair use does not fall into the latter camp: "[A]nyone who . . . makes a fair use of the work is not an infringer of the copyright with respect to such use." Given that 17 U.S.C. § 107 expressly authorizes fair use, labeling it as an affirmative defense that excuses conduct is a misnomer. . . .[143]

This treatment of fair use fundamentally departs from the conventional reading of fair use as an affirmative defense that "excuses impermissible conduct." The Ninth Circuit grounded its

> excused – this is presumably why it was treated as a defense. As a statutory doctrine, however, fair use is not an infringement. Thus, since the passage of the 1976 Act, fair use should no longer be considered an infringement to be excused; instead, it is logical to view fair use as a right. Regardless of how fair use is viewed, it is clear that the burden of proving fair use is always on the putative infringer.

Id. at 1542 n.22.

[138] 364 F.3d 471, 485 (2d Cir. 2004) (Jacobs, J., concurring) (alteration in original) (quoting Campbell v. Acuff-Rose Music, Inc., 510 U.S. 569, 575 (1994)).

[139] *See, e.g.*, *Campbell*, 510 U.S. at 575 ("From the infancy of copyright protection, some opportunity for fair use of copyrighted materials has been thought necessary to fulfill copyright's very purpose, '[t]o promote the Progress of Science and useful Arts . . .'") (alteration in original) (quoting U.S. Const. art. I, § 8, cl. 8); Feist Publ'n, Inc. v. Rural Telephone Service Co., 499 U.S. 340, 349–50 (1991) (holding that "[t]he primary objective of copyright is not to reward the labor of authors, but '[t]o promote the Progress of Science and useful Arts.'") (citations omitted). For similar judicial opinions, *see* Fogerty v. Fantasy, Inc., 510 U.S. 517, 526 (1994); Sony Corp. of Am. v. Universal City Studios, Inc., 464 U.S. 417, 429 (1984); Twentieth Century Music Corp. v. Aiken, 422 U.S. 151, 156 (1975); U.S. v. Paramount Pictures, 334 U.S. 131, 158 (1948); Fox Film Corp. v. Doyal, 286 U.S. 123, 127 (1932); Computer Assocs. Int'l v. Altai, Inc., 982 F.2d 693, 711 (2d Cir. 1992).

[140] Patry, *supra* note 74, § 10:1.50 (2018) ("'Limitations and exceptions to copyright,' a phrase much in current use, posits the issue backwards; that phrase assumes a grant of rights that is checked only on occasion, and in derogation of a presumed default of unfettered rights. Limitations and exceptions will be allowed, it is argued, if there is a public interest that justifies overriding the private rights of authors in their works in particular circumstances.").

[141] *See, e.g.*, Bateman v. Mnemonics, Inc., 79 F.3d 1532, 1542 (11th Cir. 1996).

[142] 815 F.3d 1145 (9th Cir. 2015).

[143] *Id.* at 1152–53 (citations omitted). The Ninth Circuit also concluded that "[f]air use is therefore distinct from affirmative defenses where a use infringes a copyright, but there is no liability due to a valid excuse, e.g., misuse of a copyright and laches." *Id.* at 1153.

opinion in fair use as a concept legally permitting the public to use copyrighted works, a concept deeply ingrained in copyright law. Given that the public is entitled to make legally permitted uses, copyright holders cannot unduly interfere unless uses go beyond the bounds set in section 107. Therefore, the Ninth Circuit's opinion implicitly proffers a legal basis for treating fair use as a substantive positive right under sections 107 and 108 of the US Copyright Act.

Furthermore, the Ninth Circuit moved to explicitly accept fair use as a right.[144] The court considered and agreed with the opinion of Judge Birch that fair use should be treated as a right rather than an affirmative defense, and subsequently altered the burden of proving fair use in notice-and-takedown proceedings.[145] The Ninth Circuit required the copyright holder in question to evaluate whether a fair use of his work existed before he sent a takedown notice to an internet service provider. A normal takedown notice requires proof of the nonexistence of fair use from the copyright holder, not the user.[146]

At the same time, the treatment of fair use as a user right also gains strong support from several Canadian court rulings defining the Canadian fair dealing doctrine as equivalent to the fair use doctrine. In *CCH Canadian Ltd. v. Law Society of Upper Canada*,[147] for example, the Supreme Court of Canada delivered a groundbreaking opinion on the nature of fair dealing. It decided that the fair dealing doctrine under the Canadian Copyright Act should be regarded as "a user's right."[148] For that purpose, the doctrine "must not be interpreted restrictively"[149] so as to achieve balanced protection of the rights of both copyright holder and user. In a subsequent case, the Supreme Court further justified its definition of fair dealing as a user right on the grounds of public interest protection, stating that "users' rights are an essential part of furthering the public interest objectives of the [Canadian] Copyright Act."[150]

iii Fair Use As a Collective User Right

As discussed above, I believe it is legally sound to treat fair use as a user right according to the plain language of the US Copyright Act and the growing tendency among circuit courts to depart from the affirmative defense approach. There has also been a surge in commentators adamantly arguing the case for redefining fair use as a user right.[151]

In my view, the public interest principle requires fair use to be treated as a *collective* user right. As discussed in Section 3 of this chapter, according to that principle, only public interest uses

144 *Id.* at 1153.

145 *Id.*

146 *Id.* (holding "that because 17 U.S.C. § 107 created a type of non-infringing use, fair use is 'authorized by the law' and a copyright holder must consider the existence of fair use before sending a takedown notification under § 512(c).").

147 [2004] 1 S.C.R. 399, ¶¶ 48, 51 & 63 (Can.), *available at* www.canlii.org/en/ca/scc/doc/2004/2004scc13/2004scc13.html?autocompleteStr=%5B2004%5D%201%20S.C.R.%20399&autocompletePos=1.

148 *Id.* ¶ 48.

149 *Id.*

150 *See* Soc'y of Composers, Authors and Music Publishers of Canada v. Bell Canada, 2012 SCC 36, ¶ 27 (Can.).

151 For theoretical discussion about how to treat fair use and fair dealing as a user right, *see* Abraham Drassinower, *Taking User Rights Seriously*, *in* In The Public Interest: The Future of Canadian Copyright Law 462, 463 (Michael Geist ed., 2005); Niva Elkin-Koren, *Copyright in a Digital Ecosystem: A User Rights Approach*, *in* Copyright Law in an Age of Limitations and Exceptions 132 (Ruth Okediji ed., 2017); Niva Elkin-Koren, *The New Frontiers of User Rights*, 32 Am. Univ. Int'l L. Rev. 1 (2016); Wendy J. Gordon & Daniel Bahls, *The Public's Rights to Fair Use: Amending Section 107 to Avoid the "Fared Use" Fallacy*, 2007 Utah L. Rev. 619, 626 (2007) ("[F]air use is a 'right' in all these senses: it is an existing liberty, to which the public has an enduring entitlement, and which deserves significant weight."); Joseph P. Liu, *Copyright Law's Theory of the Consumer*, 44 B.C. L. Rev. 397, 426 (2003) ("Instead, the law sets entitlements to give recognition to these interests, to provide breathing space for others to interact with copyrighted works.").

that comport with group or societal interests are protected by the fair use right.[152] Therefore, such public interests are by nature collectively shared by users as members of a group or society. Given the collective nature of users' interests, fair use should be characterized as a collective user right. Concomitantly, copyright holders have a collective duty to make their works freely available to serve fair users' right to achieve their collective interests.[153] The substantive dimension of the fair use doctrine comprises both a collective right conferred on users and a collective duty imposed on copyright holders.

Accordingly, the public interest principle reshapes the procedural dimension of the fair use doctrine. While serving as a substantive right, fair use also protects users' interests as a procedural right, which requires them to prove that they have exercised their right within the doctrine's ambit. In response to users' assertion of their right, copyright holders have a procedural duty to prove that they are *not* legally required to fulfill users' interests. The integration of users' procedural right and copyright holders' procedural duty thus plays a determining role in reallocating the burden of proof in fair use cases.

As a matter of procedure, a user, as a holder of the right to fair use, only needs to prove in judicial proceedings that he or she has exercised that right in the public interest. In terms of the four fair use factors, therefore, the user bears the burden of proof only under the first factor, which requires him or her to provide evidence demonstrating that he or she used the copyrighted work in question in the public interest. If he or she fails to meet that burden of proof, then the use of the work will be deemed to have been made for his or her own private interests.

At the same time, a copyright holder has a procedural duty to demonstrate that he or she does not bear a substantive duty to fulfill the fair use interest alleged by the user. In discharging that duty, he or she bears the burden of proving that the use made of his or her work in the public or private interest has exceeded the ambit of the fair use doctrine. Accordingly, the burden of proof for the three other fair use factors, particularly the fourth factor concerning market harm, is placed on the copyright holder.

Based on the public interest principle, the user right approach can produce positive effects in protecting the public interest in fair use cases. First, it provides a rights-based mode for protecting the public interest procedurally, correcting the inequality in legal status caused by the affirmative defense mode. In essence, the user right approach comports with the procedural premise of the operation of judicial proceedings in copyright cases.

Normally, when a copyright holder lodges a legal complaint with a court, he or she is procedurally required to prove that he or she has a right to the work he or she created because the work is copyrightable. Similarly, when a user claims that he or she has a fair use right, he or she needs to prove that he or she has such a right in the sense that the use of the work is made in the public interest. The public interest principle thus offers a procedurally equal status to the user and the copyright holder. Each bears a substantive right in judicial proceedings, namely, a copyright for the plaintiff and a fair use right for the defendant. Therefore, the user right approach rectifies the inequality in legal status under the affirmative defense mode, which regards the plaintiff as a copyright holder but potentially discriminates against the defendant as an alleged infringer or defense invoker who has no legal right that is expressly recognizable under copyright law.

[152] *See supra* text accompanying notes 51–62.

[153] According to the interest theory of rights, a person having a right to something means that the right serves his or her interest, and meanwhile someone else has a duty to provide it. *See, e.g.*, JOSEPH RAZ, THE MORALITY OF FREEDOM 180 (1986) ("The specific role of rights in practical thinking is . . . the grounding of duties in the interests of the other beings . . . . Rights ground requirements for action in the interest of other beings.").

Second, the user right approach necessitates a corresponding procedural duty for copyright holders, that is, a duty to prove, among other factors, that their economic interests have been significantly harmed. Their discharge of that duty alleviates users' burden of proof without requiring them to prove the nonexistence of significant market harm. As noted earlier in this section,[154] it is often very difficult indeed for users to prove that their uses of works do not cause market harm. The proposed approach responds to that difficulty by shifting the burden of proving the existence of significant market harm to copyright holders.[155] This modification of the procedural rule would in turn protect users' interests in two primary ways.

First, by removing the burden of proving the nonexistence of market harm from users, the user right approach procedurally implements the requirement that copyright holders must fulfill their collective duty to serve the public interest in using their works. To that end, they should tolerate public interest uses to the extent required by the fair use doctrine. As discussed in Section 3, the significant market harm standard excludes public interest uses from the scope of the market for a copyright holder's works.[156] Second, the user right approach reduces litigation costs for users because it requires copyright holders to bear the cost of proving all fair use factors other than the first, particularly the fourth, which requires market research and the collection of evidence and can thus be costly. The legal fees incurred in defending one's fair use right are thus greatly reduced, meaning a user is less likely to shy away from asserting that right for financial reasons.

In a nutshell, treating fair use as a collective user right procedurally addresses the major problems with the affirmative defense approach.[157] By modifying the procedural rules for allocating the burden of proof, this user right approach in turn promotes the protection of fair use as a substantive legal right under copyright law.

C Can Courts Protect the Public Interest Proactively?

As shown in Section 2 of this chapter, the Beijing High Court ruled against Google on the grounds that it had failed to fulfill its burden of proving fair dealing. Against the backdrop of that ruling, the proposed procedural treatment of fair use as a collective user right gives rise to concerns over whether courts should have the power to protect the public interest proactively, a power that has the potential to result in judicial activism and courts abandoning their impartial role in adjudicating fair use cases. These concerns can be encapsulated in two questions. First, can courts proactively identify the public interests involved in the use of a work that a user has not proved with evidence? Second, can they do so even if the user provides no evidence of the existence of a public interest use?

These issues are of pivotal importance. Under the public interest principle, identifying public interests in the use of copyrighted works determines the outcome of first factor analysis. It also has direct bearing on assessment of the fourth factor, as the scope of a copyright holder's market hinges upon the scope of public interest use thereunder.

154 *See supra* text accompanying notes 120–24.

155 *See, e.g.*, Cambridge Univ. Press v. Patton, 769 F.3d 1232, 1279 (11th Cir. 2014) ("Fair use is an affirmative defense, and the evidentiary burden on all four of its factors rests on the alleged infringer. However, Plaintiffs – as publishers – can reasonably be expected to have the evidence as to availability of licenses for their own works. It is therefore reasonable to place on Plaintiffs the burden of going forward with the evidence on this question.") (citation omitted).

156 *See supra* text accompanying note 69.

157 Loren, *supra* note 126, at 701 (arguing that the assignment of the burden of proof "could work a radical change in the meaning and effect of the doctrine of fair use").

A recent copyright case decided by the Beijing First Intermediate Court casts light on how courts can deal with the two issues. In *Beijing Sogou Information Service Co., Ltd. v. Wenhui Cong*,[158] the copyright holder, Mr. Cong, lodged a complaint with the Beijing Haidian District Court alleging that Sogou had infringed his copyright by circulating the web cache of the webpage that originally published his article.[159] The intermediate court held that the use of the copyrighted article for web caching constituted fair use under Chinese copyright law because Sogou's web caching service satisfied substantive fair use requirements and promoted the public interest.[160] This fair use ruling was rendered without any consideration of whether the defendant, Sogou, bore the burden of proving fair use. Sogou did not raise a fair use defense because it claimed that it had not committed any act tantamount to an infringement of Mr. Cong's right to make his article available to the public via the Internet.

Despite the defendant failing to provide any evidence proving public interest use, the Beijing First Intermediate Court buttressed its fair use ruling by elaborating upon such use, noting that the defendant's web caches contributed three indispensable public benefits. First, web caches ensure consistency in helping users to locate information on the Internet. When original websites cannot be loaded owing to technical or connection difficulties, internet users can still acquire information through the web caches stored on servers belonging to search engine service providers. Second, because web caches are not updated in a timely manner, internet users can have a quick view of them even after the relevant information has been deleted from the original websites. Third, the defendant's web caches highlight the keywords that internet users search for to enhance search efficiency. Consequently, the Beijing First Intermediate Court proactively examined the various public interests afforded by the defendant's web caching services even through the defendant had furnished no evidence proving that those services promoted the public interest.

In my view, the Beijing First Intermediate Court acted rightly in this case. First, when courts proactively examine the existence of a public interest use with regard to the purpose and character of that use, they will still have to further consider the extent to which the use harms the copyright holder's economic interests. Therefore, courts' exercise of judicial power in making additional public interest considerations is still checked by the fourth fair use factor or Article 21 of the Copyright Implementation Regulation, which protects the market value of copyrighted works.[161]

Second, the proactive examination of public interest by courts comports with social justice, a value that serves as the bedrock of any judicial system.[162] Fair use, by its very nature, is designed to promote social justice.[163] It prevents the knowledge and information embodied in works from being monopolized by copyright holders at the expense of the public interest. If courts do not examine whether a work was used in the public interest simply because a user fails to submit any

[158] Beijing First Intermediate Court, 2013 Yi Zhong Min Zhong Zi No. 12533 (Dec. 10, 2013).

[159] *See* Haochen Sun & Johnny Xuyang Han, *Requirements for Recognizing a New Type of Fair Use under PRC Copyright Law*, *in* ANNOTATED LEADING COPYRIGHT CASES IN MAJOR ASIAN JURISDICTIONS 257, 259 (Kung-Chung Liu ed., 2019).

[160] *Id.* at 263–64.

[161] Art. 21 provides that an unauthorized use of a work "shall not impair the normal exploitation of the work concerned, nor unreasonably prejudice the legitimate interests of the copyright owner."

[162] As John Rawls points out, "the principles of social justice . . . provide a way of assigning rights and duties in the basic institutions of society and they define the appropriate distribution of the benefits and burdens of social cooperation." JOHN RAWLS, A THEORY OF JUSTICE 4 (rev. ed. 1999).

[163] *See, e.g.*, Haochen Sun, *Copyright and Responsibility*, 4 HARV. J. SPORTS & ENT. L. 263, 299 (2013) (discussing how copyright law can promote social justice); SUNDER, *supra* note 50, at 105–19 (considering examples of how fair use can promote social justice).

or sufficient evidence, they will legally permit a copyright holder to override public interests beneficial to a particular group of users or to society at large. Against this backdrop, social justice demands that courts call the copyright holder's claim of infringement into question. Doing so further allows them to make proactive inquiries into the extent to which the public interest would be impaired should they uphold the claim.

In deciding the web caching case, the Beijing First Intermediate Court undertook such a proactive inquiry in considering whether a total ban on the provision of web caching services would severely jeopardize the public interest. According to the court, without the shield of fair use, web caching would be deemed an infringement of copyright. To avoid potential legal liabilities, search engine service providers would have to shoulder the unnecessarily troublesome burden of carrying out numerous preliminary and time-consuming checks to remove web caches that infringe copyright. The Beijing First Intermediate Court reasoned that, given the current level of technological development, it would be infeasible to delete web caches simultaneously with website changes. Nor would it be feasible for search engine service providers to obtain permission proactively from all copyright owners to offer a web caching service. All such providers would cease providing web caches if they were held liable for copyright infringement, which would seriously harm the public interest. Accordingly, for the sake of certain copyright owners' interests, the public would be deprived of the benefits brought about by web caches, and search engine service providers would have to bear an unnecessary burden.

3 INVIGORATING THE PUBLIC INTEREST PRINCIPLE DOMESTICALLY AND GLOBALLY

Like many legal principles and standards, the proposed public interest principle and its substantive and procedural standards are by no means perfect. In this section of the chapter, I respond to the major concerns over both the public interest principle and its subsidiary standards. Furthermore, I consider how and why the principle could play a uniquely important role in bridging the gaps between the fair use and fair dealing doctrines.

A *Preventing the Public Interest Principle from Becoming a Leviathan*

i Against an Over-capacious Principle

The first criticism that might be leveled against the public interest principle is that the principle is so capacious that it might easily infringe upon private interests in the name of protecting the public interest. Were that to occur, copyright holders would end up sacrificing too much financially. As the US Supreme Court has aptly cautioned, "[a]ny copyright infringer may claim to benefit the public by increasing public access to the copyrighted work. But ... we see no warrant for judicially imposing a 'compulsory license' permitting unfettered access."[164] The single-minded prioritization of the public interest would render copyright as a private right meaningless. It would deprive copyright holders of their economic interests in circulating their works in the marketplace, ultimately deterring them from creating or disseminating new works,[165] which would in turn impair the public interest.

164 Harper & Row, Publishers, Inc. v. Nation Enterprises, 471 U.S. 539, 569 (1985).

165 *See* Authors Guild v. HathiTrust, 755 F.3d 87, 95 (2d Cir. 2014) ("A fair use must not excessively damage the market for the original by providing the public with a substitute for that original work.").

In response to these valid concerns, I argue that the public interest principle actually requires courts to take copyright holders' economic interests seriously. To that end, it places the first factor, which carries the public interest use standard, under the scrutiny of the other fair use factors. Although the public interest principle situates the overall fair use analysis within the context of the public interest at large, it does not deviate from the traditional judicial practice of applying fair use factors in a holistic and balanced manner.[166] The principle by no means empowers the first factor to override the other fair use factors, the fourth factor in particular. Instead, it guards against the harmful disruption of copyright holders' market by maintaining the fourth factor on an equal footing with the first. It also rules out consideration of the market benefits to copyright holders to ensure an appropriate assessment of the potential market harm to them.[167] With these built-in limits on its application, the public interest principle thereby serves as a vehicle for courts to achieve the balanced application of all four fair use factors by permitting them to serve as a check on one another.

The US courts' fair use rulings in digital library cases demonstrate that the public interest principle, if properly applied with meticulous weighing up between the first and fourth factors, poses no major threats to copyright holders. After all, despite Google Library and the HathiTrust Digital Library now having existed for more than a decade, the publishing industry is still enjoying healthy growth.[168] Even the university presses, whose imminent demise was widely predicted in the social media age, are prospering.[169] What really matters today is whether copyright holders can adapt to take full advantage of digital technologies as an important means of marketing their works.[170]

At the same time, the public interest principle also forbids misuse of the fourth factor. As market harm is always a matter of degree,[171] it prevents courts from interpreting the scope of the protectable market of a work in an overly broad fashion. Instead, it forces courts to draw a line between the scope of unauthorized uses of the work in the public interest and the scope of the work's protectable market for issuing valid licenses for its use or the creation of its derivatives. On the one hand, courts must consider the scope of public interest uses in terms of the first factor, as they have long done in cases involving transformative uses.[172] On the other, they must consider whether the scope of the protectable market claimed by the copyright holder is reasonable under

[166] Peter Letterese & Assocs., Inc. v. World Inst. of Scientology Enters., 533 F.3d 1287, 1308 (11th Cir. 2008) (quoting Stewart v. Abend, 495 U.S. 207, 236–37 (1990)) ("The fair use doctrine is an 'equitable rule of reason'; neither the examples of possible fair uses nor the four statutory factors are to be considered exclusive."); Cambridge Univ. Press v. Patton, 769 F.3d 1232, 1283 (2014) (ruling that section 107 requires "a holistic analysis which carefully balanced the four factors").

[167] *See supra* text accompanying notes 85–107.

[168] *See* Julie Bosmanaug, *Publishing Gives Hints of Revival, Data Show*, N.Y. TIMES (Aug. 9, 2011), www.nytimes.com/2011/08/09/books/survey-shows-publishing-expanded-since-2008.html.

[169] *See* Chris Plattsmier, *University Presses Are Thriving, Not Broken*, ACLS (Oct. 29, 2018), www.humanitiesebook.org/university-presses-are-thriving-not-broken.

[170] *See* Pamela Samuelson, *Google Book Search and the Future of Books in Cyberspace*, 94 MINN. L. REV. 1308, 1132 (2010) ("In the digital era, authors are in a better position than in the past to grow their own audiences, cultivate reputations that attract readers, and provide their works to readers through alternative distribution channels . . . ."); Mike Shields, *"Growth Has Been Significant": Publishers Are Falling in Love with Apple News*, BUS. INSIDER (May 9, 2018), www.businessinsider.com/publishers-are-falling-in-love-with-apple-news-2018-5.

[171] Campbell v. Acuff-Rose Music, Inc., 510 U.S. 569, 590 n.21 (1994) ("Market harm is a matter of degree, and the importance of [the fourth] factor will vary, not only with the amount of harm, but also with the relative strength of the showing on the other factors.").

[172] *See, e.g.*, *Campbell*, 510 U.S. at 579 (ruling that parody "provide[s] social benefit, by shedding light on an earlier work . . .").

the fourth factor.[173] Meticulous examination of both matters is essential for courts to decide whether an unauthorized use has caused significant market harm to the copyright holder.[174] Should courts deviate from this pattern of reasoning, their application of the fourth factor will be detrimental to the public interest.[175]

The US Supreme Court's *Harper & Row* ruling exemplifies the incorrect application of the first and fourth fair use factors without any consideration of the public interest. In *Harper & Row*, the Supreme Court held that *The Nation*'s unauthorized publication of approximately 300 words of a direct quotation from President Gerald Ford's then-unpublished memoirs did not constitute a fair use.[176] The court's overly restrictive interpretation of the first and fourth fair use factors is quite problematic. Overly emphasizing the commercial nature of the use concerned, the court failed to grasp the significance of the public interests involved in the use concerned. As Justice Brennan pointed out in his dissenting opinion, such use was vital to lending authenticity to the magazine's news reporting on a historical event, i.e., the resignation and pardon of President Richard Nixon. Keeping the public informed of the details of that event undoubtedly "furthered the public interest"[177] in "[the] broad dissemination of principles, ideas, and factual information [that] is crucial to ... robust public debate and [an] informed citizenry."[178]

Moreover, if it had recognized *The Nation*'s use as a public interest use, the court would have had to modify its ruling on the fourth factor. It ruled in favor of the copyright holder on the fourth factor on the grounds that its interest had been harmed by the single cancellation of an offer to publish the memoirs as a magazine serial and subsequent refusal to pay it $12,500.[179] However, the court's finding that this single cancellation qualified as significant harm to the copyright holder's interests is dubious to say the least. In fact, the copyright holder failed to demonstrate that the use in question caused any harm to the work's potential market.[180] Although the defendant used the heart of that then-unpublished work, in weighing up all four factors, analysis of the first and fourth factors should still have led the court to rule in its favor. Had the public interest principle guided the court, it would have ruled the use concerned to constitute a fair use.

ii Against an Over-ambiguous Principle

One could further argue against the public interest principle by pointing out that public interest is a deeply troubling concept given the tremendous difficulty of defining its nature and scope. As the concept still remains ill-defined, the application of the public interest principle to fair use

173 Cambridge Univ. Press v. Patton, 769 F.3d 1232, 1277 (11th Cir. 2014) ("Put simply, absent evidence to the contrary, if a copyright holder has not made a license available to use a particular work in a particular manner, the inference is that the author or publisher did not think that there would be enough such use to bother making a license available. In such a case, there is little damage to the publisher's market when someone makes use of the work in that way without obtaining a license, and hence the fourth factor should generally weigh in favor of fair use.").

174 *Id.* at 1276 ("The goal of copyright is to stimulate the creation of new works, not to furnish copyright holders with control over all markets. Accordingly, the ability to license does not demand a finding against fair use."); Am. Geophysical Union v. Texaco Inc., 60 F.3d 913, 929 n.17 (2d Cir. 1994) ("[A] copyright holder can *always* assert some degree of adverse [effect] on its potential licensing revenues as a consequence of the secondary use at issue simply because the copyright holder has not been paid a fee to permit that particular use.") (citations omitted).

175 *See, e.g.*, Lydia Pallas Loren, *Redefining the Market Failure Approach to Fair Use in an Era of Copyright Permission Systems*, 5 J. Intell. Prop. L. 1, 30 (1997) (pointing out that the inappropriate application of the fourth factor "can inappropriately skew the fair use analysis to favor the rights of copyright owners").

176 Harper & Row Publishers, Inc. v. Nation Enters., 471 U.S. 539, 542–45 (1985).

177 *Id.* at 591.

178 *Id.* at 582 (Brennan, J., dissenting).

179 *Id.* at 567.

180 *See* Fromer, *supra* note 80, at 625.

cases would lead to myriad unintended negative consequences, thereby further aggravating the extant uncertainties surrounding the fair use doctrine.[181]

However, the law itself has been replete with legal terms that are ambiguous in nature since its inception.[182] History is witness to the positive evolution of the law over time despite the ambiguity deeply embedded into its every verbal ingredient. For that matter, language itself is fraught with ambiguities. As long as the law relies on language to convey its prescriptions, the problem of ambiguity will persist.[183] For example, under the US Constitution, it is legal for the government to exercise its eminent domain power to take private property for public use provided that fair compensation is paid to the owner.[184] This takings clause has been implemented for ages without any proper delineation of the public interest in the taking of private property.[185]

Hence, it makes no sense to argue against the public interest principle simply by faulting it for its ambiguity. Rather, the issue of ambiguity should be understood as a double-edged sword. While dealing with its negative effects, we can also take advantage of its positive effects in protecting the public interest. On the one hand, we can take measures to moderate the ambiguity of the public interest principle to the greatest extent possible. In Section 3, I discussed how courts can ascertain public interests by identifying the group- or society-based interests in using a given work.[186] Therefore, it is quite feasible to inject a proper degree of certainty into the judicial application of the principle.

On the other hand, it could be argued that the public interest principle's ambiguity is actually necessary to ensure that the principle is sufficiently broad-based to accommodate a wide range of socially beneficial interests in using copyrighted works. At the policy level, the public interest principle's ambiguity may help create a relatively flexible environment that supports technological innovation[187] and cultural development.[188] At the doctrinal level, the principle's ambiguity would help courts to protect public interests that are still underserved by the prevailing interpretation of the fair use doctrine. The US Supreme Court has designated satire as far less worthy than parody of receiving fair use protection.[189] In so ruling, the court has handed down a clear definition of the public interest in the parodic use of a work, stating that it is deserving of

[181] *See e.g.*, Sun, *supra* note 3, at 303–4 (discussing the indeterminacy of the fair use doctrine); Beebe, *supra* note 15, at 16 (asserting that "fair use is such an amorphous body of doctrine and its outcomes so unpredictable").

[182] Sun, *supra* note 3, at 304.

[183] *Id.*

[184] The Fifth Amendment states that "nor shall private property be taken for public use, without just compensation." U.S. Const. amend. V.

[185] Sun, *supra* note 3, at 319–20.

[186] *See supra* text accompanying notes 51–62.

[187] *See, e.g.*, Chander, *supra* note 14, at 664 ("The American concept of 'fair use' ... proved conducive to various innovations in the digital realm."); Fred von Lohmann, *Fair Use As Innovation Policy*, 23 Berkeley Tech. L.J. 829, 862 (2008) (arguing that "fair use as a component of innovation policy suggests that courts and policy-makers must strive to make fair use something on which innovators may more easily rely"); Robin A. Moore, *Fair Use and Innovation Policy*, 82 N.Y.U. L. Rev. 944, 946–47 (2007).

[188] *See, e.g.*, Jack M. Balkin, *Digital Speech and Democratic Culture: A Theory of Freedom of Expression for the Information Society*, 79 N.Y.U. L. Rev. 1, 50 (2004) ("To make intellectual property consistent with the idea of free speech as democratic culture, there must be a robust and ever expanding public domain with generous fair use rights."); Neil Weinstock Netanel, *Copyright and a Democratic Civil Society*, 106 Yale L.J. 283, 288 (1996) (arguing that copyright law functions to support "a sector of creative and communicative activity that is relatively free from reliance on state subsidy, elite patronage, and cultural hierarchy").

[189] Campbell v. Acuff-Rose Music, Inc., 510 U.S. 569, 580–81 (1994) ("Parody needs to mimic an original to make its point, and so has some claim to use the creation of its victim's (or collective victims') imagination, whereas satire can stand on its own two feet and so requires justification for the very act of borrowing."); *see also* Sunder, *supra* note 50, at 120 (explaining why courts and scholars have treated satire and parody differently).

protection because it informs the public of a "new expression, meaning, or message"[190] that can be added to the work. However, a broader, albeit more ambiguous understanding of the public interest could produce the positive effect of requiring courts to consider the larger social benefits that satirical uses may confer. For example, the Second Circuit held in *Blanch v. Koons* that Jeff Koons's satirical use of a portion of a photograph in a collage should be deemed fair use.[191] The court pointed out that the photo concerned was "fodder for [the user's] commentary on [the] social and aesthetic consequences of mass media."[192] As satire carries society-based public interests, it is regarded as a fair dealing exemption under the copyright laws of a number of countries, including the UK[193] and Australia.[194]

iii Against an Over-monolithic Principle

A further ground for criticism of the public interest principle is that its emphasis on the public interest would rule out private uses of works that serve users' individual interests but have long been deemed legal under copyright law. Examples of such private uses include recording television programs for the time-shifting purpose of viewing them at a later time[195] and downloading music from a computer for the space-shifting purpose of listening to it at another location of the user's choosing.[196] Private uses preserve users' anonymity, which "permits these activities to go forward, and allows fair users to decide later whether to reveal their identities when releasing their work."[197] Therefore, private uses legally protect the right to privacy, an individual interest that is actually dear to the public.[198]

To be sure, private uses can hardly satisfy the public interest use standard under the fair use factor, as they primarily serve users' individual interests in a private setting. However, it does not necessarily follow that if courts were guided by the public interest principle, the fair use doctrine would disallow all private uses. Instead, it would protect noncommercial private uses that do not cause significant market harm to the copyright holders. For instance, the private use of a work for the aforementioned time-shifting purpose would still be deemed legal. As the US Supreme Court's ruling in *Sony* shows, such use does not cause "any likelihood of nonminimal harm to the potential market for, or the value of, their copyrighted works."[199]

B Bridging the Gaps between Fair Use and Fair Dealing

By nature, the fair dealing doctrine plays the same role as the fair use doctrine by allowing the public to use copyrighted works without authorization from the copyright holders and without

190 *Campbell*, 510 U.S. at 579.
191 Blanch v. Koons, 467 F.3d 244, 246 (2d Cir. 2006).
192 *Id.* at 253.
193 Copyright, Designs and Patents Act 1988, c.48, s 30A (U.K.).
194 Australian Copyright Act 1968, § 41A (Austl.).
195 Sony Corp. of Am. v. Universal City Studios, 464 U.S. 417, 454–56 (1984) (ruling that "time-shifting" of copyrighted television shows with videotape recorders (VTR) constituted fair use primarily because it did not have negative effects on the current as well as the potential market for the copyrighted works).
196 Relying upon *Sony*, the court in Recording Industry Ass'n of America v. Diamond Multimedia Systems, Inc. held that copying for space-shifting purposes is "paradigmatic noncommercial personal use entirely consistent with the purposes of the [Copyright] Act." 180 F.3d 1072, 1079 (9th Cir. 1999); *cf.* A&M Records, Inc. v. Napster, Inc., 239 F.3d 1004, 1019 (9th Cir. 2001) (rejecting the ruling that space-shifting is fair use); UMG Recordings, Inc. v. MP3.com, Inc., 92 F. Supp. 2d 349, 351 (S.D.N.Y. 2000).
197 *See* Julie E. Cohen, *DRM and Privacy*, 18 Berkeley Tech. L.J. 575, 598 (2003).
198 Paris Adult Theatre I v. Slaton, 413 U.S. 49, 65–66 (1973).
199 *Sony*, 464 U.S. at 456.

paying them royalties. The striking discrepancies between the two doctrines lie chiefly in the structure of their legislative format and responsiveness to the role of courts. Fair dealing has entrenched an exhaustive list of exemptions and the rigid application of legal factors. Fair use, in contrast, is known for its flexibility owing to its non-exhaustive itemization of exemptions and open-ended application of legal factors.[200] Consequently, the fair use doctrine affords courts greater latitude in deciding the outcomes of disputes on a case-by-case basis and more power to come up with additional legal standards for judicial decision-making.[201]

Despite these differences, I argue that the public interest principle can guide courts toward applying the fair dealing doctrine, in addition to the fair use doctrine. In this way, the principle would serve as a meaningful alternative approach to bridging the gaps between fair use and fair dealing, an issue that has long troubled copyright scholars and practitioners.[202] The principle obviates the need to reform fair dealing by adopting open-ended fair use standards and the need to reform fair use by injecting the kinds of certainty that fair dealing affords. Application of the principle would thus steer the discourse away from whether the flexible fair use doctrine or the rigid fair dealing doctrine is more advantageous. I do not argue the case for the former to replace the latter on its own merits, or vice versa. Instead, I propose that the public interest principle can serve as a commonly shared principle for adjudicating fair use and fair dealing cases and developing further legislative reforms aimed at fixing the major problems with both doctrines.

i Acting As a Guiding Principle

First and foremost, what matters most for both the fair use and fair dealing doctrines, in my view, are the principles that can guide the courts in interpreting those doctrines. Despite the differences in their overall legislative structure, a commonality between fair use and fair dealing is the direct application of legal factors without the concomitant adoption of a guiding principle for such factor-based application. The fair use doctrine routinely entails judicial inquiries into the four fair use factors. Similarly, the fair dealing doctrine operates in a two-tier cluster of factors in common law jurisdictions. It first triggers a judicial inquiry into whether a given use of a work falls into any of the statutory factors enumerated in the various fair dealing exemptions. Then, following the *Hubbard v. Vosper* ruling in the UK, it further requires courts to consider whether the use is fair by applying a few additional factors.[203] In Canada, those factors include (1) the purpose of the dealing;

[200] *See, e.g.*, Burrell & Coleman, *supra* note 14, at 252.

[201] Pamela Samuelson, *Justifications for Copyright Limitations and Exceptions*, *in* Copyright Law in an Age of Limitations and Exceptions 45 (Ruth L. Okediji ed., 2017) (pointing out that one of the reasons why "civil law countries have generally been reluctant to adopt a flexible and open-ended [limitation and exception], such as fair use" is that "legislatures in those countries are expected to define the balance of rights between copyright owners and the public").

[202] *See id.* (arguing that "a key advantage of a flexible [limitation and exception]" is that "it enables the law to adapt to new circumstances and evolve over time without the need for continual statutory amendments").

[203] Hubbard v. Vosper [1972] 2 Q.B. 84. per Lord Denning at 1027. In this ruling, Lord Denning explicated factors for weighing on fairness as follows:

> It is impossible to define what is "fair dealing". It must be a question of degree. You must consider first the number and extent of the quotations and extracts. Are they altogether too many and too long to be fair? Then you must consider the use made of them. If they are used as a basis for comment, criticism or review, that may be a fair dealing. If they are used to convey the same information as the author, for a rival purpose, that may be unfair. Next, you must consider the proportions. To take long extracts and attach short comments may be unfair. But, short extracts and long comments may be fair. Other considerations may come to mind also. But, after all is said and done, it must be a matter of impression. As with fair comment in the law of libel, so with fair dealing in the law of copyright. The tribunal of fact must decide.

Id.

(2) the character of the dealing; (3) the amount of the dealing; (4) alternatives to the dealing; (5) the nature of the work; and (6) the effect of the dealing on the work.[204]

Without a guiding principle, the factor-based application of the fair use and fair dealing doctrines has resulted in diametrically opposing rulings. Despite the open-ended, flexible nature of fair use and the public interest–oriented *Campbell* ruling, US courts have still rendered copyright holder–centric rulings by interpreting the fair use factors restrictively. The US Supreme Court's ruling in *Harper & Row* is a case in point.[205] Conversely, despite the widely held belief in the fixed, rigid nature of the fair dealing doctrine and judicial assertions that the doctrine has been interpreted strictly,[206] the Supreme Court of Canada's rulings in *CCH* and its progeny have rendered liberal interpretations of the doctrine by applying public interest considerations.[207] Similarly, the Court of Justice of the European Union has defined parody broadly on the basis of freedom of expression, allowing the parodic use of a work to function as a satire with social and political criticism.[208]

Given that the issue of interpretation is central to both doctrines, the public interest principle would play a pivotal role in guiding courts to not only interpret the legal factors thereunder but also to determine the outcomes of hard cases after weighing those factors. To be sure, courts can rely on the fair use or fair dealing factors to settle easy cases adequately. However, they encounter severe difficulties in attempting to settle hard cases by relying solely on those factors.

In hard cases, courts are confronted with the thorny issue of how to apply the fair use or fair dealing doctrine to address the conflict between the public interest in sharing the information contained in a copyrighted work and the private interest in controlling the exclusive ownership of that work.[209] They have to deal with such bewilderingly complex tasks as drawing a line between the transformative use of a work and preparing a derivative of that work[210] and defining

204 *See* CCH Canadian Ltd. v. Law Soc'y of Upper Can., [2004] 1 S.C.R. 399, ¶ 53 (Can.).

205 Sun, *supra* note 3, at 321 (pointing out that the *Harper & Row*-type judicial practice of treating fair use as an affirmative defense "would give rise to the problem that [the public's] rights are automatically 'ranked' lower than copyrights" and that "courts actually water down the importance of protecting public interest"); Neil Weinstock Netanel, Copyright's Paradox 64–65 (2008) ("Since *Harper & Row*, the Blackstonian property-centered view of fair use has steadily gained ground.").

206 *See, e.g.*, Case C-201/13, Deckmyn v. Vandersteen, 2014 E.C.R. ¶ 43 (ruling that "the conditions set out in Article 5 [of the EU Copyright Directive that governs exceptions and limitations to copyright] must generally be interpreted strictly"); Case C-5/08, Infopaq International A/S v. Danske Dagblades Forening, 2009 E.C.R. I-0000 (ruling that fair dealing exceptions must be interpreted strictly).

207 *See* Giuseppina D'Agnostino, *Healing Fair Dealing? A Comparative Copyright Analysis of Canada's Fair Dealing to UK Fair Dealing and US Fair Use*, 53 McGill L.J. 309, 309 (2008).

208 In *Deckmyn*, the court offered a broad definition of parody as follows:

> [T]he concept of parody in the Directive ought not to be confined to the case of a parody having no meaning beyond the original, work parodied. It could perhaps be argued that, from the point of view of literary theory, the most deeply-rooted type of parody is that which, whatever the intention, is essentially designed to refer to the original work. Irrespective of that, it cannot be denied that criticism of customs, social criticism and political criticism have also, from time immemorial and clearly for the purpose of conveying a message effectively, made use of the privileged medium entailing the alteration of a pre-existing work, which is sufficiently recognisable to the public at which that criticism is directed.

Deckmyn, C-201/13, ¶ 64; *see also* Graeme W. Austin, *EU and US Perspectives on Fair Dealing for the Purpose of Parody or Satire*, 39 UNSW L.J. 684, 688 (2016) (noting that the court "interpreted the concept 'parody' quite broadly").

209 *See, e.g.*, Ronald Dworkin, Taking Rights Seriously 81 (1977) (arguing that in a hard case, "the judge has, accordingly to that theory, a discretion to decide the case either way").

210 *See, e.g.*, Paul Goldstein, *Fair Use in Context*, 31 Colum. J.L. & Arts 433, 442 (2008); Jane C. Ginsburg, *Letter from the US: Exclusive Rights, Exceptions, and Uncertain Compliance with International Norms – Part II (Fair Use)* 4–19 (Columbia Law and Economics, Working Paper No. 503, Jan. 2015), http://ssrn.com/abstract=2539178.

the scope of the market for the work.[211] In these circumstances, the public interest principle would serve to guide courts in dealing with hard cases by shedding light on how best to address the conflict between public and private interests. Its subsidiary public interest use standard would require courts to consider whether a work was used in the public interest or for the user's own private interest. If they find the former to be the case, then they can simultaneously identify the extent to which the use serves group- or society-based public interests. Moreover, the principle's significant market harm principle would dictate that courts protect a public interest use only if such protection would not cause significant harm to the market value of the work.

ii Paving the Way for Adoption of the Public Interest Principle

There are very good prospects that the public interest principle can be adopted in both fair use and fair dealing jurisdictions because courts there are increasingly embracing the practice of deciding cases in light of the public interest. By spelling out the concept of transformative use, the US Supreme Court's *Campbell* ruling paved the way for applying the fair use factors with public interest considerations. Since *Campbell*, the US courts have decided a large number of fair use cases in the public interest.[212] Their rulings in the Google Library and HathiTrust Digital Library cases not only epitomize this steadily growing judicial practice but have also developed new dimensions of fair use adjudication that are compatible with the legal standards embodied in the public interest principle I propose herein.

Meanwhile, courts in jurisdictions following the fair dealing doctrine are also increasingly applying that doctrine in the public interest. The 1988 UK Copyright, Designs and Patents Act contains a general provision mandating the application of the fair dealing doctrine with public interest considerations. It states that "[n]othing in this Part affects any rule of law preventing or *restricting* the enforcement of copyright, on grounds of public interest or otherwise."[213] With regard to the "reporting current events" defense, the UK courts have decided that it should be interpreted liberally[214] "to reflect the public interest in freedom of expression and, in particular, the freedom of the press."[215] Similarly, there have been very positive developments in court decisions on fair dealing cases in China in light of the public interest. Despite the rulings against Google Library, as shown in Section 4 of this chapter, the Beijing First Intermediate Court boldly examined the nature and scope of Chinese fair dealing provisions in light of the public interest in those rulings.[216] Most importantly, the Supreme Court of Canada, as noted in Section 4 of this chapter, has adopted a more liberal approach to defining fair dealing as a user right.[217]

iii Making the Principle Compatible with Fair Dealing

Third, the public interest principle is not necessarily incompatible with the exhaustive enumeration of fair dealing exemptions. Rather, it can play a positive role in helping courts to interpret

[211] Regarding the circularity problem in defining the scope of market, *see, e.g.*, Princeton Univ. Press v. Mich. Document Servs., 99 F.3d 1381, 1387 (6th Cir. 1996); Am. Geophysical Union v. Texaco Inc., 60 F.3d 913, 929 (2d Cir. 1994).

[212] *See supra* text accompanying notes 18–30.

[213] Copyright, Designs and Patents Act 1988, § 171(3) (U.K.) (emphasis added).

[214] Pro Sieben A.G. v. Carlton Television Ltd [1999] 1 WLR 605 at 614G.

[215] Ashdown v. Telegraph Group Ltd [2001] EWCA Civ 1142, ¶ 66 (July 18, 2001). The court also pointed out that this defense "is clearly intended to protect the role of the media in informing the public about matters of current concern to the public." *Id.* ¶ 64.

[216] *See supra* text accompanying notes 159–161.

[217] *See, e.g.*, Michael Geist, *Fairness Found: How Canada Quietly Shifted from Fair Dealing to Fair Use*, *in* The Copyright Pentalogy: How the Supreme Court of Canada Shook the Foundations of Canadian Copyright Law 157, 169 (Michael Geist ed., 2013).

specific fair dealing exemptions and the criteria for evaluating fairness. Take the fair dealing doctrine in the UK as an example. Fair dealing exemptions therein such as "research" and "study,"[218] "criticism or review,"[219] "reporting current events,"[220] and "caricature, parody, or pastiche"[221] are crudely enumerated without having their contours properly defined, which calls into question exactly how the UK courts should interpret the nature and scope of those exemptions.

In this context, the public interest principle can help courts to shed light on each enumerated exemption. Take the research exemption for instance. Without taking the public interest into account, the UK courts have ruled that this exemption permits only noncommercial research.[222] By contrast, the Supreme Court of Canada has decided to interpret it in light of the public interest. By defining the scope of research in "a large and liberal"[223] manner, the Canadian court held that the research exemption allows commercial research performed in the public interest.[224] Similarly, as discussed in the earlier part of this section, the public interest principle can guide courts' evaluations of fair dealing.[225]

iv Setting Common Goals and Agendas for Further Reforms

Last but not least, the public interest principle sets common goals and agendas for initiating more constructive reforms of both doctrines in the public interest.[226] Compatible with the relevant international copyright treaties,[227] the principle affords courts sufficient latitude to capitalize on public interest considerations in fair use or fair dealing cases.

Akin to the fair use doctrine, the burden of proving fair dealing is placed on the defendant in judicial proceedings.[228] Therefore, it would be desirable to apply the public interest principle to usher in a legislative or judicial reform that would reallocate the burden of proof between the plaintiff and defendant in the manner I suggest in Section 2.

It would also be desirable to reconsider whether fair dealing should maintain its exhaustive enumeration of exemptions, although such reconsideration may not be needed to inquire into whether the open-ended merits of fair use should be transplanted into fair dealing. What really matters in effectuating the public interest principle is to determine whether the legislature should give the judiciary more power to apply the principle to adjudicate fair dealing cases

[218] Copyright, Designs and Patents Act 1988, ch. 48; § 29 (U.K.).
[219] *Id.* § 30.
[220] *Id.*
[221] *Id.* § 30A.
[222] *See, e.g.*, Controller of HM Stationery Office & Anor v Green Amps Ltd [2007] EWHC 2755 ¶ 21 (Ch).
[223] CCH Canadian Ltd. v. Law Soc'y of Upper Can., [2004] 1 S.C.R. 399 ¶ 51 (Can.).
[224] *Id.* (holding that "[l]awyers carrying on the business of law for profit are conducting research").
[225] *See supra* text accompanying notes 203–208.
[226] Professor Rochelle Dreyfuss has argued for the need to set common goals and agendas for reforming both fair use and fair dealing doctrines around the world. *See* Rochelle Cooper Dreyfuss, *TRIPS – Round II: Should Users Strike Back?*, 71 U. Chi. L. Rev. 21, 34 (2004) ("[I]t is worth comparing the traditional intellectual property regimes of developed countries to find commonalities (such as fair use and fair dealing) that are not currently phrased as affirmative rights, and that may not reflect identical guarantees, but that nonetheless assure that users have access to innovations.").
[227] Samuelson, *supra* note 201, at 53 ("Although some scholars have questioned whether open-ended [limitations and exceptions], such as fair use, are consistent with international treaty obligations, many European as well as US scholars make compelling arguments that fair use and other flexible [limitations and exceptions] are compatible with treaty obligations.").
[228] *See* Lionel Bently et al., Intellectual Property Law 226 (2018) (pointing out that the fair dealing defense "only comes into play once a claimant has established that copyright has been infringed. Where this occurs, the onus of proof [then] falls on the defendant to prove that one of the exceptions applies").

competently.[229] One possible pathway to such reform would be the inclusion of a provision providing that fair dealing permits public interest uses in the statutory enumeration of fair dealing exemptions.[230] The Chinese government is already considering this type of reform to fair dealing in China. The latest draft amendment proposes that the exhaustive list of fair dealing exemptions under Article 22 of the Chinese Copyright Law should be broadened by incorporating a provision expressly allowing the Chinese courts to recognize new fair dealing exemptions not listed under that article.[231]

CONCLUSION

The public interest principle, as I have shown, is intended to reshape both the fair use and fair dealing doctrines to ensure that they can better serve the larger social needs of the globalized digital world. The consistent application of the principle by courts around the world would develop collective wisdom about maximizing usage of the merits of both doctrines while minimizing the effect of their demerits.

By embracing the proposed public interest principle, both the judiciary and the legislature would ensure that copyright law gains a more pertinent role in shaping the new age of big data and artificial intelligence in which the use of knowledge and information is more important than ever before.[232] Hence, the public interest principle, if properly applied, could serve as a powerhouse dedicated to revolutionizing copyright law as a legal engine of public interest protection.

[229] Robert Burrell, *The Changing Judicial Politics of Copyright Exceptions in the UK*, Chapter 9 of this book ("Judges in copyright cases may not be merely weighing the interests of copyright owners and users. They may also be involved in the ultimately more important tasks of holding the executive to account, setting the limits of executive rulemaking and establishing the relationship between national law and supranational legal obligations."). For arguments about conferring more power on the judiciary in fair dealing jurisdictions, *see* Martin Senftleben, *The Perfect Match: Civil Law Judges and Open-Ended Fair Use Provisions*, 33 AM. U. INT'L L. REV. 231, 233 (2017) (arguing that "civil law judges are capable of applying open-ended fair use norms adequately and consistently").

[230] *See, e.g.*, Michael Handler & Emily Hudson, *in* Chapter 3 in this volume (proposing to expand fair dealing with "the addition of new fair dealing purposes or the development of other closed provisions that utilize a less prescriptive drafting style").

[231] Edward Chatterton & Horace Lam, *Amendments to the PRC Copyright Law .... The Practical Implications for Rights Owners* (Aug. 1, 2014), *available at* www.lexology.com/library/detail.aspx?g=6d3a69f3-e558-4fba-ae7b-88140cd3b322.

[232] *See* Ruth Okediji, *Givers, Takers, and Other Kinds of Users: A Fair Use Doctrine for Cyberspace*, 53 FLA. L. REV. 107, 114 (2001) (predicating the necessity to reform the fair use doctrine so that it "will be a superior mechanism for safeguarding the public interest in a way that facilitates dispersion of the new benefits that the Internet offers to society as a whole"); Benjamin L. W. Sobel, *Artificial Intelligence's Fair Use Crisis*, 41 COLUM. J.L. & ARTS 45, 97 (2017) (concluding that although "[t]he fair use dilemma is a genuine dilemma [in the age of artificial intelligence], ... it offers an opportunity to promote social equity by reasserting the purpose of copyright law").

15

An Empirical Review of the Copyright Limitations and Exceptions for Educational Activities

Daniel Seng

INTRODUCTION

The axiomatic importance of education in any society needs no further elaboration. Article 26(1) of the 1948 UN Universal Declaration of Human Rights asserts that "everyone has the right to education."[1] In fact, the very first modern copyright legislation, the Statute of Anne 1709, was entitled "An Act for the Encouragement of Learning." While the Statute of Anne is more commonly remembered for the fact that it replaced the monopoly in printed books granted to printers with rights granted to authors, it should not be forgotten that the Statute also placed emphasis on the continued accessibility of books in public libraries and their affordability to university staff and students.[2]

Even where the focus of the first draft of the Berne Convention was "to constitute a general Union for the protection of the rights of authors in their literary works and manuscripts,"[3] a philosophy subsequently embodied in Article 1 of the Berne Convention,[4] the special status of educational usage of copyright materials was not forgotten. The drafters enshrined this in Article 8 of the Berne Act, which specifically reserves for countries of the Berne Union the power to enact legislation to permit "the ability to make borrowings from literary or artistic works for use in publications designed for teaching or scientific purposes."[5]

At the Stockholm Conference, Article 8 of the Berne Act was succeeded by Article 10(2), which reads:

> It shall be a matter for legislation in the countries of the Union, and for special agreements existing or to be concluded between them, to permit the utilization, to the extent justified by the purpose, of literary or artistic works by way of illustration in publications, broadcasts or sound or visual recordings for teaching, provided such utilization is compatible with fair practice.

[1] Universal Declaration of Human Rights, G.A. Res. 217A(III), U.N. Doc. A/810w [hereinafter *UN UDHR*].

[2] U.K. Copyright Act 1709, 8 Anne c.19, ss. 4 and 5.

[3] HISTOIRE *(1889), 161.*

[4] Art. 1, Paris Act of July 24, 1971 of the Berne Convention for the Protection of Literary and Artistic Works [hereinafter the "Berne Convention"].

[5] "Art. 8, Berne Act of September 9, 1886 of the Berne Convention". The Berne Convention consists of a successive series of instruments, and this reference is to a historical version of the Berne Convention not currently in force.

As Article 10(2) is the product of thoughtful discussions and measured consensus between the delegates, the key features of this provision must be noted.

First, wide latitude is to be given to the "for teaching" purpose of the limitation. At the Stockholm Conference, the conference delegates explained the meaning of the word "teaching" as follows:

> The wish was expressed that it should be made clear in this Report that the word "teaching" was to include teaching at all levels – in educational institutions and universities, municipal and State schools, and private schools.[6]

As envisaged by the conference delegates, the limitation does not distinguish between public instruction and private, and necessarily commercial, instruction. The limitation therefore encompasses all forms of profit and nonprofit instruction and at "all levels" of education, including continued adult education.[7]

Secondly, the use of the work for teaching purposes is described as being "by way of illustration." The conference delegates agree not to hamper the extent of the use of a work to illustrate a concept, an idea, or a point for teaching purposes. Thus, the carefully calibrated language of Article 10(2) delimits the scope of such usage "to the extent justified … for teaching," and confirms that the limitation does *not* preclude the use of the whole work in appropriate circumstances.[8]

Thirdly, the source works that could be used for teaching purposes encompass "works," "publications,[9] broadcasts[10] [and] sound [and] visual recordings,"[11] the entire spectrum of works addressed in the Convention. Notably, Article 10(2) is the *only* provision in the Convention that explicitly references works, publications, broadcasts, and recordings as the sources for the limitation.

[6] Records of the Intellectual Property Conference of Stockholm (1967) 1134 (W.I.P.O. 1971), at 1148. The quote goes on to state, "Education outside these institutions, for instance general teaching available to the general public but not included in the above categories, should be excluded." This has been interpreted by some commentators to equate to formal education at elementary, intermediate and tertiary institutions of learning, which would lead to the award of an "official" degree. Sam Ricketson and Jane C. Ginsburg, The Berne Convention for the Protection of Literary and Artistic Works: 1886–1986 at § 13.45 (2d ed. 2006) [hereinafter Ricketson & Ginsburg – The Berne Convention]. However, there is an alternative view that educational institutions offering adult education programs such as language proficiency courses, literacy programs and vocational training will come within its ambit, while continuing education or refresher programs generally will not. *Cf.* Ricketson and Ginsburg – The Berne Convention, at § 13.45; *see* Sam Ricketson, WIPO Study on Limitations and Exceptions of Copyright and Related Rights in the Digital Environment (SCCR/9/7) at 15 (WIPO, 2003) [hereinafter Ricketson – Study on Limitations and Exceptions].

[7] Records of the Intellectual Property Conference of Stockholm (1967) 1134 (W.I.P.O. 1971), at 886–87.

[8] Ricketson & Ginsburg – The Berne Convention, *supra* note 6, at § 13.45. *See also* Ricketson – Study on Limitations and Exceptions, *supra* note 6, at 14.

[9] The term "publications" is drawn from the expression "published works" as defined in Art. 3(3) to mean copies of works published with their authors' consent to satisfy the reasonable requirements of the public. This encompasses all permanent forms of fixation of a work, "whatever may be the means of manufacture of the copies." Ricketson and Ginsburg – The Berne Convention, *supra* note 6, at §§ 6.29–6.30 at 260–62.

[10] "Broadcasts" would be the wireless transmission for public reception of sounds or images and sounds of the representations. International Convention for the Protection of Performers, Producers of Phonograms and Broadcasting Organizations, October 26, 1961 496 U.N.T.S. 43 [hereinafter Rome Convetion], art. 2(f). Though this term is not defined in the Berne Convention, from the records of the Brussels Conference, it was clear that the delegates felt no need to define the term as they accepted that it was one means of wireless communication to the public. *See also* Ricketson and Ginsburg – The Berne Convention, *supra* note 6, at § 12.34 at 732.

[11] "Sound and visual recordings" would include tapes, videograms, phonograph records and cinematographic films. Ricketson and Ginsburg – The Berne Convention, *supra* note 6, at § 13.45 at 793.

Finally, Article 10(2) does not only permit the "reproduction" of literary or artistic works, it permits the "*utilization*" of such works. As the only provision in the Berne Convention that uses the term "utilization,"[12] Article 10(2) thereby sanctioned the creation of limitations and exceptions that go beyond "reproduction" and "communication."

For all these reasons, it has been persuasively argued that Article 10(2) is an "open, flexible and technology-neutral exception"[13] which lends itself to not just reproductions and face-to-face instruction but also communications to the public, to enable and facilitate distance learning, correspondence courses, and teaching on demand.

But Article 10(2) is not the only provision that engages education and education-related activities. The Stockholm Conference and the Stockholm Main Committee confirm that quotations for "scientific, critical, informatory or educational purposes" are within the scope of Article 10(1),[14] which enabled not just books, articles, visual works, and other printed matters, but also lectures, performances or broadcasts[15] to be quoted for scholarship purposes. The purpose of the scholastic exposition or the robustness of the scholarship in turn determines if a lengthy quotation is necessary and is thus "compatible with fair practice."[16]

Moreover, Article 10(1) and 10(2) are not the only provisions relevant to educational activities in the Berne Convention. As a general exception to the reproduction right set out in Article 9(1), Article 9(2) is also broadly worded to encompass various education-related activities. The Stockholm Conference referred to the licit making of a small number of photocopies of published works without payment for individual, private, personal, family, or domestic use, for internal use of libraries, and for use by scientific institutes,[17] and it subsumed all these uses by adopting what is now known as the three-step test in Article 9(2) in an attempt to encapsulate and generalize all of these specific exceptions.[18] The discussion at the Stockholm Conference showed that the committee members were fully cognisant that teaching not only took place in schools, but also in private and at all levels.[19] The end product was Article 9(2), which was formulated to be not only consistent with the other provisions in the Convention, but also with the limitations and exceptions identified by the Committee which were to be enacted by the member states in their public and cultural interests, many of which are education-related.[20]

[12] In contrast, Art. 10*bis*(1) permits the *reproduction, broadcasting* or *communication to the public* of works for informational purposes.

[13] Copyright Law Handbook, at 379.

[14] Records of the Intellectual Property Conference of Stockholm (1967) 1134 (W.I.P.O. 1971), at 116–17 (Document S/1), 860-1 (minutes).

[15] Ricketson and Ginsburg – The Berne Convention, *supra* note 6, at § 13.41 at 786.

[16] *Id.*, at 788. Both free uses for quotations in Art. 10(1) and for teaching purposes in Art. 10(2) are subject to the requirement set out in Art. 10(3), that mention should be made of the source and the name of the author if it appears thereon. After all, to the extent that it is feasible and practical, attribution of the source and authorship is consistent with robust research, good scholarship, and sound academic practice.

[17] Records of the Intellectual Property Conference of Stockholm (1967) 1134 (W.I.P.O. 1971), at 857–58 (Document S/1).

[18] *United States – Section 110(5) of the US Copyright Act*, para. 6.109, Report of the Panel, June15, 2000, document WT/DS/160/R.

[19] Records of the Intellectual Property Conference of Stockholm (1967) 1134 (W.I.P.O. 1971), at 886–87.

[20] Out of the 14 existing exceptions identified, 5 of them relate to educational activities. These were noted to be quotations in school books and chrestomathies, private use, reproduction by photocopying in libraries, reproduction in special characters for the use of the blind, and sound recordings of literary works for the use of the blind. *Id.*, at 42 (Document S/1).

Moving beyond the Berne Convention,[21] similar education-related limitations and exceptions allowed under the Rome Convention[22] are compendiously set out in Article 15 of the Convention. Its provisions regarding private use (Article 15(1)(a)) and teaching and scientific research (Article 15(1)(d)) mirror equivalent limitations and exceptions in the Berne Convention. In addition, Article 15(2) provides member states with an alternative set of allowable "limitations," to be of the "same kind" as that provided for copyright works, with regard to the protection of performers, producers, and broadcasting organizations.

Finally, it should be noted that permissible limitations and exceptions pertaining to educational activities as set out in the Agreement on Trade-Related Aspects of Intellectual Property Rights (TRIPS) are also pegged to the Berne Convention and the Rome Convention.[23] Likewise, in "recognizing the need to maintain a balance between the rights of authors and the larger public interest, particularly education,"[24] the WIPO Copyright Treaty (WCT) and the WIPO Performances and Phonograms Treaty (WPPT) also leverage on, and do not detract from, the limitations and exceptions inscribed in the Berne Convention and the Rome Convention.[25]

SCOPE OF REVIEW

This brief overview of the provisions shows that the copyright limitations and exceptions for the benefit of educational activities have always received the full attention of law- and policymakers in international copyright conventions and instruments. As member states implement limitations and exceptions in their national legislation based on their treaty obligations, this in turn shapes the language of the education-related provisions in the Berne Convention.

In this regard, it is instructive to examine how WIPO member states[26] have, in their national legislation, enabled various limitations and exceptions to the use of copyright works to address the multifaceted nature and breadth and scope of modern-day education, and done so in a way that is simultaneously forward-looking and retrospective, yet compatible with fair practice, to reflect the enabling language of Article 10(2) and other relevant provisions in international conventions and instruments.

[21] The Stockholm Conference was also notable for its introduction of the Appendix to the Paris Act as a special concession to the needs of developing member states with the facilities to award compulsory licenses for translations (Art. II) and for reproductions (Art. III). A developing member state is defined as one regarded as such by the General Assembly of the United Nations, "having regard to its economic situation and its social or cultural needs, does not consider itself immediately in a position to make provision for the protection of all the rights as provided for in [the Paris] Act." *See* Berne Convention, Appendix, Art. I(1). This epitomizes the consensus between developed member states as net exporters of intellectual works and developing member states as net consumers of such works, that it is in the common interests of all member states to promote and further the education of their populace.

[22] Rome Convention, *supra* note 10.

[23] Agreement on Trade-Related Aspects of Intellectual Property Rights, Apr. 15, 1994, Marrakesh Agreement Establishing the World Trade Organization, 1869 U.N.T.S. 299, 33 I.L.M. 1196 (1994) [hereinafter, TRIPS Agreement], Arts. 9(1), 14(6),

[24] Preamble, WIPO Copyright Treaty (1996) [hereinafter WCT], Preamble, WIPO Performances and Phonograms Treaty (1996) [hereafter WPPT].

[25] WCT, Art. 1(2) provides that "nothing in this Treaty shall derogate from existing obligations that Contracting Parties have to each other under the Berne Convention for the Protection of Literary and Artistic Works." A similar proviso is found in WPPT, Art. 1(1).

[26] The WIPO Convention provides that membership is open to any state that is: a member of the Paris Union for the Protection of Industrial Property, or member of the Berne Union for the Protection of Literary and Artistic Works; or a member of the United Nations, or of any of the United Nations' Specialized Agencies, or of the International Atomic Energy Agency, or that is a party to the Statute of the International Court of Justice; or invited by the WIPO General Assembly to become a member state of the Organization.

This chapter incorporates the findings of two studies, conducted in November 2016 and August 2017 respectively, which undertook this examination. The first study[27] reviews the copyright limitations and exceptions that deal with educational activities in the national legislation of all 189 member states of WIPO.[28] The second study[29] extends the first study to examine additional issues relating to the operation of copyright limitations and exceptions as applied to educational institutions. This chapter attempts to state the law as of August 2017.

Categories of Limitations and Exceptions

In this review of national copyright legislation for limitations and exceptions for the benefit of educational activities, the limitations and exceptions are classified[30] into eight categories.[31]

The first category pertains to the private or personal use exceptions for copyright works and entrepreneurial works.[32] It recognizes the private and self-actualization aspect of education and acknowledges that private research is an individually driven and self-edifying process.[33] For instance, the national legislation of many member states has enumerated various categories of permissible uses of works for "research or private study."[34] The licit private or personal use may even encompass private or family performances, in conjunction with preparations for various aspects of schooling curriculum, especially in the arts and humanities. However, where such

[27] Daniel Seng, Study on Limitations and Exceptions for Educational Activities (SCCR/33/6), Nov. 9, 2016, available at www.wipo.int/edocs/mdocs/copyright/en/sccr_33/sccr_33_6.pdf.

[28] The first study also updates and consolidates the five 2009 regional studies on the same subject: Daniel Seng, WIPO Study on the Copyright Exceptions for the Benefit of Educational Activities for Asia and Australia (SCCR/19/7), Oct. 26, 2009, available at www.wipo.int/meetings/en/doc_details.jsp?doc_id=130249; Joseph Fometeu, WIPO Study on Limitations and Exceptions for Copyright and Related Rights for Teaching in Africa (SCCR/19/5), Oct. 26, 2009, available at www.wipo.int/meetings/en/doc_details.jsp?doc_id=130241; Raquel Xalabarder, WIPO Study on Copyright Limitations and Exceptions for Educational Activities in North America, Europe, Caucasus, Central Asia and Israel (SCCR/19/8), Nov. 5, 2009, available at www.wipo.int/meetings/en/doc_details.jsp?doc_id=130393; Victor Nabhan, WIPO Study on Limitations and Exceptions for Copyright for Educational Purposes in the Arab Countries (SCCR/19/6), Oct. 7, 2009, available at www.wipo.int/meetings/en/doc_details.jsp?doc_id=130302; and Juan Carlos Monroy Rodríguez, WIPO Study on the Limitations and Exceptions to Copyright and Related Rights for the Purposes of Educational and Research Activities in Latin America and the Caribbean (SCCR/19/4), Nov. 30, 2009, available at www.wipo.int/meetings/en/doc_details.jsp?doc_id=130303.

[29] Daniel Seng, Updated Study and Additional Analysis of Study on Copyright Limitations and Exceptions for Educational Activities (SCCR/35/5 Rev.), Nov. 10, 2017, available at www.wipo.int/edocs/mdocs/copyright/en/sccr_35/sccr_35_5_rev.pdf.

[30] To facilitate the ensuing analysis in this review, effort has been made to make these categories mutually exclusive. However, in practice, a single educational activity undertaken by an educational institution may engage limitations and exceptions across multiple categories.

[31] Thse eight categories draw from, and are guided by, five inclusionary categories and one residual category of educational activities identified in the APEC–IPEG Survey on Copyright Limitations & Exceptions (July 2009), available at http://publications.apec.org/publication-detail.php?pub_id=971 [hereinafter *APEC Study*]. These are performances and displays of a work, transmissions of a work for purposes of distance learning, copying of materials by educational organizations or for educational use, copying and distribution of works for classroom use, copying of works for use in collections and textbooks, and other limitations and exceptions related to educational uses.

[32] Limitations and exceptions as to the importation of works or their material embodiment for personal reasons are considered to be outside the ambit of this chapter since these are not necessarily or directly relatable to educational activities.

[33] For instance, the *APEC Study* itself identified its lack of scrutiny of the personal use exceptions as a lacuna to be addressed. *See APEC Study*, at 5.

[34] *See, e.g.*, Copyright Act, R.S.C. 1984 c. C-42 § 29 (Can.) (referring to fair dealing for the purpose of "research, private study, [and] education"); Art. 53(2) first sentence, item 1, Act on Copyright and Related Rights (Copyright Act, as amended up to Law of October 1, 2013), Germany (permitting the making of single copies of a work for one's own "scientific use" ("wissenschaftlichen Gebrauch"), in contradistinction with "personal use" ("eigenen Gebrauch").

private or personal uses "conflict with the normal exploitation of the work," the review also briefly examines the mechanisms by which equitable remuneration is provided to the authors and owners of various related rights.

The second category deals with the use of quotations or "excerpts" as an integral part of education and study, which largely involves learning and instruction through illustration, argumentation, referral, comments, and criticisms. Among the issues evaluated are the condition and extent of the quotation, its preclusions, as well as the attribution requirement.[35]

The third category deals with the ways in which reproductions, single and multiple, by reprographic or by non-reprographic means, with or without remuneration or licensing, are permitted under the limitations and exceptions for various educational purposes and activities.[36]

The fourth category recognizes the existence of specific limitations and exceptions existing in national copyright legislation to provide for the development and publication of anthologies, compilations, and other composite works for use in educational activities.[37]

The fifth category deals with the limitations and exceptions that permit school performances. Under this category, the review examines limitations and exceptions that permit "semi-public" showings in clubs or societies, particularly prevalent as part of humanities studies or the extracurricular activities of schools.

The sixth category deals with the limitations and exceptions that permit broadcasts, cable transmissions, or other forms of communication of educational programs as part of school instruction, as well as recordings of these broadcasts, transmissions, programs, and communications by educational establishments. Provisions in member states' legislation that "make available" programming for teaching purposes are classified under this category. Other member states have enacted specific provisions that deal with online transmissions for distance learning. To the extent that these provisions engage both reproduction and the communication to the public, the provision will be classified under both the third category (scientific and educational reproduction) and the sixth category (educational broadcasts, communications and recordings). Because the making of aural and visual recordings is closely connected to the use of broadcasts and communications, limitations and exceptions that deal with such recordings are also brought under the sixth category.

For historical and teleological reasons, this review draws a distinction between the playing of sound recordings to an audience on-site (considered a performance) and the playing of sound recordings to an audience off-site (considered a communication). This distinction is maintained by Article 11 of the Berne Convention, which provides that authors of dramatic, dramatico-musical and musical works shall enjoy the exclusive right to authorize "the *performance* of their works, including such public performance by any means or process"[38] and "any *communication* to the public of the performance of their works."[39] Therefore, this suggests that performance and

[35] The line however is drawn at parodies, works of satire, spoofs, and similar works, since such works pertain more to humour, comedic effect, and political and social commentary rather than to academic and educational studies.

[36] This study groups together the two separate classes of "copying of materials by educational organisations or for educational use" and "copying and distribution of works for classroom use," as set out in the *APEC Study*. *APEC Study*, at 29, 31. As the terms suggest, these two activities actually represent a continuum of classroom instructional activities, and grouping them together reflects these activities in educational institutions in a more realistic way.

[37] This is separate from the third category, because the entity exercising this limitation or exception is not usually an educational institution, but a publishing body or entity providing instructional material for use by educational institutions.

[38] Art. 11(1)(i).

[39] Art. 11(1)(ii).

communication to the public are two separate and distinct exclusive rights. However, technological advancements have served to narrow that distinction: "As a rule, performing a work means to represent it by sight or sound, or both."[40] But as a performance can be conveyed "by any means or process," some jurisdictions such as the United States give this term a very expansive interpretation.[41]

Notwithstanding the narrowing of this historical distinction, to reflect the bifurcated nature (and origins) of these two exclusive rights, this review retains the distinction adopted in the Berne Convention that a "performance" concerns "on-site" performances, and a "communication" concerns "off-site" "performances." This distinction was retained in the European Commission (EC) Copyright in the Information Society Directive.[42] For this review, this means that a limitation or exception solely about an "acting" or a "school performance" will be interpreted to refer to an on-site performance by students or staff of an educational establishment and be brought under the fifth category of school performances. However, where the limitation or exception refers to a "*performance*, cinematographic projection and *communication*" of the same performance, it will be classified as two separate limitations or exceptions relating to both "performance" (under the fifth category as a school performance) and "public communication" (under the sixth category as a school broadcast).

The seventh category examines the limitations and exceptions in national legislation that enable the various uses such as reproductions and publications of copyright materials for purposes of educational adaptations or translations. Even though Article 12 of the Berne Convention grants to authors of literary or artistic works the "exclusive right of authorizing adaptations, arrangements and other alterations of their works," as was noted at the Stockholm Conference, "there could be little doubt that the exceptions introduced in ... Article 10(2) ... for the right of reproduction should also apply to the right of translation."[43] So this category supplements the review undertaken in the earlier categories of limitations and exceptions, but excludes a review of similar provisions that are supported by a compulsory licensing regime in the Berne Appendix.[44]

The eighth category examines the interplay between the existing limitations and exceptions for educational activities and the provisions on technological protection measures (TPM) and rights management information (RMI). In particular, this category examines the provisions that circumscribe the application of TPM and RMI in relation to the limitations and exceptions for educational activities, or restrict their application so as to enable or facilitate educational

[40] Goldstein & Hugenholtz, International Copyright: Principles, Law, and Practice (3d ed. 2013), at 327.

[41] §101 of the US Copyright Act defines the term "perform" to mean "to recite, render, play, dance, or act it, either directly or by means of any device or process or, in the case of a motion picture or other audiovisual work, to show its images in any sequence or to make the sounds accompanying it audible." It further defines the term "publicly" in the expression "to perform or display a work publicly" to mean "(1) to perform or display it at a place open to the public or at any place where a substantial number of persons outside of a normal circle of a family and its social acquaintances is gathered; or (2) to transmit or otherwise communicate a performance or display of the work to a place specified by clause (1) or to the public, by means of any device or process, whether the members of the public capable of receiving the performance or display receive it in the same place or in separate places and at the same time or at different times." This has the effect of fusing the exclusive rights of performance and communication to the public under one exclusive right.

[42] Directive 2001/29/ EC of the European Parliament and Council of 22 May, 2001 on the Harmonization of Certain Aspects of Copyright and Related Rights in the Information Society, 2001 O.J. L/ 167, Recital 23.

[43] Records of the Intellectual Property Conference of Stockholm (1967) 1134 (W.I.P.O. 1971), at 921–22.

[44] Arts. II and III of the Berne Appendix have provisions that provide for compulsory licenses for reproductions and/or translations for educational purposes.

activities. This is particularly pertinent for those member states who have acceded to the WCT and WPPT.

The following classes of limitations and exceptions and their attendant activities are not addressed:[45]

- importation of works for personal consumption and their use by natural persons;
- parodies, works of satire, spoofs, and similar works;
- informational, cultural, and news provisions;
- lending of works and the making of copies of works by libraries for the private study of individuals;[46]
- usage of works for the benefit of educational activities of institutions that assist persons with intellectual disabilities;[47] and
- private or personal use of databases and traditional knowledge and uses of databases and traditional knowledge by educational institutions, and generally, the use of computer software.

THE METHODOLOGY

Member States and National Legislation

The process of conducting this review was divided into four phases. In phase one, the author had to locate, identify, and access the copyright legislation from official resources for each member state, which could be the legislative branch or the relevant intellectual property office of each state. The version of the accessed legislation also had to be checked to ensure it was revised and updated. Where the original language of the legislation was not in English, the official (or more typically, the semi-official) English translation of the legislation from the legislative branch or intellectual property office was sought and used, if available. In the absence of this, the review relies on WIPOLex.[48] Where English translations of the member state's legislation were not available, with the assistance of the WIPO Secretariat, translations were made of the legislation by WIPOLex and various expert copyright consultants to WIPO. The author is indebted to the tremendous efforts of colleagues and experts at WIPO whose contributions are totally vital to promoting the transparency of intellectual property laws and optimizing the use of intellectual property in the global IP system.

All in, 2,048 pieces of national copyright legislation from 189 member states[49] were examined for this review.

[45] Many of these are "free access" and "right to access" provisions that are more related to the public citizen's right to information. These are the reporting of current events, press reviews, public reading/recitation, public broadcasts, and publication or broadcast of articles on current economic, political, scientific (including academic gatherings), social, or religious topics which are the focus of public opinion, and the publication of portraits for scientific, educational, or cultural purposes.

[46] *See* Kenneth Crews, WIPO Study on Copyright Limitations and Exceptions for Libraries and Archives (SCCR/29/3), Nov. 5, 2014, available at www.wipo.int/edocs/mdocs/copyright/en/sccr_29/sccr_29_3.pdf.

[47] *See* Judith Sullivan, WIPO Study on Copyright Limitations and Exceptions for the Visually Impaired (SCCR/15/7), Feb. 20, 2007, available at www.wipo.int/edocs/mdocs/copyright/en/sccr_15/sccr_15_7.pdf.

[48] WIPOLex, available at www.wipo.int/wipolex/en/ (last accessed May 7, 2016). WIPOLex is the publicly accessible database of national laws and treaties on intellectual property of WIPO, WTO and UN members maintained by WIPO.

[49] This is as of August 2017. Since September 2017, WIPO membership has risen to 191 member states. The complete list of WIPO member states can be found at WIPO, Member States, September 2017, available at www.wipo.int/members/en/.

TABLE 15.1 *List of fields for analysis of provisions*

Field	Description
Scope [of educational activity]	the nature of the educational activity characterized as a permissible copyright activity
Type(s) of source works(s)	the copyright works that are the subject of the educational activity for the limitation or exception, including the scope of the use of such works for the educational activity
Entity exercising [educational activity]	the entity or beneficiary of the limitation or exception
Purpose of [educational activity]	the legislative purpose or objective for the educational activity
Condition of [educational activity]	the conditions to be satisfied to qualify for the limitation or exception
Frequency/copies and limits	restrictions and limits placed on the the permissible activity, such as the frequency of the activity, the number of copies that could be made and prohibitions on dealings with the copies made
Preclusions (not part of [educational activity])	activities or actions that fall outside of the limitation or exception, or cannot be considered to be part of the limitation or exception
Subject to Attribution	any requisite attribution as to the source, title of the work and authorship of the work to qualify for the limitation or exception
Subject to Remuneration	whether any remuneration is required to conduct the excepted educational activity ("not required" or subject, inter alia, to "equitable remuneration")

Reviewing the Legislation

Phase two of this review examines of all the located legislation identified as being relevant, and places each of the relevant provisions into one of the eight categories of provisions used in this review.

Phase three involves a detailed legislative identification of each element in every categorized provision.[50] Each of the elements identified is placed into a field that represents the issues under consideration relevant to that category of activity.

Phase four consolidates and standardizes these tables of fields and their elements. The standardization is required to ensure consistency in the categorization of provisions and in the treatment of the elements of each provision. To minimize subjectivity in the categorization and characterization, and ensure consistency, this review has been undertaken by the author alone, and augmented by at least three passes through the provisions through automated and semi-automated processes developed by the author.

The tables of fields and their elements are set out in Table 15.1. In addition to the usual fields such as "provision" to identify the source of the provision and its section or article number, the other fields are as set out in this table.

Not all the fields are used for each category. For instance, the "Frequency/copies and limits" field is not used for Quotations and School Performances, because these elements do not typically feature in the provisions.

The fields used to analyze the TPM and RMI provisions are set out in Table 15.2.

[50] For this purpose, a purely literal interpretation is adopted of all the provisions reviewed. This is to preserve the language of the provisions. However, where available, this legislative review is supplemented by case law.

TABLE 15.2 *List of fields for analysis of exceptions against TPM and RMI*

Field	Description
Scope of TPM/RMI exception	the nature and scope of the exception to the protection of TPM and RMI
Type(s) of source work(s)	the copyright works that are the subject of the exception
Beneficiary exercising restriction	the entity or beneficiary of the exception
Purpose of restriction	the legislative purpose or objective for the exception
Condition of restriction	the conditions to be satisfied to qualify for the exception

Classifying the Limitations and Exceptions

The categorization of these provisions can be challenging, because member states may enact provisions that encapsulate two or more of these categories for an educational activity in a copyright limitation or exception. For instance, in Slovakia, Article 25 of Act No. 618/2003 on Copyright and Related Rights (as amended up to Act No. 283/2014 Coll.) reads:

> No consent of the author is necessary for the use of a short part of a released work in another work in the form of a quotation exclusively for the purpose of the review or critique of the released work or for teaching, scientific and research purposes or artistic purposes.

In dealing with exempting the "use of a short part of a released work in another work in the form of a quotation," the Slovakian legislature characterizes this as "for the purpose of the review or critique of the released work," which brings it within Article 10(1) of the Berne Convention as a permissible quotation. However, the same activity is also characterized as "for teaching, scientific and research purposes or artistic purposes," which also brings it within Article 10(2) of the Berne Convention as a use by way of illustration for teaching. The same provision is therefore analyzed under two different categories in this review.

Where the national legislation does not follow the language of the Berne Convention, the expressed object or purpose of the national legislature prevails. For instance, Article 49 of Law on Copyright and Related Rights 2011 of Serbia reads:

> Short excerpts of a work of authorship, or individual short copyright protected works, may be reproduced or be communicated to the public (right of quotation), without the author's permission and without paying remuneration, on the following conditions . . .[51]

While Article 49 at first sight appears to relate to enabling educational reproduction, it is ultimately classified as pertaining to quotations since the "right of quotation" as the purpose or object of was expressly referred to. It is also classified as pertaining to educational communications and recordings made pursuant to the qualifying conditions.

This approach is quite typically taken by member states with open-ended "fair use" exceptions that apply across different educational activities. Examples of similar fair use provisions can be

[51] This is based on the official English language translation of the Copyright and Related Rights 2011 of Serbia, from the Intellectual Property Office of the Republic of Serbia, available at www.zis.gov.rs/upload/documents/pdf_en/pdf_ap/copyright_law.pdf.

found in the United States,[52] Israel,[53] Liberia,[54] the Philippines,[55] the Republic of Korea,[56] and Singapore.[57]

Similarly, as envisioned by the broad term "utilization" in Article 10(2) of the Berne Convention, a legislative provision may use the term "use" to describe the permissible activity for a limitation or exception. In such a case, since "use" is not restricted to "reproduction," such a provision will be categorized as permitting educational reproduction, performance, broadcasting, communication, and recording. However, to the extent that there is already an existing legislative provision that addresses one of the categories of educational "use," the generic "use" provision will not be classified to encompass that specific category, following the Latin maxim *lex specialis derogat legi generali*. For instance, the educational use provision in section 19(2) ("use") is classified as encompassing the educational broadcast, communication, and recording activities ("as illustration for teaching and scientific research") but not educational performances, because there is a separate educational performance provision in section 22 ("public performance") of the Copyright Act 1992 of Estonia.

Throughout this review, effort has been made to replicate the literal language of the provision in extracting its relevant elements. This avoids any ensuing substantive interpretation issues (subject, of course, only to the accuracy of the English translation of the legislation), and enables the language of the provision to be literally read from each field of each category of provisions.

"Free Use" and Remuneration

For this review, a limitation or exception is classified as *not requiring* remuneration, if the activity that fell within the scope of the limitation or exception was described as "lawful" or "permitted without the rightholder's (or author's) authorization." This classification exercise turned out to be surprisingly difficult. For instance, a provision may exist which provides for the private and personal use of a copyright work "for free" or "without payment of author's remuneration." But a subsequent provision may provide for the remuneration of authors for the ostensibly "free use" of a copyright work, such as the use of recording media or photocopying services, or afford equitable remuneration to performers and phonogram producers whose rights have been affected by the "free use" or use which "the author may not prohibit" of the aforesaid work.[58]

[52] Copyright Act of 1976, 17 U.S.C. §107 (2012).

[53] Copyright Act of 2007, 2007 LSI 34 §19 (Isr.).

[54] § 2.7 of the Copyright Law of the Republic of Liberia.

[55] Intellectual Property Code, § 184.1(a), Rep. Act 8293 (Phil.).

[56] Chojakkwonbop [Copyright Act], Act No. 432, Jan. 28, 1957, art. 35 *amended by* Act No. 12137, Dec. 30, 2013 (S. Kor.) [hereinafter, Korean Copyright Act].

[57] § 35 and 109 of the Copyright Act (Cap. 63, 2006 rev. ed.) of Singapore.

[58] *See, e.g.*, Art. 17(1) of the Law of the Republic of Azerbaijan on Copyright and Related Rights, which refers to "free use" and "without payment of author's remuneration," and Arts. 17(3), (4), which refers to remuneration for, authors, performers and phonogram producers collectively, through levies on reproduction equipment and material media; Art. 14 of Law No. 2005-30 of April 5, 2006, relating to Copyright and Related Rights of the Republic of Benin, which sanctions personal and private use of reproductions of copyright and derivative works which "the author may not prohibit," and Arts. 74, 75, and 79, which pertain to the remuneration of authors, performers, and phonogram producers; § 19 of the Copyright Act 1992 of Estonia, describes the permitted reproduction as being "without payment of remuneration," and § 27[1], which subjects all forms of "reprographic reproductions" in s 19 to remuneration payable by the Government. In other words, only non-reprographic reproductions are outside the scope of remuneration and can be made "without payment of remuneration."

As such, this review is subject to the presumption that it had conducted an exhaustive examination of not just the limitation or exception provision in question, but also any other relevant provision in any other piece of legislation, subsidiary legislation, or regulation.

THE ANALYSIS

The examination above is tabulated and placed into tables. Using statistical software, the information in the tables is counted and analyzed.

1 *Summary*

An analysis of the count of the number of provisions for each member state, as classified into all the categories of educational activities (except that for adaptations and translations), is set out in Table 15.3. The statistics are very instructive.

Looking first at the limitations and exceptions (first to sixth categories), Table 15.3 shows that a total of 189 member states have enacted a total of 1,553 provisions to address any one of the first six categories of educational activities. This means that each member state has at least *one* provision in its legislation that is a limitation or exception as regards the use of copyright works and subject matter for educational activities. In fact, the average number of limitations and exceptions pertaining to educational activities in each member state is 8.22 (median is 8). Figure 15.1 demonstrates the qualitative and quantitative significance of this statistic.

The histogram and cumulative frequency table demonstrate clearly the distribution of the limitations and exceptions among member states. While 5 member states have one provision relating to educational activities in their national legislation, and only 4 member states have two such provisions, these statistics rise rapidly thereafter. A total of 11 member states have three such provisions, 8 member states have four, and 19 member states have five. Based on the cumulative frequency distribution, 50 percent or 94.5 member states will have up to 7.20 provisions in their national legislation. 75 percent or 141.8 member states will have up to 9.44 provisions in their national legislation, and 90 percent or 170.1 member states will have up to 13.02 provisions in their legislation. (See Figure 15.1.)

The distribution of these provisions among member states can be further observed by a review of the total number of limitations and exceptions among the top 25 member states (by the total number of such provisions in the first six categories of educational activities) (Table 15.4).

Listing the member states by the count of the total number of limitations and exceptions (for the first to sixth categories) in their national legislation, the top member state (Australia) had 32 such limitations and exceptions for educational activities, with Canada, New Zealand and Singapore following closely behind. (See Table 15.4.) In fact, the top 25 member states by total number of limitations and exceptions all have more than 13 provisions in their legislation. This explains why, on average, each member state has around 8.2 such limitations and exceptions in its copyright legislation. (See Table 15.3.)

The number of such limitations and exceptions could be a reflection of the importance that the member state gives to educational limitations and exceptions. It could also be a function of the legal heritage and the legal system of the member state. Of the top 25 member states, 12 of them (Australia, Brunei Darussalam, Canada, Fiji, Jamaica, Malaysia, New Zealand, Saint Kitts and Nevis, Saint Lucia, Saint Vincent and the Grenadines, Singapore, and the United Kingdom) are members of the Commonwealth of Nations, and two others (Ireland, Niue) are formerly members or British protectorates. (See Table 15.4.) These member states have numerous limitations and exceptions in their

TABLE 15.3 *Summary statistics of all provisions for all categories for each WIPO member state*[59]

	Provisions	Provisions per member state					Member States in Study (189)	
	Total	Max	Min	Avg	SD	Median	States	%
Limitations and Exceptions	1,553	32	1	8.22	4.42	8	189	100.0%
Private/Personal Use	332	7	0	1.76	1.13	2	177	93.7%
Quotations	251	4	0	1.33	0.63	1	183	96.8%
Reproduction	379	12	0	2.01	1.79	2	154	81.5%
Publications	149	8	0	0.79	0.80	1	127	67.2%
Performances	189	8	0	1.00	1.09	1	123	65.1%
Broadcasts/Communications/Recordings	257	10	0	1.36	1.41	1	135	71.4%
TPM/RMI Restrictions	93	7	1	1.89	1.43	1	49	25.9%

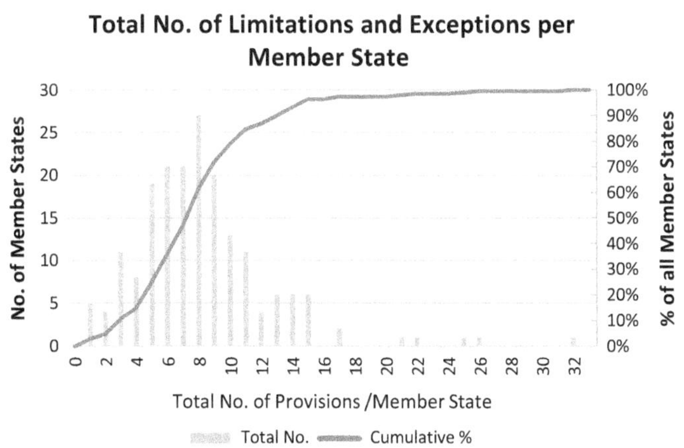

FIGURE 15.1 Distribution of limitations and exceptions provisions among WIPO member states (by first six categories)

national legislation to deal with very specific situations where works and subject matter may be used for particular education-related activities.

59 Note that the summary statistics for compulsory licenses are based on those developing member states that have implemented the licenses, and not on the total number of developing member states that are WIPO members or the total number of WIPO member states. Likewise, the summary statistics for TPM/RMI exceptions are based on those member states that have implemented the restrictions, not on the total number of WIPO member states.

TABLE 15.4 *Top 25 member states by total number of limitations and exceptions*

Position	Member state	Member of Commonwealth of Nations?	Total No. of Limitations and exceptions
1st	Australia	Yes	32
2nd	Canada	Yes	26
3rd	New Zealand	Yes	25
4th	Singapore	Yes	22
5th	Austria		21
6th (joint)	Ireland	former member	17
	Malaysia	Yes	17
8th (joint)	Belgium		15
	Fiji	Yes	15
	Saint Lucia	Yes	15
	Saint Vincent and the Grenadines	Yes	15
	United Kingdom	Yes	15
	United States of America		15
14th (joint)	Brunei Darussalam	Yes	14
	Gambia		14
	Germany		14
	Hungary		14
	Norway		14
	Sweden		14
20th (joint)	Honduras		13
	Jamaica	Yes	13
	Niue	former Protectorate	13
	Philippines		13
	Republic of Korea		13
	Saint Kitts and Nevis	Yes	13

This may be illustrated by the example from Australia, which has multiple provisions enabling educational reproductions, that range from the open-textured, "fair use"–inspired factor-based approach to fair dealing,[60] to specific ones such as fair dealing for an enrolled external student of an educational institution for an approved course of study or research.[61] It even has a "catch-all" for any other use that does not fall within any other provision of the Australian Copyright Act, as long as the use is made for the purpose of giving educational instruction, amounts to a special case, does not conflict with a normal exploitation of the work, and does not unreasonably prejudice the legitimate interests of the copyright owner.[62]

Together with the United States, there are a total of 15 member states with common law systems in the top 25 member states list. The high total count for the United States of America

[60] *Copyright Act* 1968 ss 40, 103C (Austl.).
[61] *Id.* s 40(1A).
[62] *Id.* s 200AB(3).

deserves further explanation. While the United States only has, in substance, two statutory provisions that address the issue of limitations and exceptions for educational activities, the fair use provision in section 35 of the Copyright Act is very broad and it can potentially encompass every educational activity in question. In fact, the generality of the fair use statutory exception has engendered numerous US Congress–approved agreements and guidelines that attempt to particularize the instances of "fair use" of literary and musical works and recording of broadcast programs for educational purposes, which further add to the numbers of provisions in this group of limitations and exceptions. In contrast, the other provision (section 110 from the TEACH Act) has very detailed elements and is of much narrower application, which is more characteristic of the provisions enacted by the other common law member states.

Yet, the formulation of detailed limitations and exceptions provisions is not exclusive to common law jurisdictions. Austria, Armenia, Germany, the Republic of Korea, Belgium, Hungary, Montenegro, Norway, and Sweden have very detailed provisions to provide for various uses of copyright works for educational activities. For instance, section 42(6) of the Austrian Federal Law on Copyrights on Literary and Artistic Works and Related Rights provides that "[s]chools, universities and other educational institutions may, for purposes of instruction or teaching and to the extent justified, make copies in the number necessary for a particular school class or course (reproduction for one's own school use) and distribute them [subject to conditions]," while section 42g provides that "Schools, universities and other educational institutions may, for purposes of instruction or teaching, reproduce published works for illustration for instruction for a precisely confined circle of participants of the instruction or teaching and make them available to the public [subject to conditions and equitable remuneration]." The difference appears to be based on the target of the circulation: in the former, the limited circulation is based on the number of students and is for the student's "own school use," but in the latter, the circulation is based on the "confined circle of participants of the instruction or teaching" and is "made available to the public." Another example of nuanced and specific educational limitations and exceptions can be found in the Korean Copyright Act which distinguishes, for instance, the reproduction of the whole or parts of a work *by schools* to support classes implemented in those educational institutions, for which equitable remuneration is to be paid (for their use by institutes of higher learning), and the reproduction of the whole or parts of a work by a person who receives instruction from educational institutions, "recognized as necessary for the purpose of the lessons," for which no equitable remuneration is required.[63]

Therefore, the quantity of these limitations and exceptions appears to be as much a function of the number of educational activities that national legislatures sought to address in their copyright legislation, as it is also a function of nuanced differentiations between the purpose, object, nature, and policies behind these educational activities, especially in relation to the issue of equitable remuneration for these activities.

2 *Private/Personal Use*

a Private/Personal Use and Educational Instruction

At first sight, it may appear that private or personal use of works is not associated with educational instruction. For instance, at the Stockholm Conference, after considerable discussion among the conference delegates, the private and personal use of works was eventually treated as falling

[63] *Cf.* Korean Copyright Act, Arts. 25(2), (3).

within the reworded phraseology of "certain special cases" in Article 9(2) rather than Article 10(2) of the Berne Convention.[64]

However, any distinction between the private and personal use of works and the use of works in educational instruction is artificial since private and personal use of works elides into self-edification and self-instruction. WIPO member states do recognize the close association between private and personal use and educational instruction, and have adopted a pragmatic approach to this activity in their national legislation. For instance (emphases added):

- section 58(1), Copyright Act, 1998 (CH.323) (as amended by the Copyright (Amendment) Act, Act No. 2 of 2004) of the Bahamas states that "fair dealing with a copyright work, including such use by reproduction in copies or phonorecords for purposes such as *research, private study, scholarship* or *teaching* does not infringe copyright in the work," emphasizing the proximity of research, private study, scholarship and teaching as aspects of fair dealing; and
- section 18, Copyright Act 2013 of the Cook Islands permits the translation of a work by "[a] person giving or receiving instruction . . . for *private* educational, teaching, or research purposes," associating the role of the instructor and the student with teaching or research, and also emphasizing the role of "private education" which the translated materials serve.

Nor is this limited to common law jurisdictions. Prominent illustrations from civil law jurisdictions include (emphases added):

- Article 38.3, Law No. 1328/1998 on Copyright and Related Rights of Paraguay ("in the case of *single, personal copies* that are used solely for *teaching purposes* by teaching staff at educational establishments") highlights the personal use of materials by teaching staff;
- Article 35(3) item 2, Act on Copyright and Related Rights (Copyright Act, as amended up to Law of October 1, 2013) of Germany ("permissible to make copies for *personal use* of small parts of a work . . . for state examinations and examinations in schools, higher education institutions, noncommercial training and further training institutions, as well as vocational training institutions in the required quantity") highlights the personal use of materials for educational purposes;
- Article 20 of the Royal Decree No. 65/2008 promulgating the Law on Copyright and Related Rights, Oman ("Reproduction . . . by reprographic means of protected works *by . . . educational establishments* and scientific and cultural institutions, provided that such reproduction shall be . . . to meet the *need of a natural person* for use in a study or research") emphasizes that the reproduction of works by educational establishments is to meet "the need of a natural person for use in a study or research."

b Difference between Private and Personal Use

At first glance, there appears to be a sharp difference between the *personal* use of content for educational purposes, and the *private* use of content for similar purposes. By this suggestion, *personal* use refers to the consumptive use of copyrighted work by a natural person for *his or her* own purposes, but *private* use refers to such uses within the family circle, which could not relate to educational activities.

The legislation of some member states indeed appears to make that distinction.[65] However, this review declines to draw this distinction because the *travaux préparatoires* of the Berne

[64] Records of the Intellectual Property Conference of Stockholm (1967) 1134 (W.I.P.O. 1971), at 857–58, 1144–46.

[65] *See, e.g.*, Art. 19.1(a), Federal Act of October 9, 1992 on Copyright and Related Rights (status as of January 1, 2011); s 10(a)(i) ("user's own personal or private use") and s 39(a) ("private use") of Copyright Act, 1989 of Malawi.

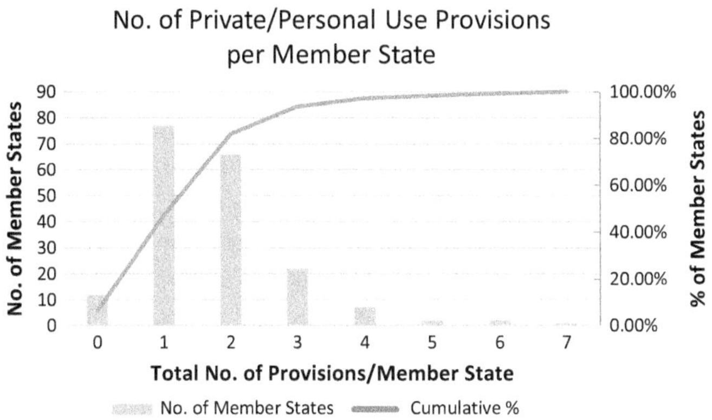

FIGURE 15.2 Distribution of private/personal use provisions among member states

Convention showed that there was no consensus on the issue.[66] Also, a review of member states' national legislation shows that a majority use the terms "private use" and "personal use" interchangeably.[67] Furthermore, any analysis that turns on the perceived difference between "personal use" and "private use" would turn on the language of the provisions, which in turn places too much emphasis on the accuracy of the English translations of the provisions. For these reasons, this review does not seeks to distinguish between the "private use" and "personal use" limitations and exceptions.

c Analysis

There are 332 provisions from 177 member states that deal with private or personal use. (See Table 15.3.) On average, each member state has 1.76 provisions that deal with private or personal use. The standard deviation of 1.13 (median: 2) together confirms that while 50 percent of member states have 1.08 private or personal use provisions, this number rises rapidly because a substantial number of member states have 2 private or personal use provisions in their legislation. Thus, by the cumulative distribution, 75 percent of member states have up to 1.80 provisions and 95 percent of member states have up to 3.12 provisions that sanction the private or personal use of works. (See Figure 15.2.) Conversely, only 12 (6.35 percent) of member states have no provisions that sanction the private or personal use of works. At 177 member states (93.7 percent), the category of provisions for private and personal use of copyright and derivative works represents the second-largest category of limitations and exceptions for educational activities. It also highlights the significance of this category of educational limitations and exceptions.

These limitations and exceptions are variously characterized. A total of 42 such provisions use the "fair use" or "fair dealing" formulation, 49 such provisions describe the purpose of the limitation or exception as being for "study," and 56 such provisions describe the purpose as for "research."

[66] Records of the Intellectual Property Conference of Stockholm (1967) 1134 (W.I.P.O. 1971), at 857–58, 1144. The delegates at the Stockholm Conference had subjected the meaning of the expression "private use" to close debate. Some delegates had sought to replace it with the expression "individual or family use" or even "personal use," and yet others were concerned that that was capable of too broad an interpretation. Ultimately, the delegates assiduously avoided reference to this expression in the Berne Convention and simply referred to these as "certain special cases." Id. *at* 1145.

[67] *See, e.g.*, s 27, Copyright Act, 2004 of Gambia; Art. 20.1 ("for his individual use"), 20.4 ("for personal use") and 20.5 ("for private use") of Law on Copyright and Related Rights No. VIII-1185 of May 18, 1999 (as amended on October 7, 2014 – by Law No. XII-1183) of Lithuania appear to use these three terms interchangeably; s 15(1)(a), The Copyright and Neighbouring Rights Act, 2006 of Uganda conflates "private use" and "personal use," as originally defined.

Many member states subject this private or personal use to conditions such as the making of a single copy (68 provisions) or a few or limited copies (12 provisions), the requirement that there be no commercial gain or profit-making purpose, income or revenue etc. from the copying (87 provisions). As to the latter, various formulations are used such as "non-commercial purpose," "no profit/income/revenue/interest/economic benefit," "free of charge," "without payment," or "gratuitous." Other member states use the "fair use factors" to guide the determination of whether the private or personal use is "fair" (18 provisions).

Another delimiter is to preclude certain works from being the source works for the private and personal use. A total of 102 provisions exclude architectural works, musical works, artistic works, computer programs, and databases from the scope of the limitations and exceptions. A total of 94 provisions delimit the private or personal use provision with elements from the three-step test set out in Article 9(2) of the Berne Convention: that the use must be confined to certain special cases, that it must not conflict with a normal exploitation of the work, and that it must not unreasonably prejudice the legitimate interests of the author.

d Attribution and Remuneration

There are only relatively few provisions (40 provisions) that require this private or personal use to be attributed. (See Figure 15.3.)

Most of the private or personal use provisions do not require any form of remuneration (236 provisions). However, a small but significant number (90 provisions) require some form of remuneration or fair compensation to the author or related rights holder, either in the form of a levy on the recording media or reproduction equipment, for the private or personal use.

3 *Quotations*

a Analysis

There are 251 provisions from 183 member states that deal with quotations. On average, each member state has 1.33 provisions that deal with quotations. The relatively small standard deviation of 0.63 suggests a very narrow distribution of provisions among member states. Based

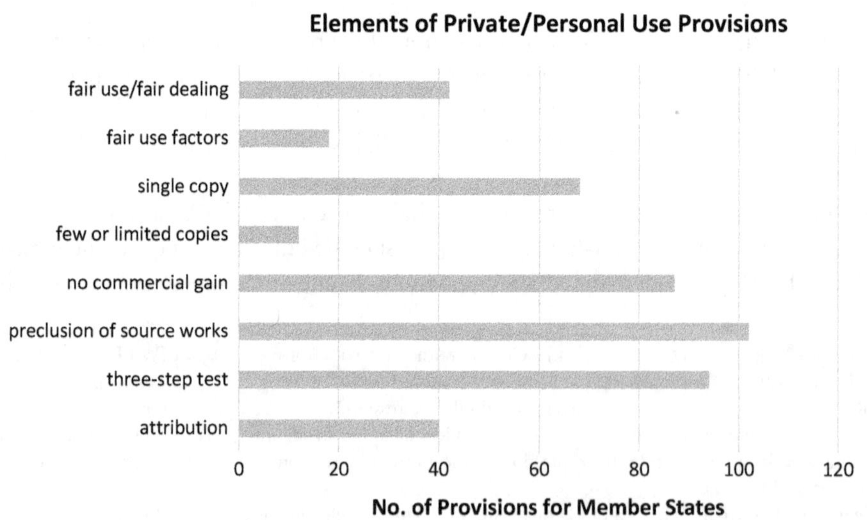

FIGURE 15.3 Distribution of elements of private/personal use provisions

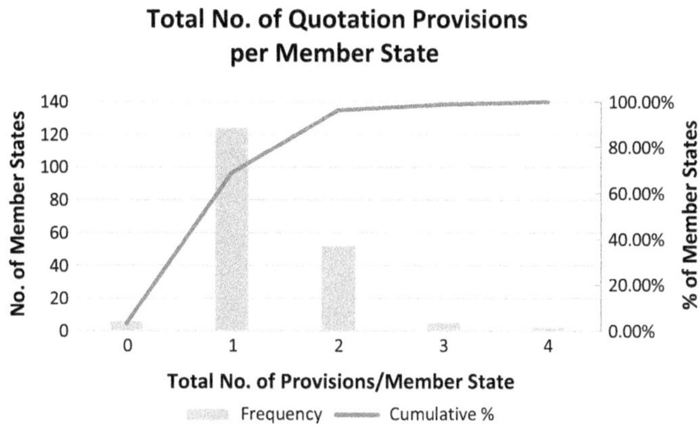

FIGURE 15.4 Distribution of quotation provisions among member states

on the cumulative distribution, it is estimated that 95 percent of member states will have between 0 and 1.95 provisions that sanction the private or personal use of works.[68] (See Table 15.3.) Similarly, with 183 member states (96.8 percent of all member states) represented, this means that almost every member state has at least one provision to address the use of quotations for educational purposes. (See Figure 15.4.)

Like the private and personal use provisions, 46 of these limitations and exceptions use the "fair use" or "fair dealing" formulation to describe the use of quotations. Most of the provisions are simply referred to as permitting "quotes" or "quotations" (139 provisions) as the scope of the provision, although other equivalent formulations include "citations," "excerpts," "extracts," "citations," and "illustrations."

The purpose of using quotations has been variously described as for "criticism" (122 provisions), "review" (60 provisions), "science" or "scientific" (37 provisions), "polemic" (30 provisions), "research" (26 provisions), "information" (26 provisions), "education" (18 provisions), "teaching" (16 provisions), "comment" (13 provisions), or "illustration" (10 provisions).

The scope and extent of use of works as quotations is frequently not spelt out explicitly in the provisions: this is because the concept of a quotation, citation, excerpt, and so on connotes a limit to reproduction or use of the source work. Some member states use "fair/proper/good/customary/reasonable practice" (85 provisions) or the "fair use factors" (18 provisions) to assess whether the quotation is "fair," while others use the more open-ended yardstick of a quotation "justified by its purpose" (105 provisions).

Unlike private or personal use however, there are few preclusions to the works that can be quoted: those that are typically excluded are performances and phonograms (10 provisions) and architectural works, computer programs and databases (9 provisions). Most of the preclusions operate by way of the three-step test (46 provisions).

At least 195 of these provisions require attribution to the quotations, as required by Article 10(3) of the Berne Convention. This figure is a marked increase from that for private and personal use. The actual figure is probably higher because many member states recognize the author's moral rights as to attribution and thus require the identification of the author when the quotation is used.

[68] The median number of quotation provisions is 1.

b *Remuneration*

Remuneration is required in only very few provisions (7 provisions). And where it is required, the provisions are limited to those instances where the quotations constitute the main or significant part of the new work. Examples of these provisions can be found in Article 10 of the Argentinian Law No. 11.723 of September 28, 1933, on Legal Intellectual Property Regime (Copyright Law, as last amended by Law No. 26.570 of November 25, 2009) and Article 31 of the Colombia Law No. 23 of 1982 (January 28) – On Copyright.

4 *Research/Educational Reproduction*

a *Analysis*

The provisions for research and educational reproduction represent the largest group of provisions by educational categories. At 379 provisions, there are more research and educational reproduction provisions than there are private and personal use provisions (332 provisions) and quotation provisions (251 provisions), as befits the mandate of this review. However, it is noteworthy that there are *fewer* member states with research and educational reproduction provisions (154 member states) than there are private and personal use (177 member states) and quotation (183 member states) provisions.

On average, each member state has 2.01 provisions (median 2 provisions) dealing with research or educational reproductions. On the other hand, the range of provisions across member states is very wide, ranging from 0 provisions (35 member states have no educational reproduction provisions) to 12 provisions (New Zealand). Australia is not far behind at 10 provisions. The relatively large standard deviation of 1.79 suggests that there is quite a lot of variability among member states in their implementation of educational reproduction provisions. Based on the cumulative frequencies, 50 percent of member states have between 0 and 1.2 educational reproduction provisions, 75 percent have between 0 and 2.40 provisions, and 95 percent of member states have between 0 and 4.59 provisions. The high variability of the distribution of these provisions is illustrated by Figure 15.5.

The many different ways in which research and educational reproduction is permitted by member states can be seen from an examination of the provisions themselves. Only 21 are "fair use" or "fair dealing" provisions for "research or study" or extended versions of "research or

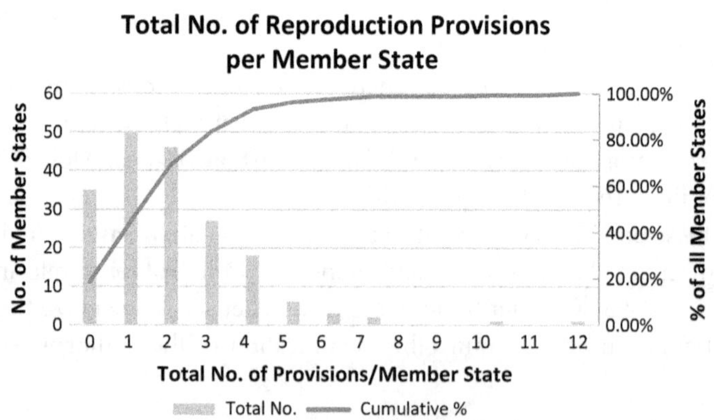

FIGURE 15.5 Distribution of research and educational reproduction provisions among member states

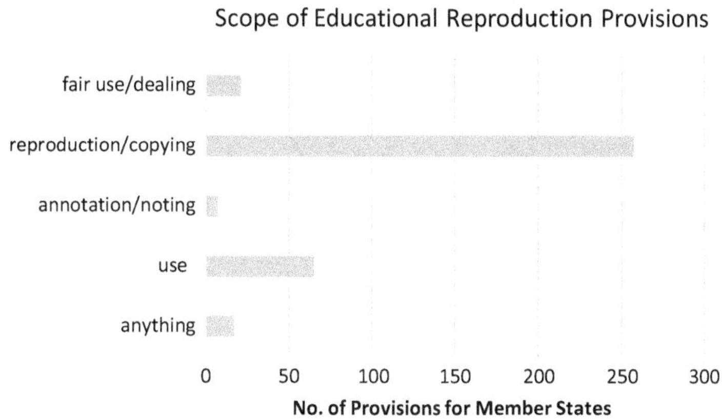

FIGURE 15.6 Distribution of scope of educational reproduction provisions

private study."[69] Member states have tended to use other formulations to scope the research and educational reproduction provision: the narrower "reproduction/copying/duplication" (257 provisions) or "annotate/notes" (7 provisions) formulations, or the broader "use" (65 provisions) or "anything" (17 provisions) formulations. Reprographic reproduction, as part of reproduction/copying/duplication, accounted for 32 provisions. (See Figure 15.6)

A majority of the provisions do not circumscribe the type of entity who may use the limitation or exception (212 provisions). For those that do, the permitted entities are instructors (41 provisions), students (36 provisions), *both* instructors *and* students (53 provisions), or the schools and educational institutions themselves (97 provisions).

The purposes for which the works are used are formulated widely to capture the diverse forms in which education can be conducted: "teaching" (125 provisions), which is the expression used in Article 10(2), is the most popular, but "education" (105 provisions), "instruction" (60 provisions), "class/lecture/lesson" (23 provisions), "examination/question" (58 provisions), "research" (100 provisions), and "science" (70 provisions) are also addressed. Interestingly, the specific use of works for courses in "films/film making" (9 provisions) is also addressed. (See Figure 15.7.)

A significant number of provisions do not prescribe any additional conditions for their use that supplement the existing scope and purpose restrictions (161 provisions). However, where they do, the primary restriction is that the educational reproduction not be conducted for commercial gain or advantage (106 provisions). Other restrictions include the unavailability of a commercial license or knowledge of its existence for the educational reproduction (39 provisions), the requirement that such reproduction be fair (35 provisions, of which 13 provisions rely on the fair use factors), the prohibition against the publication or distribution of the reproduction (19 provisions) or against the use of reprography or the making of reprographic copies (unless the provision specifically allows it) (6 provisions).

However, a significant number of provisions (106 provisions) do prescribe limits or restrictions on the extent of the copying and the frequency of the making of copies. A total of 73 provisions

[69] *See, e.g.*, *Copyright Act 1968* ss 40, 103C, 248A (Austl.) (outlining fair dealing for "research or study"); Bahamas, Copyright Act, 1998 (CH.323) (as amended by the Copyright (Amendment) Act, Act No. 2 of 2004), s 58; Copyright Act of 2007, 2007 LSI 34 §19 (Isr.); Liberia, Copyright Law of the Republic of Liberia, s 2.7; Singapore, Copyright Act (Cap. 63, 2006 rev. ed.) (consolidated as of March 31, 2015) ss 35, 109; and Uganda, The Copyright and Neighbouring Rights Act, 2006, s 15(1)(j).

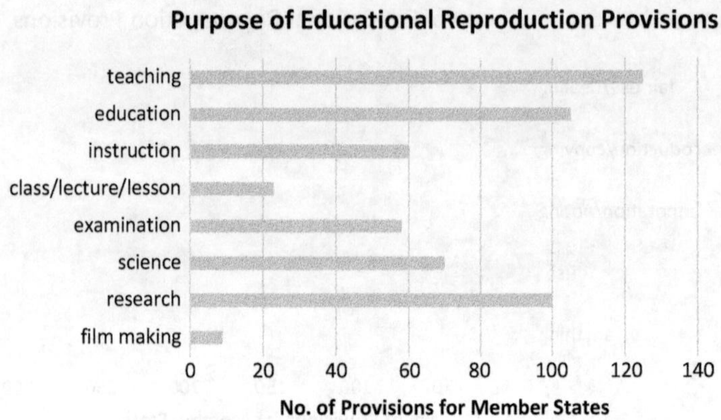

FIGURE 15.7 Distribution of purpose of educational reproduction provisions

apply an open-ended limit such as "to the extent justified by the purpose."[70] Other limits are more quantitative in nature. For instance:

- section 44(3), New Zealand Copyright Act 1994 (No. 143) (reprint as at January 1, 2014): no more than the greater of 3 percent of the work or edition or three pages of the work or edition or 50 percent of the whole work or edition, whichever is less
- Article 50(3), Copyright and Related Rights Act of 30 March 1995 as last amended on December 15, 2006, of Slovenia: no more than three copies
- section 36(1), Copyright, Designs and Patents Act 1988 of the United Kingdom: not more than 5 percent of any work/recording in twelve months

In addition, 59 provisions provide that the ensuing copies made pursuant to the provision may not be disposed of or dealt with commercially, ensuring that the first sale doctrine does not apply to these copies.

Unlike the private and personal use provisions, there are very few subject matter preclusions for the research and education reproduction provisions. Instead, the operative preclusion here is the three-step test (70 provisions). Alternatively, the preclusion can take the following form: they prohibit the reproduction of source works which have been "published as teaching or instructional materials."[71] A similar restriction against the copying of "educational consumables" is also found in the Guidelines for Classroom Copying in Not-for-Profit Educational Institutions with respect to books and periodicals and the Guidelines for Educational Uses of Music of the United States. The review has found 7 such provisions.

b Attribution and Remuneration

All good scholarship usage should be supported by references and citations. Article 10(3) of the Berne Convention reinforces this practice, although any attribution should not detract from or defeat the educational context in which the source works are used. In this regard, 133 provisions mandate that the educational reproduction be attributed, but 54 provisions prescribe some kind of waiver of the attribution requirement.

[70] *See, e.g.*, Art. 40, Law Supporting the Rights of Authors, Composers, Artists and Researchers (Copyright Law) of Afghanistan; Art. 6(3), Regulations on the Protection of the Right to Network Dissemination of Information Networks (promulgated by the State Council, May 10, 2006, effective July 1, 2006) (China).

[71] *See, e.g.*, s 29(c), The Copyright & Related Rights Act of the Maldives; s 26(c), Copyright Act (Act No. 12 of 2002) of Tonga.

A substantial majority of the provisions (319 provisions) do not prescribe any kind of remuneration for the use of works for research or educational purposes. Of the 44 provisions that do, 32 are premised on the making of copies or the use of reprographic equipment or the reproduction by third parties, 2 afford remuneration through levies on storage media or reprographic equipment[72] and 1 requires remuneration only on the continued retention of the copy made.[73] Other provisions seem to require remuneration because the source works could be both reproduced and made available to the public. These would describe provisions from Austria,[74] China,[75] France,[76] and the Netherlands.[77]

Of the 44 provisions that require remuneration, 5 explicitly envisage the making of reproductions in the digital environment. These provisions are from Canada,[78] China,[79] France,[80] Liechtenstein,[81] and Singapore.[82]

5 *Educational Publications/Anthologies/Compilations/Composite Works*

The category of provisions for educational publications, anthologies, compilations, and other composite works constitutes the smallest of the categories of educational limitations and exceptions, with only 149 provisions identified in the legislation of 127 (67.2 percent) member states. This category is separate and distinct from the earlier category of provisions for educational or research reproductions, because the purposes served by this category are overtly commercial in nature. It is however considered in the public interest to support the educational materials industry to ensure that there is adequate availability of instructional materials for educational purposes at affordable prices.

a Analysis

The relative paucity of provisions that deal with educational publications can be seen from the low average of 0.79 provisions per member state (median of 1). However, the standard deviation of 0.80 belies the fact that 95 percent of the member states have between 0 and 1.42 educational publication provisions, as illustrated in Figure 15.8.

It will be clear from this histogram that save for one member state, there are no member states with more than 3 provisions that deal with educational publications. The outlier here is Austria, which has a total of 8 distinct provisions to deal with the distribution and making available of educational compilations, depending on whether they pertain to works in general, musical works or artistic works, with special conditions ascribed for each type of publication.

[72] Art. 19.1.b, Federal Act on Copyright and Related Rights, Oct. 9, 1992, SR 231, art 19.1.b, (Switz.); Copyright Act (Chapter C.28, as codified 2004), second schedule, para. (h) (Nigeria).

[73] Copyright Act, R.S.C., 1985, c. C-42 §29.7 (Can.).

[74] Federal Law on Copyrights on Literary and Artistic Works and Related Rights (Copyright Act) [BGBL] No. 99/2015 as amended, §42g.

[75] Regulations on the Protection of the Right to Network Dissemination of Information Networks (promulgated by the State Council, May 10, 2006, effective July 1, 2006), art. 8.

[76] Code de la Propriété Intellectuelle [Intellectual Property Code] art. L211–3.

[77] Arts. 16.1, 16.2, Wet van 23 september 1912, Stb. 1912, 308.

[78] Copyright Act, R.S.C. 1984 c. C-42, §§ 29.7, 30.02(a) (Can.).

[79] Regulations on the Protection of the Right to Network Dissemination of Information Networks (promulgated by the State Council, May 10, 2006, effective July 1, 2006), art. 8

[80] Code de la Propriété Intellectuelle [Intellectual Property Code] art. L122–5.3(e).

[81] Art. 22(1)(d), Law on Copyright and Neighboring Rights (Copyright Law) (version as of June 1, 2016) Regulation on Copyright and Neighbouring Rights (Copyright Regulation), Liechtenstein.

[82] Part III, Division 6, s 52, Copyright Act (Cap. 63, 2006 rev. ed.) (consolidated as of March 31, 2015), Singapore.

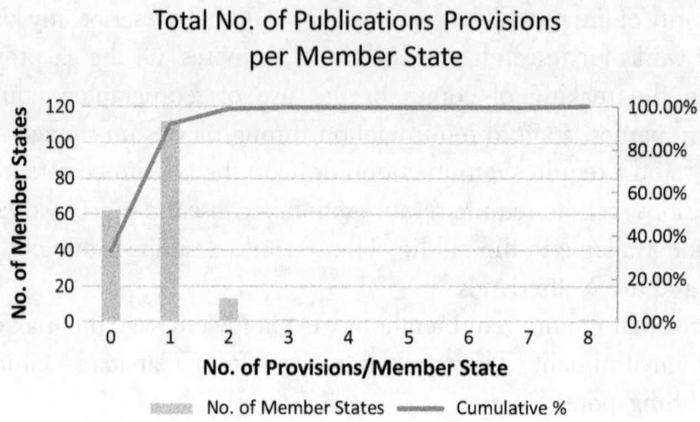

FIGURE 15.8 Distribution of educational publication provisions among member states

There is generally relatively little variation in the nature of the educational publication provisions. Most of the provisions mirror the language of Article 10(2) of the Berne Convention closely, in that they permit the utilization of works in publication (59 provisions), sound or visual recordings or films (11 provisions). The provisions operate by "using" (51 entries), "reproducing," "copying" or "borrowing" parts of source works (79 entries), transcribing them or using them for illustration (41 entries), and through selections, quotations and passages (9 entries). Many of the provisions also emphasize that the entirety of the source work cannot be used: only "part" of (22 provisions) or "minor/short/small/limited/isolated/few" (70 provisions) works can be used.

The purpose of these publications is predominantly education, teaching and instruction (128 provisions), although reference is also made to enabling publications for science or research (20 provisions).

There are also predominantly no restrictions against the entity who may be able to publish the publications and anthologies (139 provisions).

The conditions prescribed for sanctioning educational publications are quite varied: that the collection be comprised primarily of noncopyright material (21 provisions), that the publication be for noncommercial purposes (19 provisions), that fair/customary use/practice be observed (29 provisions), and that the collection be described and advertised as being for use in places of education (14 provisions). Other restrictions include limiting or justifying the extent of the use of the source work (50 provisions), limiting it to a small or reasonable part (3 provisions) or to what is necessary or essential (6 provisions), limiting the source works to no more than 2 in quantity, typically within a five-year period (26 provisions), or requiring a lapse of five years from first publication of the source work (5 provisions).

As with the other categories of provisions, published collections that use precluded source works such as buildings and software (7 provisions), and that use source works that are themselves prepared for use in education (3 provisions) are disallowed, as are collections delimited by the three-step test (32 provisions).

b Attribution and Remuneration

In almost all of these provisions, there must be proper attribution for such use of the source works (125 provisions), unless to do so will be impracticable or infeasible (30 provisions).

In 110 provisions, remuneration for these educational publications is not required. For the remaining 38 provisions in twenty-seven member states, either a statutory license or some form of remuneration or payment to the copyright owner is required.

6 School Performances

a Analysis

There are 189 performance-related provisions for educational activities identified in the legislation of 123 member states. (See Figure 15.9.) The average and median figures both indicate that most member states will have only 1 such provision in their legislation. The member state with the largest number of school performance provisions is Canada, with 8 provisions.

As would be expected, a majority of the provisions are directed at performance (120 provisions), although some member states have defined "communication" or "making available to the public" to include performance (11 provisions). Other manifestations of these provisions include showing or playing sound recordings, films, broadcasts and cable programs (54 provisions), or screening or causing such works to be heard or seen (10 provisions). Recitals (2 provisions) and exhibitions/presentations (4 provisions) are also described. In addition, some member states adopt the broad "use" formulation set out in Article 10(2) of the Berne Convention to justify the conduct of school performances (31 provisions), or apply the generic "fair use" or "fair dealing" formulation for school performances (4 provisions).

Analysis of national copyright legislation shows that there are generally two classes of school performance provisions: provisions that specifically address the schools and educational institutions (63 provisions) and their teachers, students and instructors who conduct school performances (36 provisions), and nonprofit clubs and societies (such as quasi-formal interest group associations in schools formed by students to advance their extracurricular activities) (16 provisions). For the first class of provisions, school performances are conducted for purposes of education or school (83 provisions), teaching (45 provisions), instruction or learning (23 provisions), training (10 provisions), and examination (5 provisions). They may also be conducted for research or scientific purposes (30 provisions). For the second class of provisions, the performances are conducted in support of, or for the benefit of the club or society.

There are typically six different conditions which apply to sanction school performances: the composition of the audience is limited to teachers, students, instructors, and, occasionally, family members of students (59 provisions), the performance is conducted on the premises of the educational institution (16 provisions), the performance is given free of charge or the proceeds to be applied solely for the organization of the performance (73 provisions), no remuneration is given to the performers (19 provisions), the extent of the work used in the performance is limited or restricted (8 provisions), or the use is subject to fair use or fair dealing

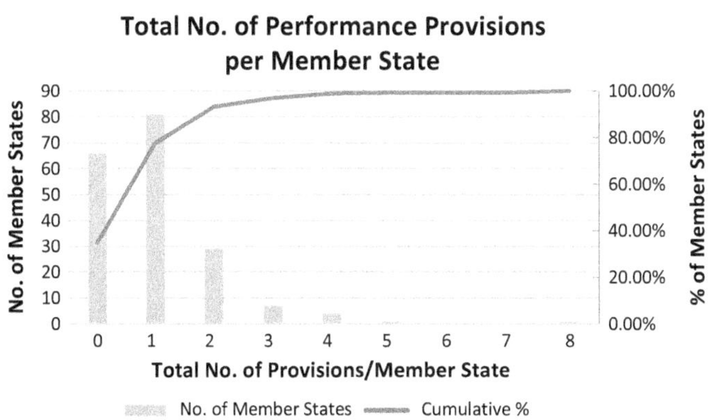

FIGURE 15.9 Distribution of school performance provisions among member states

(4 provisions). The operation of 23 provisions is further subject to the three-step test, and 21 provisions are subject to further preclusions as to the types of source works which can be used (such as phonograms, cinematographic works, computer programs, and performances).

b Attribution and Remuneration

A total of 45 provisions require attribution as to the source and/or authorship (with 10 provisions qualifying the attribution requirements).

For 118 provisions, no remuneration is required. For 7 provisions (from Canada, Finland, Germany, Iceland, Netherlands, Sweden, and the Republic of Korea), compensation to the authors and other right holders is payable by way of royalties, extended collective license or equitable remuneration (excepting the instances where a levy is payable for the use of storage media and recording equipment and devices).[83]

7 Educational Broadcasts/Communications/Recordings

a Distance Learning, Online Instruction and Communication to the Public

The category of limitations and exceptions for "educational broadcasts, communications and recordings" is based on Article 10(2) of the Berne Convention, which provides that member states may permit the utilization of works by way of illustration for teaching purposes, in "broadcasts or sound or visual recordings." Even though Article 9(3) provides that sound or visual recordings shall be considered as reproductions,[84] because recordings are exempted with broadcasts in Article 10(2), recordings for educational purposes will be considered under this category rather than the third category of research and educational reproductions.[85] Likewise, "transmissions of a work for purposes of distance learning"[86] will fall within this category.

The review of this category is complicated for the following reasons. First, although some member states have provisions that enable the "communication to the public" or "making available" of online content for educational purposes,[87] a few member states have *sui generis* provisions that address the dissemination of such content for instructional purposes *via computer networks*.[88]

[83] It is however of interest to note that the Korean Copyright Act, Art. 25(2), qualifies the remuneration payable.

[84] Records of the Intellectual Property Conference of Stockholm (1967) 1134 (W.I.P.O. 1971), at 927.

[85] Some member states such as Australia and Singapore have defined "recordings" to encompass the fixation in material form of broadcasts or other communications, comprising material which may or may not have been previously fixed in material form. *Copyright Act* 1968 s 248A(1) (Austl.); *cf. Copyright Act* 1968 s 200(1); s 246(1), Copyright Act (Cap. 63, 2006 rev ed.) (consolidated as of March 31, 2015), Singapore.

[86] *See* APEC, Asia-Pacific Economic Cooperation Intellectual Property Experts' Group Survey on Copyright Limitations and Exceptions: Report on Copyright L&E in APEC Economies, July 2009, available at publications.apec.org/publication-detail.php?pub_id=971 (examining the "transmissions of a work for purposes of distance learning").

[87] *See, e.g., Copyright Act* 1968, Part VB, Division 2A, ss 135ZMB, 135ZMC, 135ZMD, 135ZMDA, (Austl.); Copyright Act, R.S.C. 1984 c. C-42 (Can.); Code de la Propriété Intellectuelle [Intellectual Property Code] art. L122–5.3(e) (Fr.); Copyright Act, Law No. 48 of 197, arts. 34, 35(2), 36 (Japan); Liberia (ss 2.10(2), 2.19, Copyright Law of the Republic of Liberia); Mauritius (s 19(1)(a), Copyright Act 2014); Portugal (Art. 75.2(o), Code of Copyright and Related Rights (as last amended by Law No. 16/2008 of April 1, 2008)); Korean Copyright Act, Arts. 25(2), (3), 35*ter*; Singapore (Part III, Division 6, s 52, Copyright Act (Cap. 63, 2006 rev. ed.) (consolidated as of March 31, 2015)); (Art. 32.2, Consolidated Text of the Law on Intellectual Property, Regularizing, Clarifying and Harmonizing the Applicable Statutory Provisions art. 32.2 (R.D. 1996, 1/1996) (Spain); Copyright Act of 1976, 17 U.S.C. §110(2) (2012) (U.S.).

[88] *See, e.g.*, Regulations on the Protection of the Right to Network Dissemination of Information Networks (promulgated by the State Council, May 10, 2006, effective July 1, 2006), art. 6(3); s 11(1), Copyright Act (Cap 67, Act No. 21 of 2011) of Grenada; 1999 évi. LXXVI Art. 38(5), (Hung.); Legge 30 Aprile 2010, n. 633, Art. 701.1*bis* (It.).

Second, member states like Germany,[89] Norway,[90] Portugal,[91] North Macedonia,[92] and Tunisia[93] have broad "communication to the public" or "making available" *rights* that could enable the online dissemination of digital content in their educational *limitations and exceptions*, even though there is no explicit reference to online dissemination in the limitations and exceptions themselves.

Alternatively, distance learning in the form of public service broadcasts or cable program services on special education and instructional channels, such as those in Qatar[94] and Venezuela,[95] may or may not enable online distance learning. To leave this matter open for further discussion, this review flags these provisions as enabling a "communication to the public" or a "broadcast." It could be argued that online distance learning is very different from public service broadcasts or cable program services because online disseminations will invariably involve digital reproductions of source works, in whole or in part, for a transient period of time. To this end, some member states like Canada[96] and Finland[97] have provisions that exempt both the reproduction and communication rights in their educational limitations and exceptions.

Third, member states like Moldova[98] have "making available" exceptions for educational purposes, but only where such content is part of the collection of libraries or archive services, which suggests that educational institutions can only provide such content interactively for their students through the library department of the educational institution.

Finally, electronic transmissions for educational instruction will invariably involve the use of hyperlinks to enable access to the relevant sources. The current case law pertaining to the provision of hyperlinks is not uniformly settled in all member states: whether the provision of hyperlinks amounts to a communication of the underlying electronic resource is still being resolved by apex courts in various jurisdictions.[99]

For these reasons, this review will only proceed to describe the limitations or exceptions that enable educational broadcasts, communications or recordings, and will not engage in the further analysis of whether the provisions address online distance learning.

b Analysis

The 257 provisions in 135 member states' legislation for educational broadcasts, communications and recordings represent the third-largest category of educational provisions. But there are *fewer* member states with broadcast/communication/recording provisions than there are educational

[89] Gesettz über Urheberrecht und verwandte Schutzrechte [Urheberrechtsgesetz] [Law on Copyright and Related Rights] Sept. 9, 1965, BGBL I at 1273, art 46 (Ger.).

[90] s 16(2), Copyright Act (Act No. 2 of May 12, 1961, relating to Copyright in Literary, Scientific and Artistic Works) (consolidated version of 2015), Norway.

[91] Art. 75.2(f), (o), Code of Copyright and Related Rights (as last amended by Law No. 16/2008 of April 1, 2008), Portugal.

[92] Art. 52(1).17, Law on Copyright and Related Rights (Aug 31, 2010), Republic of North Macedonia.

[93] Art. 10(a), Law No. 94-36 of February 24, 1994, on Literary and Artistic Property, Tunisia.

[94] Art. 18(2), Law No. 7 of 2002 on the Protection of Copyright and Related Rights ("using the work by way of illustration for teaching, through publications, broadcasts, sound or visual recordings, films *or by any other means*").

[95] Art. 40.9, Law on Copyright (of August 14, 1993), Venezuela (Bolivarian Republic of), Art. 40.1-8, Law on Copyright (of August 14, 1993).

[96] Copyright Act, R.S.C. 1984 c. C-42 § 30.02(b) (Can.)

[97] s 14 (14.10.2005/821), Copyright Act (Act No. 404 of July 8, 1961, as amended up to 608/2015) of Finland.

[98] Art. 28(p) of Law No. 139 of July 2, 2010, on Copyright and Neighbouring Rights of the Republic of Moldova.

[99] *See, e.g.*, Case C-160/15 GS Media BV v Sanoma Media Netherlands BV, 2016 E.C.R. *Cf.* Case C-466/12 Svensson and Others 2014 E.C.R.; Perfect 10, Inc. v. Amazon.com, Inc., 508 F.3d 1146 (9th Cir. 2007), Pearson Education, Inc. v. Ishayev, 963 F.Supp.2d 239 (S.D.N.Y. 2013). Various organizations such as AIPPI and ALAI have conducted or are currently conducting detailed studies on this issue.

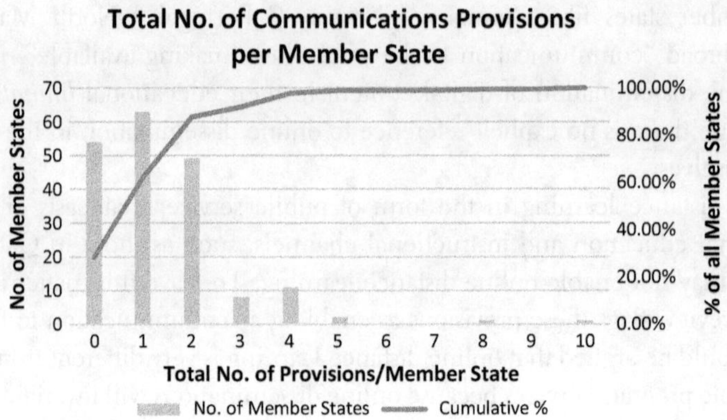

FIGURE 15.10 Distribution of educational broadcasting, communications and recording provisions among member states

reproduction provisions, suggesting that the reproduction is still envisaged as the primary means for supplying works for educational activities. Nonetheless, there are more provisions and more member states with provisions for educational broadcast/communication/recording provisions than there are for educational publications (149 provisions, 127 member states) and performances (189 provisions, 123 member states), suggesting that broadcasts, communications and recording for educational purposes are significant.

This observation is also reflected in the higher average of 1.36 provisions per member state for this category of educational provisions, when compared with the averages for publications (0.79 provisions) and performances (1.00 provisions). Although the medians for broadcasts/communications/recordings, publications and performances are the same (at 1 provision each), 50 percent of member states have between 0 and 0.64 educational reproduction provisions. This is indicative of the lack of adoption of such provisions in the legislation of member states, a situation which contrasts unfavourably with the distribution of the reproduction provisions, and with all the limitations and exceptions provisions, as illustrated in Figure 15.10.

Reference was earlier made to the 25 provisions that arguably permit the communication (and their attendant reproduction) of works for educational activities. Provisions also qualify their scope by referring to the "recording" (108 provisions), "communication" (76 provision), "broadcast" (70 provisions), "fixation" or "filming" (16 provisions), "making available" (15 provisions), or "performance" (7 provisions) of the works. (As previously noted, the "performance" provisions here refer to the communication of the works.[100]) Member states have also formulated the provisions more generally as pertaining to "use" (81 provisions), "fair use" or "fair dealing" (10 provisions), and "anything" (4 provisions) in relation to the source works.

Provisions may additionally circumscribe the entity who may rely on the limitation or exception by confining it to a school, university or educational establishment (74 provisions), or to a teacher, staff member or student (18 provisions). The purposes for which the educational communications, broadcasts and recordings are made are variously identified as for education, teaching, illustration, instruction and classroom purposes (213 provisions), for science or research (78 provisions), for examinations and questions (18 provisions), for film studies (8 provisions), and in the public interest (3 provisions). It is noteworthy that only 34 provisions specifically cited "illustration" as a purpose to justify the provision.

[100] *See* discussion in main text at *supra*, note 38.

The conditions that have to be observed for educational broadcasts, communications and recordings include: doing so without profit or for noncommercial reasons (57 provisions), observing custom or fair practice for its use and extent (36 provisions), subjecting the availability of the use of the provision to any relevant licensing terms (14 provisions), or limiting the use to a course, program or study (17 provisions). Further restrictions include prohibiting commercial dealings in the copies made (30 provisions), destroying the copies after they have been used (5 provisions), confining the online access to restricted or secure networks (7 provisions), implementing technical measures to limit or prevent infringement (9 provisions), limiting the access to a physical place (14 provisions), or to a limited audience such as staff and students (10 provisions), limiting the copies or extent made or accessed (8 provisions), or to the extent or amount that is justified (52 provisions).

Further preclusions from the application of the provision include the use of works such as computer programs and performances (15 provisions) and the three-step test (45 provisions).

c *Attribution and Remuneration*

A total of 107 provisions require some form of proper attribution to be made for such use of the source works, unless to do so will be impracticable or infeasible (30 provisions).

In 225 provisions, remuneration for these educational publications is not required. For 29 provisions in 23 member states, either a statutory license or some form of remuneration or payment to the copyright owner is required.

8 *Adaptations and Translations*

This category reviews the limitations and exceptions that enable adaptations and translations for educational activities, and finds that they operate principally in three ways, through the use of three different formulations: the "adaptation or translation" formulation, the "source work" formulation and the "use" formulation.

With the "adaptation or translation" formulation, the provisions enable the adaptation or translation of the work, in addition to the excepted activity such as reproduction or communication of the work. This review found 128 provisions (66 member states)[101] that adopt this formulation. Most of these provisions are provisions that enable the private use of works (42 provisions, 40 member states),[102] the reproduction of works for educational purposes (36 provisions, 23 member states),[103] and the use of the works for quotations (24 provisions, 21 member states).[104]

For instance, Article 71M of Chile's Law on Intellectual Property provides that:

> It shall be lawful, without remunerating or seeking the authorization of the author, to reproduce and *translate* for educational purposes, within the framework of formal education or with the consent of the Ministry of Education, small fragments of works or isolated works of a three-dimensional, photographic or figurative nature, excluding school textbooks and university manuals, where such acts are performed solely to illustrate educational activities, insofar as this is warranted and is not for profit, provided that the works in question have already been disclosed and include the name of the author and the source, except in cases where this is impossible. [emphasis added][105]

[101] *See* Table 15.5, column 2, row 8.
[102] *See* Table 15.5, column 2, row 2.
[103] *See* Table 15.5, column 2, row 4.
[104] *See* Table 15.5, column 2, row 3.
[105] Law No. 17.336, Intellectual Property, art. 71M, Abril 23, 2010, Diario Oficial [D.O.] (Chile).

Another common implementation of the "adaptation or translation" formulation is to tag activities such as adaptations, translations, and transformations onto the existing limitations and exceptions. A good example[106] of this can be found in section 106 of the Copyright and Related Rights Act, 2000 (No. 28 of 2000) (as amended up to the Copyright and Related Rights (Amendment) Act 2007 (S.I. No. 39 of 2007)) of Ireland:

> Adaptation of a work
> 106. It is not an infringement of the copyright in a work to make an adaptation of the work by any act which may otherwise be done without infringing the copyright in a work under this Chapter.

With the "source work" formulation, the provisions extend the excepted activity to the original source work, in addition to enabling the excepted activity with the translated work. Its effect is that the limitations and exceptions operate to absolve the beneficiary of liability for an action from the translator of the work, but also from the original author whose work has been translated. A total of 153 such provisions (33 member states)[107] were found in this review. Not unexpectedly, this formulation is most widely found in provisions that enable quotations (34 provisions, 30 member states),[108] but it has also been adopted for limitations and exceptions that enable research and educational reproductions (33 provisions, 18 member states)[109] and private and personal use (29 provisions, 24 member states).[110]

For instance,[111] section 40 of the Australian Copyright Act provides that:

> Fair dealing for purpose of research or study
> (1) A fair dealing with a literary, dramatic, musical or artistic work, or with *an adaptation of* a literary, dramatic or musical work, for the purpose of research or study does not constitute an infringement of the copyright in the work.[112] [emphasis added]

The "adaptation or translation" formulation may be used with the "source work" formulation to broaden the scope of the limitation or exception. For instance, section 12(1) of the Copyright and Neighbouring Rights Act, 1999 of the United Republic of Tanzania reads:

> 12.-(1) Notwithstanding provisions of section I, the following uses of a protected work, *either in the original or in translation*, shall be permissible without the authors' consent and the obligation to pay remuneration for the use of the work.

In other words, combining section 12(1) with the "adaptation or translation" formulation in section 12(2), it is permissible to translate, adapt, arrange, or transform a work for a user's own personal and private use, for not just the protected work in its translated version, but also the original protected work.

The "adaptation or translation" and "source work" formulations should be contrasted with the provisions that adopt the "use" formulation, which is drawn from the language of Article 10(2) of the Berne Convention in that it permits the "utilization" of the work for educational purposes.

[106] *See also*, Copyright Act, Law No. 48 of 197, art. 43, 35(2), 36 (Japan).
[107] *See* Table 15.5, column 3, row 8.
[108] *See* Table 15.5, column 3, row 3.
[109] *See* Table 15.5, column 3, row 4.
[110] *See* Table 15.5, column 3, row 2.
[111] *See also* Copyright Order 1989 from Lesotho, s 9, wherein the limitation or exception enables an adaptation of the source work, which could itself be an adapted work.
[112] *Copyright Act* 1968 s 40(1) (Austl.).

At first sight, it may seem that both the "adaptation or translation" formulation and the "source work" formulation are different from the "use" formulation. However, the delegates at the Stockholm Conference accepted that the "use" formulation in Article 10(2) of the Berne Convention has to apply to create an exception to the right of adaptation/translation, provided the conditions for the original exception are met.[113] While there was some dissent, the delegates also accepted that Article 10(2) as formulated is wide enough to encompass use of a work not only in its original version but also in translation.[114] As many of the delegates at the Stockholm Conference observed, the utility behind the "use" formulation in Article 10(2) will be largely lost if the limitation or exception is limited to the translated work, and permission is still required from the author of the original work.[115] In other words, the effect of the Stockholm deliberations is that the "use" formulation is a fusion of the "adaptation or translation" formulation *and* the "source work" formulation.

Therefore, a careful examination of the "use" formulation is required. As illustrated in Table 15.5, the "use" formulation in provisions predominates, particularly in relation to research and educational reproductions (69 provisions, 59 member states)[116] and educational broadcasts and communications (77 provisions, 62 member states).[117] This is unsurprising, because this formulation is directly derived from the language of Article 10(2). Indeed, many member states closely follow this formulation in their laws.[118] Thus, the total number of states that have adopted the "use" formulation and the total number of such provisions (96 member states, 283 provisions)[119] are about the same as that for the "adaptation or translation" formulation and the "source work" formulation and the total number of such provisions (80 states, 267 provisions).[120]

Some member states have taken this approach one step further, by combining the "use" formulation with either the "adaptation or translation" formulation or the "source work" formulation (24 provisions, 10 member states).[121] Examples of this can be found in Cuba[122] and Poland.[123] Section 12 of the Copyright Act, 1978 (Act No. 98 of 1978, as amended up to Copyright Amendment Act 2002) of South Africa deploys *all* three formulations. The relevant provisions read:

> (4) The copyright in a literary or musical work shall not be infringed by *using* such work, to the extent justified by the purpose, by way of illustration in any publication, broadcast or sound or visual record for teaching: Provided that such use shall be compatible with fair practice

[113] Records of the Intellectual Property Conference of Stockholm (1967) 1134 (W.I.P.O. 1971), at 921–22, paras. 1565.1 *et seq.* (stating that the Main Committee unanimously approved S/248 para. (1), which states, in relation to, among others, Art. 10(1) and (2), "it seems normal that the exceptions introduced into the provisions for the right of reproduction should also apply to the right of translation, that is to say, should also apply to the translated version of the work.").

[114] Records of the Intellectual Property Conference of Stockholm (1967) 1134 (W.I.P.O. 1971), at 922, paras. 1570–81, 926, paras. 1652.2, 927, para. 1662 (stating that the Main Committee approved S/269 Addendum, with two abstentions).

[115] Records of the Intellectual Property Conference of Stockholm (1967) 1134 (W.I.P.O. 1971), at 926, paras. 1652.2, 1653.1, 1655.

[116] *See* Table 15.5, column 6, Row 4.

[117] *See* Table 15.5, column 6, row 7.

[118] *See, e.g.*, section 15(4) of the Copyright and Neighbouring Rights Protection Act, 1994 (Act No. 6 of 1994) of Namibia; Law No. 17.336, Intellectual Property, art. 71Q, Abril 23, 2010, Diario Oficial [D.O.] (Chile).

[119] *See* Table 15.5, column 6, row 8.

[120] *See* Table 15.5, column 4, row 8.

[121] *See* Table 15.5, column 7, row 8.

[122] *See also* Arts. 38(b), 39 of the Law on Copyright (Law No. 14 of 1977) of Cuba.

[123] Art. 27 of Act No. 83 of February 4, 1994, on Copyright and Neighboring Rights (as amended up to the Act of July, 19, 2016) of Poland.

TABLE 15.5 *Summary of adaptation and translation provisions, source work provisions, and educational "use" provisions in copyright legislation of WIPO member states*

Limitations and Exceptions	**No. of "adaptation or translation" formulation Provisions (No. of member states)**	**No. of "source work" formulation Provisions (No. of member states)**	No. of "adaptation or translation" formulation OR "source work" formulation Provisions (No. of member states)	No. of "adaptation or translation" formulation AND "source work" formulation Provisions (No. of member states)	**No. of "use" formulation Provisions (No. of member states)**	No. of "use" formulation WITH "adaptation or translation" formulation OR "source work" formulation Provisions (No. of member states)
Private/Personal Use	42 (40)	29 (24)	43 (55)	6 (6)	44 (42)	4 (4)
Quotations	24 (21)	34 (30)	57 (50)	0 (0)	23 (21)	5 (5)
Reproduction	36 (23)	33 (18)	66 (38)	3 (2)	69 (59)	4 (3)
Publications	9 (8)	24 (22)	32 (29)	0 (0)	41 (36)	4 (4)
Performances	6 (5)	11 (9)	17 (14)	0 (0)	28 (26)	1 (1)
Broadcasts, Communications and Recordings	11 (6)	22 (14)	32 (19)	0 (0)	77 (62)	6 (5)
Total	128 (66)	153 (33)	267 (80)	9 (8)	283 (96)	24 (10)

and that the source shall be mentioned, as well as the name of the author if it appears on the work.

(9) The provisions of subsections (1) to (7) inclusive shall apply also with reference to the *making or use of an adaptation* of a work.

(11) The provisions of subsections (1) to (4) inclusive and (6), (7), and (10) shall be construed as embracing the right to use the work in question *either in its original language or in a different language*, and the right of translation of the author shall, in the latter event, be deemed not to have been infringed.
[emphasis added]

And as noted in Table 15.5, the "use" formulation has been applied to the private and personal use provisions (44 provisions, 42 member states),[124] educational reproduction provisions (69 provisions, 59 member states),[125] and educational broadcast, communications and recording provisions (77 provisions, 62 member states).[126]

[124] *See* Table 15.5, column 6, row 2.
[125] *See* Table 15.5, column 6, row 4.
[126] *See* Table 15.5, column 6, row 7.

9 TPM/RMI Exceptions for Educational Purposes

A total of 63 member states (33.3 percent) have enacted 124 provisions that provide for exceptions to TPM and RMI protection for educational purposes. (See Figure 15.11.) A total of 48 of these member states have ratified or acceded to the WCT and WPPT. It is therefore interesting that 15 member states that are not WCT and WPPT members, but nonetheless have these flexibilities, limitations or exceptions in their national legislation.[127]

Of these, 105 provisions from 59 member states pertain to flexibilities, limitations or exceptions to TPM protection to facilitate educational activities. Of these 59 member states, 46 are also members of WCT and WPPT. In contrast, there are only 16 provisions[128] from 14 member states that permit the removal and alteration of RMI for educational purposes. Of these 14 member states, 11 are also members of WCT and WPPT. This is noteworthy because these member states have not only enacted flexibilities, limitations or exceptions to TPM or RMI protection, but they have also done so specifically to facilitate educational activities, notwithstanding the absence of explicit obligations to enact the same in the WCT and WPPT.

This is borne out in part by examining the number of such flexibilities, limitations or exceptions enacted by WIPO member states. As can be seen from Figure 15.11, the average number of such provisions per member state is 0.66,[129] suggesting a low rate of acceptance of these flexibilities, limitations, and exceptions among WIPO member states. However, among member states that have enacted such provisions, the average number of provisions rises to 1.97.[130] In other words, member states that have enacted flexibilities, limitations, or exceptions to TPM or RMI protection to facilitate educational activities have seen it necessary to enact (about) two such flexibilities, limitations, or exceptions per member state.

Limiting the analysis to only provisions that clearly provide for exceptions to TPM protection, the average number of such provisions per member state is 1.76 (standard deviation is 1.36, median is 1). Interestingly, confining this analysis to those provisions enacted by WIPO member states who are also members of the WCT or WPPT results in no changes to the aforesaid statistics. This strongly suggests that member states ascribe to the utility of enacting at least 1 flexibility, limitation, or exception (that applies to educational activities) to TPM protection, and that this policy was adopted independent of the member states' membership in the WCT or WPPT.

The purposes for the flexibilities, limitations, and exceptions identified in these provisions include: teaching (7 provisions), private or personal use (5 provisions), educational purchase or acquisition decisions (11 provisions), encryption research (18 provisions), security testing (17 provisions), interoperability (9 provisions), legitimate access (17 provisions), and realization for beneficiaries of the limitations and exceptions enacted for their benefit (30 provisions).

The manner in which each provision provides that TPM/RMI may be circumvented, removed, or disabled, or access granted, varies considerably. A total of 43 provisions oblige or require the rightholder to lift the TPM, alter their works or make available appropriate means to enable the purposes to be achieved. Many of these provisions further require the aggrieved

[127] Cook Islands, Grenada, Holy See, Iceland, India, Liberia, Malawi, Mauritius, New Zealand, Norway, Rwanda, Sao Tome and Principe, Seychelles, Thailand, and Zimbabwe.

[128] The rest of the provisions are drafted widely and not specifically with respect to TPM or RMI, but have the effect of enabling specific types of activities such as interoperability, encryption, and security research which would not be possible if TPM or RMI were applied to the work.

[129] The standard deviation is 1.33, median is 0.

[130] The standard deviation is 1.67, median is 1.

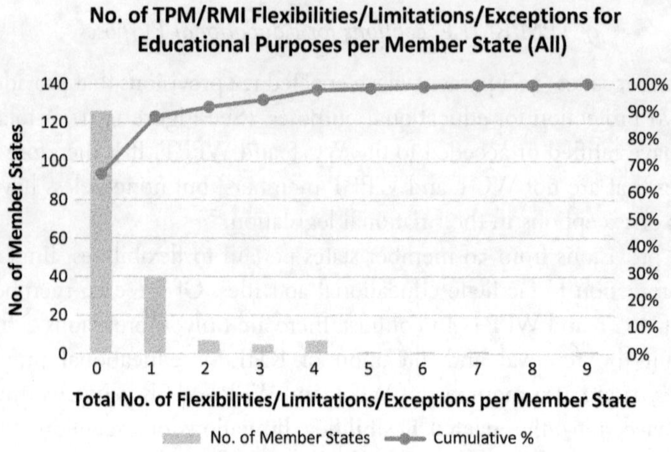

FIGURE 15.11 Distribution of number of TPM/RMI flexibilities/limitations/exceptions for educational purposes per member state

beneficiary to engage the rightholder to negotiate a solution to the impasse. A total of 73 provisions entitle the beneficiary to simply circumvent, remove, disable, or destroy the TPM or RMI without penalty or damages. The rest of the provisions variously entitle the beneficiary to reproduce or conduct activities on the work and be absolved of infringement.

The most typical conditions imposed on the exercise of these provisions are that the source work in question be a lawfully acquired copy of the work (14 provisions), and that the beneficiary act in good faith or without an intent to infringe copyright (28 provisions).

SUMMARY

The review demonstrates that WIPO member states have enacted in national legislation quite a variegated collection of limitations and exceptions for educational activities, and these limitations and exceptions need not be confined to provisions that apply only to educational institutions. The significance of the private or personal use provisions as they relate to self-edification and self-instruction is demonstrated not only by the large numbers of these provisions and their varied implementations, but also their nexus to educational instruction. In general, where there is adverse economic impact stemming from such private or personal uses which may extend beyond use for educational purposes, national legislatures have made efforts to ameliorate that impact with a combination of conditions such as requiring that such use be either fair or not for profit, precluding certain categories of works from private or personal uses, or even imposing levies on recording media and reprographic equipment to ensure equitable remuneration for right holders.

Limitations and exceptions to enable quotations, educational publications and school performances are generally quite uniformly adopted in member states, both by way of their general acceptance in national legislation, and also in their implementational details. For instance, no remuneration is generally prescribed for quotations and school performances, because of the narrow educational focus of such uses. A different scheme is adopted for educational publications, for which there is a commercial market for such uses. Either no remuneration is required of the publishers because the (occasionally detailed) provisions limit the extent to which source works may be used in collections for publication purposes, or alternatively, some form of statutory license from or remuneration for the right holder is required.

In contrast, there are wide-ranging and diverse implementations of the limitations and exceptions for educational reproductions, and educational broadcasts, communications, and recordings, arguably guided by Article 10(2) of the Berne Convention. The purposes behind these provisions are generally unambiguous (for teaching, education, instruction, science, and research). Because the usage of the educational reproduction is primarily institutional, the provisions generally impose no restrictions on the type of entity who may use the limitation or exception or do not prescribe any additional conditions for their use that go beyond the scope and purposes of these provisions. For provisions that do impose such restrictions, the primary restriction is that the reproductions not be conducted for commercial gain or advantage, or that limits or restrictions, both qualitative and quantitative, on the extent and frequency of making copies of such works be observed.

In comparison, the broadcast, communications, and recordings provisions exhibit a larger spectrum of implementational variations. Provisions in member states' legislation may refer to not just "communication" or "broadcast," but also "recording," "fixation," "filming," "making available," "performance," or even "use" or "anything." Interestingly, notwithstanding the language of Article 10(2) of the Berne Convention, relatively few member states have used the "by way of illustration" language or its variations to formulate their educational broadcasts, communications and recordings provisions. The conditions, limits, and restrictions that are placed are also quite varied, although conditions such as requiring the broadcast, communications, and recordings to be used for teaching purposes, and to be used without profit are the most common.

For the most part, educational reproduction, broadcast, communications, and recordings provisions do not attract the payment of equitable remuneration to authors and right holders. However, educational reproduction provisions that do prescribe equitable remuneration are primarily directed at the making of multiple copies, the use of reprographic equipment, and the reproduction of source works by third parties. No such clear patterns have been observed in relation to the provisions requiring equitable remuneration for educational broadcasts, communications, and recordings.

On the issue of online distance learning, only a few member states have provisions that specifically envisage the making of reproductions in the digital environment. Likewise, very few member states have specifically provided for *sui generis* provisions that explicitly address the distribution of online content for instructional purposes. While this does not mean that other member states do not have provisions that do not address the issue, it is a matter for the substantive treatment in the member states as to whether existing provisions in member states' legislation that enable "communication to the public" or "making available" rights do encompass the online dissemination of digital content. In addition, as online distance learning will invariably engage in some form of reproduction of the source works that are being communicated, some member states additionally have linked the enabling of the availability of source works online with the implementation of technological measures to manage possible unauthorized reproductions and distributions. On the other hand, provisions that impose restrictions by requiring the educational communication to be received in classrooms or require the communication equipment to be physically sited in educational establishments must surely be revisited.

As to the issue of adaptations and translations, this review has found that the "adaptation or translation" formulation and the "source work" formulation are actually complementary aspects of the third formulation – the "use" formulation – which has been adopted by many member states. The "adaptation or translation" formulation and the "source work" formulation address different aspects of the issues relating to adaptations or translations, and the Stockholm Conference clearly sought to address these issues by way of the "use" formulation, which is variously reflected in the hybridized formulation approach adopted by many member states.

Finally, a sizable number of member states have enacted provisions in national legislation to provide for restrictions to the protection of TPM and RMI. Some of the purposes of these provisions include teaching, private or personal use, making educational purchase or acquisition decisions, encryption research, security testing, and interoperability. Other provisions restrict TPM and RMI to protect and preserve the legitimate access to the works and to enable the full realization and use of the limitations and exceptions in national legislation, including the educational provisions discussed above. These qualifications to the general TPM and RMI protection provisions are noteworthy, especially since almost all of these member states are WCT and WPPT signatories. These member states have deemed it necessary, notwithstanding the absence of guidance in the WCT and WPPT, to enact limitations and exceptions to the protection of TPM and RMI, especially where doing so prejudices the use of works for educational activities. And this represents a remarkable development where national legislation has interceded to fill the perceived lacuna in our recently concluded internet copyright treaties.

CONCLUSIONS

This review confirms while the starting point for educational limitations and exceptions is largely Article 10(2) of the Berne Convention, there are considerable disparities between member states in the scope and treatment of different categories of educational activities. For instance, there are more member states with provisions that address private and personal use, quotations and educational reproduction, than there are member states with provisions that address educational publications, performances and educational communications. In addition, there is room for modernizing the provisions that deal with educational communications, broadcasts, and recordings, especially where the limitations and exceptions do not deal with the issue of incidental electronic reproductions, and where the imposed conditions are not technology neutral, as that would be an impediment to enabling online distance learning.

Nonetheless, in this review that surveyed the educational limitations and exceptions of member states, the review has found that by and large, member states have indeed taken advantage of the flexibility of the international copyright framework and enacted provisions that explicitly address issues such as the personal use of educational materials for self-studying, the publication of collections for educational purposes, the dissemination and use of online distance learning materials, the use of copyright materials for adaptations and translations, and the impediments that TPM and RMI may have on educational activities. There is much to be said for other member states to draw upon the experiences of these member states and revise and modernize their own copyright laws. After all, if these revisions are possible within the existing international framework, this is a testament to the robust discussions and the foresight and wisdom of the delegates and their acceptance of the importance of education that underlie the education limitations and exceptions in the Berne Convention.

The only area of concern would be that for TPM and RMI, where national legislation has interceded to fill the perceived lacuna in the WCT and WPPT. This strongly suggests that international consensus may be developing around the necessity for flexibilities, limitations, and exceptions, to the protection of TPM and RMI, especially for educational purposes. And this also reflects the pressing need to ensure that TPM and RMI do not displace the robust regime of copyright limitations and exceptions that form the very basis of the Berne Convention.

16

Copyright and Academic Photocopying: The Delhi University Case

Arpan Banerjee[*]

INTRODUCTION

In 1982, eleven days before Christmas, major American publishers tried to play Grinch and stop the popular practice of photocopying course readings. The publishers sued New York University (NYU) and a photocopying shop for copyright infringement, for compiling course packs.[1] Reportedly, this was the first such legal action against universities, with NYU being "not necessarily the worst violator" but a "representative" target.[2] Critics viewed the lawsuit as a tactic to force a settlement and "panic university libraries into signing up" with a collecting society.[3] Eventually, a settlement was reached, and a new photocopying policy adopted by NYU.[4] NYU agreed to seek permissions where none was previously taken.[5] This sent ripples across US

* This chapter draws from a paper presented at the Conference on Copyright and Fair Dealing in the Education Sector, July 21–22, 2016, National University of Singapore (NUS). I thank the professors who led the conference – Ng-Loy Wee Loon, Shyam Balganesh, and Haochen Sun– for their kind invitation to participate and contribute to this book. I also thank the other participants for their comments.

1 Addison-Wesley Publishing v. New York University, Copyright L. Dec. (CCH) ¶ 25,544 (S.D.N.Y. 1983). *See also* Eric D. Brandfonbrener, *Fair Use and University Photocopying: Addison-Wesley Publishing v New York University* 19 U. Mich. J.L. Reform 669 (1986) (discussing the impact of this case).

2 Edwin McDowell, *Nine Publishers Sue NYU Charging Copyright Violation*, N.Y. Times (Dec. 15, 1982), www.nytimes.com/1982/12/15/books/nine-publishers-sue-nyu-charging-copyright- violation.html?mcubz=0 (quoting an industry representative).

3 Edwin McDowell, *Ideas and Trends; College "Copy Mills" Grind Quickly, So Publishers Sue*, N.Y. Times (Dec. 19, 1982), www.nytimes.com/1982/12/19/weekinreview/ideas-and-trends-college-copy-mills-grind-quickly-so-publishers-sue.html?mcubz=1.

4 Policy Statement on Photocopying Copyrighted Materials for Classroom and Research Use (May 9, 1983), www.nyu.edu/content/dam/nyu/provost/documents/Archived%20Policies/University%20Policy%20on%20Photocopying%20Copyrighted%20Materials%20May%201983%20-%20ARCHIVED.pdf. The policy adopted a previous set of guidelines, framed by publishers and included in a House of Representatives Report. H.R. Rep. No. 94-1476, at 68, Sept. 3, 1976). The 1976 *Guidelines* laid down, among other things, tests concerning "brevity," "spontaneity," and "cumulative effect," all of which would have to be fulfilled. Brevity was defined with respect to quantitative limits– 250 words from a poem and 1,000 words or 10 percent, whichever is less, from a work of prose. Spontaneity was defined to mean copying "at the instance and inspiration of the individual teacher" and at a moment of use for "maximum teaching effectiveness" that is "so close in time that it would be unreasonable to expect a timely reply to a request for permission." Cumulative effect was defined to mean: (a) copying "for only one course," (b) copying of a maximum of one short poem, article, story, or essay or two excerpts by the same author, and of a maximum of "three from the same collective work or periodical volume during one class term," and (c) a maximum of nine instances of such multiple copying for one course during one class term. *See id.*

5 Andrew Schaffer, NYU's general counsel, told the press, "What will change is that, in many instances where photocopying was previously done, the prior permission of the publisher will be required." *See* David Margolick, *Publishers and NYU Settle Suit on Colleges' Photocopying Rights*, N.Y.Times (Apr. 15, 1983),

academia. Professors shied away from prescribing photocopied materials,[6] while many universities emulated NYU.[7]

Thirty years later, a similar incident threatened to replay in India, attracting national media attention. Three global publishing giants sued the University of Delhi (DU) before the Delhi High Court.[8] However, unlike the NYU litigation, events took a different turn. The defendants contested the case and received a favorable order from the court, while the plaintiffs chose not to appeal. Arguably, at least three factors contributed to this outcome. First, there were widespread protests that were waged against the plaintiffs. Second, a "bottom-up" transnational movement emphasizing intellectual property (IP) limitations has taken shape in developing countries.[9] In the *DU Case*, academicians invoked various sources on users' rights, which seemed to partly influence the court's decision. Third, the Indian Reprographic Rights Organisation (IRRO)[10] found itself in a crisis of governance.

This chapter discusses the *DU Case* referencing these developments. Section 1 discusses the relevant provisions of Indian copyright law, along with enforcement-related issues. Section 2 chronicles events leading up to the decision, including submissions by the parties. Section 3 analyzes the decision. Section 4 discusses the role of the Indian Reprographic Rights Organisation. The chapter concludes with comments on the impact of the decision, including possible future strategies by publishers.

1 COPYRIGHT LAW IN INDIA: AN OVERVIEW

A Political Background

Indian copyright laws originated during colonial times.[11] British publishers lobbied for copyright laws in India, then a "net importer" of Western knowledge.[12] Post independence, the Indian government advocated limitations and exceptions in the Berne Convention for the Protection of Literary and Artistic Works to facilitate access to works.[13] During negotiations in connection with the Agreement on Trade-Related Aspects of Intellectual Property Rights (TRIPS), the government's Book Promotion Division, mandated with making literature available "at moderate prices

www.nytimes.com/1983/04/15/nyregion/publishers-and-nyu-settle-suit-on-colleges-photocopying-rights.html. While Schaffer's statement did not elaborate further, presumably the 1976 *Guidelines* were not previously complied with by NYU, and publishers would henceforth grant certain permissions conditional on the payment of licensing fees.

6 Kathy Olmsted, *New York University Case Settled but Photocopy Law Still a Mystery*, STANFORD DAILY (May 19, 1983), at 1, http://stanforddailyarchive.com/cgi-bin/imageserver/imageserver.pl?oid=stanford19830519–01&getpdf=true.

7 Brandfonbrener, *supra* note 1, at 674, 708.

8 Chancellor, Master and Scholars of the University of Oxford v. Rameshwari Photocopy Services (2016) 235 D.L.T. 409.

9 Gregory Shaffer & Susan Sell, *Transnational Legal Ordering and Access to Medicines*, *in* PATENT LAW IN GLOBAL PERSPECTIVE 97, 118–22 (Ruth Okediji & Marco Bagley eds., 2014) (discussing Indian patent jurisprudence). *See also* Lawrence Liang, *Paternal and Defiant Access: Copyright and the Politics of Access to Knowledge in the Delhi University Photocopy Case*, INDIAN L. REV. 36 (2017).

10 The IRRO is the sole copyright collective in India in the field of literary works. *See infra* Section 4.

11 Lionel Bently, *Copyright, Translations, and Relations between Britain and India in the Nineteenth and Early Twentieth Centuries* 82 CHI.-KENT L. REV. 1181, 1183–85, 1217–18. (2007).

12 *Id.* at 1188–89, 1196–1205.

13 *See* MARTIN SENFTLEBEN, COPYRIGHT, LIMITATIONS, AND THE THREE-STEP TEST 78–81 (2004); Eva Hemmungs Wirtén, *Colonial Copyright, Postcolonial Publics: The Berne Convention and the 1967 Stockholm Diplomatic Conference Revisited* 7 SCRIPT-ED 3(2010); Jaman H. Shah, *India and the International Copyright Conventions* 8 ECONOMIC AND POLITICAL WEEKLY 645 (1973).

to the public,"[14] was entrusted with copyright-related negotiations.[15] India also became the first country to ratify the Marrakesh Treaty to Facilitate Access to Published Works for Persons Who Are Blind, Visually Impaired or Otherwise Print Disabled, stressing the importance of access to knowledge.[16] Until recently, the government delegated copyright-related matters to the Ministry of Human Resource Development (HRD), which oversees education.

A former TRIPS negotiator has acknowledged that India's "ideological position" was historically divorced from "national interest" and "weighted too far against the rights of copyright owners."[17] Nevertheless, subtle shifts have taken place. Today, India's publishing industry is one of the world's largest, and receives increasing foreign direct investment (FDI).[18] The industry has lobbied to protect its interests in copyright amendments.[19] Recently, the government transferred copyright-related matters from the HRD Ministry to the Department of Industrial Policy and Promotion (DIPP), whose mandate includes the "promotion, approval and facilitation of FDI."[20]

B Research and Instruction Provisions

The Copyright Act of 1957 ("Act") governs copyright law in India.[21] The Act ostensibly follows a "fair dealing" model rather than a "fair use" model.[22] The fair dealing provision of the Act covers three situations: (i) "private or personal use, including research," (ii) "criticism or review," and (iii) "the reporting of current events and current affairs, including the reporting of a lecture delivered in public."[23] Here, the Act resembles its counterparts in the UK[24] and other Commonwealth countries.[25] The UK statute, for example, exempts "[f]air dealing with a work for the sole purpose of illustration for instruction," with additional conditions such as the dealing being noncommercial and "by a person giving or receiving instruction."[26]

[14] Ministry of Human Res. Dev., *Book Promotion: Overview* (Apr. 19, 2016), http://mhrd.gov.in/book-promotion (last accessed Sept. 12, 2017).

[15] Jagdish Sagar, *Copyright: An Indian Perspective, in* THE MAKING OF THE TRIPS AGREEMENT (Jayashree Watal & Anthony Taubman eds., 2005) 341.

[16] *See* G. R. Raghavender, Closing Statement by India at the WIPO Diplomatic Conference to adopt a Treaty to Facilitate Access to Published Works by Visually Impaired Persons and Persons with Print Disabilities at Marrakesh (June 28, 2013) (transcript available at www.pmindiaun.org/pages.php?id=374).

[17] Sagar, *supra* note 15 at 342, 348.

[18] *See generally* NIELSEN, THE INDIA BOOK MARKET REPORT (2015).

[19] *See* Department-Related Parliamentary Standing Committee on Human Resource Development, Report on the Copyright (Amendment) Bill, 2010, No 227 of 2010 (Nov. 23, 2010) paras. 7.5–7.8, 13.5 http://164.100.47.5/newcommittee/reports/EnglishCommittees/Committee%20on%20HRD/227.pdf (listing proposed amendments concerning international exhaustion and access by persons with disabilities).

[20] Dep't. of Indus. Pol'y and Promotion, *Role and Functions of the DIPP* (2016), http://dipp.nic.in/about-us/role-and-functions-department-industrial-policy-promotion.

[21] Indian Copyright Act, No. 14 of 1957, INDIA CODE (2012). The Act's salient features include the recognition of (i) a work-for-hire rule (§17), (ii) rights of reproduction and distribution (§14(a)(i), (ii)), and (iii) civil and criminal remedies (§§ 55, 63, 63A).

[22] A fair dealing model circumscribes uses exempt from copyright infringement, while a fair use model is open-ended and flexible. Fair dealing involves first examining whether a use of a work falls within a permitted list of purposes, and then examining whether its use is fair. *See* Michael Geist, *How Canada Quietly Shifted from Fair Dealing to Fair Use, in* THE COPYRIGHT PENTALOGY (Michael Geist ed., 2013) 157, 157–58.

[23] Indian Copyright Act, No. 14 of 1957, INDIA CODE (2012) § 52 (1)(a).

[24] Copyright, Designs and Patents Act 1988, c.27, § 29.

[25] *See, e.g.*, Copyright Act, R.S.C. 1985, c. C-42 § 29 (Can.); *Copyright Act* 1968 s 40 (Austl.); Copyright Act 98 of 1978 §12(1)(a) (S. Afr.).

[26] Copyright, Designs and Patents Act 1988, c.27, § 32.

The Act's fair dealing provision is actually a subprovision subsumed within a broader provision. The broader provision lists various copyright exceptions and limitations (scattered across around thirty subprovisions), but without using the term "fair dealing."[27] For instance, a subprovision permitting the reproduction of works to facilitate access by visually impaired persons (under certain conditions) exists independently of the fair dealing subprovision, and does not have "fair dealing" mentioned as a built-in restriction within the subprovision.[28] Similarly, in a subprovision uniquely tailored to Indian social traditions, performing works during marriages and religious ceremonies is deemed not to be an infringement of copyright, without the inclusion of the term "fair dealing."[29] The Copyright Bill of 1956, from which the Act was originally derived, was drafted very similarly.[30] An obvious question, seemingly not answered during legislative discussions over the Copyright Bill of 1956,[31] is whether some sort of fairness standard, which weighs in the interests of copyright owners, is still inherent within these thirty-odd subprovisions. Or, whether these subprovisions are blanket exceptions permitting even uses of works that may not be fair dealing. This question would assume importance in the *DU Case*, with respect to a provision concerning educational instruction.

In an early case on the fair dealing provision, involving the reproduction of literary works in academic guidebooks, the Madras High Court observed that, for a dealing to be considered unfair, "one has to have regard to the substantiality of the quantity and the quality of the matter reproduced."[32] In a later case, involving a parody, the Kerala High Court referred to *Hubbard v. Vosper*, where Lord Denning termed fair dealing as "a matter of impression" that is "impossible" to define, but suggested that using long extracts of a work for a rival purpose may be unfair.[33] Similarly, the Delhi High Court cited Denning's remarks in two later cases (involving guidebooks) where Oxford University Press (OUP) and Cambridge University Press (CUP) were the respective plaintiffs.[34] However, the Delhi High Court combined this with references to US law. In the first case, the plaintiff and defendant both used "fair dealing" and "fair use" interchangeably.[35] The court considered whether "the defendants sufficiently made out a 'fair dealing' *or* a 'fair use' defence."[36] The court went on to discuss cases interpreting the four statutory fair use factors in the US,[37] and then applied them to lift an interim injunction against the defendant (whose guidebooks the court found "transformative").[38] In the second

[27] Indian Copyright Act, No. 14 of 1957, India Code (2012) § 52 (1).

[28] *Id.* at § 52 (1)(zb).

[29] *Id.* at § 52 (1)(za).

[30] Copyright Bill 1956 § 54 (1) (Oct. 1, 1955, Rajya Sabha).

[31] *See* Report of the Joint Committee of the Houses on the Copyright Bill, 1956.

[32] Blackwood v. Parasuraman A.I.R. Mad. 410, ¶ 86 (1959).

[33] Civic Chandran v Ammini Amma 16 P.T.C. 670, ¶ 13 (1996) (citing Hubbard v. Vosper 2 Q.B. 84, 94 (1972)).

[34] *See* University of Oxford v. Narendera 38 P.T.C. 385, ¶ 27 (2008); University of Cambridge v. Bhandari 39 P.T.C. 642, para. 72 (2009).

[35] *Id.* at paras. 7, 8, 12, 14.

[36] *Id.* at para. 15 (emphasis added).

[37] Under US copyright law, fair use 'for purposes such as ... teaching (including multiple copies for classroom use), scholarship, or research, is not an infringement of copyright' (Copyright Act 1976 §107). The same section adds four factors to consider fair use:

(1) the purpose and character of the use, including whether such use is of a commercial nature or is for nonprofit educational purposes;
(2) the nature of the copyrighted work;
(3) the amount and substantiality of the portion used in relation to the copyrighted work as a whole; and
(4) the effect of the use upon the potential market for or value of the copyrighted work.

[38] 38 P.T.C. 385, paras. 22–26, 34–38.

case, the court followed a similar approach and reached a similar conclusion.[39] The court remarked that the Act's fair dealing provisions "must receive a liberal construction in harmony with the objectives of copyright law."[40] In subsequent cases, the court persisted with this approach.[41]

Thus, the Delhi High Court's approach seemingly resembled the Canadian Supreme Court's ruling in *CCH Canadian v. Law Society of Upper Canada*[42], where the Supreme Court found the defendant, who was sued for providing photocopying services to researchers, to be protected under fair dealing. Citing Denning's opinion in *Hubbard*, the Canadian Supreme Court had observed that "whether something is fair is a question of fact and depends on the facts of each case," but "the purpose of the dealing, the character of the dealing, the amount of the dealing, the nature of the work, available alternatives to the dealing and the effect of the dealing on the work are all factors that could help determine whether or not a dealing is fair."[43] This six-factor test was derived from the Federal Court of Appeal's judgment in the same case. (Justice Linden had found the US fair use model to be more favorable to users than the Canadian fair dealing model,[44] but held that Canadian courts could seek assistance from the US, and thus framed the six-factor test "in combination with the American and British factors.")[45] Hence, although fair dealing in Canada still requires the two-stage analysis of whether there is a permitted dealing and whether the dealing is fair, the model is a "hybrid" requiring "a more extensive analysis of the purposes of the copier and recipient of the beneficiary."[46]

However, there exists a problem in India, in another respect. As mentioned earlier, the Act exempts fair dealing for purposes of, inter alia, research or private study, but also contains separate copyright exception and limitation provisions independent of the fair dealing provision. With regard to the latter, the Act exempts reproduction "(i) by a teacher or a pupil in the course of instruction; or (ii) as part of the questions to be answered in an examination; or (iii) in answers to such questions."[47] Thus, the Act includes "fair dealing" in its *research* provision, but not its *instruction* provision. Here, the Act resembles Canadian legislation.[48] In *Alberta (Education) v. Access Copyright*, involving the use of copyrighted material in guidebooks, the Canadian Federal Court of Appeal applied the *CCH* factors with respect to Canada's research provision, finding the dealing concerned unfair.[49] But the court held that fair dealing did not apply to the instruction provision, which "stands on its own as a separate provision."[50] Yet, in Canada's instruction provision, the copyrighted works must not be "commercially available," meaning, inter alia, "available on the Canadian market within a reasonable time *and* for a reasonable price *and* may be located with reasonable effort."[51]

39 University of Cambridge v. Bhandari 39 P.T.C. 642, paras. 33, 71, 73–76 (2009).
40 *Id* at para. 58.
41 *See, e.g.*, ESPN v. Global Broadcast News 38 P.T.C. 477 (2008) (holding that broadcasting reproduction rights are a special class of rights that coexist with copyright); Super Cassettes v. Hamar Television 45 P.T.C. 70 (2011) (holding that the qualitative test is as important as the amount used when considering fair dealing).
42 [2004] 1 S.C.R. 339.
43 *Id.* at paras. 52–60.
44 [2002] 4 F.C.R. 213, at para. 148.
45 *Id.* at paras. 148–50.
46 Geist, *supra* note 22, at 176–78.
47 Indian Copyright Act, No. 14 of 1957, INDIA CODE (2012) § 52 (1)(i).
48 Copyright Act, R.S.C. 1985, c. C-42 § 29.4(1), (2) (Can.).
49 [2010] F.C.A. 198, at paras. 22–48.
50 *Id.* at para. 49.
51 *Id.* at §§ 2, 29.4(3) (emphasis added).

The court held that a work was "commercially available" if it could be used via a license.[52] Such a proviso is absent in the Act.

Thus, some important questions that arose in the *DU Case* were: (a) whether the Act's research provision protected the course packs as fair dealing, (b) whether the Act's instruction provision protected reproduction of a work irrespective of fair dealing (such as the copying of a substantial amount), (c) if not, whether there was fair dealing in the present case, and (d) whether the prices of the plaintiffs' books were relevant. Unfortunately, the Delhi High Court's answers were far from comprehensive.

C *Enforcement*

Criminal and civil IP enforcement in India is hampered by problems such as weak infrastructure and delays, outside a few major cities.[53] However, through an assorted set of laws, forum-shopping in civil copyright and trademark infringement cases is possible. A plaintiff can engage in: (a) "horizontal" forum selection where the plaintiff domiciled, even if the cause of action did not occur there and the defendant is not based there, and (b) "vertical" forum selection in four major High Courts at first instance (Delhi, Bombay, Calcutta, and Madras) via "ordinary original civil jurisdiction."[54] Over the years, lawyers have strategically filed civil infringement suits directly before these four High Courts. Civil infringement cases in India tend to proceed slowly. Thus, what most plaintiffs in civil infringement cases look for is an interim injunction. Over the past decade, the Delhi High Court has been unusually liberal (and uncritical) in granting *ex parte* interim injunctions and Anton Piller orders,[55] instructing "local commissioners" (usually lawyers) to carry out searches and seizures with police assistance.[56] These orders have usually been granted promptly. Thus, the Delhi High Court has become an incredibly popular forum, hearing almost 70 percent of all IP cases in India.[57]

India has long had a culture of photocopying among students, with entire books often being photocopied at shops. Prior to the *DU Case*, publishers appear to have been largely resigned to these practices.[58] In contrast, the software and entertainment industries have been aggressive copyright litigants at the Delhi High Court. Why it took so long for the publishing industry to

52 *Id.* at paras. 127–28. The court remitted the case to the Canadian Copyright Board. On appeal to the Supreme Court, only fair dealing under the research provision was discussed. *See* [2012] 2 S.C.R. 345.

53 *See* Arpan Banerjee, *Copyright Piracy and the Indian Film Industry: A "Realist" Assessment*, 34 CARDOZO ARTS & ENT. L. REV. 608, 661–63, 669 (2016).

54 *See* Arpan Banerjee, *Forum Shopping in Intellectual Property Rights Infringement Cases in India*, ATRIP (2014), http://atrip.org/wp-content/uploads/2016/12/2014-3.-Arpan-Banerjee-Forum-Shopping-in-IP-rights-infringements-in-India.pdf.

55 Anton Piller orders are derived from Anton Piller v. Manufacturing Processes Ltd. [1975] EWCA (Civ) 12 (Eng.). The English Court of Appeal held that "in the very exceptional circumstances," a court could pass an order allowing a plaintiff to enter the premises of a defendant to inspect and remove material which the latter might destroy or dispose of.

56 *See* Prashant Reddy,*A Critical Analysis of the Delhi High Court's Approach to* ex parte *Orders in Copyright and Trade Mark Cases*, 3 MANUPATRA INTELLECTUAL PROPERTY REPORTS 171 (2011).

57 Banerjee, *supra* note 55, at 19–20.

58 I could locate only one court order, prior to the *DU Case*, where a publisher filed a criminal case against a "Xerox shop" over photocopying and selling textbooks, which failed due to lack of sufficient evidence. State v. Puttegowda, (2015) Criminal Case 18304 of 2012, Court of the Additional Chief Metropolitan Magistrate, Bangalore. I could similarly locate only one civil court order (in a Delhi lower court) on the subject, filed the year before the *DU Case*. The court found the defendant to have "blatantly infringed" copyright, and awarded damages. John Wiley v. Noble Book Stall, (2011) Court of the Additional District Judge, Delhi. However, a district court order arguably lacks the precedential and psychological weight of a High Court order, and one doubts whether the decision had much of an impact beyond the defendant.

similarly target photocopying, despite its wide prevalence, can only be a matter of conjecture. In the two guidebook cases, discussed earlier, the interim injunctions obtained by OUP and CUP were both awarded *ex parte*, along with Anton Piller orders.[59] Although the injunctions were eventually lifted, and the defendants found to be protected under fair dealing, it is unlikely that this would have made the plaintiffs wary of suing DU. On the contrary, as the course packs comprised mechanical copies of the plaintiffs' works, unaccompanied by original notes and commentaries like in guidebooks, the plaintiffs should have fancied their chances of obtaining an interim injunction, and then pushing the parties into a settlement. Yet, there was still a gap of a few years between the guidebook cases and the *DU Case*.

It could be that the plaintiffs waited for the IRRO, which was granted government recognition in 2002, to consolidate itself for some years, and proceeded only after the IRRO struggled to collect royalties from universities.[60] Or, perhaps the lawsuit was part of an ongoing global strategy by the plaintiffs to target universities, following the US case of *CUP v. Becker*.[61] That the plaintiffs filed the lawsuit only a few months after the trial court's decision in the US case (where the court had suggested a 10 percent limit to determine fair use[62]) could indicate that the plaintiffs, at the very least, hoped to secure a judgment imposing a similar limit in India.

2 THE *DU CASE*: A CHRONICLE OF EVENTS

A *Claims in the Lawsuit and Anton Piller Order*

The plaintiffs in the *DU Case* were OUP, CUP, and Taylor & Francis, and the defendants DU and Rameshwari Photocopying Services, a photocopying shop situated within the premises of the Delhi School of Economics (DSE), a renowned DU college. The lawsuit invoked the ordinary original civil jurisdiction of the Delhi High Court.[63] The lawsuit claimed that the plaintiffs had made trap purchases at Rameshwari and discovered course packs with photocopied extracts from 134 works by the plaintiffs (mostly books), as well as "cover to cover" photocopies of books.[64] As illustrations, the plaintiffs provided details of four course packs.[65] Numerically, the largest number of pages copied from a book was 184.[66] As a percentage, the largest was roughly

59 University of Oxford v. Narendera, (2008) Civil Suit 1656; University of Cambridge v. Bhandari 39 P.T.C. 642, para. 97 (2009).

60 On the role of the IRRO, *see infra* Section 4. Interestingly, the IRRO's website, www.irro.org.in, appears to have been registered only on Oct. 5, 2011. *See* WHOIS, www.whois.com/whois/irro.org.in (last accessed Aug. 29, 2017).

61 The lawsuit was filed by CUP, OUP, and SAGE in 2008, before the US District Court for the Northern District of Georgia. The plaintiffs claimed that Georgia State University had infringed copyright in their works through an online electronic resources system. On May 11, 2012, the court issued an order finding most of the alleged infringements to be protected by fair use. CUP v. Becker 863 F. Supp. 2d 1190 (N.D. Ga. 2012). In 2014, the Court of Appeals for the Eleventh Circuit affirmed and reversed different portions of the decision, and remanded the case to the District Court. CUP v. Patton 769 F.3d 1232 (11th Cir. 2014). In 2016, the lower court issued its decision on remand, finding four instances of infringement (out of 49). CUP v. Becker Case 1:08-cv-01425-ODE Document 510 (N.D. Ga, Mar. 31, 2016).

62 CUP v. Becker 863 F. Supp. 2d 1190 (N.D. Ga. 2012) (stating, inter alia, that "Congress intended that use of a smaller portion would be more apt to be acceptable than use of a larger portion," and that an excerpt representing 10 percent of a copyrighted work would "cause substantial damage to the potential market for the copyrighted work," as "the 10 percent excerpt would not substitute for the original, no matter how many copies were made.").

63 Chancellor, Master and Scholars of the University of Oxford v. Rameshwari Photocopy Services (2016) 235 D.L.T. 409.

64 *Id.* at para. 8.

65 *Id.*

66 *Id.* (the fourth book cited in relation to the fourth course pack).

28 percent, in two instances.[67] The plaintiffs alleged substantial copying, "both qualitatively and quantitatively."[68] No instance of a book being photocopied in entirety was cited. However, the local commissioner's report stated that eight books, outside the course pack, had been copied in entirety.[69]

The plaintiffs claimed that DSE faculty members were "directly encouraging students" to purchase the course packs.[70] The plaintiffs further pointed to an agreement between DSE and Rameshwari, under which Rameshwari was exclusively allocated space inside DSE through an open tender and was required to photocopy 3,000 pages for the DSE library free of cost every month.[71] They thus accused DU of "illegally profit[ing] from such unauthorised reproduction."[72] The plaintiffs built their claim as follows: Rameshwari was "regularly and knowingly" reproducing and distributing the course packs for a "commercial purpose," causing the plaintiffs financial loss.[73] DU was aiding these acts.[74] This constituted "a clear case of profiteering" and "not a case of a teacher or student making photocopies of a work in the course of instruction or a fair dealing in the course of private study."[75] The plaintiffs made two additional points of note. First, the plaintiffs had authorized the IRRO to collect license fees on their behalf,[76] the unwritten suggestion being that the defendants should obtain an IRRO license. Second, the defendants were also causing losses to the *authors* of the plaintiffs' books.[77]

The plaintiffs sought an Anton Piller order and the appointment of a local commissioner to visit Rameshwari's premises, without prior notice and with police assistance. A day after the lawsuit had been filed, Justice Kailash Gambhir of the Delhi High Court granted the plaintiffs an order on these terms.[78] Following the execution of the order, DU and Rameshwari appeared before the court and sought time to file responses.[79] Justice Gambhir directed DU to consider the option of an IRRO license, which had now been formally proposed by the plaintiffs.[80]

B Responses by DU and Rameshwari, Interim Injunction

In their respective responses, Rameshwari and DU both advanced rather facile contentions challenging the plaintiffs' copyright ownership.[81] More significant were submissions claiming protection under the Act's research and instruction provisions, pointing out that the plaintiffs' books were highly priced and held in limited quantities by DSE, and that Rameshwari was charging students merely forty paisa a page (less than a US cent).[82] DU added that the Act

[67] *Id.* (the second book cited in relation to the second course pack (45 out of 160 pages), and the first book cited in relation to the third course pack (120 out of 416 pages)).

[68] *Id.* at para. 12.

[69] Chancellor, Master and Scholars of the University of Oxford v. Rameshwari Photocopy Services (2016) 235 D.L.T. 409, at para 6.

[70] *Id.* at para. 9.

[71] *Id.* at para. 10.

[72] *Id.* at para. 11.

[73] *Id.* at para. 14.

[74] *Id.* at para. 15.

[75] *Id.*

[76] *Id.* at para. 16.

[77] *Id.* at para. 17.

[78] Order in *DU Case* (Aug. 14, 2012), http://delhihighcourt.nic.in/dhcqrydisp_o.asp?pn=159532&yr=2012.

[79] Order in *DU Case* (Aug. 27, 2012), http://delhihighcourt.nic.in/dhcqrydisp_o.asp?pn=166420&yr=2012.

[80] Order in *DU Case* (Sept. 26, 2012), http://delhihighcourt.nic.in/dhcqrydisp_o.asp?pn=193462&yr=2012.

[81] Written Statement filed by Rameshwari Photocopy Services in *DU Case* ("*Rameshwari Response*") paras. 1–5 (on file with the author); Written Statement filed by Delhi University in *DU Case* ("*DU Response*"), paras. 3, 10–12 (on file with the author).

[82] *Rameshwari Response*, *id.* at ¶ 6; *id.* at ¶¶ 6–7.

should be viewed as a "welfare legislation" linked to the Fundamental Right to education[83] and two Directive Principles of State Policy, under the Indian Constitution.[84] In contrast to the Fundamental Rights in the Constitution, which grant citizens rights and freedoms against the state, the Directive Principles are judicially unenforceable,[85] but have been held by the Supreme Court to carry "considerable moral force and authority"[86] and to be "fundamental in the governance of the country."[87] DU argued that both the Fundamental Rights and Directive Principles "operate on a higher pedestal than . . . any legislation."[88]

However, DU and Rameshwari's responses took a problematic turn on one count. Both sought protection under a provision of the Act granting immunity to acts done in good faith.[89] Rameshwari claimed that it had merely acted under instructions from the DSE.[90] DU claimed that it had always tried to comply with the law and did not exercise control over Rameshwari.[91] Thus, both parties appeared to be subtly pinning blame on the other. DU further claimed that it was forming a committee to draft a photocopying policy, and would not commit any infringement.[92]

Following these responses, the plaintiffs produced evidence of copyright ownership, easily defeating the defendants' opening contention. Justice Gambhir found it "quite manifest" that the course packs seized by the local commissioner included the plaintiffs' copyrighted material, and that Rameshwari had no right to reproduce them.[93] The judge also noted DU's stance that it did not intend to breach the law.[94] The judge accordingly passed an interim injunction restraining Rameshwari.[95] Thus, DU's attempt to distance itself from Rameshwari ostensibly tilted the court in favor of the plaintiffs – a decision open to criticism, since the vicarious liability argument was seemingly employed *arguendo*, secondary to more significant arguments.[96]

C Campaign by Students and Academicians

The interim injunction – widely reported in the media – handed the plaintiffs a strong advantage. In the following months, the IRRO sent letters to over 400 colleges asking them to

83 INDIA CONST. art. 21 ("No person shall be deprived of his life or personal liberty except according to a procedure established by law"). In *Francis Coralie Mullin v. Administrator*, (1981) A.I.R. S.C. 746, the Supreme Court expanded the scope of the article to include "the right to live with human dignity and all that goes along with it," including "reading, writing and expressing."

84 *DU Response*, *supra* note 81, at paras. 8–9. The first Directive Principle cited requires the state to ensure "that children are given opportunities and facilities to develop in a healthy manner" (INDIA CONST. art. 39(f)). The second requires it to "within the limits of its economic capacity and development, make effective provision for securing the right . . . to education" (INDIA CONST. art. 41).

85 *See* M. P. Singh, *The Statics and the Dynamics of the Fundamental Rights and the Directives Principles*, 5 SUP. CT. CASES J. 1 (2003).

86 Swaraj Abhiyan v. Union of India A.I.R. SC 2953 (2016), at para. 20.

87 Akhil Bharatiya Soshit Karamchari Sangh v. Union of India A.I.R. S.C. 298 (1981), at para. 45.

88 *DU Response*, *supra* note 81, at para. 9.

89 Indian Copyright Act, No. 14 of 1957, INDIA CODE (2012) § 85.

90 *Rameshwari Response*, *supra* note 81, at para. 6.

91 *DU Response*, *supra* note 81, at para. 20.

92 *Id.* at paras. 21–22.

93 Order in *DU Case* (Oct. 17, 2012), http://delhihighcourt.nic.in/dhcqrydisp_o.asp?pn=212892&yr=2012.

94 *Id.*

95 *Id.*

96 *See also* Shamnad Basheer, *Copyright Aggression vs. Educational Access: The "Grammar" of Justice?*, SPICY IP (Oct. 26, 2012), https://spicyip.com/2012/10/copyright-aggression-vs-educational.html (criticizing drafting by DU's lawyers).

acquire licenses, with some obliging.[97] Amid speculation that DU would follow suit, CUP confirmed that the plaintiffs would withdraw the lawsuit were that to happen.[98] CUP clarified that a blanket IRRO license would only cost INR 24,000 (around USD 370) a year.[99] For students, this would mean paying INR 300 (around USD 4.5) for a 200-page course pack instead of the prevailing INR 200 (around USD 3).[100] The additional amount, CUP claimed, would be distributed among authors.[101] Hence, central to the dispute was the issue of students merely having to pay the additional costs of "about two cups of tea or coffee a semester."[102]

In fairness to CUP, the DSE and a few other DU colleges include many affluent students who anyway pay subsidized tuition fees. However, CUP's arguments were still problematic, if expanded to cover all schools and colleges. Many institutions are severely underfunded and cater to students from low-income groups. Moreover, an IRRO blanket license limits photocopying of a work to a maximum of twenty copies (a severe restriction in India, where class sizes tend to be large) and not more than one chapter or 10 percent of a book (another difficult restriction).[103] There were also no judicial or legislative guidelines in India that had imposed quantitative limits on academic photocopying. Assuming the applicability of a 10 or 15 percent cap, an IRRO license would not be required if universities maintained this limit. In the course packs cited in the lawsuit, some extracts involved copying of less than 10 percent, and the overall average was around 17 percent.[104]

As news of universities acquiring IRRO licenses spread, a string of protests ensued. An influential student union, affiliated to the ruling party then in government, urged the Indian government to intervene.[105] DU students submitted a memorandum to the vice chancellor opposing a settlement with the IRRO.[106] The students expressed "great dismay at the weak stance taken by" DU in court, which in their view "amounted to an admission" of wrongdoing and then led to the injunction.[107] On social media, creative protests were employed.[108] Meanwhile, multiple legal scholars supported the defendants. Shamnad Basheer sought at least a 20 percent photocopying cap,[109] while Lawrence Liang argued that no quantitative restriction

97 Soma Das & Urmi Goswami, *Copyright Organisation Asks Colleges to Buy Licence to Photocopy Book Portions*, Economic Times (Apr. 22, 2017), http://economictimes.indiatimes.com/articleshow/19670429.cms.

98 Prashant Reddy, *Is This a "Fair" Solution to the OUP/CUP–DU Copyright Infringement Lawsuit?*, Spicy IP (Sept. 11, 2012), https://spicyip.com/2012/09/is-this-fair-solution-to-oupcup-du.html (quoting the managing director of CUP's India office).

99 *Id.*

100 *Id.*

101 *Id.*

102 *Id.*

103 Indian Reprographic Rights Organisation, *Licence Limitations*, https://web.archive.org/web/20110721162727/ http://www.irro.in/limitations.php (cached copy).

104 Smita Chandra, *Book-Wise Analysis*, https://docs.google.com/spreadsheets/d/1NpDWCzQb1ejZwTiLx32v6gz1Kp GNPXSZ72hdQNEjylU/edit#gid=0 (documenting calculations of the percentages copied).

105 Letter from Rohit Choudhary, National President, National Students' Union of India, to Kapil Sibal, Minister for Human Resource Development (Sept. 11, 2012), https://drive.google.com/file/d/0B3UBa-WkvhlOQlRteDZBa G9oNoo/view.

106 Anshul Kumar Pandey, *Memorandum to the Vice Chancellor: Campaign to Save D School Photocopy Shop*, Youth Ki Awaaz (Nov. 9, 2012), www.youthkiawaaz.com/2012/11/memorandum-to-the-vice-chancellor-campaign-to-save-d-school-photocopy-shop.

107 *Id.*

108 A Facebook protest urged students to boycott the plaintiffs. Laurence Tidy, *Delhi University Students Enraged by Cambridge University Press Legal Action*, Cambridge Student (Oct. 4, 2012, www.tcs.cam.ac.uk/news/0019054-delhi-university-students-enraged-by-cambridge-university-press-legal-action.html). On YouTube, a song satirizing the plaintiffs was shared. John Daniel, *Pay Up!* (Dec. 26, 2012), www.youtube.com/watch?v=WM64BMobQ2c.

109 Shamnad Basheer, *Publishers vs Students*, Indian Express (Aug. 30, 2012), http://archive.indianexpress.com/news/publishers-vs-students/994981/0.

applied under the instruction provision.[110] The dissenting voices soon morphed into a signature campaign, spearheaded by eminent academicians, urging the plaintiffs to withdraw the lawsuit.[111] Its supporters included authors of the plaintiffs' works, thus weakening the argument about authors being adversely affected. One academic declared that is was "absolutely essential" for his writings to be photocopied and made available in India, due to high prices.[112] Meanwhile, the Nobel laureate Amartya Sen directly urged OUP not to pursue the case.[113]

In March 2013, the plaintiffs were formally sent the signature petition, with the above statements annexed.[114] In reply, the plaintiffs reiterated their case for copyright infringement, adding that an IRRO license would be a "legitimate and accessible method" for securing permissions.[115] The signatories, through Basheer, responded with three main arguments.[116] First, the Act's research provision protected the defendants, and its instruction provision was not qualified by fair dealing, making "*any* dealing" exempted.[117] Second, a quantitative cap, if applicable, ought to be greater than 10 percent. Third, arguments about unaffordability.[118] The signatories also drew attention to an observation in *CCH*, describing fair dealing as a "user's right" that should be interpreted liberally.[119] The signatories went on to accuse the IRRO of coercing universities, and claimed that the IRRO could progressively hike its licensing fee. The plaintiffs did not yield.

D *Impleadment Applications*

Some of the plaintiffs' opponents formed themselves into two associations, the Association of Students for Equitable Access to Knowledge (ASEAK) and the Society for Promoting Educational Access and Knowledge (SPEAK), comprising academicians and DU students, respectively. ASEAK and SPEAK both applied to the Delhi High Court to implead themselves as defendants. Both associations were assisted by legal academicians, including Basheer and Liang, and lawyers acting pro bono.

ASEAK's application mostly reiterated previous arguments against the plaintiffs. ASEAK argued that it represented the "class of persons most affected."[120] SPEAK, which comprised signatories to the letter against the plaintiffs, reproduced their earlier arguments. SPEAK argued

[110] Lawrence Liang, *Oxford and Cambridge University Publishers v. Students of India*, Kafila (Aug. 27, 2012), https://kafila.online/2012/08/27/oxford-and-cambridge-university-publishers-v-students-of-india/.

[111] *Appeal to Publishers to Withdraw Suit Filed against Delhi University*, Change.org (2012), www.change.org/p/academics-appeal-to-publishers-to-withdraw-suit-filed-against-delhi-university; Anshul Kumar Pandey, *Who Is Afraid of Copyright Infringement? Campaign to Save D School Photocopy Shop*, Youth Ki Awaaz (Oct. 11, 2012), www.youthkiawaaz.com/2012/10/who-is-afraid-of-copyright-infringement-a-public-meeting-organised-by-campaign-to-save-d-school-photocopy-shop-held-at-delhi-school-of-economics/.

[112] Statement by Kaushik Sunder Rajan, Oct. 27, 2012, *available at* South Asia Citizens Web, www.sacw.net/IMG/pdf/Relevant_section_of_Email_from_Prof_Kaushik_Sunder_Rajan_on_the_issue.pdf.

[113] Letter from Amartya Sen to OUP, Sept. 17, 2012, *available at* South Asia Citizens Web, www.sacw.net/IMG/pdf/Amartya_Sen.pdf.

[114] Email from Nivedita Menon to OUP, Mar. 10, 2013, *available at* Spicy IP, https://spicyip.com/docs/DU%20Photocopying%20case/email-reply-publishers-association-limited.pdf.

[115] Email from Emma House, Director of Publisher Relations, The Publishers Association Limited to Nivedita Menon, 14 March 2013, *available at* Spicy IP, https://spicyip.com/docs/DU%20Photocopying%20case/email-reply-publishers-association-limited.pdf (last accessed Sept. 11, 2017).

[116] Email from Shamnad Basheer to Emma House, Mar. 29, 2013, *available at* Spicy IP, https://spicyip.com/docs/DU%20Photocopying%20case/email-reply-publishers-association-limited.pdf.

[117] *Id.*

[118] *Id.*

[119] 1 S.C.R. 339 (2004), at para. 48.

[120] Application for Impleadment by ASEAK (Feb. 25, 2013), at para. 9 (l), (o) (on file with the author).

for impleadment as a permanent injunction would potentially bind faculty members throughout India.[121] In April 2013, ASEAK's application was heard by Justice Rajiv Sahai Endlaw, now hearing the case after Justice Gambhir. The plaintiffs contended that ASEAK could be allowed to intervene and make arguments, but could not be impleaded as a defendant.[122] Justice Endlaw accepted ASEAK's application, citing an earlier judgment of his where he had held public interest to be relevant in determining the appropriateness of an interim injunction.[123] Justice Endlaw also accepted SPEAK's application the following month.

E Further Submissions

In November 2014, the plaintiffs submitted a set of further arguments, classifiable into five main arguments. SPEAK filed a submission countering each of these arguments. First, the plaintiffs argued that the Act's research and instruction provisions could only be availed of by persons actually engaged in such use, precluding DU and Rameshwari.[124] Against this argument, SPEAK cited a dissenting judgment in a US case, where the majority found photocopying course packs not protected by fair use.[125] The dissenting judge held that it was incorrect to distinguish between photocopying by a shop for students and photocopying by a student, as the former is merely a faster and cost-effective substitute for the latter.[126] The judge also permitted "incidental private sector profit" in the course of photocopying.[127]

Second, the plaintiffs argued that the instruction provision ought to be interpreted in light of India's obligations as a Berne and TRIPS member.[128] That the defendants' acts were incompatible with the "Three-step Test,"[129] and that the Berne Convention also subjected instruction exceptions to "fair practice."[130] Against this, SPEAK contended that references to international law were inappropriate since the Act already had a fair dealing provision, that international law should be interpreted in light of local requirements, and that domestic law should take precedence in case of conflict.[131]

Third, the plaintiffs submitted that the instruction provision should permit only "a singular instance of copying by a teacher or pupil," rather than multiple copies.[132] Against this, SPEAK cited *Longman v. Carrington*, a New Zealand decision where the term "course of instruction,"

[121] Application for Impleadment by SPEAK (Mar. 12, 2013), at para. 6 (on file with the author).

[122] Order in *DU Case* (Mar. 1, 2013), at para. 6, http://delhihighcourt.nic.in/dhcqrydisp_o.asp?pn=45772&yr=2013.

[123] *Id.* at para. 6 (citing Ishmali Devi v. Delhi Development Authority, MANU/DE/1838/2009 (Del. H.C.)).

[124] Written Submission by Plaintiffs in *DU Case* (Nov. 19, 2014) (on file with the author) (hereinafter "*Plaintiff Submission*").

[125] Written Submission by SPEAK in *DU Case* (Dec. 10, 2014) (on file with the author) (hereinafter "*SPEAK Submission*"), citing Princeton University Press v. Michigan Document Services 99 F.3d 1381 (6th Cir. 1996).

[126] 99 F.3d 1381 at 1393.

[127] *Id.* at 1393–94.

[128] *Plaintiff Submission*, *supra* note 124 (citing Entertainment Network v. Super Cassette 9 SCALE 69 (2008), ¶ 78).

[129] Berne Convention art. 9(2) ("It shall be a matter for legislation in the countries of the Union to permit the reproduction of such works in certain special cases, provided that such reproduction does not conflict with a normal exploitation of the work and does not unreasonably prejudice the legitimate interests of the author."); TRIPS Agreement art. 13 ("Members shall confine limitations or exceptions to exclusive rights to certain special cases which do not conflict with a normal exploitation of the work and do not unreasonably prejudice the legitimate interests of the right holder.").

[130] Berne Convention art. 10(2).

[131] *SPEAK Submission*, *supra* note 125 (citing Handicrafts Emporium v. Union of India A.I.R. S.C. 2340 (2003) at para. 53, and Gramophone Company v. Pandey A.I.R. S.C. 667 (1984) at para. 12).

[132] *Plaintiff Submission*, *supra* note 124.

in New Zealand's copyright legislation, was defined to include "anything in the process of instruction," including preparation and copying of course materials.[133]

Fourth, the plaintiffs argued that fair dealing, unlike fair use, is "exhaustive and inflexible," and the Act's research and instruction provisions should be read narrowly.[134] Furthermore, even applying the US and Canadian fair use factors, the defendants' acts were commercial, non-transformative, causing losses to the plaintiffs, and involved qualitatively and quantitatively substantial copying (such as entire chapters and articles).[135] There also existed an alternative to the dealing, in the form of an IRRO license.[136] Against this, SPEAK pointed to the *CUP Guidebook Case*.[137] SPEAK argued that all four factors weighed in the defendants' favor. First, the photocopying was noncommercial and students were charged a meagre amount. Second, the nature of the work enabled access to knowledge.[138] Third, the amount copied was not qualitatively or quantitatively substantial, even if entire articles were copied.[139] Fourth, the course packs were not in competition with the plaintiffs' works.[140] SPEAK also argued that an IRRO license was no alternative to the dealing, as the IRRO could hike tariffs at its discretion.[141]

Finally and fifth, the plaintiffs contended that the defendants' acts should not be permitted in the "larger public interest," as they would cause huge losses to the publishing industry.[142] Against this argument, SPEAK pointed out that the Indian publishing industry had grown enormously, despite the existence of widespread photocopying for many years, and was unlikely to suffer financially if the court ruled against it.[143]

The case stretched on for many months, amid adjournments and delays. On September 16, 2016, Justice Endlaw finally delivered his decision, more than five years after the initial Anton Piller order.

3 The Delhi High Court's Decision

A *Single Judge Decision*

Justice Endlaw began by emphasizing that copyright was not a "natural right" but a "statutory right" subject to the Act's exceptions, and that the Act maintained a balance between the interests of copyright owners and the public.[144] Moving on to the instruction provision, he observed that although the provision uses the expression "by a teacher or a pupil," the legislature intended the provision to include educational institutions, rather than just individuals, and a contrary interpretation was not in keeping with ground realities.[145] Furthermore, "instruction"

133 *SPEAK Submission*, *supra* note 125 (citing Longman v. Carrington 2 N.Z.L.R. 574 (1991) (N.Z. H.C.)).

134 *Plaintiff Submission*, *supra* note 124.

135 *Id.*

136 *Id.*

137 *Supra* notes 34 to 40 and accompanying text.

138 *SPEAK Submission supra* note 125 (citing *CCH* (2004) 1 S.C.R. 339, at para. 58 ("The nature of the work in question should also be considered by courts [. . .] the dealing may be more fair in that its reproduction with acknowledgement could lead to a wider public dissemination of the work – one of the goals of copyright law.")).

139 *Id* (citing *CCH*, *id.* at para. 56 ("for the purpose of research or private study, it may be essential to copy an entire academic article")).

140 *Id.*

141 *Id.*

142 *Plaintiff Submission*, *supra* note 124.

143 *SPEAK Submission*, *supra* note 125.

144 *DU Case* 68 P.T.C. 386 (2016), at paras. 28, 41.

145 *Id.*

included activities beyond lectures.[146] Thus, the "reproduction of any copyrighted work by the teacher for the purpose of imparting instruction to the pupil as prescribed in the syllabus during the academic year would be within the meaning" of the instruction provision.[147]

Moving on to the Act's research provision, Justice Endlaw postulated that if a DU student photocopied pages from books in DU's library, or took images with a mobile phone, this would be protected under the provision, if done for purposes of research or private study.[148] In the present case, all that was happening was that DU was itself carrying out such copying, through Rameshwari, as it held limited copies of books.[149] Justice Endlaw thus stated:

> [W]e are a country with a bulging population and where the pressure on all public resources and facilities is far beyond that in any other country or jurisdiction. While it may be possible for a student in a class of say 10 or 20 students to have the book issued from the library for a month and to laboriously take notes therefrom, the same is unworkable where the number of students run into hundreds if not thousands. According to me, what is permissible for a small number of students cannot be viewed differently, merely because the number of students is larger.[150]

Justice Endlaw cited the US case of *Williams & Wilkins v. United States*,[151] which held that it was a fair use for libraries to photocopy articles for patrons engaged in scientific research. It was held that a "library is in the same position" as an individual researcher making a photocopy "when responding to the demands of individual researchers acting separately."[152] Justice Endlaw added that Rameshwari could only be "functioning commercially" if it was "charging for a reproduction of the book of the plaintiffs at a price competing with the price fixed by the plaintiffs for the books."[153]

Justice Endlaw further referred to the three-step test. He felt that the Indian legislature should be "deemed to have kept the said international covenants in mind" while enacting the instruction provision, and that the court should not impose its own interpretation.[154] Thus, as the legislature had not imposed any limitation on the extent of reproduction, the court could not do so.[155] Justice Endlaw also remarked that the judgments cited by the parties could not form the basis of interpreting the Act.[156] The judge accordingly ruled in favor of the defendants and held that there was no triable issue of fact.[157]

Justice Endlaw's decision was understandably welcomed by activists and academicians. In my opinion, however, the judgment can be criticized on a few counts. The judge did not explicitly state whether the instruction provision was subject to fair dealing. Nor did he address the plaintiffs' submission that it was subject to "fair practice." He simply avoided interpreting the Berne Convention. Therefore, the judge did not clarify whether the absence of a statutory provision concerning a quantitative limit in the instruction provision (as well as research provision) meant that there was no limit to what could have been copied. Considering that the local commissioner found some books photocopied in entirety, such a clarification by the

146 *Id.* at para. 60.
147 *Id.*
148 *Id.* at paras. 73–78.
149 *Id.* at para. 89.
150 *Id.*
151 487 F.2d 1345 (Ct. Cl. 1973).
152 *DU Case* 68 P.T.C. 386, at para. 77 (2016).
153 *Id.* at para. 88.
154 *Id.* at para. 97.
155 *Id.*
156 *Id.* at paras. 99–100.
157 *Id.* at para. 101.

court would have been helpful. Moreover, the judge also missed an opportunity to clarify whether the price of a book and availability of an IRRO license should be deemed relevant in considering the instruction provision (like in Canada), and could also be weighed in a fair dealing analysis. It may further be said that the judge did not systematically apply a four-factor or six-factor test, preferring to make scattered observations about the course packs not being in competition, or Rameshwari not operating commercially. The judge also did not comment on the relationship between the Act and the Fundamental Rights and Directive Principles, which may (or may not) have strengthened jurisprudence on users' rights in the Act.

Thus, for those expecting a judgment that would clarify the scope of fair dealing, engage extensively with foreign case law, and discuss constitutional law principles, the decision was anticlimactic. The judgment ran into a whopping ninety-four pages and recapitulated the submissions of the various parties, but the judge did not analyze them with the detail that was perhaps expected. Nevertheless, it can equally be said that social justice principles loom large over the judgment, that a systematic application of the four-factor test in India is not strictly necessary (and Denning did not do so in *Hubbard* either), that the issue of a quantitative limit in fair dealing is best addressed on a case-by-case basis, and that the Berne Convention's requirement of fair practice, as well as the three-step test, adds little to the Act's existing provisions. In this context, Liang has remarked that those who believe that "the court should have been more proactive" should appreciate that the judgment "moves beyond the rhetoric of balance of interest alone."[158] Basheer praised Justice Endlaw's departure from the recent tradition of "atrociously one sided and skewed IP decisions" from the Delhi High Court.[159]

B *Interventions by the Publishing Industry*

The plaintiffs appealed against the judgment to a division bench (i.e., a two-judge bench) of the Delhi High Court. During this time, three parties representing the publishing industry – the Association of Publishers in India (API), the Federation of Indian Publishers (FIP), and the IRRO – filed intervention applications. The parties were represented by the same law firm, and their respective applications contained identical submissions. The applications advanced seven main contentions. First, that international publishers had made books available in India "at possibly the lowest prices anywhere in the world," through special India editions, and further ensured greater access by allowing the IRRO to issue licenses at "nominal rates."[160] Second, the single judge's order had effectively "legitimised the act of photocopying entire books" and granted a "blanket permission" to all educational institutions, as well as for-profit institutes like private coaching and test preparation centres.[161] This would have "adverse ramifications" for the Indian publishing industry and the thousands it employed.[162] Third, this, in turn, was "tantamount to interference with" the fundamental right of publishers to carry on business.[163] Fourth, that it was wrong to interpret the Act's educational instruction provision as a "standalone

158 Lawrence Liang, *The Radical Significance of the DU Photocopy Case for Global Copyright*, Kafila (Sept. 20, 2016), https://kafila.online/2016/09/20/the-radical-significance-of-the-du-photocopy-case-for-global-copyright.

159 Shamnad Basheer, *Breaking News: Major Victory for Students and Educational Access in DU Photocopy Case!*, Spicy IP (Sept. 16, 2016), https://spicyip.com/2016/09/breaking-news-major-victory-for-students-and-educational-access-in-du-photocopy-case.html.

160 Intervention Application by API in *DU Case* (Nov. 5, 2016), at para. 8 (on file with the author).

161 *Id.* at paras. 10, 22.

162 *Id.* at para. 10.

163 *Id.* at para. 12.

section," where fairness was not a requirement, as fairness was "built into" the provision.[164] Fifth, the instruction provision and research provision were both applicable only to natural persons, specifically teachers and pupils.[165] Sixth, Rameshwari was operating commercially, as it was making a profit.[166] Seventh, the judgment was incompatible with the three-step test.[167] The intervening applications were accepted by the division bench.[168] Its judgment, however, did not dwell on all the arguments raised in the applications.

C Division Bench Decision

The Division Bench comprised Justices Pradeep Nandrajog and Yogesh Khanna, with the former delivering the judgment on behalf of the court. The court agreed with the single judge's interpretation of the term "course of instruction."[169] Before the court, case law from the US, UK, Canada, and New Zealand was cited.[170] But the court advised "care and caution" in applying foreign case law.[171] The court held that US, UK, and Canadian cases had "no relevance" and "no persuasive value in the Indian context."[172] Here, the court pointed to the existence of a fair dealing requirement in the UK's instruction provision and a statutory fair use provision in the US, along with the *1976 Guidelines*.[173] The court also acknowledged the approach taken in the *CUP Guidebook Case*, but held that the case was "distinguishable on its peculiar facts."[174] However, the court found "special relevance" in *Longman*, as it interpreted the instruction provision in New Zealand's erstwhile copyright statute, which was very similar to the Act's.[175]

In *Longman*, the court held that New Zealand's instruction provision did not place any quantitative restrictions on photocopying, and that agents could photocopy material on behalf of teachers and students. The division bench agreed with this view, holding the Act's corresponding provision to be a similar "standalone" provision[176] However, the court departed from *Longman* by holding that a "general principle of fair use" was still applicable in the Act's instruction provision, as "unless the legislative intent expressly excludes fair use... fair use must be read into the statute."[177] Here, the court held that "the four factors on which fair use is determined in jurisdictions abroad" would not apply, and neither would a "qualitative and quantitative test."[178] Rather, fairness would have to be determined on the basis of "extent justified by the purpose," i.e., "so much of the copyrighted work can be fairly used which is necessary to ... make the learner understand what is intended to be understood."[179] The court felt that this would warrant

[164] *Id.* at paras. 14, 20.
[165] *Id.* at para. 14.
[166] *Id.* at para. 18.
[167] *Id.* at para. 21.
[168] Order in *DU Case* (Nov. 8, 2016) http://delhihighcourt.nic.in/dhcqrydisp_o.asp?pn=213879&yr=2016 1 (last accessed Sept. 1, 2017).
[169] Chancellor, Master and Scholars of the University of Oxford v. Rameshwari Photocopy Services (2016) 235 D.L.T. 409, at paras. 39, 60 (2016).
[170] *Id.* at para. 20.
[171] *Id.* at para. 19.
[172] *Id.* at paras. 64–68.
[173] *Id.* at paras. 64–66. *Supra* note 4 and accompanying text.
[174] *Id.* at para. 72.
[175] *Id.* at paras. 40–56 (discussing Copyright Act 1962, s 21(4) (N.Z.)).
[176] *Id.* at para. 47.
[177] *Id.* at paras. 31, 56.
[178] *Id.* at paras. 33, 35.
[179] *Id.* at para. 33.

a detailed analysis of each course pack, requiring expert evidence, and thus remanded the case to the single judge on this point.[180]

The court also ruled that the single judge had been wrong to hold that there was no triable issue of fact, as the local commissioner's discovery of eight fully photocopied books would lead to an issue of "whether photocopying of entire books" in the course of instruction "would be a permissible activity."[181] The court thus restored the suit, although denying the plaintiffs an injunction.

Turning to the research provision, the court, in contrast to the single judge, held that the provision had "no relevance" in such situations, as the instruction provision had "so outstretch [ed] itself" that it "muted" the research section.[182] Like the single judge, the court did not refer to the Directive Principles and Fundamental Rights. The court "simply noted ... for record" submissions regarding copyright policy in developing countries with low purchasing power.[183] Nevertheless, the court acknowledged that education was "fundamental ... to a society" and warranted "the promotion of equitable access to knowledge," with "the more indigent the learner, the greater the responsibility to ensure equitable access."[184] With reference to the three-step test, the court followed the single judge's view on the sovereignty of the Indian legislature.[185]

The court's finding that fair use is implicit in the educational instruction provision (although through a necessity test) distinguished its ruling from that of the single judge, and arguably acts as a potential curb against unrestricted photocopying. However, the court's reluctance to follow a quantitative test, not even explicitly declaring the copying of an entire textbook as unfair, arguably gives copyright owners a raw deal. Although the court relied on *Longman*, New Zealand's copyright statute at the time has long been repealed, and several changes made in light of the TRIPS Agreement. New Zealand's existing instruction provision imposes strict quantitative limits.[186] The court acknowledged this and even cited a later New Zealand case citing the newer provision, but held that this had "no relevance in the Indian context" (in my view, without precisely clarifying why, but hinting that fairness should not be interpreted through quantitative limits).[187]

In January 2017, hearing the case on remand, Justice Endlaw rejected an intervention application by the IRRO, and two impleadment applications by the API and the FIP.[188] Meanwhile, a group of academicians and students submitted a fresh plea to OUP urging it not to proceed with an appeal to the Supreme Court against the division bench's decision.[189]

[180] *Id.* at paras. 56, 80.
[181] *Id.* at para. 79.
[182] *Id.* at paras. 75, 77
[183] *Id.* at para. 62.
[184] *Id.* at para. 30.
[185] *Id.* at para. 63.
[186] Copyright Act 1994, s 44 (N.Z.). On copying "done by or on behalf of an educational establishment," the limit is a maximum of three percent or three pages of a work, whichever is greater. In doing such copying, if a whole work is copied then no more than 50 percent of that work may be copied. There additionally exists a 14-day embargo on subsequent reproduction of a work.
[187] Chancellor, Master and Scholars of the University of Oxford v. Rameshwari Photocopy Services (2016) 235 D.L.T. 409, at paras. 58–59 (citing Copyright Licensing Authority v. University of Auckland, 2 N.Z.L.R. 574 (H.C.) (1991).
[188] Order in *DU Case* (Jan. 20, 2017), http://delhihighcourt.nic.in/dhcqrydisp_o.asp?pn=12384&yr=2017.
[189] Pankhuri Agarwal, *Oxford University Students and Others Urge OUP to not Appeal to the Supreme Court in the DU Copyright Case*, SPICY IP (Jan. 24, 2017), https://spicyip.com/2017/01/oxford-university-students-and-others-urge-oup-to-not-appeal-to-the-supreme-court-in-the-du-copyright-case.html.

In March 2017, the plaintiffs announced their decision to withdraw the lawsuit. A statement issued by the plaintiffs offered no reasons for this decision.[190] The IRRO, through a petition before the Supreme Court, appealed against the division judge bench's decision. The court held that the petition could not be entertained, as the plaintiffs had withdrawn from the case and the IRRO was merely an intervenor.[191] This conclusively brought an end to the case, after nearly six years.

4 Role of the IRRO

The IRRO was formed in 2000. In 2002, it was granted registration by the government. Until recently, there was little information available on who the IRRO's members and board members were, and just how representative the authors were of India's cultural and academic community. The IRRO's website had also been suspended, after inactivity for several months. Even cached copies of the website (on archive.org) offered very limited information about the IRRO. The IRRO's shoddy governance became evident when, in December 2014, the IRRO's registration under the Act was not renewed the by the HRD Ministry, after it failed to hold elections to its governing body.[192] Thus, even if the court gave a finding that DU would require a photocopying license, the plaintiffs would have had to directly collect royalties from DU and other universities, posing a great obstacle. This may well have been a factor in the plaintiffs' decision to withdraw from the lawsuit.

However, at the time of writing (mid-2019) the IRRO has revamped its website, provided information about it that was hitherto unavailable, and started a fairly active Twitter handle (on New Year's Day in 2019). According to its revamped website, the IRRO's membership comprises seventy-one publishers and 207 authors (both lists being quite diverse), with a governing body that includes a representative of CUP.[193] The IRRO claims to have entered into agreements with twenty-four collecting societies abroad, with four more in the pipeline.[194] While information about the IRRO's revenues seems absent, an archived copy of the website of the International Federation of Reprographic Rights Organisations (IFRRO), updated in 2014, reveals that the IRRO earned EUR 544,935.03 through licensing worldwide the preceding financial year. Of this, as much as EUR 537,755.58 originated from collecting societies abroad, with the remainder coming from India.[195]

Prior to the *DU Case*, the IRRO acknowledged that "not a single university or college" in India had acquired an IRRO license, despite attempts by the IRRO, and only some corporate houses had.[196] Presumably, therefore, the *DU Case* was of great importance to the IRRO, and cruelly dashed its hopes of greater earnings. However, if a recent, alarmist tweet by the IRRO is an indication – "Whether it's cheating on your taxes or publishing without an IRRO copyright

190 Joint statement by Oxford University Press, Cambridge University Press and Taylor & Francis (Mar. 9, 2017), http://fdslive.oup.com/asiaed/News%20Items%20and%20Images/Joint%20Public%20Statement.pdf.

191 Shamnad Basheer, *Breaking News: Supreme Court Refuses IRRO Appeal in DU Photocopy Case*, Spicy IP (May 9, 2017), https://spicyip.com/2017/05/breaking-news-supreme-court-refuses-to-admit-irro-appeal.html.

192 Basant Kumar Mohanty, *Photocopy Licensing Agency Loses Licence*, The Telegraph (Jan. 14, 2014), www.telegraphindia.com/1140114/jsp/nation/story_17785667.jsp.

193 List of IRRO Members 2018–19: Publishers, www.irro.org.in/wp-content/uploads/2019/01/IRRO-Members-Publishers-2018-19.pdf; List of IRRO Members 2018–19: Authors, www.irro.org.in/wp-content/uploads/2019/01/IRRO-Members-Authors-2018-19.pdf; Governing Body, www.irro.org.in/about-us/governing-body/ (last accessed June 19, 2019).

194 Bilateral Agreements, www.irro.org.in/about-us/bilateral-agreements/ (last accessed June 19, 2019).

195 Indian Reprographic Rights Organisation (cached copy), https://web.archive.org/web/20170626163221/http://ifrro.org/members/indian-reprographic-rights-organisation (last accessed June 19, 2019).

196 Basant Kumar Mohanty, *Photocopying of Books Stops in Delhi University after raid*, The Telegraph (Aug. 28, 2012), www.telegraphindia.com/1120828/jsp/odisha/story_15905658.jsp.

license, chances of you ending up in a legal trouble are high!," the tweet claims, with pictures of handcuffs and prison cell bar in the background[197] – the IRRO could well be plotting another battle. Interestingly, the tweet tags a few expensive private universities in India (perhaps existing or prospective licensees). In this regard, it is not explicitly clear from the IRRO's website if it has now renewed its registration under the Act. Not long ago, the IRRO had, in fact, petitioned the Delhi High Court challenging (unsuccessfully) the constitutionality of various copyright provisions, including one granting the Indian Copyright Board (a statutory government body) powers to intervene with the IRRO's tariff structure, one giving members of the IRRO equal voting rights, and one permitting compulsory licensing.[198] The judgment described the IRRO as a "registered Society under the Societies (Registration) Act, 1860,"[199] which means little, as it is the Copyright Act which authorizes collecting societies.

CONCLUDING THOUGHTS

In developed countries, a persistent narrative has held that India is not hospitable to IP owners. The US Chamber of Commerce cited the decision in the *DU Case* as a factor for giving India a low rank in its global IP index.[200] Yet, there were fundamental mistakes in the plaintiffs' strategy. After tolerating photocopying for many years, the plaintiffs took aim at course packs where a lot of the material copied was around 10 percent, and assumed that the interim order would scare universities into signing up with the IRRO. The plaintiffs should have been conscious of socioeconomic realities in India and anticipated the backlash from civil society. A more incremental strategy, starting by targeting the copying of entire books, might have been wiser. The plaintiffs could also have targeted for-profit coaching centres that prepare students for competitive examinations (a lucrative and booming industry in India) instead of universities. And had the plaintiffs held wide-ranging consultations with authors before pursuing legal proceedings, an equitable solution, such as generous quantitative caps or the exemption of institutions catering to low-income groups, might still have been possible. Instead, India is now left with a precedent with a vague "fairness" criterion in the instruction provision, and uncertainty on whether copying entire textbooks in the course of instruction can be allowed, and on whether courts should be guided by *CCH*, *Longman*, or the *CUP Guidebook* case.

Recently, the Delhi High Court ruled in favor of an author whose entire book was being photocopied and sold by a private coaching centre and its publishing wing. The court did not find the division bench's decision to be of assistance to the defendants, finding the defendants to be engaged in "commercial and profit making" activity.[201] But this still leaves open questions concerning the liability of photocopying of lesser portions.

In terms of a future strategy, had the IRRO continued to be dysfunctional the publishing industry might well have given up on the idea of expecting universities to ever pay licensing fees in India, relying instead on royalties earned overseas. However, with the IRRO reorganizing itself, a future test case cannot be ruled out. Yet, even if the High Court or the Supreme Court

[197] @IRRO_Official, https://twitter.com/IRRO_Official/status/1140219410243710976, June 16, 2019 (last accessed June 19, 2019).

[198] Anand Bhushan v. Union of India 2018 Indlaw DEL 1312.

[199] *Id.* at para 1.

[200] Shreeja Sen, *India Ranks 43 out of 45 Countries in USCC Intellectual Property Index*, MINT (Feb. 9, 2017), www.livemint.com/Politics/xclc5fGhkySYU65WAI8WnL/India-ranks-43-out-of-45-countries-in-USCC-intellectual-prop.html.

[201] Neetu Singh v Rajiv Saumitra Civil Suit 935/2016 (Aug. 4, 2017), at para. 4.

interprets the instruction provision differently, the industry can perhaps expect favorable judicial outcomes only in cases of photocopying of entire books, which not many universities indulge in anyway.

Another possible strategy for the publishing industry could be to lobby for change in legislation. For example, as more Indian universities sign up for online repositories, the industry could lobby for a special, more stringent provision governing material originating from such databases. While introducing amendments to the Act, the then HRD Minister had stated, "If a student wants to do research in copyrighted material, he cannot be charged. If somebody wants to do research in copyrighted material or wants to teach something, he cannot be charged."[202] Possibly, the DIPP may lend the publishing industry a more sympathetic ear. But given the court's decision, and vocal public opposition, the best that the industry can perhaps hope for are a set of non-binding guidelines, not unlike the 1976 *Guidelines*. But here, too, the DIPP will be opening itself to criticism if organizations like SPEAK and ASEAK are not involved in deliberations. Hence, for the foreseeable future, the *DU Case* represents an emphatic victory for proponents of access to knowledge.

[202] Kapil Sibal, Discussion on the Motion for Consideration of the Copyright (Amendment) Bill 2012 (May 22, 2012).

17

Parody, Satire, Caricature, and Pastiche: Fair Dealing Is No Laughing Matter

David Tan

1 INTRODUCTION

We all love a good laugh.

But we often loathe others having a laugh at our expense. Therefore it hardly comes as a surprise when copyright owners aggressively seek to enforce their monopoly right against others who use their works for the purposes of parody, satire, caricature, and pastiche.

A parody or satire must invoke or copy a significant proportion of the original copyright work in order for it to be effective; it will invariably satisfy the substantial similarity test for copyright infringement. The question that follows is whether such works can nevertheless claim to be fair use or fair dealing. The open-ended "fair use" model, as opposed to the categorical "fair dealing" approach, is widely viewed as the most flexible limitation and exception on copyright holders' rights, given its potential applicability to any circumstance or use.[1] Both fair use and fair dealing are designed to foster creativity, enable intellectual exchange, and promote cultural expression. Parody enjoys an exalted protected status in intellectual property jurisprudence. In the United States, the First Circuit Court of Appeals described parody as "a humorous form of social commentary and literary criticism ... [that] seeks to ridicule sacred verities and prevailing mores,"[2] thus implicating First Amendment concerns. The Second Circuit noted "the broad scope permitted parody in First Amendment Law"[3] and that "in today's world of unrelieved solemnity, copyright law should be hospitable to the humor of parody."[4] While the critical message in a parody that comments directly on the original work or its author can be easily discerned, the ideas expressed in other forms of humorous works such as satire, caricature, and pastiche may be more obtuse. In an oft-quoted passage, the US Supreme Court in *Campbell v. Acuff-Rose Music* cryptically mused:

> Parody needs to mimic an original to make its point, and so has some claim to use the creation of its victim's (or collective victims') imagination, whereas satire can stand on its own two feet and so requires justification for the very act of borrowing.[5]

[1] Michael Geist, *Fairness Found: How Canada Quietly Shifted from Fair Dealing to Fair Use, in* The Copyright Pentalogy: How the Supreme Court of Canada Shook the Foundations of Canadian Copyright Law 157, 157 (Michael Geist ed. 2013).

[2] LL Bean Inc. v. Drake Publishers Inc., 811 F.2d 26, 29 (1st Cir. 1987).

[3] Groucho Marx Prods. v. Day and Night Co., 689 F.2d 317, 319 n.2 (2d Cir. 1982).

[4] Elsmere Music v. National Broadcasting Co., 623 F. 2d 252, 253 (2d Cir. 1980).

[5] Campbell v. Acuff-Rose Music Inc., 510 U.S. 569, 580–81 (1994).

This dictum has resulted in much confusion in US fair use jurisprudence over two decades, especially at the district court levels where certain judges drew a crude line between permissible parody and impermissible satire,[6] but more recent decisions by the Second and Ninth Circuit Courts of Appeals have obviated this distinction.[7] On the other hand, perhaps learning from the US experience, Australia and the United Kingdom have each enacted specific categorical fair dealing exceptions to protect uses for the purposes of parody, satire, caricature, and pastiche (PSCP).

The fair use defense has been disparagingly identified with the "most nebulous and unpredictable aspects"[8] in copyright law. In Commonwealth common law jurisdictions like Australia, Hong Kong, Singapore, and the UK, "fair dealing" is one of several statutory defenses in copyright law that "provide a reasonable balance between … giving copyright owners a fair return for the investment expended … [and] the interests of copyright users to have access to and to make use of the works and information contained therein."[9] This chapter presents an overview of how PSCP is protected through the fair use and fair dealing defenses in five jurisdictions: the US, Australia, the UK, Singapore, and Hong Kong. Section 2 explores the definitions of "parody," "satire," "caricature," and "pastiche," and the perceived values of PSCP to society. Section 3 examines how PSCP is treated under the US fair use approach and under the various fair dealing regimes in a selection of Commonwealth common law jurisdictions. In particular, it will focus on a discussion of the "transformative use" doctrine as presently applied by the US courts, in an attempt to discover its relevance, if any, to fair dealing jurisprudence in Australia, the UK, Singapore, and Hong Kong. It argues that US fair use jurisprudence is significantly influenced by the ascendancy of free speech interests as enshrined in the First Amendment, and that one should be wary of transplanting the "transformative use" doctrine into the Commonwealth jurisdictions. Section 4 offers some suggestions on the way ahead for other jurisdictions to adopt a more nuanced evaluation of the fairness factors in order to strike that reasonable balance between the copyright owners and users in contemporary times.

2 PARODY, SATIRE, CARICATURE, AND PASTICHE – WHAT'S IN A NAME?

The courts have generally avoided attempts to articulate definitions of "parody," "satire," "caricature" or "pastiche." In *Campbell v. Acuff-Rose Music*, the only fair use decision handed down by the US Supreme Court in the last twenty-five years, the court commented that:

> Modern dictionaries accordingly describe a parody as a "literary or artistic work that imitates the characteristic style of an author or a work for comic effect or ridicule," or as a "composition in prose or verse in which the characteristic turns of thought and phrase in an author or class of authors are imitated in such a way as to make them appear ridiculous." For the purposes of

[6] *See, e.g.*, Cariou v. Prince, 784 F. Supp. 2d 337 (S.D.N.Y. 2011); Dr Seuss Enterprises LP v. Penguin Book USA Inc., 924 F. Supp. 1559 (S.D. Cal. 1996). However, more recent decisions preferred to focus on whether the secondary use was "transformative." E.g. Dr Seuss Enterprises LP v. ComicMix LLC, 256 F. Supp. 3d 1099, 1106 (S.D. Cal. 2017) ("although *Boldly* fails to qualify as a parody it is no doubt transformative … the copied elements are always interspersed with original writing and illustrations that transform *Go!*'s pages into repurposed, *Star-Trek*–centric ones).

[7] *See, e.g.*, Cariou v. Prince, 714 F. 3d 694 (2d Cir. 2013); Seltzer v. Green Day, 725 F. 3d 1170 (9th Cir. 2013).

[8] J. Thomas McCarthy, The Rights of Publicity and Privacy § 8:9 (2d ed 2000). *See also* Paul Goldstein, *Fair Use in Context*, 31 Colum. J.L. & Arts. 433, 433 (2008) (describing fair use as "the great white whale of American copyright law," and a concept that is "[e]nthralling" and "enigmatic"). *But see* Pamela Samuelson, *Unbundling Fair Uses*, 77 Fordham L. Rev. 2537, 2541 (2009) ("fair use law is both more coherent and more predictable than many commentators have perceived once one recognizes that fair use cases tend to fall into common patterns").

[9] Susanna Leong, Intellectual Property Law of Singapore 9.002 (2013).

copyright law, the nub of the definitions, and the heart of any parodist's claim to quote from existing material, is the use of some elements of a prior author's composition to create a new one that, at least in part, comments on that author's works.[10]

Writing for a unanimous court, Justice Souter concluded that "parody has an obvious claim to transformative value,"[11] because "[l]ike less ostensibly humorous forms of criticism, it can provide social benefit, by shedding light on an earlier work, and, in the process, creating a new one."[12] In other words, parody is seen to be an art form that targets the original work, humorously imitating it to convey a particular message. It is given greater leeway than other forms of copying as it is perceived to be the paradigmatic kind of permissible copying that rests upon "the acknowledgement that critical and expressive speech is necessary and desirable in a healthy society"[13] and also on the assumption that the market for parodic works is different from that for the original works or their derivatives and adaptations.[14] The court also defined "satire" as a work "in which prevalent follies or vices are assailed with ridicule," or are "attacked through irony, derision, or wit,"[15] explaining that satirical works which do not directly comment on or criticize the original – unlike parodies – may require greater justification in order to qualify for fair use protection. For a period of time, some US courts have perhaps drawn an incorrect distinction between parody (fair use because it targets or comments on the original work) and satire (not fair use because it uses the original work as a weapon to comment on something else other than the original work).[16] The former is often known as "target parody" and the latter "weapon parody."[17] In arguing that there is a compelling public interest to protect both types of works, Haochen Sun suggests that "courts should give equal treatment to parody and satire. Rather than treating satire unfavorably, courts should broadly examine the political or artistic values that may underlie a satirical use of a copyrighted work."[18] The degree of market substitution is nonetheless important for both parodies and satires as Souter J cautioned:

> The [Copyright] Act has no hint of an evidentiary preference for parodists over their victims, and no workable presumption for parody could take account of the fact that parody often shades into satire when society is lampooned through its creative artifacts, or that a work may contain both parodic and nonparodic elements. Accordingly, parody, like any other use, has to work its way through the relevant factors, and be judged case by case, in light of the ends of the copyright law.[19]

In *Bourne Co v. Twentieth Century Fox Film Corporation*, it was noted that "[t]he distinction between parody and satire turns on the object of the 'comment' made by the

[10] Campbell v. Acuff-Rose Music, Inc., 510 U.S. 569, 580 (1994) ("Campbell") (internal citations omitted).

[11] *Id.* at 579.

[12] *Id.* For a detailed analysis of the critical importance of parody's cultural value, *see* David S. Roh, Illegal Literature: Towards a Disruptive Creativity 14–17 (2015).

[13] Nicolas Suzor, *Where the Bloody Hell Does Parody Fit in Australian Copyright Law?*, 13 Med. & Arts L. Rev. 218, 220 (2008).

[14] *See, e.g.*, *Campbell*, 510 U.S. 569, 592 (1994). *See also* SunTrust Bank v. Houghton Mifflin Co, 268 F. 3d 1257, 1275–76 (11th Cir. 2001) ("SunTrust Bank").

[15] *Id.* at 580 n.14 (internal citations omitted). *See also* Dustin Griffin, Satire: A Critical Reintroduction (1994); Conal Condren et al., *Defining Parody and Satire: Australian Copyright Law and Its New Exception: Part 2 – Advancing Ordinary Definitions*, 13 Med. & Arts L. Rev. 401 (2008).

[16] For an excellent analysis of these cases, *see* Suzor, *supra* note 13, at 238–43.

[17] *See, e.g.*, Anna Spies, *Revering Irreverence: A Fair Dealing Exception for Both Weapon and Target Parodies*, 34 U.N.S.W. L. J. 1122 (2011).

[18] Haochen Sun, *Fair Use As a Collective User Right*, 90 N.C.L. Rev. 125, 189 (2011).

[19] *Campbell*, 510 U.S. 569, 581 (1994).

allegedly infringing work."[20] However, the distinction can be an elusive one as the message may be a hybrid one that contains different comments targeted at different objects.

In many cultures, humor has traditionally been given significant leeway to say and do things that would otherwise not be permitted; PSCP depend on "the perceived resolution of incongruities, employing non-seriousness and irony to convey complex meanings ... and from the use of nonsense and illogic."[21] Other genres of humor such as caricature and pastiche are arguably less critical of the original work (parody) or of other follies or vices (satire), and in the parlance of the *Campbell* court, may require "[greater] justification for the very act of borrowing."[22] The *Oxford English Dictionary* defines "caricature" as "a picture, description, or imitation of a person in which certain striking characteristics are exaggerated in order to create a comic or grotesque effect." A "pastiche" is defined to be "an artistic work in a style that imitates that of another work, artist, or period"; it is a late nineteenth-century term derived from the French and Italian, which are based on the Latin word *pasta* which means "paste." A pastiche can involve an artistic work consisting of a medley of pieces imitating various sources, or literally pasting together parts of original copyright works to create a new work as seen in the works of appropriation artists Jeff Koons and Richard Prince which were the subject of litigation in *Blanch v. Koons*[23] and *Cariou v. Prince.*[24] Pastiche is said to be "a widely used but little examined term" but as a form of "aesthetic imitation" it has been the subject of a book by film studies scholar Richard Dyer.[25] Last but not least, the word "lampoon" is often used in the context of cartoons, and it means to "publicly criticise (someone or something) by using ridicule, irony or sarcasm." Satires, caricatures, and lampoons tend to feature most prominently in political cartoons. Generally these different forms of "literary disruptions" are perceived to be "driven by the advancement of culture – through form, genre, criticism, ideology, and politics ... [that] disturb reified practices."[26] David Roh, using literary works in his analysis, argues that "there should be space reserved for subversive, distinct elements for a healthy cultural system to avoid stagnation"[27] and such "deformations, though they may be of dubious aesthetic value, contribute to the whole system of texts."[28] Unlike piracy or plagiarism, PSCP generally seek to "actively transform the literary relationship between author and reader."[29]

There are three practices which often pose significant challenges for copyright law in the area of fair dealing: appropriation art, fan works, and social media.

Appropriation art has been defined as "[t]he practice or technique of reworking the images or styles contained in earlier works of art, esp. (in later use) in order to provoke critical re-evaluation of well-known pieces by presenting them in new contexts, or to challenge notions of individual

[20] 602 F. Supp. 2d 499, 504 (S.D.N.Y. 2009).

[21] Condren et al, *supra* note 15, 404–5.

[22] *Campbell*, 510 U.S. 569, 580–81 (1994). The UK Intellectual Property Office also commissioned an independent report on parody and the law in 2013. *See* Dinusha Mendis & Martin Kretschmer, The Treatment of Parodies under Copyright Law in Seven Jurisdictions: A Comparative Review of Underlying Principles (2013) ("*U.K. Parody Report*").

[23] Blanch v. Koons, 467 F. 3d 244 (2d Cir. 2006) ("*Koons II*"). Jeff Koons won this case on a ruling of fair use, but had lost an earlier lawsuit pre-*Campbell*. *See* Rogers v. Koons, 960 F. 2d 301 (2d Cir. 1992) ("*Koons I*").

[24] Cariou v. Prince, 714 F. 3d 694 (2d Cir. 2013) ("*Cariou*").

[25] *See* Richard Dyer, Pastiche 1 (2007).

[26] Roh, *supra* note 12, at 6–7.

[27] *Id.* at 9.

[28] *Id.* at 11.

[29] *Id.* at 13.

creativity or authenticity in art."[30] It is identified closely with the practice of "recoding" or "a shift in meaning" which occurs purely due to the fact that an original word, image, or object has been appropriated.[31] The Second Circuit recognized the genre of appropriation art as a "tradition [which] defines its efforts as follows: when the artist finishes his work, the meaning of the original object has been extracted and an entirely new meaning set in its place. An example is Andy Warhol's reproduction of multiple images of Campbell's soup cans."[32] Appropriation art may not be a pure parody that targets the original work; it is often a mélange of any combination of PSCP that invites the audience to rethink traditional frameworks of references in respect of popular cultural emblems.

There is much academic literature on fan communities in the digital age, both from sociocultural[33] and legal[34] perspectives. Although there has been no authoritative court ruling on the application of the fair use defense to fan activities on the Internet, the general academic consensus is that such behavior is highly transformative and should be protected under fair use. Fan communities especially in the digital age are "responsible for generating tremendous bodies of creative work – including art, music, videos, graphics, prose, fiction and poetry-based popular texts."[35] A "fan work" is generally defined as "any work by a fan, or indeed by anyone other than the content owner(s), set in such a fictional world or using such preexisting fictional characters."[36] Fans online are typically not motivated to produce a commercially marketable mass-distributed product. In addition, it is well canvassed that all fan fiction is essentially transformative, especially when slash fiction demonstrates a particular type of "contra-normative positioning of sexuality itself in our culture."[37] In his study of digital fandom, Paul Booth advances his thesis of a "philosophy of playfulness" which he observes to be prevalent in fans' use of today's digital technology.[38] In contrast to the classic readings of fandom which tended to focus on how fans *oppose* the hegemonic structures of the text, more recent scholarship have found that the dialogic practices of fans – even transformative and subversive works – tend to augment rather than resist the commercial media industry that has authored the original works.[39] For instance, the emerging phenomenon of GIF (Graphics Interchange Format) fics – like *SuperWhoLock* digital fandom that is an amalgamation of the cult television series *Supernatural*, *Doctor Who*, and *Sherlock* – which are short fan narratives constructed from animated GIFs that tell a story utilizing characters from popular movies and television series, is "based both on semantic reproduction of textual elements and syntactic appropriation of ideological moments from a media text."[40] While GIF fics do not necessarily oppose the original texts, they

[30] Emily Meyers, *Art on Ice: The Chilling Effect of Copyright on Artistic Expression*, 30 COLUM. J.L. & ARTS 219, 220 (2007).

[31] Isabelle Graw, *Fascination, Subversion and Dispossession in Appropriation Art*, *in* DAVID EVANS, APPROPRIATION 214, 214 (internal citations omitted).

[32] *Koons I*, 960 F. 2d at 304.

[33] *See, e.g.*, PAUL BOOTH, PLAYING FANS: NEGOTIATING FANDOM AND MEDIA IN THE DIGITAL AGE (2015); AARON SCHWABACH, FAN FICTION AND COPYRIGHT: OUTSIDER WORKS AND INTELLECTUAL PROPERTY PROTECTION (2011).

[34] *See, e.g.*, David Tan, *Harry Potter and the Transformation Wand: Fair Use, Canonicity and Fan Activity*, *in* AMATEUR MEDIA: SOCIAL, CULTURAL AND LEGAL PERSPECTIVES 94 (Dan Hunter et al. eds., 2012); Jane M. Becker, *Stories around the Digital Campfire: Fan Fiction and Copyright Law in the Age of the Internet*, 14 CONN. PUB. INT. L.J. 133 (2014).

[35] Becker, *supra* note 34, at 136.

[36] SCHWABACH, *supra* note 33, at 8.

[37] BOOTH, *supra* note 33, at 133.

[38] PAUL BOOTH, DIGITAL FANDOM: NEW MEDIA STUDIES 2 (2010).

[39] BOOTH, *supra* note 33, at 13–15.

[40] *Id.* at 26.

are seen to be a form of pastiche that simultaneously mirrors and subverts the original narrative through a nostalgic interaction with the texts.[41]

The continuing development of a plethora of social media platforms presents an ongoing challenge for copyright law. On the Internet, one often sees amateur reworks of well-known images – often using cartoon or superhero characters, and celebrities – to express viewpoints or meanings different from the original connotations. Social networking sites like Facebook and Instagram are filled with such irreverent images and memes, while YouTube contains countless fanvids that use the complete original iconic song from a pop singer to accompany performances by fans. In her recent study of four predominant social media sites – Facebook, YouTube, Twitter, and Wikipedia – Corinne Tan argues that by virtue of the technological features on all four sites, there are "multiple possibilities for a user to indulge in generative behaviours, such as the creation, modification and dissemination of content."[42] Moreover, the fact that such activities "can be easily undertaken on [these] sites exposes users to higher risks of copyright infringement … [and] the technological features 'nudge' users to behave in certain ways" that violate the exclusive rights of copyright holders.[43] At the same time, the GIFs available on Facebook Messages side by side with emoticon options, as well as the myriad GIFs and other images posted by users on their walls, call into question whether these may be defined as PSCP. The ready availability of video editing software, video hosting websites, and social media platforms makes it much easier today than ever before for individuals to engage in the production and dissemination of multimedia works, but it is still open for the trier of fact to differentiate legitimate parodies from illegitimate rip-offs.[44]

3 THE "TRANSFORMATIVE USE" DOCTRINE – US AND THE REST

A *The United States – Fair Use and the Transformative Use Doctrine*

The fair use defense is widely believed to have its American origins in Justice Story's test for a fair and bona fide abridgement as set out in his 1841 decision in *Folsom v. Marsh*.[45] If prima facie copyright infringement was found, the "fair use" defense as codified in section 107 of the 1976 Copyright Act can nonetheless provide a safe harbor for the defendant, especially if transformative elements may be discerned in the infringing work.[46]

Pierre Leval, then a judge of the United States District Court for the Southern District of New York, published an influential article in 1990 that considered whether imprecision – the absence of a clear standard – in the fair use doctrine was a strength or a weakness.[47] Leval was concerned that fair use "should be perceived not as a disorderly basket of exceptions to the rules of copyright, nor as a departure from the principles governing that body of law, but rather as a rational, integral part of copyright."[48] In particular, he advocated instilling a coherent and useful set of principles in the fair use doctrine, such that "the use must be of a character that serves the

[41] *Id.*

[42] Corinne H. Y. Tan, *Technological 'Nudges' and Copyright on Social Media Sites*, 1 INTELL. PROP. QUART. 62, 67 (2015). *See also* Jonathan Zittrain, *The Generative Internet*, 119 HARV. L. REV. 1974, 1980–82 (2006).

[43] Tan, *supra* note 42, at 75.

[44] Suzor, *supra* note 13, at 237.

[45] 9 F. Cas. 342, 349 (C.C.D. Mass. 1841) (No. 4901).

[46] Copyright Act 1976, 17 U.S.C. §107 (2015).

[47] Pierre N. Leval, *Toward a Fair Use Standard*, 103 HARV. L. REV. 1105 (1990).

[48] *Id.* at 1107.

copyright objective of stimulating productive thought and public instruction without excessively diminishing the incentives for creativity."[49]

In his analysis of the four statutory fair use factors, Leval was of the view that factor one – the "purpose and character of the use" – is the "soul of fair use."[50] Explaining that this consideration raises the question of justification, i.e., "Does the use fulfill the objective of copyright law to stimulate creativity for public illumination?,"[51] he emphasized that the answer turns primarily on whether, and to what extent, the challenged use is transformative. Leval frames the inquiry as follows:

> The use must be productive and must employ the quoted matter in a different manner or for a different purpose from the original . . . [If] the secondary use adds value to the original – if the quoted matter is used as raw material, transformed in the creation of new information, new aesthetics, new insights and understandings – this is the very type of activity that the fair use doctrine intends to protect for the enrichment of society.[52]

The phrase "transformative use" has surged into prominence in fair use jurisprudence ever since the US Supreme Court in 1994 embraced transformativeness as the cynosure of fair use in *Campbell*.[53] The decision is important in its emphasis on how a highly transformative use of an original work may qualify the secondary infringing work for fair use protection even if the latter was commercial in nature, rebutting presumptions in earlier cases.[54] The *Campbell* court concluded that the first factor in a fair use inquiry should be examined with reference to its transformative nature in the manner that Pierre Leval has argued in his 1990 law review article. Justice Souter held:

> The central purpose of this investigation is to see . . . whether the new work merely "supersede[s] the objects" of the original creation ("supplanting" the original), or instead adds something new, with a further purpose or different character, altering the first with new expression, meaning, or message; it asks, in other words, whether and to what extent the new work is "transformative."[55]

More emphatically, Justice Souter laid the groundwork for the transformative use doctrine – especially for commercial parodies, appropriation art, and fan communities – to flourish over the next two decades:

> the goal of copyright, to promote science and the arts, is generally furthered by the creation of transformative works. Such works thus lie at the heart of the fair use doctrine's guarantee of breathing space within the confines of copyright, . . . and the more transformative the new work, the less will be the significance of other factors, like commercialism, that may weigh against a finding of fair use.[56]

In respect of the first factor of fair use, this approach requires courts to examine the "purpose and character of the use," but neither "purpose" nor "character" is defined in the statute. Courts therefore may consider a kaleidoscope of relevant factors like what kind of transformation is

49 *Id.* at 1110.
50 *Id.* at 1116.
51 *Id.* at 1111.
52 *Id.* (internal citations omitted).
53 *Campbell*, 510 U.S. 569 (1994).
54 *See, e.g.*, Harper & Row Pubs. Inc. v. Nation Enterprises, 471 U.S. 539 (1985); Sony Corp. of America v. Universal City Studios, 464 U.S. 417 (1984).
55 *Campbell*, 510 U.S. at 579 (internal citations omitted).
56 *Id.* at 579.

present in the secondary work, the track record of the author of the secondary work, the extent of commentary or criticism present in the secondary work, the significance of the secondary use to research or study, as well as its public benefit.[57] Indeed the transformative use doctrine in the first factor of fair use is a difficult one to elucidate. Nonetheless the transformative test has become the defining standard for fair use, and has risen to the top of the agenda of the copyright academic community in the US in the last five years.[58] Jane Ginsburg concludes that the last twenty years have marked the "extraordinary expansion" of the fair use doctrine, and in particular, the concept of transformative use, with recent cases demonstrating a shift from focusing on finding a "transformative work" to discovering a "transformative purpose."[59]

Most of the Circuit Court decisions in the last decade on fair use have hailed from the Second and Ninth Circuits, with a handful from the Federal,[60] First,[61] Third,[62] Fourth,[63] Tenth,[64] Seventh,[65] and Eleventh[66] Circuits, and virtually nothing of note from the Fifth, Sixth, and Eighth Circuits. Post-*Campbell*, the transformation use doctrine as consistently articulated by the Second Circuit for over a decade obviates the distinction between parody and satire, and is broad enough for caricature and pastiche to qualify as transformative uses. It is succinctly stated as:

> If "the secondary use adds value to the original – if [copyrightable expression in the original work] is used as raw material, transformed in the creation of new information, new aesthetics, new insights and understandings – this is the very type of activity that the fair use doctrine intends to protect for the enrichment of society."[67]

The Second Circuit did not require the secondary work to comment on the original work or on the original author/artist, so long as a transformative nature may "reasonably be perceived."[68] More importantly, in 2013 the Ninth Circuit in *Seltzer v. Green Day*[69] has aligned itself with the Second Circuit in adopting Leval's formulation: whether "the quoted matter is used as raw material, transformed in the creation of new information, new aesthetics, new insights and understandings." Generally, courts have found a transformative *purpose* both where the defendant combines copyrighted expression with original expression to produce a new creative work,

57 U.S. CONST., Art. I, § 8, cl. 8.

58 *See, e.g.*, Matthew D. Bunker & Clay Calvert, *The Jurisprudence of Transformation: Intellectual Incoherence and Doctrinal Murkiness Twenty Years after* Campbell v. Acuff-Rose Music, 12 DUKE LAW & TECH. REV. 92 (2012).

59 Jane C. Ginsburg, *Copyright 1992–2012: The Most Significant Development?*, 23 FORDHAM INTELL. PROP., MEDIA & ENT. L.J. 465, 487–89 (2012).

60 *See, e.g.*, Oracle America Inc. v. Google Inc., 750 F. 3d 1339 (Fed Cir. 2014); Oracle America, Inc. v. Google LLC, 886 F. 3d 1179 (Fed. Cir. 2018).

61 *See, e.g.*, Society of Holy Transfiguration Monastery Inc. v. Gregory, 689 F. 3d 29 (1st Cir. 2012).

62 *See, e.g.*, Peter Murphy v. Millennium Radio Group LLC, 650 F. 3d 295 (3rd Cir. 2011).

63 *See, e.g.*, AV ex rel Vanderhye v. iParadigms LLC, 562 F. 3d 630 (4th Cir. 2009) ("*Vanderhye*"); Bouchat v. Baltimore Ravens LP, 737 F. 3d 932 (4th Cir. 2013) ("*Bouchat*").

64 *See, e.g.*, Shell v. DeVries, 2007 WL 4269047 (10th Cir. 2007).

65 *See, e.g.*, Kienitz v. Sconnie Nation LLC, 766 F. 3d 756 (7th Cir. 2014) ("*Kienitz*"); Brownmark Films LLC v. Comedy Partners, 682 F. 3d 687 (7th Cir. 2012).

66 *See, e.g.*, Cambridge University Press v. Patton, 769 F. 3d 1232 (11th Cir. 2014); Suntrust Bank, 268 F. 3d 1257, 1270 (11th Cir. 2001).

67 *Cariou*, 714 F. 3d 694, 706 (2d Cir. 2013); *Koons II*, 467 F. 3d 244, 251–52 (2d Cir. 2006) (quoting Castle Rock Entertainment Inc. v. Carol Publishing Group Inc., 150 F. 3d 132, 142 (2d Cir. 1998)). Note however a recent decision of the Seventh Circuit was less enamored of this approach. *See Kienitz*, 766 F. 3d 756, 758 (7th Cir. 2014) ("We're skeptical of *Cariou*'s approach, because asking exclusively whether something is 'transformative' not only replaces the list in § 107 but also could override 17 U.S.C. § 106(2), which protects derivative works.").

68 *Cariou*, 714 F. 3d 694, 707 (2d Cir. 2013).

69 Seltzer v. Green Day, 725 F. 3d 1170, 1176 (9th Cir. 2013) ("*Seltzer*").

and where the defendant uses a copyrighted work in a different context to serve a different function than the original.[70] The Second Circuit further clarifies: "Added value or utility is not the test: a transformative work is one that serves a new and different function from the original work and is not a substitute for it."[71]

The tension between copyright interests and the First Amendment is apparent. The Copyright Act, enacted by Congress under the authority of the US Constitution's Copyright Clause, grants individuals monopoly-like power to preclude others from using copyrighted material in their expression. It is this "paradox" that creates the tension: copyright laws grant a copyright owner the right to suppress or abridge another person's freedom of speech when that person seeks to express copyrighted material. In *Campbell*, the Supreme Court underscored the importance of protecting parody as fair use, but did not explicitly refer to the First Amendment. Souter J merely asserted that "parody has an obvious claim to transformative value."[72] In *Hustler Magazine v. Falwell*, where Jerry Falwell sued *Hustler Magazine* alleging that the publisher had intentionally inflicted emotional distress on him through a parody advertisement depicting him as drunk, immoral, and hypocritical, the Supreme Court reiterated that:

> At the heart of the First Amendment is the recognition of the fundamental importance of the free flow of ideas and opinions on matters of public interest and concern. [T]he freedom to speak one's mind is not only an aspect of individual liberty – and thus a good unto itself – but also is essential to the common quest for truth and the vitality of society as a whole.[73]

Although the case concerned offensive political cartoons and vulgar caricatures of public figures, Rehnquist CJ's concerns about stifling political discourse comports with prevailing judicial sentiments about the importance of parody (defined broadly).[74] While the critical message in a parody that comments directly on the original work or its author can be easily discerned, the ideas expressed in satire, caricature, or pastiche may be more obtuse. The famous comment by the Supreme Court in *Hurley* that "a narrow, succinctly articulable message is not a condition of constitutional protection"[75] appears to have been implicitly subsumed within the modified Leval test – *whether the secondary work may reasonably be perceived to have transformed the original in the creation of new information, new aesthetics, new insights and understandings* – that presently holds sway over the Second and Nine Circuits. This broader approach to transformative use allows for uses of the original work that do not comment on the original or may not even have a critical bearing on the original, so long as the original has been used in the creation of something *new*. Under this rubric, it would appear that most forms of PSCP are transformative uses. It should however be noted that the Second Circuit recently appeared to have retreated from such an expansive reading of transformative use in *TCA Television Corp v. McCollum*, where the court found the defendants' verbatim incorporation of more than a

[70] Warner Bros Entertainment, Inc. v. RDR Books, 575 F. Supp. 2d 513, 541 (S.D.N.Y. 2008) ("Warner"). In a number of recent Circuit Court decisions, fair use was not found in the absence of such a transformative purpose. *See, e.g.*, VHT, Inc. v. Zillow Group, Inc., 918 F.3d 723 (9th Cir. 2019); Brammer v. Violent Hues Prods., LLC, 922 F.3d 255 (4th Cir. 2019); Oracle America, Inc. v. Google LLC, 886 F. 3d 1179 (Fed. Cir. 2018); Fox News Network LLC v. TVEyes, Inc., 883 F. 3d 169 (2d Cir. 2018); Capitol Records LLC v. ReDigi, Inc., 910 F. 3d 649 (2d Cir. 2018); Disney Enterprises, Inc. v. VidAngel, Inc., 869 F. 3d 848 (9th Cir. 2017).

[71] Authors Guild Inc. v. HathiTrust, 755 F. 3d 87, 96 (2d Cir. 2004).

[72] *Campbell*, 510 U.S. 569, 579 (1994).

[73] Hustler Magazine v. Falwell, 485 U.S. 46, 50–51 (1988) (internal citations omitted).

[74] *Id.* at 51–55.

[75] Hurley v. Irish American Gay, Lesbian, and Bisexual Group of Boston, 515 U.S. 557, 569 (1995).

minute of the *Who's on First?* routine in their commercial production was not a fair use of the material.[76] The court observed:

> [E]ven if the Play's purpose and character are completely different from the vaudevillian humor originally animating *Who's on First?*, that, by itself, does not demonstrate that defendants' use of the Routine in the Play was transformative of the original work ... The Play may convey a dark critique of society, but it does not transform Abbott and Costello's Routine so that it conveys that message.[77]

On a number of occasions, the Supreme Court had rejected any further independent consideration of the impact of the First Amendment on copyright law, pronouncing that "copyright law contains built-in First Amendment accommodations."[78] As a "traditional contour" of copyright law, the court had held that the "fair use defense affords considerable latitude for scholarship and comment, ... even for parody."[79] I have previously argued that in many US decisions that have applied the transformative use doctrine in extending the fair use privilege to infringing works, the results might have been influenced by pertinent First Amendment considerations.[80] From the perspective of the First Amendment, these transformative uses inevitably add to the marketplace of ideas, and in certain situations can stimulate political discourse or discussion of public issues.[81] It is therefore unsurprising that once transformativeness is found, the other fairness factors pale into insignificance in the balancing.

B Australia, the United Kingdom, Hong Kong, and Singapore – Fair Dealing and the Fairness Factors

The fluidity of "parody" to morph into "satire," "caricature," "pastiche," or other related genres may result in an infringing work losing its requisite sting to enable it to fall within the protection of the categorical fair dealing exception of criticism or review of the original work.[82] The various copyright law reform reports from Australia,[83] the UK,[84] and Hong Kong[85] have all either advocated the enactment of a general fair dealing provision like in the US or a categorical fair dealing exception broad enough to cover parody and its related genres of humor. It was generally accepted that the incumbent categorical exceptions were inadequate in striking a fair balance between the different interests of rights owners, creators, and content users in the twenty-first century.

76 TCA Television Corp. v. McCollum, 839 F. 3d 168 (2d Cir. 2016). Judge Raggi commented: "Insofar as *Cariou* might be thought to represent the high-water mark of our court's recognition of transformative works, it has drawn some criticism." *Id.* at 181.

77 *Id.* at 181.

78 Eldred v. Ashcroft, 537 U.S. 186, 219 (2003) ("Eldred"). *See also* Golan v. Holder, 132 S Ct 873, 890 (2012); Harper & Row Publishers, Inc. v. Nation Enterprises, 471 U.S. 539, 560 (1985).

79 Eldred, 537 U.S. 186, 219–20 (2003).

80 *See* David Tan, *The Lost Language of the First Amendment in Copyright Fair Use: A Semiotic Perspective of the "Transformative Use" Doctrine Twenty-Five Years On*, 26 FORDHAM INTELL. PROP., MEDIA & ENT. L.J. 311 (2016).

81 *Id.* at 357–58, 372–73.

82 *See* Copyright, Designs and Patents Act 1988 s 30 (U.K.); Copyright Act 1968 (Cth) s 41 (Australia); Copyright Act (Cap 63) s 36 (Singapore); Copyright Ordinance (Cap 528) s 39(1) (Hong Kong).

83 AUSTRALIAN LAW REFORM COMMISSION, COPYRIGHT AND THE DIGITAL ECONOMY: FINAL REPORT, ALRC REPORT 122 (2013) ("ALRC Report").

84 IAN HARGREAVES, DIGITAL OPPORTUNITY: A REVIEW OF INTELLECTUAL PROPERTY AND GROWTH (2011) ("Hargreaves Report").

85 LEGISLATIVE COUNCIL PANEL ON COMMERCE AND INDUSTRY, TREATMENT OF PARODY UNDER THE COPYRIGHT REGIME, 18 MARCH 2014 ("HK LegCo Report").

Singapore responded first in 2004 by introducing the open-ended US approach in Singapore to complement the categorical Australian and UK models.[86] Singapore's fair dealing provision has undergone several changes since its original enactment in 1987. Originally, section 35(2) was modeled largely on section 40 of the Australian Copyright Act,[87] thereby inheriting the UK categorical model where fair dealing is permitted only for specific enumerated purposes, as opposed to the US open-ended model. However, the simultaneous incorporation of the third Australian fairness factor into Singapore's general fair dealing suggests that the Singapore Parliament had not intended to transplant wholesale the US approach.[88] It was emphasized by the then law minister that the amendment was "not connected with the [US–Singapore Free Trade Agreement]."[89] Rather, the Ministry of Law had undertaken a comprehensive review of foreign fair dealing jurisprudence before arriving at the current section 35(2),[90] and a deliberate decision was made to retain the categorical fair dealing approach together with the Australian fairness factors while adopting the more open-ended US model for purposes falling outside these categories. To date, there has been no case relating to PSCP that has invoked this general fair dealing in the Singapore courts.

In the UK, the Gowers Review in 2006 had earlier recommended the creation of a fair dealing exception for the purpose of caricature, parody, or pastiche ("parody exception").[91] But it was not till the release of the Hargreaves Report in 2011 that the UK government responded positively to introduce section 30A(1) to the Copyright, Designs and Patents Act 1988 which states: "Fair dealing with a work for the purposes of caricature, parody or pastiche does not infringe copyright in the work."[92] This new fair dealing provision came into force on October 1, 2014,[93] and it has yet to be argued before the English courts. The reasons – as well as objections – for including this fair dealing provision are well canvassed in the Gowers Review, the Hargreaves Report, and the UK Parody Report and will not be further discussed here.[94] They are generally aligned with the issues raised in the ALRC Report, which culminated in Australia adding section 41A to the Copyright Act 1968, which states: "A fair dealing with a literary, dramatic, musical or artistic work, or with an adaptation of a literary, dramatic or musical work, does not constitute an infringement of the copyright in the work if it is for the purpose of parody or satire." This provision came into force on 11 December 2006.[95] While there have been a number of academic

[86] Copyright Act (Cap 63), s 35(2).

[87] Copyright Act 1968 (Cth), s 40.

[88] *See* Copyright Act (Cap 63) s 35(2)(e); Copyright Act 1968 (Cth) s 40(2)(c). The third Australian fairness factor to be evaluated in considering fair dealing for the purpose of research or study is also Singapore's current fifth fairness factor for general fair dealing. This factor requires the court to consider "the possibility of obtaining the work or adaptation within a reasonable time at an ordinary commercial price."

[89] Singapore Parliamentary Debates, Official Report (Nov. 16, 2004) vol. 78, col. 1070 (Prof. S. Jayakumar, Minister for Law) [*Parliamentary Debate (16 Nov 2004)*]; David Tan, *The Transformative Use Doctrine and Fair Dealing in Singapore: Understanding the "Purpose and Character" of Appropriation Art*, 24 Sing. Acad. L.J. 832, 833–34 (2012).

[90] *Parliamentary Debate (Nov. 16, 2004)*, *supra* note 89, at col. 1052.

[91] Gowers Review of Intellectual Property 4.90 (2006) at [4.90] ("Gowers Review").

[92] *Hargreaves Report*, *supra* note 84.

[93] Copyright and Rights in Performances (Quotation and Parody) Regulations 2014 (No. 2356/2014).

[94] For academic commentaries on the parody fair dealing provision, *see* Ronan Deazley, *Copyright and Parody: Taking Backward the Gowers Review?*, 73 Mod. L. Rev. 785 (2010); Jonathan Griffiths, *Fair Dealing after Deckmyn – the United Kingdom's Defence for Caricature, Parody or Pastiche*, *in* Research Handbook on Intellectual Property in Media and Entertainment 64 (Megan Richardson & Sam Ricketson eds., 2017).

[95] Copyright Amendment Act 2006 (Cth) s 2. Section 103AA, which covers fair dealing of an audiovisual item for the purpose of parody or satire, shares similar wording with section 41A, and will not be separately discussed here. *See* Copyright Act 1968 (Cth) ss 41A and 103AA.

commentaries on section 41A,[96] this provision has not been tested in the Australian courts. In Hong Kong, the road to a similar categorical fair dealing exception is a rocky one fraught with political difficulties since extensive public consultations commenced in 2006.[97] Another round of public consultations resumed in 2013 when the new Legislative Council (LegCo) took office, and views regarding a parody exception were polarized. Nevertheless, the LegCo introduced the Copyright (Amendment) Bill 2014 in June 2014 which contained a new fair dealing exception in the proposed section 39A(1): "Fair dealing with a work for the purpose of parody, satire, caricature or pastiche does not infringe any copyright in the work."[98] Unfortunately, the bill generated a new wave of public antagonism as the debate shifted to one advocating a copyright exception to user-generated content (UGC) on the Internet.[99] As at today, Hong Kong lags behind its Commonwealth counterparts without a fair dealing exception broad enough to cover PSCP, and authors of works that contain elements of PSCP can only seek limited refuge under section 39(1) of Copyright Ordinance (Hong Kong), which covers fair dealing with a work for the purpose of criticism or review.

Although there is a dearth of cases in the UK and Australia on the new fair dealing exception, it is important to note that the European Court of Justice (CJEU) in *Deckmyn v. Vandersteen* has recently considered the interpretation of Article 5(3)(k) of the EU Directive 2001/29, which provides for exceptions and limitations to copyright and article 22(1) of the Belgian Law of June 30, 1994 on copyright and related rights (*Belgisch Staatsblad*) which states that: "Once a work has been lawfully published, its author may not prohibit … caricature, parody and pastiche, observing fair practice."[100] Willy Vandersteen was the author/creator of the drawing at issue; the original drawing – a representation of one of the comic book's main characters wearing a white tunic and throwing coins to people who are trying to pick them up – had appeared on the cover of the *Suske en Wiske* comic book entitled *De Wilde Weldoener* (which may roughly be translated as *The Compulsive Benefactor*), which was completed in 1961. The defendant Johan Deckmyn was a politician. At a reception, Deckmyn handed out calendars where on the cover page of those calendars, the central character was replaced by the mayor of the city of Ghent and the people picking up the coins were replaced by people wearing veils and people of color.

Deckmyn and his codefendants submitted that the drawing at issue is a political cartoon which falls within the scope of parody under Belgian law, and the issue of what constituted a parody was referred to the CJEU. The CJEU emphasized that the law must aim to strike a fair balance between, on the one hand, the interests and rights of authors, and, on the other, the freedom of expression of the user of a protected work who is relying on the exception for parody.[101] As a result, the court ruled that parody should be given a broad interpretation, and that the "essential characteristics of parody, are, first, to evoke an existing work, while being noticeably different from it, and secondly, to constitute an expression of humour or mockery."[102] More importantly, the court held the concept of "parody," within the meaning of that provision,

96 *See, e.g.*, Suzor, *supra* note 13; Graeme W. Austin, *Four Questions about the Australian Approach to Fair Dealing Defenses to Copyright Infringement*, 57 J. Copy. Soc'y U.S.A. 611 (2010).

97 *See* Wenwei Guan, *When Copyrights Meet Human Rights: 'Cyberspace Article 23' and Hong Kong's Copyright Protection in the Digital Era*, 42 H.K.L.J. 785 (2012).

98 Copyright (Amendment) Bill 2014, cl. 19, www.legco.gov.hk/yr13-14/english/bills/b201406131.pdf.

99 For an analysis of the issues surrounding this debate, *see* Wenwei Guan, *Fair Dealing Doctrine Caught between Parody and UGC Exceptions: Hong Kong's 2014 Copyright Amendment and Beyond*, 45 H.K.L.J. 1 (2015).

100 Deckmyn v. Vandersteen, Case C-201/13 (CJEU, September 3, 2014) at [5]–[6].

101 *Id.* at [27].

102 *Id.* at [33].

is *not* subject to the following conditions: (i) the parody should display an original character of its own, other than that of displaying noticeable differences with respect to the original parodied work; (ii) it could reasonably be attributed to a person other than the author of the original work itself; (iii) it should relate to the original work itself or mention the source of the parodied work.[103] This broad interpretation of "parody" arguably covers the other genres like "satire," "caricature," and "pastiche." But the national court still had to determine, in the light of all the circumstances of the case in the main proceedings, whether the application of the exception for parody, on the assumption that the drawing at issue fulfills the essential requirements of parody, preserves that *fair* balance; a weighing exercise must still be conducted by the court.[104]

It has also been argued by academic commentators, at least in the Australian context, that "parody or satire" in section 41A should not be construed narrowly.[105] If "parody" was interpreted to mean only "target parody" and "satire" to be only "weapon parody," then other forms of artistic expressions such as "pastiche" might not be capable of being categorized as fair dealing under section 41A. This would render the Australian provision narrower than the UK provision. As a form of intentional unconcealed aesthetic imitation, which Richard Dyer explains is different from "reproduction," pastiche is an "evaluatively open" form of imitation that is sometimes assimilated within the term "parody."[106] If one accepts Dyer's analysis of pastiche in that by referencing genres of works, it encourages "intellectual reflection" of "frameworks of understanding and feeling in a culture,"[107] then pastiche may well be seen to have changed the purpose or character of the original material in "the creation of new information, new aesthetics, new insights and understandings."[108]

It is often said that the fairness of dealing is "a question of degree and impression."[109] In respect of what is "fair" dealing, jurisprudence in the UK, Australia, and Singapore indicates that courts must first determine which categorical exception the infringing use falls into, and then weigh the fairness factors in light of all the circumstances to make a determination whether the unauthorized use is ultimately fair.[110] This stands in contrast to the US approach post-*Campbell*, where the first factor – supplanted by the "transformative use" doctrine – may trump all the other factors. Generally, the four fairness factors are: the purpose and character of the dealing, including whether such dealing is of a commercial nature or is for nonprofit educational purposes; the nature of the work or adaptation; the amount and substantiality of the part copied taken in relation to the whole work or adaptation; the effect of the dealing upon the potential market for, or value of, the work or adaptation.

i Purpose and Character of the Dealing

The first factor, of "purpose and character of the dealing," features in the majority of UK cases decided before the 2014 parody amendment. This phrase is similarly used in the first

[103] *Id.*
[104] *Id.* at [34].
[105] Condren et al., *supra* note 15.
[106] Dyer, *supra* note 25, at 23–25.
[107] *Id.* at 179–80.
[108] *Cariou*, 714 F. 3d 694, 706 (2d Cir. 2013); *Koons II*, 467 F. 3d 244, 251–52 (2d Cir. 2006).
[109] Bently & Sherman, *infra* note 112 at [2.1].
[110] This is the approach adopted for examining whether a use is fair for the purpose of "criticism or research." Most academic commentators have suggested that a similar balancing of fairness factors should be conducted for PSCP fair dealing. *See, e.g.*, Suzor, *supra* note 13; David Tan & Benjamin Foo, *The Unbearable Lightness of Fair Dealing: Towards an Autochthonous Approach in Singapore*, 28 Sing. Acad. L.J. 124 (2006). For a recent application of the general fair dealing defense in Singapore where the Singapore Court of Appeal weighed all the factors, *see* Global Yellow Pages Ltd v. Promedia Directories Pte Ltd, [2017] SGCA 28 at [73]–[91] (Sing.).

factor of the US general fair use provision, which the courts there have virtually supplanted with the "transformative use" doctrine. Lord Ellenborough first conceived this notion in *Cary v. Kearsley*, observing that "a man may fairly adopt part of the work of another ... *for the promotion of science, and the benefit of the public*."[111] Later cases expanded this principle and consistently found fair dealing more likely where "the defendant can show that they have added to or recontextualized the part taken ... [or] if they can show that the dealing was transformative."[112] Contrastingly, the courts have rejected the fair dealing defense when the defendant's work was "not a mental operation involving thought and labour and producing some original result, but a mechanical operation with scissors and paste, without the slightest pretension to an original result of any kind."[113] I have also argued elsewhere that a change in purpose or change in character is essentially what makes the secondary use "transformative," and courts in the Commonwealth common law jurisdictions might be able to draw some guidance from the US "transformative use" doctrine in the interpretation of the first fairness factor.[114] In most PSCP scenarios, the secondary work, borrowing from the judgment in *Campbell*, can be said to add "something new, with a further purpose or different character, altering the first with new expression, meaning, or message." Condren et al. have also observed that satire is "defined primarily by *purpose* rather than structure or technique."[115] In uses of PSCP, audiences who are culturally familiar with the semiotic markers of the original works and the humorous play-frames in which the secondary uses are situated are "forewarned about what to expect" and "such expectations affect the reception of the stimuli which follow";[116] they may or may not like the resulting humor, but if the play-frame was clear, they are reasonably likely to perceive the difference in purpose from the original.[117]

Whether the infringing work has a commercial purpose is another aspect of this factor.[118] In *De Garis v. Neville Jeffress Pidler*, the Federal Court of Australia, citing the US Eleventh Circuit, went as far as to say that "commercial nature of the use militates quite strongly against a finding of fair use ... a commercial purpose makes copying ... 'presumptively unfair.'"[119] These two dimensions to the first factor highlight a tension between the proprietary rights of the copyright owner and the need for unimpeded access to works for the creation of new works. Although the assessment of fairness is fact-specific, the trend in UK and Australian decisions shows that the utilitarian objectives of copyright law in advancing creativity and innovation often trump the commerciality of the dealing.[120]

111 Cary v. Kearsley, (1802) 4 Esp. 168, 170 (Eng.).

112 Lionel Bently & Brad Sherman, Intellectual Property Law, at [2.1.2] (4th ed. 2014).

113 Walter v. Steinkopff, [1892] 3 Ch. 489, 495 (Eng.); Time Warner Entertainment v. Channel Four Television Corporation, [1994] EMLR 1, 13 ("*Time Warner*") (Eng.).

114 Tan, *supra* note 89, at 852–53, 862–66. The Singapore Court of Appeal appeared to have accepted the relevance of US and Australian decisions when evaluating fair dealing. Global Yellow Pages Ltd v. Promedia Directories Pte Ltd, [2017] SGCA 28, at [76] (Sing.).

115 Condren et el., *supra* note 15, at 406 (emphasis added).

116 *Id. See also* Booth, *supra* note 38.

117 Such a perception would also render the work "transformative." *See Cariou*, 714 F. 3d at 707.

118 Newspaper Licensing Agency v. Meltwater Holding BV, [2011] EWCA Civ 890 at [41]; De Garis v. Neville Jeffress Pidler Pty Ltd, (1990) 18 IPR 292, 302 ("De Garis").

119 *De Garis*, 18 IPR at 301 (citing Pacific Southern Co, Inc. v. Duncan, 744 F. 2d 1490, 1496 (11th Cir. 1984)).

120 For cases where courts have found fair dealing because the dealing involved a distinct purpose from the original work despite the defendants' commercial use of the work, *see* Time Warner, [1994] EMLR 1 (Eng.); British Broadcasting Corporation v. British Satellite Broadcasting Ltd, [1990] Ch 141 (Eng.) ("BBC").

ii Nature of the Work

The second factor appears in Commonwealth case law as synonymous with whether the work is unpublished.[121] Courts consistently find the use of an unpublished work to be a more substantial infringement of copyright than publication of a published work. This greater protection given to unpublished works recognizes the author's "right to prevent its being published at all"[122] or the "right to control the first public appearance of his undisseminated expression."[123] The underlying concern in affording unpublished works additional protection is one of fairness as "it would be manifestly unjust that an unpublished literary work should, without the consent of the author, be subject of public criticism, review or newspaper summary."[124] In US case law, this factor calls for "recognition that some works are closer to the core of intended copyright protection than others with the consequence that fair use is more difficult to establish when the former works are copied."[125] The US Supreme Court noted that this factor is unlikely "to help much in separating the fair use sheep from the infringing goats in a parody case, since parodies almost invariably copy publicly known, expressive works."[126]

iii Amount and Substantiality of the Part Copied

Frequently raised in case law, the starting point of this analysis is to "consider first the number and extent of the quotations and extracts. Are they altogether too long and too many to be fair? . . . To take long extracts and attach short comments may be unfair. But short extracts and long comments may be fair."[127] However, the quantity taken does not resolve the matter as the quality of the part taken is equally important. Another consideration is the necessity of the taking to achieve the defendant's purpose.[128] Where more is taken than is necessary, the factor tends to weigh against fair dealing.[129] In *Campbell*, the US Supreme Court commented that if 2 Live Crew "had copied a significantly less memorable part of the original, it is difficult to see how its parodic character would have come through" but also cautioned that "context is everything, and the question of fairness asks what else the parodist did besides go to the heart of the original."[130] The addition of other creative elements in works of PSCP is going to be important in the balancing exercise. Even in *Cariou*, the Second Circuit was only prepared to rule summarily that twenty-five of Richard Prince's paintings were fair use, and remanded five paintings which contained "relatively minimal alterations" to the district court for determination.[131]

[121] Bently & Sherman, *supra* note 112, at [2.1.4].

[122] Beloff v. Pressdram, [1973] FSR 33, 62 (Eng.); Hyde Park Residence v. Yelland, [2001] Ch 143, 158–59 (Eng.) ("*Hyde Park Residence*").

[123] This was a point made in the US decisions. *See, e.g.*, Harper & Row Publishers Inc. v. Nation Enterprises, 471 U.S. 539, 555 (1985); Monge v. Maya Magazines, 688 F.3d 1164, 1177 (9th Cir. 2012).

[124] British Oxygen v. Liquid Air, [1925] 1 Ch. 383, 393 (Eng.).

[125] *See, e.g.*, *Campbell*, 510 U.S. at 586. For instance, literary, dramatic, musical and artistic works are "closer to the core" than compilation works.

[126] *Id.*

[127] *De Garis*, 18 IPR at 302; Associated Newspapers Group plc v. News Group Newspapers, [1986] RPC 515, 518 (Eng.).

[128] *Hyde Park Residence*, [2001] Ch. at 159; *BBC*, [1990] Ch. at 150. *See also* Bently & Sherman, *supra* note 112, at [2.1.7].

[129] *Hyde Park Residence*, [2001] Ch. at 159; *British Oxygen*, [1925] 1 Ch. at 393.

[130] *Campbell*, 510 U.S. at 588–59.

[131] *Cariou*, 714 F. 3d at 710–11. The lawsuit was later settled. *See Art in America*, www.artinamericamagazine.com/news-features/news/landmark-copyright-lawsuit-cariou-v-prince-is-settled, July 10, 2017.

iv Effect of the Dealing on Potential Market or Value

This factor requires courts to consider not only the extent of market harm caused by the particular actions of the alleged infringer, but also whether unrestricted and widespread conduct of the sort engaged in by the defendant would result in a substantially adverse impact on the potential market for the original and its adaptations. Although UK and Australian cases do not use the label "effect or consequence of the dealing,"[132] the equivalent of this factor is considered under the rubric of preventing unfair competition and unjust enrichment. In a strongly worded statement, Lord Denning succinctly captured the crux of this factor, observing that "[i]t is not fair dealing for a rival in the trade to take copyright material and use it for his own benefit."[133] The court's ultimate concern is to ensure that defendants do not "reap where they have not sown, and to take advantage of the labour and expenditure of the Plaintiffs . . . for the purpose of saving labour and expense to themselves."[134] However, where the defendant's work has a different purpose or character from the original, this factor is less likely to weigh against fair dealing.[135] There is a virtually irrebuttable presumption in prevailing US case law that when the secondary use is transformative, market substitution is unlikely.[136] However courts should be more circumspect as some copyright owners engage in commercial self-parodies, and an appropriately nuanced fair dealing analysis should be undertaken in such scenarios.[137]

4 WHO HAS THE LAST LAUGH? – THE WAY FORWARD

The fair use jurisprudence in the US today stands apart from the Commonwealth common law jurisdictions of Australia, the UK, and Singapore, with its "First Amendment accommodations" resulting in a heightened protection for PSCP. As Pamela Samuelson notes, notwithstanding the Supreme Court's unwillingness in *Campbell* to presume that parodies are fair, every subsequent parody case has been adjudged a fair use.[138] Moreover, it appears that the prevailing "transformative use" standard adopted by a majority of Circuit Courts of Appeals – particularly the Second and Ninth – privileges the first fairness factor over the other factors: so long as a use was found to be highly transformative, its commerciality does not appear to matter, and the market for such a transformative work is presumptively different from that for the original work or its derivatives/adaptations.[139] Fair use is widely perceived to be an essential doctrine in US

[132] "Effect of the dealing" is the terminology used in both section 35(2) of the Singapore Copyright Act and section 40(2) of the Australian Copyright Act. Bently and Sherman refer to this factor as "consequences of the dealing": BENTLY & SHERMAN, *supra* note 112, at [2.1.3].

[133] Hubbard v. Vosper [1972] 2 QB 84, 93 (Eng.).

[134] Walter v. Steinkopff [1892] 3 Ch 489, 495 (Eng.).

[135] *BBC* [1990] Ch. at 157, 159.

[136] Ginsburg is especially critical, observing that "if the market is 'transformative,' there is no cognizable harm because impairment to a transformative, as opposed to a traditional, market doesn't count. Thus, if the use is 'transformative,' the four-factor statutory test effectively reduces to a single factor." Jane Ginsburg, *Fair Use for Free, or Permitted-but-Paid?*, 29 BERKELEY TECH. L.J. 1383, 1400 (2014). See also Jane Ginsburg, Fair Use in the United States: Transformed, Deformed, Reformed?, [2020] Sing. J. L. S. 265, 268.

[137] For instance, Lucasfilm has a series of officially licensed self-parody merchandise which includes humorous "Expressions of Vader" and "Wookiee Photo Bomb" T-shirts. *See Top Five Best Funny Star Wars T-Shirts For Sale*, http://heavy.com/entertainment/2015/04/top-best-funny-star-wars-t-shirts-designs-gifts-merchandise-official-for-sale-mens-womens, July 6, 2017.

[138] Samuelson, *supra* note 8, at 2550.

[139] Samuelson also argues that "[c]onsistent with First Amendment values, courts should also heed market failure-based arguments that licensing markets are unlikely to develop to authorize critical commentary or unwelcome transformations." *Id.* at 2567.

copyright law that "counterbalances what would otherwise be an unreasonably broad grant of rights to authors and an unduly narrow set of negotiated exceptions and limitations."[140]

For Singapore, which has a general fair dealing provision in section 35(2) that is similar to the US fair use provision, it is possible that the Singapore courts will look at how the PSCP scenarios have been evaluated under the "transformative use" doctrine in case law. But the courts are likely to be cautious in privileging the first fairness factor over the other statutory fairness factors contained in section 35(2) since Singapore has not embraced a robust free speech culture comparable to that engendered by the First Amendment in the US.[141] Indeed while other Commonwealth common law jurisdictions might want to embrace a more liberal interpretation of the first fairness factor, they should be careful not to transplant the consequential effect of a finding of "transformative use" doctrine into their legal systems. For Australia and the UK, the parody exception contained in section 41A and section 30A(1) of their respective copyright legislation is broad enough to cover different genres of parody or PSCP, and across different media. This is where one may find some convergence with US law such that works which *may reasonably be perceived to have transformed the original in the creation of new information, new aesthetics, new insights and understandings* will fall within the categorical definition of "parody or satire" (Australia) or "parody, caricature or pastiche" (UK). However, the critical difference, as illustrated by the CJEU's decision in *Deckmyn*, is that the courts in Australia and the UK will have to systematically balance the fairness factors in each case rather than rely on a finding of transformative use as a trump card.[142] Michael Spence has noted that "the conflict between free speech and intellectual property is far more difficult to resolve in the situation exemplified by weapon parody than it is in the situation exemplified by target parody."[143] Despite the legislative amendments in Australia and the UK that have obviated distinctions between different forms of parody (or as between parody and satire which the US Supreme Court in *Campbell* had highlighted), the national courts may nonetheless take into account the relative differences when weighing the fairness factors, perhaps according commercial target parodies greater leeway than commercial weapon parodies since the latter is arguably avoiding the drudgery of creating something new and free-riding on the success of the original work.

Hong Kong presents a more interesting problem since it had not enacted a parody exception for fair dealing. It is open to the Hong Kong courts to follow the famous 1996 Canadian decision involving a parody of the Michelin Man which rejected the contention of "parody" under the category of "criticism" as a fair dealing defense to copyright infringement,[144] or to view PSCP as being covered by the freedom of speech under Article 27 of the Basic Law and Article 16 of the Hong Kong Bill of Rights, thus availing these works protection under the broad "public interest"

[140] *Id.* at 2618.

[141] While the Singapore Court of Appeal referred with approval to the finding of transformative use in *Campbell* and *Authors Guild*, the court cautioned: "the inquiry under s 35(2), in the final analysis, is necessarily fact-sensitive. … the issue of whether there has been fair dealing is one of fact and impression having regard to all the circumstances." Global Yellow Pages Ltd v. Promedia Directories Pte Ltd, [2017] SGCA 28, at [86] (Sing.).

[142] The US Supreme Court has also noted that: "[t]his is not, of course, to say that anyone who calls himself a parodist can skim the cream and get away scot free." *Campbell*, 510 U.S. at 579.

[143] Michael Spence, *Intellectual Property and the Problem of Parody*, 114 L.Q.R. 594, 613 (1998).

[144] Compagnie Générale des Établissements Michelin-Michelin & Cie v. National Automobile, Aerospace, Transportation, (1996) 71 CPR (3d) 348, 381 (Canada). *But see* Productions Avanti Ciné Vidéo Inc. v. Favreau, [1999] 177 DLR (4th) 568 (H.K.). *See also* AGL Sydney Ltd v. Shorthand County Council, (1989) 17 IPR 99 (Aust.) (not allowing the "criticism or review" fair dealing provision to be invoked for parody). However, it would appear from the Supreme Court of Canada's pentalogy of copyright decisions handed down in July 2012 that the categorical exceptions should be interpreted expansively. *See* Geist, *supra* note 1, at 171–81.

exception in section 192 of the Copyright Ordinance.[145] In any event, Hong Kong would have the benefit of the 2004 decision of the Supreme Court of Canada in *CCH Canadian Ltd v. Law Society of Upper Canada* to support a liberal reading of existing categorical fair dealing provisions to cover PSCP.[146]

Copyright is ultimately an economic incentive for creative activity that benefits society. Corporate copyright owners like Disney and Warner Brothers who have invested significantly to promote their various fictional characters and associated franchises may have a strong motivation for refusing to license in order to protect their brands and reputation. In Wendy Gordon's terms, this would constitute a secondary market failure as leaving licensing to rights owners will not ensure the most efficient use of their works.[147] PSCP may not necessarily decrease the demand for the original work and its derivatives by negatively influencing consumers' views of the original work; through mocking imitation and irreverent evocation, it can also increase demand by heightening consumer awareness of the original work. On the other hand, as Jane Ginsburg warns, when a US court perceives the use to be socially beneficial, the court may overemphasize its "transformativeness," and correspondingly underestimate the market consequences, in order to prevent the copyright owner from frustrating the social benefit.[148] Perhaps, as Ginsburg points out, there may be merit in recognizing in a certain class of cases "where the use is 'fair' only because it supposedly cannot reasonably be licensed, then permitted-but-paid should replace fair use for free."[149]

As Martin Senftleben points out, "[b]reathing space for quotations, parody and other transformations of copyright material is central to any copyright system . . . [and] in the furtherance of the cultural inspiration cycle."[150] Appropriation art and fan fiction, while borrowing heavily from the original works and canonical universe, maintain a "critical distance" in introducing many more new cultural productions and rarely intrude on the economic market of the originals and their derivatives.[151] Users on social media platforms like Facebook, Instagram, and YouTube who upload silly images and inane videos can hardly be said to be adversely impacting the demand for the original works.

Ultimately, any copyright system seeking to support the cultural innovation cycle "must provide for both rights broad enough to spur investment and creativity, and limitations broad enough to provide sufficient breathing space for freedom of expression and information."[152] PSCP tend to bruise a few egos more than they make a hole in the pockets of rights owners.[153] In

[145] Copyright Ordinance (H.K.), s. 192(3) ("Nothing in this Part affects any rule of law preventing or restricting the enforcement of copyright, on grounds of public interest or otherwise.").

[146] CCH Canadian Ltd v. Law Society of Upper Canada, [2004] 1 SCR 339, at [48] (Canada). Eight years after the *CCH Canadian* decision, Canada introduced a parody exception via the Copyright Modernization Act 2012. *See* Copyright Act 1985, s. 29 ("Fair dealing for the purpose of research, private study, education, parody or satire does not infringe copyright.").

[147] Wendy J. Gordon, *Market Failure and Intellectual Property: A Response to Professor Lunney*, B.U. L. Rev. 1031, 1033 (2002).

[148] Ginsburg, *supra* note 136, at 1385.

[149] *Id.* at 1387.

[150] Martin R. F. Senftleben, *Quotations, Parody and Fair Use*, *in* A Century of Dutch Copyright Law: Auteurswet 1912–2012 345, 345–46 (Bernt Hugenholtz et al. eds., 2012). In a similar vein, Samuelson comments that "[c]ourts should, however, be more willing to consider whether a second author's use is reasonable and customary in the authorial community in which he or she creates." Samuelson, *supra* note 8, at 2578.

[151] Condren et al, *supra* note 15, at 421. Christina Chung also argues that while substitutes may harm the economic incentives of the original author, such complementary fan works maintain a "strict dichotomy" from the original canon and may in fact enhance the authors' abilities to recapture profits. Christina Chung, *Holy Fandom, Batman! Commercial Fan Works, Fair Use, and the Economics of Complements and Market Failure*," 19 B.U. J. Sci. & Tech. L. 367, 393–96 (2013).

particular, multinational corporations who own the intellectual property rights to a panoply of works and fictional characters often continue to exploit lucrative economic opportunities unaffected by PSCP. Instead of threatening legal action to suppress irreverent and denigrating representations, perhaps rights owners should just chill,[154] and continue laughing all the way to the bank!

[152] Senftleben, *supra* note 150, at 389.

[153] Susan Linehan Faaland, *Parody and Fair Use: The Critical Question*, 57 WASH. L. REV. 163, 191 (1981) ("When a parody victim sues, one may wonder then what was really hurt: copyright or pride.").

[154] In an acrimonious lawsuit between Mattel and MCA Records over the parodic treatment of Barbie, Kozinski J, bemused by the public invectives the parties hurled at each other in the media, concluded his judgment with the apropos line: "The parties are advised to chill." Mattel Inc. v. MCA Records Inc., 296 F. 3d 894, 908 (9th Cir. 2002).

18

Cultural Impact on Copyright Exceptions: Parody in Germany and Japan

Christoph Rademacher

The battleground between copyright protection and parody exceptions is not new. The US Supreme Court tested the fair use framework provided for under US copyright law in its well-known 1994 decision regarding a parody of Roy Orbison's title song to the blockbuster movie *Pretty Woman*;[1] arguably, no other single court decision had a similar impact on the copyright law treatment of parodies both in the US and internationally. The notion that the use of copyright-protected content in a parody should be generally permissible under copyright law has gained widespread traction across most jurisdictions. At the same time, the question of what exactly constitutes a parody varies from country to country and from culture to culture. This chapter provides an overview of the development of copyright exceptions related to parody under German and Japanese law, and highlights how a different tradition of parody can result in different copyright law interpretation.

1 BACKGROUND: WHAT IS A PARODY?

Literature and dictionaries recognize several definitions of parody. The English-language version of Wikipedia defines a parody as "*a work created to imitate, make fun of, or comment on an original work – its subject, author, style, or some other target – by means of satiric or ironic imitation.*"[2] Quite similarly, the German literature professor Rotermund defined a parody as a "literary work that adopts formal stylistic properties and often content from other works, but modifies the adopted parts to create a clear and often comical distance between the different layers."[3] Both the notion and the term parody date back to ancient Greek literature, which mentioned a *parodia*[4] as a narrative poem imitating the style and prosody of epics "but treating light, satirical or mock-heroic subjects."[5] Traditional culture and literature in Japan developed a somewhat different sense of parody. Rather than to mock or to otherwise ridicule former works, certain types of pre-Meiji literature would explicitly refer to former well-known poems to "lighten" such originals and to add significance and depth to the adopting work.[6] That said,

[1] Campbell v. Acuff-Rose Music, 510 U.S. 569 (1994).

[2] *Parody*, Wikipedia, https://en.wikipedia.org/wiki/Parody, last accessed August 2017.

[3] Erwin Rotermund, Die Parodie in der modernen deutschen Lyrik [The Parody in Modern German Lyric Poetry] 9 (1963).

[4] The word parody derives from the Greek terms *para* (παρά = beside, counter, against) and *oide* (ᾠδή = song).

[5] Simon Dentith, Parody 10 (2000).

[6] R. H. Blyth, Oriental Humor 245 (1959).

both Western and traditional Japanese forms of parody require two basic elements for being effective: (1) the existence of a prior work that is referenced or "parodied," and (2) knowledge of the existence of such prior work by the target audience of the parody. Other than such a very basic common understanding, the Japanese and the German approach to parody and both countries' application of copyright protection toward works that become subject to "parody" differ significantly.

2 PARODY UNDER GERMAN COPYRIGHT LAW UNTIL 2016

German copyright law does not have a general fair use exception like the US. Also, there is no specific exception for parodies under German law. Commentators and courts point to the constitutional law freedom of expression and art[7] as a legal basis for a parody exception.[8] German copyright law has two statutory exceptions to copyright owners' exclusion rights that could be applicable in the case of parody: the free use exception under Article 24 of the Copyright Act and the copyright exception for the purpose of quotation under Article 51 of the Copyright Act.

A *Free Use under Article 24 German Copyright Act*

Article 24 of the Copyright Act[9] allows an author to freely use the work of another person for the creation of an independent work. In assessing whether or not a parody can be covered by the free use exception under Article 24 of the Copyright Act, a court has to define the scope of protection of the original work and compare such original work with the parody. Evolving case law has provided guidance regarding the required degree of difference from the original work.

B *The* Disney *Guideposts and Their Application*

In its 1971 *Disney* decision,[10] the Federal Court of Justice provided the first comprehensive guideposts[11] according to which a parody can qualify as free use. With the intention of commemorating Walt Disney's death, a German cartoonist had published a comic strip of

[7] GRUNDGESETZ [GG] [BASIC LAW], art. 5 (Ger.), *translation at* www.gesetze-im-internet.de/englisch_gg/index.html.

(1) "Every person shall have the right freely to express and disseminate his opinions in speech, writing and pictures, and to inform himself without hindrance from generally accessible sources. Freedom of the press and freedom of reporting by means of broadcasts and films shall be guaranteed. There shall be no censorship."
(2) [. . .]
(3) "Arts and sciences, research and teaching shall be free."

[8] *See* SABINE STUHLERT, DIE BEHANDLUNG DER PARODIE IM URHEBERRECHT [THE TREATMENT OF PARODY UNDER COPYRIGHT LAW] 5 (2002) (pointing out that the intellectual property rights of authors are also guaranteed by the Basic Law and that any kind of legal assessment of a parody must balance the constitutionally guaranteed property rights of the prior work's author and the freedom of art and expression of the parodying author).

[9] Article 24 (1) Copyright Act: "An independent work created in the free use of the work of another person may be published or exploited without the consent of the author of the work used." Urheberrechtsgesetz [UrhG] [Act on Copyright and Related Rights], Sept. 9, 1965, BGBL I at 1273, last amended by Gesetz [G], Sept. 1, 2017, BGBL I at 3346, art. 24(1) (Ger.), www.gesetze-im-internet.de/englisch_urhg/englisch_urhg.html#p0013.

[10] Bundesgerichtshof [BGH] [Federal Court of Justice] March 26, 1971, NEUE JURISTISCHE WOCHENSCHRIFT [NJW] 2169, 1971 (Ger.). A partial English translation of the decision can be found at IIC 70, 1972.

[11] Article 24 of the Copyright Act had been enacted in 1961; that said, predecessors of the Copyright Act had provided for similar exceptions allowing a free use of copyright-protected content. Thus, it is somewhat surprising that the applicability of the free use exception for parody was invoked so rarely.

thirty-one picture frames that contained illustrations of one or more famous Disney characters such as Mickey Mouse or Donald Duck.[12] To qualify as a parody, the second work in question must use the content of the original work in an anti-thematic context. Such anti-thematic treatment must further be objectively recognizable by the audience. The relevant audience here is an observer who is aware of the original work and has the intellectual capabilities of understanding the parody.[13] In the specific case in question, the Federal Court of Justice found the cartoon was not objectively recognizable anti-thematic-treatment. The court held that the depicted characters overshadowed the accompanying and arguably independent text bubbles, making it too difficult to recognize anti-thematic treatment.[14] Further, the court held that even if a parody can be recognized as anti-thematic treatment, it must not use more of the content of the original work than necessary to achieve the purpose of the parody in order to be considered a free use pursuant to Article 24 of the Copyright Act.[15]

Being provided with the rather restrictive guidelines for assessing a parody defense to assertions of copyright infringement, lower courts as well as the Federal Court of Justice started to develop the free use requirements. In the 1972 decision "From tip to toe [*Von Kopf bis Fuß*]," the Regional Court of Berlin decided that a parody must intend to ridicule the specific work that is the basis for the parody to be considered a free use.[16] The daily tabloid newspaper *Bild* had published a cartoon with a figure resembling the Red Army Faction (RAF) terrorist leader Ulrike Meinhof, accompanied by the text line "From tip to toe, we focus on murder; this is our world and nothing else";[17] such text was a persiflage of the refrain line from a well-known song composed by Friederich Hollaender that went, "From tip to toe, I focus on love; this is our world and nothing else."[18] The court held that such persiflage of the song's refrain line did not qualify as anti-thematic treatment as the ridicule was directed only against Ms. Meinhof and the RAF and not against Hollaender's original song. Another example of the rather restrictive approach of German courts post-*Disney* was the decision "Laughing Sun" [*Lachende Sonne*], in which the Regional Court of Frankfurt decided that changing the text of the anti-nuclear-energy activists' logo from "Nuclear Energy – No Thanks" to "Democracy – No Thanks" did not constitute an anti-thematic treatment.[19] In 1991, the Higher Regional Court of Munich found that large parts of two comics published under the title "Anniversary-Persiflage"[20] ridiculing

[12] 1971 NJW 2169 (Ger.); in one of these frames Walt Disney himself is shown; in three others he is not actually shown himself, but is addressed by his characters. Four frames contain figures from paintings by Michelangelo and Raphael. The text accompanying these illustrations is given in speech bubbles. The deceased Walt Disney summons Donald Duck with his three nephews before him in heaven, and with their help starts transforming its inhabitants, figures of Renaissance paintings, into Disney characters. As a result, in one frame Mickey Mouse is shown posing as an angel of Raphael's paintings. After this experiment has succeeded (to an extent), a hand appears from out of a cloud, with a pointed finger touching the tip of Walt Disney's brush. There is a bang. The whole sequence turns out to be Donald Duck's dream. The story ends with the sentence: "Why don't you admit it: you all would be terribly relieved if it were Walt Disney who designs the other world."

[13] *Id.*

[14] *Id.*

[15] *Id.*

[16] Landgericht Berlin [LG Berlin] [Regional Court of Berlin] Dec. 13, 1972, Gewerblicher Rechtsschutz und Urheberrecht [GRUR] 231, 1974 (Ger.).

[17] The German original read: "*Wir sind von Kopf bis Fuß auf Morde eingestellt, denn das ist unsere Welt – und sonst gar nichts.*"

[18] The original lyrics from the song composed by Hollaender were "*ich bin von Kopf bis Fuß auf Liebe eingestellt, denn das ist unsere Welt – und sonst gar nichts.*"

[19] Landgericht Frankfurt am Main [LG Frankfurt a. M.] [Regional Court of Frankfurt] July 23, 1981, 94 Archiv für Medienrecht und Medienwissenschaft [UFITA] 334, 1982 (Ger.).

[20] The German title was "*Die hysterischen Abenteuer von ISTERIX. Jubiläums-Persiflagen" [The Hysterical Adventures of Isterix. Anniversary-Persiflage]*, mimicking the title of the original comic, *The Adventures of Asterix*.

certain features of the French comic series "Asterix"[21] did not constitute an anti-thematic treatment of the original characters or the original comic series.[22] In this case, the publisher of the allegedly infringing comics appealed to the Federal Court of Justice, providing the Federal Court of Justice with the opportunity to review its own standards more than twenty years after *Disney*.

C Asterix *Decision and Subsequent Case Law*

In *Asterix*, the Federal Court of Justice reviewed and revised the restrictive decision practice that German courts had developed.[23] Instead of strictly requiring an objectively recognizable anti-thematic treatment that authors relying on a parody defense were usually unable to prove in legal proceedings, the court introduced the new concept of internal distance between the original work and the parody as the decisive criterion. Accordingly, a parody can gain internal distance to the original work when the author of the parody employs original and creative authorship, in particular with respect to the borrowed peculiar features of the original work. In such case of original and creative authorship which can be achieved, e.g., by extensive appropriation of the protected work, the original work's features would usually "fade" in the parody as they would have superimposed on them the new and original content of the parody. As the court recognized the potential necessity to use the peculiar features of the original work to achieve the purpose of the parody, it held that it may be permissible to have such original and peculiar features visibly remaining in the parody as long as the creative authorship of the author of the parody results in a sufficiently high internal distance.[24]

Applying this criterion to the *Asterix* case, the Federal Court of Justice upheld some of the assessments of the Higher Regional Court and reversed others. It upheld the finding that the title cover of the persiflage had not developed sufficient internal distance, as it merely depicted the clearly identifiable original characters as members of a motorcycle gang.[25] It reversed, however, much of the findings of the Higher Regional Court with respect to the internal distance developed by the stories published in the persiflage. In particular, those stories that mixed contemporary political reality with the comic figures, resulting both in political comedy and a parody of the original comic heroes, were held to be independent creations of the author of the anniversary-persiflage that had developed sufficient internal distance from the original comic.

The Federal Court of Justice continued the application of the criteria of internal distance developed in *Asterix* in subsequent decisions. In the 2000 decision *Mattscheibe*,[26] it expressly

[21] The original *Adventures of Asterix* comics star the title character Asterix and his friend Obelix as part of a village of indomitable Gauls resisting Roman occupation.

[22] Oberlandesgericht München [OLG München] [Higher Regional Court of Munich], Sept. 13, 1990, ZEITSCHRIFT FÜR URHEBER- UND MEDIENRECHT [ZUM] 252, 1992 (Ger.); Oberlandesgericht München [OLG München] [Higher Regional Court of Munich], July 4, 1991, ZEITSCHRIFT FÜR URHEBER- UND MEDIENRECHT [ZUM] 252, 1992 (Ger.).

[23] Bundesgerichtshof [BGH] [Federal Court of Justice] Mar. 11, 1993, GEWERBLICHER RECHTSSCHUTZ UND URHEBERRECHT [GRUR] 191, 1994 (Ger.); a partial English translation of the decision can be found at IIC 610, 1994.

[24] *Id.*

[25] The court held that while the appearance of the characters had "been distorted in a manner which might be found amusing by a considerable number of readers," such distortion itself would not "constitute a parodic treatment of these figures." The court rejected the defendant's argument that "the statement inherent in the title drawing is that Asterix and Obelix as members of a motorcycle gang, are rebelling against modern middle-class values just as the Gauls objected to the lifestyle of the Romans," finding such interpretation "far-fetched." *Id.*

[26] Bundesgerichtshof [BGH] [Federal Court of Justice] Apr. 4, 2000, GEWERBLICHER RECHTSSCHUTZ UND URHEBERRECHT [GRUR] 703, 2000 (Ger.).

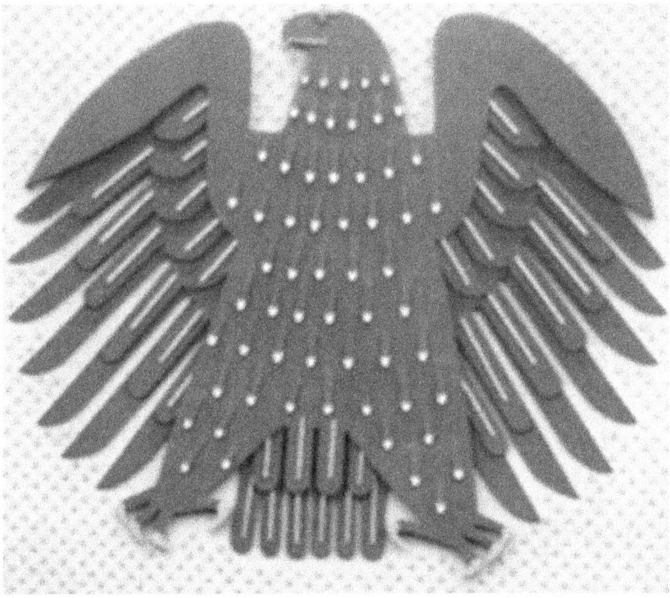

FIGURE 18.1 The Gies Eagle

criticized the appellate court[27] for failing to observe the *Asterix* framework, and decided that the defendant's satire format, *Mattscheibe*, would be a free use of a well-known German TV show despite the established fact that 68 percent of the content of the satire format came directly from the original TV show. In making this ruling, the Federal Court of Justice further moved away from its *Disney* precedent by explicitly giving up the criterion that a parody may not use too much of the mimicked original work.[28]

Three years after *Mattscheibe*, the Federal Court of Justice continued to loosen the requirements for the free use defense in the widely noted *Gies Eagle* decision.[29] Leading to the *Gies Eagle* decision, the collective society representing the estate of the sculptor Ludwig Gies asserted infringement of copyright by the weekly news magazine *Focus*. Gies had created the sculpture of the eagle shown in Figure 18.1. A reproduction of this eagle had adorned the plenary hall of the German parliament in Bonn since 1955. *Focus* referenced Gies's eagle on the cover of a 1999 issue shown in Figure 18.2, to announce a story alleging an illegitimate use of taxation measures to meet the government's budget needs, illustrated by a greedy federal eagle. The Federal Court of Justice held that the cover transformed the "dignified and somewhat lethargic but always good-natured Gies Eagle" into a "grasping and malicious bird of prey that has little in common with the original."[30] In doing so, the *Focus* parody – according to the court – maintains a clear internal distance from the borrowed created features of the older work and therefore should be regarded as an independent creation. The court, however, continued to make reference to the criterion of fading originally established in *Disney*, stating that the individual

[27] Oberlandesgericht München [OLG München] [Higher Regional Court of Munich] Oct. 23, 1997, MULTIMEDIA UND RECHT [MMR] 254, 1998 (Ger.).

[28] *Id. See also* Bernhard v. Becker, *Grenzenlose Freiheit der Satire? [No Limits for Satire?]*, 2001 NEUE JURISTISCHE WOCHENSCHRIFT [NJW] 583, 584 (Ger.).

[29] Bundesgerichtshof [BGH] [Federal Court of Justice] Mar. 20, 2003, GEWERBLICHER RECHTSSCHUTZ UND URHEBERRECHT [GRUR] 956, 2003 (Ger.); a partial English translation of the decision can be found at IIC 984, 2004.

[30] *Id.*

FIGURE 18.2 Cover: the "greedy" state

features of the older work "fade into the background" in the more recent work.[31] In allowing the free use defense for the parody of the Gies Eagle, the Federal Court of Justice extended the permissible use of parody to allow not only commentary or criticisms of the parodied work itself, but also commentary or criticisms of groups or persons for whom the copyrighted work functions as a symbol.[32]

D Parody As Quotation?

German copyright law allows the use of copyright-protected content without authorization of the author for the purpose of quotation. The relevant statute is Article 51 of the German Copyright Act,[33] which allows quotations so long as the extent of the work used for quotation

[31] *Id.*

[32] *See, e.g.*, for commentary: Bernhard v. Becker, *Parodiefreiheit und Güterabwägung - Das „Gies-Adler"-Urteil des BGH [Freedom of Parody and Balancing of Interests – the Gies Eagle Decision of the BGH]*, 2004 GEWERBLICHER RECHTSSCHUTZ UND URHEBERRECHT [GRUR] 104 (Ger.).

[33] Article 51 of the German Copyright Act: "It shall be permissible to reproduce, distribute and communicate to the public a published work for the purpose of quotation so far as such use is justified to that extent by the particular purpose. This shall be permissible in particular where

1. subsequent to publication individual works are included in an independent scientific work for the purpose of explaining the contents,
2. subsequent to publication passages from a work are quoted in an independent work of language,
3. individual passages from a released musical work are quoted in an independent musical work."

is justified and the work that quotes another work constitutes an independent creation. The question of whether or not quotation can be a defense to copyright assertions against parodies had been – at least in dicta – discussed in a number of court decisions;[34] in the past, a number of scholars had also argued for employing a quotation defense to allow parodies.[35] Nevertheless, the view that the free use defense would be more applicable to parodies has prevailed during the last decade. The one exceptional case that should be noted here was the *Germania* 3 decision that was decided on constitutional law grounds by the Federal Constitutional Court in 2000.[36] The play *Germania* 3, by the German dramatist Heiner Müller, discussed politics and society between 1914 and 1956 and had used about four pages of the text of two plays written by Bertolt Brecht; the text that was copied from Brecht's plays was marked as another author's work by being printed in italics. The Higher Regional Court of Munich had enjoined the publisher of *Germania* 3 from selling the book that contained the texts written by Brecht, triggering a constitutional complaint by the publisher who alleged a violation of the constitutional freedom of art guaranteed in Article 5(3) of the German Basic Law. The Federal Constitutional Court followed the reasoning of the publisher and held that the lower court had misunderstood the constitutional freedom of art when assessing the quotation defense under Article 51 of the Copyright Act.[37] In coming to this conclusion, the court stated that Brecht's works were representative of a certain era in Germany. Use of the text elements would not cause any significant financial consequences to Brecht's estate. In light of such circumstances, Müller's interest in making and publishing artistic expressions would prevail over the intellectual property rights of Brecht's estate. Looking at the prominent and strong defense of the quotation right established by the Federal Constitutional Court, at least one commentator forecasted an increasing relevance of the quotation defense for parodies.[38] Seventeen years after the *Germania* 3 decision, one can safely state that that forecast did not come true.

3 THE "EUROPEAN" PARODY EXCEPTION

In many areas of intellectual property law, German courts' decision-making is strongly influenced by European sources of law and their respective interpretation by European courts. As explained above, German copyright law does not contain any explicit copyright exception for parodies. The Information Society Directive (also often referred to as the InfoSoc Directive),[39] which was enacted in 2001 in order to implement the World Intellectual Property Organization (WIPO) Copyright Treaty and to harmonize certain aspects of copyright law across Europe, including but not limited to copyright exceptions, explicitly mentions parodies as a recognized

Urheberrechtsgesetz [UrhG] [Act on Copyright and Related Rights], Sept. 9, 1965, BGBL I at 1273, last amended by Gesetz [G], Sept. 1, 2017, BGBL I at 3346, art. 51 (Ger.), www.gesetze-im-internet.de/englisch_urhg/englisch_urhg.html#p0013.

34 1974 GRUR 231, *supra* note 15; 1994 GRUR 191, *supra* note 22.

35 Hans-Heinrich Schmieder, *Die Freiheit der Kunst [The Freedom of Art]*, 93 ARCHIV FÜR MEDIENRECHT UND MEDIENWISSENSCHAFT [UFITA] 63 (1982) (Ger.); Bernhard v. Becker, *Zitat und Kunstfreiheit – Das «Brecht-Zitate»-Urteil des Bundesverfassungsgerichts [Quotation and Freedom of Art – The "Brecht-Quote" Decision of the Federal Constitutional Court]*, 2000 ZEITSCHRIFT FÜR URHEBER- UND MEDIENRECHT [ZUM] 864, 866 (Ger.).

36 Bundesverfassungsgericht [BVerfG] [Federal Constitutional Court] June 29, 2000, GEWERBLICHER RECHTSSCHUTZ UND URHEBERRECHT [GRUR] 149, 2001 (Ger.).

37 The Federal Constitutional Court did not comment on the lower court's refusal to allow incorporation of Brecht's text into the play *Germania* 3 as permissible free use under Article 24 Copyright Act.

38 Becker, *supra* note 34, at 866.

39 Council Directive 2001/29/EC, 2001 O.J. (L 167) 10.

FIGURE 18.3 *BZ News* adaptation of the Zimmermann photo

category of copyright exceptions in Article 5(3).[40] In 2014, the Court of Justice of the European Union (CJEU), for the first time, had to provide further guidance as to the requirements of a parody exception under the InfoSoc Directive.

A *Background of* Deckmyn v. Vandersteen

On New Year's Eve 2011, the Belgian Flemish nationalist political party handed out 2,000 calendars. The calendar cover contained significant elements of the cover page of a 1961 "Spike and Suzy" comic titled De Wilde Weldfoener [The Wild Benefactor], shown in Figure 18.3. On the calendar cover, a figure who resembles Daniël Termont, at that time mayor of the Belgian city of Ghent – depicted as the wild benefactor – is hands out money presents to a group of dark-skinned people wearing head scarfs and turbans Figure 18.4. The heirs of Willy Vandersteen, the creator of the the "Spike and Suzy" comic series, and the series' publisher were not amused and filed a copyright infringement lawsuit against Vlaams Belang politician Johan Deckmyn and the party's gift association agency Vrijheidsfonds VZW. The Court of First Instance of Brussels held that the parody exception would not apply and that the calendar cover constituted copyright infringement. Johan Deckmyn and Vrijheidsfonds appealed to the Brussels Court of Appeals, which confirmed that Belgian copyright law had implemented the parody defense within the framework of the InfoSoc Directive.[41]

[40] Council Directive 2001/29/EC, art. 5(3), 2001 O.J. (L 167) 10, 16: "Member States may provide for exceptions or limitations to the rights provided for in Articles 2 and 3 in the following cases: . . . (k) use for the purpose of caricature, parody or pastiche."

[41] Hof van Beroep [HvB] [Court of Appeals] Brussel, 8e ch. Apr. 8, 2013, Case No. 2011/AR/914 & 915.

FIGURE 18.4 Vandersteen comic cover

It noted that any interpretation of the parody concept under Belgian law might have to follow the concept of parody as outlined in the InfoSoc Directive, and therefore referred the following questions to the CJEU:[42]

1) Is the concept of "parody" an autonomous concept in European Union law?
2) If so, must a parody satisfy the following conditions or conform to the following characteristics:
   - display an original character of its own (originality);
   - display that character in such a manner that the parody cannot reasonably be ascribed to the author of the original work;
   - seek to be humorous or to mock, regardless of whether any criticism thereby expressed applies to the original work or to something or someone else;
   - mention the source of the parodied work?
3) Must a work satisfy any other conditions or conform to other characteristics in order to be capable of being labeled as a parody?

[42] *Id.*

B CJEU Decision

The advocate general appointed to the case, Pedro Cruz Villalón, delivered his opinion on May 22, 2014; the CJEU delivered the court's opinion a few months later,[43] largely following the findings and the framework of the opinion of the advocate general.

With respect to the first question, the court held that the concept of "parody" is indeed an autonomous concept under EU law, and that it is for the CJEU to ensure a harmonized interpretation throughout the EU.[44] This answer was not unexpected, given that the CJEU had over the years prior to 2014 delivered similar decisions when holding that other exceptions and limitations set forth in Articles 5(2) and (3) of the InfoSoc Directive are subject to interpretation of the CJEU.[45]

The court went on to provide a definition of parody, holding that in "everyday language" a parody's essential characteristics are, "first, to evoke an existing work while being noticeably different from it, and, secondly, to constitute an expression of humor or mockery."[46] The CJEU further held that none of the four conditions suggested by the referring Belgian court would have to be satisfied for a work to constitute a parody, arriving at a much more liberal definition of parody than German courts had developed even post-*Asterix*.

The CJEU, however, went on to hold that the parody exception under Article 5(3) of the InfoSoc Directive has to strike a "fair balance" between the interests of the copyright holder and the "freedom of expression of the user of a protected work who is relying on the exception for parody."[47] The balance of the interests of the copyright holder and the parodist has to be assessed on a case-by-case basis. Here, the CJEU decided that in this case the drawing conveyed a discriminatory message,[48] and the estate of Willy Vandersteen had a legitimate interest in not being associated with such message. The CJEU left it for the national courts to decide whether or not the parody would indeed serve to associate the original work with a discriminatory message, in which case the fair balance would tip in favor of the original work's copyright holder.

C *Reception of* Deckmyn *in Germany*

The *Deckmyn* decision received mixed reviews from German commentators. One particularly harsh review criticized the CJEU for interpreting Article 5 of the InfoSoc Directive too broadly when it created the requirement of a fair balance test between the copyright owner's and the parody's author's interests; in doing so, it failed to even mention the three-step test incorporated in Article 5(5) of the InfoSoc Directive and basically ignored aspects of freedom of opinion.[49]

43 Case C-201/13, Deckmyn v. Vandersteen (Sept. 3, 2014), http://curia.europa.eu/juris/celex.jsf?celex=62013CJ0201&lang1=en&type=TXT&ancre=.

44 *Id.* at 15.

45 Case C-467/08, Padawan v. Sociedad Gen. de Autores y Editores de España, 2010 E.C.R. I-10098 ¶¶ 29–37; Case C-510/10, DR, TV2 Danmark v. NCB – Nordisk Copyright Bureau, ¶¶ 34–35 (April 26, 2012), http://curia.europa.eu/juris/celex.jsf?celex=62010CJ0510&lang1=en&type=TXT&ancre=; Case C-435/12, ACI Adam BV v. Stichting de Thuiskopie, ¶ 49 (April 10, 2014), http://curia.europa.eu/juris/celex.jsf?celex=62012CJ0435&lang1=en&type=TXT&ancre=.

46 Deckmyn, *supra* note 42, ¶ 20.

47 *Id.* at ¶ 27.

48 Here, the CJEU referenced the principle of nondiscrimination based on race, color, and ethnic origin that was defined in the Council Directive 2000/43/EC of June 29, 2000, implementing the principle of equal treatment between persons irrespective of racial or ethnic origin, *id.* at ¶ 30.

49 Karl Riesenhuber, *EuGH: Parodie als eigenständige Kategorie des Unionsrechts [CJEU: Parody As an Independent Category of EU Law]* 2014 Lindenmaier-Möhring-Kommentierte BGH-Rechtsprechung [LMK] 363019 § 3 (Ger.).

Another commentator attested that the introduction of a political correctness test by the CJEU would have the potential to eliminate parodies from public discussion.[50] While finding some similarities between the CJEU's newly established fair balance test and former requirements set by German courts to balance between the constitutionally guaranteed freedoms of expression and art on the one hand and the intellectual property owner's property right on the other hand, the general consensus among German commentators was that the German free use approach refined in *Disney*, *Asterix*, and subsequent decisions would not be compatible with the directions under *Deckmyn*.[51]

The Federal Court of Justice had the opportunity to realign the German test for free use with the parody test developed by the CJEU in July 2016.[52] The photographer of the prominent German actor Bettina Zimmermann, who held a copyright in the photograph shown as Figure 18.5, had sued the operator of the Internet-based magazine *BZ News* that had invited submissions for comedic adaptations of prominent figures' photographs, resulting in the adaptation shown in Figure 18.6. The Regional Court had found for the copyright owner;[53] the appeals court had considered the adaptation a free use under Article 24 of the Copyright Act and had reversed the decision of the first instance.[54] The Federal Court of Justice acknowledged the structural differences between its own prior case law and the *Deckmyn* decision. It recaptured the two principal requirements for a parody under *Deckmyn* being (1) to "evoke an existing work, while at the same time being noticeably different from that work," and (2) to present "an expression of humour or mockery."[55] The court abolished the long-established requirement for a parody to have its own original character or to be a personal intellectual creation[56] and went on to clarify that a parody does not need to be an anti-thematic treatment of the parodied work or the subject matter portrayed by that work.[57] It also referenced the fair balance test introduced in *Deckmyn* and incorporated it into the parody test under German copyright law.[58]

In the matter at issue, the Federal Court of Justice largely sided with the internet magazine operator; it found that the "adaptation evoking an existing work contains an expression of humor or a mockery."[59] The court further concluded that it could not find any interest of the copyright owner that would be particularly harmed by the parody. Here, however, the court noted that the appellate court had not conducted a proper balancing of interests, and therefore remanded the decision back to the appellate court.

[50] Christopher Unseld, Note on Council Directive 2001/29/EC, 2014 EUROPÄISCHE ZEITSCHRIFT FÜR WIRTSCHAFTSRECHT [EuZW] 914 (Ger.).

[51] Anne Lauber-Rönsberg, *Parodien urheberrechtlich geschützter Werke – Eine Bestandsaufnahme nach der »Deckmyn«-Entscheidung des EuGH [Parodies of Copyright-Protected Works – Assessing the Situation after the CJEU's* Deckmyn *Decision]*, 2015 ZEITSCHRIFT FÜR URHEBER- UND MEDIENRECHT [ZUM] 658 (Ger.); Bernhard von Becker, *Die entstellende Parodie: Das EuGH-Urteil „Vrijheidsfonds/Vandersteen" und die Folgen für das deutsche Recht [The Defacing Parody – The CJEU Decision "Vrijheidsfonds/Vandersteen" and the Consequences for German Law]*, 2015 GEWERBLICHER RECHTSSCHUTZ UND URHEBERRECHT [GRUR] 336 (Ger.).

[52] Bundesgerichtshof [BGH] [Federal Court of Justice] July 28, 2016, GEWERBLICHER RECHTSSCHUTZ UND URHEBERRECHT [GRUR] 1157, 2016 (Ger.); a partial English translation of the decision can be found at IIC 474, 2017.

[53] Landgericht Hamburg [LG Hamburg] [Regional Court of Hamburg] Feb. 25, 2011, BECK RECHTSPRECHUNG [BeckRS] 15634, 2016 (Ger.).

[54] Oberlandesgericht Hamburg [OLG Hamburg] [Higher Regional Court of Hamburg] Dec. 4, 2014, GEWERBLICHER RECHTSSCHUTZ UND URHEBERRECHT RECHTSPRECHUNG [GRUR-RS] 12244, 2015 (Ger.).

[55] 2016 GRUR 1157, *supra* note 51.

[56] *Id.*

[57] *Id.*

[58] *Id.*

[59] *Id.*

FIGURE 18.5 Vlaams Belang calendar cover

4 PARODY UNDER JAPANESE LAW

Like in Germany, Japanese copyright law does not recognize a specific exception for parody; again, like its German counterpart, Japanese copyright law also does not provide for a general fair use provision.[60] The specific exception that is usually applied to attempt to shield parodies from copyright infringement liability is the right to quote that is provided for under Article 32 of the Japanese Copyright Act. As a starting point, parodists can also point to the constitutional guarantees for free speech and all other forms of expression that have to be balanced against copyright holders' interests in the protection of their intellectual property rights.

60 *See* Tatsuhiro Ueno, *supra* Chapter 12 in this volume.

FIGURE 18.6 Original photograph of Bettina Zimmermann

A Constitutional Law Basis for Parody?

Article 21 of the Japanese Constitution provides, among others, for the freedom of speech, press, and all other forms of expression. While this constitutional guarantee was rarely explicitly invoked as a balancing factor by Japanese courts, there are a few infringement actions that highlight the tension between a parodist's freedom of speech and expression and a copyright holder's intent to assert broad copyright protection.

Frequently cited as an example of how Japanese courts have applied a parody defense to copyright infringement in modern times, the Tokyo District Court was asked to decide on a preliminary injunction motion during a dispute between the Japanese publisher and translator of the US bestselling motivational business fable *Who Moved My Cheese?*[61] and the publisher of a satirical adaptation titled *Where Has My Butter Gone?*[62] The Japanese version of *Who Moved My Cheese?* was published in November 2000, and became a bestseller in Japan. The satirical version, *Where Has My Butter Gone?*, was published in Japan in April 2001; as shown in Figures 18.7 and 18.8, the color tone and the fonts of the cover of *Where Has My Butter Gone?*

[61] The title of the Japanese version of *Who Moved My Cheese?* was "Chīzu wa doko e kieta," which could be literally translated as "Where did the cheese disappear?" SPENCER JOHNSON, CHĪZU WA DOKO E KIETA [WHO MOVED MY CHEESE?] (Misuzu Kadota trans., 1999).

[62] The original Japanese title was "Batā wa doko e toketa."

FIGURE 18.7 Cover of *Who Moved My Cheese?*

resemble those of the cover of the widely noted bestseller *Who Moved My Cheese?* The content of *Where Has My Butter Gone?* was written to be an antithesis of *Who Moved My Cheese?*: the original text describes changes in the lives of four characters and the reaction to such changes during their hunt for cheese. The original text has been referred to as portraying change in an optimistic fashion. In *Where Has My Butter Gone?*, the author arrives at the conclusion that change should be avoided, and that the characters are better off not embracing change and instead waiting out certain challenges. The text of Where *Has My Butter Gone?* references *Who Moved My Cheese?* in the resemblance it has to it in style and structure.

The court first confirmed that the translator of *Who Moved My Cheese?*, who was one of the plaintiffs, owned a copyright in the translation of the English original as far as the translation contained creative expressions.[63] It went on to find that fifteen passages in *Where Has My Butter Gone?* that mirrored passages from *Who Moved My Cheese?* constituted an infringement of the plaintiff's copyright. It rejected the defendant's argument that these mirror references constituted a parody protected by the constitutional right of free expression, holding that the intention of

[63] Tōkyō Chihō Saibansho [Tokyo Dist. Ct.] Dec. 19, 2001, Hei 13 (yo) no. 22103.

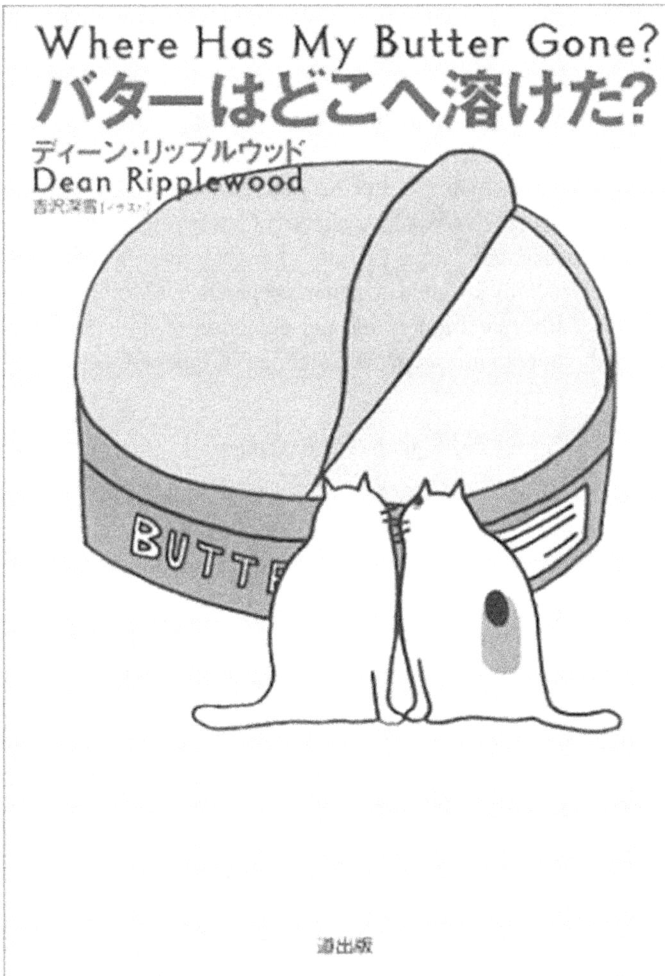

FIGURE 18.8 Cover of *Where Has My Butter Gone?*

mocking the original work does not justify these instances of copyright infringement, as the effect of mocking or criticizing could also have been achieved without infringing these passages. In its holding, the Tokyo District Court indicated that the concept of parody was a stylistic concept to be found in literature rather than a concept applicable in Japanese copyright law.

Another, more recent, copyright infringement case in which the accused infringer raised concerns of free speech rights was the so-called *High Score Girl* proceedings. The well-known Japanese comic series *High Score Girl* published a number of editions in which the hero was shown as playing different video games. In doing so, the comic depicted – among others – video game characters from the games *The King of Fighters* and *Samurai Showdown* that were subject to copyright protection by the game company SNK Playmore Corporation. In May 2014, SNK Playmore filed a criminal complaint with the Osaka prefectural police against the comic's publishing company Square Enix Co., Ltd.; in October 2014, SNK Playmore also filed a civil lawsuit at the Osaka District Court, alleging copyright infringement by Square Enix. The Osaka prefectural police searched the offices of Square Enix and required sixteen named individuals, including *High Score Girl*'s author Rensuke Oshikiri, to make themselves available for further questioning and submission of information by the prosecutor. As a reaction to this highly unusual level of interest by the police in initiating criminal proceedings for copyright infringement, Square Enix decided to stop sales of the issues alleged to infringe the character copyright, and eventually settled with SNK Playmore, agreeing to republish the editions in a revised format. In reaction to this case, which received a significant amount of attention from interested groups and the comic culture, Japanese academics argued that Rensuke Oshigiri's conduct should not amount to copyright infringement but rather be protected by his free expression right under the constitution, making the case that Japanese copyright law would be unconstitutional and pose a threat to the diversity of Japanese arts and cultural development if interpreted too broadly.[64] A group of artists and academics signed a paper prepared by Meiji University's Intellectual Property Law and Policy Institute arguing that the depiction of the video games in the comic should be covered by the quotation exception contained in Japanese copyright law.

B Quotation Exception

Among other exceptions provided for in Japanese copyright law, Article 32 of the Japanese Copyright Act allows the quotation of publicly available works for certain purposes, including for the purpose of criticism.[65] When Japanese copyright law was established in 1899, it was designed as a tool of protection for foreign printing companies that were concerned about copyright protection of Japanese translations of their works. Article 30 of the 1899 Copyright Act contained a number of exceptions, including an exception for quotations[66] that was based on the citation exception that eventually would become Article 10 of the Berne Convention. Unlike the current law, the 1899 Copyright Act's quotation exception did not mention any permissible purposes for which quotations could be made. Interestingly, no parody cases that were litigated under the 1899 Copyright Act were reported until the 1960s.

i Montage Picture Case

The *Montage Picture* litigation was triggered by a photomontage made by Japanese artist Mad Amano. He modified the original photograph, shown in Figure 18.9, of six alpine skiers skiing down a snowy alpine slope in St. Christoph, Austria, leaving parallel zigzag ski tracks. Mad Amano's adaptation showed the same slope, but added a giant black Bridgestone tire rushing down the slope and threatening to crush the skiers. The adaptation was published in a Japanese magazine with the intention of raising awareness of the environmental dangers of overdeveloping ski resorts.

The infringement action was brought in the name of the original photo's photographer, Yoshikazu Shirakawa. In the first instance, the Tokyo District Court sided with Mr. Shirakawa and found Mr. Amano's photo adaptation to be a copyright infringement.[67] On appeal, the Tokyo High Court reversed and held that a permissible free use of the copyright-protected work should be assessed based on the extent, character, and purpose of the use.[68] The High Court

[64] *See, e.g.*, Masahiko Kinoshita & Takeshi Maeda, *Chosakukenhō no kenpō tekigō-teki kaishaku ni mukete – haisukoagāru jiken ga tsukitsukeru kadai to sono kokufuku [The Interpretation of the Constitutional Compliance of the Copyright Law – Overcoming Problems Posed by the* High Score Girl *Incident]*, 1478 JURIST, at 46 (2015).

[65] Chosakukenhou [Copyright Act], Law No. 48 of 1970, art. 32, para. 1 (Japan): "It shall be permissible to make quotations from a work already made public, provided that their making is compatible with fair practice and their extent does not exceed that justified by purposes such as news reporting, criticism or research."

[66] Chosakukenhou [Copyright Act], Law No. 39 of 1899, art. 30: "The reproduction of works already published shall not be considered as infringements in the following cases: ... (2) To make extracts, or to cite passages provided that the citations are within due limits."

[67] Tokyo District Court, Decision of November 20, 1972, Case No. Sho 46 (wa) 8643.

[68] Tokyo High Court, Decision of May 19, 1976, Case No. Sho 47 (ne) 2816.

〈原告作品〉

〈被告作品〉

FIGURE 18.9 Original photograph of ski slope (on the left) and adaptation by Mad Amano (on the right)

found that for the purpose of preparing a critical parody, the extent and the character of the portions used by Mr. Amano were appropriate, and thus upheld the quotation defense raised.[69] The High Court also held that the parody work prepared by Mr. Amano would be protected under the constitutional right of free expression.[70]

The copyright holder appealed to the Japanese Supreme Court, which reversed the High Court decision and found in favor of the copyright holder.[71] The Supreme Court first explained that criticism would be a permissible purpose for quotation also under the 1899 Copyright Act that governed the dispute. It then went on to state that the montage photograph's production and publication had to be considered copyright infringement "if it is possible to directly perceive the essential characteristics of the other person's photograph from this montage photograph."[72] The court further explained that it considered the snowy alpine slope and the skiers an essential part of the original photograph, and that such essential characteristics are directly perceivable from the montage photograph to a sufficient extent. While the court recognized that the montage photograph expressed "ideas and feelings different from" the original photograph,[73] such difference in purpose was not significant enough to overcome the direct perception of the essential elements that pushed the montage picture outside the permissible range of quotation.

The Supreme Court's decision created a very difficult standard for works of parody; even early German case law had conceded the fact that perceiving the essential characteristics of the original is almost a requirement for an effective parody. The majority of the deciding bench of

69 *Id.*; the High Court even used the term "fair use" to emphasize the concept of a permissible quotation constituting free use.

70 *Id.*

71 Saikō Saibansho [Sup. Ct.] Mar. 28, 1980, Sho 51 (O) no. 923, 34 SAIKŌ SAIBANSHO MINJI HANREISHŪ [MINSHŪ] 244 (Japan). An English translation is available at the Supreme Court's website at www.courts.go.jp/app/hanrei_en/detail?id=60, last accessed August 2017.

72 *Id.*

73 *Id.*

the Supreme Court obviously disagreed with this concept and found that only those parodies that identify an original work in a sufficiently light or indirect way may be considered as a quotation under copyright law.[74]

ii Subsequent Case Law

Japanese courts in Japan have to follow precedential decisions by the Supreme Court,[75] and – in the absence of legislative action – only the Supreme Court would have authority to modify the standard under which parodies would qualify for the quotation exception under Article 32 of the Copyright Act. In light of the strict requirements set by the Supreme Court, it is not too surprising that not many defendants accused of copyright infringement tried to raise a parody defense. One court decision that has been mentioned by Japanese commentators as a subsequent test for parody[76] was the *Tokimeki Memorial* case decided by the Tokyo District Court in 1999.[77] *Tokimeki Memorial* is a popular dating-simulation video game developed and distributed by Konami Digital Entertainment; the first edition of the *Tokimeki Memorial* game series was released in 1994. The defendant produced a short video that was described in the trial as a "parody video" of the popular video game. The video depicted the game's main character Shiori Fujisaki, albeit without using the character's name. The video – a ten-minute short animation that contained adult content involving the Fujisaki character – was released under the name "Dogimagi Imagination," with "Dogimagi" making a noticeable phonetic reference to the title of the game. Konami alleged infringement of its character's copyright, and the court agreed and awarded damages. It should be noted that the defendant did not even raise a quotation defense under Article 32 of the Copyright Act, but merely relied on non-infringement and non-validity defenses that were rejected by the court.[78]

Another dispute that may provide some guidance on the application of parody-test elements was decided by the Tokyo District Court in 2004.[79] The copyright holder of the classic Japanese movie *Seven Samurai* directed by Akira Kurosawa alleged that the samurai drama *Musashi* that was produced by Japan's national broadcasting service NHK and that was aired weekly throughout 2003 incorporated copyright-protected elements of Kurosawa's work such as Kurosawa's legendary style of movie cutting, sound elements, and other stylistic expressions, making *Musashi* an infringing adaption of Kurosawa's *Seven Samurai*. The District Court disagreed, and found that the stylistic elements used in *Musashi* did not cause the viewer to directly perceive the essential parts of *Seven Samurai*. While NHK did not pursue a parody defense and prevailed on grounds of non-infringement, a parody defense might have been equally successful

[74] The Supreme Court decisions triggered significant criticism among Japanese commentators; *see, e.g.*, Tatsuhiro Ueno, *Inyō o meguru yōken-ron no saikōsei [Reconstructing the Theory of Requirements on Quotation]*, in CHOSAKUKENHŌ TO MINPŌ NO GENDAITEKI KADAI: HANDA MASAO SENSEI KOKI KINEN RONSHŪ [CONTEMPORARY ISSUES IN COPYRIGHT LAW AND CIVIL LAW: WRITING IN HONOR OF PROF. MASAO HONDA], Hōgakushoin, at 307 (Akira Moriizumi ed., 2003); NOBUHIRO NAKAYAMA, CHOSAKUKENHŌ [COPYRIGHT LAW], Yuhikaku, 2d ed., at 322 (2014); Toshiaki Iimura, *Saibanrei ni okeru inyō no kijun ni tsuite [About the Standards for Quotation in Court Cases]*, 26 ANNUAL OF COPYRIGHT LAW, at 91 (1999).

[75] For a brief note on the power of precedence in Japan, *see* Toshiaki Iimura, Ryu Takabayashi, & Christoph Rademacher, *The Binding Nature of Court Decisions in Japan's Civil Law System*, STANFORD LAW SCHOOL CHINA GUIDING CASES PROJECT, https://cgc.law.stanford.edu/commentaries/14-iimura-takabayashi-rademacher, last accessed August 2017.

[76] Makoto Ito, *Guteiteki jirei kara miru – Nihon ni okeru parodi mondai [Reviewing Concise Sample Cases – Japan's Problem with Parodies]*, 66-6 Patent, at 7 (2015).

[77] Tokyo District Court, Decision of August 30, 1999, Case No. Hei 10 (wa) 15575.

[78] *Id.*

[79] Tokyo District Court, Decision of December 24, 2004, Case No. Hei (wa) 25535.

when applying the Supreme Court's 1980 test. A takeaway from the court's analysis is that under the *Montage Picture* test, it may be quite difficult to draw the line between an infringing adaptation and a parody failing the test for the permissible scope of citation under Article 32 of the Copyright Act.

Finally, the most recent case decided by a Japanese court that at least remotely touched on parody under copyright law aspects was the *Web Satomi* case decided by the Tokyo District Court in 2007.[80] Here, the plaintiff was the operator of the internet game site *Satomi Gakuen Hakkenden*; the defendant was a frequent user of the plaintiff's game site who had made his own game site that incorporated certain elements of the plaintiff's site, such as chat rooms named in reference to "Satomi Gakuen." While the defendant characterized his website as a "parody game site" and stressed the comic nature of his site, the court did not entertain this line of argument as it rejected the infringer's claim of copyright infringement.

C Alignment of "Japanese Parody" and Western-Style Copyright Law

The concept of what constitutes a parody differs between cultures and languages. Japan, with its complex set of rather unique cultural norms, has a significantly different humor than European cultures such as Germany have; such different humor reflects on the Japanese understanding of parody. The primary example of traditional Japanese parody established as stylistic means prior to the Meiji era is certain types of *waka* poetry[81] such as *kyōka*.[82] Unlike European parody, *kyōka* references other work not in order to generate laughter through ridicule or criticism of the referenced work, but to lighten the mood by merely referencing the original. In doing so, it makes use of the *honkadori* technique, which creates an allusion to an older poem that readers would be expected to recognize. Below is an example of an ancient famous Japanese poem and a *kyōka* based on such a poem, illustrating the application of *honkadori* in a Japanese *kyōka*:[83]

Original poem by Saigyo (Japanese priest, twelfth century)

吉野山	Yoshinoyama	Mount Yoshino
去年の枝折の	Kozo no shiori **no**	From last year's broken twig
道かへて	**Michi** Kaete	I will change my path
まだ見ぬ方の	Mada minu kata no	I have not yet seen
花をたづねん	Hana o tazunen	And view cherry blossoms

Kino Sadamaru, eighteenth-century *kyōka* "parody"

吉野山	Yoshinoyama	Mount Yoshino
去年の枝折を	Kozo no shiori **o**	I broke last year
見ちがえて	Mi chigaete	I wander around
うろつくほどの	Urotsuku hodo no	Having mistaken the twig
花盛りかな	Hanazakari kana	The flowers are in full bloom

The reference to the old poem comes in the first two lines of Sadamaru's *kyōka*; that said, while the Japanese words used in the first two lines are almost identical,[84] Sadamura changed

[80] Tokyo District Court, Decision of January 31, 2007, Case No. Hei 18 (wa) 13706.

[81] *Waka* can be literally translated as "Japanese poem," which is a type of poetry from classical Japanese literature dating back to the eighth century AC. *See Waka*, WIKIPEDIA, https://en.wikipedia.org/wiki/Waka_(poetry), last accessed August 2017.

[82] *Kyōka* can be literally translated as "mad poetry."

[83] Translation found in Rokuo Tanaka, *Forgotten Women: Two Kyōka Poets of the Temmei Era*, *in* UNDERSTANDING JAPANESE HUMOR 113–14 (Jessica Davis ed., 2006).

[84] When just listening to the two poems, the first three lines would sound almost identical.

the content of the second line and thus the direction of the entire poem significantly by changing just one seemingly minor word in the first two lines, replacing a "no" with an "o." This kind of soft wordplay[85] is a prime example of what even modern Japanese culture understands as humor or as parody. The *Montage Picture* decision – which seems to be based on an entirely illogical test from the perspective of a Western commentator – starts to make more sense when looked at through the lens of traditional Japanese parody that derived from techniques that required only a somewhat thin perception of the referenced original work.

5 COMPARATIVE THOUGHTS

The comparison of the parody exception under Japanese and under German copyright law yields interesting results. Neither Germany nor Japan has a broad fair use provision, and both tend to rely on a catalogue of specific copyright exceptions to maintain a balance between copyright holders' interests and the public interest in certain permissible free uses of copyright-protected content. Neither jurisdiction's copyright law mentions the word "parody." Germany traditionally used the free use exception to allow works of parody, albeit imposing rather strict requirements for recognizing free use. By acknowledging the CJEU's framework for a parody exception outlined in *Deckmyn* and modifying the German free use test to fit the *Deckmyn* test, the German Federal Court of Justice established different tests for a parody free use and for other forms of free use; given the broad definition of parody provided by the CJEU and accepted by the German Federal Court of Justice subsequently, parody free use seems to be subject to an easier test than other forms of free use.[86] Under Japanese copyright law, parody can be exempted from being infringing by being classified as a subcategory of a quotation. The governing test that dates back to 1980 is – compared to the standards for parody exceptions of most other major jurisdictions – very rigid and difficult to meet. At the same time, the test for the quotation exception outside the world of parody has been significantly broadened by Japanese courts in the last few years.[87] The Japanese government has considered introducing a revised and less rigid test as a basis for a specific parody exception over recent years, but has (to date) refrained from making any adjustment to the standard issued by the Supreme Court in 1980.

Humor is deeply embedded in a culture and is part of the society that decides its legal norms. The German culture – or German humor – generally allows for jokes that generate laughter at the expense of others. One example that every German and probably also other European cultures would be familiar with is blonde jokes. Japan, on the contrary, is a uniquely harmonious

[85] Ms. Tanaka quotes a definition of *kyōka* as creating a "satirically humorous perspective" by invoking "the heart of a poet who wears a 'robe made of silk brocade but who ties it with a sash made of straw'"; *see* Tanaka, *supra* note 82, at 114.

[86] Gerhard Schricker & Ulrich Loewenheim, Urheberrecht: Kommentar [Copyright Law: Commentary] §24, n. 28 (5th ed. 2017) (Ger.).

[87] A comparatively liberal interpretation of the quotation exception had been provided by the IP High Court in a 2010 decision regarding art authenticity certificates (IP High Court, Decision of October 13, 2010, Case No. Hei 22 (ne) 10052). When preparing art authenticity certificates for two painters, the art appraiser had attached reduced color photographs of the assessed paintings to the back of the certificates. While the Tokyo District Court had found the photographs of the paintings infringing (Tokyo District Court, Decision of May 22, 2010, Case No. Hei 20 (wa) 31609), the IP High Court reversed on appeal and provided the following test factors that should be considered when reviewing a quotation defense: (1) the purpose for which the alleged infringer uses the work; (2) the method and manner of such use; (3) the type and nature of the work used; and (4) the existence or nonexistence of any influence of such use on the author of the work and the extent of such influence. When applying this test (which closely resembles the test for fair use under US copyright), the court found that attaching color photographs would be helpful for the purpose of appraising the authenticity of the paintings, which would eventually benefit the copyright holder.

society, and at least within organizations direct confrontation that could lead to open conflict is usually avoided as much as possible. This harmonious nature of Japanese society results in a type of mainstream humor that does not have the same tolerance for jokes that target specific groups or persons in mean or potentially offensive ways. The presence or absence of a culture of laughing at the expense of others has an impact on how much parody a society's copyright owners want and have to accept.

19

From Fair Dealing to User-Generated Content: Legal La La Land in Hong Kong

Alice Lee & Brendan Clift

Here's to the ones who dream
Foolish as they may seem
Here's to the hearts that ache
Here's to the mess we make[1]

In March 2016, the Hong Kong government abandoned its latest attempt to reform copyright law for the digital era. Notwithstanding strong support from the business sector, opposition to the Copyright (Amendment) Bill 2014 had become a crusade for civil rights activists and Internet-user interest groups, who protested it online and outside the legislature, and also for pro-democracy lawmakers, who filibustered tirelessly until the bill's demise.

Had the bill become law, copyright users would have gained new fair dealing exceptions covering parody, satire, caricature, pastiche, comments on current events, and quotation – provisions and protections they had requested when the predecessor Copyright (Amendment) Bill 2011 was rejected – along with greater clarity on various technology-related matters. Instead, Hong Kong retains a limited and dated range of exceptions in the areas of education, journalism, and public administration.

To understand this counterintuitive result, it is necessary to consider not only the copyright reform process – all ten fruitless years of it – but also Hong Kong's political climate. Since the return to Chinese sovereignty in 1997, the mood in the city has shifted from intermittently tense to frequently tumultuous. By the time the 2014 bill was proposed, political conflict had reached a high point as the public lost patience with Beijing's refusal to countenance democratic reform. Hundreds of thousands took to the streets and occupied them from September to December 2014.

Amid the prevailing atmosphere of confrontation and mistrust, the bill's opponents proclaimed it a threat to free speech and internet freedom and demanded broader protections for user-generated content (UGC), which had by then become a notable mode of anti-establishment expression. A shell-shocked government, seemingly lacking the wherewithal to sell the reform package or mediate between copyright owners and users, moved the controversial item to the back of the legislative agenda to allow the budget and other essential business through.

Thus copyright remains analogue and decreasingly fit for purpose in Hong Kong. But, despite the political stalemate over its future, the impetus for reform has not evaporated. With treaty

[1] Emma Stone, *Audition (The Fools Who Dream), on* La La Land (Summit Entertainment 2016).

obligations unmet, and with copyright owners and users stubbornly staking out their claims, there will be further chapters to this saga. It remains to be seen whether the next attempt at reform will be incremental in nature or, bowing to popular opinion, if it will revolutionize Hong Kong copyright law by architecting a UGC utopia.[2]

BACKGROUND: HONG KONG'S UNIQUE CONSTITUTIONAL CONTEXT

On July 1, 1997, the British Crown Colony of Hong Kong became a Special Administrative Region of the People's Republic of China. The territorial handover took place in accordance with a treaty between the outgoing and incoming sovereigns.[3] Recognizing Hong Kong's success as a freewheeling hub for international trade and a global financial center, the United Kingdom and China agreed that the city's established ways of life and commerce, and many of its core institutions, would remain unchanged for at least fifty years.[4]

Hong Kong's de facto constitution is the Basic Law.[5] It guarantees fundamental rights and freedoms in the territory.[6] It provides for the continuation of laws in force at the time of the handover, judicial independence, the common law legal system, and the use of overseas precedent.[7] And, in the political sphere, it promises Hong Kong a high degree of autonomy, independent legislative and executive branches, and gradual and orderly progress toward elections via universal suffrage.[8]

Despite the trappings of a liberal democratic state, Hong Kong is subject to a superior, undemocratic governing body: the Central Government of the People's Republic of China. The Basic Law reserves certain powers to China, including acts of state and the powers to amend and finally interpret the Basic Law itself.[9] "Interpretations" can be, and have been, issued by the Chinese government to guide or override decisions of Hong Kong's highest court.[10]

Hong Kong is not a state in a federal system with clearly delineated jurisdictional boundaries between regional and national governments. It is a hybrid regime, enjoying limited regional autonomy which can be overridden at the discretion of the national government.[11] Although the Basic Law sets out discrete areas of responsibility, its underlying "One Country, Two Systems" concept[12] accommodates the view that Hong Kong's

[2] Alice Lee, From Fair Dealing to Fair Use to UGC – Three Steps to Copyright Reform or Pseutopia?, Presentation at NUS–UPenn–HKU Conference on Comparative Dimensions of Limitations and Exceptions in Copyright Law (July 21–22, 2016).

[3] Joint Declaration of the Government of the United Kingdom of Great Britain and Northern Ireland and the Government of the People's Republic of China on the Question of Hong Kong, Dec. 19, 1984, U.K.–P.R.C., 1984 Gr. Brit. T.S. No. 20 (Cmd. 9352).

[4] *See further* Yash Ghai, *Hong Kong's New Constitutional Order: The Resumption of Chinese Sovereignty and the Basic Law* (2d ed. 1999).

[5] XIANGGANG JIBEN FA (H.K.) [hereinafter Basic Law].

[6] Basic Law Ch. III.

[7] Basic Law arts. 8, 81, 84–85. *See also* Basic Law arts. 82 and 94 which provide, respectively, that overseas judges may be invited to sit on the Hong Kong Court of Final Appeal, the territory's apex court, and that overseas lawyers may be admitted to practice in the region.

[8] Basic Law arts. 12, 16–18, 68.

[9] Basic Law arts. 13–14, 158–59.

[10] For a description of this power and examples of its exercise, *see* Anthony Mason, *The Rule of Law in the Shadow of the Giant: The Hong Kong Experience*, 33 SYDNEY L. REV. 623 (2011).

[11] *See* Yash Ghai, *The Imperatives of Autonomy: Contradictions of the Basic Law*, *in* HONG KONG'S CONSTITUTIONAL DEBATES 29 (Johannes Chan & Lison Harris eds., 2005).

[12] For an official account of this state policy, which is applied in the Special Administrative Regions of Hong Kong and Macao, *see* WU BANGGUO, THE BASIC LAW AND HONG KONG: THE 15TH ANNIVERSARY OF REUNIFICATION WITH THE MOTHERLAND (2012), www.basiclaw.gov.hk/en/publications/15anniversary_reunification.

integrity as a self-contained autonomous system may be overridden in the interests of "one country."[13]

POLITICS: THE BASIC LAW AND ELECTIONS

Since the early days of the Special Administrative Region, the inherent contradictions of this "schizophrenic" constitutional set up[14] have been apparent in the wrangling over electoral models. The topic can flare up at any time but reliably does so around the election of the chief executive, Hong Kong's de facto leader, scheduled to occur every five years.

The Basic Law describes the method for selecting the chief executive, a method which may be amended by China's National People's Congress if the amendment is consented to by two-thirds of Hong Kong's legislature, the Legislative Council.[15] The Basic Law states that the "ultimate aim is the selection of the Chief Executive by universal suffrage upon nomination by a broadly representative nominating committee in accordance with democratic procedures."[16]

Currently, the chief executive is chosen by a committee of 1,200 members which is divided into subsectors largely representing commercial and professional interests.[17] Although members are elected, this is not by universal suffrage. The representatives of the general public – legislators and district council members – constitute only around 10 percent of the committee. Many seats on the committee are decided solely by corporate voters and many are uncontested.[18]

The opaque and undemocratic nature of this committee, which reliably produces chief executives from the pro-establishment side of politics, has long been a source of agitation. In 2014, the Hong Kong government acceded to calls to reconsider the process and ran a consultation on the electoral model to be used in 2017. Public engagement was high – an online survey by the University of Hong Kong attracted more than half a million votes. Pro-democracy groups openly advocated universal suffrage, and some announced plans to stage civil disobedience campaigns unless genuine progress toward democracy was made.

When the consultation closed, Beijing announced its decision on the new model: the selection committee would remain in place to vet the candidates for chief executive. Those who were not screened out by the committee would be eligible to stand for election by the Hong Kong public. Outraged opposition legislators vowed to use their veto to block the half-hearted reform. University and school students launched an extended strike, which tipped into the streets when police blocked access to protest sites around government offices. When police resorted to

[13] This is the current policy position of the Central Government as described in its White Paper, *The Practice of the 'One Country, Two Systems' Policy in the Hong Kong Special Administrative Region. See* INFORMATION OFFICE OF CHINA'S STATE COUNCIL, THE PRACTICE OF THE 'ONE COUNTRY, TWO SYSTEMS' POLICY IN THE HONG KONG SPECIAL ADMINISTRATIVE REGION (2014), www.fmcoprc.gov.hk/eng/xwdt/gsxw/t1164057.htm. As to the search for coherence in China's Basic Law interpretation methodology, *see* Lin Feng & P. Y. Lo, *One Term, Two Interpretations: The Justifications and the Future of Basic Law Interpretation*, *in* INTERPRETING HONG KONG'S BASIC LAW: THE STRUGGLE FOR COHERENCE 143 (Hualing Fu et al. eds., 2007). For an argument that China's approach is mere *ipse dixit*, *see* Robert Morris, *The 'Replacement' Chief Executive's Two-Year Term: A Pure and Unambiguous Common Law Analysis*, 35 HONG KONG L.J. 17 (2005).

[14] Todd Schneider, *David v Goliath: The Hong Kong Courts and China's National People's Congress Standing Committee*, 20 BERKELEY J. INT'L L. 575 (2002).

[15] Basic Law art. 159.

[16] Basic Law art. 45.

[17] Basic Law annex I.

[18] *See generally* ELECTING HONG KONG'S CHIEF EXECUTIVE (Simon N. M. Young & Richard Cullen eds., 2010). It is noteworthy that only half of the seats in the Legislative Council are elected by universal suffrage, the other half being functional constituencies with restricted voting, some of it corporate. This too is an ongoing source of controversy.

batons, pepper spray, and eighty-seven canisters of tear gas, hundreds of thousands of ordinary Hong Kongers joined the students and flooded the city streets. The Umbrella Movement, a mass protest which would blockade the Central, Causeway Bay, and Mongkok districts for seventy-two consecutive days, had begun.[19]

This was the backdrop against which the latest copyright reform consultation was launched.

COPYRIGHT: THE LAW AND EXCEPTIONS

At the time of the handover, a raft of new, local laws took effect in Hong Kong. These included the territory's first comprehensive copyright statute, the Copyright Ordinance.[20] The Ordinance filled the void left by the UK Copyright Act 1956, which had applied in the colony until that point, and was based in most respects on the successor to the 1956 Act: the Copyright, Designs and Patents Act 1988.[21]

Under the Ordinance, copyright subsists in a work of a prescribed type if it is original and fixed in material form.[22] The jurisprudence on these criteria remains English in origin. Thus the originality requirement has a low threshold focused on independence of creation rather than inventiveness; a minimum degree of skill, judgment, labor, or investment is required; and copyright ultimately protects not an idea but its expression.[23]

The exclusive rights of copyright owners, set out in terms of "restricted acts," include the right to reproduce the work in any material form, in whole or substantial part.[24] Both physical and electronic reproductions fall within this restriction, and the copyright owner enjoys exclusive rights of first issue of the work to the public and of making it available online.[25] Infringements of these rights are termed "primary" infringements.

"Secondary" infringements involve dealing with infringing items in connection with a trade or business. This category also proscribes the distribution of an infringing item, not in connection with a trade or business, to an extent that prejudicially affects the copyright owner.[26] It is a defense to secondary infringement to prove reasonable belief, on the facts subjectively known, that the copy was not an infringing copy.[27]

Certain infringements are offenses under the Ordinance, mostly those done in connection with a trade or business. The primary infringement of making available online does not attract criminal liability, however, whereas the secondary infringement of prejudicial non-commercial distribution does.[28] Damages are available to the copyright owner unless it is

[19] For an account of the movement, *see* JASON Y. NG, UMBRELLAS IN BLOOM: HONG KONG'S OCCUPY MOVEMENT UNCOVERED (2015).

[20] Copyright Ordinance, (1997) Cap. 528 (H.K.). This is not the same as the short Copyright Ordinance, (1973) Cap. 39 (H.K.) (repealed 1997) which merely supplemented the UK Copyright Act 1956 when it still applied in the colony.

[21] MICHAEL D. PENDLETON ET AL., INTELLECTUAL PROPERTY RIGHTS: HONG KONG SAR AND THE PEOPLE'S REPUBLIC OF CHINA, Div. IV, paras. [1], [5]–[50] (2d ed. 1994) (loose-leaf updated Oct. 2018); KENNY K. S. WONG & ALICE S. C. LEE, INTELLECTUAL PROPERTY LAW AND PRACTICE IN HONG KONG para. 3.003 (2010). The 1956 Act remains influential: Cap. 528 § 193(2) provides that a provision which "corresponds to" a provision of the 1956 Act shall be construed in accordance with the previous law, notwithstanding a change of expression.

[22] Copyright Ordinance, (1997) Cap. 528, §§ 2, 4–10 (H.K.).

[23] *See, e.g.*, McMillan & Co. Ltd. v. Cooper (1924) 40 T.L.R. 186 (P.C.) (appeal taken from Ind.); Interlego A.G. v. Tyco Industries Inc. [1988] 1 A.C. 217 (P.C.) (appeal taken from H.K.); Designers Guild Ltd v Russell Williams (Textiles) Ltd [2001] F.S.R. 113 (H.L.) (appeal taken from Eng.).

[24] Copyright Ordinance, (1997) Cap. 528, § 22 (H.K.).

[25] Copyright Ordinance, (1997) Cap. 528, §§ 23–24, 26 (H.K.).

[26] Copyright Ordinance, (1997) Cap. 528, § 31(1)(d) (H.K.).

[27] Copyright Ordinance, (1997) Cap. 528, § 36 (H.K.).

[28] Copyright Ordinance, (1997) Cap. 528, § 118 (H.K.).

shown that the infringer did not know and had no reason to believe copyright subsisted in the work.[29]

Largely based on the UK Copyright, Designs and Patent Act 1988, the Ordinance contains a long list of "acts permitted in relation to copyright works,"[30] ranging from fair dealing to education, libraries, and archives. It may be said that the Hong Kong exceptions are comparable to those found throughout Europe and the Commonwealth.[31] There is an explicit provision that, in determining whether an act may be done in relation to a copyright work notwithstanding the subsistence of copyright, the primary consideration is whether the act conflicts with a normal exploitation of the work by, or unreasonably prejudices the legitimate interests of, the copyright owner.[32]

FAIR DEALING AND PARODY: WHERE LAW MEETS POLITICS

The major exceptions to copyright infringement are found in the fair dealing provisions of the Copyright Ordinance.[33] Before 2007, fair dealing was confined to the purposes of research and private study;[34] criticism, review, and news reporting.[35] The range of exceptions was expanded after criticisms that the Copyright Ordinance was unfairly tilted in favor of copyright owners, and it now includes acts done for the purposes of giving or receiving instruction[36] and public administration.[37]

The 2007 amendments liberalized the education exceptions by making them medium-neutral[38] and added a fourth fair dealing factor, the effect of the dealing on the potential market for or value of the work.[39] Despite these moves to broaden fair dealing, its specific heads or purposes still have their own further criteria, contributing to the granularity of the current law. For example, fair dealing for the purposes of criticism, review and news reporting must contain "sufficient acknowledgement" identifying the copied work and its author.[40]

The Ordinance contains no express exception or defense for a work of parody that reproduces the whole or a substantial part of a copyright work. There is no reason why copyright cannot subsist in a work of parody if it meets the standard criteria; in the case of an artistic work,

29 Copyright Ordinance, (1997) Cap. 528, § 108 (H.K.). Other remedies, including an account of profits, may still be available.

30 Copyright Ordinance, (1997) Cap. 528, Pt. II, Div. III, §§ 37–88.

31 Based on Art. 9(2) of the Berne Convention for the Protection of Literary and Artistic Works.

32 Copyright Ordinance, (1997) Cap. 528, § 37(3) (H.K.). The wording is reminiscent of the international "three-step test." *See infra* note 64 and the accompanying main text. *See, e.g.*, Kevin H. Pun, *Reform of Copyright Law in Hong Kong: Time to Redraw the Balance*, 32 Hong Kong L.J. 83 (2002).

33 Copyright Ordinance, (1997) Cap. 528, §§ 38–39, 41A, 54A (H.K.).

34 Copyright Ordinance, (1997) Cap. 528, § 38 (H.K.).

35 Copyright Ordinance, (1997) Cap. 528, § 39 (H.K.).

36 Copyright Ordinance, (1997) Cap. 528, § 41A (H.K.) (added in 2007).

37 Copyright Ordinance, (1997) Cap. 528, § 54A (H.K.) (added in 2007).

38 Copyright Ordinance, (1997) Cap. 528, §§ 41–45 (H.K.). The education exceptions used to be medium-specific, with separate provisions for reprographic copying (§ 45) and non-reprographic copying (§ 41). Now, under § 41A, anything could be done for the purposes of giving or receiving instruction provided that it is fair. *See* Alice Lee, Butterworths Hong Kong Copyright Handbook (3d ed. 2011).

39 Under the original fair dealing provisions, the court shall take into account all the circumstances including (a) the purpose and nature of the dealing, (b) the nature of the work, and (c) the amount and substantiality of the portion dealt with in relation to the work as a whole. Since 2007, a fourth factor has been added: (d) the effect of the dealing on the potential market for or value of the work.

40 If the author's identity can be ascertained by reasonable inquiry. *See* Copyright Ordinance, (1997) Cap. 528, §§ 39, 198 (H.K.).

irrespective of its quality.[41] A mere tracing may not meet the threshold for protection; a painted or sculpted reproduction may.[42] However, an unauthorized derivative work is liable to infringe the original copyright, even if the copying is unintentional or inadvertent.[43]

Despite the lack of a dedicated exception, it has been suggested that the terms "criticism" and "review" are broad enough in scope to encompass parodic works, particularly given the underlying assumption that the fair dealing provisions provide for copyright exceptions justifiable in the public interest. On the other hand, it has also been observed that the requirement for acknowledgment does not sit well with many forms of parody.[44]

In the UK, a 2014 amendment to the Copyright, Designs and Patents Act 1988 introduced a new fair dealing exception for "caricature, parody or pastiche"[45] – without any acknowledgment requirement – as well as adding a new category of "quotation" to the existing exception for criticism, review, and news reporting.[46] These exceptions were legislated in recognition of the public interest in parody and the adoption of such exceptions in several European countries.[47]

Similar exceptions have been legislated elsewhere, including Australia[48] and Canada,[49] while courts in the United States have held that a right of parody exists within the fair use exception.[50] More so than fair dealing, fair use has proven to be broad and flexible in judicial hands, able to be sculpted to the circumstances on policy grounds without legislative intervention, although it comes with a corresponding lack of certainty.[51]

FIRST ATTEMPT: THE COPYRIGHT (AMENDMENT) BILL 2011

In 2008, Hong Kong signed the World Intellectual Property Organization (WIPO)'s Copyright Treaty and Performances and Phonograms Treaty, instruments which had spurred widespread modernizations of copyright law including the US Digital Millennium Copyright Act in 1998 and the EU Copyright Directive in 2001. In anticipation of following suit, the Hong Kong

[41] Copyright Ordinance, (1997) Cap. 528, § 5 (H.K.).

[42] British Northrop v. Texteam (Blackburn) [1974] R.P.C. 57 (Ch.); Martin v. Polyplas [1969] NZLR 1046 (HC); *see* Pendleton et al., *supra* note 21, Div. IV, para [552].

[43] Michael D. Pendleton & Alice Lee, Intellectual Property in Hong Kong 145 (2008); Chow Wai Man Vivian v. Easy Finder Ltd., HCA 4042/1995 (H.C. July 28, 1995) (Legal Reference System) (H.K.).

[44] et al., *supra* note 21, Div. IV., paras. [2152]–[2153]; *see* UK Intellectual Property Office, Taking Forward the Gowers Review of Intellectual Property: Proposed Changes to Copyright Exceptions para. 200 (2007), https://webarchive.nationalarchives.gov.uk/20140603152127/http://www.ipo.gov.uk/consult-copyrightexceptions.pdf.

[45] Copyright, Designs and Patents Act 1988, c. 48, § 30A (Eng.).

[46] Copyright, Designs and Patents Act 1988, c. 48, § 30 (Eng.).

[47] Parody exceptions are provided for by Art. 5(3) of the Information Society Directive (Directive 2001/29/EC of the European Parliament and of the Council of 22 May 2001 on the Harmonisation of Certain Aspects of Copyright and Related Rights in the Information Society). *See* UK Intellectual Property Office, *supra* note 44, para. 195; Dinusha Mendis & Martin Kretschmer, The Treatment of Parodies under Copyright Law in Seven Jurisdictions: A Comparative Review of the Underlying Principles – Parody and Pastiche: Study II (2013).

[48] *Copyright Act 1968* (Cth) s 41A (Austl.).

[49] Copyright Act, R.S.C. 1985, c C-42, § 29 (Can.).

[50] Campbell v. Acuff-Rose Music, Inc., 510 US 569 (1994). Other countries employing fair use doctrine include the Philippines and Israel.

[51] Ian Hargreaves, Digital Opportunity: A Review of Intellectual Property and Growth para. 5.9 (2011), https://assets.publishing.service.gov.uk/government/uploads/system/uploads/attachment_data/file/32563/ipreview-finalreport.pdf. For a statement of the US view on the public interest in parody, *see* SOFA Entm't, Inc. v. Dodger Prods., 709 F. 3d 1273 (9th Cir. 2013). The Hong Kong government noted that US courts are less likely to regard satire as fair use than they are parody. *See* Commerce and Economic Development Bureau, Treatment of Parody under the Copyright Regime: Consultation Paper (2011), www.cedb.gov.hk/citb/doc/en/Consultation_Paper_English.pdf [hereinafter Treatment of Parody under the Copyright Regime: Consultation Paper].

government had launched a consultation, entitled "Copyright Protection in the Digital Environment," in 2006.

The consultation led to the 2008 "Preliminary Proposals for Strengthening Copyright Protection in the Digital Environment"[52] and, after further consultation, the 2009 "Proposals for Strengthening Copyright Protection in the Digital Environment."[53] This process laid the foundations for the Copyright (Amendment) Bill 2011, which was introduced with the declared aims of technology neutrality, strengthened protection against online infringement, and the facilitation of new modes of uses.[54]

The centerpiece of the 2011 bill was a new right of communication to the public: a technology-neutral right wide enough to encompass future developments in electronic transmission. The right would be infringed by any person who, without the license of the copyright owner, communicated the work to the public (1) for the purpose of or in the course of any trade or business that consisted of communicating works to the public for profit or reward, or (2) to such an extent as to affect prejudicially the copyright owner.[55] In addition to civil liability, infringement was to carry criminal sanctions.

This communication right would have superseded the extant "making available" provision of the Ordinance, which carries no criminal sanction, substantially toughening online copyright protection. Such a right is envisioned by Article 8 of the WIPO Copyright Treaty and appears in the copyright laws of various jurisdictions, including the UK.[56] Its scope elsewhere, however, is less broad. For example, European jurisprudence has incorporated the additional requirement that profit has been made from the communication to the public.[57]

Between the 2008 and 2009 proposal documents, the overall reform proposition was softened. Limitations were placed on online service provider (OSP) liability for infringing materials via "safe harbour" provisions. The proposed criminalization of unauthorized transmission through streaming technologies was amended to remove criminal liability for peer-to-peer file-sharing and unauthorized downloading except for acts which involved actively making unauthorized communications to the public. And exceptions were added for temporary reproductions and media shifting between formats.[58]

But the communication right remained unaltered, and it became the focus of debate. Copyright owners supported criminal sanctions which were technology-neutral and applied regardless of commercial motivation, arguing that this was the most effective way to combat online piracy and would not affect legitimate use of the Internet. Users objected, suggesting that the criminalization of noncommercial activities would inhibit the free flow of information, stymie Hong Kong's development as an internet services hub, and chill speech.[59]

[52] Commerce and Economic Development Bureau, Preliminary Proposals for Strengthening Copyright Protection in the Digital Environment (2008), www.ipd.gov.hk/eng/intellectual_property/copyright/Consultation_Document_Prelim_Proposals_Eng(full).pdf.

[53] Commerce and Economic Development Bureau, Proposals for Strengthening Copyright Protection in the Digital Environment (2009), www.cedb.gov.hk/citb/doc/en/consultation/Panel_Paper_Digital_Eng_Full.pdf.

[54] Commerce and Economic Development Bureau, Legislative Council Brief: Copyright (Amendment) Bill 2011, CITB 07/09/17, para. 3 (2011), www.legco.gov.hk/yr10-11/english/bills/brief/b35_brf.pdf [hereinafter Legislative Council Brief on Copyright (Amendment) Bill 2011].

[55] Copyright (Amendment) Bill 2011 (H.K.), www.legco.gov.hk/yr10-11/english/bills/b201106033.pdf (amending Copyright Ordinance, (1997) Cap. 528, § 118 (H.K.)).

[56] Copyright, Designs and Patents Act 1988, c. 48, § 20 (Eng.).

[57] Case C-306/05, Sociedad General de Autores y Editores de España (SGAE) v. Rafael Hoteles SA, 2006 E.C.R. I-11519.

[58] Legislative Council Brief on Copyright (Amendment) Bill 2011, *supra* note 54, para. 4.

[59] *See* Wenwei Guan, *When Copyrights Meet Human Rights: 'Cyberspace Article 23' and Hong Kong's Copyright Protection in the Digital Era*, 42 Hong Kong L.J. 785 (2012).

Concerns over the bill's effect on freedom of speech saw it labeled "Cyberspace Article 23" by its detractors. This was a reference to a deeply unpopular Hong Kong government proposal to enact a draconian national security law in accordance with Article 23 of the Basic Law. In July 2003, half a million residents took to the streets in protest against the perceived authoritarian thrust of that law. Presaging the fate of copyright reform, the government lacked sufficient support in the Legislative Council to push through the security law which was withdrawn and indefinitely shelved.[60]

Hong Kong's political opposition, comprising an array of community groups, political parties and legislators – the latter informally affiliated under the "pan-democrats" banner – thus took copyright into its stable of causes. There it sits alongside – and now intertwined with – issues including Hong Kong autonomy, the implementation of universal suffrage, remembrance of the 1989 Tiananmen Square massacre, and local concerns from housing to graft.

Perhaps with democratic ideals in mind, parody and satire were identified as activities deserving of protection, activities which were not addressed by the proposed amendments but had been expressly protected elsewhere. Pan-democrat lawmakers, urged on by emerging organizations of internet users,[61] held up the bill by raising the suggestion that a parody exception be added.[62] The goalposts having shifted, the bill was allowed to lapse at the expiry of the 2012 Legislative Council term.

SECOND ATTEMPT: THE COPYRIGHT (AMENDMENT) BILL 2014

Following the abandonment of the 2011 bill, another round of consultation was held to address the unresolved concerns. This was entitled "Treatment of Parody under the Copyright Regime."[63] With the resultant Copyright (Amendment) Bill 2014, the government proposed to introduce a range of new fair dealing exceptions to the Copyright Ordinance in terms not dissimilar to the then-imminent amendments to the UK Copyright, Patents and Designs Act 1988.

Fundamentally, the government deemed each of the newly proposed exceptions to be acceptable because their scope was clear and confined, affording a reasonable degree of legal certainty. The government was especially concerned that exceptions comply with Hong Kong's international obligations under the Agreement on Trade-Related Aspects of Intellectual Property Rights (TRIPS) – particularly Article 61, requiring deterrent criminal penalties in cases of commercial piracy, and Article 13, providing that limitations or exceptions must be confined to certain special cases which do not conflict with a normal exploitation of the work or unreasonably prejudice the legitimate interests of the rights holder (the "three-step test").[64]

[60] Under Article 23 of the Basic Law of the HKSAR, Hong Kong "shall enact laws on its own to prohibit any act of treason, secession, sedition [or] subversion" against the Central Government of the People's Republic of China. *See* Wong Yiu-chung, *'Super Paradox' or 'Leninist Integration': The Politics of Legislating Article 23 of Hong Kong's Basic Law*, 30 ASIAN PERSPECTIVE 65 (2006).

[61] Such groups include Keyboard Frontline, Netizens Power and the Copyrights and Derivative Works Alliance. Members of these groups, active on social media sites and internet discussion forums, are increasingly vocal in the offline world. Of the 2,455 written submissions received in the lead-up to the 2014 Bill, 2,387 were from internet users and netizen groups, of which 2,125 originated or were generated from online templates. *See* COMMERCE AND ECONOMIC DEVELOPMENT BUREAU, LEGISLATIVE COUNCIL BRIEF: COPYRIGHT (AMENDMENT) BILL 2014, CITB 07/09/17, para. 4 (2014), www.ipd.gov.hk/eng/intellectual_property/copyright/LegCo_Brief_2014_e.pdf [hereinafter LEGISLATIVE COUNCIL BRIEF ON COPYRIGHT (AMENDMENT) BILL 2014].

[62] *Id.* para. 3.

[63] TREATMENT OF PARODY UNDER THE COPYRIGHT REGIME: CONSULTATION PAPER, *supra* note 51.

[64] LEGISLATIVE COUNCIL BRIEF ON COPYRIGHT (AMENDMENT) BILL 2014, *supra* note 61, para. 5.

Addressing parody directly, a new section exempted fair dealing for the purpose of "parody, satire, caricature or pastiche."[65] In determining whether dealing was fair, all the circumstances were to be taken into account, in particular the purpose and nature of the dealing, whether it was nonprofit-making or commercial, the nature of the work, the amount and substantiality of the portion dealt with, and the effect of the dealing on the potential market for or value of the work.

The government expressed the view that the amendments were justified because the acts were well-recognized practices which had been accommodated in overseas copyright regimes; they were common means for the public to express views or comment on current events and may promote freedom of expression; they may encourage creativity, nurture new talent, and boost the entertainment business, contributing to economic and cultural development; and they were commonly critical or transformative in nature and would be unlikely to compete with or substitute the original works.

Beyond citing dictionary definitions and opining that the acts taken together constituted a broad exemption, the government did not define parody, satire, caricature, or pastiche.[66] In doing so it was aware of the lack of a unified approach to parody in the corresponding provisions in Australia, the US, Canada, and the UK.[67]

Addressing parody-related acts, the bill proposed to expand the section covering fair dealing for the purposes of criticism, review and news reporting, a move intended to clarify the rights of internet users in particular.[68] First, a provision was to be added exempting fair dealing for the purpose of commenting on current events, on the basis that users commonly used copyright works when commenting on political or social matters. Second, a quotation exception, to no greater an extent than necessary for the specific purpose, allowing users to quote copyright works in facilitating discussion, providing information, or expressing opinions, for example on blogs and social media.[69] These two additions were aimed at addressing internet users' concerns. While "commenting" is clearly wider than "reporting," the proposed quotation exception may be invoked "whether for the purpose of criticism, review or otherwise."

However, the consultation revealed that respondent users believed the scope of permitted acts should include a wide range of common internet activities involving the use of copyright works as well as the circulation of the results on social media sites like YouTube and Facebook or discussion forums or blogs. Products and acts cited included mashups, altered pictures or videos, doujinshi, image or video capture, streaming of video game playing, posting of earnest performances of copyright works, and rewriting song lyrics.[70] Criticism of the bill focused on the contention that such acts would fall outside the exemptions if not done for the purposes covered by the fair dealing provisions. The concern was also raised that there was no "contract override" provision to prevent copyright owners from contractually excluding the exceptions.[71]

Most problematically, despite offering up the previously requested exceptions, the 2014 bill could not shake off the pejorative tag of "Internet Article 23." Its coincidence with the Umbrella

65 The proposed § 39A.

66 LEGISLATIVE COUNCIL BRIEF ON COPYRIGHT (AMENDMENT) BILL 2014, *supra* note 61, paras. 1 and 19.

67 TREATMENT OF PARODY UNDER THE COPYRIGHT REGIME: CONSULTATION PAPER, *supra* note 51, para. 25.

68 Copyright Ordinance, (1997) Cap. 528, § 39 (H.K.).

69 LEGISLATIVE COUNCIL BRIEF ON COPYRIGHT (AMENDMENT) BILL 2014, *supra* note 61, para 13.

70 *Id.*

71 Stuart Lau, *Hong Kong copyright bill explained: why are people so concerned about this?*, SOUTH CHINA MORNING POST (Dec. 17, 2015), www.scmp.com/news/hong-kong/politics/article/1888931/hong-kong-copyright-bill-explained-why-are-people-so.

Movement exposed the bill to the skepticism and boiling resentment that had been engendered by broken promises of democracy and the sting of tear gas.[72] Satirical imagery – inserting the chief executive into Cultural Revolution – style propaganda posters, or superimposing his leadership team's faces onto a movie poster for *The Avengers* retitled "The Suppressors" – featured in the anti-bill campaign. Ironically, such examples would likely have fallen within the proposed fair dealing exceptions.

But they, and the overall message, struck a chord. An online petition opposing the bill attracted more than 55,000 signatures ahead of the second reading. Online user groups clamoured for greater protection, by introducing fair use or blanket exception for noncommercial UGC. Pan-democrat lawmakers came on board and promised to filibuster the bill,[73] one of them duly proposing over 1,000 amendments.[74]

Despite its anxiety to see digital copyright reforms passed into law,[75] the government – claiming to have the support of copyright owners – rejected the suggestion of a UGC exception.[76] First, it stated that the exception may not comply with TRIPS Article 13, not being confined to certain special cases – an objection equally applicable to the open-ended doctrine of fair use. Second, it was unclear on which acts might be covered by a UGC exception that were not covered by the proposed fair dealing exceptions, and why those acts deserved protection. Third, it opined that the concept was unsettled and developing, with only Canada having adopted it in legislation.[77]

After three months of filibustering and negotiations,[78] with all sides bemoaning the others' unwillingness to compromise,[79] the bill was moved to the back of the agenda and effectively

[72] The association is also drawn by Peter K. Yu, *The Quest for a User-Friendly Copyright Regime in Hong Kong*, 32 Am. U. Int'l L. Rev. 283 (2016).

[73] Kris Cheng, *Gov't Says New Copyright Law Will Not Restrict Speech Amid Concerns of Parody Ban*, Hong Kong Free Press (Dec. 3, 2015), www.hongkongfp.com/2015/12/03/govt-says-new-copyright-law-will-not-restrict-speech-amid-concerns-of-parody-ban.

[74] Stuart Lau, *Hong Kong Government's Shelving of Controversial Copyright Bill: What Went Wrong?*, South China Morning Post (Feb. 26, 2016), www.scmp.com/news/hong-kong/politics/article/1917070/hong-kong-governments-shelving-controversial-copyright-bill.

[75] The Legislative Council Brief on Copyright (Amendment) Bill 2014 warned: "We are not free from the watchful eyes of the international community. Some US copyright owners associations have made submissions to the Office of the United States Trade Representative (USTR) suggesting that Hong Kong should be put under a list of 'Deserving Special Mention' and 'Watch List' in the Special 301 Report as they allege that the existing copyright legislation of Hong Kong provides inadequate copyright protection in the digital environment." *See* Legislative Council Brief on Copyright (Amendment) Bill 2014, *supra* note 61, para. 2.

[76] *Id.*, para. 19. Note that some submissions on UGC used the term "secondary creations." The government observed that such a term is not commonly used in copyright jurisprudence and may cover a wider range of activities, including the creation of derivative works by adaptation or modification. It declined to take the analysis of secondary creations any further. *Id.*, para 5.

[77] Copyright Modernisation Act, S.C. 2012, c 20, § 29.21 (Can.). The Hong Kong government observed that Australia and the UK had declined to adopt the concept for the time being, while the US and the EU were examining it. *See* Legislative Council Brief on Copyright (Amendment) Bill 2014, *supra* note 61, para 19. The same concerns have been raised by the Hong Kong Bar Association in its *Position Paper on the Copyright (Amendment) Bill 2014*. *See* Special Committee on Intellectual Property, Hong Kong Bar Association, Position Paper on the Copyright (Amendment) Bill 2014 and the 3 Amendments Proposed by Certain LegCo Members (2016), www.hkba.org/sites/default/files/Copyright%20(Amendment)%20Bill%202014%20. . .%20(E).pdf. In a statement, the Law Society of Hong Kong said UGC or contract override provisions required "serious and thorough evaluation" which should not delay the passing of the bill. *See* Lau, *supra* note 71.

[78] Kris Cheng, *Copyright Bill Officially Withdrawn after Months of Filibustering*, Hong Kong Free Press (Apr. 15, 2016), www.hongkongfp.com/2016/04/15/copyright-bill-officially-withdrawn-after-months-of-filibustering.

[79] Eric Cheung, *Copyright Owners, Netizens Fail to Reach Consensus in Copyright Bill Talks*, Hong Kong Free Press (Feb. 18, 2016), www.hongkongfp.com/2016/02/18/four-sides-fail-to-reach-consensus-on-copyright-bill.

dropped for the remainder of the government's term.[80] Optimistic appraisals were few and far between as stakeholders lamented a lose–lose result.[81]

ANALYZING THE OUTCOME

Copyright has always contained a tension between restrictive rights in private property and the right to freedom of speech. If a fair balance is to be maintained, the law must adapt to changing circumstances. The in-tandem evolution of the digital economy, on the one hand, and norms of netizen behavior, on the other, presents a major challenge to the fragile equilibrium that copyright law seeks to maintain between competing interests. The longer copyright reform is delayed in Hong Kong, the longer parties on both sides of the debate must tolerate an increasingly uncertain and inapposite legal framework.

Did the 2014 bill fairly balance these competing interests? The government and copyright owners appeared to be satisfied that it did, even after conceding on additional exemptions. The opposition's objections – and the calls for UGC exceptions and fair use – largely focused on the risk that users might inadvertently incur criminal liability for noncommercial infringement of the communication right. This raises the question whether the proposed reform cast the criminal net wider than was necessary to protect the interests of copyright owners.

The answer seems to be no. In the "prejudice" limb of the communication right in the 2014 bill, the government dropped the previous wording "more than trivial economic prejudice," which had been criticized as unclear and overly broad.[82] The revised provision described specific economic considerations: the purpose of the communication; the nature of the work including its commercial value; the amount and substantiality of the portion communicated in relation to the work as a whole; the mode of communication; and the economic prejudice caused to the copyright owner including the effect on the potential market for or value of the work.[83] The scope and specificity of these factors would exclude the vast majority of noncommercial and nonpiratical activity by ordinary internet users.[84]

It is apparent that a real issue, if not the real issue, behind the hostile reception to "Cyberspace Article 23" was the conflation of copyright law with the perceived government interest in controlling speech. This position was understandable but misconceived. It has been suggested that, as against the government, copyright owners and users have a commonality rather than a conflict of interest: copyright's protection of ideas is a critical element of the freedom of speech. A law which enhances copyright protection while protecting parodic expression creates dual

[80] Chantal Yuen, *Copyright Bill Fails to Pass before Gov't Imposed Deadline*, Hong Kong Free Press (Mar. 4, 2016), www.hongkongfp.com/2016/03/04/copyright-bill-fails-to-pass-before-govt-imposed-deadline.

[81] Stuart Lau & Vivienne Chow, *Blame Game Begins As Hong Kong Copyright Bill Shelved Indefinitely*, South China Morning Post (Mar. 4, 2016), www.scmp.com/news/hong-kong/politics/article/1920593/blame-game-begins-hong-kong-copyright-bill-shelved.

[82] It was once proposed that the infringing communication must cause "more than trivial economic prejudice" to the copyright owners. It was hoped that the proposed wording could "allay netizens' concerns regarding the possible impact of the criminal liability for the proposed prejudicial communication offence." *See* Legislative Council Brief on Copyright (Amendment) Bill 2014, *supra* note 61, para. 9. It turned out to be a false hope.

[83] *Id.*, para. 10. *See also* Alice Lee, Submissions to the Legislative Council (July 26, 2011), www.legco.gov.hk/yr10-11/english/bc/bc10/papers/bc100723cb1-2825-1-e.pdf.

[84] During the public debates over the bill, Ada Leung Ka-lai, director of the Hong Kong SAR Intellectual Property Department, gave assurances that the public could rely on the new exemptions and would not be targeted, saying: "We target large-scale copyright infringement, not individual users." *See* Lau, *supra* note 71.

limitations on government authority, with the rights of the individual being the ultimate beneficiary.[85]

Guan suggests, convincingly, that the government's possible interference with free speech is a serious constitutional issue which should be hashed out elsewhere, not in the copyright amendment process.[86] The fact that the issues were conflated shows that the most unlikely of matters can snowball when tensions between the rulers and the ruled are running high.[87] The case of copyright reform reveals that, in Hong Kong, those conflicts are being addressed in a manner which can ultimately negate progress. That may be explained by the city's unusual constitutional set up.

Yam posits that hybrid regimes are inherently unstable and prone to generating political conflict due to their governments' ineffectiveness at suppressing opposition. In a purely authoritarian state, the ruling party dominates all arenas of contestation. Hong Kong, by contrast, enjoys a free press and a legislature which is partially democratically elected, granting a voice to the political opposition. The opposition cannot form a government, but it can filibuster, thus forcing the government to the negotiation table. It can also defend against attempts to ban this tactic by filibustering away proposed changes to the procedural rules of the legislature.[88] Copyright reform is not the only worthwhile initiative to fall by the wayside as genuine legislative deliberation is replaced with bickering and gamesmanship.

WHERE DO WE GO FROM HERE?

Hong Kong copyright law is not entirely bereft of digital adaptations. The Copyright Ordinance ushered in a range of innovations to an outdated British law that had been superseded in Britain almost a decade earlier. The "making available" right, though now dated by international standards, appears to have been the first such provision in Asia.[89] Where the express terms of the Ordinance are ambiguous in their application to the online realm, the courts have been willing to step in and innovate. This occurred in the case of a BitTorrent seeder who was held to have infringed the distribution right, rather than the noncriminal and online-specific right of making available, facilitating criminal liability for online piracy.[90]

But useful innovations, many of which reflect common sense and accepted norms of digital conduct, are not reflected in the law. A media-shifting exemption, permitting conversion of CDs to MP3 files for personal use, would validate a widely practiced activity lacking in detriment to copyright owners.[91] OSP provisions regulating notification and takedown of infringing materials would be a sensible addition clarifying proper procedures and allocating responsibility appropriately. Both media-shifting and OSP codes of practice were proposed in the decade-long digital copyright consultation, but they have lapsed with the 2014 bill. It may be argued that

85 Guan, *supra* note 59.

86 *Id.*

87 For example, medical practitioners demanded that lawmakers reject legislation reforming the Hong Kong Medical Council, citing suspicions as to the chief executive's intentions for appointments to the Council. *See* Albert Cheng, *Hong Kong Doctors' Advice: Reject Medical Reform Bill, and Then Get Rid of CY Leung*, South China Morning Post (July 14, 2016), www.scmp.com/comment/insight-opinion/article/1989806/hong-kong-doctors-advice-reject-medical-reform-bill-and-then.

88 Julius Yam, *The Role of Courts in Hybrid Regimes and a Reconceptualisation of Separation of Powers: The Case of Filibuster in Hong Kong*, 17 Australian J. Asian L. Art. 3 (2016).

89 Pendleton et al., *supra* note 21, Div. IV, para. [1803].

90 Chan Nai Ming v. HKSAR, (2007) 10 H.K.C.F.A.R. 273, [2007] 3 H.K.C. 255 (C.F.A.).

91 Legislative Council Brief on Copyright (Amendment) Bill 2014, *supra* note 61, para. 12. At the time of the 2014 bill, such an exception had been legislated in Australia and New Zealand.

acquiescence or voluntary codes of practice could fill the breach. But, as was pointed out in submissions to the UK's Hargreaves Report, copyright law should be relevant to consumers and provide certainty to the creative and the technology industries which innovate within the limits of the regulatory framework.[92]

There are legitimate arguments that the dynamic, participative nature of the Internet requires some form of UGC protection[93] which may not contravene TRIPS,[94] and the Hong Kong government has left open the possibility of returning to the idea should it gain wider international acceptance.[95] Many regard the UGC model as the only way to achieve a digital utopia. In Hong Kong, as in many other jurisdictions, the copyright conversation has boiled down to "UGC or no UGC." Innovative and powerful provisions such as those for "commenting on current events" and "quotation" have been brushed aside. As has been seen, the former is broader than the existing fair dealing exception for "reporting current events" and should facilitate freedom of expression.[96] The latter goes even further in leaving the purpose of quotation open. Had it been enacted, quotations of all kinds of copyright work would have been permitted, provided that the work had been released, the use of the quotation was fair, the extent of the quotation was no more than was required by the specific purpose for which it was used, and the use was accompanied by a sufficient acknowledgment (unless it was not reasonably practicable to do so).[97]

Such an exception would cover common uses of copyright works whether they were altered or not, whether there was any parodic element or not. Possible examples include quotations of literary or artistic works, films or sound recordings for the purposes of facilitating discussions, providing information or expressing opinions as used on blogs and social media websites.[98] It is hard to see why such a broad exception cannot do what the UGC model can.

Perhaps the ultimate question is not a legal one. Even if UGC or similar exceptions had been written into the bill, the filibustering would not have subsided. It is political stalemate that has condemned copyright reform in Hong Kong, at least for now.[99]

92 Hargreaves, *supra* note 51, para. 5.12 (Consumer Focus submission).

93 *See* Peter K. Yu, *The Quest for a User-Friendly Copyright Regime in Hong Kong*, 32 Am. U. Int'l L. Rev. 283 (2016); Wenwei Guan, *Fair Dealing Doctrine Caught between Parody and UGC Exemptions: Hong Kong's 2014 Copyright Amendment and Beyond*, 45 Hong Kong L.J. 719 (2015).

94 If confining the exemption to noncommercial copying satisfies the requirement of restriction to "certain special cases": Jojo Y. C. Mo, *The Copyright (Amendment) Bill 2014 in Hong Kong: A Blessing or a Curse?*, 38(2) Statute L. Rev. 211 (2017).

95 Legislative Council Brief on Copyright (Amendment) Bill 2014, *supra* note 61, para. 19.

96 *Id.* para. 13. Copinger and Skone James on Copyright (Kevin Garnett et al. eds., 16th ed. 2011), *cited in* Legislative Council Brief on Copyright (Amendment) Bill 2014, *supra* note 61, para. 13 (even the existing exception for reporting current events has been construed liberally in the UK).

97 The proposed §§ 39(2) and (6), which were modeled on the newly added "quotation" provisions in the UK, which were in turn based on Art. 10 of the Berne Convention. *See* Legislative Council Brief on Copyright (Amendment) Bill 2014, *supra* note 61, para. 13 (citing The Copyright and Rights in Performances (Quotation and Parody) Regulations, 2014, SI 2014/2356 (Eng.)).

98 Legislative Council Brief on Copyright (Amendment) Bill 2014, *supra* note 61, para. 13. *See also* Tanya Aplin, The Case for Mandatory, Global Fair Use, Presentation at NUS–UPenn–HKU Conference on Comparative Dimensions of Limitations and Exceptions in Copyright Law (July 21–22, 2016).

99 Stuart Lau, *Five Reasons the Hong Kong Copyright Bill Failed*, South China Morning Post (Mar. 4, 2016), www.scmp.com/news/hong-kong/politics/article/1920569/five-reasons-hong-kong-copyright-bill-failed.

20

Rights, Exceptions, and the "Work" of News

Graeme W. Austin[*]

So, a lot of my information doesn't come from the news. It comes from what I see on the Internet.[1]

1 INTRODUCTION

This chapter considers whether the rise of citizen journalism should provoke a reassessment of the public goods problem that copyright seeks to solve. Both consumption patterns and methods of production of news are changing as social media platforms become more prominent. There is now an extraordinary array of content purporting to be news,[2] and people are increasingly turning to social media for news content, rather than to traditional media institutions.[3] Case laws on copyright exceptions and defenses appear to be catching up. Recent English cases have recognized that the fair dealing exception for news and current events should extend to citizen journalism.[4]

This shift in thinking about what counts as news for the purposes of fair dealing does not exhaust the social policy issues that need to be considered as copyright responds to today's media environment and to changes in the wider information ecosystem. As a result of lowered technological and economic barriers to production and dissemination, we are now awash with content purporting to be news.[5] We are also witnessing the rise of "fake news," including politically or financially

* The author is grateful to Professors Haochen Sun, Shyam Balganesh, and Wee Loon Ng-Loy for the invitation to participate in this research project and acknowledges the excellent research assistance of Scott Fletcher, Carlos Smith Diaz, and Lucy Kenner. Thanks are also due for feedback provided by the many experts participants in the symposium on copyright exceptions held at the National University of Singapore Faculty of Law in 2016, and to Nicole Moreham, and my colleagues at Victoria University of Wellington, where this paper was presented as a faculty seminar.

1 *Six Virginia Residents Share their Election Perspectives and Voting Plans*, PBS NEWSHOUR (Aug. 16, 2016), www.pbs.org/newshour/bb/six-virginia-residents-share-their-election-perspectives-and-voting-plans/.

2 *See generally* IAN CRAM, CITIZEN JOURNALISTS: NEWER MEDIA, REPUBLICAN MOMENTS AND THE CONSTITUTION (2015).

3 In 2016, for example, the Pew Research Foundation noted that over 60 percent of Americans get news from social media. *See News Use Across Social Media Platforms 2016*, PEW RESEARCH CENTER (May 26, 2016), www.journalism.org/2016/05/26/news-use-across-social-media-platforms-2016/.

4 *See infra* Section 2.

5 *See* Mark A. Lemley, *IP in a World without Scarcity*, 90 N.Y.U. L. REV. 460, 486 (2015). The phenomenon is not of course confined to news. *See* JEREMY RIFKIN, THE ZERO MARGINAL COST SOCIETY: THE INTERNET OF THINGS, THE COLLABORATIVE COMMONS, AND THE ECLIPSE OF CAPITALISM (2014).

motivated promulgation of false information purporting to be news.[6] Given this glut of "news" content, the production of content itself might not be the most relevant focus of the public goods problem to which systems of intellectual property rights are conventionally directed. Today, encouraging the production of *reliable* content may be more important than calibrating rights and exceptions in order to encourage the production of content alone.

The question explored in this chapter is whether our understanding of the public goods issues that copyright addresses should extend to the task of facilitating more efficient internalization of investment in verification and authentication of news content. In recent years, we have seen firms entering a new market niche for verifying content that purports to report current events. These efforts sit alongside initiatives by social media platforms themselves to filter "fake news" from their sites.[7] In an information ecosystem where there is plenty of content but a premium on truth and reliability, should copyright norms be more aligned with the work of these new third-party initiated "veracity markets"? That question implicates a larger set of issues related to how we think about incentives as the information ecosystem evolves – and about the continued salience of orthodox copyright norms in an information ecosystem that is no longer defined by scarcity.[8]

In modern Anglo-American copyright law, we largely take it for granted that expressions of authorial subjectivity are the "work" whose production both rights and exceptions should be directed at encouraging.[9] Beyond *sui generis* schemes, such as the EU Database Directive,[10] other kinds of "work," including investment in verifying data, count for less and less.[11] As we confront the implications of this content glut for the prospects of receiving reliable news information, it may be useful to recall that copyright policies in the news context have sometimes been directed at issues other than encouraging the production of content.[12] For example, in the news context, the 1870s brought the emergence of statutory protections for "Telegraph Copyright," which aimed to encourage the investment in the telegraph infrastructure necessary to bring news content to distant colonies and dominions, in a number of British Commonwealth jurisdictions.[13] "Telegraph Copyright" is a useful reminder that different kinds of approaches to the calibration of rights and exceptions have been necessary in the light of prevailing technological and economic conditions. The copyright doctrines and policies that we now treat as orthodox do not necessarily offer all the answers.

2 CITIZEN JOURNALISM AND FAIR DEALING

From copyright's beginnings, legal prohibitions against unlicensed exploitation of others' creative work have been directed at preventing free-riding on the investment in the creation and

[6] *See generally* Mark Verstraete et al., *Identifying and Countering Fake News* (U. Ariz. James E. Rogers C.L., Report No. 20017), https://law.arizona.edu/report-identifying-and-countering-fake-news (setting forth a detailed taxonomy of "fake news").

[7] *See id.*

[8] *See, e.g.*, Lemley, *supra* note 5, at 460; Jon M. Newman, *Copyright Freeconomics*, 66 VAND. L. REV. 1409 (2013).

[9] *See infra* Section 3.

[10] *See* Council Directive 96/9, 1996 O.J. (L 77) (EC). In 2016, the European Commission announced a public consultation on the possibility of extending related rights protections for publishers. *See Digital Single Market*, EUR. COM., https://ec.europa.eu/digital-single-market/en/news/public-consultation-role-publishers-copyright-value-chain-and-panorama-exception.

[11] *See, e.g.*, Feist Publications, Inc., v. Rural Telephone Serv. Co., 499 U.S. 340 (1991).

[12] *See generally* LIONEL BENTLY & BRAD SHERMAN, THE MAKING OF MODERN INTELLECTUAL PROPERTY LAW (2008) (tracing the rise of creativity as copyright's key organizing principle and discussing different kinds of policies pursued by earlier intellectual property laws).

[13] *See infra* Section 3.

dissemination of goods that are non-rivalrous, and, for the most part, non-excludable.[14] The Preamble to the first copyright statute, the 1709 Statute of Anne, described this public goods problem in the following terms:

> Whereas Printers, Booksellers, and other Persons, have of late frequently taken the Liberty of Printing, Reprinting, and Publishing, or causing to be Printed, Reprinted, and Published Books, and other Writings, without the Consent of the Authors or Proprietors of such Books and Writings, to their very great Detriment, and too often to the Ruin of them and their Families.[15]

The Act was aimed at "Prevent[ing] ... such Practices for the future."[16]

Legal prohibitions against copying create an artificial scarcity, thereby allowing markets in copyright-protected content to emerge.[17] From those markets, rewards for creative endeavor can be derived. So understood, copyright exemplifies the familiar theme that property rights facilitate the internalization of investment.[18] Across the Atlantic, the framers of the US Constitution pursued similar themes. When justifying the proposal to grant the US Congress legislative power to enact national copyright laws, James Madison wrote that, with copyright (as with patents), "[t]he public good fully coincides ... with the claims of individuals."[19]

Because the broader public interest is not necessarily captured fully by the impulse to privatize *everything* that would otherwise be in the commons, limitations on property owners' exclusive rights usually evolve.[20] Again, copyright is no different. As other chapters in this volume explore, copyright statutes typically include a large number of exceptions and limitations on the rights of copyright owners. Together, these comprise a set of policy levers that "balance"[21] the exclusive rights of copyright owners with the wider public interest.

In the Anglo tradition, an important set of exceptions is known as "fair dealing." Fair dealing has the same legal provenance as the US "fair use";[22] the difference is that fair dealing was originally tethered to specific uses and remains so in most jurisdictions adopting the fair dealing model. A fair dealing with a copyright-protected work does not require a license from the copyright owner, nor does it require the party dealing with the work to pay any compensation for the use.[23] Exceptions of this kind are typically explained in terms of market failure and societal benefit. Relevant market failure occurs most often when the transaction costs associated with negotiating licenses to use copyright-protected material are higher than the value of the use,

14 *See* Yochai Benkler, The Wealth of Networks: How Social Production Transforms Markets and Freedom 311 (2006).

15 *See* Copyright Act 1709, 8 Ann. c 19, pmbl. (Gr. Brit.).

16 *Id.*

17 *See* Paul A. Samuelson, *The Pure Theory of Public Expenditure*, 36 Rev. Econ. & Stat. 387, 387 (1954).

18 *See* Harold Demsetz, *Toward a Theory of Property Rights*, 57 Am. Econ. Rev. 347, 348 (1967). Because of the non-rivalrous character of copyright-protected works, copyright is not obviously justified by the need to prevent overuse. *See* Carol M. Rose, *Romans, Roads, and Romantic Creators: Traditions of Public Property in the Information Age* 66 L. & Contemp. Probs. 89 (2003).

19 The Federalist No. 43 (James Madison).

20 For a classic analysis of the evolution of rights and limitations on those rights, *see* Carol M. Rose, *Crystals and Mud in Property Law*, 40 Stan. L. Rev. 577 (1988).

21 The "balance" rhetoric begs more questions than it answers. As the Preamble to the Statute of Anne underscores with its reference to the "Advancement of Learning," the creation of exclusive rights in creative work is itself understood to be in the public interest.

22 *See generally* Graeme W. Austin, The Two Faces of Fair Use, 25 N.Z.U. L.R. 285 (2012).

23 *Cf.* Jane Ginsburg, *Fair Use for Free, or Permitted-but-Paid?* 29 Berkeley Tech. L.J. 1383 (2014) (discussing "permitted but paid" fair use categories, under which copyright owners receive equitable remuneration for unlicensed uses).

leading to the possibility that the use will be foregone,[24] and subsequent creative activity will be inhibited. Consider the exception for dealings for the purposes of research and study. The costs of securing licenses for material that scholars wanted to use in new scholarship would likely be prohibitive, and, as a result, much research activity would not occur. Research and study also have an obvious social utility,[25] and are consistent with values of freedom of expression as well as those furthered by academic freedom.[26]

Technological and societal changes can affect the normative evaluation of the balance between rights and exceptions. For example, technological innovations can significantly increase the efficiency of transactions and ameliorate market failure problems.[27] And shifting perceptions of the value of different forms of creative work can change our understanding of how the copyright balance ought to be struck. For example, a number of software products now make it relatively easy to create audiovisual "mashups," or works that combine preexisting material from diverse sources into new, unified video productions. With diminishing costs of creation, the externalities produced by prohibitions against reusing others' material in the creation of these kinds of pastiche works might be regarded as more significant than in the past. Contrariwise, on the exceptions side, public interest claims supporting the fair dealing exception for research and study might be weaker in the context of research conducted within or for a private firm, including for-profit educational institutions. The appropriation of copyright-protected material for the benefit of a private entity's bottom line might provoke more careful scrutiny of the claim that copyright owners ought to subsidize others' business endeavors.

Similarly, the lowering of technological barriers to the production and dissemination of news content is causing a shift in our thinking about rights and exceptions.[28] Both the creation and wide dissemination of current events content are significantly easier and much less costly than ever before. Early this century, the Court of Appeal of England and Wales explained the purpose of the "current events" exception as being to protect the "role of the media" in informing the public about matters of current concern to the public,[29] language that reinforces the importance of the institutional origins of current events reporting.[30] Yet, when video, blogs, photos, vlogs, and tweets can all be disseminated by anyone with an internet connection, the character of the "role of the media" will increasingly be called into question in the fair dealing context, just as it has been in other areas of the law in which traditional media receive special treatment.[31]

In a high-profile 2016 decision, the High Court for England and Wales confirmed that the exception for fair dealing for the purposes of reporting current events is not limited to traditional new media outlets and extends to the work of citizen journalists. *England and Wales Cricket*

[24] *See* Wendy Gordon, *Fair Use As Market Failure: A Structural and Economic Analysis of the "Betamax" Case and Its Predecessors*, 82 Colum. L. Rev. 1600, 1618 (1982).

[25] Kienitz v. Sconnie Nation LLC, 766 F.3d. 756, 759 (7th Cir. 2014) (suggesting that academic research might not be possible if researchers were required to find and negotiate copyright owner consent). Academic research thus has a dual fair use claim: public benefit and market failure.

[26] *See generally* Ann Monotti & Sam Ricketson, Universities and Intellectual Property: Ownership and Exploitation 42–49 (2003).

[27] Tom Bell, *Fair Use vs. Fared Use: The Impact of Automated Rights Management on Copyright's Fair Use Doctrine*, 76 N.C. L. Rev. 557, 584 (1998) (arguing that automation of licensing reduces transaction costs of licensing access, thus reducing the scope of fair use insofar as it is a market failure response).

[28] *See generally* Cram, *supra* note 2.

[29] Ashdown v. Telegraph Group Ltd. [2001] EWCA (Civ) 1142 [64] (Eng.).

[30] *See also* the observation of Salmon J. in Copyright Licensing Ltd. v. University of Auckland [2002] 3 NZLR 76 (HC) at [41] (N.Z.) (suggesting that it would be difficult to imagine the legitimate reporting of current events in some other circumstance than by a section of the news media).

[31] *See generally* Cram, *supra* note 2.

Board Ltd. v. Tixdaq Ltd.[32] involved the posting of eight-second clips from broadcasts of cricket matches to the defendants' website, www.fanatix.com, and various apps for electronic devices, including the iPhone and iPad. When sued for copyright infringement, the defendants alleged that the activities were within the UK fair dealing defense for the reporting of current events.[33] Rejecting this argument, Arnold J. held that the dealings were not fair, and that the infringement claim was made out. Of particular interest here is his Lordship's observation that citizen journalism is the kind of "news" that falls within the fair dealing exception. He reasoned that the exception is "not restricted to traditional media" and that "citizen journalism" can qualify as reporting current events. His Lordship elaborated:

> If a member of the public captures images and/or sound of a newsworthy event using their mobile phone and uploads it to a social media site like Twitter, then that may well qualify as reporting current events even if it is accompanied by relatively little in the way of commentary.[34]

A similar issue arose some two months later in *Heythrop Zoological Gardens Ltd. v. Captive Animals Protection Society*, a decision of the UK Intellectual Property Enterprise Court. The claimants operated a private zoo that supplied animals to the film and television industry. They applied for a preliminary injunction against an animal rights organization, "CAPS," claiming inter alia that its posting of photographs and video footage to a website breached the claimants' rights in its employee zookeepers' performances. Rights in certain kinds of performances, including "variety acts," are granted and protected by the UK Copyright, Designs, and Patents Act 1988.[35] The images showed various performances by the claimant's zookeepers, together with tigers and lions. CAPS claimed that these depicted mistreatment of the animals and indicated that the animals were exhibiting recognizable signs of stress. The images were captured by CAPS during an open day. Other images posted by CAPS were supplied to it by members of the public and by a former employee of the zoo.

As for the performers' rights claim, Birss J. considered that the claimants presented a good case that their rights had been infringed by the taking of a substantial part of the performances. However, his Lordship also considered that CAPS had a good case that its dealing with the material was "fair."[36] The issue as to the journalistic character of CAPS's activities arose in the context of section 12 of the UK Human Rights Act 1998. This provision is triggered when a court is considering whether to grant any relief which, if granted, might affect the exercise of the right to freedom of expression set forth in the European Convention on Human Rights. In broad outline, a court must have "particular regard" to the Convention right to freedom of expression. When the proceedings relate to material that is journalistic, literary or artistic, a court must then have regard to a number of factors, including whether "it is, or would be, in the public interest for the material to be published."[37] Relevant passages from Birss J.'s analysis are as follows:

[32] England and Wales Cricket Board Ltd. v. Tixdaq Ltd. et al. [2016] EWHC (Ch) 575 (Eng.).

[33] The defendant contended the app, designed for 18- to 34-year-olds, did report on current events as individual sports fans shared their own reports, as opposed to traditional media companies, at 110, that publication caused no harm to and in fact benefited the claimants at 137, and that the extent and nature of the eight-second clips justified their use. *See also id.* at 149.

[34] *Id.* at 114.

[35] Copyright, Designs, and Patents Act 1988, § 180(2) (U.K.) [hereinafter CAPS].

[36] CAPS invoked the fair dealing exception for criticism or review, rather than the fair dealing for the purposes of news reporting. *See id.*, § 30, sch. 2, para. 2(1) (extending the fair dealing defense to rights in performances).

[37] Human Rights Act 1989, § 12 (U.K.).

> [T]he publications in this case are clearly journalistic in nature … and that is high value speech … . The issue of animal treatment is clearly a matter of current public interest. That alone demonstrates that this case is a long way from a case about celebrity gossip.
>
> … CAPS is a charity and a campaigning organisation. Today campaigning organisations carry out an important journalistic function. … The fact that such organisations are not newspapers does not mean that they do not carry out a vital role in a democratic society which is, in effect, investigative journalism.

Drawing on this analysis, Birss J. concluded that the application for the interim injunction should be declined.

These cases expand the notion of "news" beyond traditional formats, something for which a number of leading commentators have been agitating.[38] The expansion is not merely about the character of the content – whether, for example, "infotainment" today counts as news.[39] These cases signal an expanding understanding of who creates news content in the new media environment. For the purposes of fair dealing (and, as in *Heythrop*, also in the remedial context) news creators are no longer to be confined to traditional news outlets. This fair dealing defense appears no longer "intended" *only* to "protect the role of the media in informing the public about matters of current concern to the public," to quote language from an earlier decision of the Court of Appeal.[40]

If the purpose is to inform, then the expansion of the vehicles that may legitimately rely on the fair dealing exception in order to achieve that purpose seems entirely sensible, a point that is underscored by consideration of the purpose of the exception. With many kinds of news reporting, the kind of market failure that justifies fair dealing will often be present. The speed of news cycles may make negotiating a license impractical (or weight the transactions too much in favor of the copyright owner). In the case of scoops, the target is unlikely to willingly license the use of copyright-protected material that will help substantiate claims made in news reports.[41] The inability to rely on a functioning market for copyright-protected material will often justify the application of an exception,[42] and this will be so whatever kind of news platform is involved. In addition, the reporting of news and current affairs is of enormous social value and contributes to democratic accountability and freedom of expression. Discussions of citizen journalism typically emphasize the disruptive and participatory potential of these flows of uncensored communication, which, in turn, contribute to the rise of new kinds of cultural citizenship that do not depend on resources from official or traditional sources. During the Arab Spring, for instance, ordinary citizens could record and distribute news faster than governments could adopt measures to control it.[43] The new case law thus aligns with both the rise in consumption of citizen journalism and the widespread celebration of the potential of citizen journalism to

[38] *See, e.g.*, Melissa de Zwart, *"Seriously Entertaining":The Panel and the Future of Fair Dealing*, 8 Media & Arts L. Rev. 1 (2003); Michael Handler & David Rolph, *'A Real Pea Souper': The Panel Case and the Development of the Fair Dealing Defences to Copyright Infringement in Australia*, 27 Melb. U.L. Rev. 381 (2003).

[39] Graeme W. Austin, *Four Questions about the Australian Approach to Fair Dealing Defenses to Copyright Infringement*, 57 J. Copyright Soc'y. U.S.A. 611, 617 (2010).

[40] Ashdown v. Telegraph Group Ltd. [2001] EWCA Civ 1142 at 64. For a similar characterization, *see also* Copyright Licensing Ltd. v. University of Auckland [2002] 3 N.Z.L.R. 76 at 41.

[41] Graeme W. Austin, *EU and US Perspectives on Fair Dealing for the Purpose of Parody or Satire*, 39 U.N.S.W. L.J. 684, 710–11 (2016).

[42] *Id.* at 708–9.

[43] Naila Hamdy, *Arab Citizen Journalism in Action: Challenging Mainstream Media, Authorities and Media Laws*, 6 Westminster Papers in Comm. and Culture 92, 93 (2009).

liberate both the consumers and producers of news from traditional institutional contexts and government control.[44]

The kinds of challenges posed by citizen journalism are not of course unique to copyright exceptions. In a variety of contexts, the rise of new information platforms has required courts, policymakers, and legislators to consider how far special privileges afforded to the media extend. These privileges largely evolved in response to the media's key role in democratic governance. Whether citizen journalism "counts" as media in contexts such as defamation, access to the legislature, and privacy is preoccupying courts and policymakers in many jurisdictions. As the US Supreme Court has noted, even the very power to define what is and what is not media can raise difficult constitutional questions. Justice Berger observed in 1978, long before the rise of the blogosphere, "[a]lmost any author may quite accurately assert that he is contributing to the flow of information to the public."[45]

In recent commentary, it has been suggested that media that is analogous to traditional formats will remain important in courts' understanding of the privileges afforded to the media.[46] Birss J.'s observations as to the "journalistic function" of campaign organizations might, however, anticipate a more functional approach, one that emphasizes substance over form. In the immediate context, the recognition of the role of citizen journalists in furthering the purposes of fair dealing might also provoke some rethinking of the English Court of Appeal's analysis of the relationship between copyright protections and human rights protections for freedom of expression and information. In *Ashdown v. Telegraph Group Ltd.*, the court famously suggested[47] that some unlicensed uses of copyright-protected material beyond the parameters of fair dealing might be required in the light of the protections for freedom of information set forth in Article 10 of the European Convention on Human Rights.[48] The court went on to say, however, that such a dealing would not necessarily be without compensation and that a court-ordered license fee might be an appropriate remedy.[49] For present purposes, we can leave aside the propriety of creating a liability rule out of traditional property concepts,[50] as well as the suggestion that the appropriate way of navigating between freedom of expression and copyright is to impose a fee. It might nevertheless be useful to note that the holding did not anticipate the differential burdens of the ruling on different kinds of producers of news. It is one thing to require an established newspaper or television channel to pay a court-ordered license fee, but possibly quite another for the operator of a small blogsite. As the influence of human rights principles on intellectual property continues to grow, the relationship between this part of the court's analysis in *Ashdown* and the expanded notion of what counts as news may need some further thought.

3 NEWS AND THE COPYRIGHT "WORK"

Traditional media outlets are themselves turning to social media and citizen journalism for news content. In 2012, the director of a prominent news organization was quoted as saying, "you can make the most amazing films using content from social networks, sometimes with the

[44] *See generally* DAN GILMOR, WE THE MEDIA: GRASSROOTS JOURNALISM BY THE PEOPLE, FOR THE PEOPLE (2004).

[45] First National Bank v. Bellotti, 435 U.S. 765, 801–2 (1978).

[46] *See generally* CRAM, *supra* note 2. *See also* Jared Schroder, *Focusing on How Rather Than on Whom: Constructing a Process-Based Framework for Interpreting the Press Clause in the Network-Society Era*,19 COMM. L. & POL'Y 509 (2014).

[47] Ashdown v. Telegraph Group Ltd. [2001] EWCA Civ 1142 at 39–45.

[48] The European Convention on Human Rights, art. 10, Nov. 4, 1950, Europ. T.S. No. 5, 213 U.N.T.S. 221.

[49] Ashdown v. Telegraph Group Ltd. [2001] EWCA Civ 1142 at 46.

[50] Guido Calabresi & A. Douglas Melamed, *Property Rules, Liability Rules, and Inalienability: One View of the Cathedral*, 85 HARV. L. REV. 1089 (1972).

permission and sometimes without the permission of the people who shot them."[51] When unlicensed uses are the subject of legal challenges, we might expect traditional media outlets to invoke the fair dealing exception. In such a case, many of the same issues are at play as in cases of citizen journalists' *own* unlicensed uses of content. In one respect, however, such uses of content from social networks will implicate a different set of issues: When citizen journalism has been used without a license, how should a court apprehend the character of the work?

The easy answer is simply to describe what has been taken, adopting the conventional fair dealing or fair use lens – that is, to consider the proximity of the work taken to copyright's "core." Raw video footage might be at one end of the spectrum, and heavily edited material at the other. If the appropriated material is of "low" authorship,[52] containing principally "facts," that will likely weigh in favor of a dealing or use being regarded as fair.

The conventional analysis may not, however, accommodate all the important policy issues that arise in the news context. Today, consumers seeking news that is reliable and accurate confront an information asymmetry problem. With news content, credence is a crucial public good – and it is expectations around the reliability of the content that provide a key plank in the normative justification for the special treatment of the media in various legal contexts. We cannot always ascertain, however, the reliability of news content from the content itself. One corollary of this is it might not only be the *production* values that are the most important characteristic of the work – or the extent to which the content manifests "originality" in the conventional copyright sense. Rather, the valuable attributes of the content might include the extent to which consumers of the content can rely on its veracity.

A notorious episode from 2013 illustrates the concern. It arose out of the intense debate that surrounded the involvement of the United States in the Syrian civil war and its use of force against the Assad regime.[53] In 2013, the *New York Times* published a story with the title "Brutality of Syrian Rebels Posing Dilemma in the West," which described a profoundly disturbing video that had been smuggled out of Syria by a former rebel fighter. The video was said to show the execution of seven Syrian rebel soldiers summarily executed by their leader. The *New York Times* story referenced the video in making the case that Al Qaeda and other extremist groups were growing among the ranks of the rebels whom the United States was supporting,[54] arguing that the US military assistance to those resisting the Assad regime could inadvertently strengthen "Islamic extremists and criminals."[55] It transpired, however, that the video footage had been made a year earlier, and the executioner had no connections with Al Qaeda or other known Jihadist groups. While the video depicted the brutality and depravity of some of the rebel soldiers, it did not support the specific thesis that providing military assistance to those fighting the Syrian government jeopardized the security interests of the United States. This episode, involving a reporter without accurate information about the video's provenance, and a content-maker who was apparently prepared to mislead in this way, raises serious questions about the

[51] Kate Buckley, *The Rise of Citizen Journalism*, The Guardian (June 11, 2012) (quoting Chris Shaw, editorial director ITN Productions), www.theguardian.com/media/2012/jun/11/rise-of-citizen-journalism. For a scholarly treatment of the same phenomenon, focusing on the effect of the institutional context of traditional news media on the use of citizen journalism, *see* Steve Paulussen & Pieter Ugille, *User Generated Content in the Newsroom: Professional and Organisational Constraints on Participatory Journalism*, 5 Westminster Papers in Comm. & Culture 24 (2008).

[52] Jane C. Ginsburg, *Creation and Commercial Value: Copyright Protection of Works of Information*, 90 Colum. L. Rev. 1865, 1916–35 (1990).

[53] Matt Sienkiewicz, *Start Making Sense: A Three-Tier Approach to Citizen Journalism*, 36 Media, Culture & Soc'y 691 (2014). The analysis that follows in the main text draws from the account set forth in this article.

[54] *Id.* at 692.

[55] C. J. Chivers, *Brutality of Syrian Rebels Posing Dilemma in the West*, N.Y. Times (Sept. 5, 2013).

capacity of citizen journalism (and its use by mainstream media) to be trusted to enhance our understanding of current events.[56]

With raw video footage of atrocities occurring in the context of armed conflict, we are a long way from the kind of characterization of the interests protected by the copyright in broadcasts of cricket matches that was set forth by Arnold J. in *England and Wales Cricket Board Ltd. v. Tixdaq Ltd.*:

> At least in the case of broadcasts and first fixations of films of sporting events, broadcasters and producers invest in the production of broadcasts and first fixations knowing, first, that some parts of the footage of an event (e.g. wickets in the case of cricket matches and goals in the case of football matches) will be more interesting to viewers than other parts and, secondly, that there is a market for highlights programmes and the like in addition to the market for continuous live coverage. It is for these reasons that broadcasters and producers invest, among other things, in the technology to produce action replays of particular events, which often involve editing footage from multiple camera angles, close-ups, slow motion and the like.[57]

On the production side, citizen journalism is not always the result of significant investment in the production of content. On the consumption side, the interest is partly in the content, but its more significant value is in its contribution to our understanding of domestic and international affairs. The veracity and reliability of the content is therefore key. For the purposes of the fair dealing analysis, therefore, when thinking about the nature of the copyright-protected work, some sensitivity to these aspects of the material that has been taken might be helpful.

The mainstreaming of citizen journalism has conventionally been understood in terms of a two-tier information ecology. One tier comprises the creators of the content itself; the second tier comprises the traditional media outlets, such as the *New York Times*, that make use of this content. As Matt Sienkiewicz explains, in the citizen journalism context there has now emerged what he describes as a middle "interpretive tier," one that is directed at credence concerns.[58] This tier comprises a group of semiprofessional journalists characterized by extensive knowledge of particular regions of the world from which much of the significant citizen journalism has been produced. They work collaboratively using online tools, sometimes drawing on academic support, to establish the reliability of news content through detailed verification processes. These kinds of processes enhance the trustworthiness of the content. As Sienkiewicz explains, this kind of work is increasingly necessary, given the sheer volume of user-generated content that vies for attention.[59] More recently, we have seen the emergence of firms such as Storyful, which seek to professionalize this tier,[60] acting as broker between content producers and mainstream users of content.[61] This is a new kind of "work" that can significantly enhance the value of the content.

In terms of copyright policies and doctrines, according value to this kind of endeavor may be difficult to accommodate with the new copyright orthodoxy that increasingly emphasizes the importance of subjective authorial activity. In the past several years the understanding of "originality" in copyright law has brought the "author" to the center of the analysis.[62] This

[56] Sienkiewicz, *supra* note 53, at 692.
[57] England and Wales Cricket Board Ltd. v. Tixdaq Ltd. et al. [2016] EWHC (Ch) 575 at 66.
[58] Sienkiewicz, *supra* note 53, at 692.
[59] *Id.* at 695.
[60] *Id.* at 693.
[61] *See generally* STORYFUL., https://storyful.com.
[62] In the United Kingdom, the immediate impetus has been the alignment of domestic and EU copyright law. *See* Case C-5/08, Infopaq International A/S v. Danske Dagblades Forening, 2009 E.C.R. I-6569 (U.K.). In Australia, a decision of the High Court of Australia emphasized the centrality of authors in the copyright system, emphasizing that

approach limits the relevance of other kinds of "work" to the law's apprehension of the appropriate subjects for copyright law.[63] It may well be that this evolution in what "counts" for the purposes of copyright law bolsters the normative case for copyright protection in useful ways.[64] Even so, it is possible that the approach does not sufficiently accommodate the effort expended by these information intermediaries in enhancing the veracity and reliability of citizen journalism news content. Recognizing the value of other aspects of content will attract the criticism that rights should not follow from investment[65] – the "if value, then rights" fallacy.[66]

This is only a fallacy, however, if we assume that protection of subjective expression always aligns with appropriate public policy goals. In the news context, earlier systems of private rights targeted aspects of content that were quite different from this kind of subjective expression. As Lionel Bently has explained,[67] in the 1870s in the British Empire, there emerged a kind of copyright protection that was aimed at protecting the investment in telegraph infrastructure that was necessary to bring news content to colonies and dominions.[68] This became known as "Telegraph Copyright." As Bently recounts, these schemes provided short-term protection for telegraph messages published in newspapers (usually for a matter of hours), which expired if the information was not used quickly. The protection was only for information received from outside the country, and was conditioned on publication with notice. Most importantly, protection extended beyond literal copying to reuse of the substance of the telegraph communication as well as commentary on the "intelligence" that had been communicated. There were few if any exceptions to the right to communicate information conveyed through a telegraph.

For present purposes, the detail of the telegraph copyright schemes is less important than what the scheme suggests about different conceptions of the object and purpose of the legal protections. The relevant enactments were the result of petitions by leading newspaper proprietors in far-flung colonies who were concerned about the very high cost of receipt of telegraph communications, particularly those from Great Britain. Lead time advantage was insufficient to recoup the costs if subsequent publication of the information – even by way of paraphrase – were

copyright protections should be trained on the expression manifest in the part of the work alleged to have been infringed. *See* IceTV Pty Limited v. Nine Network Australia Pty Limited (2009) 239 CLR 458 (Austl.). That analysis has recently been adopted by the Singaporean Court of Appeal in Global Yellow Pages Ltd. v Promedia Directories Pte Ltd. *See* [2017] SGCA 28. In US copyright law, similar ideas are advanced by the Supreme Court's rejection of "sweat of the brow" as a basis for copyright protection. *See* Feist Publications, Inc. v. Rural Telephone Service Co., 499 U.S. 340 (1991).

63 *Cf.* Ladbroke v. William Hill [1964] 1 All ER 465 (Eng.); Walter v. Lane [1900] AC 539 (HL). While the works at issue in these House of Lords cases manifested some authorial creativity, parts of the analysis emphasized in their Lordships' speeches acknowledged the significance of effort and investment that were not necessarily directed at the expression of the works' final form.

64 It also aligns with the human rights basis for copyright. *See* Graeme W. Austin, *Authors' Human Rights and Copyright Policy*, 40 Colum. J.L. & Arts 405 (2017).

65 *See* Shyamkrishna Balganesh, *"Hot News": The Enduring Myth of Property in News*, 111 Colum. L. Rev. 419 (2011).

66 *See* Ralph S. Brown Jr., *Advertising and the Public Interest: Legal Protection of Trade Symbols*, 57 Yale L.J. 1165 (1948); Rochelle Cooper Dreyfuss, *We Are Symbols and Inhabit Symbols, So Should We Be Paying Rent? Deconstructing the Lanham Act and Rights of Publicity*, 20 Colum. J.L. & Arts 123 (1996).

67 *See* Lionel Bently, *Copyright and the Victorian Internet: Telegraphic Property Laws in Colonial Australia*, 38 Loy. L.A. L. Rev. 71 (2004). The discussion in the main text draws extensively from Professor Bently's article.

68 *See The Telegraphic Messages Copyright Act* 1871 (Cth) 414 (Vict.); *The Telegram Copyright Act* 1872 (Cth) 10 (S. Austl.); *The Telegram Copyright Act* 1872 (Cth) 7 (W. Austl.).

permitted.[69] It was also thought at this time that newspapers were excluded from copyright protection,[70] a fortiori the information itself.[71] The telegraph copyright scheme is very difficult to accommodate within modern conceptions of copyright concerned with protecting only the subjective expression of authors, rather than "facts."[72] Indeed, within the current orthodoxy, putting facts beyond copyright protections aligns with concerns for freedom of expression and avoiding the privatization of the building blocks of knowledge. And yet, in the particular social and geographical context of British colonies in the latter decades of the nineteenth century, this species of protection was considered necessary to encourage investment in the technology required to communicate the precious commodity of "news" to populations located at considerable distance, usually from Great Britain, a place that many in the colonies considered to be "home" until well into the twentieth century.

The telegraph copyright statutes advanced values and priorities that were considered appropriate for the characteristics of the information ecology for particular places in a particular time. Even if, by protecting the substance of the communication, telegraph copyright took facts out of the public domain, albeit for a short period; the broad aim of the scheme was the same as the earliest justification for copyright: the advancement of knowledge. The way of achieving that end was, however, quite different. What was considered valuable was the promulgation of current events content through a new technology that was costly to operate. This value was not apparent on the face of "work." It was not, in modern terms, what we would describe as its expression: it was a characteristic of how the work was produced.

4 CONCLUSION

If, in the contemporary information ecosystem, there is a premium on the accuracy and verifiability of news, this might influence our understanding of the object of copyright protection. While the contemporary focus on the surface of the text might enhance the conceptual integrity of protections afforded to creative endeavor through copyright, it is possible that, in some contexts, this might cause important "value" to be overlooked – including, in the news context, the crucial value in the content's veracity.

It is too early to tell whether the evolution of content verification services – what Sienkiewicz describes as the "interpretive tier" in the new information ecology – will pose any specific new challenges for contemporary copyright policy. And it is possible that other forms of protection may be appropriate, such as certification trademarks.[73] Examination of the need for specific incentives to encourage this kind of investment needs to await another opportunity. Credence markets are yet to develop sufficiently for free-riding concerns to be identified with any

[69] *See* Bently, *supra* note 67, at 75–88.

[70] *See* Cox v. Land & Water Journal [1869] 9 LR Eq. 324 (Eng.).

[71] The problem was exacerbated by the 1868 ruling of the House of Lords in *Routledge v. Low* that works first published in the colonies were not protected under Imperial copyright legislation. Pre-suit registration requirements were also an impediment. *See* [1868] 3 LRE & I App. (HL) 100. *See also* Bently, *supra* note 67, at 93–96.

[72] For similar reasons, there is controversy about recent proposals within the European Union to add to the rights of press publishers (and, possibly, other publishers) by way of a right to remuneration for both linking to news websites and the production of short summary textual previews of news content. *See Proposal for a Directive of the European Parliament and of the Council on Copyright in the Digital Single Market*, COM (2016) 593 final (Sept. 14, 2016). The relevant parts of the proposal build on, and extend, legislative initiatives already in Germany and Spain. As Ula Furgal explains, this kind of initiative would enable press publishers to monetize aspects of their business activity that may not currently be protected by conventional copyright prerogatives. *See* Ula Furgal, *Ancillary Right for Press Publishers: An Alternative Answer to the Linking Conundrum* 18 J. INTELL. PROP. L. & PRAC. 1 (2018).

[73] *See, e.g.*, Margaret Chon, *Marks of Rectitude*, 77 FORD. L. REV. 2311 (2009).

precision. Even so, with lowered barriers to production and dissemination of content, it is possible that underinvestment might result from inadequate opportunities to internalize the investment in verification.

Verification may be a new kind of public good in the news context. Once a story is verified and published, it may be difficult to exclude others from appropriating the investment in verification – possibly leading to a pernicious race to the bottom, increasing the extent to which all content purporting to be news is regarded as fungible. Similarly, with telegraph copyright, once a telegraph-sourced news story had been published, it was impossible to exclude other news agencies from using that content in their own publications. Whether that is perceived to be a sufficient problem to warrant legislative intervention is of course a different matter and might depend on the level of governmental concern with the veracity of news content. The untethering of news from truth can be a useful political strategy – at least in the short term.

There might, however, be greater scope for responding to the work done in the intermediate tier in news verification in the parts of copyright law that are in the control of the judiciary, including fair dealing. When conceiving of the work that has been copied, it might be possible to take account of characteristics that are not necessarily manifest on the surface of the text. In an information ecology characterized by a glut of content purporting to be news, valorizing subjective authorship risks causing us to overlook other things of value.

21

Copyright and Religion: An Exemption for the Use of Music and Songs in Worship?

Ng-Loy Wee Loon[*]

1 INTRODUCTION

Malaysia and Singapore are alike in many respects. Both are melting pots of cultures of three main ethnic groups, namely the Chinese, the Indians, and the Malays. Singapore was even once part of Malaysia,[1] and quite a few living on either side of the Causeway[2] are related by blood and family ties. Both countries also inherited the common law system, a legacy from the days when they were under British protection and rule.[3] More specifically in the realm of copyright law, Singapore and some states in Malaysia had once applied the UK Imperial Copyright Act 1911.[4] In fact, this imperial legislation remained in force in Singapore and those states in Malaysia for many years after these two countries became sovereign states.[5] On the international front, both countries are World Trade Organization (WTO) members as well as contracting parties to the Berne Convention for the Protection of Literary and Artistic Works ("the Berne Convention"),[6]

[*] I am very grateful to Associate Professor Arif Jamal (my colleague) and Emeritus Professor Alison Firth (University of Surrey) for giving me such insightful comments on an earlier draft of this chapter. All errors remain mine, of course.

[1] This was between September 16, 1963, and August 9, 1965.

[2] The Causeway is the road and rail link which was built by the British government in 1923 to connect Singapore with mainland Malaysia across the Straits of Johor.

[3] The following is a very brief account of British protection and rule in Singapore and Malaysia. Singapore was a British Crown colony from 1826 to 1963 (when it became part of Malaysia). In the case of Malaysia, which is a federation with thirteen states, the rule and/or protection of the British varied from state to state: two states (Penang and Malacca) were British Crown colonies from 1826 to 1957; one state (Sarawak) was a British protectorate from 1888 to 1946, and then a Crown colony from 1946 to 1963; and the remaining ten states were British protectorates from the late nineteenth century to 1957.

[4] The UK Imperial Copyright Act 1911, as an imperial legislation, was intended to apply beyond the United Kingdom to the rest of "His Majesty's dominions." But for this imperial legislation to come into force in a British colony, it was necessary for the governor of that British colony to issue a proclamation. *See* Imperial Copyright Act 1911, 1 & 2 Geo. 5 c. 46, § 37(1)(d) (UK). In the case of Singapore and the two states of Malaysia, which were British colonies at the material time (namely, Malacca and Penang), this was done on July 1, 1912. In the case of the other states of Malaysia, which were British protectorates at the material time, six of them (Pahang, Perak, Negri Sembilan, Sabah, Sarawak, and Selangor) enacted copyright legislation in the 1930s which was modeled on the UK Imperial Copyright Act 1911. For a more detailed tracing of the history of the copyright law of Malaysia, *see* KHAW LAKE TEE, COPYRIGHT LAW IN MALAYSIA 2–6 (3d ed. 2008).

[5] Malaysia became a sovereign state in 1957, and it enacted its own (federal) copyright legislation in 1969. Singapore became a sovereign state in 1965, and it enacted its own copyright legislation in 1987.

[6] Berne Convention for the Protection of Literary and Artistic Works, *opened for signature* Sept. 9, 1886, 828 U.N.T.S. 221, S. Treaty Doc. No. 99-27, 99th Cong. (1986) (revised at Paris, July 24, 1979) (hereinafter Berne Convention). Malaysia acceded to the Berne Convention in 1990, while Singapore acceded to it in 1998.

the World International Property Organization (WIPO) Copyright Treaty and the WIPO Performances and Phonograms Treaty.[7]

Not surprisingly, therefore, the current copyright legislation of these two countries – the Singapore Copyright Act 1987 and the Malaysia Copyright Act 1987 – shares many features in common. On exceptions and limitations to copyright infringement, both pieces of legislation adopt the same approach: each enumerates a list of permitted uses of copyright works for specific purposes (e.g., research, criticism, review, reporting of current events) and the enumerated list is then supplemented by a provision permitting any other "fair dealing" with a copyright work. The latter provision, which for convenience I shall refer to as the "general fair dealing" exemption, was enacted by Singapore and Malaysia in 2005 and 2012, respectively, and was modeled on the US fair use doctrine. Thus, the general fair dealing exemption does not confine the use to any specific purpose, and the only issue is whether the use is "fair" in the light of certain factors. Just like in the US, these factors include:[8]

(a) the purpose and character of the dealing, including whether such dealing is of a commercial nature or is for nonprofit educational purposes;
(b) the nature of the copyright work;
(c) the amount and substantiality of the portion used in relation to the copyright work as a whole; and
(d) the effect of the use upon the potential market for or value of the copyright work.

In the case of Singapore, there is a fifth factor, namely the possibility of obtaining the copyright work within a reasonable time at an ordinary commercial price.[9]

The reasons for, and the advantages and disadvantages of, Malaysia's and Singapore's move to adopt the US-style fair use doctrine are the subject of discussions elsewhere.[10] In this chapter, I want to explore what I see as a difference in the two countries' approach to one particular type of use of copyright works: the use of songs and music in religious services. For such use, the Singapore Copyright Act 1987 crafted out a specific exemption in section 42:

> A performance of a literary, dramatic or musical work of a religious nature, or an adaptation of such a work, in the course of services at a place of worship or other religious assembly shall not constitute an infringement of the copyright in the work.

Section 42 has been in the Singapore Copyright Act 1987 since its inception. As we will see later, its presence was the result of representations made by two Christian groups – a church called the Trinity Christian Centre (arguing for exemption) and the Christian Booksellers Association (arguing against exemption) – to the Select Committee in 1986 during the copyright reform exercise.

[7] Malaysia acceded to the WIPO Copyright Treaty and the WIPO Performances and Phonograms Treaty in 2012, while Singapore acceded to these treaties in 2005.

[8] *Compare* Singapore Copyright Act 1987, ss.35(1), 35(2)(a)–(d), *and* Malaysia Copyright Act 1987, ss.13(2)(a), (13)(2A)(a)–(d), *with* US Copyright Act, 17 U.S.C. § 107 (1976) (listing the factors).

[9] *See* Singapore Copyright Act 1987, s.35(2)(e). This fifth factor is derived from section 40(2)(e) of the Australia Copyright Act 1968. *But see* SINGAPORE COPYRIGHT REVIEW REPORT 26–27 (Jan. 17, 2019) where the Singapore government has proposed the deletion of the fifth factor.

[10] For a discussion of Singapore, *see* Ng-Loy Wee Loon, *Defences – Restoring the Balance in IP Law, in* SINGAPORE ACADEMY OF LAW CONFERENCE 2006: DEVELOPMENTS IN SINGAPORE LAW BETWEEN 2001 AND 2005 245–68 (2006). For a discussion of Malaysia, *see* Ida Madieha Azmi, Chapter 13 in this volume.

TABLE 21.1 *Religious make-up of the populations of Malaysia and Singapore in the 1980s*

	Buddhism/ Taoism	Christianity	Hinduism	Islam	Other religion or no religion	Total
Malaysia	26.3%	7.3%	6.7%	55.8%	3.9%	100%
Singapore	55.3%	11.4%	3.7%	15.5%	14.1%	100%

The Malaysia Copyright Act 1987 does not have an exemption similar to the Singapore section 42. Some will say that this absence is immaterial (at least since 2012) because the noncommercial and nonprofit nature of the performances of religious songs and music in worship services would bring such use within the general fair dealing exemption. Others will caution that a justification under the general fair dealing exemption is not a given because the performance is invariably of the entire song or piece of music, and very often in a non-transformative manner.[11] I do not propose to add to the debate on whether the general fair dealing exemption in Malaysia can achieve the same outcome as the Singapore section 42. I am interested in two other questions.

The first question is: When the two countries were revising their copyright laws in the 1980s, was their approach vis-à-vis the use of music and songs in worship influenced by any religio-cultural reason? I have mentioned that Malaysia and Singapore are culturally very alike because of the presence of the same three ethnic groups in their population. In this part of the world where the ethnic identity of a person has a strong influence on his or her religious identity, the major religions in Malaysia and Singapore are the following: Buddhism/Taoism[12] (mostly among the Chinese), Hinduism (mostly among the Indians), Islam (mostly among the Malays), and Christianity.[13] However, precisely because the ethnic composition of the two populations is different, the dominant religion in the two countries is also different. In Malaysia, where the Malays are the majority, the dominant religion is Islam;[14] in fact, Islam is the state religion in Malaysia.[15] In Singapore, where the Chinese are the majority, the dominant religions are Buddhism/Taoism. Table 21.1 shows the religious distributions in the two populations in the 1980s.[16]

The role of music and songs in Buddhism/Taoism, Christianity, Hinduism, and Islam is investigated in Section 2 of this chapter. In brief, the investigations reveal that the playing of musical instruments and singing are a critical part of worship in all these religions except Islam. In worship services in the mosque, there are no musical instruments nor singing; in fact, the use

[11] The role of the "transformative use" doctrine in determining whether a use is fair or not is discussed by other authors in this book. *See, e.g.*, Azmi, *supra* note 10; David Tan, Chapter 17 in this volume.

[12] Buddhism and Taoism are two different religions, but the distinction between them is often blurred among the Chinese in Malaysia and Singapore. Prof Chee-Beng Tan, an anthropologist and expert on Southeast Asia, has argued that the majority of the Chinese in Malaysia and Singapore are not followers of Buddhism or Taoism; rather, theirs is a syncretic religion, which he calls "Chinese Religion," involving the worship of Chinese deities of both Taoist and Buddhist origins, natural spirits and the ancestors. *See* Chee-Beng Tan, *Chinese Religion in Malaysia: A General View*, 42 ASIAN FOLKLORE STUD. 217 (1983). It has also been observed that "[t]he strictly Buddhist temple is a rarity in Singapore. In most temples both Taoist and Buddhist images are likely to be found, although usually in different rooms or shrines." *See* Maurice Freedman & Majorie Topley, *Religion and Social Realignment among the Chinese in Singapore*, 21 J. ASIAN STUD. 3, 8 (1961).

[13] The term "Christianity" is used in this chapter to refer to both Catholicism and Protestantism.

[14] Islam is so integral to the Malay community in Malaysia that the Federal Constitution, Art. 160 (Malaysia) deems Islam to be the faith of a person who is ethnically Malay.

[15] *See* Federal Constitution, Art. 3(1) (Malaysia).

[16] These figures represent the average of two sets of statistics obtained from the population census conducted by Malaysia in 1980 and 1991, and by Singapore in 1980 and 1990.

of music or singing in worship may even be regarded as heresy. This unique stance of Islam is significant. It may well account for why Malaysia, where Islam was (and still is) the dominant religion, did not see the need to have a specific exemption in its Copyright Act 1987 to permit the use of music and songs in worship. The situation in Singapore was (and still is) different. The vast majority of the Singapore population are Buddhists/Taoists, Christians, or Hindus who habitually engage in musical performance and singing in their worship. Thus, in 1986 when the Trinity Christian Centre and the Christian Booksellers Association made representations to the Select Committee arguing, respectively, for and against an exemption for religious use, they were speaking not only for the Christian community in Singapore but also for the Buddhist/ Taoist and Hindu communities.

The second question that this chapter addresses is: does the fact that music and songs play a critical role in worship per se justify the state in providing in its copyright law a specific exemption for such use? This is a question of more than merely academic interest. Not all the compositions used in worship in churches and temples today are the work of composers who are long dead and which have fallen into the public domain. On the contrary, there are many contemporary artists who compose worship music in this part of the world, including: Imee Ooi, a Malaysian composer and performer who has released more than fifty albums of Buddhist music and songs;[17] the New Creation Church, the nondenominational church in Singapore which has a music ministry dedicated to composing, performing, and producing Christian songs;[18] and Padmini Chandraskekar, a Singapore-based composer and singer of Indian devotional songs.[19] What are the arguments for and against free use of their copyright works by their fellow faithful worshippers? Section 3 of this chapter is dedicated to this investigation. In brief, the main thrusts of the arguments can be found in the representations made by the Trinity Christian Centre ("Surely the church is not expected to pay when these works are written for the glory of God.") and by the Christian Booksellers Association ("Surely the church must pay, just as it pays salaries to its pastor and other church staff all of whom labor for the glory of God.") to the Select Committee in 1986. I will also refer to the US and the UK models in Section 2.

2 MUSIC AND SONGS IN WORSHIP IN THE MAJOR RELIGIONS IN MALAYSIA AND SINGAPORE

This section investigates how the major religions in Malaysia and Singapore view the use of music and songs in worship. On this issue, Buddhism/Taoism, Christianity, and Hinduism all share the same stance: that is, music and singing are an important, and even vital, part of the worship ritual. In Islamic law, the role of music and songs in worship is an extremely controversial issue. As Islam's stance is unique, it is discussed under a separate subheading.

(i) Buddhism/Taoism; Christianity; Hinduism

The use of music in worship in these religions is uncontroversial. For some of them, their holy scriptures explicitly endorse and encourage the use of vocal and instrumental music in worship rituals.

[17] *See Imee Ooi*, FACEBOOK, www.facebook.com/imeeooi.immmusic (where music albums can be purchased) (last accessed July 15, 2020).

[18] *See* NEW CREATION CHURCH, www.newcreation.org.sg/resources/#worship-albums (where music albums can be purchased) (last accessed July 15, 2020).

[19] *See Padmini Chandraskekar*, https://music.apple.com/gb/artist/padmini-chandrashekar/569625811 (where music albums can be purchased) (last accessed July 15, 2020).

In Buddhism, one of the holy scriptures, Amitabha Sutra, teaches that listening to melodious sounds can move the devotee to become mindful of the *Dharma* (that is, the teachings of Buddha).[20] In Taoism, hymns were composed as early as the Han dynasty.[21] It has also been noted that in ancient China, learning how to play the Chinese musical instrument called the *ch'in* was considered an obligatory study among Buddhists and Taoists because of the belief that the playing of this musical instrument was a means of attaining their spiritual goal.[22] Today, Chinese Buddhist worship no longer involves only 梵呗 (the chanting of prayers) – which is strictly not regarded as music – but also encompasses the singing of 佛教音乐歌曲 (Buddhist devotional music and songs).[23] In 2016, three Buddhist associations in Singapore, Malaysia, and Indonesia even co-organized a concert in Singapore to celebrate Vesak Day (Buddha's birthday) through devotional music and dances.[24]

In Christianity, the Bible abounds with explicit and unambiguous references approving the use of music and songs as a means of offering love and devotion to God. For example, the Book of Psalms records the use of the trumpet, harp, lyre, timbrel, strings, pipe, and cymbals to praise God,[25] and Saint Paul in the Book of Ephesians urged Christians to "[s]ing and make music from your heart to the Lord."[26] Thus, church worship services in Malaysia and Singapore invariably incorporate music and singing, differing only in the type of musical instruments used (from the organ to the electric guitar) as well as the genre of songs sung (from the very traditional hymns to contemporary songs of praise). The Methodist Church in Singapore has a School of Music dedicated to Christian music education where it conducts, for example, a certificate course to train Christians in the use of music as an act of worship.[27] Music and songs have always been an integral part of worship for the Methodists. The cofounder of the Methodist movement, Charles Wesley (1707–1788), composed more than 6,000 hymns, one of which is the very popular Christmas carol "Hark! The Herald Angels Sing."

In Hinduism, worship includes the singing of devotional songs such as *bhajans*, many of which are based on verses from the Ramayana. According to a scholar of Hinduism, for the Hindus "the act of making contact with God and participating in a divine interaction has something intrinsically to do with the realm of song."[28] There is also a Hindu goddess of art, music, knowledge and wisdom (Saraswathi) who is often portrayed holding a stringed musical

[20] *See Protecting Our Environment*, PURIFYMIND.COM, www.purifymind.com/WritingTeachings1.htm (last accessed July 15, 2020).

[21] *See* Kristofer Schipper, *Vernacular and Classical Ritual in Taoism*, 45 J. ASIAN STUD. 21, 33 (1985). *See also* Tsao Penyeh & Shi Xinming, *Current Research of Taoist Ritual Music in Mainland China and Hong Kong*, 24 Y.B. TRADITIONAL MUSIC 118 (1992); Michel Strickmann, *The Longest Taoist Scripture*, 17 HIST. RELIGIONS 331, n.29 (1978).

[22] *See* Shui-Cheng Cheng, *Permissions and Prohibitions Concerning the Playing of the Ch'in*, 21 WORLD OF MUSIC 81, 83 (1979).

[23] Various scholars have written about the important role that musical instruments, songs, and even dances play in Buddhism. *See, e.g.*, Pi-yen Chen, *Buddhist Chant, Devotional Song, and Commercial Popular Music: From Ritual to Rock Mantra*, 49 ETHNOMUSICOLOGY 266 (2005); Ian Mabbett, *Buddhism and Music*, 25 ASIAN MUSIC 9 (1993).

[24] *Sadhu for the Music*, FACEBOOK, www.facebook.com/SadhuForTheMusic/ (last accessed July 15, 2020) (providing details of the concert). The word "Sadhu" (which, in Pali, means virtue) is often pronounced thrice by Buddhists at the end of a teaching or sermon to express their happiness or approval.

[25] *See* Psalms 150:3–5. Note that in the Torah, the Jewish Bible, the Book of Psalms is entitled *Tehillim* which means "songs of praise."

[26] Ephesians 5:19.

[27] *See* METHODIST MUSIC OF SCHOOL, http://msmusic.edu.sg/ (last accessed July 15, 2020).

[28] John Stratton Hawley, *The Music in Faith and Morality*, 52 J. AM. ACAD. 243, 245 (1984). Professor Hawley is the Claire Tow Professor of Religion at Columbia University.

instrument called the *veena*.[29] The importance of music in Hinduism can also be seen during the Thaipusam procession where live singing and music played on Indian drums traditionally accompany the devotees as they carry their *kavadi*[30] during their journey by foot from one temple to another in fulfillment of their vows or to seek blessings. So important is drum music and singing at this Hindu festival that in Singapore in 2015, a scuffle ensued between some Hindus and the police when a group of people was stopped from playing drums during the Thaipusam procession. The incident provoked a fair amount of unhappiness among the Hindu community, prompting the government to take quick action to ensure that playing live music and singing during Thaipusam is no longer an issue.[31]

(ii) Islam

The role of *samā'* (religious music) in Islam is extremely controversial, provoking an "interminable debate" among Islamic legalists, theologians, and spiritual leaders.[32] There is no explicit reference to music in the Qur'an, but it has been argued that some verses therein have music in mind. The real debate is whether these verses approve or disapprove of music. Opponents of the integration of music into worship rely on the command to avoid "diverting talk" (verse 31:5) as an implicit prohibition against singing, whereas proponents rely on the command to "give good tidings to my servants who listen to the Word and follow the fairest of it" (verses 39:17–18) as an implicit approval of singing.[33] This debate cannot be conclusively resolved by the second most authoritative source of Islamic law, the Hadith (the traditions of Prophet Muhammad), since both sides in the debate have interpreted different traditions, and even the same tradition, in a way that advances their respective case.[34]

At the core of this controversy lies the belief that the one true path to Allah is via the text – and only the text – in the Qur'an. The Sufi mystics,[35] who argue that music acts as an inspirational force to the faithful on this path, are said to breach this belief because:

> The inspirational power that the mystics attributed to music presupposes the use of man's inner resources for his spiritual experience rather than dependence on the words of the scriptures which, according to the "nomos" doctrine, should be the only way leading to the true knowledge of God and all He created.[36]

[29] In Singapore, Saraswathi is among the deities worshipped in various temples such as the Sri Siva Krishna Temple and the Sri Veerma Kaliamman Temple.

[30] A *kavadi* is a structure made of wood and steel rods and hooks which are pierced into the carrier's body.

[31] There was, in fact, an application for judicial review of the police's decision to stop the playing of musical instruments during the Thaipusam procession. *See* Vijaya Kumar s/o Rajendran v. Attorney-General [2015] SGHC 244. It was argued that the police's decision breached the right of freedom of religion protected by the Singapore Constitution. The High Court's judgment, dismissing this challenge, was issued in September 2015. Not long after that in early December 2015, on the recommendation of the Hindu Endowments Board in Singapore, the Singapore government decided to allow the playing of live religious music during the Thaipusam procession. *See Thaipusam to Have 'Live' Music for the First Time in 42 Years*, TODAY (Dec. 2, 2015), www.todayonline.com/singapore/7-music-points-added-thaipusam-2016 (last accessed July 15, 2018).

[32] *See* AMNON SHILOAH, MUSIC IN THE WORLD OF ISLAM: A SOCIO-CULTURAL STUDY 31 (1995). *See also* HENRY GEORGE FARMER, A HISTORY OF ARABIAN MUSIC 22 (1929) ("One of the most perplexing points about Islam is its attitude towards music, and for centuries its legalists have argued the question whether listening to music (*al-samā'*) is lawful or not.").

[33] *See, e.g.*, SHILOAH, *supra* note 32, at 32; FARMER, *supra* note 32, at 22–23.

[34] *See* SHILOAH, *supra* note 32, at 32–33; FARMER, *supra* note 32, at 24–28.

[35] Note that even among the Sufis, the acceptance of *samā'* is not unanimous. *See* Arthur Gribetz, *The* Samā' *Controversy: Sufi vs. Legalist*, 74 STUDIA ISLAMICA 43 (1999).

[36] SHILOAH, *supra* note 32, at 35.

In Malaysia and Singapore, the vast majority of Muslims are Sunnis, and the four Sunni legal schools of thought – the Hanafī, the Mālikī, the Shafi'i, and the Ḥanbalī – broadly prohibit *samā'*.[37] Thus in the worship services in the mosque in Malaysia and Singapore, there is no playing of any musical instrument nor singing of songs.

What then about the *adhān* (the call to prayer) and the recitation of the Qur'an during a worship service? To the ear of a non-Muslim, this may sound melodic, but to the Muslim this is not music or singing. To Muslims, this is "cantillation," which has been described by a scholar of musicology as a form of "tensed speech" that "avoids regularity of rhythmical organization and remains entirely subordinated to the division, fluidity and accents of the text" of the Qur'an.[38] Another scholar of musicology explained it in this way:

> Islam has no mosque music comparable with the music service of the Christian Church. There is neither priesthood nor choir in the mosque, in the Occidental sense. Islām is far too personal a religion for that . . . The Qur'ān lent itself to cantillation, since most of it consisted of what of has been loosely termed "rhymed prose," the assonance of which tempted the voice into modulated sound in "reading." The word for "reading" in Arabic is *qirā'a*, a label which lifts this cantillation out of any suspicion that it was "singing" (*ghinā'*). To have suggested that would have been rank heresy . . .[39]

The sentiment expressed in the last sentence of this quotation – having music and songs in a mosque would be "rank heresy" – illustrates how fundamentally differently Islam sees the role of music and songs in worship, compared to Buddhism, Christianity, and Hinduism.

3 COPYRIGHT EXEMPTION FOR RELIGIOUS USE OF MUSIC AND SONGS

This section investigates the question of whether a state where the majority of people profess and practice a religion(s) that sanctions and encourages the use of music and songs in worship – such as Buddhism, Christianity, and Hinduism – should enact an exemption for such religious use.

It would be a mistake to assume that the answer to this question must be yes, because an exemption must surely be in line with what authors of religious music and songs intended when they composed these works. Whilst this is indeed their purpose and hope, it does not necessarily mean that these authors would spurn financial compensation from the community of their faith. Some of these authors depend on their writings and compositions for their livelihood and their ability to provide for their families. I will refer to the Singapore experience where the arguments for and against an exemption were canvassed by two Christian groups in their representations to the Select Committee in 1986. I will also refer to the UK experience because on two occasions, in 1833–41 and 1911, when its Parliament debated whether to extend the term of copyright protection, Christian writings and hymns were used by both supporters and opponents to advance their case for and against extension. The policy concerns raised in these debates are equally applicable to the issue at hand.

(i) The Singapore Experience

As mentioned in Section 1, the UK Imperial Copyright Act 1911 remained the copyright law in Singapore for many years after Singapore became an independent state. This imperial statute

[37] *See* FARMER, *supra* note 32, at 29.
[38] *See* SHILOAH, *supra* note 32, at 37.
[39] *See* Henry George Farmer, *The Religious Music of Islam*, 1 J. ROYAL ASIATIC SOC'Y G.B. & IR. 60, 62 (1952).

was a milestone in the copyright law of the UK and its dominions because it was the first UK copyright statute to provide a list of permitted uses of copyrighted works (e.g., fair dealing for the purpose of private study, research, criticism, review, or newspaper summary). But, this list did not include an exemption for religious use. In 1986, when Singapore decided to repeal this 1911 Act, its drafters looked to the Australian Copyright Act 1968 as a model. The latter did not contain any exemption for religious use of music and songs either.[40] Unsurprisingly, the first draft of the new law – the Copyright Bill 1986 – did not contain an exemption for religious use.

The Copyright Bill 1986 was committed by Parliament to a Select Committee for closer examination. When the Select Committee invited the public to give their views and comments on the bill, two Christian groups responded. One group argued for an exemption for religious use, and its reason was essentially: why should the church pay Christian authors when they are composing for the glory of God? The other group argued for full copyright protection of Christian music and songs, and its reason was essentially: Why shouldn't the church pay Christian authors when it pays its church staff for laboring for the glory of God? The full arguments of both sides are outlined below.

Arguing that all religious organizations should be exempted from the new copyright law was the Trinity Christian Centre, a church of the Assembly of God denomination. Its reasons were the following:[41]

(a) Religious organizations such as churches are nonprofit-making entities.
(b) Religious hymnals and songs which are copyrighted are used weekly. These hymnals and songs are written for a spiritual purpose. To impose copyright permission would therefore counteract the primary intent of the songwriters in writing their songs and hymns.
(c) Church choirs present special singing items every week. They practice from photostatted copies of songs because it is a mammoth task to write for permission on a weekly basis.
(d) Christian hymnals and songs are photostatted on transparencies and screened so that congregations can sing and worship. Some of these songs, even though copyrighted, are anonymous. Therefore copyright permission in such cases would be even more difficult to obtain.
(e) The number of religious literary works is usually limited, especially the older ones. In order to use them, churches therefore resort to photostatting in order to teach catechism classes and Sunday Schools.
(f) Musical and dramatic presentations are organized by churches for Easter, Pentecost Sunday, Father's Day, Mother's Day, Christmas, and other Christian festivals. Many of these presentations are produced by combining extracts from numerous sources (some of which are traditional, e.g., Handel's *Messiah*). Therefore having to obtain copyright permissions for every separate extract would make these presentations nonfeasible.

Arguing for full protection of religious works was the Christian Booksellers Association whose members dealt in Christian books, music, and sound and video recordings. It welcomed Singapore's move to enact a new copyright law,[42] saying that the new law raised "a moral aspect

[40] Note, though, that there was an exemption for playing a *sound recording* in public as part of the activities of a nonprofit organization that was concerned with, inter alia, the advancement of religion. *See* Australian Copyright Act 1968 (Cth) s 106. This provision was subsequently amended by the Australian Charities and Not-for-profits Commission (Consequential and Transitional) Act 2012.

[41] *Report of the Select Committee on the Copyright Bill [Bill No. 8/86]* at p A 148.

[42] While the Christian Booksellers Association welcomed this move, it also alerted the Select Committee that the Christians in Singapore were disadvantaged because its members could not import the cheaper American editions of

TABLE 21.2 *Comparing the Singapore and US copyright provisions*

Singapore section 42	US section 110(3)
A performance of a literary, dramatic or musical work *of a religious nature*, or an adaptation of such a work, *in the course of services at a place of worship or other religious assembly*	Performance of a nondramatic literary or musical work or of a dramatico-musical work *of a religious nature*, or display of a work, *in the course of services at a place of worship or other religious assembly*

to the question of copyright,"[43] i.e., the importance of respecting the rights of others, including authors of Christian works. The explanation was delivered in these terms:

> Too often, churches and religious organizations feel they are exempt from the laws regarding the use of copyrighted music. Choir music and church songbooks and song sheets seem to be an area in which some pastors and church music directors want exemption from having to pay that which is due the copyright owner(s). These same people, however, do not neglect to pay salaries for the church staff, utility bills, robes for the choir, pews for the church, and other related expenses of church operation. Why should the composer and publisher not be treated equally?
>
> Booksellers, music publishers, and composers frequently hear the expression, "But the music is going to be used in our ministry and the Lord's work." The owners of copyrighted music appreciate that, and are pleased that their music is to be used in that manner. They are also willing to work with churches or religious organizations on special requests. However, when people use copyrighted music without permission in order to save their "ministries" from additional expense, they have in fact reduced the income needed for the ministries of the composers and publishers who own those copyrighted works. Christian composers and publishers consider the music they write and publish to be their ministry, but they have bills to pay, kids to feed, and house payments to make – just like everyone else.[44]

The deliberations of the Select Committee on this issue resulted in a revision of the Copyright Bill 1986 to include the exemption which is now section 42 of the Singapore Copyright Act 1987.[45] The Select Committee did not indicate how it came to adopt the text of section 42, but it is likely that the committee looked to section 110(3) of the US Copyright Act 1976. The text of the two countries' exemptions is set out side by side in Table 21.2 for easier comparison:

Two points should be noted. First, the Select Committee did not accede to the full request of the Trinity Christian Centre which was essentially for an exemption for all uses of copyright works by a religious organization. For example, the Trinity Christian Centre also had in mind an exemption to allow the copying of the lyrics of hymns and songs on transparencies – those were the days before PowerPoint slides – which were projected onto a screen so that the congregation could sing along. Section 42 does not go so far as to exempt such copying. Second, there are differences between the Singapore provision and the US provision. In particular, whilst both

books due to arrangements made between British and American publishers which prevented the latter from selling directly to retailers in Singapore. As a result of this representation from the Christian Booksellers Association (and from other quarters), the Select Committee made revisions to the Copyright Bill 1986 to allow parallel importation of copyright works.

[43] *See Report of the Select Committee on the Copyright Bill*, *supra* note 41, at A 37.

[44] *See id.* at A 39. This explanation is found in a document entitled "Copyright and Wrongs" that was annexed to CBA's submissions. This document was prepared by the Church Music Publishers Association in the US and sought to educate church leaders what constituted copyright infringement (e.g., photocopying a song sheet) and why churches should not infringe copyright.

[45] *See Report of the Select Committee on the Copyright Bill*, *supra* note 41, at D 14.

provisions have a limitation that the music and song must be "of a religious nature," the US limitation applies only to "dramatico-musical works" such as oratorios, cantatas, and musical settings of the mass and choral services.[46]

(ii) The UK Experience

The UK Imperial Copyright Act 1911 did not exempt use of music and songs in worship. Neither does the current UK Copyright Designs and Patents Act 1988.[47] This deliberate omission is intriguing, to me at least, because the history of the UK was so profoundly affected by Christianity. Furthermore, the UK is the birthplace of the first copyright statute in the world (the Statute of Anne 1709); indeed there is a view[48] that English copyright law was conceived through Catholic Queen Mary and King Philip's desire to suppress the spread of the "detestable heresies against the faith and sound doctrine of Holy Mother Church"[49] found in Protestant teachings.

More pertinent for our purposes is the influence that Christianity exerted in another area of English copyright law, namely the copyright term of protection. On two occasions when Parliament debated whether to extend the copyright term, Christian writing and music were used in the arguments for and against this extension.

The first occasion was in 1838–41. At that time, the governing UK Copyright Act 1814 provided that the term of protection was twenty-eight years or the lifetime of the author, whichever was longer. In 1838, a bill was presented in Parliament by the Member of Parliament Sir Thomas Talfourd to extend the term of protection to the life of the author and sixty years thereafter. Arguing for this extension, Talfourd spoke of how Christian clergymen, who expended their intellect writing and composing for "the sacred cause of the Church,"[50] were so scantily paid by the church that their only hope of providing for their family after their death was the earnings from the use of their writings and hymns. He mentioned one specific case that came to his attention, namely, the pecuniary plight of the great-grandson of Dr Philip Doddridge (1702–1751), a church leader whose book *The Rise and Progress of Religion in the Soul* was what led William Wilberforce, the anti–slave trade campaigner, to become a Christian.[51]

[46] *See* H.R. Rep. No. 94/1476, at 84 (1976).

[47] The UK used to have an exemption for public performance of a *sound recording* for religious purposes. *See* Copyright Act 1956, 4 & 5 Eliz 2 c. 74, § 12(7) (UK); Copyright, Designs and Patents Act 1988, § 67 (UK), *repealed* by (Amendment) Regulations 2010 (S.I. 2010/2694) (effective Jan. 1, 2010).

[48] Lyman Ray Patterson, Copyright in Historical Perspective (1968). More recently, the UK Supreme Court said that the Statute of Anne 1709, which put an end to the stationer's copyright, was enacted partly for "the control of unlicensed (and possibly subversive) publications." *See* in Lucasfilm Ltd v. Ainworth [2011] 3 WLR (Civ) 487 [15] (Eng.). There is also a view that Queen Mary and King Philip did not rely on the stationer's copyright to censor Protestant writings; rather, it was done through various royal proclamations and statutory instruments. *See* Ronan Deazley, *Commentary on the Stationers' Royal Charter 1557*, *in* Primary Sources on Copyright (1450–1900) (Lionel Bently & Martin Kretschmer eds., 2008), www.copyrighthistory.org/cam/tools/request/showRecord?id=commentary_uk_1557.

[49] The preface of the Royal Charter granted by Queen Mary and King Philip in 1557 to the Stationers' Company to regulate the printing of books. *See* Charles Robert Rivington, The Records of the Worshipful Company of Stationers 2 (1883). The full preface reads, "Know ye that we considering and manifestly perceiving that certain seditious and heretical books, rhymes, and treatises are daily published and printed by divers scandalous, malicious, schismatic, and heretical persons, not only moving our subjects and lieges to sedition and disobedience against us, our Crown and dignity, but also to renew and move very great and detestable heresies against the faith and sound doctrine of Holy Mother Church, and wishing to provide a suitable remedy in this behalf."

[50] *Hansard* volume 45 column 929 (February 27, 1839).

[51] *Hansard* volume 45 column 930 (February 27, 1839).

However, the majority in Parliament voted against Sir Thomas's bill.[52] One of them, Mr. Macaulay, was against it because of his concern that Christian doctrinal writings would remain in private hands for a longer time and hence would not be available to the Christian community at low cost. In a speech in Parliament in 1841, Mr. Macaulay used the writings of John Wesley, the other cofounder of the Methodist Church, to illustrate this point:

> Suppose that the works of [John] Wesley were suppressed. Why, Sir, such a grievance would be enough to shake the foundations of Government. Let Gentlemen who are attached to the Church [of England] reflect for a moment what their feelings would be if the Book of Common Prayer were not to be reprinted for thirty or forty years, – if the price of a Book of Common Prayer were run up to five or ten guineas. And then let them determine whether they will pass a law under which it is possible, under which it is probable, that so intolerable a wrong may be done to some sect consisting perhaps of half a million of persons.[53]

John Wesley was the brother of Charles Wesley, the prolific composer of Christian hymns whom I have mentioned in Section 2. Incidentally, Charles Wesley's family did benefit from the copyright of his hymns: they received a payment of £50 per annum from the Methodist Church for the sales of the hymnbook comprised of his compositions.[54]

The second occasion was in 1911. At that time, the UK Copyright Act 1842 provided that the copyright term was the lifetime of the author and seven years thereafter or forty-two years, whichever was longer. Having ratified the Berne Convention in 1887, the UK government had to revise the country's copyright law to comply with the minimum standards mandated by the Berne Convention, including a minimum term of protection lasting the lifetime of the author and fifty years thereafter. In 1911, a new copyright bill, which provided for these minimum standards, was presented in Parliament. This new bill eventually became the Imperial Copyright Act 1911. In the course of this new law's passage through Parliament, one Member of Parliament, Mr. Joynson-Hicks, opposed the copyright term extension, asking:

> Has it ever occurred to the right hon. Gentleman [the Minister who presented the bill] what a blessing – I am perfectly serious – to millions of the public there has come from some well-known editions of hymns in the English language? Is it not a fact that a year or two ago there were considerable difficulties in the publication of a new hymn book, the compilers of which desired to include certain well-known old hymns, and they had to wait two years until they could get a copy of the hymns for publication; that is, to get rid of the copyright. I think it was "Rock of Ages," and they had to wait until the copyright ran out in order to include it in the hymn book. [He was corrected that the hymn was not "Rock of Ages" but "Lead, Kindly Light."]
>
> It may have been "Lead, Kindly Light," but at any rate they wanted to include a well-known hymn and were not allowed to do so. The proposal here is asking for practically forty or fifty years to be added to the existing copyright, during which the public is to be deprived of the right of having these hymns, which may have been published in many millions of copies, included in a new hymnbook. Of course, there are different collections of hymns which are made from different standpoints, and from different shades of religious thought. They may be High Church, Low Church, and Congregational hymnbooks, and so far as a hymn is published, they may have

52 The vote was 73 (no) against 37 (yes).

53 *Hansard* volume 56 column 356 (February 5, 1841).

54 This is recorded in a biography of Charles Wesley's son, Samuel Wesley who was also a musician. *See* PHILIP OLLESON, SAMUEL WESLEY: THE MAN AND HIS MUSIC 212 (2003). *See also* THOMAS JACKSON, RECOLLECTIONS OF MY OWN LIFE AND TIMES 229–31 (1874). Thomas Jackson, who was the president of the Methodist Conference, befriended the adult children of Charles Wesley in the 1830s and bought from them all the papers and manuscripts of Charles Wesley for the benefit of the Methodist Church. This allowed the Methodist Church to prepare and publish the Supplement to the Wesleyan Hymn Book, for which it secured a copyright, and, from the sales of this hymn book, the Methodist Church was able to pay the annuity to Charles Wesley's family.

the copyright in only one particular combination, and I think it is very hard upon the general public to be deprived of having that hymn in their book because it is in another combination, for that long term of years.[55]

Mr. Joynson-Hicks did not succeed in persuading Parliament to vote against the longer copyright term. A supporter of this extension, Mr. Arthur Lynch, rebuked Mr. Joynson-Hicks with these words:

> I was aroused by what I regarded as [Mr Joynson-Hicks's] very Philistine attitude and my desire to smite him hip and thigh like Samson of old, if possible, though not, I hope, with the same weapon. He seemed to be opposed to copyright altogether in any shape or form.[56]

Mr. Lynch was obviously attentive in Sunday School to have remembered the account in the Book of Judges in the Bible where Samson killed 1,000 Philistines with a "fresh jawbone of a donkey."[57]

4 CONCLUSION

Countries vary in how they treat the use of music and songs in worship. Even two countries like Malaysia and Singapore, which share much of a common cultural and legal heritage, have different approaches. The copyright law in Singapore has a specific exemption for such use, but Malaysia does not. I advanced a hypothesis that perhaps it is more important for Singapore to have this specific exemption as the majority of its population are Buddhists/Taoists, Christians, or Hindus and in these religions, music and songs are an integral part of the worship ritual. On the other hand, in Malaysia, where Islam is the state religion and where the majority of the population are Muslim, there is no music or singing during worship in the mosque. This anthropological approach helps us better appreciate why other countries have or do not have a specific exemption for religious performances. For example, I have mentioned in Section 2 that the US also has an exemption for religious performances. When we consider that Christianity is the dominant religion in the US, we see that the exemption is to enable and support an important religio-cultural practice in the country.[58] Other examples in Asia are India (Hinduism is the dominant religion)[59] and Thailand (where Buddhism is the dominant religion).[60]

55 *Hansard* volume 23 columns 2617–18 (April 7, 1911).

56 *Hansard* volume 23 column 2626 (April 7, 1911).

57 Judges 15:15. *See also* Judges 15:16 (where Samson says, "With a donkey's jawbone, I have made donkeys of them. With a donkey's jawbone, I have killed a thousand men.").

58 *See, e.g.*, Christopher Geiger, Jonathan Griffiths & Reto Hilty, Declaration on *a Balanced Interpretation of the "Three-Step Test" in Copyright Law*, 39 INT'L REV. OF INTELL. PROP. AND COMPETITION L. 707, 708 (2008) (urging individual states to shape their copyright law to their own "cultural, social and economic development needs.").

59 India is the birthplace of Hinduism and 80 percent of its population are Hindus. The exemption for religious performances is found in section 52 of the India Copyright Act 1957 which permits "the performance of a literary, dramatic or musical work or the communication to the public of such work or of a sound recording in the course of any bona fide religious ceremony or an official ceremony held by the Central Government or the State Government or any local authority." There is also an explanation in this provision to clarify that "religious ceremony includes a marriage procession and other social festivities associated with a marriage."

60 In Thailand, about 94 percent of the population are Buddhists. The exemption for religious performances is found in section 36 of the Thailand Copyright Act 1994, which provides that "[t]he public performance of a dramatic work or musical work, as appropriate, which is not organized or conducted to obtain profit from such activity and without a direct or indirect charge for watching the performance and with no remuneration for the performers shall not be deemed an infringement of copyright provided that it is conducted by an association, foundation or another organization which has objectives of public charity, education, religion or social welfare and that the first paragraph of Section 32 is complied with [i.e. the performance does not conflict with normal exploitation of the copyright work by the owner of the copyright and does not unreasonably prejudice the legitimate rights of the owner of the copyright]."

However, my hypothesis is only a starting point, and it cannot and does not account for every country's model. One exception is the UK, which I also mentioned in Section 2. The UK is a country where Christianity is the state religion, yet it does not have a specific exemption for religious performances. At the time of writing, the UK is already taking steps to leave the European Union, but it is still worth noting that the absence of this exemption in the UK is not attributable to any constraint imposed by its EU membership.[61] I believe it is also unlikely that this issue did not occur to UK policymakers; after all, I pointed out how Christian writings and hymns were raised in their parliamentary debates on the issue of copyright term extension. Ultimately, when a state considers whether to allow some free use of copyright music and songs in worship, it approaches this issue like any other issue in copyright law; that is, it balances the need to recognize and reward the author for his or her creativity with the desire of the community to have access to the work. In the UK, the absence of an exemption shows that the policymakers were more persuaded by the argument that although authors of religious music and songs compose for the glory of God, this does not mean that these authors should find their reward only in Heaven.

[61] In fact, Art. 5(3)(g) of the EU Directive on the Harmonization of Certain Aspects of Copyright and Related Rights in the Information Society allows EU member states to provide for an exception for "use during religious celebrations or official celebrations organized by a public authority." The Netherlands, for example, has an exemption for religious use. *See* Dutch Copyright Act, *Stb.* 1912, 308, Art. 17c (permitting "congregational singing and the instrumental accompaniment thereof during a religious service.").

PART V

Copyright Exceptions and Technology

22

Security Measures and the Future of Fair Use

David Nimmer[*]

1 PREDICTING (WHAT ELSE?) THE FUTURE

When the plaintiff has made a case of copyright infringement under US law, the defendant can still avoid liability by showing fair use.[1] The defense comprises four factors, arguably the most important[2] of which is the fourth, namely "the effect of the use upon the potential market for or value of the copyrighted work."[3] The word "potential" connotes a focus on the future, a need for courts to evaluate how events could unfold in days to come and what effect will thereby arise in that future world.

But the future itself can be carved up into different dimensions. The trend in existing cases has been to examine the current utilization and to predict what effect it would exert on a going-forward basis. In other words, assuming that the defendant's exploitation continues and becomes generalized (through identical conduct by others, for example), how will the market for the work be affected?[4] That sense of "potential" evaluates the future as a continuous extrapolation from the present.

[*] © 2016 by David Nimmer. These ruminations matured during preparation for a panel at the USC Intellectual Property Institute, held at Santa Monica, California, on February 9, 2016. The subject panel was a discussion of fair use featuring Judge Pierre Leval, Judge Alex Kozinski, and this writer, moderated by Professor Jane Ginsburg of Columbia University. I thank my fellow panelists for their private and public interventions, exposing hidden fault lines and forcing me to clarify my thoughts on this subject. In particular, I am indebted to the inaugural exploration in Jane C. Ginsburg, *Security Failure Fair Use Analysis*, THE MEDIA INSTITUTE (Jan. 25, 2016).

[1] 17 U.S.C. § 107. This chapter treats the doctrine under the rubric of a "defense," although ferment continues over whether it should be actually classified as an affirmative defense or something more fundamental. *See* Lenz v. Universal Music Corp., 815 F.3d 1152–53 (9th Cir. 2016); Bateman v. Mnemonics, Inc., 79 F.3d 1532, 1542 n.22 (11th Cir. 1996).

[2] At one point, the Supreme Court labeled this fourth factor "undoubtedly the single most important element of fair use." Harper & Row, Publishers, Inc. v. Nation Enters, 471 U.S. 539, 566 (1985). *See* Stewart v. Abend, 495 U.S. 207, 238 (1990) (same). Later, it retreated from that pronouncement. "The task is not to be simplified with bright-line rules, for the statute, like the doctrine it recognizes, calls for case-by-case analysis. . . . [All four] statutory factors are to be explored, and the results weighed together, in light of the purposes of copyright." Campbell v. Acuff-Rose Music, Inc., 510 U.S. 569, 577–78 (1994) (reversing decision below that had quoted above language from *Harper & Row v. Nation*). Nonetheless, courts continue to trot out the old formulation. *See, e.g.*, Oracle Am., Inc. v. Google Inc., 750 F.3d 1339, 1376 (Fed. Cir. 2014); BWP Media USA, Inc. v. Gossip Cop Media, LLC, 87 F. Supp. 3d 499, 509 (S.D.N.Y. 2015).

[3] 17 U.S.C. § 107(4).

[4] As reflected by the Supreme Court, "to negate fair use one need only show that if the challenged use should become widespread, it would adversely affect the potential market for the copyrighted work." Harper & Row, Publishers, Inc. v. Nation Enters, 471 U.S. 539, 568 (1985) (internal quotations omitted). It added, "Isolated instances of minor infringements, when multiplied many times, become in the aggregate a major inroad on copyright that must be prevented." *Id.* (same).

But a discontinuous perspective yields a different vision. In other words, the seeds germinated today may sprout tomorrow to grow radically different organisms. Conduct performed today, even if not harmful to the copyrighted work when undertaken by the defendant and even if generalized to others, nonetheless could be seen to threaten the "potential market for or value of the copyrighted work" when combined with the intervention of new elements in the future.

In ages past, US copyright cases posing the question of fair use typically posed the first inquiry. But technology threatens upheaval to that scheme (along with countless others) – recent cases to arise in the realm of mass digitization have brought the second inquiry to the fore.[5] This chapter examines that progression

2 SUPREME COURT RETROSPECTIVE

To illustrate through the prism of fair use cases under the current Act that have reached the United States Supreme Court, consider the following progression.[6] In a case decided in 1985,[7] the question of fair use arose when the *Nation* magazine ran a scoop containing a portion of President Ford's forthcoming autobiography. Specifically, the question arose what effect that appropriation would exert on the work's publisher, including any adverse effect on that company's first serialization rights. The majority's inquiry[8] did not extend to historical discontinuities[9] – for instance, what would the effect be if a new technology called "the Internet" were to become widespread after 1985 and individuals began in that new era to exploit those excerpts in an online environment?[10]

Moving ahead to a 1990 case,[11] the question arose about Universal Pictures continuing to screen its movie *Rear Window* after the revocation of rights in the underlying short story on which the film was based. Here, the investigation was less historical than in the previous case, in which the primary harm caused by *The Nation* occurred at the moment of the scoop, by which it deprived *Time* magazine of its contractual right to be the only party to exercise first serialization rights. In the instant case, Universal Pictures previously owned all necessary rights in the short story, so that its historical conduct was wholly non-infringing. The question, instead, was whether its continued exploitation of the film, after reversion of renewal rights in that story had

[5] *See infra* Section 3.

[6] The discussion below begins with the second fair use case to reach the United States Supreme Court under the current Act. Later, it circles back to consider the first one, decided the previous year. *See infra* Section 6.

[7] *See* Harper & Row, Publishers, Inc. v. Nation Enters, 471 U.S. 539 (1985).

[8] Even the dissent concentrated its efforts entirely on the effect of past conduct rather than looking to the future. According to Justices Brennan, White, and Marshall, *Time* magazine may have canceled its contract not because *The Nation* published a few quotations consisting of copyrightable expression, but instead because the latter published "significant information and ideas from the Ford manuscript," which stand outside of copyright protection. *Id.* at 602 (Brennan, J., dissenting).

[9] This case actually focused exclusively on past harm, rather than looking to potential damage.

> Rarely will a case of copyright infringement present such clear-cut evidence of actual damage. Petitioners assured *Time* that there would be no other authorized publication of any portion of the unpublished manuscript prior to April 23, 1979. Any publication of material from chapters 1 and 3 would permit *Time* to renegotiate its final payment. *Time* cited *The Nation*'s article, which contained verbatim quotes from the unpublished manuscript, as a reason for its nonperformance.

Id. at 567. As such, it did not look to the future at all.

[10] Even at that time, the ARPANET afforded a vehicle that later was to mature into today's Internet. *See* Brett Frischmann, *Privatization and Commercialization of the Internet Infrastructure: Rethinking Market Intervention into Government and Government Intervention into the Market*, 2 Colum. Sci. & Tech. L. Rev. 1, 10 (2001).

[11] *See* Stewart v. Abend, 495 U.S. 207 (1990).

taken place, would cause harm to that story in the future. An element of prediction was thereby ineluctably at play. But that prediction inhered simply in the extrapolation of present conduct into the future.[12] Again, there was no investigation into discontinuities – for instance, if new technology called DVDs and Blu-Rays were developed for future viewing of motion pictures, how would that circumstance play into the fair use analysis?[13]

Concluding with the last time that the court has addressed fair use, the question arose in 1994 concerning 2 Live Crew's unauthorized version of Roy Orbison's "Pretty Woman."[14] The investigation in that instance centered on the effect on the copyright owner of Luther Campbell's rap version of that song, considered in light of current events.[15] Again, discontinuities were off the table – for instance, how would these circumstances play out in a hypothetical future world of vending music through iTunes or exploitation of snippets by the likes of Girl Talk.[16]

In each of the above cases, the operative question centered around current utilizations to predict what effect they would exert on a going-forward basis. The cases investigated what effect the defendant's conduct would exert on the potential market for, respectively, the literary, audiovisual, and musical works at issue in those three cases. In contrast stand the recent digitization cases.

3 THE FUTURE AIN'T WHAT IT USED TO BE

By contrast to the way that the above cases proceeded, consider a pair of recent Second Circuit cases. Both involved immense projects to digitize book collections, one undertaken by a consortium called HathiTrust, the other by Google, the world's largest search engine. Focusing on the latter case,[17] the court validated the scanning and indexing of more than 20 million books.[18] The Google Books project allowed users to search those volumes, displaying to them three snippets, each consisting of three lines of text, containing hits to the appropriate search terms.[19] To prevent users from thereby accessing the entirety of a given book, Google blacklisted one page out of every ten and otherwise disallowed repeat searches.[20] After extensive analysis, the

[12] The entirety of the court majority's discussion of this factor was the following: "The record supports the Court of Appeals' conclusion that re-release of the film impinged on the ability to market new versions of the story. Common sense would yield the same conclusion." *Id.* at 238. Although three justices dissented from the statutory construction of the reversion right, they did not address fair use in their opinion.

[13] As those future technologies developed, later courts had to address them. *See* Universal City Studios, Inc. v. Corley, 273 F.3d 429, 459 (2d Cir. 2001) (concluding that there is no fair use defense to anti-circumvention violation of DVD movies). *See also* Neil Weinstock Netanel, *First Amendment Constraints on Copyright after* Golan v. Holder, 60 UCLA L. Rev. 1082, 1115 (2013) (calling that conclusion into question based on later Supreme Court authority).

[14] *See* Campbell v. Acuff-Rose Music, Inc., 510 U.S. 569 (1994).

[15] Of signal importance to this opinion was that the defendants made a parody, given that "the parody and the original usually serve different market functions." *Id.* at 591. The court focused on the fact that the defendant's use was transformative, with the consequence that "market substitution is at least less certain, and market harm may not be so readily inferred." *Id.* ("as to parody pure and simple, it is more likely that the new work will not affect the market for the original in a way cognizable under this factor, that is, by acting as a substitute for it"). But it remanded for further consideration "of the market for a nonparody, rap version of" the defendant's song. *Id.* at 593.

[16] *See* Brian Pear, *Girl Talk, Fair Use, And Three Hundred Twenty-Two Reasons For Copyright Reform*, 1 N.Y.U. Intell. Prop. & Ent. Law Ledger 19 (2009).

[17] To explain the sequence, the former case did not allow display of the snippets to be described below. In addition, the former case involved defendants distinct from Google, Inc., one of the world's largest corporations acting for its own commercial advantage. Given that the latter case presented the harder fair use challenge to its defendant, its facts are highlighted above.

[18] *See* Authors Guild v. Google, Inc., 804 F.3d 202, 208 (2d Cir.2015).

[19] *Id.* at 209–10.

[20] *Id.* at 210.

opinion validated the new forms of research afforded by the Google Books project as falling within the scope of fair use.[21]

In each case, the plaintiff copyright owners argued against fair use under the fourth factor not on the basis of past exploitation, but rather by invoking future threats. In the first case, the plaintiff authors "speculate[d] that, if hackers were able to obtain unauthorized access to the books stored [by HathiTrust], the full text of these tens of millions of books might be distributed worldwide without restriction, 'decimating' the traditional market for those works."[22] By the same token, the plaintiff authors in the second case advanced the parallel argument "that Google's storage of its digitized copies of Plaintiffs' books exposes them to the risk that hackers might gain access and make the books widely available, thus destroying the value of their copyrights."[23]

In other words, the plaintiffs in those two cases constructed their arguments based not on current events, but instead on speculation about events that might transpire in the future. Not being able to point to current adverse effects on their potential market, they argued that hackers could come upon the scene in the future and devastate their market at that later point in time.

Both these Second Circuit cases rejected the plaintiff's challenge to fair use. To consider that defense on its merits, those courts both had to investigate future harm. The particular paths that each followed differ somewhat.

In *HathiTrust*, Judge Parker detailed "the extensive security measures the Libraries have undertaken to safeguard against the risk of a data breach."[24] Given that the plaintiffs failed to rebut that showing, the court concluded that no security breach was likely to occur.[25] It thereupon concluded that factor four favored fair use.[26]

But the opinion then added a final consideration acknowledging the prospective orientation of the claim: "Without foreclosing a future claim based on circumstances not now predictable, and based on a different record, we hold that the balance of relevant factors in this case favors the Libraries."[27] The discussion below returns to those twin points about matters not now predictable and about the possibility that a different record could arise.[28]

In *Google Books*, Judge Leval began by labeling the security concern "theoretically sound."[29] The opinion conceded:

> If, in the course of making an arguable fair use of a copyrighted work, a secondary user unreasonably exposed the rights holder to destruction of the value of the copyright resulting from the public's opportunity to employ the secondary use as a substitute for purchase of the

[21] *Id.* at 225. Notable here are "ngrams" that track the frequency of given terms over time. *Id.* at 209 & n.5.

[22] Authors Guild, Inc. v. HathiTrust, 755 F.3d 87, 100 (2d Cir. 2014).

[23] 804 F.3d at 227.

[24] 755 F.3d at 100. Just to cite one example,

> a mass download prevention system called "choke" is used to measure the rate of activity (such as the rate a user is reading pages) by each individual user. If a user's rate of activity exceeds certain thresholds, the system assumes that the user is mechanized (e.g., a web robot) and blocks that user's access for a set period of time.

Id.

[25] "[W]e see no basis in the record on which to conclude that a security breach is likely to occur, much less one that would result in the public release of the specific copyrighted works belonging to any of the plaintiffs in this case." *Id.* at 100–101

[26] *Id.* at 101.

[27] *Id.*

[28] *See infra* Section 7.

[29] 804 F.3d at 227.

> original (even though this was not the intent of the secondary user), this might well furnish a substantial rebuttal to the secondary user's claim of fair use.[30]

But notwithstanding its "reasonable theoretical basis," the opinion rejected the claim as lacking support in the evidence tendered to the district court.[31] Google had documented that its "digital scans are stored on computers walled off from public internet access and protected by the same impressive security measures used by Google."[32] By contrast, the plaintiffs could not identify any past thefts from Google Books or the company's library project.[33] The Second Circuit therefore concluded that "Google has made a sufficient showing of protection of its digitized copies of Plaintiffs' works to carry its burden on this aspect of its claim of fair use . . ."[34]

4 THE ISSUE AS REFLECTED IN THE COPYRIGHT ACT

There is a dearth of copyright authority addressing the novel issues raised in those mass digitization cases. Two sources must be considered regarding security and potential breaches: First, how has the governing statute treated the matter? Second, how have past cases handled it? The following section addresses the latter point.[35] Meanwhile, let us examine here the Copyright Act 1976 to see how it addresses the topic.

The question posed by the mass digitization cases concerns security measures adopted to forestall copyright infringement and their potential defeat by intermeddling third parties. The Act addresses various matters arising out of the same nexus of concerns, but with fundamental differences that render them inapposite to the current question.

As we have seen, both HathiTrust and Google employed strong security measures to protect the resulting book scans. The Second Circuit cases recognized those steps as potent enough to forestall third parties from invading the corpus and thereby infringing the subject copyrights. There is a portion of the statute, added by the Digital Millennium Copyright Act in 1998, that addresses technological steps taken to safeguard copyrighted works against invasion, and that further contains specifications regarding security.[36] On inspection, though, it is wholly inapplicable here. That provision largely addresses technological measures taken by *copyright owners* to protect their works, as opposed to the measures adopted by *defendants* over those owners'

[30] *Id.* The opinion relied here on two Ninth Circuit opinions, which will be confronted below. *See infra* Section 5.

[31] 804 F.3d at 227.

[32] *Id.* at 228. Indeed, "Plaintiffs' own security expert praised these security systems, remarking that 'Google is fortunate to have ample resources and top-notch technical talents' that enable it to protect its data." *Id.* (internal quote as altered by court).

[33] *Id.* Although the plaintiffs quoted from Google's SEC filings admitting the possibility that "security breaches could expose it to a risk of loss due to the actions of outside parties, employee error, malfeasance, or otherwise," the court concluded that this "prudent acknowledgment" fell "far short of rebutting Google's demonstration of the effective measures it takes to guard against piratical hacking." *Id.*

[34] *Id.* Interestingly, the next portion of the opinion revisited security concerns in a distinct context:

> Plaintiffs contend that Google's distribution to a participating library of a digital copy of Plaintiffs' books is not a fair use and exposes the Plaintiffs to risks of loss if the library uses its digital copy in an infringing manner, or if the library fails to maintain security over its digital copy with the consequence that the book may become freely available as a result of the incursions of hackers.

Id. The court rejected the prospect that libraries might misuse their digital copies, calling this "sheer speculation." *Id.* at 229. Correlatively, it labeled the chance that those libraries would leave those digital copies "unreasonably vulnerable to hacking" as also "nothing more than a speculative possibility." *Id.*

[35] *See infra* Section 5; *see also infra* Section 6.

[36] *See* 17 U.S.C. § 1201(a).

objections in the mass digitization cases.[37] In one narrow particular, the statute affords immunity to defendants who undertake specified security testing, as opposed to regulating how much security a defendant must implement to protect against future intermeddlers.[38] For both these reasons, that superficial similarity to the matter under investigation leads to a dead end.

Another mention of "security" in the Copyright Act relates to the exception for ephemeral recordings.[39] Specifically, it allows qualifying transmitting organizations to make a single copy (or phonorecord) of a particular transmission containing copyrighted material, when the purpose of making the copy is for "archival preservation or security."[40] At least that language refers to "security" undertaken with regard to a copyrighted work by an erstwhile defendant – to that extent, it is congruent with the current inquiry.[41] But, beyond the failure to explicate what "security" means in the Act itself, in its legislative history,[42] or in any case decided under it over the past four decades,[43] that provision says nothing about how much security is requisite or what the effect on fair use might be were a defendant to adopt inadequate security measures. Identical considerations apply to a comparable feature of the 1976 Act allowing libraries and archives to make up to three copies (or phonorecords) of unpublished works when "duplicated solely for purposes of preservation and security."[44]

In sum, the drafting of the current statute lies far afield from any issues raised in the mass digitization cases. If the past is any guide for how to deal with these issues, it must therefore arise in the case law.

5 CONTRAST WITH PAST CASES

Following the above statutory investigation,[45] it is time to see how case law has addressed the matter. The answer is that no case is squarely on point.[46]

HathiTrust cited to the Supreme Court's *Sony* opinion,[47] which will be discussed below.[48] Meanwhile, *Google Books* cited to two Ninth Circuit cases to support the proposition that if "a

[37] *See supra* Section 3.

[38] *See* 17 U.S.C. § 1201(j). *See generally* 4 Nimmer on Copyright § 12A.04[D].

[39] *See generally* 2 Nimmer on Copyright § 8.06.

[40] 17 U.S.C. § 112(a)(1)(B). A parallel feature applies to governmental bodies and nonprofit organizations who make up to ten copies (or phonorecords) for the same "purposes of archival preservation or security." 17 U.S.C. § 112(d)(2).

[41] *See supra* Section 3.

[42] Both the House Report and Senate Report simply repeat the language without explicating it. Elsewhere, both reports, in the context of preemption of state causes of action, offer that "a person having no trust or other relationship with the proprietor of a computerized data base should not be immunized from sanctions against electronically or cryptographically breaching the proprietor's security arrangements and accessing the proprietor's data." H. R. Rep. No. 94-1476 at.132 (1976); S. Rep. No. 94-473 at.116 (1976). But that snippet offers no standards at all regarding fair use.

[43] Very few cases have even cited to the provision in question – and none offers any explication at all regarding what the "security" language might mean. *See* Bonneville Int'l Corp. v. Peters, 153 F. Supp. 2d 763, 770 (E.D. Pa. 2001), *aff'd*, 347 F.3d 485 (3d Cir. 2003); Agee v. Paramount Communs., Inc., 59 F.3d 317, 321–22 (2d Cir. 1995); Capitol Records, LLC v. BlueBeat, Inc., 765 F. Supp. 2d 1198, 1202 (C.D. Cal. 2010).

[44] 17 U.S.C. § 108(b). Again, very few cases have even cited to the provision in question – and the few that quote the "security" language fail to offer any explication at all regarding what the term might mean. *See* N.Y. Times Co. v. Tasini, 533 U.S. 483, 503 & n.12 (2001); Vault Corp. v. Quaid Software, Ltd., 847 F.2d 255, 265 & n.20 (5th Cir. 1988); Atari v. JS & A Group Atari, Inc. v. JS & A Group, Inc., 597 F. Supp. 5, 10 & n.5 (N.D. Ill. 1983).

[45] *See supra* Section 4.

[46] A somewhat similar issue arose in Fox News Network, LLC v. TVEyes, Inc., 43 F. Supp. 3d 379, 396 (S.D.N.Y. 2014) (plaintiff failed to demonstrate market harm absent evidence that people were actually using defendant's clips of plaintiff's broadcasts as substitute for watching those broadcasts).

[47] 755 F.3d at 101.

[48] *See infra* Section 6.

secondary user unreasonably exposed the rights holder to destruction of the value of the copyright resulting from the public's opportunity to employ the secondary use as a substitute for purchase of the original (even though this was not the intent of the secondary user), this might well furnish a substantial rebuttal to the secondary user's claim of fair use."[49] It construed those past cases to support its ruling:

> For this reason, the *Arriba Soft* and *Perfect 10* courts, in upholding the secondary user's claim of fair use, observed that thumbnail images, which transformatively provided an Internet pathway to the original images, were of sufficiently low resolution that they were not usable as effective substitutes for the originals.[50]

It is therefore necessary to investigate those two rulings.

Both the cited *Arriba Soft* and *Perfect 10* cases involved internet search engines, geared at pictures rather than text or other content. In *Arriba Soft*, the defendant's program crawled the Web seeking out images. It initially downloaded full-sized copies of the images onto Arriba's server.[51] But it used those copies to generate smaller, lower-resolution thumbnails of the images.[52] "Once the thumbnails were created, the program deleted the full-sized originals from the server."[53]

The Ninth Circuit upheld the search engine's fair use defense. It treated the subject copying as the entire work, but nonetheless held the third fair use factor (inquiring as to the amount copied from the copyrighted work)[54] to be equivocal.[55] Nevertheless, when it considered the fourth factor, the opinion relied on the degraded quality of the reproductions available to the public to conclude that the copyright owner's potential market had not been adversely affected.[56]

The result in that case was entirely appropriate.[57] Initially, the defendant made an entire copy of the protected work. But the product was solely an intermediate copy, later destroyed, that was used for pro-social purposes – thus warranting a holding of fair use under prior Ninth Circuit authority.[58] Under that typology, the third fair use factor inclines against the defendant (the copying constituted 100 percent of the original) but the fourth weighs entirely in the defendant's favor, as there was no public exploitation at all of the copyrighted work (the intermediate copy having been destroyed after serving its purpose).

On the other hand, if viewed through the prism of adopting security mechanisms (which is how *Google Books* cited the Ninth Circuit's case), then *Arriba Soft*'s analysis should run differently. Now, the thumbnail quality of the reproduction means that only a small percentage

[49] 804 F.3d at 227.
[50] *Id.*
[51] *See* Kelly v. Arriba Soft Corp., 336 F.3d 811, 819 (9th Cir. 2003).
[52] *Id.*
[53] *Id.* "Although a user could copy these thumbnails to his computer or disk, he cannot increase the resolution of the thumbnail; any enlargement would result in a loss of clarity of the image." *Id.*
[54] 17 U.S.C. § 107(3).
[55] 336 F.3d at 821.
[56]
> Arriba's use of Kelly's images also would not harm Kelly's ability to sell or license his full-sized images. Arriba does not sell or license its thumbnails to other parties. Anyone who downloaded the thumbnails would not be successful selling full-sized images enlarged from the thumbnails because of the low resolution of the thumbnails. There would be no way to view, create, or sell a clear, full-sized image without going to Kelly's websites. Therefore, Arriba's creation and use of the thumbnails does not harm the market for or value of Kelly's images.

Id. at 821–22.
[57] An earlier version of the case treated deep linking. *See* 280 F.3d 934 (9th Cir. 2002). This writer criticized that ruling. *See* 4 Nimmer on Copyright § 12B.01[A][2][a]. The court later withdrew that aspect. *See* 336 F.3d 811 (9th Cir. 2003).
[58] *See* Sega Enters. Ltd. v. Accolade, Inc., 977 F.2d 1510 (9th Cir. 1992).

of the subject pixels have been copied. The third factor therefore inclines sharply in favor of fair use (the copying constituted but a small percentage of the original). The fourth factor may do likewise, for the reason cited by the Ninth Circuit.

Yet, so viewed, this case has nothing to do with security *breaches*. One could imagine a different universe in which defendant Arriba Soft not only made an entire copy of each image but also offered those complete copies as part of its searching capabilities – but only subject to technical protections that choked usage down to seeing only 10 percent of the pixels from any image and prevented repeat searches from evading that limitation. That hypothetical matches the later Second Circuit mass digitization cases.[59] Under those circumstances, Mr. Kelly theoretically could have complained that the security measures adopted were inadequate to safeguard his works. But given the actual fact patterns of his case, there was no occasion for him to raise any security concern.

Turning to the other cited Ninth Circuit case, the facts were different – in that case users could obtain the entire image. But that availability arose through a process called in-line linking, meaning it emanated from the plaintiff owner itself rather than from the defendant.[60] (It so happens that the principal defendant in this case was Google in its capacity as a search engine – as distinct from the Google Books service at issue in the later case.) Google did not even store those photographic images, and therefore was not liable for infringement relating to the full images (without the need even to consider any defense, such as fair use).[61]

Nonetheless, another aspect of that case likewise implicated thumbnails used for the purpose of imaging. This aspect of the case unfolded by reliance on the earlier *Arriba Soft* opinion – the Ninth Circuit cited that case to uphold the fair use defense.[62] Given that Google evidently did not store the full images on its servers[63] (even temporarily, as did Arriba Soft),[64] the plaintiffs in this case likewise could not urge any complaint about putative security breaches affording access to their entire works.

In sum, the previous Ninth Circuit cases afford no insight into the question of security breaches, and other courts have failed to confront the issue.[65] But the question still remains whether the other case citation may fill that breach.

[59] *See supra* Section 3.

[60] *See* Perfect 10, Inc. v. Amazon.com, Inc., 508 F.3d 1146, 1156 (9th Cir. 2007). *See generally* 4 NIMMER ON COPYRIGHT § 12B.01[A][2][b].

[61] 508 F.3d at 1161.

[62] *Id.* at 1165.

[63] The facts are more thoroughly ventilated in the district court's opinion. There, one learns that because Google's "web page index is based entirely on the textual part of web pages and not the images, [its] web page cache contains only the text pages, and not the images that those pages include when displayed." Perfect 10 v. Google, Inc., 416 F. Supp. 2d 828, 833 (C.D. Cal. 2006). The material that Google stored consisted of thumbnails, "in order to present the results of the user's query." *Id.*

[64] 336 F.3d at 819.

[65] One outlying case deserves mention. In Rubin v. Brooks/Cole Publ'g Co., 836 F. Supp. 909 (D. Mass. 1993), the court held that defendant's past printing of plaintiff's copyrighted psychological instrument in textbooks constituted fair use. Nonetheless, the opinion enjoined the defendant from undertaking the same conduct(without a license) in the future. *Id.* at 922. It concluded that

> while Brooks/Coles use may have been "fair" in the necessarily inchoate world of private ordering, once the historic rights of the parties are balanced by this Court, the very fact of judicial decision affects private conduct in ways that, if continued, will not be fair to Rubin. Accordingly, while Rubin is entitled to no damages from this action, the future unauthorized use of the Love Scale will be enjoined.

Id. That reasoning seems to invoke a sort of legal analogue to Heisengerg's uncertainty principle. Cf. Laurence Tribe, *The Curvature of Constitutional Space: What Lawyers Can Learn from Modern Physics*, 103 HARV. L. REV. 1 (1989). Suffice it to say that later cases have not followed the lead of that sole ruling.

6 LAST PIECE OF SUPREME COURT PRECEDENT

The final case cited by the Second Circuit's mass digitization opinion was the famous *Betamax* case,[66] which was the first case to reach the Supreme Court under the 1976 Act (and also its first occasion to address that statute's codification of fair use).[67] Like the Ninth Circuit cases just confronted, this case treated a technological innovation and its effects on copyright owners pursuant to fair use doctrine.[68]

At issue in *Betamax* was a new device that allowed television viewers to tape shows off the air for later viewing. The Supreme Court validated home taping as fair use, rejecting the plaintiffs' predictions of harm from that conduct as being hinged on "speculation about audience viewing patterns and ratings, a measurement system which Sidney Sheinberg, MCA's president, calls a 'black art' because of the significant level of imprecision involved in the calculations."[69] The majority determined, to the contrary of that prediction, that time-shifting of programs which audience members had already been invited to watch produced benefits to that audience, and that its supposed harm was "speculative and, at best, minimal."[70]

HathiTrust quoted that language as support for its ruling.[71] Although the technological base of *Betamax* makes it seem superficially apposite to that later ruling, further inspection dispels that conclusion. In two of the Supreme Court cases addressing fair use under copyright law, the majority concluded that the use was fair and unlikely to damage the copyrighted work; in the other two, it reached the opposite conclusion.[72] At base, though, the exercise was identical in all four – with respect to President Ford's memoirs and *Rear Window*, the court concluded that widespread exploitation of the work along the lines of the defendants' utilizations would adversely affect the potential market for the work. With respect to *Pretty Woman*, by contrast, the court reached the opposite conclusion; by the same token, the *Betamax* majority concluded that the evidence failed to show adverse effects on the potential market for the shows at issue. That conclusion arose independently of the technological nature of the VCR at issue in that case, instead it followed from the speculative nature of Nielson ratings and like metrics.

As noted above, the court's focus in its other three fair use cases always examined "potential" harm as a continuous extrapolation from the present,[73] never from the perspective of such discontinuities as what would happen if the future saw the development of the Internet, DVDs, or Girl Talk.[74] The same story unfolded in the *Betamax* case – the majority examined the

[66] *See* Sony Corp. v. Universal City Studios, Inc., 464 U.S. 417 (1984).

[67] This discussion therefore completes the treatment started in *supra* Section 2.

[68] *See supra* Section 5.

[69] 464 U.S. at 452 (quoting district court opinion).

[70] *Id.* at 454 (quoting district court opinion). Justices Blackmun, Marshall, Powell, and Rehnquist rejected that manner of proceeding:

> Proof of actual harm, or even probable harm, may be impossible in an area where the effect of a new technology is speculative, and requiring such proof would present the "real danger … of confining the scope of an author's rights on the basis of the present technology so that, as the years go by, his copyright loses much of its value because of unforeseen technical advances." Register's Supplementary Report 14. Infringement thus would be found if the copyright owner demonstrates a reasonable possibility that harm will result from the proposed use.

Id. at 482 (Blackmun, J., dissenting).

[71] 755 F.3d at 101. *See supra* Section 3.

[72] *See supra* Section 5.

[73] *See supra* Section 1.

[74] *See supra* Section 2.

product as it was employed in consumers' hands when the record was compiled in 1976 rather than to future developments.[75]

To be sure, the technological nature of the VCR could have elicited altogether different treatment. One could have examined what would eventuate in the future were new refinements to be added to video recordation – from commercial squelching[76] to remote storage[77] to digital technology.[78] But that task falls more on the congressional than the judicial side of lawmaking.[79] In any event, when the Supreme Court addressed the case in 1984, it raised none of those issues – it simply determined, based on the 1976 record before it, whether harm to the copyright owner's potential market was established, without delving into any discontinuities that could arise *in futuro*.

7 FUTURE: TENSE TO PREDICT

To recap, past fair use cases analyzing the fourth factor have had to engage in prediction along only one axis[80] – assuming that the defendant's utilization continues and becomes generalized (through identical conduct by others, for example), how will the market for the work be affected?[81] But the recent Second Circuit cases involving mass digitization push the inquiry to a second level: assuming that future events transpire that are different in kind from anything happening at present, then how will the market for the work be affected? In other words, *HathiTrust* and *Google Books* pose the same challenges of prediction of traditional cases – but only after a separate level of inquiry has been vaulted, which itself poses its own challenges of prediction.

Focusing on that new layer, the possibilities are manifold. Table 22.1 envisions some of situations that could emerge, based on the Second Circuit's determination that the defendant applied a very high degree of protection to its Google Books Project.

To confront the chart's particulars, row 1 reflects *sub silentio* the Second Circuit's prediction as to how events will unfold. But there is no track record in existing cases or experience to reach that conclusion, so it represents but one possibility.[82] It is beyond commonplace to reflect that events often unfold outside anyone's expectations.[83] We therefore reach row 2 – to the extent that a small coterie of techno-cognoscenti are able to hack their way into the 20 million volumes and read them at their leisure, the copyright owners may lose some marginal revenue, but the effect is likely to be small.

On the other hand, row 3 envisions that the heirs to Eric Corley and David LaMacchia[84] will adopt as their next cause célèbre the wide-scale dissemination of all tools to allow the world to

[75] The compilation of that case's factual record as of events that took place in 1976 emerges from the district court opinion. *See* Universal City Studios, Inc. v. Sony Corp. of Am., 480 F. Supp. 429, 439 (C.D. Cal. 1979), *rev'd in part*, 659 F.2d 963 (9th Cir. 1981), *rev'd*, 464 U.S. 417 (1984).

[76] *See* Fox Broad. Co. v. Dish Network, L.C.C., 905 F. Supp. 2d 1088, 1094–96 (C.D. Cal. 2012). *See generally* Peter S. Menell & David Nimmer, *Unwinding Sony*, 95 CAL. L. REV. 941, 1019 (2007).

[77] *See* Cartoon Network LP, LLLP v. CSC Holdings, Inc., 536 F.3d 121 (2d Cir. 2008).

[78] *Id.* As part of the Digital Millennium Copyright Act, Congress legislated the holding into law – but specifically limited to analogue technology, inapplicable to digital technology. *See* 17 U.S.C. § 1201(k).

[79] *See generally* 4 NIMMER ON COPYRIGHT § 12A.07[B].

[80] At times, even that one level of prediction is not required – to the extent that the evidence clearly shows harm to have arisen in the past, it may not even be necessary to investigate future potential harms. *See supra* note 9.

[81] *See supra* Section 1.

[82] *See supra* Sections 5–6.

[83] As these words are written, a man lacking any governmental or military service has just secured the Republican nomination for president of the United States, a feat that all the pundits long derided as impossible.

[84] We have already met the former. *See supra* note 13. The latter prevailed in United States v. LaMacchia, 871 F. Supp. 535 (D. Mass. 1994). Congress closed that loophole by enacting the NET Act. *See generally* 5 NIMMER ON COPYRIGHT § 15.01[B][2].

TABLE 22.1 *Possibilities based on record*

No.	Technology adopted by Google	Third-party hacking	Effect on copyright owner
1	State-of-the-art security as of 2014	Nobody ever hacks it	None
2	State-of-the-art security as of 2014	It is hacked within two years, but only by select individuals	Minimal
3	State-of-the-art security as of 2014	It is hacked within two years by cyberarnarchists	Potentially massive
4	State-of-the-art security as of 2014 that is continually updated	It is hacked by cyberarnarchists in 2034	Significant
5	State-of-the-art security that is never updated	It is hacked by cyberarnarchists in 2034	Uncertain

TABLE 22.2 *Some other possibilities*

No.	Technology adopted by target defendant	Third-party hacking	Effect on copyright owner
6	Adequate security as of 2014	Nobody ever hacks it	None
7	Adequate security as of 2014	It is hacked within two years by cyberarnarchists	Potentially massive
8	Deficient security as of 2014	Nobody ever hacks it	None
9	Deficient security as of 2014	It is hacked within two years by cyberarnarchists	Potentially massive

access the 20 million encrypted volumes that form the Google Books corpus.[85] Under those circumstances, the loss to their respective copyright owners could be incalculable.

Turning to rows 4 and 5, we are now addressing events of two decades hence. One can only guess at the effect on the marketplace of events that far distant. To the extent that the cat-and-mouse game between technology companies and hackers continues into that time frame, if the latter win then it is readily imaginable, as in row 4, that the effect on the copyright owners will be significant. Moving to row 5, perhaps nobody will be using today's book-reading technology in that future world, so there would be neither the incentive to maintain the current encryption to protect that technology nor much harm to content owners should that encryption be breached then.

It is important to reflect that Table 22.1 represents only the possibilities that follow from the factual record as developed in the *Google Books* case itself. As the court recognized, the concerns expressed over security breaches are "theoretically sound." Therefore, if another defendant instead adopted less robust protection over its project, then different fair use conclusions would ensue. Moreover, the consequences could vary if that protection were merely adequate, on the one hand, or were positively deficient (or nonexistent), on the other. The universe of possibilities is wide, indeed. A few possibilities (Table 22.2) must stand in for what could be a massive chart.

Rows 8 and 9 represent the antithesis of the robust security actually used in the *HathiTrust* and *Google Books* cases. Given the former's recognition that a future claim "based on circumstances not now predictable, and based on a different record" could come out the opposite way,

[85] *See supra* Section 2.

it would seem that row 9 represents the paradigm of unfair use.[86] The same conclusion follows from the latter's recognition that "a substantial rebuttal to the secondary user's claim of fair use" would arise when a secondary user unreasonably exposed the rights holder to destruction of the value of the copyright from inadequate security technology.[87]

If row 9 represents the paradigm of unfair use, row 7 at least arguably deserves the same treatment. After all, the defendant in that case had the option of securing its product fully yet failed to do so, to the copyright owner's loss. In Judge Leval's words, this hypothetical defendant (unlike Google in the actual case) "unreasonably exposed the rights holder to destruction of the value of the copyright resulting from the public's opportunity to employ the secondary use as a substitute for purchase of the original (even though this was not the intent of the secondary user) . . ."[88] Even if the defendant be viewed as nonnegligent by virtue of having adopted (merely) adequate security precautions, the copyright owner is even more unambiguously nonnegligent – and has now massively suffered from the defendant's inadequate safeguards. The risk of loss in that instance sensibly belongs on the defense side.[89]

8 PROBLEMS WITH EXPEDITIOUS RESOLUTION

It follows that the plaintiff should win when rows 7 and 9 are concretely presented in given cases. But now a fundamental problem supervenes: to the extent that the case is litigated expeditiously, a court has no way of predicting how the future will unfold. In other words, a suit for copyright infringement filed after adequate (but not robust) security was adopted may indeed eventuate along the lines of row 7; the same case, filed after deficient security was adopted, may indeed eventuate along the lines of row 9. But the problem is that this state of affairs will not be known for two years.

When the case is filed, the state of affairs may be that the defendant "unreasonably exposed the rights holder to destruction of the value of the copyright." But that exposure may not be known, as it will not occur until after judgment has already been entered, as actual events later unfold.[90]

Conversely, it may never come to pass. In particular, even though it may not be terribly difficult for hackers to defeat the adequate security employed by the defendant, they may simply not bother to do so (row 6). Even if it were trivially easy to defeat the defendant's manifestly deficient security, hackers may focus their ingenuity on juicier targets and leave those minimally encrypted books alone (row 8). After all, many of the digitized volumes at stake in the litigation are available on Amazon.com for $1 or less.[91] Given "the fact that the normal purchase price of a book is relatively low,"[92] the risk of loss to copyright owners may never reach fruition. In other words, the future may witness the advent of row 6 or row 8 in lieu of row 7 or row 9.

We thereby reach the danger that liability may be drawn too broadly. In other words, even though it seems, in the abstract, that the defendant has created an unreasonable danger to the

[86] 755 F.3d at 101.
[87] 804 F.3d at 227.
[88] *Id.*
[89] As observed in a different context, "as between two innocent parties (*i.e.*, the copyright owner and the innocent infringer) the latter should suffer inasmuch as he, unlike the copyright owner, has the opportunity to guard against infringement." 4 NIMMER ON COPYRIGHT § 13.08[B][1].
[90] We revert to the proposition that even the experts routinely fail at predicting how future events will unfold. *See supra* note 83.
[91] Judge Leval made this point publicly at our panel at the USC Intellectual Property Institute. *See supra* note *.
[92] 804 F.3d at 224.

plaintiff's works, it may be that no harm will ever eventuate. Under those circumstances, how should the law react? Although the immediate context favors a holding of liability under those circumstances (with the concomitant possibility of an injunction), the end result would be to enjoin conduct that is actually pro-social, based on a danger that was never destined to come to pass.[93] The public is the loser in that scenario.

Looking through the opposite end of the telescope brings the converse danger into focus. For this purpose, we revert to row 3 of Table 22.1. Just because Google built high security into its book scans scarcely renders them inviolate – we regularly learn about breaches of the most seemingly impregnable systems.[94] The possibility must therefore be acknowledged that the catastrophe that the plaintiffs fear may come to pass, despite all the safeguards that Google historically has taken. The question arises how to allocate responsibility under those circumstances.

Google Books absolves Google of liability in row 3, based on the reasonable steps it took to avoid harm to the copyright owners. Yet those steps are cold comfort to these proprietors, in the world of row 3, who have suffered massive damage as a consequence. If there is any culpability for the state of affairs, it falls on Google's shoulders as opposed to those plaintiffs', who resisted setting up the state of affairs that occasioned the loss. Once again, between two largely innocent parties, the onus must fall on the one that could have prevented the damage from having arisen, which is the defendant rather than the plaintiffs in this instance.[95]

In sum, a quick resolution without taking into account what will actually transpire in two years threatens disadvantages in both directions:

- Given high security, the defendant will avoid immediate liability, even though it should be held responsible in the not altogether unlikely contingency that future events develop (per row 3) that cause massive damage to the plaintiffs;
- Given low security, the defendant will be held immediately liable, even though the public would actually be the winner in the not altogether unlikely contingency that future events develop (per rows 6 or 8) without any harm to the plaintiffs.

9 PROBLEMS EVEN WITH DELAYED RESOLUTION

To redress the difficulties just noted, one solution would be to decline to resolve the case within the relatively expedited two-year window. Given that civil litigation often stretches over many years, perhaps a languid schedule of four to five years would yield more just results.

The rub arises in rows 4 and 5 of Table 22.1.[96] It could be that harm is threatened to the copyright owners by the security that Google employs today, but the threat may not be realized until decades into the future. Although it may make sense to hold off resolution for several years, the case can scarcely be maintained in limbo until 2034. Plus, that date is itself arbitrary – actual harm, if it comes, may occur in 2037, or 2042, or any other given date. An endless delay in resolving the case is tantamount to denying the plaintiffs any relief. Better for them to have an expeditious resolution, even if they lose the case in rows 1–5, as long as they win the cases in rows 6–9.

[93] In some sense, this state of affairs represents the looking-glass world of that reached in *Rubin v. Brooks/Cole*. *See supra* note 65.

[94] "Technical experts continue to believe that for every technological lock placed within the work product, there will be a pirate locksmith ready and willing to break in, if not for the financial reward, then merely for the joy of accomplishment." Anne Wells Branscomb, *Who Owns Information?* 90 (1994).

[95] *See supra* note 89.

[96] *See supra* Section 7.

Another challenge brought into focus by considering the long term is that of collateral estoppel. Rows 1–5 highlight that one result may inure today, another tomorrow. What happens if a lawsuit is resolved before the change in status?

Taking the actual *Google Books* litigation, its resolution in 2014 means that defendant Google has been adjudicated innocent of copyright infringement, based on the expectations reflected in row 1. What happens if reality upsets that expectation? If we imagine that row 3 instead eventuates, what is the effect of the security breach two years after final judgment has been entered in the litigation?

As a matter of collateral estoppel, that judgment would not be considered binding under US law against new plaintiffs. A victorious litigant cannot employ that doctrine against a third party who was uninvolved in the first suit; therefore, Google will not be able to use collateral estoppel as a sword against future copyright owners who file suit for infringement of their works.[97] On the other hand, Google can use collateral estoppel as a shield to protect itself from claims brought by the same plaintiffs who originally litigated against it.[98] Initially, the *Google Books* case was brought as a class action, meaning that it would bind all authors who might be potentially aggrieved.[99] But, as part of the procedural twists and turns of the case, it was eventually decided only as to specified author-plaintiffs.[100] Accordingly, if Jim Bouton refiled a claim against Google for copying his baseball memoir *Ball Four*, he would be collaterally estopped by the previous judgment against him from proceeding;[101] but if a new author were to file suit, the doctrine would not come into play.

Nonetheless, the practical effect on that new author might not be much different. Let us imagine that Jim Brosnan were to file suit in the future for copying *The Long Season*, another baseball memoir. Although defendant Google could not get the suit tossed based on collateral estoppel, it could certainly rely on *stare decisis* for the proposition that the ruling in *Google Books* binds future courts in the Second Circuit. Thus, it would seem straightforward to argue, in 2016, that the exact same conduct adjudicated as fair use in 2014 continues to qualify as immune from liability.

In response, author Brosnan could argue that circumstances had changed.[102] His position would be that the Second Circuit had reached a conclusion of fair use based on its prediction in 2014 that nobody would be able to hack into the collection – but subsequent events have debunked that expectation. He would style his claim, in the words of *HathiTrust*, "a future claim based on circumstances not [then] predictable, and based on a different record."[103] He would further distinguish *Google Books* on the basis that, pointedly unlike his own situation, the plaintiffs in that case could not identify any past thefts.[104]

97 *See* Blonder-Tongue Lab. v. University of Illinois Found., 402 U.S. 313 (1971).

98 *See* Whimsicality, Inc. v. Battat, 27 F. Supp. 2d 456 (S.D.N.Y. 1998).

99 *See* Authors Guild v. Google, Inc., 282 F.R.D. 384 (S.D.N.Y. 2012), *vacated*, 721 F.3d 132 (2d Cir. 2013).

100 804 F.3d at 208 n.1.

101 For a potential view to the contrary, see the next footnote.

102 In fact, reverting to actual plaintiff Jim Bouton, perhaps he could urge the same argument. In other words, even though Bouton lost his case in a final judgment entered in 2015, to the extent that new circumstances on the ground pertained in 2017 (or thereafter), there might be room for him to maintain that collateral estoppel no longer binds him. That topic lies beyond current bounds, so suffice it to cite the Supreme Court's observation long ago about collateral estoppel: "That both suits involved 'essentially the same course of wrongful conduct' is not decisive." Lawlor v. National Screen Service Corp., 349 U.S. 322, 327 (1955). More recently, the Second Circuit has clarified that "claim preclusion will not bar a suit . . . 'based on legally significant acts occurring *after* the filing of a prior suit that was itself based upon earlier acts.'" TechnoMarine SA v. Giftports, Inc., 758 F.3d 493, 501 (2d Cir. 2014).

103 755 F.3d at 100.

104 804 F.3d at 227.

In sum, it must be concluded that hypothetical plaintiff Brosnan could advance powerful arguments that were not available to actual plaintiff Bouton. Of course, given how notoriously unpredictable the fair use doctrine has proven to be, it remains unclear whether those distinctions would prove dispositive. In other words, courts adjudicating those fact patterns under Second Circuit law could distinguish the prior cases to determine that the 2016 utilizations were fair use – or could adhere more woodenly to the holdings of those past cases and continue to vindicate fair use, given that Google made a valiant effort to protect the corpus against hacking.

Now, let us imagine instead that events match row 4, namely that the breach takes place in 2034. What is the effect then? Logically, there is no reason that the lapse of twenty years, rather than two, should make a difference. If Google continued to maintain state-of-the-art security yet a fiendish cyberarnarchist was still able to defeat those measures, then the same countervailing arguments arise as were rehearsed in the preceding paragraph. In other words, the usage should preferably be deemed unfair, but the contrary position is also cognizable.

Finally, let us instead imagine that events match row 5, such that the breach takes place in 2034 because Google never updated its security settings past 2014 standards. In that event, Google's already weak argument in favor of fair use is further undercut. As events change on the ground, the fair use doctrine must be correspondingly recalibrated.[105] Even the perspective that validated fair use above – concluding that Google made a valiant effort to protect the corpus against hacking, and so should be deemed to fall within the protection of the fair use doctrine, notwithstanding that a third party ultimately defeated those measures – must now acknowledge that the predicate for that finding no longer pertains (in other words, it can no longer be stated that Google made a valiant effort to protect the corpus against hacking; instead, its efforts over time were severely lacking).

10 CONCLUSION

Predicting the future is a complex task. As this chapter has shown, premising copyright liability – or the absence thereof – on that prediction is even more complicated. And yet, when confronted with the need to predict as part and parcel of the necessary fair use analysis, courts have done little more than assume away the issue.

With the advancement of technology, these issues are likely to recur with greater frequency. For that reason, courts need to grapple overtly with the basis on which their predictions rest. Perhaps it will aid analysis for them to state explicitly the extent to which their fair use analysis is predicated on measures deriving from extant security measures and their reasoning about how those measures are likely to evolve and get progressively better – or indeed, worse. The first wave of opinions on that score have relied on tacit assumptions. Shining light on the process may yield greater refinement when the next wave of cases arises. The minuet between technological progress and court rulings is endless. It is hoped that more sophisticated dance steps may emerge out of the considerations urged above.

[105] The advent of new licensing collectives converted library photocopying of magazine articles, held to be fair use in the 1970s, into unfair use two decades later. *Compare* Williams & Wilkins Co. v. United States, 487 F.2d 1345 (Ct. Cl. 1973), *aff'd by an equally divided court*, 420 U.S. 376 (1975), *with* American Geophysical Union v. Texaco Inc., 60 F.3d 913 (2d Cir. 1994).

For EU product safety concerns, contact us at Calle de José Abascal, 56–1°,
28003 Madrid, Spain or eugpsr@cambridge.org.

www.ingramcontent.com/pod-product-compliance
Lightning Source LLC
LaVergne TN
LVHW060019210926
848481LV00013B/3746

* 9 7 8 1 0 0 9 2 9 3 1 4 3 *